All Mapped Out

Also by Dave Bartram
The Boys of Summer

ALL MAPPED OUT

The UK tour of a lifetime

DAVE BARTRAM

Every day is a journey, and the journey itself is home.
(Matsuo Basho, 1644-1694)

fantom
publishing

First published in 2015 by Fantom Films
fantomfilms.co.uk

A catalogue record for this book is available from the British Library.

Hardback edition ISBN: 978-1-78196-133-9

Typeset by Phil Reynolds Media Services, Leamington Spa
Printed and bound by CPI Group (UK) Ltd, Croydon, CR0 4YY

Jacket design by Robert Hammond

Dedicated to Sue Townsend (1946-2014)
My home town's greatest ever author

Contents

Contents

Preface

'TO BOLDLY GO WHERE no man has gone before' articulates the robust voice-over to each intergalactic episode of TV's cult phenomenon *Star Trek*; and, though perhaps not as intrepidly as Captain Kirk and the crew of the Starship Enterprise, it could be argued that in the course of my professional life I've been to the moon and back… not just once, but by any stretch of the imagination a highly improbable four times!

Two million miles is a staggering approximation of the distance I and my associates have covered during a migratory musical adventure spanning four decades over air, land and sea by means of just about every conceivable mode of transport known to man. Aeroplanes (from light aircraft to gravity-defying jets), helicopters (military and civilian), cars, double-decker buses, executive coaches, trucks, motorcycles, scooters, trains, monorails, luxury cruise liners, rowing boats, army tanks, tuk-tuks, a human-powered rickshaw (through the overpopulated streets of Hong Kong), a trishaw (in Singapore), a raft (to traverse a small creek across to a beach party), an ox-cart (to a remote hotel) and a mountain-hugging armed-services vehicle that sped, caterpillar-like, almost vertically to an isolated Falklands reconnaissance site where a hermit-like platoon of just twenty-two forces personnel awaited a rare blowout, which needless to say was accomplished in raucous style.

Two million miles filled with endless traffic jams, road repairs and diversions, breakdowns, freezing one's nuts off in the fetid waiting room of a railway station, propping up my tired head against a pile of luggage following a missed connection, or simply twiddling thumbs in a hotel room biding time when a pre-booked taxi had for whatever reason failed to show.

Two million miles of struggling to stay awake behind the wheel of a myriad of motor vehicles ranging from a clapped-out 1960s Bedford van to an eye-catching, shiny black Mercedes sports convertible posing around many a busy shopping street with the soft-top down (in January), right elbow rested on the driver's door, sporting an unnecessary pair of Ray-Ban shades.

In reality, though, and notwithstanding any or all of the above gripes, the practised traveller's lot seldom fails to raise the spirits: confronting an open road to who knows where, uplifted and lost in thought, admiring each contrasting landscape or shadowing the stars in the night sky above the deserted highway home.

During a fascinating chat with a remarkably sprightly eighty-nine-year-old acquaintance of my wife's, the worldly-wise lady expressed: 'I feel truly blessed to have had the opportunity of visiting some fascinating places in almost every corner of the globe and have seen many extraordinary things; but, David, I envy you, as I can't honestly say I really know my own country – so perhaps it's high time I made a start!'

True to say as we spoke I'd roamed the streets of almost every UK city, the exceptions being Lichfield in the West Midlands along with the recently sanctioned community of St Asaph in North Wales (I completed the full set in the spring of 2012), with each piece of hallowed ground possessing a distinct uniqueness in its own culture, architecture and most of all idiosyncratic characters, many of whom lost no time in contributing a tale or two.

Whilst begging forgiveness for the odd tendency towards name-dropping (which family, friends and business colleagues strongly urged me to include), unlocking this treasure trove of reminiscences and anecdotes has afforded me immeasurable untold pleasure, serving as a cheerful reminder of how Lady Luck so often smiled when it seemed the long road ahead was lined with broken promises and dreams.

NB Each chapter is footnoted with a mini tourist guide based purely on the opinions of not only myself but a whole host of travelling musicians, friends and acquaintances.

Chapter 1
Sunderland

THE NIGHT WAS BLACK AS I reclined uncomfortably in a time-ravaged armchair, analysing the peeling, nicotine-tainted wallpaper of a dilapidated room by candlelight and seething at the deplorable and grimy disrepair of the hovel in which, due to my struggling band's impecunious state of affairs, I had been given little choice but to bed down.

Glancing over at the metal-framed bed I could clearly see, even in the ill-defined, murky light, the yellowing stains of some previous occupant's lustful satisfaction hardened on the threadbare, tide-marked sheets.

The blackout due to industrial action wasn't helping matters at all, with no TV, radio or heating to soften the blow and serve as a distraction from the wintry despair, and scarcely sufficient light to read or even attempt the crossword in the out-of-date, dusty copy of *Weekend* magazine that I'd discovered peeping out from halfway underneath the bed.

The fierce wind rustled through the trees causing the dustbins in the rear yard of the guest house to rumble like a dramatic timpani roll at the tautest moment of a scary movie, accompanied by an eerie hissing as the gale draughtily percolated through the ill-fitting and rotting window-frames where ice had begun to form in the beading.

Earlier on in the evening my band 'Choise' had laboured through a couple of cruelly interrupted forty-five-minute sets at the Birtley Rex Social Club, close to Chester-le-Street in County Durham. The initial disruptions came courtesy of two sudden blackouts due to the strikes, and were rounded off by a third unexpected rift an hour or so later when the lank-haired compère (bestowed with the official title of Honorary Entertainments Secretary) clanged his bell, blurting into the microphone that the band urgently needed to curtail our performance with immediate effect and make way for the bingo, now running an unforgivable fifteen minutes late.

Humbled and downcast, the sneering performers loaded up the van, eager to cut and run from the ensuing mayhem. Picking up the princely sum of twenty pounds in cash as scant reward for our efforts, we were left in no doubt as to the evening's main attraction and humiliated at playing second fiddle to a crappy game of housey-housey!

Back at the digs a scruffy, pallid and bespectacled landlord going by the name of Jimmy Butler offered the returning quartet a warming nightcap, with hot water poured from a huge, tarnished aluminium kettle onto a selection of second-hand teabags plucked from an interior washing-line. In truth something far more potent and medicinally fulfilling than limescale-seasoned tea served in chipped, discoloured mugs was desperately needed to awaken the sagging spirits and provide the faintest touch of light relief. But whatever: beggars couldn't be choosers and on such a cold and depressing night the brew provided a welcome tonic, made even sweeter at the mention of a pair of match tickets, compliments of our host and handed over to co-guitarist Trevor, for the Sunderland game set to take place at Roker Park the following afternoon, as raining-off Jimmy explained he was much too busy to go along under his own steam.

Quite what was keeping the grubby proprietor occupied will forever remain a mystery, with little evidence to suggest any time or effort spent on maintenance or cleaning duties at his shabby establishment. In all fairness this was reflected in the weekly room rate of seven pounds and fifty pence (in the form of a ten-bob note), payable first thing on a Saturday morning prior to the man himself rustling up an oily breakfast.

****

Having been an ardent footie fan – a Leicester City supporter – since the age of six, it may be fair to say I've attended getting on for a thousand matches spanning more than half a century. For reasons unknown, however, this particular encounter remains indelibly etched in the scrapbook of my mind, due largely to the bitterly cold weather and quagmire of a pitch, though the fare served up was every bit as unpalatable in one of the dullest and most dire spectacles of the great game I've ever had the misfortune to witness.

'The Mackems', as the residents of Sunderland are informally known, must surely lay claim to the title of the most hostile supporters in British football. Throughout an awfully tedious ninety minutes ending in a nil-nil draw with Preston North End – continually referred to as Preston Knob End by those in close proximity – the spectators constantly berated and abused not only the match officials, but every last one of the twenty-two players on the pitch, in the kind of game where both sides were lucky to score nil. Chilled to the bone and with a thumping headache after an afternoon whose highlight had been the infamous 'Roker Roar', we trudged back to the pigsty along the road.

Never in my wildest dreams could I have imagined that I was in fact feasting my eyes upon the season's FA Cup winners. Only months later in May 1973 Sunderland's heroic line-up defeated hot favourites Manchester United, in what is still regarded as one of the biggest shocks ever known in the competition.

****

Littered with club gigs on virtually every corner, the north east of England became a magnet for early-seventies working bands and proved the saving grace for a number of professional musicians on the breadline, many of whom uprooted from the south and Midlands often for weeks on end when the diary was looking blank.

The philosophy was simple: if a band grafted hard and came up to the mark the fervent audiences soon made known their approval in a boisterous show of appreciation. This came, though, at a small price, with many diehard punters insisting any artist of worth give an interpretation of the rhythm-and-blues classic 'The Hunter', originally by legendary guitar player Albert King, but popularised locally by Free in the late sixties.

The sleazy oldie's haunting rhythm turned the track into something of a Tyne and Wear anthem, prompting such comments as: 'Yers are shite if yer cannie pley "The Hoonta"!' Arriving early at one venue on a wintry afternoon, we found ourselves bombarded with requests to perform the song that evening, and were only too happy to oblige. Within a couple of hours the song had transformed our repertoire, keeping the north-south divide in check from that moment on.

On the back of several excursions to the region over a period of two or three years the hard-working four-piece built up a healthy following, upheld as the demand for gigs went through the roof, boosting not only the income but the boys' alcoholic intake, with the local beer rarely more than ten pence a pint. Deeply serious about their music, the warm welcome afforded the young hopefuls by a fraternity of working-class clubgoers left a profound impression, along with the perfect grounding for what lay just around the corner.

****

Twenty-first-century Sunderland paints a vastly different picture, being almost unrecognisable from those dark dank days of 1972. Wholesale changes have completely rejuvenated the newly sanctioned city, including the demolition of the old Roker Park football ground to make way for a brand spanking new, state-of-the-art arena christened 'The Stadium of Light' (with no prizes for guessing what the away supporters call it – though it does rhyme with light!), which proudly opened its gates to the 'Black Cats' fanatics for the first time in 1997.

A keen observation, picked up on during successive visits to the city, is the profusion of teenage girls out on the streets to party, squeezed into the shortest, skimpiest skirts pretty much anywhere in the UK, flaunting their charms while evidently immune to goose pimples even in the polar winter months, with much of the flesh on display enriched by a kind of orange hue courtesy of regular sunbed treatments or fake tan.

The town itself, together with neighbouring Houghton-le-Spring and Washington, was granted its prestigious status in 1994, though gratifyingly in the midst of the huge modernisation programme it seems to have retained much of its former gritty charm and character.

****

A giant leap from the humble setting barely ten miles away in which we played poor relations to a bingo caller, the centrally located Empire Theatre is one of an old breed of classic concert halls, in which the band played to packed houses on a number of occasions.

Boasting a curious reputation, the maze of dressing rooms to the rear of the auditorium is said to be haunted by the ghost of the *Carry On* films legend Sid James, who suffered a heart attack whilst performing at the venue in 1976, sadly passing away en-route to hospital; and palpably, a spooky iciness prevailed in the backstage corridors as the entourage prepared for each of our visits, often resulting in the entire cast and crew relocating next door to the rambunctious Dun Cow pub, essentially to warm up for the show.

Apparitions apart, the Empire manifested a rarefied ambience found only in a select few time-honoured, lovingly constructed theatres and which purpose-built modern entertainment complexes somehow clinically lack. Coupled with the deafening Mackem roar, it never failed to raise the temperature.

In more recent times I was delighted to hear that the old place had undergone a costly makeover in 2004, thanks to a group of prudent, forward-thinking local councillors, thus ensuring its long-term future as a live entertainment venue.

Causes célèbres (a selection of famous personalities born in the city)

Kate Adie – intrepid BBC international reporter
James Bolam – *When the Boat Comes In* and *Likely Lads* actor
Bob Paisley – legendary Liverpool FC manager
Dave Stewart – record producer and Eurythmics co-founder

Bob Willis – hostile England bowler (cricket)
Bryan Ferry – Roxy Music frontman
Nat Jackley – music-hall comedian (once likened to the band's rhythm
    guitarist, Trevor)

Essential travelling band info

Favourite live music venue: Empire Theatre, Quayside
Favourite curry house: Backwaters, Thomas Street – 70%
Favourite pub: Fitzgeralds, Green Terrace – 72%
Don't miss: National Glass Centre, Liberty Way – 80% (if you like things made
    of glass!)
Sense of humour/friendly welcome: 63%

Chapter 2
Aberdeen

THE CONSTANT GRIND OF TOURING as part of a band can be draining at the best of times, hampered by the daily upheaval of unpacking and repacking one's things before setting off for yet another town, drinking until all hours in local clubs and watering holes, followed by a nightcap in the hotel bar, and surviving largely on junk food and cooked breakfasts. It all takes its toll, even leading occasionally to fugue states.

On a miserable, drizzly morning in early springtime I rose from my pit, stretched and drew back the faded, ineffective curtains of my hotel room, which had leaked in daylight from the very moment when the dawn chorus struck up, around the time I'd finally hit the sack after a foolhardy soirée with the boys in the downstairs bar. As the beginnings of a severe hangover preyed on the impaired brain cells floating around the innards of my uncoordinated cranium, I wiped away the condensation from the window with my sweatshirt sleeve and observed what appeared to be row upon row of derelict sheds adjacent to a railway siding. In the distance through the haze I could just about make out a conglomeration of imposing-looking granite buildings. As I discharged a long, gaping yawn and rubbed my rheumy eyes, an odd sense of loss swept through my befuddled skull, as the realisation dawned that I had no recollection whatsoever as to where I physically was.

The large old Victorian hotel, albeit grand in stature, was clearly trading on past glories, furnished with chipped antiques, straggly carpets and a toiling central heating system that gurgled and clunked throughout the night. Crouching forwards, I caught my finger opening a splintering bedside drawer in the hope of finding a sheet of stationery or indeed anything that may help identify the unknown location, unearthing nothing but a lone Gideon Bible.

Casting an eye towards the clock I saw that the hour had crept around to 11.30am. By now the breakfast leftovers would be long consigned to the waste-bins and, though my churning constitution hankered for a bacon sandwich, a small pack of Bourbon biscuits represented the only nourishment on offer to kick-start what would doubtless pan out into a tiresome day.

As I tottered towards the en-suite loo, the wall-mounted telephone chirruped into life, its shrill tone penetrating through my grey matter like a pneumatic drill. In a pained stupor I plucked the receiver from its rest.

'Excuse me sir, but checkout time is supposed to be eleven o'clock!' the receptionist related with an air of authority in a snooty Scottish twang.

'Pardon me for asking, but would you mind telling me where I am?' I quizzically croaked, paying little heed to her plea.

'This is the Station Hotel,' the girl haughtily replied.

'Yes but where actually are we? What town?' I inquired with a hint of desperation.

'Don't be silly now, I wasn't born yesterday, you're trying to pull my leg aren't you?' she implied with a prudish titter.

'B… but, I honestly d… don't…' I stammered, only to be put in my place as the girl interrupted:

'You have an unpaid bar bill for £67.40p. I'd appreciate it if you could vacate the room and settle this account as soon as possible.'

'How the hell did I spend that amount? It's no wonder I have a bloody thick head! Look, I'm sorry, but I'm being deadly serious – what city is this hotel in?' I gasped, letting slip a muffled expletive into the mouthpiece.

'Good lord man! You're in Aberdeen in Scotland – are you having an attack of amnesia?' she blurted out, immediately hanging up.

****

Known as the Granite City, Aberdeen's most high-profile theatre during the 1970s went by the name of The Capitol, prominently positioned on Union Street and erected on the site of an old cinema in 1933. Fashioned on three levels highlighting the Art Deco interior, hidden to the rear spiralled a warren of narrow corridors and dressing facilities accessed by a precarious concrete staircase and situated over four floors.

The most spacious of the designated changing areas and the only room capable of accommodating a full complement of eight band members sat atop the multi-storeyed building, perched like a crow's nest with uninterrupted panoramic views opening up from the high-sided windows across the sprawling city. Once we had energetically scaled the lofty stairway to make ourselves at home, the enclosure quickly resembled the set of a *Teletubbies* TV episode, illuminated by a blinding array of brightly coloured Teddy-boy outfits dangling conspicuously from a long metallic clothes rail to create a Crimplene rainbow across the rear wall.

****

Working on a theory based on hitting our audiences 'right between the eyes', the band's rousing opening gambit shook the old foundations, featuring Eric Coates' *Dambusters Theme*, interspersed with explosions and a piercing pre-recorded tannoy announcement blasting into the auditorium at a huge rate of watts through the mountainous PA rig. Powering into a guitar-laden rendition of Edvard Grieg's classical epic *In the Hall of the Mountain King*, the five instrumentalists acquitted themselves with aplomb, niftily sidestepping through a neatly choreographed stage routine to screams of anticipation from a caboodle of excited teenage girls, interlaced with a plentiful din of whoops and hollers from the majority of fervid attendees making up the crowd.

With the overture's crescendo drawing near, the three featured vocalists on the introductory song – myself included – awaited our cue, nervously adjusting our bootlace ties, hearts palpitating nineteen to the dozen in an immeasurable adrenaline rush. Reverberating around the hall, the final strident chord petered out beneath a tumultuous cacophony of cheers whilst the up-tempo intro to the first vocal number burst into life, heralding the arrival of the lingering trio, set to emerge from the wings to take centre stage and launch in triplicate into the opening verse.

To the frantic backbeat of Little Richard's *Ready Teddy* pumping lustily from the pulsating sound system, we three muppets appeared through a side door that we had foolishly assumed led to the main platform but which in fact brought us directly onto the first-floor balcony, startling the chock-full turnout of shocked and equally disoriented concertgoers.

As we halted dead in our tracks, the spotlight frenziedly veered upwards attempting to latch onto the misguided, red-faced strays, who – peering down to the level below – could only watch the stunned band improvise, allowing ample breathing space for the three stooges to scamper, tails between legs, to the correct access point.

Suffice to say an exuberance of ironic cheers augmented the shrill girlish screams as the humbled threesome finally made our big entrance, eager to put the Keystone Cops charade behind us and go about our business with a degree of panache.

The sheer scale of the hysteria in evidence at those heady late-seventies shows at times bordered on frightening, underlined when a botched getaway added to the woes of the earlier humiliation thanks to a preoccupied driver failing to notice I hadn't quite made it into the vehicle's rear seat. As I teetered backwards from the open door, a group of maniacal teeny-boppers gripped onto a lock of my hair apiece, dragging me deliriously to the floor. A pair of muscular minders hurried to the rescue, heroically tearing into the pack of untamed hellcats to wrestle free their prey, prior to manhandling my shaken torso into the car, which in a cloud of burning rubber dramatically screeched from the loading bay.

The case in point illustrated but one of a catalogue of close shaves where the majority of band personnel flirted with physical injury, raising genuine fears for our safety and prompting a major rethink, essentially in an effort to outfox the rampant hordes by devising a range of incognito methods of getting to and from the venues. Before long the familiar grimy theatre changing rooms had given way to plush hotel suites from which the band were transported in full regalia directly to each venue's stage door courtesy of blacked-out vans and minibuses, allowing ample time to tune up and deliver the goods, prior to frantically bolting from the building as the final chord sounded, giving the hordes little time to gather and allowing us to make the return sortie in one piece.

****

With the band undertaking a further string of concerts north of the border some eighteen months later, the back-to-back schedule again included the oil-rich Granite City, paving the way for a return to the Capitol with the added bonus of a more comfortable stopover on the outskirts of the city in the snazzy and upmarket Holiday Inn hotel.

Once more riding high in the charts with our lucky thirteenth single 'I Wonder Why', we observed as we pulled into the drop-off zone that the gathering of pimply-faced adolescents armed with items of memorabilia for signing had taken on a somewhat different look, being swelled by a posse of heavily pierced, sombre-looking disciples clad from head to toe in black. It transpired that jetting in from Germany at some point in the day for a one-off gig at the city's University was none other than heavy metal band Black Sabbath, complete with frontman Ozzy Osbourne, whose headline-gracing escapades in recent times had earned him the tag of the Wild Man of Rock, and who just so happened to be booked into the same hotel.

While we passed the time autographing a mishmash of album sleeves and body parts ahead of checking in, the faithful metalheads looked on, indulging in a spot of good-natured ribbing, accentuated by wolf-like howls together with a feeble chant of: 'Ozzy Ozzy Ozzy,' to which the sheep responded: 'Oi-Oi-Oi!'

Bedraggled from their early start, the weary Brummie boys eventually arrived mid-afternoon, receiving short shrift from our own cluster of devotees. Slouching towards reception, they set down their belongings, in sore need of a pick-me-up and craving refuge in the lobby bar. Acknowledging their poppy counterparts happily ensconced at a corner table and pulling up a chair, the haggard rockers engaged in a similarly wacky line of conversation, sharing a touch of common ground by also hailing from the Midlands and swapping a few home truths, belying the deep, dark satanic personae prevalent among the gossipmongers, prior to both bands being cajoled into heading our separate ways.

****

Spurred on by a moonstruck audience and after yet another sell-out concert the buoyant mood in the camp extended to the hotel bar, resulting in a prolonged session that extended way past 2am until, gallingly, the surly barman put up the towels and drew down a protective metal cage, thus preventing any forbidden access to the bar.

'You've got to be joking mate! The party's just getting started, and your gaffer's bound to be over the moon with the takings – give us another hour… please,' Geoff beseeched.

'It's alright for you lot, you'll be sleeping in 'til lunchtime. Some of us have got homes to go to!' the bolshie steward griped. Ignoring all bribes and adamant that the bar would under no circumstances be reopened, he clicked a padlock into place at the top of the enclosure and flitted off, accompanied by a less than complimentary chorus of disapproval.

Holding back until the coast was clear, we remained inconspicuous behind a tableful of empty glasses. A hint of mischief pervaded the room, foreshadowing a cunning plan hatched to breach the offending grille ahead of pilfering an emergency supply of urgently needed bottles, displayed enticingly on a row of glass shelves barely a metre from our grasp.

Opening each night's show with a thirty-minute set, a four-piece Bay City Rollers spin-off going under the name of Rosetta Stone made up the bill, featuring the tartan heart-throbs' former member Ian Mitchell, who – seeking a little recognition in his own right as well as cashing in on the Scots' magic formula – had opted to go his own way, forming the offspring in tandem with the Rollers' renowned one-time manager Tam Paton.

Priding himself on an engaging, albeit puckish personality, Ian's fraternal instincts endeared him to the boys on the few occasions we'd met during his BCR years, never taking life too seriously and well-liked by one and all. Lithely fit, slight of frame and always up for a dare, here was the lucky break needed and in seconds flat it was unanimously decided to put our young partner in crime's friendship to the test.

To the top of the metal grille lay the tightest of openings; however, with the padlock attached to the far right-hand side, should the cage be forced from the opposite end it appeared there may just be sufficient space to prise through the head and shoulders of a slender human being, a task for which Ian fitted the bill perfectly.

With all hands on deck gripping the cage rim, the thirsty pranksters tugged and yanked with all our might until finally the framework buckled, leaving a tapered gap in the top corner, after which Ian was hoisted aloft similar to a corpse on a sea of hands at a fanatical religious rite and propelled towards the aperture like a human battering ram. His eyes tightly closed, and skin scraping against the abrasive metal, remarkably the scapegoat's head popped through the recess, though on the brink of reaping our just desserts the rigid torso halted, budging no further and rendering the hoodlums high and dry. We shoved hard one more time in frustration, and – amid a clatter and pained yell – Ian's bruised torso suddenly thrust forward through the top of the cage in a nosedive towards the tiled floor, thankfully coming to a stop as every hand on deck clung on for dear life, preventing the scallywag from landing on his head.

Suspended upside down, Ian athletically twisted his upper body back towards the interior of the grille, heaving his feet from our grasp and somersaulting inside, triggering high-fives amongst his joyful accomplices.

Suddenly, in an unexpected blaze of activity akin to a big-screen drugs bust, dazzling lights filled the dimly lit room announcing the arrival of a grim-faced column of armed men decked from head to toe in blue combats.

'What the fuck is going on down here?' barked a stocky senior officer, whose broad London accent seemed oddly out of place.

'We're in deep shit now!' I muttered, motioning through the grate to the incarcerated Ian to duck down out of harm's way.

'We're searching for a fourteen-year-old female named Jackie, who we understand may be in one of your rooms… The girl's parents have reported her as missing, informing us she was last seen at a rock concert here in Aberdeen. We've also received a tip-off she was invited back to this hotel by a long-haired musician!' the head honcho boomed.

Stunned, we warily eyeballed one another, knowing full well not a soul present had any inkling whatever as to the girl's whereabouts. The lawman's beady eyes diverted briefly to the act of vandalism perpetrated barely a hair's breadth away, arousing visions of a sharp rap on the knuckles for a violation not remotely connected with the case at hand. Thankfully, it prompted nothing more than a dismissive sigh before the abusive diatribe continued: 'I and my enforcement team are about to turn your fucking rooms downside-up. What's more I expect your full cooperation, and if there's just so much as a fuck… C'mon let's get started!'

Deserting the hapless Ian, still stranded in the cage, the suspects were led via a disorderly route march into reception. One by one our surnames were bawled out in schoolmasterly fashion by one of the badges and checked against the register, after which the marked men, resembling an unshackled chain gang, were chaperoned in single file to our bedchambers.

'Hey, hold on a sec,' Geoff suddenly called out, taking everyone by surprise. 'We're not the only band staying here tonight: Black Sabbath checked in this afternoon!'

'What? Well somebody had better get all their fucking names and room numbers including the road crew... *now!*' the main man demanded.

In macho style reminiscent of a Schwarzenegger movie, the heavy-handed cops crashed through the fire doors adjacent to the lift, scaled the emergency staircase three steps at a time and galloped along the corridors, unnecessarily kicking at doors with their hefty boots to rouse the unsuspecting guests, all in the hope of earning a few brownie points and snaring a shamefaced performer with the underage adolescent.

Meanwhile, personally shepherding a splinter group into an available lift, the chief firebrand metamorphosed into a chatty and approachable individual, making light of the situation which apparently served as a welcome distraction from the treadmill of domestic violence and drunken disorderliness regularly ascribed to his watch.

The lift had barely halted at the third floor when a perspiring, florid-faced deputy, who had evidently sensed a breakthrough, came hurtling along the hallway and darted through the opening doors, breathlessly accosting the main man and indicating the girl may be in room 301.

'Wait here and don't move a muscle,' the top dog ordered, hotfooting along the corridor in pursuit of his colleague and pausing outside of the said room, gaining entry using a pass key and tiptoeing as quietly as a mouse into the chamber.

Shuffling a little closer to eavesdrop on the dialogue taking place, all we could hear was a burst of spontaneous laughter from the mouths of the police guys, who soon reappeared back onto the landing clutching their stomachs.

'What the fuck's going on man?' asked a disoriented, lily-white-skinned specimen, clad in nothing but a pair of odd socks and pince-nez spectacles, turning the air blue with a tirade of further obscenities in a slurred Black Country accent before wandering aimlessly down the corridor in the opposite direction.

'God only knows what he's been on, we just had to scrape him off the ceiling,' laughed the chief, allowing us in on the joke and nodding towards Ozzy, whilst with his hands full the second officer ushered the apparition back to his sleeping quarters.

Contrary to the slapstick spectacle down below, the over-the-top SWAT team wreaked havoc on the fourth floor, tossing mattresses upside down, turning drawers inside out and rummaging through wardrobes in a scene of utter chaos, much to the displeasure of the swarm of paying guests spilling out into the passageway incensed at the awakening.

Undaunted and defiant the sneering Gestapo pressed on, searching every nook and cranny until at last the operation ground to a halt, confirming neither touring party had abducted the missing teenager, if indeed she was in the building at all.

'It would appear we've been on a wild goose chase – sorry to have bothered you chaps,' was the best the CO could offer, turning tail and summoning his troops, who obeying orders disappeared in a blur down the fire escape and out of the hotel. Watching from an upstairs window as the armoured car screamed from the car park akin to a movie trailer from *The French Connection*, someone asked the obvious question: 'What happened to Ian? Surely he can't still be locked in the cage… can he?'

With Rambo and his band of extras making themselves scarce, the relieved mob sped down to the basement where we chanced upon a variation of a drunken comedy routine. The sound of clinking bottles and barely audible gaga chat, embellished by baby-like squeals of delight and the odd hiccup, could all be heard emanating from the floor of Ian's pen where he sprawled, surrounded by screwed-up crisp packets and a row of scattered empties and best described as paralytic!

Left little choice but to come clean and face the music, Geoff tottered off to alert the night porter, who appeared to be shirking his duties and lying low. Stumbling with a faltering gait towards the bar, the old boy gasped in horror whilst surveying the rat's nest before turning back towards his cubbyhole to raise the alarm.

'Whoa there… I'm really sorry mate, we all know this is bang out of order, but I guess you could say it's been one of those nights,' I owned up, lightly grabbing the guy's shoulder and slipping him a twenty-pound note.

'In the light of all the disturbances tonight, if you'll help me get this mess cleaned up I'll be willing to overlook the matter,' he acquiesced, looking sheepishly either side of him and discreetly pocketing the note, as jangling keys at the ready he stooped to remove the padlock, ducking underneath the flap and sneaking into the bar. 'I might need a little help here lads, your pal's in a bit of a state,' he cackled, quietly adding in Ian's ear: 'Come on sonny, let's get you out of here.'

Out cold from toppling backwards and clouting his head, Ian was now a dead weight which the rescuers dragged through the narrow gap, dumping the carcass onto a sofa before rummaging in his pockets for the room key and preparing to haul the body into the lift.

Third-floor bound, the elevator pinged to a halt at the ground level, where rooted in all their finery a well-groomed couple looked on aghast at the debauched carry-on before their eyes, recoiling a metre or more as the man shielded his spouse from the iniquity.

'Hold fire darling, there's sure to be another one along any second,' the dinner-suited toff reacted, shying away as the doors closed to, thus allowing the unruly brigands to dispose of the body in its final resting place for the night.

****

Barely six months on from his drunken confinement in north-east Scotland, Ian Mitchell walked out on Rosetta Stone. The news of his departure saddened his abettors, revealing that the young bass player had relocated to Los Angeles to try his luck (and libido) in the booming late-seventies US erotic film industry.

Just a few months later we found ourselves once again rubbing shoulders with the Sabbath boys, for a co-appearance on *Top of the Pops* at the BBC Television Centre. In his unique and endearing West Midlands drawl Ozzy somehow recalled the night in question, humorously commenting: 'I tell you what, my arsehole was going half-a-crown-sixpence when those coppers stormed into me room. I could hardly believe it when they didn't cart me off in their paddy wagon, 'cause they must've known I was high as a fucking kite!'

Causes célèbres

Annie Lennox – charitable female singer
Isobel Barnett – TV celebrity (who also resided in Leicestershire for many years)
Graeme Garden – of *The Goodies*
Denis Law – Manchester United footballing legend
Lou Macari – Manchester United footballer
Billy Bremner – guitarist (who played on a handful of my solo recordings)

Essential travelling band info

Favourite live music venue: The Lemon Tree, West North Street
Favourite curry house: Echt Tandoori, Echt, near Aberdeen – 80%
Favourite pub: Moorings, Trinity Quay – 77%
Don't miss: Footdee, a quaint fisherman's village a little way along the coast, absolutely enchanting – 89%
Sense of humour/friendly welcome: 58%

Chapter 3
Armagh

THE 'TWIN' CATHEDRAL CITY OF Armagh in Northern Ireland could never in idealistic terms be described as the most favoured of the seventy townships featured in this journal. Putting it bluntly I possess an inherent dislike of the place, based solely on my own experiences in the course of one too many visits to the area spanning the previous three decades.

'If anyone should ask what you're doing in the vicinity you must *not* at any cost divulge you are working for the armed forces,' ordered an army officer during a briefing prior to entertaining Her Majesty's troops stationed in the province some years ago, at a time when the Troubles remained a serious threat. Fair to say the introduction to the region was far from ideal, but even during peacetime the city seems to retain a kind of restlessness and hostility no longer prevalent in most of Ulster's other large towns, unsettlingly far removed from the outgoing welcome afforded the band during frequent visits to the territory over a number of years.

****

'I've booked the entire party into the Charlemont Arms in Armagh for three nights – it's a half-decent hotel and a good central location for you to travel from,' crowed promoter Mickey at the beginning of a mid-noughties tour, believing he'd done everyone a favour.

'Bloody hell, do we have to?' groaned Trevor disapprovingly. 'I can't stand that town!' Having taken the words out of my mouth he spun around and lurched off, cantankerously muttering beneath his breath, unaware the majority of the guys empathised totally.

The same afternoon the rented people-carrier jammed full of personal effects pulled up outside the hotel, with the party instantly brought to task by a tubby, overzealous employee running out onto the street and bossily blurting: 'You can't park that vehicle there! It's just a drop-off point. It'll have to be moved immediately!'

'Do you mind if we just unload our stuff first, or perhaps you might even like to help us if your blood pressure is up to it!' I snapped, my words falling on deaf ears as, tail between his legs, the jumped-up underling scuttled away.

'He was just a bacon-faced kid; don't you think you came down a bit hard on him?' Rod preached, watching me sign the register.

'What, Billy Bunter? He was in my face from the word go and wasn't exactly blessed with the best of manners himself... Mind you, there's something about this town that puts me on edge!' I explained, fighting my corner.

'Yeah, I know what you mean. Anyway, do you fancy something to eat before we leave for the gig?' my pal enquired.

'Yep, I could eat a scabby donkey – shall I see you down here in fifteen minutes? Something cheap and cheerful will do me!' I replied, looking in vain for assistance and struggling up the narrow staircase with my bags.

Downstairs in the deserted café, skipping a starter I opted for a high-carb spaghetti bolognese while a voracious-looking Rod plumped for two courses, consisting of homemade vegetable soup followed by a mixed grill. The soup quickly arrived and I looked on, slurping at a refreshing cup of strong sweet tea and with stomach rumbling, as he shovelled spoonful upon spoonful of liquidised carrots and potatoes into his gaping orifice, making satisfied grunts whilst savouring each mouthful.

Suddenly a waiter wearing yellow oven-gloves sprang through the kitchen's swing-doors, frantically rushed to the table with two piping hot plates of food, shoved one right under my nose and plonked the other down just to the side of my colleague's soup bowl.

'Excuse me, but I'm still eating my starter – I'm not ready for the main course yet!' Rod scowled, tearing a strip off the attendant, who unhesitatingly fired back: 'Well, when you are, there it is,' before sloping off back to the cookhouse.

Unable to contain myself I burst into a fit of the giggles. This accidentally resulted in an unwanted morsel of pasta escaping from my lips to decorate the top of Rod's platter, drawing a distraught response: 'Oh, that's just fucking great – somebody tell me this isn't happening!' Performing a surgical dissection on the bespattered piece of meat and pushing the defiled cut to the edge of his plate, the bass player further bellyached: 'Besides, you could scarcely call this a mixed grill, two bloody bangers and a lamb chop; still I suppose it'll have to do!'

Precariously rattling on their hinges the saloon doors again swung open forerunning the *garçon*'s presence at the tableside armed with an unmarked bottle of mineral water, which suspiciously looked to be straight from the tap.

'How can you call this a mixed grill? There's only two different items on the plate!' my grumpy senior admonished.

'Ah well now, if you look at the menu it actually says "Mick's Grill", and Mick is the Christian name of the chef,' the waiter audaciously replied.

Disbelieving, mouth agape, I grabbed for the menu and scanned it in haste. Sure enough in black and white there it was: *Mick's Special Grill – a sumptuous feast of spicy sausage, gammon steak and tender Irish lamb chop, freshly prepared at our grill-bar.*

'There's no way I would've swallowed that if I hadn't seen it with my own two eyes; but where's the bloody piece of gammon?' Rod bickered, before listening to a string of excuses topped off with: 'Ah well, you won't have to swallow anything of the sort – we ran out of bacon at breakfast, but to make up for it you got an extra sausage!'

'Gammon isn't the same as bacon you dodo! You must get some fucking wankers coming in here and putting up with this kind of service,' Rod flipped, looking to the heavens.

After pausing for the briefest of moments, the smartass waiter delivered a crushing knockout blow: 'Not before today, sir,' stirring images of a boxing match where the referee is obliged to rush in to stop the fight and prevent any further punishment.

Adding insult to injury the conquering hero subsequently returned, plonking down the bill on a tarnished silver platter accompanied by two sweaty After Eight mints evidently purloined from the Rowntree's 1962 launch party. Balking at the outrageous prices, arms folded and utterly deflated, Rod somehow remained silent, whilst from my own perspective the sheer entertainment value had been worth every penny.

****

The greasy morning fry-up followed in much the same fashion, miserably failing to satisfy the taste buds and more resembling the fare at a run-down transport café, though contrary to the previous afternoon the service was cordial and on the ball.

Having slipped surreptitiously from the bar, hoarse as a crow in the wake of the previous night's gig and anxious to rest my overtaxed vocal chords, I was now refreshed from eight hours' shut-eye. Armagh's streets awaited and, with time on my hands to take a good look around prior to an early-evening soundcheck, I headed towards the hotel's main entrance, zipping up my thick winter jacket.

'You wouldn't happen to have such a thing as a tourist map… would you?' I enquired of the receptionist, soon wishing I hadn't bothered.

'Uh… a what?' the frosty assistant asked, gawping at me as if I'd grown a second nose. Assuming the answer to be a resounding *no*, I scurried through the squeaking revolving doors to brave the great outdoors.

Barely having scratched the surface but finding little of real interest, I momentarily drew to a halt, fascinated by the sight of an unkempt man hopping awkwardly on the pavement outside the clothiers from which he'd emerged, removing his shoes and socks. As I looked on, mesmerised and enjoying the diversion, the itinerant produced a fresh pair of chequered hose from a brown paper bag, slipping the items onto his callused feet and lacing up his badly scuffed footwear, before dumping the cast-offs into a nearby litter-bin. Ambling past the humming receptacle I became aware of a ghastly, aged-cheesy smell emanating on the breeze, causing the passers-by to screw up their noses. Clamping my fingers over my own nostrils, I made to cross the road for a breath of unpolluted air.

Just away from the main drag accessed by a pathway down into a sprawling dip stood the hugely impressive modern twin-spired cathedral. Putting on a spurt I set off towards it, though becoming a trifle confused whilst passing a street sign depicting *St Patrick's Cathedral* pointing in the opposite direction. Paying little heed, figuring it to be the work of practical jokers, I strode on purposefully, wending my way up the steps to the arched entrance eager to take a peek inside.

I stepped to one side to make way for a heavily robed priest ambling slowly towards the exit. The holy man faltered, tilting his head to one side whilst analysing my confused expression, and piously enquired: 'Is something troubling you, my son?'

'Not so much troubling me Father, but I couldn't help but notice a sign indicating that St Patrick's Cathedral is over on the other side of town; surely there can't be more than one in Armagh… can there?' I humbly pried.

'Ah, now you're asking; there are many folk in this diocese that would have you believe that, but I can assure you that this beautiful edifice is the one and only official Catholic cathedral!' he confirmed in a robust Ulster twang, cleverly bypassing the question.

Offering my thanks with a rueful smile I lingered on, peacefully sauntering along the pristine aisles between polished oak pews. As I sneaked by so as not to disturb the smidgen of devotees kneeling in prayer, all of a sudden the penny dropped: 'Ah, I get it – what if…?' and I strode back outside to check out the ancillary Church of Ireland building.

A small gathering of bystanders partially blocked the untidy thoroughfare, where upon closer inspection I saw a young boy of eleven or twelve lying literally in the gutter, hands clamped over his right eye and obviously in agony.

'Is he okay – is there anything I can do to help? What happened?' I asked of the woman kneeling over the wailing kid.

'That chubby little bastard Connor fired a pebble from his catapult straight into the lad's eye, but I already called an ambulance. If you catch the beggar maybe you could give 'im a good tompin' on my behalf!' she cussed, breathing fire.

'I'm sorry… a good what?' I asked, narrowing my eyes.

'A tompin'… T-H-U-M-P… be Jesus don't you understand fuckin' English?' she countered, jumping down my throat.

'Ah, you mean give him a thump?' I fathomed out with a snigger.

'That's what I bloody well said, didn't I?' she snapped, comforting the boy and contemptuously waving me away.

****

The unquestionably more ancient though less awe-inspiring sanctuary stood rather wistfully, tucked away atop a hillside behind a mini-matrix of back streets. Draped above the entrance was a weather-stained banner canvassing for funds, which from the look of it were desperately needed for the decrepit building's upkeep.

As I ducked inside the cheerless edifice a forbidding shivering sensation seeped beneath my skin, oozing through to my bones. Sensing my ecclesiastical cup had run empty, within minutes I made tracks back to the main street, craving a warming brew. I opted for a tucked-away greasy spoon, anxious to steer clear of the scene of Rod's earlier humiliation.

I instantly realised I'd chosen badly as a dozen or more heads twisted around, each one giving me the eagle eye, chatting furtively under their breath as if caught in the middle of an underhanded deal I'd by chance uncovered. I scanned the room for a place to sit and a scornful couple sidled along from the adjoining row of seats spreading out onto the sole unoccupied table, mumbling hoarsely to their companions and causing my hackles to rise. Wisely deciding against making a scene I exhaled a huge sigh, gritting my teeth whilst clocking the culprits studying my reaction.

'What-do-you-want?' a slovenly, obese girl snorted from behind the counter, coming as a stark reminder that perhaps the service may not be up to scratch and prompting a facetious response: 'I don't suppose there's any chance of a snog…!' as I darted for the door to make for the hotel, where hopefully the company may be more agreeable.

****

Falling short of expectations the gig had been at best an uphill struggle, though in truth an under-par band had failed to fire on all cylinders, hampered by a sub-standard rented-in sound system and a tight-fisted theatre administration content to skimp on its heating bills, all making for a disappointingly uninspiring spectacle.

Opting for a couple of late beers as opposed to a post-mortem, pleasingly we found the ambience in the hotel lounge was both lively and convivial. That was until Romeo caught my attention from the far end of the bar, drawing a finger across his throat and disdainfully raising his eyebrows.

'What's up?' I queried, squeezing in alongside and hailing a barman.

'Oh, there was just some drunken arsehole giving the English a right slagging-off, but with a bit of luck he may have pissed off,' the drummer explained.

Regrettably, the firebrand hadn't left at all and within seconds came shoving his way back to the space he'd vacated, visibly aggrieved to come across another trespasser before grunting: 'Do you belong to that fucking English band?'

'Mm, I'm not sure I'd quite use the same terminology, but yes I am a singer in a band; why do you ask?' I calmly countered.

'You bastards killed my great-great-grandfather,' he moronically claimed.

'Oh really, that's interesting; did he suffer a heart attack at tonight's concert?' I sarcastically rallied, shifting uncomfortably.

'Huh, my family wouldn't waste their money lining your fucking pockets,' the busybody responded malevolently, putting my patience severely to the test.

'Listen sunshine, you believe what you want to believe but please don't try and drag me or my fellow countrymen into your little debate; now here's to Oliver Cromwell!' I retaliated, raising my glass and snubbing the idiot.

Having none of it, the ruffian ignorantly threatened: 'What did you just fucking say? That's fighting talk where I come from!'

Enough was enough, and with tempers fraying at the end of a tiresome day I was swivelling back round to voice my displeasure when, from out of nowhere, a crushing left hook landed squarely on the guy's chin, poleaxing him to the floor.

'You don't have to put up with that crap – my mother's half English,' conveyed a buck-toothed man draped from head to toe in black, standing over his prey whilst the night staff scurried over to revive the recumbent fool.

'Thanks for that mate! You're right though – he was bang out of order,' I yawped above the confusion, patting the peacemaker on the shoulder and taking a shufti backwards as the unconscious carcass was dragged from the bar.

'I was at your concert tonight and you guys worked your balls off; if it hadn't been bloody freezing in there you would've wrecked the place,' he complimented, slowly buttoning up his Crombie overcoat.

'Well, at least there's someone in Armagh with a good word to say – everyone's been grouchy as hell all day long,' I offered in jest.

'Christ almighty man, I'm not from this dump – I come from along the way in Portadown!' he bade, making for the exit.

Causes célèbres

Reverend Ian Paisley – vociferous ex-leader of the Democratic Unionist Party
(died 2014)
William McCrum – inventor of football's penalty kick

Essential travelling band info

Favourite live music venue: Groucho's Café, The Square, Richhill.
Favourite curry house: Shapla, Lower English Street – 36%
Favourite pub: Victoria Bar, Barrack Street – 13%
Don't miss: The road out of town!
Sense of humour/friendly welcome: 6%

Chapter 4
Bangor

TOWARDS THE END OF THE 1970s a wide variety of flourishing musicians, under the guidance of a savvy breed of financial advisors, spread their wings and booked studio time in a wealth of exotic climes to which they would jet off, sometimes for weeks on end, to record their eagerly awaited modern classics inspired by sandy beaches and wall-to-wall sunshine. Stimulated by a mushrooming tax-avoidance industry, accountants sought ways to skirt around the punishing income-tax rates (running as high as eighty-three pence in the pound) implemented by an incumbent Labour government under the leadership of Jim Callaghan, whose policies seemed hell-bent on driving the nation's most talented exports into exile to an extent that had become untenable.

Displaying an indifferent attitude towards escalating treasury demands and simply hankering to escape yet another winter of discontent, whilst most of the band's contemporaries were busy living it large in the Caribbean, Florida or at worst the south of France, Showaddywaddy were sent packing to Ireland's capital, Dublin.

Although I'd thus far enjoyed my visits to the fair city, undoubtedly one of Europe's great capitals, in early February the thought of donning shorts and a T-shirt beneath a clear blue sky seemed a vastly more enticing proposition. As if that were not enough, the potential headache of a pile of distractions virtually on the studio's doorstep looked set to prolong the task in hand at no little expense, thus defeating the original object of the exercise.

One such diversion came in the shape of a basement nightclub, concealed at the bottom of an alleyway just off O'Connell Street and situated midway between the studio and the band's hotel accommodation. Licensed until 3am the small venue possessed more of a pub ambience than that of its neighbouring glitzy city-centre establishments, proving the ideal place to unwind and relax after a long day's recording. Working the late bar shift the owner's pretty daughter Marina instantly caught my eye, and we hit it off over a post-session nightcap on more than one occasion.

By the time I finally plucked up the courage to make my move, I was dishearteningly unable to commit myself until the album was complete when a return trip to Dublin would be on the cards. Once back home, washed up from a fortnight of back-to-back eighteen-hour sessions and sorely in need of a little rest and recuperation, I took advantage of a few days' downtime during which a return to the home of Molly Malone seemed to fit the bill perfectly, providing not only a pick-me-up but a chance to get to know the young Irish head-turner. In a moment of madness and overly eager to impress I blundered badly, though, opting to show off my swanky set of wheels by driving all of two hundred miles to the port of Holyhead in Anglesey.

The ferry to Dun Laoghaire (pronounced *dun leery*) departed from the Anglesey port at 7.30pm, with the crossing expected to take around four hours. Should everything go according to plan I'd be ensconced in the fair city by 1am, clutching a pint of the black stuff with the damsel I'd travelled so far to see on the other arm. I was destined, however, on this occasion at least, not to make it to the Irish capital. An unexpected turn of events saw myself and my shiny Jaguar spending the night in what is affectionately known as 'the Athens of Wales', that being the tiny cathedral city of Bangor (though it would appear the town of Aberdare lays claim to a similar sobriquet).

****

The torturous journey commenced at the rather un-rock-and-roll hour of 7am, since I'd figured out the travel to Holyhead alone may take six or seven hours, disregarding a chance to stretch the legs and refuel both the tank and my innards, perhaps in some other out-of-the-way place of interest en route.

Four hours into the hike and still stuck on the M6 motorway, I cursed and swore at the constant stream of slow-moving traffic, deciding on an alternative route and weaving my way onto the old A55 road just outside of Chester. Shades wrapped round to shield my peepers from the blinding sunshine, relieved to be eating up the miles, I powered the five-litre engine ahead, curbed only by the low fuel warning light signalling a pit stop may be way overdue.

With visions of refuelling, taking a leak and grabbing a life-saving cup of tea, I spied an old milestone jutting from the grass verge depicting '*Rhuddlan 1 Mile*', soon after which I happened on a roadside garage. After I'd interrupted a pair of grease monkeys halfway underneath a rotting old Vauxhall, the more helpful of the twosome grudgingly rolled onto his knees, eyeing me with suspicion before rising and grunting in a Neanderthal tone: 'Uugh?'

'Can you fill her up please?' I asked civilly.

This was met with a further stream of indecipherable jabber, prompting a silver-haired old stager of eighty or more to hobble over and save the day, mumbling gutturally: 'Up to the brim eh?'

'Yes, if you don't mind… You wouldn't happen to know of a café in town where I might get a cup of tea and something to eat, would you?' I asked hopefully. My enquiry triggered off a hacking bout of coughing as, clunking the pump nozzle firmly into its berth, the old boy sloped away throatily chuntering to himself.

I followed in the man's footsteps over to a rickety old lean-to where the dust-bound till looked destined for *Antiques Roadshow*, and handed over a twenty-pound note. Like a bolt from the blue the human relic hoarsely growled: 'Two 'undred yards on yer roight,' stepping outside and waving his fist towards the main street.

'Have you thought about sucking a Fisherman's Friend?' I taunted, drawing on a well-used *double entendre*. I was swiftly forced to take evasive action as, clearing his throat and lurching forward, the yokel emitted a foul dollop of green phlegm onto the arid ground.

Sure enough, as the patriarch had so gruffly pointed out, barely a stone's throw along the street nestled between a small row of shops stood a secluded little café. Trapped within its walls I again felt strangely out of place, tuning into a light hubbub of conversation centring round the true purpose of the young outsider's visit. As I sat daydreaming and slurping at a mug of stewed builder's tea to help wash down a stodgy local delicacy known as a Welsh cake, the docks of Holyhead beckoned, while further afield on the far side of the Irish Sea hopefully a more cordial welcome awaited.

****

Crawling at a snail's pace on the outskirts of Bangor in yet another tailback, and watching the clock tick towards 4pm, I had just switched on the radio to catch up with the news when I felt the Jag judder alarmingly, followed by a bout of coughing and spluttering. This in turn gave rise to an outburst of foul-mouthed obscenities as I realised something untoward may have taken place forty miles back at the unwelcoming refuelling stop.

The temporary lights eventually blinked to green, goading the queue of vehicles over the uneven surface, but as I hit the throttle the car violently hiccupped, pointing towards mechanical problems. With thirty-odd miles to go and knowing less than nothing about engines and the like, I plumped to chance my arm, praying the glitch may miraculously correct itself.

Bearing left I caught my first glimpse of the infamous Menai Suspension Bridge, while glancing sideways I could see the white-capped Snowdonia peaks zigzagging on the distant horizon, all the while keeping tabs on the gridlock pottering towards the historic old structure. At last the hold-up began to abate, allowing the frustrated commuters to make their way home.

As I traversed the crossing apprehensively, the Menai Strait opened up to either side. Meanwhile beneath the bonnet the ailing mechanism hemmed and hawed, stubbornly indisposed, as nose to tail the convoy edged closer to Anglesey.

'Uh-oh,' I fretted when, roughly halfway across, the engine choked and stalled. This enraged the queuing motorists, most of whom honked impatiently and shouted a few choice words from behind the wheel as, alighting from the car, I despairingly held my hands aloft.

Fully twenty minutes passed before the first jam-sandwich weaved onto the scene, acting effectively to ease the mounting chaos and keep the traffic moving along unhindered. Meanwhile, I could do nothing but peer out over the strait, coerced as I was into a two-hour wait for the summoned tow-truck. Any hopes I harboured of making the ferry were dead and buried.

Not until twenty-four hours later did the XJS receive a clean bill of health when, garbed in freshly laundered white overalls, the sympathetic chief mechanic pointed out that the malfunction had been caused by an excess of water and red diesel accidentally finding its way into the fuel tank, adding that the system had been drained clean.

'I'm not so sure it was an accident!' I admitted, describing in detail my earlier encounter with the unscrupulous 'Rhuddlan Hillbillies'.

'Oh no, I've heard all about that family! It's the interbreeding, you know,' he divulged. Shaking his head in despair he pointed me in the direction of the Esso filling station, warning me in future to steer clear of 'cowboys' in rustic backwaters.

****

A little while later I was able to pour my heart out in a lengthy, apologetic phone-call to Marina after checking into a simple but comfortable guest house. Here my impromptu Bangor stopover took a turn for the better as I found myself killed with kindness, in total contrast to the boondocks barely an hour away along the coast, and the welcome afforded restored my faith in the human race.

Taking to the street I strolled to the city's main landmark, to be informed by a sightseeing egghead that the sixth-century cathedral had once been laid in ruins by the dastardly English as far back as 1211. Happily after centuries of committed renovation work it now stands proudly if unobtrusively within spitting distance of the town centre. Dazed from the earful and licking my lips, having savoured nothing but a lead-weight Welsh cake all day, I moved on.

Tagging along behind a clique of university students, most of whom bore strong Far-Eastern features, I happened on a bustling Italian diner, singling out the house speciality in the form of a delicious bowl of homemade ravioli.

With the hour fast approaching 10pm and figuring a flagon or two of ale may provide the perfect send-off to my digs, I dropped into a lively kerbside hostelry. Half expecting the chit-chat to shift from English to Welsh the moment I opened my mouth, I was pleasantly surprised to find instead a good-humoured cosmopolitan clientele. Climbing up onto a stool I ordered a jar of the local tipple from the trendy young barman.

As I gazed around, indulging in a spot of people-watching, a cluster of beaming faces acknowledged my presence, moving to one side to make room for a rotund Pavarotti lookalike who burst into the middle of the floor and powerfully belted out in his best dulcet tones: '*Let's go for a little walk, under the moon of love,*' presumably as a gesture of goodwill aimed at the unexpected new kid in town.

To my acute embarrassment, the entire pub – with the exception of a handful of addled senior citizens – erupted into song, pumping out their chests to make a helluva racket as they bellowed the lyrics to the band's chart-topping hit, led by the portly tenor. By now his veins were bulging from his head as, wearing a crazed expression, he sang right into my face.

Acknowledging their endeavours whilst laughing like a drain, I felt the woes of the day fading into oblivion, subdued by a bellyful of hops and barley. The sing-song continued well past the bewitching hour until, after singing myself hoarse in a half-crocked rendition of The Eagles' 'Hotel California', I staggered back in the direction of the hotel.

****

Up bright and early the next morning anticipating a prompt getaway, I overindulged on a full Welsh breakfast before shuffling to the payphone to call for a progress report on the car, only to be informed the mechanics were still working on the problem and estimating the vehicle may be ready just prior to the lunch break.

Again cursing my luck I set off along the city's outstretched High Street, essentially to kill a little time. I soon discerned that word was out the 'Show-wobbly-wobbly chap' (as a jovial baker put it) was in town, with virtually the entire local community bidding me good morning or 'yaki dah' ('*iechyd da*', literally 'good health'), whilst chirpily going about their daily chores.

The clutch of dexterous mechanics performed a sterling job on my pride and joy, which – boding well for the return journey – sounded as sweet as a nut. To my relief, although there for the taking I was far from skinned alive.

I subsequently rearranged my tryst in Dublin for later in the month, when unhesitatingly I opted to fly.

Causes célèbres

Dewi Bebb – Welsh international rugby player of renown
Harry Parry – jazz musician
Aled Jones – high-pitched child warbler and TV host
Sasha – internationally renowned club DJ

Essential travelling band info

Favourite live music venue: Theatr Gwynedd
Favourite curry house: Spicy Voujon, High Street – 50%
Favourite pub: Tap and Spile, Garth Road – 74%
Don't miss (or break down on): Menai Strait and Suspension Bridge – 69%
Sense of humour/friendly welcome: 81% (not including Rhuddlan)

Chapter 5
Bath

FEW VISITORS TO THE CULTURALLY rich World Heritage City of Bath would argue that as a historic centre of interest this architectural gem truly takes some beating. Majestic in its beauty, it provides the perfect setting for a brief getaway, always taking care to allow for the endless coachloads of blue-rinsed day-trippers converging on the main access routes.

Having visited the city on a number of occasions, taking in concert dates, corporate functions and even a high-society ball, it was clear that here was a place I needed to explore in far more detail. I had been seeking solace during a gruelling series of back-to-back tour dates in the autumn of 2004, and a gap in the calendar soon after the final date made this possible.

For the purpose of persuading any prospective rolling stones to drop anchor in this rewarding part of Britain, here follows an account of a leisurely twenty-four-hour jaunt around this most dignified of cities.

A day-tripper's unofficial guide to the city of Bath

Thursday

10.30am: Arrive at the outskirts where a bombardment of heavy traffic has ground to a frustrating standstill.

11.10am: Queue at car park some distance from the centre and locate space before digging deep for the pricey daily prepaid rate.

11.20am: Stroll briskly from the parking facility onto the busy Pierrepoint Street catching sight of the attractive Abbey, where on the west side angels can be seen escalating stone ladders on a stairway to the stars.

11.40am: Amble past the nearby bustling Grand Pump Room, but decide against a coffee in favour of returning to car to collect bags and check in at hotel.

12.30pm: Sample a scrumptious Bath bun washed down with a proper cuppa at Sally Lunn's Tea House, reputedly the oldest building in the city. Fully sated, amble over to join the not-too-lengthy queue for the Roman Baths Museum.

2.30pm: Having come highly recommended from various sources, the city's premier attraction, albeit costing an arm and a leg, did not disappoint at all, providing my other half and me with a fascinating hour or two of all things ancient Roman. Observing the pea-green waters of the Great Bath (which in truth looked a tad murky) I was transported back to an ostentatious era of opulence and greed, visualising a small bevy of milky-white, semi-naked nubile goddesses soaping down a battle-scarred centurion or pot-bellied consul, beatific in their reverie as the purifying liquid soothed their fatigued muscles or corpulent spare tyres.

Mounted upright and peering down upon the green-algae-covered pool stand a body of weather-stained statues (remarkably only erected in Victorian times) representing the illustrious Roman emperors including Vespasian, Agricola, Augustus and the mighty Caesar himself, creating a mystifying aura, whilst poised alongside the less celebrated governors of Britannia look on in begrudging awe.

In a second complex of baths located in the west wing, the beautifully preserved stumpy tiled pillars (which once produced the original concept of an underfloor heating system) aroused images of canoodling well-to-do public bathers, perhaps afflicted by other unsociable diseases but nonetheless unlikely to complain of chilblains.

Epitomising perhaps the most influential historical era of them all, the incomparable piece of Roman Britain in my view stands head and shoulders above the large majority of the UK's high-ranking tourist attractions.

3pm: Following a caffeine fix and a shared sandwich, a browse around the spanking new and tastefully constructed shopping mall seemed like a good idea. After admiring scores of antique Singer sewing machines assembled in a clothes store's unique window display, we moved on to the Jane Austen Centre which, with its meagre collection of relics and memorabilia, disappointingly paled into insignificance.

3.50pm: Bath's most famous and prestigious address, the Royal Crescent, in tandem with the nearby Circus represent two genuine masterpieces of Georgian architecture. The former's Number One residence provides an engrossing insight into eighteenth-century England and just how the city's aristocratic elite actually conducted their affairs, complete with original items of ornate furniture and staff attired in period costume; whilst within shouting distance the latter, said to be inspired by Rome's Coliseum, houses thirty-three outstanding mansions, once again demonstrating the decadent lifestyle of the period's upper-crust society.

4.45pm: With time pressing on and forgoing the 'must see' Assembly

Rooms, where historically the city's socialites gathered, it was briefly back to our brush-cupboard of a hotel room to pick up our swimwear and test out the recently renovated Thermae Bath Spa, an open-air rooftop pool in which the waters are purported to possess therapeutic qualities. Irritatingly, though, the facility was partially closed for maintenance with the sole functioning indoor pool booked out to a private party, who presumably wished to indulge in a Roman orgy of their very own!

5pm: Rolling back the years whilst passing the familiar and fabulous old Theatre Royal, it was off to the grandly named Royal Avenue for a peaceful stroll in the park away from the hullabaloo and carbon monoxide fumes of the rush-hour traffic. After gasping at the perilous antics of a trio of fearless skateboarders, we headed back to the hotel to freshen up.

6pm: The Old Green Tree pub, or 'the treehouse' as the cordial barman referred to the watering hole, became the chosen refuge for an evening heart-starter, extending to more than one as the subject of rugby union reared its head, along with a reminder of the long-standing rivalry between my hometown club 'The Tigers' and the old enemy Bath RFC. A friendly debate ensued, amounting to little more than facetious banter, until a nudge in the ribs from my glum-faced good lady emphasised the time was nigh to strap on the nosebag.

6.45pm: After some indecision we plumped for lisping Essex-boy Jamie Oliver's city-centre restaurant, an Italian-themed, informally stylish diner which ticked all the boxes without stinging the pocket too severely. Tucking into a sumptuous pasta dish my wife commented: 'You see that guy on the next table? I'm sure I know him from somewhere!'

As I indiscreetly turned my head, the blood drained from my face. There, perched together with his family and sipping a post-prandial coffee, was a man whose artistry and vocal ability I'd long admired and envied: namely, Peter Gabriel.

Throughout my career I'd rubbed shoulders with some extraordinarily famous people, many of whose names I've dropped in various chapters of this journal; but somehow this encounter was different as, dumbfounded and shifting uncomfortably in my chair, I failed even to acknowledge the virtuoso as our eyes briefly met. With the boot firmly on the other foot, like so many admirers for whom I'd signed cards, scraps of paper and even restaurant menus to appease, I was reduced to a startled, babbling wreck jolted by the normality of a musical paladin. Shortly afterwards he rose and sauntered from the clattering room, ruffling his young companion's hair on the way out.

'I should've nipped out to the car and got him to sign that CD we were playing on the way down,' I wittered to my unimpressed spouse.

'Stop acting like a child – the car park's a good mile from here. Besides, I'm sure he's got far more important things to do than hang around waiting for a star-struck fan!' she lambasted, bringing me tumbling down to reality with a resounding bump.

9.30pm: Suffering blurred vision whilst perusing the tourist guide in a dimly lit wine bar, and running on empty from fourteen hours of non-stop travelling and sightseeing, I sensed the hotel room calling. Time to put our feet up and plan the day ahead. With the woes of the world on the national news, within minutes the lights had gone out.

Friday

9am: Weaving out of the city adjacent to the River Avon and traversing the border into neighbouring Wiltshire brings the avid traveller to the enchanting market-town of Bradford on Avon, a place I'd vowed to revisit some years before whilst passing through pressed for time en-route to a one-off gig in nearby Trowbridge.

Kissed by the morning sunlight, the rambling sandstone buildings etched a glorious picture of rural England as, caught in slow-moving traffic, we crossed the ancient bridge, eventually parking up just a short stroll away from the township's heartbeat.

Worth a couple of hours of anyone's time and home to 'The UK's top tea place', a refreshing cup of char in the renowned Victorian Tea Shop provided a fitting finale to an absorbing twenty-four hours spent in a time-honoured neck of the woods, where old traditions have been upheld for centuries and stunning architecture in no need of a hare-brained fix stands supremely proud in all its untouched glory.

****

On a previous visit to the bewitching city as part of an arduous fifty-date package, the eclectic mix of street entertainers spread throughout the busy central zone proved irresistible to the eye. They included denim-clad Dylan-esque buskers; soaring divas bellowing out an aria from Puccini's *Turandot*; contemporary dancers skipping across the pavement in the midst of a parlous acrobatic routine; and, most noticeable of all, a plethora of outrageously robed and heavily made-up mime artists, each of whom spends hour upon hour literally perched still as stone on top of a wooden box. In recent years this has become a hugely popular activity and additional source of income amongst students the world over, but Bath's old-world byways provide the perfect backdrop and could arguably lay claim to being the UK's hotspot for partakers of this fascinating stoical art form.

On a personal note, it was without a doubt home to the most cunning daddy of them all. A small crowd had gathered, intrigued by a stock-still gallant knight complete with chain mail, mace, iron helmet and a glistening steel sword drawing parallels with King Arthur's Excalibur, perhaps intended as a mock-up of the bold monarch. I watched in fascination as, without so much as a twitch or blink of the eye, the skilled exponent took street mimicry to another level.

Dropping some items of loose change into the trouper's collection box, my bandmates and I forged ahead along the scenic lane before, disrupted by the shrill tone of my cell phone, I was forced into lingering behind. Dawdling and deep in conversation, from afar I noted that, despite a dwindling crowd, the swordsman remained still as stone. Suddenly I clocked a sheepish, hirsute guy scamper from a nearby antique shop to retrieve the cash from its overflowing container.

'No!' I huffed under my breath, sniffing a rat and curtailing the call, anxious to spill the beans to my companions. By now, though, they were long gone, and rather than catch them up I felt compelled to return to the statuesque dead ringer's pitch, where a fresh new crop of enraptured easy pickings had assembled, audibly praising the efforts of the Arthurian hero and rewarding him in kind. Keen to put my theory to the test, I lurked in a nearby café to lie in wait.

Yet again at a peaceful juncture the hippy sprinted towards the kitty, making off with a heap of coins and a handful of notes, gleeful at the afternoon's take, whilst the trilby hat belonging to a talented busker only yards away barely contained his bus fare home.

Stealthily tiptoeing from my hiding place, I squeezed behind a splintering plywood barrier protecting the warrior from the clutches of the philanthropic public. Snooping beneath the long purple robes draped across the figure's lower body and feet I found nothing more than a crudely erected wooden frame attached to the upper torso of a plastic mannequin.

As I scuttled back underneath the rail with the hem of the robe in one hand, the ear-piercing sound of Velcro ripping from the frame exposed the barefaced fraud to the stunned huddle, a sprinkling of whom scurried to the pot anxious to retrieve their donations before traipsing away grumbling in utter disgust.

Unperturbed by the exposure of his mean-spirited prank, within moments the money-grabber sped to his golden goose, quickly rectified the problem and prepared for the next batch of suckers, as shuffling guiltily away I could only admire his audacity and entrepreneurial nous.

Causes célèbres

Bill Bailey – comedian/actor
Tears for Fears – '80s electronic rock band
Ann Widdecombe – obese ex-politician
Jeremy Guscott – rugby pundit
Russell Howard – comedian
Ken Loach – film director

Essential travelling band info

Favourite live music venue: Theatre Royal, Saw Close
Favourite curry house: Panahar, Moorland Road – 67%
Favourite pub: Old Green Tree, Green Street – 84%
Don't miss: The Roman Baths, Stall Street – 90% (pricey admission fee)
Sense of humour/friendly welcome: 67%

Chapter 6
Belfast

ANYONE ABOVE THE LEGAL AGE of alcohol consumption hailing from Northern Ireland's intriguing capital may justifiably claim that their home city plays host to perhaps the finest of all of the United Kingdom's drinking establishments, namely the magnificent Crown Tap (a.k.a. the Crown Liquor Salon) situated in all its splendour on Great Victoria Street. Located within a hair's breadth of the notorious Europa Hotel (which during the hostilities carried the dubious tag of the world's most bombed place to stay), the grandiose inn fast became a familiar haunt of the band's entourage during a succession of visits to the province.

The Crown was once one of the most prominent of all the prospering, gaslit gin-palaces of the late nineteenth century; and, notwithstanding its visual allure from the street, the showpiece Victorian architecture of the interior exemplifies a long-lost era of meticulous craftsmanship, with a mind-blowing array of patterned wall tiles set against an ornately chequered mosaic floor, further complemented by an arresting vision of etched windows and mirrors, elaborate wood-panelling and highly polished brass taps. Ten elegant oak-carved cubicles run along either side of the capacious barroom, each complete with swing-doors, padded seats and a long table, thus allowing small groups of customers seeking a modicum of peace and quiet a little privacy away from the conviviality of the bustling lounge area.

On one particular excursion the band were based on the outskirts of the city in a comfortable contemporary hotel, sworn to secrecy as to the purpose of our visit (as guests of the British military forces). A joint task force of around twenty strong, consisting of off-duty army personnel, leggy dancing girls and four band members old enough to be their fathers, farted our merry way into the city courtesy of an unidentified khaki-green bus putting the passing public's lives at risk by emitting a fog of carbon monoxide fumes out onto the busy streets. Arriving through the lavish old watering hole's impressive pillared façade and fortuitously stumbling upon two vacant booths, we split up into two groups, with the avuncular quartet, a pair of showgirls and a trio of infantrymen sidling into the first snug within a whisker of the straggling nymphets and servicemen crammed next door.

'Who likes oysters? They're irrefutably the speciality of the house,' recommended old-school team leader Richard in a plummy radio voice, suggesting a dozen of the molluscs washed down with a pint of Irish stout was quite simply a match made in heaven and cueing a show of hands from more than half of the shebang.

In typically boisterous fashion as the flowing black stuff took effect, a selection of airborne bread-rolls, oyster shells and other garbage soon found its way over the partition into the neighbouring throng, who retaliating in kind slung missiles of their own, transfiguring the bibulous luncheon into a gleeful bun-fight.

'Shove up,' asked one of the girls, freeing herself from the mayhem of the adjacent cubicle but unnervingly looking on the verge of tears.

'What's wrong – why the long face? Are you missing your pals?' I pried, showing a hint of concern and making room for her curvy rear.

'No, no, it's not that at all; the loud-mouthed officer with the fair hair just got his dick out under the table and tried to put my hand on it,' she let on in disgust.

'Did he now?' I exclaimed, attracting the attention of my bandmates and intimating a little assistance was needed to tackle a spot of bother. 'You know how oysters are said to be an aphrodisiac? Well, it seems they worked their magic on that cocksure NCO,' I snitched.

'I've heard your neck goes stiff as you swallow one. I can't stand the bloody things; they're like giant dollops of phlegm!' Geoff distastefully portrayed.

'Never mind all that; what that knobhead just did to young Lucy was bang out of order. Officer or not, the jumped-up prick deserves a lesson,' I niggled.

Leaning into the abutting cubbyhole, I summoned the buzzcut braggart seated in the far corner. 'What can I do for you, sunshine?' he self-importantly snapped, put out at having to battle through a sea of legs.

I edged over towards the bar, where a crowd of dishevelled tipplers had assembled ready to put the world to rights. 'Sorry to bother you guys, but this virile young feller here has got something to show you!' I announced, instantly familiarising myself.

'Is that raight?' countered a cheery Ulsterman in an intrigued Northern tone, beckoning for his colleagues to join in the fun.

'Okay mate, here's your big chance. If you like getting your knob out in public, do it now and give us all a good laugh!' I urged the military man.

'What the fuck!' he replied, astonished at the brash request.

'Oh, I'm with you now – he's a fuckin' flasher is he? Come on then, son, this is no taime for modesty,' the local man enthused, entering into the spirit of things.

'Have you lost your fucking mind?' the young officer snarled, staring me down.

'Oh, that's rich that is! It's okay for you to go flaunting your dick to an innocent young woman but you're not man enough...'

'Dave, Dave,' interrupted the dancer, waving her arms frantically. 'It's not him – you've got the wrong guy!' In a cloud of dust, a similar-looking brother-in-arms could be seen surreptitiously making haste towards the exit.

Tightening on the spot and wishing the ground would swallow me whole, I gasped 'Oops!' and glanced apologetically at the wrongly accused man, whose clenched fists and hate-filled eyes displayed the most burning of desires to punch out my lights.

'Easy, tiger! Just put it down as a case of mistaken identity, son. Besides, you wouldn't want to strike a man who plainly needs glasses, now, would you?' the Irishman intervened, restraining the bruiser and taking some of the heat out of the situation. The offer of a conciliatory handshake was flatly refused, though, as my new adversary irately stormed from the taproom, blowing a gasket at the culpable sidekick in full view of the startled passers-by and a watchful Geoff stood on the pavement puffing at a gasper.

Back inside, a mini-session was well under way with the best part of the gang enjoying the craic with the quick-witted local wags busy reeling off gag after gag, mostly at my own expense, with all and sundry cracking up as each punchline was delivered.

'So Saddam Hussein out there thought you'd like to see his weapon of mass destruction, did he?' an unshaven guy put to the danseuse who, timidly nodding her head, burst into a prolonged fit of the giggles.

'That bloody show-off is thinking of retiring soon you know... but he's decided to stick it out a while longer!' ribbed the jovial ringleader.

'Haha! I personally thought he showed real balls!' another lad pitched in as the good-humoured banter continued unabated for the next half-hour or so.

Thinking better than to stir up a hornet's nest and perturb our hospitable employers, we quickly agreed for the matter to be swept under the carpet with no further action deemed necessary. Away from the spotlight, though, the blameworthy poseur received a stern ticking-off from his senior officer, along with an unexpected name-check during the evening's performance, when – also referred to as 'Private Parts' and 'Flash Harry' – the culprit's true identity was revealed, receiving his comeuppance at the hands of a gaggle of piss-taking cohorts.

****

The band's inaugural visit to the province in 1975 could only be described as a baptism of fire, again involving a strong military presence whose sole purpose was to ensure their high-profile visitors' safe passage from and back to a low-profile country retreat.

Knowing precious little as to the genuine impact of 'The Troubles', other than from contradictory media footage, we found the robust city's make-up seemingly plagued by a large, permanent storm-cloud hung over the dour surroundings. The effect was intensified by the paucity of taciturn residents scurrying to and fro, burdened with the weight of their own struggles.

The setting for our Ulster debut was to be the imposing Queen's University of Belfast. At a time when a majority of performers (at the beck and call of their cagey advisors) sidestepped the province, undaunted travellers were virtually assured of an indebted welcome, though what actually lay in wait was nothing short of astonishing.

Transferred from the out-of-town hideaway in two presidential-style limousines to a covert backstreet location, the troupe (conspicuously garbed in a range of splendiferous stage costumes) was ushered towards a brace of camouflaged armoured vehicles in which we crammed tightly together for a rocky diversion en route to the main campus. After bumping along a rutted back-road we pulled up outside the complex, where two enormous metal gates topped out with roll upon roll of barbed wire clanged apart. Behind them, it seemed, lay an entire battalion of armed fighting men clad in combats and padded protective gear, whilst fluttering deafeningly in a cloud of debris and dust a see-sawing military helicopter touched down, sliding back its doors for the dumbfounded gang to leap inside and strap ourselves to the inner chassis before plonking our twitching backsides onto the bench seats. Whirling back into the air, within a matter of seconds the chopper descended upon a flat gravelled rooftop where yet another subdivision of animated soldiers snaked in all directions remaining vigilant to face any imminent threat.

'Now!' yelled a crouched commando shielding an automatic weapon, urging the concert party with a forceful wave of the hand to sprint for our lives across the uneven asphalt and make for a concealed service entrance, where behind closed doors lay the relative tranquillity of the designated dressing rooms.

The gig itself sticks in the memory mostly for the right reasons, with in excess of a thousand formally attired undergraduates affording their visitors a euphoric welcome, culminating in a large assemblage of ecstatic revellers clambering up onto the stage to lend their support in a riotous rendition of our closing anthem 'Hey Rock and Roll'.

As we departed the stage to relentless cries of *more, more, more!* all of a sudden the building rocked on its foundations accompanied by a thunderous boom within close proximity to the university campus, serving as a chilling reminder of our true whereabouts and dampening any feelings of elation in a New York minute.

As we quaked in our brothel-creepers, relieved to be homeward bound in just a matter of hours, the equally grim-faced task force readied their shaken visitors for the return leg before fast-tracking the party in reverse, up above the chimney pots and back down to reality, deeply grateful to be out of harm's way.

****

2012 saw the sad loss of two much-loved and prominent celebrity characters, both of whom had graced the UK's TV screens for going on half a century.

An incessant jokester, Belfast-born Frank Carson's inexhaustible supply of gags fuelled a career spanning in excess of sixty years. He frequently worked alongside the band at club and corporate functions from way back in his *Comedians* days, sadly for the final time just eighteen months before his passing.

Frank's affable and approachable personality endeared the man to everyone around him. Scarcely pausing for breath between each 'cracker' both offstage and on, he bombarded his audiences with a brand of effervescent humour which, in an age of precious few genuinely funny men, will doubtless leave a gaping hole in the sphere of stand-up comedy. After all, in the words of the Ulsterman himself: 'It's the way you tell 'em!'

A special mention also goes out to *Coronation Street* actor Bill Tarmey, better known to millions of TV soap addicts as Jack Duckworth, with whom the boys and myself had the pleasure of spending a little time at an extraordinarily glitzy affair held at Belfast's cavernous King's Hall on New Year's Day back in 1985.

A diverse galaxy of stars from the fields of music, television, entertainment and sport descended on the capital, jetting in at no little expense from all corners of the UK to assemble for a huge corporate bash at the invitation of mobile-phone giants Vodafone. Latching onto our crowd, Bill – whose premature departure came during the writing of this chapter in late 2012 – displayed all the qualities of a true gentleman, perfectly content to take time out, chat and sign items for all comers, but feet firmly on the ground remaining notably modest about his unrivalled popularity as a global soap star, an attribute which was highlighted the following morning at the city's Aldergrove airport.

Boarding passes in hand, an array of luminaries hung back awaiting the nod to proceed through an all-embracing security scan, when a poker-faced bulky woman in uniform remarked to her fastidious colleague: 'Hey Maggie, look who we've got here – it's that guy from *EastEnders*!'

Swinging round, pivoting on his heel and looking me directly in the eye, through clenched teeth and with a rueful smile Bill jested: 'That's how bloody famous I am lad!'

The man's legend lives on as repeats of the long-running insight into English northern life continue to be screened in countless far-flung corners of the world, which incredibly include Cyprus, the Middle East and Asia.

Causes célèbres

Frank Carson – comedian
Ciaran Hinds – actor
Kenneth Branagh – actor/film director
C.S. Lewis – writer
Van Morrison – stalwart singer/songwriter
George Best – glamour-boy footballer (often referred to as the fifth Beatle)
Eamonn Holmes – tubby TV presenter
Gary Moore – guitarist
Alex Higgins – bad-boy snooker star
James Galway – flautist
Ruby Murray – '50s singer

Essential travelling band info

Favourite live music venue: Grand Opera House, Great Victoria Street
Favourite curry house: The Raj, Lisburn Road – 48%
Favourite pub: The Crown Liquor Salon, Great Victoria Street – 95%
Don't miss: Stormont Castle, Upper Newtownards Road – 73%
Sense of humour/friendly welcome: 59%

Chapter 7
Birmingham

THE PEROXIDE BLONDE BUT VIVACIOUS landlady who compiled the weekly pub quiz prided herself on the toughness of the questions, thus attracting a regular caboodle of eggheads from the neighbouring villages ready to vie for the alluring fifty pounds first prize.

My inclusion in the six-strong home team had been based solely upon a keen knowledge of pop music, but even so the hostess's obsession with times and dates often proved beyond my chronologically challenged capabilities when it came to the music round.

It had proven to be a nail-biting contest and, as the scores were totted up, incredibly the local know-it-alls were neck and neck with the antiquated, all-conquering habitual victors, who to everyone's annoyance regularly took the money and ran the very moment the results were announced. So imagine the haughty Einsteins' consternation at being put to the test with a single, nerve-tingling tie-break question.

'So here goes, this week's winners will be decided by the following question. The first raised hand with the correct answer please: *Name both the date and one of the public houses stricken by the 1970s Birmingham pub bombings!*'

Like an Exocet missile my right arm propelled into the air, stunning the bewildered participants who, waiting with bated breath, fell completely silent.

'I must warn you, Dave, if it's the wrong answer the other team will win by default,' warned the equally surprised lady of the house.

'The twenty-first of November 1974; the afflicted pubs were "The Tavern in the Town" and "The Mulberry Bush"!' I cried out. The sound of the losers' chairs scraping across the flagstones could be heard with immediate effect once the outcome was confirmed, as my dumbfounded teammates engaged in an over-the-top display of backslapping, complete with embraces in sheer disbelief.

'Where the hell did you pluck that one from, David?' asked my knowledgeable next-door neighbour Matt, receiving a coy response: 'Let's just say it's a long story, Matt. C'mon, let's eat, or rather drink into that fifty quid!'

In truth it wasn't a long story at all, but the evening in question would remain forever etched in my memory as, at the age of twenty-two, I brushed a little too close for comfort with the true, spineless horrors of terrorism.

With the silly season of '74 fast approaching and with a brand spanking new Christmas single about to be released just the following day, an exclusive preview was aired on our local Midlands news channel ATV, featuring an audio clip of the song 'Hey Mister Christmas' over a montage of animated snowmen. The prematurely seasonal piece was complemented by a five-minute interview with band representatives Trevor Oakes and yours truly, in which our fawning hosts touted the single as a potential number one. The credits rolled hastening a quick change into our winter woollies prior to casually strolling back to the car, in no particular rush to return to base and debating whether to stay put in town for a little mosey around, perhaps boosted by an early-evening tipple.

'Let's find an Indian – I've heard there are plenty of really good curry houses around here and I'm bloody starving,' suggested Asian-food addict Trevor.

'Go on then, but let's get a bit closer to the centre and park up – there's got to be a half-decent one near to New Street!' I concurred.

With bellies bulging full of spicy fare washed down with a chilled bottle of Mateus Rosé, the stroll back to the car in the midst of the New Street hustle and bustle provided a welcome blast of fresh air, particularly in the light of Trevor's flatulent rear end imitating a brass band in between leering at the local totty togged up in their glad rags and already out to play.

'Do you fancy a pint for the road? I'm buying,' I offered, feeling the first drops of light rainfall and eyeing the bevy of beauties veering off into a nearby pub.

'You've got to be joking! I'm fit to burst – if I have anything else I'll probably throw up,' he gruffly replied, unleashing a resounding belch and upping the pace as, with me trotting behind to keep up, we scampered towards the parked car.

As we crawled away from the central area at around 8pm hampered by several sets of lights, a peculiar tremor or distant rumble of thunder emanated from somewhere in the neighbourhood just as Trevor's shiny blue Chrysler ducked into the dimly lit tunnels of the Queensway freeway, picking up the blue signs for the M6 motorway. Switching on the radio and deliberating above the melodious din some twenty minutes into the journey, the music was suddenly interrupted by an urgent newsflash:

'We have a report of two explosions, suspected to be IRA bombs, both of which were detonated between the hours of 8 and 8.30pm this evening in two public houses located in Birmingham city centre. We'll bring you further updates as they become available.'

Peering to my right, I met Trevor's eyes, but words wouldn't come. Shifting uncomfortably, I watched the blood drain from his face as we waited anxiously for the next update to uncover the true scale of the catastrophe transpiring on the busy paved area the pair of us had trodden only minutes before. It wasn't long in coming.

For the ensuing half-hour news filtered in non-stop, revealing varied accounts as to the actual number of fatalities and casualties, reckoned to run into hundreds, with the public houses identified as 'The Mulberry Bush' and 'The Tavern in the Town'. Live from the ill-fated scene, a reporter's voice cracked with emotion while he attempted with some difficulty to fill in the blanks as to the evening's tragic events.

'Wasn't that second one the pub you...?' Trevor faltered, drifting carelessly to the left and pausing in mid-sentence.

'Yes, and if you weren't such a greedy bugger we may even have gone inside,' I pondered, trembling at the thought which brought tears to my eyes as it hit home.

Pulling onto the hard shoulder for a brief respite while we struggled to make some sense of it all, my bandmate uncharacteristically leant to the side, placing one hand on my shoulder and grasping the other in my lap in a gesture of extreme tenderness, whilst almost dumbstruck I managed to croak: 'I guess I owe you one!'

****

Upon first impressions England's second city radiates an aura of prosperity, being a thriving, international business centre as well as boasting a diversified array of excellent shops, bars and restaurants, along with some of the finest theatres the United Kingdom has to offer, such as the Town Hall, the Hippodrome, the National Indoor Arena, the refurbished New Alexandra Theatre and my personal favourite the Symphony Hall (though for whatever reasons disappointingly the band never once performed there).

From the very inception of Showaddywaddy back in 1973 a number of the city's entertainment hot spots beckoned, cueing a small fleet of personal vehicles to regularly burn rubber up and down the forty-mile A47 carriageway from nearby Leicestershire, a journey which became super-quick upon the completion of the M69 motorway in 1977. For much of the late seventies and early eighties Birmingham (affectionately known as 'Brum') became like a second home with the band partaking in numerous sell-out theatre concerts, including an arduous fourteen-night stint at what for many years was arguably the UK's premier cabaret club venue, 'The Night Out.' The plush theatre-cum-restaurant fast evolved into a favourite haunt of the entourage, differing from the majority of club venues on the circuit in its slickly run enthusiastic approach headed up by a suave manager going by the slightly discomfiting name of Paul Lillicrap, but whose unquestionable professionalism came as a breath of fresh air. He grasped in no small measure that the glittering array of top-line artists booked to appear at the club put 'bums on seats', and accordingly afforded his big-name attractions the star treatment.

Taking on so many back-to-back appearances at the club, a sense of inevitability suggested that not every performance would go entirely according to plan, and indeed as the law of averages forced its hand it was there that I suffered the rare ignominy of being obliged to leave the stage mid-show in what could only be termed as an acutely embarrassing incident.

Squeezed into a pair of snug-fitting drainpipe stage trousers simulating a second skin and heeding the advice of a couple of frisky female PR assistants working alongside the band, I found myself coaxed, so as not to display an ugly 'panty line', into unabashedly taking to the stage without the security of even the skimpiest underwear.

Caught up in the excitement midway through a set of onstage exertions and failing to notice the ineffective nylon zip of my trousers had given way, from the corner of my eye I spotted a small section of the seated crowd sheepishly giggling and gesticulating towards my nether regions whilst I strutted my stuff, microphone in hand. Thanking the appreciative crowd as the song in progress drew to a close, I began the link into the next tune, when cutting through the ebbing applause a smiling, bald-headed man seated on the front row of tables caught my eye, impertinently remarking: 'Careful your knob don't pop out, son – seeing your pubes is bad enough!'

Glancing downwards and beginning to flap I shouted back to the boys: 'Shit! Play "Jailhouse Rock" ' (a song in which I took a breather and performed back-up vocals), 'I'll be back in a sec,' before fleeing in haste from the stage to the privacy of the dressing room to make the quickest costume change of my professional life.

Needless to say that random piece of exhibitionism marked the last performance I ever did without making every effort to protect my modesty and donning a pair of briefs or boxer shorts beneath my stage apparel from then on.

****

The aforementioned ATV (Associated Television) studios were the setting for the green Midlands outfit's debut TV appearance in 1973 on what was touted as a groundbreaking prime-time show called *New Faces*.

The programme's producer had taken precious time out to honour us with his presence at a live gig, and soon afterwards extended an invitation for the band to perform, with no audition necessary, on the *Britain's Got Talent* of its day. At this stage we were completely in the dark as to the show's intended format and had no inkling whatever as to what potentially lay ahead, other than that the production's sole purpose was to showcase the cream of the UK's up-and-coming talent.

In the build-up to the big day proud mothers, or in a couple of cases wives, busied themselves laundering pairs of fluorescent pink socks and pressing up frilly shirts and flared breeches together with a mishmash of multi-coloured stage suits, while the intoxicating buzz of excitement in the camp reached fever pitch. This was it – the opportunity every starry-eyed wannabe longed for: the chance to excel and become overnight sensations with the new phenomenon's name fresh on the lips of every goggle-eyed TV addict in the land.

In a pre-digitalised era of only three operative TV stations (Channel Four's first programme wasn't transmitted until 1982), the estimated audience for a popular Saturday-evening variety show often soared to the giddy heights of as many as thirty million viewers. With an earmarked slot of four minutes max, this presented the band with a dilemma: should we play it safe with a trustworthy crowd-pleaser, or go for broke and hit them hard with a pastiche of six or seven trimmed-down classics designed to leave the watching public breathless? Visualising the latter as a blueprint for success, rock-and-roll standards such as the pounding instrumental 'Wipe Out', Buddy Holly's 'Rave On', Larry Williams' 'Bony Moronie' and a couple of other upbeat titles were condensed into fifty-second teasers as a taster of the band's uniquely animated style, whilst fitting snugly into the restricted time-frame.

Looking back now, the naïve strategy could easily have backfired, bordering on overkill with the frantic mix of pumping adrenaline and youthful exuberance confusing the hell out of the viewers, though as I study old videotape recordings burnt onto DVD, the sheer unbridled energy and vigour of it all proved an endearing and potent cocktail.

The incongruous panel of judges were equally impressed, with *Crossroads* soap legend Noele Gordon visualising the band as 'vibrant young men with a bright future', whereas eccentric intellectual Clement Freud's take focused solely on a strange fixation with my own mouthful of pearly-whites as opposed to the actual routine, commenting: 'The lead singer has a remarkable set of teeth that flashed like gleaming alabaster beneath the lights!'

Making up the jury and ever the wheeler-dealer, likeable record mogul Mickie Most enthused over the performance, discreetly mentioning how he'd be keen 'to have a little chat', though getting wind of record and management deals already in place and never one to pass up a golden opportunity quickly switched his attentions to a band signed to his own RAK Records label, who in a matter of weeks took *Top of the Pops* by storm garbed in a kaleidoscope of Teddy-boy suits and belting out their latest hit 'Tiger Feet'. Viewed scathingly as an act of plagiarism by the tabloid press, with a nod and a wink to their rookie rivals little could stand in the way of either Mr Most or Mud, whose classic and defining record rocketed to number one in the UK charts. However, in an industry where treading on toes was second nature, nothing was about to deter the ambitious young Turks.

Two days after winning *New Faces* with a record-breaking score, a frenetic Monday morning saw the phone lines white-hot, with every major record company and producer in creation staking their claim to either sign or work with the nation's next big thing, promising the earth, moon and stars to entice the young hopefuls into their lairs. Contractually bound into a watertight management agreement in addition to putting pen to paper with the enormously successful Bell record label, in typically uncompromising style symbolic of a closed-shop era the hapless octet's hands were tied, unable to move a muscle in shaping a future foreshadowed to be as bright as the desert sun.

In retrospect, loved or loathed, a bunch of hungry Midlands rock-and-rollers had been the name on everyone's lips, perceived as the hottest property around with a big wide world looming large on the horizon. The calendar was filling up rapidly and the coming year would undoubtedly be hectic, but what the hell: dreams were made to fly, and visions of visits to exotic climes such as the USA, Japan and Down Under only ramped up the excitement, suggesting the air-miles would soon be stacking up… wouldn't they??

****

One year on and with four big-selling top-twenty hits on the CV, incredibly the band had performed a back-breaking three hundred live gigs, all to packed houses and taking in back-to-back seven-night shifts in workaday destinations such as Oldham, Liverpool, Blackburn, Hull, Birmingham, plus (to provide a modicum of light relief) our home town of Leicester.

Before long, murmurs of doubt began to dominate every dressing-room conversation as we faced up to a few harsh realities, centred upon the big bosses' vested interests in the very nightclubs the band had scoured the country to play. With each venue bursting at the seams as the golden goose took temporary residence for a seven-night stint, further salt was being rubbed into the wounds thanks to the hefty commission being reaped by others based on our earnings.

Foolhardily, while a host of international promoters and TV producers cried out for the band to visit far-flung destinations, the boys and I forcibly stayed put on British soil, remaining on the well-worn treadmill for in excess of twelve months, lining the pockets of our so-called advisors but feeling undermined by a total lack of foresight. In an era of dark winter days and industrial action at the drop of a hat, this spelt big trouble for the manipulative big guns by way of our making a stand.* Incessant rumblings of disquiet, coupled with the strong probability of burn-out and over-exposure to the British public, necessitated a radical rethink as even the avaricious powers-that-be began to fear for their embittered golden goose, resulting in meetings ostensibly held to discuss a new strategy for the band's long-term future.

First up on the radar was a six-week tour of the backwaters of Germany, which despite not living up to expectations at least seemed a step in the right direction. It put a renewed spring in the step of the disenthralled members and served as a much-needed break from the tedium of the constant scampi-in-the-basket grind.

In double-quick time the audiences took on a different complexion, consisting of diehard fans and record buyers from all across Europe who packed into a profusion of venues the length and breadth of the continent, even extending onto forbidden turf behind the Iron Curtain. Here, in a series of one-night-stands, we found ourselves greeted as heroes by hordes of hysterical fans, and a covey of jaw-dropping beauties flatteringly offered proposals of marriage to the boys, concealing the ulterior motive of freeing themselves from the shackles of Communism.

Big-selling international singles and albums followed as Europe's jet-setting crêped crusaders revelled in the new-found idolisation, with the ever-winding road ahead becoming a distinctly more mouth-watering prospect.

****

Located in the heart of Birmingham city centre and regarded as one of the most notorious rock-and-roll hot spots in the West Midlands, 'Barbarella's' featured early performances from the likes of Queen, the Sex Pistols, Dire Straits and AC/DC as well as a selection of breaking chart bands which, proving no exception to the rule, included SWW on a rare excursion away from the bread-and-butter sweatshop grind back in late '74. Notwithstanding that it was predominantly a rock venue, the gig had been decidedly well received and, as we towelled ourselves down and relaxed backstage, the ring-pulls from an oversized ice-bucket chock-full of lagers popped in celebration.

A stocky man sporting an expensively tailored two-piece suit and neatly trimmed beard appeared at the top of the stairs leading down into the room. Clearing his throat he politely interrupted: 'Sorry to disturb you, lads – I just

---

* See Chapter 60 – Stoke On Trent

wanted to say how much I enjoyed the gig!'

'Thanks very much, mate,' I reciprocated, parodying the obviously local man's accent and feeling a hint of recognition kick in.

'I was brought up on rock and roll, it's in my blood and does a lot more for me than all that arty-farty "Pink Side of the Moon" crap!' he amusingly went on.

'Do you play yourself?' I quizzed, none the wiser.

Astonishingly the guy replied: 'Indeed I do mate – me name's John Bonham, I'm the drummer with a band called Led Zeppelin!'

An awestruck hush descended on the room, prolonged by several pairs of roving eyes seeking some form of verification, borne out by our very own drummer Romeo who, in the presence of his all-time musical hero and clad in just a pair of briefs, stood riveted to the spot.

Blessed with an engaging personality as large as his bulky frame, the gifted powerhouse behind one of rock music's greatest ever bands displayed a down-to-earth, self-deprecating line of humour, happy to touch on a renowned hellraising reputation whilst reeling off a captivating mixed bag of ripping yarns from his extraordinary life, which would subsequently be tragically curtailed. On September 25th 1980, in the throes of preparing for an autumn tour date, news reached the entourage of Bonzo's premature passing, rendering an unearthly silence over the backstage area. Each band member quietly geared up for the matter in hand, clearly affected by the loss of one of the music industry's truly great performers.

At the midpoint of an uncommonly subdued hour-long set, as a mark of respect I stepped to the microphone to tremulously announce: 'The band would like to dedicate the next song to the greatest rock drummer that ever lived, the one and only Mr John Bonham,' fittingly followed by the jangly guitar intro to our hit, 'Three Steps to Heaven'.

****

At the pinnacle of the band's popularity as teen idols in 1977, the BBC invited a small number of high-profile artists to appear on a series of live outside broadcasts from the gardens of their Birmingham-based Pebble Mill studios, aptly entitled *Pop at the Mill*, with one of the programmes focusing prominently on their young Midlands neighbours made good.

Inundated with enquiries during the preceding weeks, the TV station generously set aside an allocation of tickets exclusively for members of the Showaddywaddy fan club, perhaps a tad in the dark as to the fervid disposition rampant amongst a pack of fanatical wildcats, with only one likely outcome – mayhem!

Throughout the day as the riggers toiled beneath the hot sun an influx of a few hundred orderly bods arrived in dribs and drabs equipped with picnic baskets, deckchairs, blankets and cool-boxes, more resembling a 'Last Night of the Proms' audience than the expected excitable mob. As the afternoon wore on, however, the numbers were swelled by splinter groups of teenage girls kitted out in scarves, bobby socks and eye-catching merchandise bearing the band's name. Their arrival was monitored by their gratified heroes from a bird's-eye view on the top floor of the studio building as they formed a semicircle like an assortment of oversized jelly-babies in a blaze of vivid colours.

A sharp rap at the door signified the arrival of two slapheaded heavies assigned the task of escorting the bill-toppers down to the stage-side, where to our amazement the crowd had ballooned to getting on for three thousand bodies, a disorderly section of whom directed a stream of sarcastic insults towards a cheesy pop outfit called 'Stephenson's Rocket' who nervously minced around the boards going through the motions of a mushy playback routine.

Opting for a rather uncool choice of host, in their wisdom the BBC's programmers plumped for veteran DJ Pete Murray, whose outmodedly eloquent style, not to mention dress sense, typified a bygone generation of dapper, silver-tongued presenters seemingly with a job for life at the corporation (Brian Matthew and David Jacobs soldiered on well into their eighties). He looked strangely out of sorts bandying around a few banal chart statistics to the disinterested revellers eagerly awaiting the headlining act.

As we kicked off with a couple of up-tempo hit tunes, the lively swarm swayed enthusiastically, pumping their fists towards the open sky. A temporary interruption between songs followed as the hoisted camera spun back to the greying anchorman, who in a timeworn tongue announced: 'And now the boys are going to play an exclusive little number from their new long-playing record...' before stopping in his tracks, caught seriously off guard as a group of frenzied kids, evading an inept cluster of idling security men, climbed like crazed chimpanzees up the scaffolding pipes and into the open on the alarmed emcee's rostrum.

A pair of barrel-chested crew riggers in black standard issue AC/DC T-shirts moved swiftly to block the rat pack's route to the band as, grabbing at Murray's microphone, a fervent adolescent hollered in a broad Lancashire tone: 'I luv Deeve, tal Deeve I luv 'eem!' However, her only reward was to be needlessly rugby-tackled to the ground by an overexcited stagehand trying to make a name for himself in the act of wrestling the device from her.

Inflamed by the unseemly response, a battery of teenagers sparked into life, violently surging towards the stage like a human bulldozer trampling over the toppling crash-barriers and any other obstacles in their path, hell-bent on breaching the already overworked security personnel to literally get a piece of their idols.

'One-two-three-four,' sounded the countdown followed by the upbeat backing track's opening bars thundering from the tall banks of speakers, while to the fore it was literally all hands on deck with members of the camera crew, technical staff and a sprinkling of boys in blue arriving at the scene all linking arms in a desperate bid to restrain the frenzied youngsters, whose unhinged demeanour by now appeared to be on a knife-edge.

Battling valiantly, the makeshift cordon just about proved up to the task as, evading a shoal of mitts and clawing fingernails, the boys and I made it through to the song's finale before fleeing the stage through a cobbled-up emergency exit to the rear. Unbelievably, a section of the possessed hordes had got wind of the diversion, crawling beneath the wooden construction on their hands and knees to form a formidable blockade with fire in their eyes.

Like a wild animal a worked-up female grabbed at my long dark locks, jerking determinedly to uproot a souvenir clump. Her efforts were foiled by a burly protector who responded with a sharp, swift karate chop, freeing me from her grip in an instant but incensing the crazed fan who retaliated in kind with a rabbit punch to the side of the man's cranium. Shrugging off the attack with a shake of his head and firmly pushing me towards safety through the narrow gap he bellowed above the din: 'Bloody hell, I never knew you guys were this big!'

'Neither did I, mate, neither did I!' I replied, thinking just what might have been, eventually making it back to the main building thankful to be in one piece.

Causes célèbres

Ozzy Osbourne – bat-munching legend
Trevor Eve – TV actor
Martin Shaw – actor
Jasper Carrot – comedian
Cat Deeley – TV presenter
Ian Lavender – actor (*Dad's Army* etc.)
Tony Iommi – guitarist
Jeff Lynne – ELO/Traveling Wilburys etc.
Barbara Cartland – novelist
Steve Winwood – musician
Jamelia – singer
Roy Wood – Wizzard/ELO/The Move
Nick Mason – Pink Floyd

Duran Duran – '80s stars
Enoch Powell – visionary politician
Murray Walker – treasured Formula 1 commentator

Essential travelling band info

Favourite live music venue: Symphony Hall, Victoria Square
Favourite curry house: Pushkar, Broad Street (expensive) – 68%
Favourite pub: Post Office Vaults, New Street – 72%
Don't miss: Thinktank Planetarium, Millennium Point – 80%
Sense of humour/friendly welcome: 70%

Chapter 8
Bradford

'WE'RE UP AT TOP O' CHARTS AGAIN,' boasted a purple-nosed Terry, the bass player and sole remaining original member of Bradford band Smokie in his inimitable West Yorkshire dialect, adding loftily: 'And it's gone to number one in Outer Mongolia, where we're off next month to play some massive arenas and telly shows!'

The record my long-standing pal spoke of was none other than the cringe-worthy risqué version of his own band's original seventies hit, 'Livin' Next Door to Alice (Who the Fuck is Alice?)', on which the rejigged line-up had mysteriously teamed up with notorious blue comedian Chubby Brown to create a one-off novelty hit.

Under-impressed by the bombast I cruelly fired back: 'What are you planning to follow it up with – perhaps a cover of Benny Hill's "Ernie, the Fastest Fucking Milkman in the West"?'

'Hey, that's uncalled for and you know it you piss-taking bastard! Besides, you're only jealous,' Terry retaliated.

'Well, at least if you're selling shedloads of records you can afford to buy me a drink, you tight git!' I countered.

'That sounds like a much better idea and would be a pressure… sorry, pleasure David,' the pudgy bassist gamely retorted.

Featuring on TV shows, festival bills and the like over a number of years the gregarious Bradford quartet had crossed our paths more than most. We had become well acquainted and shared many a late night (not to mention a barrel-load of laughs) in each other's company, frequently in hotel bars – not only post performance, but often for a touch of Dutch courage prior to clambering aboard the tour bus to depart for the gig.

Little did our northern counterparts realise but hidden beneath our cynical, mocking exterior lurked a sneaking admiration for the boys' uncanny adeptness at holding things together on stage, in spite of the excessive liquor coursing through their veins. The band and I would linger in the wings awaiting a minor catastrophe as the Bradford lads precariously tottered out before a sceptical public, only for them to defy the odds as they habitually delivered the goods. Demonstrating a huge amount of staying power, they would launch into their sweet harmonies, seemingly immune from the effects of the human liver's most feared adversary.

Hair-raisingly, in keeping with a stereotypical rock-star persona, the boys persisted in wearing stack- or Cuban-heeled snakeskin boots in which they strutted unsteadily onto the stage, legs akimbo, defying gravity and somehow remaining upright. Inevitably, though, on one occasion bass player Terry did take a nasty tumble, spending the night in a German hospital bed, hugely relieved to be discharged relatively unscathed the following morning essentially after drying out!

Putting all the antics and jibes to one side a healthy, mutual respect prevailed for each respective band's unwavering adeptness, despite the bestowal of a stream of unkind nicknames, the most amusing being 'Guts and Roses' – not necessarily as a nod to Axl Rose and company, but more as a brazen reference to the guys' comically bulging midriffs.

****

Few touring musicians could ever be pigeonholed as 'angels', but likewise the catalogue of well-documented tales concerning the supposedly questionable morals and outlandish behaviour of rock and roll's renowned wild men applies in reality to a small minority, many accounts being economical with the truth and exacerbated by equally flaunting 'Chinese whispers'. That's not to say that alcohol and the world of rock and roll don't necessarily go hand in hand; those practising the genre mostly differ little from any other male-oriented travelling parties who, freed from the shackles and prying eyes of ''er indoors' on all-expenses-paid trips, indulge in acts of uncalled-for waywardness, often making themselves ill in the process, which on the whole is where any similarity ends.

As the saying goes, though, boys for the most part will be boys; and besides, where's the harm in a few 'on the road' high jinks in the company of a fraternity of like-minded bacchanalians, often including names unheard of for years: The Mamas and the Papas, Scott McKenzie, Terry Jacks, The Turtles, Christie, Lovin' Spoonful and many more, the majority of whom believed their touring days were long over and were hell-bent on reliving the rock and roll dream!

Jamaican singer Desmond Dekker and his band The Aces (remember the blue-beat classic 'The Israelites'?) featured on a string of nostalgia-themed packages, also enjoying a spot of post-gig banter whilst hobnobbing with the other seasoned artists on the bill until all hours of the night when time was finally called.

In a chaotic Berlin hotel lobby on the morning of departure following a summer festival gig at the German capital's chasmic outdoor amphitheatre 'The Waldbuhne' (interestingly the scene of a number of Adolf Hitler's wartime addresses), Desmond emerged, beret-clad and in something of a dither, from the jolting lift and uncoordinatedly shuffled over to the main desk to receive a cordial '*guten morgen*' from the attractive receptionist, whose frumpier and disturbingly over-efficient colleague was busy attending to my good self.

'Good morning, sir; are you checking out?' the young lady courteously enquired.

'Jah, mi' name's Dekker,' the songbird replied in something of a stupor.

'Before I print off ze bill, did you have any items from ze mini-bar during your stay, sir?' the girl queried in an emphatic Teutonic twang, causing the bewildered Desmond to ponder before replying in his native Jamaican-English patois:

'*Errm, jah mon, ebrat'ting alkhallic* (interpreted as 'everything alcoholic').

Summoned to settle the damage, his right-hand man Delroy duly removed the rubber band from a wad of banknotes and handed over the cash.

Keeping the apparently carefree Desmond's company on several occasions, to learn of his hush-hush drinking binges came as doubly surprising and in a way amusing, having come to admire the man's self-discipline and dedication in bedding down ahead of the pack. Of course, one also took into account that his customary spaced-out approach to life may in part be attributed to the illegal stash concealed beneath his tight-fitting black beret.

Desmond Dekker died of a heart attack at his London home in 2006. He was sixty-four years of age.

****

First come the restless, sweaty nights tossing and turning beneath the dampening sheets, followed by the morning shakes and thunderous hangover, as the simple task of filling the kettle descends into farce, ducking to avoid uncontrollable jets of water gushing hither and thither, inauspiciously shaping the challenges of the day ahead into an uphill struggle.

The lucky ones apart, it would seem the large majority of casual barflies suffer much the same symptoms following any prolonged drinking session. The torture commonly extends well into the next day, by which time, head hung low, the trite maxim 'never again' repeatedly passes through the casualty's lips.

Personally speaking the physical, not to mention masochistic, demands of alcoholism may in such circumstances prove too painful a burden for my own lily-liver to bear, when the price to pay for frequently pushing out the boat is invariably nothing short of damaging.

The nervous jitters, throbbing cranium, heartburn and indigestion eventually subside, replaced in no small measure by an excruciatingly tender red swelling around the big-toe joint of either foot as the readjustment process begins to take hold. This condition for the uninitiated is the dreaded gout, which not only lingers agonisingly for days but, worst of all for yours truly, made the task of squeezing into a pair of brothel creepers prior to flaunting some nifty footwork onstage pretty much a hopeless one.

Disregarding the devil-may-care effects of a pre-gig skinful, a relaxing pint or even a remedial dram of the hard stuff is in no way a bad thing, loosening the inhibitions and larynx at one sitting and paving the way for a stonking performance.

As ever the exception proves the rule; and, saddled with an original complement of eight differing personalities, our very own band of merry misfits experienced its fair share of trials and tribulations, in particular during a mystifying period when the weight of constant touring took its toll on a trio of undisciplined playmates. Supposedly stone cold sober whilst taking to the stage, the individuals concerned covertly returned to the dressing rooms three sheets to the wind, feigning exhaustion from their exertions and claiming to be high on adrenaline.

Before long all was revealed when, brought to task over his continual presence on stage despite the absence of technical hitches, a member of the production crew finally spilt the beans, citing an alleged secret pact with the true instigators and claiming that their personal pint pots, to all appearances filled with Coca Cola, were replenished with generous measures of vodka at regular intervals throughout the seventy-minute show.

It was a warning sign of trouble ahead and gave a sense that the wheels may yet come off, laying a hard-earned, critically acclaimed 'live' reputation on the line. A stream of flimsy excuses followed, degenerating into heated squabbles and uncovering rifts which had lurked beneath the surface for a dog's age. In short the rot was setting in, creating irreparable divisions and ultimately leading to an acrimonious parting of the ways.

****

On the band's inaugural visit to Bradford in the winter of 1975 overtones of excitement filled the air, sustained as yearning ambitions to headline our own series of concerts were about to be fulfilled in the shape of a string of pilot dates, further stimulated by the tantalising prospect of an extensive UK tour as bill-toppers should the shows prove successful.

Attracting swarms of hysterical female followers on the back of four top-twenty singles and with a big-selling debut album tucked proudly beneath our star-spangled belts, boundless optimism had scaled an all-time high; and a herd of young fillies was already in evidence, gathered en masse at the stage door as their heroes pulled up outside of the venue.

With a resounding bump the January concert at the St George's Hall brought the whole shebang crashing back down to earth – or, more expressly, forced a section of show-goers onto their knees, brandishing an assortment of knocks, grazes and bruises when, only minutes before the final curtain, the proverbial house of cards came tumbling down.

The gig itself had been going incredibly well, with the nucleus of high-pitched teenage voices busy mouthing the lyrics to every song, interspersed with feverish screams each time a band member so much as moved a muscle, creating an exhilarating buzz of electricity reminiscent of a tumultuous mob packed into a football stadium.

Extended above the mountain of gear to their maximum height and situated to either side of the stage stood two hydraulic lighting towers, both mounted on castors atop a sturdy six-legged iron base and placed strategically by the LD (lighting designer, not lorry driver!) to cover the performance area with a multi-coloured panoply of fluorescent colours.

From the very outset the team of overworked security staff looked to be up against it, acting on impulse to intercept the scores of unruly juveniles seen attempting to scale the towers, bent on reaching the stage platform. Struggling manfully to maintain some semblance of order it seemed at last as if the battle was won as, waving farewell and setting down our instruments, the band scurried into the wings, joyfully unaware of a vicious sting lurking in the tail.

Returning to the stage in a cacophonous din, we made ready for an encore. As the baying rabble surged forwards, a dozen or more youngsters freed themselves from the crush and slipped the net, cunningly and athletically evading the frustrated minders to monkey-walk up the floodlights' telescopic shafts.

Horrifically, within seconds gravity played its part, as over to the left an overwhelmed tower toppled agonisingly like a giant redwood, crashing unmercifully into the seated stalls in a scene reminiscent of a disaster movie.

Beyond scared and fearing for those caught beneath the devastation, I backed off from the mike in dismay as hundreds of panicking bystanders rummaged beneath the grounded pylon preparing themselves for the worst-case scenario. As if by an act of God, whilst the metal beam had sluggishly lurched backwards many fans had the presence of mind to dive beneath the seats for protection, thus averting a major catastrophe.

Fortuitously only one attendee – an eighteen-year-old girl – was hospitalised, sustaining minor head and back injuries. Comfortingly, she was discharged the following day to the whole team's palpable relief. The mental image of the weeping wounded lingers on in the memory as I slipped back into the hall to survey the wreckage, observing a crew of St John Ambulance volunteers performing heroics in an area resembling the emergency facility of a war zone.

Recounting the evening's events, I wonder how different things would have been had the incident occurred in modern times. Scary images spring to mind of avaricious lawyers and ambulance chasers, climbing on the bandwagon to dispense a ream of outrageous claims for whiplash or other invisible afflictions on behalf of their traumatised clients, not to mention the quires of adverse, safety-minded publicity biased against the band banging on about the wherefores and pitfalls of attending rock-and-roll concerts, where the security of the general public clearly came second.

Whether by sheer good fortune or even a minor miracle, in averting a potential nightmare common sense for once prevailed. No broken bones. No internal injuries. No unnecessary writs. Just a mixture of bumps, bruises and bleeding hearts, proving perhaps in the words of a thriving lawyer friend, himself a Tyke: 'They built 'em tougher in those days, especially in West Yorkshire;' and who am I to disagree!

Causes célèbres

David Hockney – artist extraordinaire
Frederick Delius – composer
Ade Edmondson – actor/ TV personality (*The Young Ones* and many more)
J.B. Priestley – novelist/playwright
Michael Rennie – *The Third Man* actor (if you're old enough to remember the
    series!)
Timothy West – actor (Winston Churchill etc.)
Smokie – harmony rock band (as mentioned in this chapter)
Harry Corbett – TV personality (*The Sooty Show*)

Essential travelling band info

Favourite live music venue: Alhambra Theatre, Morley Street
Favourite curry house: Sweet Centre Restaurant, Lumb Lane – 77%
Favourite pub: New Beehive Inn, Westgate – 76%
Don't miss: Salts Mill, Shipley – 81%
Sense of humour/friendly welcome: 72%

Chapter 9
Brighton and Hove

THE WHITEWASHED HOTEL HAD KNOWN better days. Looking forlorn and weather-beaten as the glinting sunlight exposed the crumbling Georgian façade, in glorious summers past it doubtless served as a chic, upmarket retreat.

Inside, though, I was being killed with kindness by a chubby trio of mother hens (privately dubbed 'The Weather Girls'). The topic of conversation turned to bathing belles, rumoured to be found basking in all their glory at the town's renowned nudist beach.

'Now why on earth would you be wanting to go over there?' enquired the senior receptionist in a broad Somerset twang, repulsed at the thought any self-respecting pillar of society may even contemplate a visit to the resort's most famous littoral.

'The forecast for today is a sweltering seventy-five degrees (Fahrenheit), so be sure to use some sunscreen as we wouldn't want you to get your winkles burnt… now would we?' her younger colleague cheekily chipped in.

'Well, if I do, perhaps you could rub some after-sun on it later,' I teased with a twinkle in my eye, quick to point out the true voyeuristic purpose of the outing.

An instant damper was placed on the proceedings as the hotel's ancient lift abruptly juddered to a halt, the whining doors trundled apart and, with a face like thunder, the bronzed figure of Trevor emerged and strode restlessly in the direction of the main desk.

'Aye-up, what's eating Sunbed the sailor man?' Geoff offered in jest.

'I want a change of room – and can you make sure it doesn't have an adjoining door!' he abruptly demanded, failing to as much as acknowledge his bandmates.

'Really? The one I gave you has a lovely sea view; what appears to be the problem?' the girl replied, shielding her eyes from the sunshine leaking in.

'I'd like a room where I can get a bit of privacy, without the chambermaids inviting themselves in every five minutes without even having the decency to knock!' he bickered, fast approaching boiling point.

'Might I suggest you hang the "Do Not Disturb" sign on the knob outside? Then the girls won't bother you at all,' the ruffled assistant politely countered.

'Haha, I bet it was your knob getting a good polishing when they burst in on you!' chirped Rod, throwing a fly in the ointment to chuckles all around.

'What's got into you today, you grumpy old git?' I asked Trevor.

'You'd have gone apeshit; the bloody chambermaid just strolled in like she owned the place while I was stretched out on the bed reading… in the nude!' he complained with a bee in his bonnet the size of a bat.

'You fucking reading? It must've been *Men Only* or *Fiesta* while you were pulling your one-eyed monster,' Geoff exclaimed, launching into a coughing fit.

'Very funny,' the guitarist retorted, rudely snatching the replacement key from the tittering assistant and sulkily storming back into the elevator craving his own space infused with a modicum of tranquillity.

****

The much publicised naturists' paradise was situated at the eastern end of the promenade in an area known as Black Rock, roughly a two-mile hike from the hotel, and an energetic hour or two checking it out seemed the perfect antidote to a cooped-up existence of wearisome travelling, offset by the bracing sea air and a cloudless blue sky let alone the crowning glory of a bevy of local beauties topping up their all-over tans.

Barely an hour later the unappealing sight of a broad, reddening backside, its owner delving into a bulging picnic hamper, indicated our quest was at an end. Disappointingly the male-dominated dozen or more skinny-dippers on parade exhibited a wide range of pot bellies and wrinkles, with the majority of their flabby stomachs drooping due south, at least serving mercifully to shield their insignificant, shrivelled penises.

Only one aged female was visible to the eye, other than a posse of red-complexioned, sandwich-munching schoolgirls who passed nervously by, hands shading their eyes, unsure whether to giggle or simply scream out in horror. After sizing up the ugly spectacle for all of two minutes, the unpalatable display of flaccid skin caused our stomachs to churn, provoking a hasty retreat in search of greener pastures, whilst leaving the sun-kissed naturists to their unfettered freedom.

Seeking protection from the stifling midday heat we found ourselves drawn towards the town's renowned shopping area where the sheltered alleys and hidden crannies afforded a welcome respite from the intensifying UVA rays, and the opportunity of pausing for a cooling ice-lolly midstream. Barely a month away from the peak-season turmoil, a gentle ocean breeze swept over the sparsely populated promenade, caressing each of our moistening brows whilst reaching deep into my own set of wheezing lungs.

As we picked up the ornately lettered signs for the 'Lanes' complex, the thunderous sound of rock music caused the earth to shudder, booming from an ostentatious pick-up truck cruising along the main drag adorned with a framework of glinting chromium bars supporting a deafening multi-kilowatt woofer system.

'Would you credit it? I'd heard he lived around these parts,' I gasped, peering up at the oversized Tonka toy. Bare-chested and posing flamboyantly as if in a carnival parade, the well-toned ebony figure of the eccentric ex-boxing champion Chris Eubank took centre stage, flexing his taut biceps and posturing like a premier danseur.

'What a bighead! Who the fuck does he think he is?' Geoff viciously derided.

'I've heard he speaks well of you!' I joked.

'Haha! One thing's for certain – he's not backwards in coming forwards,' interjected Rod, shaking his head in disbelief.

Dwindling into a speck on the skyline, the surplus of rippling muscles, sagging buttocks and mindless self-indulgence proved quite enough for one day. Meanwhile the unmoved townsfolk, paying little heed to the apparently commonplace occurrence, pressed on with their daily routines without as much as a second glance.

In 1996, in recognition of a vainglorious self-regard, Eubank acquired the title as Lord of the Manor of Brighton, forking out a forty-five-thousand-pound purse for the privilege, presumably obtained from his prizefighting spoils. In addition the pugilist received four thousand herring, three cows per annum and one slave.

Declared bankrupt with unpaid taxes estimated at a staggering 1.3 million pounds, the status was relinquished in 2009.

****

'Our special guest live in the studio this afternoon is none other than the lead singer of the chart-topping boy band Showaddywaddy, who just so happen to be performing at the legendary Brighton Dome theatre this evening; let's give a warm welcome to the dashing Dave Barton,' the annoying radio jock babbled.

'It's Dave Bartram, B-A-R-T-R-A-M, and we're a man-band; but whatever, it's lovely to be beside the seaside!' I responded, feeling a tad mischievous.

'Oops, that's put me in my place… Anyway, everyone's excited to have you here, how long have you been on tour?' he waffled on.

'Coming up to twenty-five years now,' I kidded, which in truth wasn't far wrong.

'No, no, I mean how long has this particular tour been going on for?' he scowled, becoming a trifle uppity.

'Like I said, twenty-five years, almost anyway,' I teased.

'I don't think our guest is quite with me listeners… What I'm trying to say is, how many shows have you completed on the current tour?' the DJ persisted.

'Ah, that's a tricky one; I'd estimate around three thousand or so by now,' I taunted, getting under his skin but nevertheless stating a fact.

'Three thousand… what the hell…? Well folks, I think it's time for some music. Here for any fans tuning in is the band's biggest hit to date "Under the Blue Moon of Love",' he incorrectly announced.

As the track began playing, he completely lost his cool. 'How dare you fucking embarrass me on the air? Let me remind you this is my fucking show not yours; I didn't want you in as a guest in the first place,' he yawped, flying off the handle and showing all the signs of a bruised ego.

'Well, in that case I'd best leave you to it; and by the way the title of the song you're playing does not contain the word "blue", you jumped-up prick,' I berated, evening up the score and slinging my hook.

Breathing fire, I returned to the theatre for an early-evening soundcheck. A crouched-over figure emerged from a straggle of autograph hunters, catching my eye and posing the question: 'Hey buddy, do you remember me?'

'You'll have to forgive me, but I'm not sure I do,' I admitted, giving my first straight answer of the day.

'I was the male streaker who ran onstage with you at the Falmer campus down the road a while back. It's a night I'll never forget,' he candidly recalled.

'I'm sorry mate, I didn't recognise you with your clothes on! All I know is it was a great night,' I acknowledged.

'It certainly wasn't great for me,' he put glumly as, pulling me to one side, he began to unfold his unfortunate tale…

The band had been booked to play a university ball on the outskirts of town some years before. Out of nowhere, clad in nothing but a pair of ankle-length socks and wielding his unexceptional dangly bits, the milk-white exhibitionist swaggered coolly across the stage to a raucous but under-impressed reception, marking the band's first ever mid-gig flasher.

Coming a cropper whilst attempting to scale the high-rise drum rostrum, the show-off nosedived headfirst into Romeo's kit, drawing blood from his nether regions and letting out an excruciating shriek whilst clinging onto his manhood.

'I knew something was seriously wrong but not a soul showed the slightest touch of sympathy, especially your roadie whose size nine boot up my arse only made matters worse,' the guy persevered with a pained expression.

'Listen mate, I'm sorry you suffered and all that, but I sincerely hope you're not expecting me to kiss it better,' I remarked in jest.

'Don't be daft – I just thought you should know that after climbing on stage with you guys I had to have my right testicle amputated and I've been impotent ever since!' he recoiled, evoking a gasp of horror as my legs closed together.

'That's awful, but I hope you're not holding the band responsible. Besides, what gave you the urge to get your kit off in the first place?'

'Oh, I'm not complaining or after any money – in fact I wanted to thank you,' the oddball insisted, to a brief, stunned silence.

'Thank me…?' I gasped, stepping a pace backwards.

'Yes – the Red Cross volunteer only worked the shift that night because you guys were on; she accompanied me to hospital and we've been married now for almost two years!' he enthused, at least giving the story a happy ending.

****

Dubbed 'the gay capital of Britain', yet in years gone by just a humble fishing village, London-by-the-sea has a liberal-minded, continental ambience which understandably lures hordes of free-thinking bohemians to its shores, making for an arresting, cosmopolitan resort during the more temperate summer months.

Finding myself afforded the rare luxury of a weekend break and heading south for a breath of coastal air, the city's captivating 'Lanes' district with its abundance of individual shops and cosy cafés figured high on the agenda and I took time out to hang loose for an hour or two over tea and scones, whilst also indulging in a bout of people-watching. Filled with a sophisticated, albeit laid-back aura, Brighton's maze of alluring streets and alleys lend the place an artsy-craftsy air, attracting a wide pool of creative talent seen plying their wares in every conceivable nook and cranny.

Stopped in my tracks by the finger-picking wizardry of a gifted bluegrass banjoist, I took a pace forward to drop a pound coin into his instrument case; minutes later, I guiltily returned to increase the donation to a fiver.

'How long have you been playing the banjo?' I asked the budding virtuoso, dazzled by his seemingly effortless technique.

'For one-and-a-half hours now,' he replied in a guttural, eastern European accent, nonchalantly looking down at the strings and pitching into another tune.

'Ah well, ask a stupid question,' I muttered to myself, caught slightly off guard by the curt reply, yet nonetheless preoccupied with his God-given artistry.

Causes célèbres

Zoe Ball – TV presenter
Alexandra Bastedo – actress (*The Champions*, 60s/70s popular TV series)
Arthur Bliss – composer
Simon Cowell – *X Factor* impresario
Amanda Redman – actress
Katie Price – pumped-up celebrity
Holly Willoughby – attractive TV presenter and personality
Peter Mayle – author of *A Year in Provence*
Bella Emberg – comedy actress and sidekick
Natasha Kaplinsky – newsreader
Max Miller – bad-boy old-time comedian

Essential travelling band info

Favourite live music venue: The Brighton Centre, King's Road
Favourite curry house: Indian Summer, East Street – 66%
Favourite pub: Evening Star, Surrey Street – 77%
Don't miss: The Royal Pavilion, an extraordinary piece of architecture that once served as a royal palace. Totally unique and well worth a nose around! – 85%
Sense of humour/friendly welcome: 55%

Chapter 10
Bristol

FROM THE LATE 1950S THROUGH the mid '60s, perhaps one of the most familiar voices traversing the airwaves of the infamous Radio Luxembourg belonged to a West Country entrepreneur named Horace Batchelor, also known as 'King of the Football Pools'. On a weekly basis, cutting nasally through the white noise, crackles and other interference threatening to engulf the station's broadcasts, a bookish accentuated voice plied his wares to the gullible masses. By providing eight crosses beside the calculated selections, each participant was promised a king's ransom should Horace's expert weekly predictions come up trumps.

As the big sell drew to a conclusion, Batchelor fastidiously announced the full address to which the entries should be posted, meticulously spelling out the town's name: 'That's K-E-Y-N-S-H-A-M… KEYNSHAM.' For reasons unexplained this habit was latched onto by a vast listening audience, dictating along with Horace in the comfort of their homes whilst chuckling at the man's rustic pronunciation and readying their envelopes for the morning post.

Incredibly the deliberate, drawn-out incantation somersaulted Batchelor's business premises into one of the UK's most cherished addresses, rolling similarly off the tongue to Number 10 Downing Street. Besides affording Horace the most unlikely celebrity status, it also put the one-horse town firmly on the map as legions of curious radio buffs descended upon the whistle stop en-route to the honeypot of Bath.

Horace Batchelor ceaselessly rubbed his prophetic crystal ball from the Somerset hideaway until shortly before his death in 1977, by which time the BBC's all-powerful Radio One dominated the airwaves, effectively bringing down the curtain on the evanescent tones of the iconic Radio Luxembourg.

****

'Autograph hunters are nothing but a pain in the ass,' or so said a conceited American crooner the band had the dubious pleasure of touring with on more than one occasion; and, although I brushed his words aside as an unnecessary display of petulance, I could at least identify with where he was coming from.

The old adage that 'opposites attract' no doubt applies to the atitude a great many touring artists have towards their fans. Although often freaked out by the macabre fascination of solitary cranks found lurking amongst the groups lingering en masse outside stage doors and in hotel lobbies, most musicians are happy as a rule to engage in an ego-massaging chit-chat, except for a small minority of swollen-heads whose hectic workload apparently allows little or no margin for fraternising with the hoi polloi.

I've been called upon in my time to scrawl illegible signatures onto charity items such as musical instruments, sporting paraphernalia and even a motor car, while a wide range of body parts from bare breasts, upper thighs and buttocks to biceps and even a young woman's forehead would unabashedly be uncovered and shoved before my trembling mitt with a promise 'never to wash again', which grimly in some cases may not have been too far from the truth.

However, the distinction of the most bizarre request belonged to a young Bristolian who, armed with his bride-to-be's entire collection of erotic lingerie, showed up at the city's Holiday Inn hotel to bizarrely request a personalised dedication on each individual garment by means of a green felt-tip pen.

'That'll be me on a promise for the next few weeks! Good on you, boy,' the groom puckishly drawled with a knowing glint in his eye.

The shrewd night staff at the same establishment certainly knew the ropes when it came to handling high-profile musicians and entertainers, dropping subtle hints as to the generosity bestowed upon them by a veritable who's who of stars. Plonking down a glossy hardback album retrieved from a compartment beneath the desktop, the guileful concierge skimmed through the pages, unveiling an assortment of unreadable dedications along with the artistic scrawls of an enviable array of major celebrities ranging from Diana Dors to the Rat Pack legend Sammy Davis Junior.

Flipping over yet another yellowing leaf I halted in my tracks as, in bold black ink, a single, ovoid rubber-stamped imprint leapt out on the page, indelibly depicting the name of the much lauded American singer-songwriter Lou Reed. 'That's one of my favourites,' remarked the janitor, recounting the eccentric behaviour of the one-time Velvet Underground star, adding he'd been totally awestruck by the singer's rare and unnerving charisma.

'What about refusals from narcissistic types?' I snooped, feeling in exalted company and inscribing my moniker onto the vellum sheet.

'Narc... does that mean did any of them fall asleep?' he queried, peeping over his glasses with a look of astonishment.

'Haha, I think you're getting mixed up with the word narcolepsy. No, I mean oversized egos,' I cackled with an amused sniffle.

'Ooh yeah, we've had more than our fair share of gasbags, but it would be indiscreet of me to mention any names,' he replied with a sly grin.

'Have you ever come across Lemmy from Motorhead?' I queried.

'Why, is he a bit of a nutter?' he asked sceptically.

'I've heard he's a likeable character, though he has acquired a reputation in rock-and-roll circles for the risqué captions he's known to scrawl on the odd item of fans' memorabilia,' I let slip, cranking up the ante.

'Such as?' the nightman probed.

'Oh, I couldn't possibly go telling tales out of school!' I retorted with a devious smirk, playfully tapping the side of my nose.

Fresh from an 'off the record' heart-to-heart with my new pal and itching to air a little dirty laundry, I turned back towards the gathered throng and found myself confronted by a boorish Geordie guy, who judging by Geoff's masturbatory wrist movement over at the bar had undoubtedly been making a nuisance of himself. Unrolling a pilfered poster and forgetting his manners, the man bade: 'Here, put your moniker on this and dedicate it to my wife Sharon, then I've got the lot!'

As I fumbled around for a pen to fulfil the man's craving, showing a total disregard the ignoramus blurted: 'I don't have a clue what she sees in your band – I personally think your music is a load of fucking crap!'

'How eloquently put,' I retorted, continuing with my artistic squiggle, until the wording ultimately read:

Lots of love to Sharon
Dave B.
P.S. how did you wind up married to such a fucking moron?

Sauntering back to the porter's desk picturing the good lady's reaction to her homesick spouse's token of his devotion, I beckoned to my equally artful partner in crime and wickedly chuckled: 'Hey buddy, here's another tale to add to your Little Red Book!'

****

British geeks, along with our US counterparts, have long held a peculiar obsession to categorise or pigeonhole virtually everything in existence, a trait which extends itself to a staggering diversity of musical genres almost as far-reaching as the Great Wall of China. Beginning with the original forms of pop, jazz, blues and classical music, the predominantly African-American roots soon diversified into rock & roll, R&B, soul, funk and doo-wop, from which a small number of cult offshoots were derived which have since become extinct.

Modern-day typecasters continually seek to confuse matters, concocting an inventory of differing denominations, ranging from the sublime to the utterly ridiculous; so, no matter 'What's Your Flava', hereafter follows a miscellany:

4x4 garage, acid jazz, Afrobeat, Bhangra, blue-eyed soul, Britpop, Celtic reggae, cello rock, chillout, dance hall, darkstep, death rock, dubstep, electronica, gameware, glam punk, hard house, indie (several genres of its own), jam band, kinko, krautrock.

The list runs into hundreds, even extending to a classification of our very own, coined in the words of a bet-hedging music journalist as: 'retro rock and roll/doo-wop glam', whilst still left wanting at pinpointing the band's Fifties-influenced trademark style.

Not solely restricted to the music, the addictive tendency also applied to the performers, who as a result became grouped into two main categories: singles artists – relating to radio-friendly hit-makers – and album artists – consisting of prog-rockers and 'respected' virtuosos, many considering themselves above the mainstream and refusing to bow to the demands of commerciality in releasing edited seven-inch versions of their songs. Distinctly at odds with the status quo, Showaddywaddy remarkably broke the mould, stirring up the water by rocketing to the dizzy heights of number nine in the LP (long-playing) chart in esteemed company and thus confounding the 'expert' analysts in one fell swoop.

With the band comfortably ensconced in an upmarket Bristol hotel, the news greeted us by way of congratulatory telegrams and incredulous phone calls from industry bigwigs including our own gloating record chief, whose disbelieving voice cracked with emotion, elated that the pretentious trend had at long last been bucked.

Having woken to the glad tidings with around twelve hours to kill prior to the fifth show of a six-day stint, a joyful lightness pervaded the air, lending itself to a spontaneous interlude of fully justified conviviality. Garbed in trendy hip-hugging Speedo swimming trunks, the massed ranks joined forces at the indoor poolside, lazing wantonly on a row of teak recliners as trolleys of ice-bucketed champers and canapés arrived to further enhance the good humour.

'It's not every day a band like us makes the album charts, let alone the top ten,' commented Romeo.

'In that case we'd better make the most of it. There'll be plenty of time to sober up before the gig!' Geoff announced, raising his glass and savouring the moment.

As if by magic, and with absolutely no inkling as to where they appeared from, within the hour the pool area became awash with a bevy of giggling bimbos clad in skimpy bikinis as the bacchanalia stepped up a gear before the startled eyes of the gaggle of staff members assigned the task of catering to our every whim.

All around were beaming faces guzzling pricey bubbly straight from the bottle while the half-naked beauties screamed with delight, leaping into the blue water with gay abandon. The strains of loud rock music pumped tremulously into the clammy, chlorine-tainted cauldron of animated bodies, bringing to life the rock-and-roll dream.

Skirting cautiously around an area of broken glass, I located the health spa and tugged back the handle of the Finnish sauna. A blast of woody heat pinched at my nostrils, awakening my senses to a feverish panting emanating from up on the top deck where, coupled together with an open-minded young filly, a red-faced band-member was sweating buckets, reeling from the exertions of a steamy workout.

'Oops, sorry to disturb you,' I gulped, averting my eyes from the perspiring Jezebel who brazenly retorted: 'Oh you can come in, I don't mind at all.'

Figuring three may be a crowd and declining the invitation I left the libertine couple to reconvene, picking up where they left off seemingly unperturbed by prying eyes or even the risk of heatstroke.

As twilight descended and the bender continued at full throttle, the trivial matter of the night's performance reared its ugly head. With a scheduled onstage time barely three hours hence, the party was brought to a swift conclusion, much to the chagrin of our scantily clad guests. The only sensible course of action now was to return to our rooms and sleep off the debauchery's effects, hoping against hope that – come the moment of truth – the challenge lying ahead may not be all uphill.

The hour onstage remains a blur; but, muddling through in a way only musicians can, by all accounts the performance went off well, jollied along by a large proportion of the paying customers being in a similarly critical condition.

Following a late-night curry at a grubby unlicensed Indian restaurant (where, to bolster trade, white wine was poured from a porcelain teapot into cups and saucers), the session picked up where it left off, this time in the hotel bar, from where I'm reliably informed a staff member assisted me back to my quarters as the dawn was breaking.

I rose from an unconscious slumber with noon fast approaching. The simple act of putting one foot in front of the other took a comical turn, not in any way helped by a thumping head and full bladder whilst stumbling to the bathroom. Relieving myself gratefully, I glanced into the mirror to survey the wreckage. A dark brown reflection I swore blind had been white as snow just hours before glowered back, making eyeball-to-eyeball contact and frightening me out of my wits.

'A-A-A-A-ARGH,' I hollered, teetering away from the WC, carelessly dribbling onto the bedroom carpet and noticing the soiled pillowcase on which my face had rested smeared from top to bottom with a cocoa-coloured substance. Chewing my upper lip I found a mysterious sickly-sweet coating tingling on the tip of my tongue, confusing the hell out of my taste buds. 'What the fuck was I drinking?'

As I deliberated I looked over to the adjoining bed where, smack in the middle of the unblemished pillow, lay an unwrapped chocolate bedtime treat.

Doddering back to the mirror for a second peek, I heard the metallic crunch of a pass key. The door swung open to reveal an elderly chambermaid sporting a sky-blue smock, who upon examining the semi-naked figure shrieked: 'Goodness gracious, for a second there I thought I'd walked in on Al Jolson in his undies!'

'Al who?' I yawned, beginning to come to.

'Al Jolson, he was one of the Black and White Min… Oh, never mind, you're probably too young; anyway what happened to you?' she gasped, eyes agog.

'I think I must've crashed out face down on the pillow when I hit the sack without even noticing the chocolate,' I surmised.

'And you woke up… without realising. Oh my God, that's the funniest thing I ever heard!' cried the housekeeper, helplessly crouching forwards and snorting loudly like a hyena in an irrepressible fit of the giggles.

She retreated through the door, and her infectious laughter echoed all the way along the corridor as she beckoned a bevy of curious chambermaids, who to my acute embarrassment – made even worse by the trail of urine spattered on the carpet – barged into the room to witness for themselves what all the fuss was about.

'Now now, girls there's no need to get excited,' the senior char reprimanded, re-entering the bathroom and handing over a dampened, soapy flannel, struggling along with her blubbering colleagues to keep a straight face.

Shooing the ladies back into the corridor and slotting the security chain in place, I decided the task of returning my skin to its natural pigmentation was beyond my capabilities for now. Tiptoeing around the spillage and doing the sensible thing, I crawled back beneath the sheets, clicking out the light for an hour or two's extra shut-eye.

Causes célèbres

James May – *Top Gear* presenter
Massive Attack – trip hop/electronica band
Justin Lee Collins – hairy TV presenter
Lee Evans – funny man
Banksy – heralded graffiti artist

Derren Brown – TV illusionist
Stephen Merchant – bespectacled comedy actor
Russ Conway – '60s pianist
W.G. Grace – cricketing legend
Cary Grant (born Archibald Leach) – silver-screen legend

Essential travelling band info

Favourite live music venue: Hippodrome, Saint Augustine's Parade
Favourite curry house: Rupsha, Regent Street, Clifton – 71%
Favourite pub: Beer Emporium, King Street – 67%
Don't miss: Brunel's SS Great Britain, Gas Ferry Road – 73%
Sense of humour/friendly welcome: 45%

Chapter 11
Cambridge

COMMENDED IN TOURIST GUIDES as a city for all seasons, the East Anglian university town of Cambridge may likely be perceived as one of the more desirable of England's municipalities in which to set up home, particularly on the evidence of a weekend stopover.

Toying with the idea of investing in an urban bolt-hole in the mid 2000s, I had drawn up a shortlist of favourable locations well suited to a change of scenery and, at first glance, the ancient fenland pearl ticked all the boxes. This initiated a spate of emails to property agents in the area ahead of knuckling down to a day or two of house-hunting, during which we would perhaps be able to throw in a smidgen of precious social time for good measure. That, anyway, was the plan!

****

Easily navigable on foot, the city's buzzing central hub boasts all the hallmarks of a classic stomping ground, from the enchanting infrastructure of the university buildings where learned students and lecturers diligently come and go, through an aberration of spick-and-span shop frontages tastefully concealed beneath the original stonework, proving easy on the eye and harbouring an Aladdin's cave of something for everyone. A mere stone's throw away, the delightful River Cam threads unremittingly between an embankment of higgledy-piggledy dwellings, lending an air of grace and tranquillity to the general scheme of things, where alongside muscular, straw-boatered punters (which I'll come to later) the lilting stream snakes past a melange of traditional waterside inns.

We arrived in town good and early, bent on a coffee infusion prior to gathering up a stack of glossy particulars, to find a swarm of pollen-gathering bees zigzagging to and fro in the form of a huge peloton of cyclists snarling up the mesh of narrow streets and lanes. Wishing I had eyes in the back of my head I yanked the steering wheel back and forth as a tailback of day-tripping motorists blocked off the arterial route, ticking over by the entrance to the central hub's sole multi-storey car park. Stiff from locating a parking berth some thirty minutes later, we hurriedly alighted from the foul-smelling stairwell to a welcome burst of untainted air that refreshed our eager lungs.

Put in Dickensian terms Cambridge offers its very own tale of two cities, divided between the innermost tourist honeypot and an unsightly matrix of white-brick suburbs visibly spilling over into the environs, in the thick of which our initial viewing was set to take place. Typically the heavens opened, making for a miserable, dank mud-heap of an introduction. The first impression was not improved by hard-hatted contractors punctuating each sentence with the f-word as they scowled down at the would-be purchasers, escorted by bleached-blonde sales reps beneath soaking umbrellas to a range of on-site show dwellings.

'The prices are a little top-heavy, aren't they?' I adjudged, nosing around a characterless two-bed apartment backing onto a block of shabbily constructed social housing and quoted at a staggering £400,000.

'I'm afraid that's the going rate to own a place in one of the country's most sought-after locations,' chirped the go-between, dampening our enthusiasm in addition to the outer lairs and throwing a monkey-wrench into the ointment.

'The city centre may be sought-after, but I'm not having it that this area's anything to write home about; plus it's a helluva long walk into town,' I responded.

Housing market statistics affirm that, along with Oxford and Guildford, the city of Cambridge takes the biscuit as the least affordable place to live in the entire United Kingdom, amazingly eclipsing the nation's capital.

As we trawled from one quagmire to the next where multi-coloured display boards beat the drum for 'Contemporary Luxury Living' within a symmetry of lavishly appointed rabbit-hutches, the incessant sales pitch soon rang hollow. Any thoughts of taking root in the Fenlands were cast aside, together with several sets of details banished to a cast-iron litter-bin.

****

For such a prominent and thriving centre of cultural excellence, astoundingly Cambridge badly lacks an outstanding modern concert arena, placing the burden of attracting big-name artists to the city on the reverberant Corn Exchange tucked away on Wheeler Street. Never figuring high on the list of the band's best-loved auditoriums, the venue nonetheless incorporates a shambolic, unrefined ambience suited to rock-and-roll events, at the same time as presenting a head-scratching acoustical nightmare predestined to challenge the most experienced of technical crews.

Back in town for the umpteenth time in 2007 and eager to escape the confines of the clattering hall post soundcheck, a stretch of the legs along the King's Parade seemed the perfect tonic coupled with the ulterior motive of satisfying my sweet tooth courtesy of 'Jim Garrahy's Fudge Kitchen' and introducing the guys to a heaven-sent delicacy.

Revived by a light summer breeze, we perused the typically English scene. The sight of fresh-faced canoodling couples pussyfooting around silver-topped senior citizens ambling contentedly arm in arm stirred the imagination, while happy-snapping international tourists and students posed for photographs from long-lensed cameras and mobile phones, ready to be forwarded on to their loved ones scattered across the globe.

As a group of smartly attired graduates assembled to 'watch the birdie', the ever-mischievous Danny tagged stealthily onto the end of the pack, grinning like a Cheshire cat whilst hoodwinking the unsuspecting subjects. The cameraman hesitated for the briefest of moments to line up the shot, and his puzzled expression alerted the clique's uppity, self-appointed top dog, decked from head to toe in light-brown tweed. Getting wind of the uninvited guest he admonished: 'Hey-hup, we don't know you, you horrible little man, go away,' looking down his nose at the prankster whilst cutting short the horseplay in a manner befitting a slave-driver.

'What a stuck up knobhead he was! No bloody sense of humour at all. There's an expensive education for you!' Dan bickered, smarting from his dressing-down, though perfectly apt in his description of the pompous ass whose over-the-top grandiosity portrayed an utter disregard for the plebeian lowborn.

Back at the theatre I was waylaid by the tubby but amiable stage-manager who asked: 'Are you Dave?' before handing over a folded, fingerprint-stained envelope. In almost indecipherable handwriting it read:

DAVE THE LEED SINGER – ERGENT

A trifle puzzled, I ripped at the gummed flap post-haste. Inside, a screwed-up piece of foolscap revealed a confusingly scrawled message:

IF YOU DON'T LET ME SEE YOU I'M GON TO KILL MESELF, BABY KYLIE IS DOOIN JUST FINE LUV ANGELA

I wracked my brain, totally flummoxed, as the eyes of the fat controller met my own. Judging my expression perfectly, he elicited: 'Problems?'

'Did you happen to see who dropped this off?' I grilled, anxious to shed just a glimmer of light on the unjust and disturbing contents.

'Indeed I did; you'd spot him a mile off, he was a right scruffy geezer. I wouldn't have trusted him as far as I could sling him. He looked like he needed a bloody good scrub and wore a dark blue donkey-jacket, with hair streaked in dandruff...' he gabbled excitedly as he reached for an inhaler, clearly unimpressed by the messenger's appearance.

'I honestly can't get my head round this one; we often get crackpots sending weird messages but I don't know anyone named Angela, and as for a baby christened Kylie... what's that all about?' I puzzled aloud, assuming it to be one big mistake.

'Do you want me to allow them backstage? I'll gladly knock them back on your say-so, especially as I didn't like his pushy attitude,' the aide asserted.

'I'm not sure what to do. All I know is, if this is a hoax I'd like to get to the bottom of it. No, let them in – if there's any trouble there's plenty of able-bodied men on hand to sort it,' I suggested a tad reluctantly.

I was noisily running up and down some scales in readiness for the gig when a light tap at the dressing-room door signalled the arrival of the straw boss, who quietly whispered: 'Dave, sorry to bother you; your guests are here – shall I show them in?'

'No you bloody well won't, I'll be out in a sec – and by the way they're not my guests,' I testily snapped, hurriedly pulling a comb through my hair.

''Ere 'e is, I told ya I'd gerrit fixed up for ya to meet 'im,' boasted the woman's inarticulate partner, living up to his reputation as the great unwashed and garbed in the same apparel as described in his former role of Postman Pat.

'So you must be Angela; what's all this nonsense about?' I put firmly, sniffing something more rancid than a rat.

'What's what all about? It's been my life's ambition to meet you, that's the honest truth; what are you so pissed off about?' she fretted, her bottom lip trembling.

'Because the letter said you were contemplating suicide if I didn't, plus it mentioned a baby named Kylie!' I protested.

'That's crazy – what letter? This is Kylie here and you can see she ain't no toddler,' the admirer bleated, acknowledging a pretty teenage girl stood right beside her, who sweetly chimed in: 'Mum's been a huge fan since she was my age; she always had your songs on when I was growing up, so I'm a fan too – it's lovely to meet you!'

Scowling at her lank-haired partner with fury in her eyes, the mother screamed: 'You cretin, you've gone and spoilt everything! No wonder he's fuming. You may not be Kylie's dad, but you know darned well he ain't either!'

'I couldn't think of any other way they'd let us backstage,' the man pleaded, under threat from his partner's handbag hovering ever closer to his thick skull. The danger was nipped in the bud in the nick of time as the dependable Kylie rushed to the rescue, tugging at the leather strap and saving the dunce from a serious battering.

'Is it okay if we pose for a quick photo with you? Then we'll be out of your way. I can't apologise enough for all the hassle; it seems my mum's boyfriend overstepped the mark this time,' the young adult rued, going out of her way to smooth things over.

As she tenderly touched my arm to express her gratitude, the girl's parting words rendered me speechless: 'It's been wonderful to meet you, and thanks not only for making my mum's life but also for being so understanding... I wish you were my real dad, but sadly I haven't seen him in fifteen years; what a scumbag!'

These few words melted my heart whilst also exposing the invisible scars so blindly inflicted by her good-for-nothing father. Ironically, his parting shot had been to forsake a radiant young woman in the making, gratifyingly different from those who'd helped shape her values and personality, including the mutton-headed stepdad-in-waiting whose thoughtlessness and slanderous words had sparked such outrage.

****

At variance with its unexceptional outlying sprawl, Cambridge remains high on my list of preferred UK destinations, though a few words of cautionary advice to would-be visitors may well come in handy for the more adventurous types wishing to partake in the popular pastime of punting along the river Cam.

What indeed could be finer than watching the world go by, cool-box at the ready, kissed by the glorious summer sun in the pastoral surroundings of a quintessential English township, pores oozing tiny beads of sweat whilst indulging in a spot of light exercise, gently drifting alongside the river's verdant banks?

'How hard can it be?' I'd said to my other half upon boarding the flat wooden vessel, unaware the rudest of awakenings lay in store which later prompted me to compile a resumé of carefully selected words of wisdom:

A bungling oaf's guide to the rights and wrongs of river punting

Correct stance: Stand sideways between the port and starboard side of the punt with one foot placed in front of the other.
DB method: Stand facing the boat's bow, legs akimbo.
Correct: Raise the pole vertically using hand-over-hand method until the butt is clear of the water.
DB: Jolt the pole out of the water at a 45-degree angle.
Correct: Place weight on front leg and slide pole smoothly through hands until it finds the river bed.

DB: Drop pole into water losing balance and tottering backwards.

Correct: Grip pole with both hands and push against river bed moving hands smoothly along the pole.

DB: Shove down on pole and propel punt in a circular motion.

Correct: Transfer weight from front foot to rear leg taking care not to use excessive force whilst pushing through the stroke.

DB: Use brute force and topple over, dropping pole into water.

Correct: Successful stroke ensures natural upward movement of pole to surface from river bed.

DB: Kneel down to retrieve pole from water and lose balance, struggling to return to upright position.

Correct: Steer pole to rear as with a rudder and sweep to right to turn to the right, then vice versa to bias towards left.

DB: Clumsily push down on pole to manoeuvre to left, yet again lose balance and leap from stern onto quayside to avoid falling into water, stranding wife and daughter literally up a creek without a paddle.

Athletic young boatmen scattered like shepherdless sheep, undergoing the effects of a sudden panic attack and clambering aboard a half-dozen vacant punts in pursuit of the abandoned craft cutting adrift my nearest and dearest, as hanging my head in abject disgrace I nervously looked on from the embankment.

Somewhat fortuitously a wiry, nimble water-boy gained on the stray punt, teetering on the brink yet managing to pluck up the courage to leap onto the vessel, finally traversing the metre-wide gap by the skin of his teeth before clinging onto a pole tossed over to him from the grassy bank.

Crestfallen and utterly humiliated, I returned to the landing pier where a whiskery, finger-wagging head honcho delivered a stern ticking-off, stressing that, had I simply requested a trial run, his beefy crew would gladly have assisted.

A little while later we had stumbled across a pleasantly situated riverside restaurant and were basking on the decked terrace in the warm sunshine. Studying the extensive menu my wife commented: 'Pricey, isn't it; shall we go somewhere else?'

Without thinking, eyes closed and enjoying my peaceful reprieve, I inadvertently replied: 'No, this is just perfect – let's push the boat out a little!'

Causes célèbres

Richard Attenborough – esteemed actor
Nigel Davenport – actor
Douglas Adams – author
Jack Hobbs – cricketing great
Oliver Cromwell – born in nearby Huntingdon
Dave Gilmour, Roger Waters and Syd Barrett – original Pink Floyd founder
    members

Essential travelling band info

Favourite live music venue: Corn Exchange, Wheeler Street
Favourite curry house: Taj Tandoori, Cherry Hinton Road – 67%
Favourite pub: St Radegund, King Street – 88%
Don't miss: King's College (and Chapel) – 84%
Sense of humour/friendly welcome: 42% (add a further 30% for property prices)

Chapter 12
Canterbury

THE RISKY SPHERE OF CONCERT promotion has long attracted a wealth of bloodsuckers entertaining thoughts of making a quick killing by basically dabbling in a megabucks industry, often compromising the reputation of the artists actually putting the bums on seats.

Briefly breaking the mould, businessman Derek Taylor fell into a different category, creating an impression of integrity and trust when we met over coffee to discuss a possible run of theatre dates, predominantly in the south of England. We hit it off from the word go, rubber-stamping the foundations of a lucrative deal. Within a month, however, on the back of three unsuccessful tour projects, nice-guy Derek's company fell into financial difficulty, forced into liquidation whilst he funded a plague of debts from his own pocket, and the chances of us working together were eliminated.

As fate would have it, whilst holidaying on the Spanish island of Menorca and taking a peaceful stroll through the capital Mahon, my wife and I chanced upon Derek and his family. After a brief catch up we arranged to meet for dinner, winding up enjoying each other's company for the best part of seven days.

Recently turned all of seventeen, son Nigel had grudgingly joined them on the trip. Spending much of his time wrestling with a hand-held game console, he could be briefly distracted away from the device at the mention of football, or more accurately his beloved West Ham United – a passion shared by DT and the real apple of his eye, absent daughter Annie.

'She went through university at Brunel and then shacked up with an Iranian lad over in Paris. He comes across as an okay kind of guy, but together they're like driftwood, just bumming around and going nowhere,' he explained, pouring out his heart over a gin and tonic while seated at an outdoors marina-side bar in the evening twilight.

'The same could be said of a lot of youngsters these days; you have to allow them their own space. Things have changed a lot since we were kids Derek. Let her get it out of her system,' I expounded like a fountain of knowledge.

'I know all about that, Dave, but she's a switched-on kid and could go far. I'm afraid she's a chip off the old block and can't stay focused on anything for long. She'll wind up just like me, doing this and trying that without any real purpose,' he reflected.

'Don't give me that. I know the concerts didn't quite work out but you're not exactly down on your uppers. If she's intelligent she'll set her sights far higher than the Eiffel Tower; and as for her soulmate, he'll probably get itchy feet and move on,' I banged on, sensing there may be other issues with Annie's Arabian boyfriend.

After losing touch for the best part of twelve months a surprise call from Derek confounded any such assumptions, suggesting to my astonishment I contact his future son-in-law: 'He's working for a small indie record label, permanently on the lookout for up-and-coming bands. When I told him you'd ventured into the management game he said he'd be well up for a chat; it's got to be beneficial to you both,' he enthused, speaking of his admiration for the young Iranian and pre-empting something quite extraordinary.

Teaming up for a week-long studio project we hit it off both musically and personally. The dusk 'til dawn sessions unveiled an enlightening, jaw-dropping account of epic proportions, detracting partially from the job in hand, though nonetheless enthralling in its brutal portrayal of the barbaric forces of tyranny.

****

Nasri's harrowing yet heart-stirring story began in the dust-ridden suburbs of the Iranian city of Isfahan. He was born the only son of pious parents beholden to the teachings of the peace-loving Baha'i faith, a religion unrecognised in the region and condemned by successive nefarious Islamic regimes, declaring its followers as 'Enemies of God'.

Coiled up in the foetal position beneath a wooden bed-frame, powerless to stifle the blood-curdling screams of his tortured father, the terrified seven-year-old quaked with fear, while only yards away in broad daylight the innocent victim suffered the most savage of assaults at the hands of a heinous lynch mob. Tragically far worse was to come when, upon squeezing his head through an open skylight, the horror-struck youngster witnessed the cold-blooded execution of his blindfolded Papa, booted to his knees in the middle of a side road where a bullet to the skull from point-blank range took the defenceless man's life.

Beset by inconceivable grief and shock, young Nasri and his mother were warned by neighbours of a sweeping radio announcement from the evil governmental hierarchy declaring their intent to hunt down every Baha'i 'criminal' in the country, in what amounted to a genocidal free-for-all against human rights. Abandoning all hope of remaining in their homeland, the indomitable mother and son swiftly took their leave, packing a bare minimum of essential belongings before embarking on a daring, tortuous three-month journey into bordering Pakistan, seeking the right of asylum and safe passage into the more hospitable surrounds of the UK.

****

Aided by the generosity of friends and acquaintances, the outcasts slipped away under cover of darkness heading for the small city of Herat in the Yadz province, where temporary shelter and an emotional reunion with close family beckoned. Mother Maryam's sister Kiana had met her match with a go-getting Shia Muslim man and converted to Islam some five years previously; now she laid eyes on her widowed sibling for the first time in almost a decade, introducing the overwhelmed aunt to her niece and two nephews, whilst lurking in the background Naz eyed the brood with a stoic frown.

Providing a roof over their heads and a chance to recuperate from a strength-sapping eighteen-hour journey, the days that followed instilled a renewed vigour for the ordeal that undoubtedly lay ahead. Faced with a backbreaking six hundred miles to the border nothing less than a superhuman effort would ensure a favourable outcome.

With favours called in from useful contacts to allow a smooth transition into Pakistan, fake documents were organised courtesy of artful brother-in-law Ali. Despite the occasional dent in the journey provided by the assistance of close allies, a realisation dawned that much of the trek would have to be covered on foot, perhaps getting lucky and being able to cadge a ride when weariness or worse still malnutrition came calling.

Transfixed and on the edge of my seat, I listened as Nasri recalled the countless scrapes they'd encountered along the way, creating a vivid image of a circumspect, courageous humankind willing to risk life and limb for those they scarcely knew, undertaking chivalrous tasks to speed their compatriots to a safe haven immune to the forces of fanaticism.

As the exhausted pair footslogged through remote hills and hollows for close on six weeks, bedding down in bushes and hedgerows beneath freezing night-time temperatures, the debilitating effects of starvation began to take hold, hampering a final push towards the city of Anbarabad where provisions would be supplied by a trusted source.

Stumbling upon the prostrate Baha'is in the emerging daylight cloistered beneath the ruins of an ancient settlement, a pair of wily kidnappers gagged the comatose boy before swaddling him in rags and blankets and making off into the empty desert, unbeknownst to his enervated, dead-to-the-world guardian angel. Dumped mercilessly inside a crudely erected wooden outhouse and bound from head to toe in parcel tape and knotted strands of string, the mummified bundle received strict instructions not to move a muscle, although – haunted by the descending darkness and shaking like a leaf through fear, hunger and cold – no such thoughts entered the captive's mind.

Hours later the padlocked door creaked open to reveal a young woman garbed in a filthy tunic and chequered headscarf draped to shield her features. She explained she had no intention of letting the boy starve, and uncovered an earthenware dish containing half a dozen cubes of fatty meat mixed in with a portion of soggy rice.

'Have no fear, we'll be moving from here in a few days to a new home where you will see things in a different light. You must learn to trust us: we wish you no harm,' the woman emphasised, further disorienting the infant.

'But where is my mother? What am I doing here?' the kid implored, shuddering at the cruel words that shattered his heart into tiny pieces:

'Your mother is dead! We are your new family and we will take care of you from now on!'

****

Pounding his thin bony hands against the mud-packed floor and crying himself into a stupor, the boy's imagination ran riot as he visualised in his mind a traumatic scene reminiscent of his father's brutal last rites, tormented by the nagging thought of his dear mother suffering a similar fate whilst assuming he may well be next in line.

At first light, as the sun crept through the slats and into his eyes, he came to in a daze as the scarfed woman returned toting a serrated carving knife in her right hand, spooking the breathless prisoner. Shutting his eyes tight and fearing the worse, he sensed the blade's coldness hovering ever closer to his goosed flesh. As he awaited his fate still as stone, humanely the abductor ripped through the taut binding, freeing up the infant's sore wrists before gently dabbing unclean water on the discoloured burn marks with a soiled castoff of underclothing.

'My father forbade me to untie you, but as you are part of our family now I begged his permission. Just be patient and remain here until it's time for us to leave,' she chided, ruffling the fledgling's hair. Grateful to be momentarily cut loose, he acknowledged the small act of mercy with a rueful nod of the head.

Feeding him scraps of unleavened bread and more chunks of chewy meat – thought to be goat – along with the odd can of warm cola, the girl returned at irregular intervals, working at gaining the boy's trust and reassuring him a better life awaited his new family upon ridding themselves of such a barren and depressing place.

Wrapped in a shroud of darkness and smitten by sleeplessness, tenaciously

82

Naz wriggled free of the tightly bound knots biting into his ankles. He thrust the balls of his feet at the outhouse walls incarcerating him, only to be thwarted by the impregnable battens. Sinking back down onto the grubby floor the orphan's heavy eyes finally closed as he mouthed a silent prayer for his departed mother, snuggling up beneath the thick wad of blankets and reliving the nightmare through a veil of tears.

As he lay chilled to the bone a hissing draught deadened the night's sounds making neither sleep nor peace possible, rattling both the captive and the hut's wooden framework, until instinctively perking up and putting two and two together Naz reasoned: *If something's tap-tapping, then surely a couple of slats must have worked their way loose!*

Blindly fumbling around, he made out an old wardrobe silhouetted in the murk. Forcing a leg into the gap to the rear the boy deduced: *If I can somehow get the damn thing to move, there may just be a couple of broken battens at the back.* Using every ounce of strength he could muster he struggled to get the trunk to budge; but the obstruction stood firm, dashing the kid's hopes until, briefly losing his footing and pulling away from the cabinet, he hurtled backwards onto the earthen surface as fortuitously a side-panel split clear of the main body. Carefully lifting the splintering plank and sliding it into the gap between the chest and the outhouse wall, he repositioned himself on the floor. Knees bent and back bolt upright the gritty young buck placed the soles of his hardened feet against the partition, taking a deep breath and looking to the heavens above, cramped into a rowing position and pumping for all he was worth, praying the bulky obstacle would dislodge.

Encouraged as the heavy coffer inched tantalisingly across the floor, the young lionheart collapsed backwards into a tearful heap, sapped of every last drop of energy and realising a bullish show of strength may not be enough. Incensed by the injustice of it all a renewed wave of grim determination stirred the boy into one last effort, gritting his teeth and pumping out his chest, when lo and behold the trunk creaked but a hair's breadth more.

Again crippled with exhaustion yet mindful the process would be prolonged and tiresome, he continued to strain every sinew whilst sensibly easing off between attempts. Gradually the formidable obstacle edged away from the wall, shifting sufficiently to force in a small limb, indicating that one final valiant push may expose the slats to the rear. As he heaved repeatedly with all his might, infuriatingly the lever snapped, noisily splitting in two and rendering the juvenile's spent body motionless at the prospect of an angry backlash from his awakening captors.

For a moment he stayed glued to the spot as, through the night's eerie blackness, silence prevailed; and though embittered by the breakage a huge sense of relief swept over the youngster, making him all the more determined to go for broke and devise a master plan to work his slender torso into the widening gap he'd so unflinchingly created.

Able to wedge his small figure into the recess in the tightest of squeezes, he thrust his back and arms against the rear of the trunk, shoving bullishly against the upright panels. The cumbersome cabinet gave a few more precious centimetres, suggesting one last full-blooded shove may surely do the trick. Devastatingly, at the key moment the boy's puny, overburdened physique finally failed him.

As he hit out in frustration at the battens above his head, the middle beam splintered, working itself loose. The sight re-energised his aching muscles just enough to cling onto the lifeline before tugging with renewed hope. Watching with anticipation as the roof timbers fragmented, squinting in the dimness he saw that a cleft to the top right-hand corner appeared to have opened up, sending an exhilarating breeze brushing across the appreciative internee's brow.

As he hoisted himself up onto the storage unit, to his dismay a faded exterior light suddenly sparked into life, flickering threateningly like a muddied beacon and casting shadows across the dusty expanse to the hut's rear. He stiffened like a board as chattering voices echoed from an upstairs window of the solitary hovel next door, spelling out that the game was well and truly up. The freezing seven-year-old despondently descended once more and, as his goose-pimpled legs buckled, he swathed himself in the woollen blankets and rested his head back against the chest, praying for a miracle... hoping... and drifting off into a deep, dark sleep.

****

The low moon created a misty, golden twilight as dawn's first glow crept over the horizon, stirring the inmate from a profound slumber. Up above him a low whistle trilled through the ruptured aperture, rekindling a faint memory of the heated exchange he'd eavesdropped on just a couple of hours before.

Surely they mustn't have heard me, he excitedly reflected, eyeing the cranny and hatching a quick-witted plan to make good his escape, knowing full well speed was of the essence due to the fast-approaching sunrise. Given a new lease of life, he leaped back onto the wooden chest and thrust his right foot, karate style, repeatedly towards the damaged batten. To his amazement and relief, in seconds flat the entire plank lunged backwards onto the arid earth.

With no time to lose the intrepid kid scrambled through the breach, dragging a blanket behind him. Undeterred by the tough, craggy terrain and smelling freedom, he charged as fast as his underdeveloped legs would carry him, driving toward an isolated rocky outcrop where a much-needed breather would allow him time to plan his next move.

Pumping his arms, head slightly bowed, the minor pushed on, gaining little ground on the rock formation and imagining it to be nothing more than a mirage. As he came to a narrow tarmac road, from out of nowhere a farmer driving an antiquated tractor pulled into his path, curious as to where a panic-stricken infant was headed at such an unearthly hour.

'I was taken by some bad people who killed my mother, but I ran away,' he unravelled, panting in fits and starts.

'Hop up on the back, lad; let's get you fed and watered and then you can tell me the whole story,' the rustic offered, nodding to an empty trailer hitched to the rear and jumping down to help the passenger on board.

Covering himself with the blanket, Naz felt himself dozing off again, until the old rattletrap hiccoughed to the safety of a modest stone dwelling. In no time at all the half-starved youngster sat perched on a small Persian rug by an old iron stove, cradling a bowl of hot soup and being comforted by a wizened-faced middle-aged woman. Tenderly she stroked the back of his head, softly assuring her unexpected guest that everything would be okay.

Over the next few days the kindly couple sought to distract the kid from the memory of his harrowing ordeal, and needing little persuasion the man of the house suggested the boy tag along on the weekly jaunt to the local market. The offer was grasped with both hands by the rejuvenated youngster, thrilled at the prospect of assisting his trusty guardian. Much as anticipated the colourful, crowded marketplace provided a welcome diversion from the living nightmare of the preceding weeks; but, mistrustful of the strangers around him, the boy's mind wandered, still traumatised by his parents' slaughter and his own abduction at the hands of those whose motives he would forever question.

Naz followed hard on the man's heels through a labyrinth of stalls, determined to stick like glue and not lose sight of his protector, until the peasant halted at a fruit and veg mart. After a bout of noisy bartering and heaving a burdensome burlap sack onto his shoulders, he intimated to his young accomplice that their business was done.

Suddenly, as they made their way back to the vehicle, the boy stopped dead in his tracks and the blood drained from his face, convinced he'd recognised one of the kidnappers queuing at a butcher's stall on the adjacent aisle and alerting his chaperon.

'What is it, boy? You look like you've seen a ghost!' the rustic queried, scratching his temple and setting down the weighty sack.

'That m… m… man over there in the red k… kaftan – he's one of the men that killed my mother and snatched me away,' the boy babbled, convulsing in fright.

'Are you absolutely certain? Those are serious allegations you're making; I can't go pointing fingers unless you're one hundred per cent sure,' his confidant advised.

'It's him, it's him, I just know it is!' Naz panicked.

Lifting up the purchase and returning to the greengrocer's stall, the patron plonked down the sack to the rear of the counter and caught the ear of a man perched atop a stack of straw bales, whose wide-eyed expression spoke volumes. Shouting back, he summoned a brace of well-toned T-shirted guys who quickly emerged from the rear canopy wearing uneasy frowns. After a heated conversation and angrily spitting to the ground, the aggressors tooled up with stubby sticks and agricultural implements and marched purposefully en masse in the direction of the meat counter.

To divert his eyes from the ensuing mayhem, a matronly woman clad from head to toe in black ushered the petrified boy behind a protective tarpaulin. Leaning forward to fuss over and embrace him, she protectively clasped his hand, assuring him everything would soon be resolved. Nonetheless, Naz felt confused and alone and, with his head cradled in the woman's lap, tears again began to flow.

The Samaritan returned roughly twenty minutes later, rousing his ward from a fitful reverie and leading him by the hand to a cold, dark storeroom located just off the main market square. Nervously entering the building, he saw, encircling the squatting evildoer, a dozen or more sinister-faced men who greeted the boy with an eerie silence, broken only by a grey-bearded sagacious-looking spokesman dressed in a white kaftan.

'Is this the man you say murdered your mother?' the wise man gently probed, crouching forwards and resting his hand on Naz's shoulder.

'I didn't kill anyone – this is madness!' shouted the kidnapper, receiving a size nine boot to the small of his back courtesy of a frenzied onlooker.

Terror-stricken by the perpetrator's presence, the young accuser was lost for words. Quaking in his shoes he gesticulated towards the man in a fit of pique, observed by the hirsute mediator who quickly intervened to calm the distressed child.

'You must try your best to help us – it's wrong to go accusing someone of such a serious crime if there is no truth in what you say!' the man urged.

'There were two of them; they took me away from my mother while I was sleeping and the lady said they killed her!' the kid squealed, fighting for breath.

'What lady?' the arbiter asked in hushed tones.

'The lady who came in to feed me when I was tied up in the hut,' he revealed, eyeing the man in white edging closer to the captive.

'Why would the boy lie? I can see guilt written all over your face, you scum. You separated this child from his mother and held him against his will. I want no more lies or you will be handed over to the police in Anbarabad. Where is the woman?'

Deflated and defeated, the abductor's head slumped forward. Blubbering fitfully like a baby, he received little sympathy from the aggrieved eyewitness whose Doc Marten cracked into his right shoulder, causing the wretch to cry out in panic: 'The boy's mother is still alive! It was a hare-brained idea; I can explain everything, but no police, please. I know where she is – I can take you there... now!'

****

Sandwiched between a small army of men in the rear of a delivery van and recognising the house instantly, for the first time in days the boy's eyes filled with brightness and hope, dreaming of being reunited with the one person he truly loved.

He was ordered to remain in the vehicle for his own safety. Not a soul appeared to be at home, confirmed by a thickset warrior in camouflaged combats who, after hammering repeatedly at the door, gave the all-clear for his comrades to sprint round to the building's rear, where a thorough recce of the immediate area uncovered no trace of any accomplices.

Dragging the wretched hostage into the undulating courtyard, the men urged the chaperone to follow on with the boy. The punctured pick-up truck his wiry frame had been bundled into just days ago stood abandoned on the scorched earth, packed to overflowing with items of furniture and other assorted household junk.

'It looks as though your co-conspirators have flown the nest and left you to face the music alone,' the booted henchman implied, flinching as a pair of stray hens fluttered from an outbuilding in the adjoining enclosure.

'Shush, listen up a sec,' another helper pleaded, picking up on a high-pitched buzzing sound in the distance, bumping along the craggy approach road.

'Everyone back against the wall, and you – keep your mouth shut,' the Rambo lookalike barked, snarling at the prisoner, eager not to blow the posse's cover. The man froze on the spot as a turbaned biker skidded onto the quadrangle in a cloud of dust, screeching to a halt beside the laden pick-up.

Nasri instantly identified the man as the secondary abductor and cried out in alarm. Forewarned by the sound, the wrongdoer opted to make a bolt for it, kick-starting the moped and ramming his foot to the floor. Leaping athletically into the man's path, one of the strapping T-shirted males courageously put his body on the line, colliding with both contraption and rider in mid-air and bringing the sideshow crashing to the ground in one fell swoop.

'Where is the woman?' the fired-up hero bellowed, legs akimbo, glaring down threateningly at the pathetic creature lying prostrate on the deck.

'I haven't a clue what you're talking about,' the miscreant blubbered, quivering and shielding his eyes from the blistering sun, unaware of the presence of an angry lynch mob wanting answers and manhandling his kinsman to his side.

'The game's up, Farrokh; I told them everything. It's over. You just wouldn't listen. I said from the start it was wrong to take the boy!' the captive admitted, dropping to his knees. As his partner in crime turned away from the sun's glare the conspirators' eyes met, wracked by guilt and the knowledge their ill-deeds had come back to haunt them. Collapsing onto his side and thumping his fists against the hardened soil the grazed biker looked to the cloudless sky, unleashing a gut-wrenching, agonised roar that within moments digressed into fitful sobbing.

Pointing to the rear of the courtyard where a decrepit stable block stood tucked away behind a wooden shack, the bound man insinuated this was where Maryam was held, alerting the boy who slipped from the clutches of his minder and charged in a straight line towards the barn, somersaulting spectacularly over a protruding clump of grass.

'Easy, tiger – I have to make sure it's safe in there first,' the right-hand man in pursuit shouted, helping the boy to his feet.

Cautiously the pair of them entered the tumbledown shelter, balking as the putrid stench of rotting animal carcasses hit like a sledgehammer. Shoving aside the soiled bales of straw strewn untidily across the uneven floor they tiptoed around a distasteful rubble of age-old cow pats and spilt grain. More worryingly, neither hide nor hair of the seized woman presented itself.

They stumbled and tumbled their way through an agricultural obstacle course to the derelict far end of the outbuilding, coming to a halt beneath a crudely erected hayloft. A mound of bales lay stacked in a skew-whiff step formation, which the supremely fit helpmate scaled with impressive agility before pushing a rickety partition to one side and happening upon a bound and gagged female nestled in a bed of straw.

Meeting her defiant eyes, the saviour spoke softly to put her at her ease: 'Please be still – I am not here to harm you. Your son is down below and can't wait to see you.' Drawing a penknife from his jeans pocket, he cut loose the binding around her feet and hands before carefully unsealing the adhesive bandage covering her mouth.

'Nasri is here?' she gasped disbelievingly, hands clasped together as she uttered an inaudible prayer to the heavens above. Her question was met with a reassuring nod and a smile. Conscious of her immobility as the woman tottered to her feet, the hero of the hour signalled down to his compatriots to arrange the bales to break their fall. This done, he hauled Maryam over his shoulder and prepared for lift-off. Landing in a heap, buried up to their chins in the cushioning straw, the emancipated couple wheezed a huge sigh of relief as their glowing eyes again met, before erupting into a bout of spontaneous joyful laughter.

'How can I ever repay you for your kindness?' the indebted woman whispered, her voice faltering, hoarse with raw emotion.

'Mama, Mama, is that you?' an ecstatic wee voice cried out, echoing off the barn walls in the sweetest dulcet tones imaginable, filling his loved one's ears with inexpressible gladness. A second later the animated sprog vaulted into the bosom of the weeping Maryam; and this time, thankfully, the glistening droplets were tears of joy.

****

Fatigued from an all-night studio session, Naz and I flopped into two plastic chairs as the sunrise's burning orange hue seemed to stir up a resonance of memories, loosening my colleague's tongue and transporting him back to a scarred, yet character-building childhood.

An epic journey of such proportions would indeed fill the pages of a bestseller in its own right, no doubt delving into the resourceful pair's hazardous exploits in the restive Sistan-Baluchestan province, where mistaken for illegal aliens in the border town of Mirjahve the couple were detained for forty-eight hours.

Suffice to say that, blessed with a superhuman will to survive and aided and abetted by the admirable fortitude of a multiplicity of big-hearted compatriots, the castaways ultimately crossed into Pakistan where, provided with the necessary legal documentation, the authorities opened the door to a new and unassailable life in England.

****

A Catholic church in the picturesque Kentish city of Canterbury on a flaming June afternoon in 2006 became the joyful setting for the marriage of Annie and Nasri. As the most radiant of brides strolled arm in arm down the aisle with Derek, the proud father lightly dusted his watery eyes with a handkerchief as he prepared to give away his life's blood.

Mingling with a cross-section of guests at the stylish reception held in the rose gardens of a plush hotel perched on the banks of the pretty Stour River, I

89

found myself chewing the fat with the groom's stout-hearted mother. She sensed my genuine interest as I turned the conversation to Naz's incredible account in the hope that a flute or two of vintage champagne may loosen her tongue and bring light to a couple of gaps in the story. As she talked freely, enraptured by the day's splendour, extraordinarily a further heart-rending tale began to unfurl:

'The last thing I wanted was for the police to be involved, so I cut a deal with the kidnappers to arrange transport to a town closer to the border. On the way the driver revealed all, explaining that the young son of the abductors' family had been caught up in a tragic accident, shot and killed when a foolhardy footsoldier handed his rifle to a reckless gung-ho youth who, unwittingly releasing the safety catch, indiscriminately fired the weapon, hitting a teenage girl in the arm but sadly taking the infant's life.'

'But where on earth did Naz figure in all this? Surely they couldn't have seen him as a ready-made replacement?' I gasped, totally engrossed.

'That's exactly what they did. Riding by on his moped one of the kidnappers spotted Nasri trailing behind me at the roadside; and, together with his brother-in-law, came up with a dim-witted plan to present his distraught wife with an orphan of similar age and matching features. My boy was earmarked as that surrogate child, but by the grace of God and with no little fortune he lived to fight another day,' Maryam concluded.

Causes célèbres

Orlando Bloom – film actor
Fiona Phillips – TV host
Freddie Laker – cheap flights originator
Thomas Becket – murdered in the cathedral in 1170

Essential travelling band info

Favourite live music venue: Marlowe Theatre, The Friars
Favourite curry house: The Ancient Raj, North Lane – 41%
Favourite pub: Foundry Brew Pub, White Horse Lane – 63%
Don't miss: St Augustine's Abbey – 63%
Sense of humour/friendly welcome: 42%

Chapter 13
Cardiff

DISILLUSIONED WITH SCHOOL LIFE AND sorely in need of ready cash to fuel a burgeoning semi-professional career in rock and roll, in keeping with my father's wishes when a livelihood in telecommunications beckoned I followed my head instead of my heart, ditching the blackboard jungle and any ongoing academic ambitions at the tender age of sixteen.

Three months into my apprenticeship (which provided me with a paltry take-home pay of seven pounds and ten shillings) I found my backside parked, along with twenty equally green trainees, on a battered military-style coach as we headed, like convicted criminals banished to a foreign outpost, across the Welsh border to the capital city of Cardiff. Over the next fortnight of intense tuition the band of fresh-faced rookies were expected to acquire the basic skills of telephone engineering necessary to stand each and every one of us in good stead for the remainder of our working lives.

Meanwhile, barely half a mile away at our board and lodgings, the quiz of egg-headed tutors appeared oblivious to a quite different curriculum of education high on the landlady's agenda. Mrs Butterworth was what may be aptly described as a full-figured woman, blessed with assets any regular guy would refer to as amply proportioned, along with a mind perhaps even broader than her distinguishing features. The proud owner of a three-storey semi-detached townhouse, the fortysomething lady of the house had for some time been accommodating wet-behind-the-ears recruits, clearly enjoying the company of youthful males despite her protestations regarding the pittance she received from the college administrators, cussing the tight-fisted money men and bitching: 'They think because I'm a lonely divorcee they can take liberties!'

One Friday evening after hanging back to wait for a member of staff who lived in the same vicinity as our digs, a group of us piled into his Vauxhall Victor estate wagon, bent on making the most of the weekend ahead. However, the genial lecturer beat us to it: 'I think it's time you boys earned your stripes and took a look at our fair city. I'll pick you up at 7.30 and with any luck you'll be spewing your brains up by midnight!'

'Is it okay if I stay in, sir? I don't drink, and besides I promised my parents I'd write,' in-house geek Michael crawled, frowning deeply as the remaining stragglers pumped the air excited by the prospect of painting the town red.

The next morning, after sleeping like babies on the back of a shedload of the local tipple 'Brains', the bleary-eyed flock of night-birds arrived down to breakfast to find a dejected Michael sitting alone in the corner, still as stone and white as a sheet.

'What the hell's wrong? You look like you've seen a bloody ghost!' my new best mate Fozzie pried, patting a hand onto the youth's slight shoulders.

'If you don't mind I'd rather not say,' he politely responded, rising from the table and forlornly traipsing off to his room.

'What he needs is a fucking good blow-out and a few pints down his neck,' scoffed Kevin, the wise owl at the old age of seventeen, quickly minding his Ps and Qs as Mrs Butterworth glided into the lounge full of the joys of spring.

'Good morning, boys; I hope you slept well? Would you like a nice fry-up? I say, your friend Michael's a lovely lad, isn't he? Real breeding. I was… chatting with him for a while before I turned in last night!' she let on.

'He looks a bit under the weather today to me; I think he's suffering from a bout of homesickness,' acknowledged Fozzie.

'Not at all! He told me he's not used to late nights; perhaps he's just a little tired, that's all. Anyway, I'm sure he'll be fine!' she concluded.

Satiated after breakfast and anticipating a chilled-out weekend, the group lingered on the stairs making plans for the evening. The possibility of a further jaunt into the big city entered the equation, but doubts were raised as we assessed just how much cash we'd need. The discussion was cut short when Michael poked his head through his room door, urging irrationally: 'Don't worry, I've got plenty of dosh. For God's sake don't go anywhere without me tonight!'

Following a revitalising soak in the top floor bathroom, and seeing the darkening dusk clouds roll in through the skylight, I raced down the staircase to catch the afternoon's football results, passing by the open door to the kitchen where a perky Mrs Butterworth serenaded herself as she busily prepared the evening meal. Diverting into the TV lounge, I stopped dead in my tracks. There, sprawled across the old velour settee covered in a rash of red smudges, lay a spent-looking Fozzie who, suddenly aware of my presence, came to spluttering: 'Aye-up Dave! Wow, I was a goner there; what time is it?'

'It's ten to five. What the hell happened to you? You look like you've been dragged through a haystack backwards!' I observed.

'You wouldn't believe me if I told you!' he remarked.

'Try me – I'm all ears…' I pitched, somewhat intrigued.

'If you don't mind me asking, are you a virgin?' he inquired, getting personal.

'I'm not actually, but I only ever did it once and it lasted all of thirty seconds… Are you?' I probed after spilling the beans.

'Not any more I'm not,' he confessed, eyes twinkling like fairy lights and bursting into a fit of the giggles.

'What you… just…?' I clammed up.

'Yep: twice inside half an hour, not bad going eh – but keep it to yourself!' he boasted, erring on the side of caution.

'How did it… why… with her?' I stuttered, totally gobsmacked.

'I was lying on the bed with the pillows stacked up reading and she just sauntered into the room like she owns the place!' he blabbed.

'She does!' I chipped in.

'Silly me – of course! Anyway, she excused herself saying she needed to hang some lining curtains; and when I next looked she was halfway up a stepladder with her glory hole winking at me! She wasn't wearing any drawers!' he unravelled breathlessly.

'You're having me on! So, what…?' I yapped, mouth agape.

'For crying out loud, use your imagination will you?' he snapped, shifting across to make room on the sofa and fill in the blanks.

****

Latching onto a bunch of friendly locals we made the rounds of the city's pubs. The mini route march took us to a lively watering-hole named the Buccaneer, described by our new playmates as the 'in' place for any red-blooded male to hang out and feast their eyes on the local talent.

And feast our eyes we did, cold-shouldered by a bevy of stuck-up Welsh beauties who had far bigger fish to fry, referring to their visitors as 'kids fresh out of nappies' before blanking the quintet of pimply-faced wishful-thinkers with a dismissive sneer. Taking it firmly on the chin and content to simply ogle, we scratched together barely enough for a beer. Pretty soon the meagre kitty dried up, leaving the wannabe Don Quixotes little choice but to step out into the night and leg it back to the boarding house, pondering whether the amorous landlady may still be on dick patrol.

Following another of Mrs Butterworth's legendary fry-ups the Sunday morning promised little in the way of excitement, other than fulfilling a promise to straddle the touchline of the local recreation ground and cheer on instructor Mr Crowe who was donning his hooped jersey for a rugby match just a stone's throw from our lodgings.

'I can't stand that thuggish game; I'd much sooner stay here and catch up on some homework,' the baby of the group Ricky avowed, moping off to his room and entrusting his brown-nosing pals to show a face and keep our macho tutor sweet.

Bored witless throughout eighty minutes of ill-tempered mud-wrestling and craving a warming cuppa, we unlocked the latched door to our digs to be hit like a dose of smelling salts by the rank aroma of boiled cabbage, bubbling away on the stove, while conspicuous by their absence the hostess with the moistest and my young room-mate seemed to have vanished off the face of the earth.

'Shush,' Kevin begged, pressing a finger to his lips as, all ears, the gang tuned in to a rhythmical whimper emanating from the room above, accompanied by an intermittent creaking sound presumably stemming from the see-sawing bedstead.

'Sounds like Ricky's having a lot more fun than we did… Surely it's got to be my turn next!' mooted Kevin with a trace of envy, finally drawing a response from Michael who coyly revealed:

'While you were all out boozing on Friday night, I was busy taking a shower and before I knew it there she was climbing in with me!'

'And?' a saucer-eyed Kevin pumped.

'She dropped down to her knees and started sucking my thingy! I was shaking like a leaf and didn't know if I was coming or going,' he admitted.

'So you had your cherry popped too?' inquired Fozzie, choking on his words.

'Well, not exactly; in fact she got a little bit cross, saying I wasn't man enough and that I suffered from premature ejaculation,' he conceded, bowing his head in shame.

'So that's three down and two to go – and only five days left,' Kevin reckoned up with a self-satisfied clench of the fist.

The penultimate day, Thursday, saw a long-drawn-out recap focusing on everything covered in the two-week syllabus to prepare the students for a two-hour examination scheduled for the Friday prior to the long journey home. I returned, innocence intact, for the final time to the Butterworth residence and scampered up the stairs to begin packing. Sure enough, draped in a flimsy negligee leaving little to the imagination, there stood the wanton householder.

'W… was it me you wanted to see?' I stammered, surveying the contours of her pendulous breasts and going weak at the knees.

'You're being a little presumptuous, young man! Why would you think that? This also happens to be Ricky's room, doesn't it?' she chided, jumping right down my throat.

'Err… well yes, I suppose it is. He should be back any second. We need to swot up for tomorrow's exam,' I jabbered, all at sixes and sevens.

'Well, in that case perhaps you could clear off and watch TV for a while. I need to have a quiet word in his ear… in private!' she bossily snapped.

Hot to trot – undoubtedly; voluptuous – to the nth degree; an oil painting… most definitely not! In retrospect, the cattish claws of an opportunistic cougar dug no deeper than invisible wounds, conceivably sparing an unsullied stripling the recurring agony of psychological nightmares well into later life.

A little bit older and a whole lot wiser, four of five housemates hit the road home performing handsprings, having sailed through the exam with flying colours, yet ironically bleeding for young Ricky whose below-par performance marked him as the course's sole failure, doubtless distracted by the pleasures of a lustful floozy's excess of flesh.

Causes célèbres

Shirley Bassey – wellington-booted singer
Griff Rhys Jones – comedian/actor
Charlotte Church – crossover warbler
Rob Brydon – comedy actor/TV personality
Roald Dahl – author
Dave Edmunds – singer/guitarist/record producer
Shakin' Stevens – singer
Stereophonics – indie rock band
Underworld – techno/rock fusion band
Tanni Grey-Thompson – paralympic athlete/TV personality
Ryan Giggs – footballer

Essential travelling band info

Favourite live music venue: St David's Hall, The Hayes
Favourite curry house: Moksh, Bute Crescent – 81%
Favourite pub: City Arms, Quay Street – 70%
Don't miss: Cardiff Castle, Castle Street – 74%
Sense of humour/friendly welcome: 54%

Chapter 14
Carlisle

FIRING UP THE THROATY V8 engine of his two-seater Ford Mustang and startling the stagehands in the loading bay of Carlisle's Old Market Hall, fellow band member Buddy Gask accelerated into the darkness with me as his trusty accomplice at his side, beaming from ear to ear following a rollicking night's work in the old sweatshop of a venue back in late '74.

Going out of his way to impress a fawning clique of hangers-on in addition to the bill-topping heroes in a post-gig spree, the concert's overjoyed promoter had laid on oodles of cold beers as well as champagne on ice to celebrate a profitable venture, all ripped into with gleeful aplomb by the octet of voracious performers keen to replace a few burnt calories transuded from each dripping carcass throughout sixty-plus minutes of toil. Scarcely the perfect send-off prior to an arduous four-and-a-half-hour trek, the mismatched cocktail of seriously strong Danish lager and Moet bubbly at least provided an initial spring in the heels, which coupled with intended shared spells at the wheel would surely see us safely tucked up between the sheets well before sunrise.

Winding through the uncluttered city streets, Buddy followed the clearly marked exit route which soon brought us to an open stretch of the M6 motorway, allowing the juice-guzzling eight-cylinder beast to make light work of eating up the miles.

'I'm feeling a bit rough – I reckon I may have had one too many; any chance of pulling over soon for a breath of fresh air and a piss?' I begged, barely thirty minutes into the journey.

'I've got a feeling we may come grinding to a halt much sooner than you think – just take a look out of the rear window,' Buddy replied.

Craning my neck to peer through the glass, I could see that a police patrol vehicle appeared to be hot on the car's trail at full tilt, flashing blue lights aglow, before melodramatically sounding the alarm as the driver gestured with a wave of the arm to pull over onto the hard shoulder.

The car crawled to a standstill and I hopped clumsily out, glad of a dose of desperately needed air. A grim-faced brute of a man decked out in a blue cap and yellow fluorescent jerkin strode to my side, clipboard in hand, good and ready to read the riot act.

'Excuse me, sir, but we have reason to believe that upon leaving Carlisle you were in contravention of the Highway Traffic Act section… blah… blah… blah… and furthermore that anything you say may be used as evidence against you; are you carrying any documentation with you in the car, sir?' the humourless flatfoot reeled off.

'No, mate, I'm afraid not; I keep all my stuff under lock and key in a drawer at home. Anyway, we weren't speeding, were we?' I woozily replied, taking a deep breath and accidentally letting slip a resonant belch.

'No sir, *we* weren't speeding at all, but unfortunately *you* were doing eighty-two miles an hour,' the cocksure patrolman fired back.

'Ah well, *we* haven't done anyone the slightest bit of harm; and anyway, the limit used to be eighty until that bloody Barbara Castle woman took over as Minister of Transport and buggered it all up, so let bygones be bygones eh!' I blurted back.

'That's as may be sir, but you've just committed a serious motoring offence; and on top of that I must ask if you've been drinking?' he sussed, getting more to the point.

'As a matter of fact I have, officer – two or three of those Special Brews and then there were a couple of glasses of fizz on top!' I unfurled.

'Oh dear oh dear, sir, I'm afraid I'm going to have to ask you to sit in the back of the patrol car and undergo a breath test,' he contentedly chuckled.

'What the hell for?' I exclaimed in a tizzy.

'Because it would appear you are in no fit state to drive sir, due to an excess of alcohol in your bloodstream,' he asserted.

'Ah well, that's just it you see: I wasn't driving, was I?' I casually explained, failing to penetrate the officer's thick skull.

'Are you trying to be clever, young man? I beg to differ: both my partner and I clearly saw you alight from the car on the driver's side!' he rapped, beginning to see red.

'Bloody hell, if being daft carried a sentence you'd be serving life! It's an American Ford Mustang, you dodo; they drive on the opposite side over there, so it also happens to be left-hand drive!' I preached, nodding towards my buddy perched behind the wheel.

Inwardly squirming and smouldering in his shoes, making to talk and thinking better of it, the big fellah strutted disconsolately back to the jam-sandwich, tail firmly between his legs, muttering a stream of unpronounceable profanities.

'How the hell did you get rid of him? I was sat crapping my pants in case he got a whiff of my breath – that's why I stayed put!' my colleague gulped, half-choking on a sigh.

'You're not going to believe it... some coppers are not the brightest!' I answered, feeling him hit the gas and roaring with laughter all the way home.

****

Regular brushes with the law became part and parcel of life on the road, with the aforementioned Old Market Hall in Cumbria's county town again at the centre of a controversy when, post-performance during another visit to the acoustically unsound venue, a sextet of armed police crashed through the rear fire-doors and into the dressing area, scaring the living daylights out of the room's near-naked inhabitants in an over-the-top clandestine operation reminiscent of a macho American TV cop thriller.

'Everybody freeze! We have received a tip-off to suggest there are a number of illegal substances on these premises, so gentlemen if you could please begin by emptying all your possessions onto the floor... and I mean now!' the senior officer chillingly yapped.

We stared glumly at one another in total astonishment, knowing full well the accusations were false. A heap of upturned suitcases revealed an assortment of personal effects including bottles, hairspray canisters, brushes, combs, spare undies, bootlace-ties and a whole range of non-incriminating items, though – failing to uncover anything resembling a hidden stash – the shakedown bore all the hallmarks of a wild goose chase.

Sheepishly seeking to deceive the unwelcome visitors and assuming the search to be at an end, one of the boys (who shall remain nameless) began replacing the half-dozen essentials removed from his bag before furtively pulling on the zipper.

'Aye, Mr Wise Guy, what the hell do you think you're doing? We haven't seen inside your case, so empty the lot out right away!' barked the top dog in a ferocious tone.

'But... there's nothing out of the ordinary in here,' the nervous musician pleaded, balking as, obeying his senior officer's orders, a young commando tipped the holdall upside down sending the contents spewing out onto the deck.

Raucous laughter filled the room, with every man jack including the hit squad in stitches. Taking pride of place amongst a hodgepodge of odds and ends there lay a huge, skin-coloured dildo, glinting in the light like an overgrown glow-worm.

'What the f...?' I gulped.

'Where've you had that, you dirty bastard?' Geoff butted in, eyeing up the guilty party.

'Never mind the histrionics, lads; it would seem that, other than that disgusting sex toy, you guys are as clean as a whistle, so we'll be on our way,' the head honcho lectured, trying desperately to keep a straight face whilst strutting out of the door.

The untimely intrusion had us flummoxed for days until a close source revealed that the boys in blue had strayed only slightly off course. A part-time crew hand known as 'Dipstick' had been sighted earlier by a second-hand record stall subsidising his earnings distributing small glass ampoules of the chemical compound amyl nitrite. Outraged at the rigger's gall, and perhaps a little too eager to point the finger at his employers, a grudging market-trader squealed like a pig, blowing the lid off the devious enterprise but rendering the unknowing band members as guilty by association.

****

Continuing on the theme of law enforcement, arguably the scariest experience of them all came whilst I was trying my hand as an after-dinner speaker at the request of a prominent Police Commissioner I'd come to know, culminating in a nerve-racking thirty-minute life history before a distinguished gathering of elite police personnel and their spouses.

'It'll be far more interesting to have someone from the world of pop music as opposed to yet another burned-out sports personality; you'll have them eating from the palm of your hand in no time at all. Besides, it's all in aid of charity,' my dignified acquaintance insisted, using all his powers of persuasion to coerce me into agreeing.

Conscious from the outset of being 'thrown to the wolves' and aware the 'what ifs' far outweighed the positives, I spent hour upon hour compiling amusing anecdotes and ripping yarns based on a teenage heart-throb's on-the-road antics; but still the challenge of captivating a gathering of scoffers appeared no less daunting.

Billed as a Gala Dinner Celebration, the event was supported by two hundred or more charitable souls whose every whim was catered for as waiters scampered through the aisles of the tastefully adorned marquee replenishing an array of bottomless wine-glasses. Arriving late, I took my place at the top table, seated between a cheery senior bobby and his equally charming wife, neither of whom admitted to being familiar with the band's music.

Dabbing a serviette at his shiny pink conk, the white-haired, red-coated emcee rose unsteadily from his chair and commenced the proceedings with a stockpile of hackneyed phrases, followed by a garbled toast to the Queen signalling starter's orders as the guests proceeded to tuck gluttonously into a three-course banquet fit for a king.

Suffering butterflies in my stomach the size of dinosaurs, I picked fussily at a stringy *coq au vin*. The calming effects of a stiff brandy temporarily settled my nerves, shattered in the blink of an eye by the sharp rap of a wooden gavel, cutting short the incessant tittle-tattle and grabbing the attention of the entire throng.

'Ladies and gentlemen, your attention please! Those of you who spent their Saturday afternoons glued to ITV's *World of Sport* will no doubt... hic... be familiar with the evening's first guest... Please put your hands together for Mr TV himself... Jackie Palance!' articulated the already worse-for-wear master of ceremonies.

Unimpressed by the flawed introduction and being confused with a bygone actor, curly-haired ex-professional wrestler Jackie Pallo tore a huge strip off the reeling toastmaster before settling into a well-worn routine and proceeding to run his old muckers Mick McManus, Johnny Kwango and Billy Two Rivers into the ground. As he inarticulately prattled through thirty minutes of clichés and old chestnuts, a smattering of well-oiled hecklers began voicing their displeasure, goading the old-timer into retaking his seat whilst catching the incoherent emcee unawares.

'Order, order! Just remember our celebrity guests are here out of the goodness of their hearts, so pleesh show some respect and put a sock in it,' the anchorman slurred, stumbling to his feet and belligerently rapping his gavel. 'It's now my great pleasure to introdoosh you to a young pop artiste who sings with the world famous group "The Shoo-wobbly-wobblies". This is his first ever effort at after-dinner speaking, so don't be too hard on him. Let's hear it for Dave Bartlett!'

Nerves shot, though confident of stringing a few sentences together unlike my predecessors, with a nod to the heavens and a sharp intake of breath I referred quickly to my set of bullet points: the moment of truth had arrived.

After making headway with a scathing riposte concerning the incorrect pronunciation of my own and the band's identities, I proceeded to fill in the blanks as to my role as a performer, birthplace and beloved football team (to loud jeers from a section of West Bromwich Albion fans). The polite response came a long way from igniting the floor. Unable for once to hole up behind a protective wall of sound, the early signs pointed to an uphill battle ahead, confirmed when a tubby, balding guy in close proximity openly yawned, omitting to politely shield his mouth and slithering down in his seat.

'Sorry if I'm boring you, my friend; do you often fall asleep on the job?' I cracked with a hint of venom, abetted by the man's long-suffering wife whose rueful glance intimated I'd struck the nail squarely on the head.

'You may be surprised to know that, before I ventured into the world of sex, drugs and rock and roll, I actually completed an application to enrol in the police force,' I fabricated. My heart was pumping, but at long last I had the gallery's undivided attention. Mind racing, breathing hard and knees knocking, conscious an unfavourable response would find me dead in the water, I delivered the audacious punchline: 'But I'm sorry to say I was rejected out of hand… when the recruiting officers realised to their horror that my parents were married when I was born!'

The deafening silence left me tongue-tied. Frozen in time with nothing in the way of contingency plans, I stood, the blood draining slowly from my face, until the jovial bigwig to my side burst into a fit of raucous laughter, triggering off a spontaneous barrage of self-deprecating delight which rapidly spread throughout the marquee.

Seizing the moment with renewed confidence, I reached beneath the table for my trusted ukulele. The opening lines of the band's hit 'Three Steps to Heaven' quickly followed, augmenting into a hastily prepared rendition of 'The Laughing Policeman', provoking a mini sing-song straight out of vaudeville.

Mindful not to overstay my welcome (while also heedful of the odd disapproving glance from the sober minority), I signed off with a crescendo and my heartfelt thanks and retook my seat to warm applause. There followed – other than my wedding speech – a hiatus of twenty-odd years prior to my contemplating any form of public speaking when, succumbing to copious quantities of real ale at a fundraising beerfest, my very own larynx had some difficulty articulating.

Causes célèbres

Eddie Stobart – late haulage-company magnate
Melvyn Bragg – *The South Bank Show* broadcaster
Mary Queen of Scots – imprisoned in Carlisle Castle prior to her execution

Essential travelling band info

Favourite live music venue: The Sands Centre (city centre)
Favourite curry house: The Viceroy, Rigg Street – 59%
Favourite pub: King's Head, Fisher Street – 82%
Don't miss: Tullie House, Castle Street – 67%
Sense of humour/friendly welcome: 48%

Chapter 15
Chelmsford

THE SO-CALLED MISUNDERSTOOD BREED OF rock-and-roll artists, as in all walks of life, bear a disparate range of personalities, perceived by many onlookers outside the industry as something of a strange phenomenon. So for argument's sake, whilst in keeping with a peculiar journalistic obsession to pigeonhole almost anything that moves, hereafter follows a breakdown of the three main categories involving travelling musicians:

a) Egocentrics – A tiresome, aloof species, most of whom lead a lonely existence content to disappear slowly up their own backsides, ferried to and from every public engagement via ostentatious modes of transport consumed by an image of untouchability.

b) Arty-Farty Intellectuals – A classification reserved for cliquey avant-garde types and pretentious eggheads manifesting a desire to keep themselves to themselves, whilst looking down their noses at the incorrigible behaviour of the rank and file.

c) Unrefined Rabble-Rousers – No prizes for guessing that these constitute an exclusive club of, shall we say, more outgoing exponents bent on living life to the full; and, though every bit as passionate as *a)* and *b)* about their music and stage performance, tend towards adopting a devil-may-care approach away from the spotlight's glare.

Cleverly sidestepping the pre-eighties trend favouring so-called 'respected artists', in a plucky bid to boost dwindling attendances and finally put paid to the mud-bath mentality, a perceptive alliance of European festival promoters turned their attentions towards retro-themed events. In doing so they were looking to entice a moneyed, more mature audience whilst opening the floodgates to a torrent of mainstream artists brought out of hibernation – many reforming for the privilege – to join forces with a whole host of seasoned international performers, all seeking to cash in on a wave of nostalgia sweeping an entire continent. One-time icons such as Chubby Checker, Creedence Clearwater Revival, The Mamas and The Papas, Percy Sledge plus a cornucopia of long-in-the-tooth nine-day wonders came crawling out of the woodwork. Jetted in at great expense from across the pond, they were all poised to trade on former glories and rejuvenate a flagging crop of colourful careers.

****

Granted city status as recently as 2012, from the mid-eighties onwards 'the only way is Essex' led an eclectic mix of musicians and performers to Hylands Park and the precursor to the acclaimed V2 Festival, then known as The Chelmsford Spectacular.

Designed to showcase over four days a diverse range of bygone talent representative of the various golden eras of music and opening its gates to a twenty-thousand-strong multitude, each nostalgic occasion sought to cater to every taste, featuring Afro-topped twinkle-toed disco ensembles, glittery glam-rockers and age-old crooners, even with a smidgen of psychedelic rock (group *b*) thrown into the mix for good measure.

Buoyed by a flattering request to appear for the second year running, we arrived late afternoon for the designated soundcheck to find a bunch of self-absorbed mavericks tinkering noisily with a beat-up Hammond organ and a set of tubular bells, showing a total disregard for the earmarked schedule whilst falling foul of the onstage crew by disrespectfully ignoring their pleas to speed things along and make way for the next band.

'Surely you can see we're nowhere near ready; now how's about being a good road-thing and asking those three-chord wonders to cut us a little slack,' the keyboard player disparaged, stirring up a hornet's nest.

'Did I hear you rightly? What a bunch of pretentious wankers… Talk about disappearing up your own arse!' the crew boss icily retaliated.

'I beg your pardon!' the musician bellyached, deserving the curt response:

'You fucking heard – just get a bloody move on!'

We were eventually summoned to the stage for the briefest of run-throughs a full twenty minutes behind schedule, resigned to getting under way on a wing and a prayer. Offering no apology, the sulky anachronisms passed by on the access ramp resolved to cold-shouldering their co-performers whilst cranking up the tension to near fever pitch.

Picking up later on a heated debate emanating from within the trailer's walls and gatecrashing the party, a finger-pointing popinjay affectedly held court, sounding off to our own middle-man who was huddled over a wad of documents with a ruffled minion from the festival's organising committee.

'… And furthermore a clause in my artist's rider stipulates private restroom facilities, meaning we are about to commandeer the adjoining latrines for our own sole use; so please ensure your artists refrain from using them as of now.

In addition this ungentlemanly rabble might also consider themselves fortunate I've decided against putting in an official complaint to the promoters regarding your road crew's unnecessarily crude and insulting outbursts,' the upstart belittled, high-and-mightily laying down the law.

'So where are we expected to take a dump, in the bloody bushes?' Geoff griped, brushing past the swellhead, in need of a calming ciggy.

'There are half a dozen similar lavatories located close to the barriers on the far side of the compound – I suggest you make use of those!' the braggart haughtily bleated, swiftly removing himself out of harm's way.

'Who the fuck do these people think they are? First they overrun on their soundcheck, now we can't even take a shit without walking half a mile. This is past a joke!' I ranted, staring down the ruffled mediator with the boys' backing.

'Please don't do anything hasty; try not to use the loo for the time being. I'll get something sorted, I promise – just give me fifteen minutes,' the go-between begged.

As we cooled off beneath a bank of threatening clouds, a temporary distraction arrived in the shape of a stretch limo, unveiling an entourage of larger-than-life, shaggy-haired Kurt Cobain lookalikes sporting skintight paisley print leggings, stalked by a brace of voluptuous rock chicks and afforded the star treatment by means of a quartet of burly escorts.

'Bloody hell, look at the jugs on those dolly birds – you don't get many of those to the pound,' an open-mouthed eyewitness drooled, referring to the girls' pumped-up assets which instantly lifted the spirits in the camp.

'I'm sure I recognise that pair from a dodgy… interesting movie I once saw,' implied a crew member, provoking a barrage of lewd comments from the leering mob as, basking in the limelight, the minxes wiggled provocatively by.

****

Bestrewn with heavyset, hirsute crew-men displaying a selection of macho tattoos, the hospitality tent resembled a busy transport café, complemented by the amply stacked females propping up the well-stocked bar and turning every red-blooded male's head whilst tipsily canoodling with their long-locked gentlemen friends.

Opting for the stewed coffee, I was half-filling two white ceramic mugs for Geoff and myself when an anaemic Gollum-like gofer squeezed between us, crouching beneath the table for a twenty-four-can pack of Coca Cola whilst also making off with the one bottle of vodka on his way back up and handing the swag over to a couple of arch rivals loitering by the entrance.

'Hey, you thieving bastards,' Geoff called out, scaring the hell out of the pilferers who, under the watchful eyes of the disquieted party animals, scurried off like red-handed schoolboys to baying, unappreciative howls of derision.

Having retreated to our own refuge, I was taking forty winks while the guys put the world to rights when a sharp rap sounded on the door followed by the unannounced arrival of our highfalutin chum. With a headsetted official in tow, he ill-manneredly barged right through the door, once again making his feelings known: 'I'm up to here with you lot – it seems you're deliberately trying to make life difficult for my artists. The toilet facility that we agreed would be for our sole use has been engaged for the last twenty to thirty minutes!'

'Did you say for arsehole use? That figures! Try getting your facts straight before you go making accusations. To begin with NO ONE in our party agreed that the lavatory would be for YOUR sole use and furthermore everybody in here has been using the one provided for OUR SOLE use! Now piss off and leave us alone,' I bickered, again closing my eyes.

'This is ridiculous! Who the hell is in there then? It just has to be one of your party!' the windbag countered, not content to let it go.

'How the fuck should I know? Perhaps the door's jammed; do you need me to hold your hand while we take a look?' I fired back, leaping to my feet.

I'm chuckling as I write, recalling the priceless sight (surely worthy of rock and roll's hall of fame) of a pair of stack-heeled snakeskin boots sliding back and forth beneath the gap at the bottom of the outhouse door, accompanied by the sounds of heavy breathing and the pungent aroma of bodily fluids drifting on the cool summer breeze.

'Listen, sunshine: regardless of what you may think, neither I nor any of my colleagues would be seen dead in a pair of boots like that!' I spluttered, resolving that a stereotypical heavy-metal freak may be making hay with a busty companion.

'This is outrageous,' the knobby sidekick hollered, watching the loo door almost fly off its hinges to reveal the cherry-faced rompers who, dusting themselves down without a care in the world, ambled slowly back to their trailer.

'I think you owe me an apology,' I pressed, as Geoff arrived at my side curious as to what all the fuss was about. 'Well?' I prodded, forcing the issue.

'Ah yes… *mea culpa*, my friend, *mea culpa*!' the old hippy responded, put to shame and light-footedly tripping away.

'What the fuck is that supposed to mean?' Geoff scoffed.

'It means he's nothing other than a pompous twat!' I lamented, hoofing a stray Coke can into the nearby bushes in my exasperation.

Retribution came quick and sweet by means of a black NEC cell phone the size and weight of a house brick, when the phrase 'to take the piss' took on an entirely new meaning.

'Why the hell didn't you stick around? You would've lapped it up. I nearly came out in sympathy and wet myself!' explained the smug-sounding crew boss.

'What happened? Come on, don't keep me in suspense any longer,' I urged.

'Did you see the queues for the public bogs before you left? They stretched for bloody miles,' he chuckled throatily.

'I can't say I did; why?' I asked.

'Huh – I'll come back to that. You guys gave those punters exactly what they wanted tonight; you can be a bloody hard act to follow at times,' he begrudgingly complimented.

'Ah, I get the picture: did the audience give the prog-rockers a hard time?' I cottoned on with a touch of self-satisfaction.

'You can say that again. They bored the crowd shitless. All that lot wanted to do was party, not listen to all that self-indulgent crap!' he said bitterly.

'So where did the shithouses come into all this?' I inquired, more than a little intrigued.

'Haha, half the audience had taken a leak into those resealable sandwich packs. Once one joker had launched the first piss-bomb at the organist, a whole load of others followed soon after. The band were covered from head to toe in piss!' he signed off in hysterics.

'Priceless… just priceless,' I exclaimed, turning back to the boys.

Causes célèbres

Sarah Cracknell – singer (St Etienne)
Hazell Dean – '80s singer
Harry Judd – McFly drummer/ex-*Strictly Come Dancing* winner

Essential travelling band info

Favourite live music venue: V2 Festival, Hylands Park
Favourite curry house: Zeera, Rainsford Road – 69%
Favourite pub: Ale House, Viaduct Road – 68%
Don't miss: Tropical Wings Zoo, Wickford Road – 71%
Sense of humour/friendly welcome: 56%

Chapter 16
Chester

RIDING HIGH ON THE BACK of four top-twenty hit singles and a top-ten album, by the late spring of '75 the band had already clocked up a dozen or more *Top of the Pops* appearances. A chance invitation from the BBC show's producers, who had got wind of strong sales during the first week of release of our fifth offering 'Three Steps To Heaven', culminated in an exclusive opportunity to promote the new single live in the studio, dubbed as an exclusive preview.

Dropping down to my knees to semi-whisper the spoken passage midway into the song, backed up by a jangling rhythm of acoustic guitars and purring vocal harmonies, I displayed a facetious piece of showmanship by carefully removing the trademark shades I'd donned since the band's inception two years previously. Strategically concealed beneath the top pair's bulkier lenses lay a second, smaller set of tinted pince-nez specs. This manoeuvre proved to be something of a talking point in the show's wake, incredibly prompting reruns on the local news as well as a flurry of comments in the national tabloids.

'Dave, we've received an approach from a Manchester-based advertising agency,' the office girl interpreted from a stream of telegraphic messages relayed to her in-tray the same morning. 'They'd like you to do a screen test with a view to appearing in a lucrative TV campaign to promote a new range of sunglasses aimed at the younger end of the market!'

'Why would they want my ugly mug?' I quibbled, amazed that a simple act of tomfoolery may lend itself to a nationwide hard sell.

'I wondered that myself…' the paper-shuffler cheekily responded, quickly correcting herself with: '… but it's a fantastic opportunity.'

'Well, it certainly can't do any harm; so what's the next move?' I enquired.

'There are a few minor issues still to be sorted out, especially as we're not sure how this will go down with the other band members; in fact, we're having a meeting over lunch. Meanwhile the last telex is marked for your attention, which I'm sure you'll be happy about!' she unravelled, dictating the garbled communication:

F.A.O. Dave.

Lots of ideas to discuss, please join us as a VIP guest at Chester racecourse for the midsummer Ladies Day meeting, official invitation to follow by post.

Kind regards, Andrew.

After bedding down overnight in the midst of Manchester's hustle and bustle in readiness for a live radio interview on the local station's breakfast show, suited and booted like a dog's dinner the thirty-five-mile trip to Chester passed in a flash, leaving ample time for a glimpse around the historic city centre prior to checking in at the hotel for a 1pm champagne reception. Chuffed to bits at the likelihood of a welcome windfall for simply peacocking in a range of posy shades, I donned my own ultra-trendy Ray Bans and took to the olde-worlde streets, treading the famous 'Rows' designed to shelter erstwhile shoppers from the unpredictable elements, and captivated by a gravity-defying checkerboard of mediaeval buildings towering above a systematic clutter of cobblestone alleyways and thoroughfares.

As I meandered in the late-morning sunshine alongside the uniquely tiered walkways, a refined middle-aged lady exiting an upmarket lingerie store stopped dead in her tracks, taking time out to study my features more closely prior to unleashing a tongue-lashing of splenetic proportions, much to the bewilderment of the young visitor.

'Mr Jagger, why do you persist in putting on that dreadful cockney accent during TV interviews when it's perfectly clear you're a well-educated man?' the old maid fussed, staring me down like a priggish schoolmistress.

'I hate to disappoint you, but I'm not Mick Jagger,' I replied, quickly pulling up the biddy, much to her chagrin. Totally unconvinced and with a dismissive swat of the hand she issued a curt, snotty-nosed reprimand ahead of making her way onto the street.

Being born of malleable, rubber-lipped features, this supposed case of mistaken identity was but one of a number of striking resemblances where my own notoriety took second place to a who's who of interesting yet often ungratifying characters.

In early 1979, proudly perched at number one in the frostbound UK's album chart, I was swaggering full of contentedness by the poolside of a swish, sun-baked Rio hotel when a stereotypical American attired in a ten-gallon hat stepped directly into my path, begging a signature on a glossy tourist guide shoved tactlessly into my hand.

'You are Superman from the movie, aren't you?' he pressed in a shrill voice.

'You mean Christopher Reeve? I'm afraid not; you got the wrong guy, buddy – I'm a singer in a well-known British rock-and-roll band,' I answered with a chuckle.

'What a crock!' the J.R. Ewing lookalike noisily exclaimed, rudely snatching back the signed booklet and storming off in a huff.

I was enjoying a post-show tipple backstage with the wonderfully articulate comedian and raconteur Les Dawson (1931-1993) when the humorous northerner insisted: 'It's uncanny – you just have to be the long-lost bastard son of Barney Fife,' silencing the room and prompting a resounding chorus of 'WHO?' from the onlookers. He went on to greet me as: 'Barney… lovely to see you again,' when next our paths crossed at the BBC some eight years later, leaving me still very much in the dark as to the true identity of a little-known US actor.

Further mirror images saw me confused with my late friend Les Gray from Mud along with Freddie Mercury from Queen,* and perhaps flatteringly in recent times TV's Professor Brian Cox and the current Welsh football team manager Chris Coleman. Without a doubt, though, the most vexing dead-ringer came from the lips of a Chinese restaurateur: *'You rook rike Plime Minister Tony Brair!'* ignoring my unconstrained pleas to the contrary in what was and remains the most baffling likeness of them all.

****

I left the car in a side street just a stone's throw from the imposing Grosvenor Hotel, dodging between an opulence of Rollers, Bentleys and Mercedes Coupes garaged close to the rear entrance. The grand old place's interior oozed elegance and class, exemplified by the expertly trained personnel gliding to and fro catering to their clients' every need.

I was afforded a cheery welcome by a pudgy, top-hatted porter and a speedy check-in followed, handled courteously by two attractive members of staff, one of whom clarified with a smile: 'Your room is situated on the fourth floor and the VIP reception is scheduled to start at 1pm in the Presidential Suite just one floor below.'

The room was kitted out with a queen-sized bed bedecked with hand-embroidered cushions and satin sheets; the term 'the lap of luxury' struck a resonant chord. It was far removed from the dingy B&Bs and downmarket establishments liked or lumped over months of touring. This was emphasised again in the sumptuous bathroom where a bundle of crisp white towels lay draped alongside a gleaming marble washbasin complemented by a range of scented toiletries and lotions.

After freshening up with a sluice down followed by a quick straightening of the tie, I was ready to let loose with the high rollers as a day of hedonistic

---

* See Chapter 25 – Exeter

corporate hospitality beckoned. As chance would have it, I bumped straight into my soon-to-be employers crammed together in a lift on the way down.

'It's Dave, isn't it? Crikey – you look so much younger, and for that matter taller, than you do on *Top of the Pops*,' the main man complimented, before introducing me to his voluptuous, pouting other half standing to one side busy studying my own features.

'I didn't realise you had such lovely blue eyes; surely you're not alone... are you?' the enchantress seductively enquired.

'Afraid so – I'm not currently seeing anyone,' I confessed, keeping my own thoughts under wraps as to her own physical attributes.

Like a fish out of water I mingled with the Bollinger-swigging crème-de-la-crème of Cheshire society as introductions to advertising moguls, private bankers and a host of *nouveau riche* fat cats followed. Amongst a sprinkling of local dignitaries and celebrities were a heavily perspiring portly man sporting an enormous gold chain whom I assumed to be the city's mayor, and none other than the legendary funny man Norman Wisdom who, in keeping with his reputation for slapstick behaviour, held court before a trio of half-interested spectators.

Feeling well out of my depth as the debate turned to mega-finance, I sidled away to a quiet corner with a plate of canapés. The sweet smell of perfume bode the presence of my host's head-turning partner. Eyes glinting, she leaned aside to kindly whisper: 'John and I are about to leave for the racecourse in the Rolls; we wondered if you'd care to squeeze in alongside for a little chat before the champers starts doing the talking!'

After being captured arm-in-arm by a gaggle of photographers on hand to take snapshots of the departing glitterati, I expected the confab on the journey to focus on all things Polaroid; but an awkward silence amplified the Silver Shadow's rhythmical hum as it glided smoothly over the tarmac. At last in a husky tone the glamour puss spoke: 'We've been watching through a few of your TV performances on our new video-recorder; aren't they just the best invention ever?'

'I don't get a lot of time to watch television, so I don't really need one,' I explained, well aware such a device would cost an arm and a leg.

'Surely all the more reason to invest in one, then you can pick and choose what you care to watch exactly when you want to see it,' argued John, stifling a yawn.

'There's something about you; I couldn't help but notice how well-endowed you look in those drainpipe trousers – do you put a length of rubber hose down your left leg?' the lady teased, unperturbed by her husband's fazed reaction.

'Ah, now that would be telling! Anyway, I thought you both wanted to chat about your new range of sunglasses as opposed to oversized cod-pieces,' I replied, giving nothing away and sidestepping the leading question.

'That's Roberta's department – I can only suggest you talk it over with her!' John proposed, ordering the chauffeur to take a left turn.

'We can discuss it all later, by which time I'm sure we'll have gotten to know each other a lot better!' the temptress implied, raising her eyebrows.

****

'LADIES DAY' promoted a giant placard by the gated entrance, made more than evident by a bevy of well-groomed, hatted fillies parading their latest strappy designer dresses in the glorious late-spring sunshine in front of a rake of glossy equine beasts striding nonchalantly around the fenced-off paddock.

Setting aside the spendthrift sum (or so I thought) of a couple of hundred quid, realistically prepared to fritter it all away on the odd punt, I placed twenty pounds each way with our own bookie's runner. A group of young bankers quickly put me to shame by rushing up to the guy waving wads of cash in his face, pushing the boat out big time.

Owing to a tip from a wide boy at the hotel reception I got lucky when the unfancied nag cantered in ahead of the pack, boosting my personal coffers by a hundred smackers. I tagged on to the short queue to collect the booty, inclined toward wagering the lot on an extravagant each-way bet on the favourite for the sponsor's handicap which, at odds of four to one, appeared pretty generous. As I picked up the pink betting-slip an oafish, rat-faced guy nudged ignorantly past, stumbling to his knees after making contact and leaping to his feet in a flash.

'Who the fuck do you think you are, pushing me around?' the man viciously snapped, seemingly livid at the encounter whilst staring me down.

'Might I remind you there are ladies here, so go easy on the language, pal… In any case, it was you who bumped into me in your desperation to jump the queue!' I calmly responded, eager not to rise to the bait.

Backing off with a contemptuous sneer and drawing a thick wad of banknotes from his pocket the attention-seeking brat yelled towards the bemused bookie: 'Butcher's Boy, a monkey on the nose,' counting out the cash under the wide eyes of the startled recipient and making off with a cavalier wave of his precious betting slip.

Amidst great excitement I relocated to the reserved seating enclosure in time for the starting pistol. Reflecting the sun's bright rays the dozen or more shimmering colts stampeded from the tape, electrifyingly churning up the turf to the baying cheers of the animated crowd. Noticing my own selection lagging behind the frontrunners by a couple of furlongs, my setback was compounded as I witnessed my opposite number leaping to his feet whooping and hollering like a castrated hyena as his unfancied choice agonisingly romped home by three lengths, leading from start to finish in a deflating cakewalk.

'Bad luck, mate! I didn't want him to win either; he's nothing but a spoilt mummy's boy. What say we go back to the tent and get hammered?' urged a down-to-earth invitee I'd briefly hit it off with at the hotel bash, receiving a thumbs-up from me in reply.

'Have you known John and Roberta long?' my new buddy probed, setting a brisk pace back toward the sponsor's marquee.

'About four and a half hours, that's all,' I acknowledged with a light snicker.

'I figured as much; be careful!' he warned with a knowing look.

'Hang on a sec, you can't just leave it at that! I thought I was here to discuss a forthcoming advertising campaign, nothing else,' I let on.

'Far be it from me to go blowing the whistle; let's just say you wouldn't be the first young stud to be lured into their tangled web,' the guy levelled, playing innocent.

Back at the VIP tent the big spenders continued in much the same vein, squandering profligate amounts of hard cash via the besieged gofer who, loaded up to the gunnels with greenbacks, scurried back and forth, commenting as he passed: 'Money to bleeding burn, this lot; my gaffer's cleaning up this afternoon!'

Typically of an English summer's afternoon, with little or no notice a soufflé of darkening clouds swept across the skies intensified by lightning strikes and distant claps of thunder to herald the opening of the heavens along with the postponement of the card. Dashing hither and thither in an almighty flap, a large clique of dapper gents and sodden stunners converged on the hospitality area, taking shelter from the downpour whilst summoning a phalanx of swanky limousines to signal a mass exodus from the course, promising faithfully to meet up for dinner later on in the evening.

****

Displaying impressive staying power in the ornate bar, though fast losing the power of speech, the freeloading yuppies drank themselves into a stupor, amusing one another by emitting wind, tittering like schoolgirls at each audible belch or fart.

As she appeared like a vision from a tucked-away snug flaunting yet another figure-hugging creation, all eyes in the crowded room diverted to the provocative Roberta, thankfully waylaid whilst making a beeline for yours truly.

'Looks like you've got your hands full there, son, but watch out for peeping John and his hidden camera,' a smart-aleck offered in jest, chuckling along with his playmates.

'Are you serious?' I gulped.

'Never more, my friend… She's a bloody man-eater, that one. Just be on your guard, that's all,' the informant earnestly advised in the nick of time.

'David… I was thinking perhaps it's time we got down to some business. Here's the key to my suite; please let yourself in and I'll be up shortly,' Roberta prompted.

Guzzling down a glass of Perrier, I marched back through the lobby to drop off the said passkey. En route I passed a comatose figure catching flies, collapsed into one of the elegantly upholstered sofas doing a fine impersonation of a slumbering old sow. Mumbling an unflattering comment beneath my breath in passing, I was halted in my tracks by the reaction of a horrified lady guest, eyes popping from her head, advocating a second glance at the wasted figure left for dead on the couch.

Slouched, shirt buttons about to pop, clutching a cushion for a teddy bear lay the undignified Flash Harry I'd almost come to blows with only hours before, exposing for all and sundry to see his shrivelled, limp penis, audaciously slipped through his unzipped fly by the sleight-of-hand skills of a fiendish acquaintance, and confirming I'd been right all along when comparing his character to the tiny appendage on show.

Ambitions of a lucrative, though improbable, nationwide TV campaign in tatters, and risking life and limb in addition to a lengthy driving ban, I decided an enlightening day in the company of the north-west's swinging society had run its course, giving rise to a premature vanishing act into the night to escape the clutches of an exhibitionist wildcat.

Causes célèbres

Daniel Craig – actor (James Bond etc.)
Michael Owen – former England footballer/TV pundit
Russ Abbot – TV funny man
Emily Booth – actress
Beth Tweddle – gymnast (raised in Chester)
Keith Harris – ventriloquist (don't ask where Orville was born!)
Hugh Lloyd – actor
Martin Tyler – sports commentator

Essential travelling band info

Favourite live music venue: Alexanders, Rufus Court
Favourite curry house: Barton Rouge, Steam Mill Street – 61%

Favourite pub: Brewery Tap, Lower Bridge Street – 81%
Don't miss: Chester Zoo (amazing monkey house) – 72%
Sense of humour/friendly welcome: 57%

Chapter 17
Chichester

'BUGGER BOGNOR' WERE REPUTEDLY THE ineloquent final words to pass from the lips of His Royal Highness King George V, upon failing to heed a physician's advice to take the air and convalesce in the West Sussex town back in 1929. On the back of fourteen consecutive Sunday visits to the town some sixty-four years later, the allegedly foul-mouthed monarch's words rang loud and clear. I empathised entirely with the sentiments of a respected head of state who, disingenuously it could be said, honoured the resort with its elevated 'Regis' status (Latin for royal) whilst frequenting the same stretch of coastline prior to suffering a permanent bout of ill-health.

Ten weeks into the stint, the interminable four-hundred-mile round trip began to bleed the band dry, causing brains to scramble and perpetrating fits of fractiousness and jangled nerves as the sinews stiffened with seemingly no end in sight. In full-on party mode, and showing no inclination to settle for second best (perhaps picking up on the band's tendency to switch to autopilot), the merry-making seaside revellers pumped every last drop of gas from each of our weary carcasses, fuelled by reckless quantities of hooch whilst intent on revealing a surplus of painfully reddened flesh.

Each week the inbound crawl led through the outskirts of the sophisticated, compact city of Chichester ahead of twisting and turning along the tedious, caravan-laden A259 – once tagged the most dangerous road in south-east England – before finally descending upon the 'cheap and cheerful' neighbouring holiday resort. Keeping, as if under lock and key, a mental history comprising my all-time favourite (and most despised) venues played, each monotonous journey stirred memories harking back to the late seventies, and in particular two hugely satisfying concerts staged at the acoustically perfect Festival Theatre in Chichester's city centre.

A classic British auditorium in all respects, the hall played host to a string of high-profile rock and pop artists of the day, brought to an abrupt halt more than a quarter of a century ago by a new administration who, in their infinite wisdom, looked down their noses at touring rock-and-roll events. Stuffily they opted instead to focus on middle-of-the-road, culturally enlightening productions, blissfully unaware of the unadulterated debauchery ensuing all of seven miles away in the region's royally appointed tourist trap.

****

The summer of 2007 saw the band pay a long overdue visit to the South Downs to take part in an annual event known as the Chichester Real Ale and Jazz Festival, held in the grounds of a multi-purpose sports complex named Priory Park.

We were received at the gate by an organised, well-turned-out steward clad in a bright yellow jerkin, who announced our arrival by way of a squealing walkie-talkie. The official obeyed a command to desert his post and personally escort the bill-topping sextet along a narrow pebbled drive to a timber-framed clubhouse laying adjacent to a verdant bowling green, and set aside as a changing area for the visiting artists.

'Aye up, it looks as if The Rubettes are on too!' came a witty crack from the back-seat boys, referring to a bunch of white-capped old-timers crouching low to partake in Sir Francis Drake's favourite sport on a surface resembling a billiard table, giddily rising and clutching at their lower backs after each meticulously positioned shot.

As we retrieved our belongings, crammed in tightly beneath the vehicle's tailgate, a dignified-looking green-jacketed lady hobbled awkwardly from the structure's entrance, greeting the party with a broad smile whilst catching her breath and shuffling slowly back inside pursued by a half-dozen mickey-taking waddling ducks.

Adjusting our eyes within the dimly lit oak-panelled hallway, we could see an impressive array of polished trophies gleaming through the frontages of a row of glass display cabinets, while a mini gallery of wall-mounted certificates bore further evidence of the club's most notable past achievements.

'Are you okay to share the changing facilities with another group of show-business colleagues?' the hostess softly pleaded.

'Only if it's Hot Gossip,' Romeo quipped with a tiny hint of menace.

'Hot Gossip? Do me a favour! They'll all be well into their fifties by now,' responded our very own God's gift, Trevor.

'Listen to bloody Tom Cruise. At least they'll all have a full head of hair,' Geoff ranted. 'The trouble with you is…'

He was halted in midstream by a strangely familiar voice emanating from a doorway to the rear of the lobby, stressing: 'Do you lot ever stop bickering?'

'Well, strike me down with a feather! That's spooky – we thought we just clocked the four of you playing bowls on the green outside,' I playfully ribbed, delighted to be reunited with our long-time muckers The Rubettes.

Over three decades and then some, the two bands' paths had crossed on countless occasions, leading us to build up a mutual respect for each other's slick professionalism, notwithstanding the bouts of ribald backstage banter which often thornily centred upon the Essex ensemble's somewhat fortuitous existence courtesy of a quirk of fate dating back to late 1973.

In May of the following year the 'flat-capped southerners' took the UK charts by storm, remaining perched at the summit for all of four weeks thanks to a melodic throwback to the fifties entitled 'Sugar Baby Love', which surprisingly had been earmarked as their northerly rivals' debut single prior to the formation of the Southend-based outfit. With SWW locked into an ego-boosting tug of war between two major record labels (viz. Polydor and Bell) both hungry to secure long-term deals with the band, the latter company's enthusiasm towards a stockpile of original demos (penned by rhythm guitarist Trevor Oakes and myself) ultimately tipped the scales, forgoing the retro-inspired efforts of an alternative songwriting team and culminating only weeks later in our own chart-busting anthem 'Hey Rock and Roll'.

Back in Chichester, bright orange fragments of the evening sunshine cut like laser beams through the anteroom windows, exposing an unflattering collection of pale limbs and podgy stomachs seen squeezing into a guise of freshly laundered white suits, topped off with a millinery of matching 'Gatsby'-styled headgear.

'It's like a sauna in that marquee, so they shouldn't need much warming up,' reflected drummer and firm friend John Richardson, psyching himself up for a fifty-minute test of endurance before a well-oiled, rambunctious throng.

After indulging himself in the seventies rock-and-roll lifestyle during his band's successful formative years the dutiful John chucked it all in, receiving a spiritual wake-up call and resolving to devote his energies *post hoc* to the doctrines of the Hare Krishna movement, eventually combining the two chosen paths by reuniting with his chums some twenty years later. Never one to preach or bore the pants off those distrustful of his teachings, John's uniquely calming presence served as a godsend to many touring parties and provided a reassuring fillip when back-to-back months on the road caused tempers to fray, occasionally threatening to derail the whole process.

Blighted by a virulent bronchial infection during the relentless winter of 2006, two thirds of the way through a back-breaking run of dates, I had considered chucking in the towel. Egged on by the persuasive tongues of nervy promoters fearing a spate of refunds and against the advice of a doctor in the West Sussex town of Worthing, perhaps unwisely I soldiered on, opting to tough things out in spite of the wearisome physical demands.

Despite my keeping my cards close to my ailing chest, sensing all was not well the altruistic JR intervened in an effort to oil the rickety wheels, dragging me off to a private corner before applying his healing hands onto my infected ribcage and throat regions to gently massage away the negative antibodies by means of reiki therapy.

Up to that point I had dismissed the ramblings of white-robed 'witch doctors' and fanciful faith-healers as mumbo-jumbo. As if by magic, John's compassionate treatment dispelled all such doubts, instilling a rejuvenated pizzazz into my afflicted lungs as well as boosting my spirits tenfold in preparation for a further assault on my vocal chords.

****

Setting out our stall in the dungeon-like dressing rooms of yet another antiquated theatre just a couple of days later, we checked out the kitchenette earmarked as the catering area. An unusually pungent witch's brew bubbled ominously on the stove, causing a few raised eyebrows amongst the loitering crew.

'What the bloody hell's that stink?' Trevor fretted in disgust, alerting a burly rigger busy spreading a thick layer of Marmite over two rock-hard slices of burnt toast.

'It's some fucking weird concoction the medicine man's got on the go; it reeks like a piss-stained tramp's vest to me!' the muscleman complained, screwing up his nose before crunching bestially into his teatime treat.

'I sincerely hope that's not something he's brewing up for me!' I twigged, following behind and picking up the scent.

'Hey Dave, I gathered up some goodies from a roadside wood on the way over; I've got a special elixir fermenting that'll have you singing like a nightingale tonight!' the ever-enthusiastic guru chirped, waltzing through the doorway to attend to the simmering stew pot under the watchful eyes of the amused gathering.

'I just hope it doesn't taste as foul as it bloody well smells; what the hell's in it?' I beefed, almost choking on the noxious vapour, provoking a stifled outbreak of belly-laughs.

'Have no fear: there's dandelion and camomile leaves, nettles, wild tarragon, a mixture of herbs… it's overflowing with natural vitamins,' he enthused, playing the proper drugstore cowboy and implying I may be about to sample the nectar of the gods.

The clump of heavy boots sounded on the stone staircase cueing the arrival of a cluster of crew hands, spent and in need of sustenance following an afternoon of hard labour and seeking an hour of recuperation prior to ringing the curtain up. Each worker begged the same question: 'What the fuck is that awful smell?'

Exiting to the adjoining room laden with a tray full of goodies, checking the coast was clear and raising up the reeking vat, the unperturbed John diligently transferred the potion's contents into the empty kettle, bringing the liquid back to the boil and filling up two large mugs ahead of relocating to a quiet spot well away from the rancid kitchenette.

Delving into my debilitated memory banks, a degree of uncertainty remains as to the true efficacy of the infusion, but like the ideal patient I slurped down the contents (ingrained with two heaped spoonfuls of sugar to alleviate the tartness), refraining even from taking a single breath under the watchful eyes of my therapist.

I returned next door to the catering area where, bugging the hell out of the musicians and crew snacking on toasted pikelets and custard creams, the irksome Trevor repeatedly practised the same riff over and over on an electro-acoustic guitar. He was finally barracked into pausing for a tea break to the ironic cheers of his captive, underwhelmed audience.

Tossing two teabags into a ceramic teapot, selfishly playing mother to one, the grumpy performer neglected to check the kettle's contents. Raising the overflowing beaker to his eager lips, he consumed a healthy slurp prior to decorating the floor with a vulgar cocktail of brown fluid and churned-up leaves, while also drenching his valuable guitar from tip to toe.

'You bunch of bastards,' the guitarist snarled, incensed by a hearty round of applause from the startled yet delirious onlookers whilst arrogantly seeking retribution at the expense of the tickled, luckless guitar-tech: 'And when you've finished taking the piss those fucking strings need changing,' ill-temperedly taking his leave and slamming the door.

Entering their fortieth year in 2014 The Rubettes continue to tour, regularly donning their white caps at nostalgic overseas festivals. Meanwhile, betwixt and between his vocational duties, the inimitable John Richardson also put pen to paper, compiling a fascinating account of his chequered past entitled *The Beat of Different Drums*.

Causes célèbres

Hugh Dennis – comedian/actor
Michael Elphick – actor (*Boon*)
Charlotte Hawkins – TV presenter
Anita Roddick – founder of 'The Body Shop'

Essential travelling band info

Favourite live music venue: Minerva Theatre, Oaklands Park
Favourite curry house: Memories of India, Bosham Roundabout – 60%
Favourite pub: Bell Inn, Broyle Road – 68%
Don't miss: Fishbourne Roman Palace – 71%
Sense of humour/friendly welcome: 50%

Chapter 18
Coventry

'YOU'RE NOT THE FIRST ROCK star I've met you know,' crowed the born nuisance who'd somehow given security the slip before inviting himself into the band's basement dressing room at Bedworth's Civic Hall (near Coventry).

Feet up, well away from the noise onstage, I was attempting to enjoy a few peaceful moments alone with a book. 'Really? Which other megastar has had the unexpected pleasure of your company?' I mockingly enquired.

'Billy Fury!' he answered gloatingly.

'Wow, the first single I ever bought was by him; was he a nice guy?' I half-interestedly patronised, thumbing the page.

'Ah well… I didn't really get the chance to talk to him; the minute I walked into his changing room he told me to fuck off!' the dimwit declared with a hint of despondency.

'Well that makes two of us; now do the decent thing, there's a good boy!' I chastened, irritated by the unannounced interruption.

'I'm not quite with you, how do you mean?' he stupidly maintained.

'What I'm trying to say is, there's the door – now piss off!' I cruelly snapped, pointing a finger towards the wood in the hole.

****

Two passages contained within this text focus on what would best be described as anomalous examples of outsize manhood. The first case in point belonged to a virile young drummer who formed the backbone of a four-piece band tipped as 'one to watch' when I was in the embryonic stages of spreading my wings into artist management during the early eighties.

Beginning in '79, the city of Coventry's rather disjointed profile received a huge boost owing to the emergence of the Blue-Beat-influenced Two-Tone revolution; and it fast became a magnet for a number of aspiring artists who, however tenuous their connection, flocked to the in-vogue West Midlands town in search of recognition.

The Specials, The Beat, Selecter and even London's much touted nutty-boys Madness all signed up to the '2 Tone' record label created by Jerry Dammers (himself a Special). The label sought to create a British alternative to Detroit's legendary Tamla Motown company, whilst at the same time promoting a multi-cultural theme with strong anti-racism beliefs. Dominating the UK charts for fully three years, the concept's success speaks for itself and influenced many bigger players into climbing on the bandwagon, rushing to sign a rat pack of multiracial artists from under their noses, two such examples being Dexy's Midnight Runners and UB40.

In my capacity as a budding Svengali I was paying regular visits to the West Midlands' second city to keep tabs on any up-and-coming new bands. Upon the advice of a trusted musician friend, a rendezvous was arranged at a rambling old pub on the city's outskirts to take a peek at a promising young rhythm-and-blues band going by the name of Boom-Boom, who by a quirk of fate were made up of two black and two white guys. Blessed with the youthful looks to potentially drive adolescent female fans wild and boasting an average age of just nineteen, here lay a golden opportunity to nurture the fresh-faced foursome into a new and exciting Two-Tone sensation.

Pulling in a few favours from a fraternity of local contacts whilst preparing for an imminent two-month tour with SWW, the stage seemed set for my prodigies to gain some invaluable experience in my absence, even blagging a couple of mouth-watering support slots at high-profile club venues where a cutting-edge young band would surely set the tongues wagging, possibly alerting a circle of hankering industry scouts.

****

A rip-roaring autumn tour in the bag, I was all set to don my managerial hat when a buzz of excitement filled the air whipped up by a review in a local rag's entertainment pages: '*Making up the bill with a gutsy fusion of 2-Tone/R&B, teenage Midlands boys Boom-Boom pushed all the right buttons!*' This provoked a series of congratulatory calls to each member suggesting progress may be well ahead of schedule.

Expressing a burning desire to witness the startling transformation with my own eyes and ears, a hard sell to an agency acquaintance resulted in a one-off gig set to take place just the following weekend at a social-club venue in the town of Hinckley ten miles or so to the north of Coventry, where away from the prying eyes of any snooping opportunists the boys could run the new, all-happening repertoire.

During my travels I had put out a few feelers to a posse of active A&R contacts based in the nation's capital. As if by chance a 'thanks but no thanks' courtesy call came in from a major label's rep named Daniel, dismissing a singer-songwriter's demo tape I'd mailed to him as: 'Not quite what we're looking for!'

'Never mind; to be honest I'm not entirely convinced myself,' I responded, before taking the opportunity to drop the subtlest of hints as to my emerging stable's new addition into the mix.

'Two-Tone... good-looking kids... I like the sound of that. When are they next rehearsing?' the scout doted at the merest mention of something up-to-the-minute.

'They'll be running the rejigged set for the first time this coming Friday night; I'm trying to get them out gigging as much as possible,' I explained.

'I'll be there!' he asserted.

'Whoa, hold your horses Daniel – they're bound to be a little rough around the edges; I haven't even heard the new stuff myself!' I forewarned.

'Doesn't matter – we're not expecting the finished article. If they show sufficient promise, we can soon iron out any imperfections. I can see it already: a Two-Tone band that appeal to the screamers – they could be massive!' he enthused.

'Okay, but don't expect miracles,' I urged, agreeing to pass on some paraphernalia to whet his appetite and signing off with cautious optimism.

When we met in the arrivals hall of Leicester's railway station my blond-locked contact was accompanied by a second dapper man said to represent a rival label, intimating the cat may already be out of the bag. A head-spinning barrage of questions followed during the fifteen-mile trek, put on hold as the car swerved onto the forecourt of the red-brick building.

Inside, nerve ends tingled with anticipation as the boys added the final touches to the set-up, acknowledging the out-of-towners and myself with a wave of the hand prior to disappearing backstage fired up for the moment of truth.

Hampered by a tray-load of drinks, I weaved unsteadily between a network of wooden trestle tables where around forty half-interested regular customers clutched onto glasses of cheap frothy beer, looking up from their pint pots and frowning as if the strident opening chords hailed some form of unwanted disturbance.

The band kicked off full of vim and vigour, but midway into the upbeat curtain-raiser an outrageous interruption threatened to curb the boys' progress by way of a distorted, high-handed announcement blasting through the in-house PA system: 'Turn down the volume... *now*, if you please, or we'll be forced into pulling the plug!'

Shrugging off the intrusion with a minor tweak and a belligerent leer the boys took up the gauntlet, demonstrating a musical prowess belying their tender years as they rattled through stonking adaptations of the Freddie King instrumental 'Hideaway' and Cream's 'NSU' prior to winding things up with a contemporary twist on the Howlin' Wolf standard 'Smokestack Lightning' in a high-energy opening gambit abounding with R&B classics.

I plied my guests with yet more alcohol, and the second half began to muted applause with an uninspiring take on The Pioneers' 'Long Shot Kick the Bucket'. Sensing a dip and ignoring the anchorman's muffled warning the boys upped the ante, ripping into a frantic version of the reggae classic 'Monkey Man' (later recorded by Amy Winehouse). Hot on its heels, bandleader Daryl announced: 'We'd like to perform a brand new song that's been earmarked as our first ever single; it's called "Hair of the Dog" – hope you like it!'

'You didn't say they could write too! That song's got "hit" written all over it,' bellowed Daniel, fresh from mouthing the lyrics to the second chorus, backed up by his equally animated bedfellow who yelled through cupped hands: 'What a corking little band!'

I glanced around the hall. The change in the sparse crowd's body language spoke volumes as they gleefully punched the air and latched onto the infectious hook line: 'I need, need, need, need, need, the hair of the dog,' bearing out the words of the A&R man who, climbing into a cab some fifteen minutes later, promised faithfully be in touch first thing Monday morning.

As I moseyed back into the club, head held high, a sprinkling of punters making for the last bus home headed in the opposite direction. They missed out on a much merited encore where, after thanking those present, the boys bounded into a rollicking interpretation of the 1970 Nicky Thomas hit 'Love of the Common People,' rounding off a successful night's work with a reprise of the sure-fire blockbuster on everyone's lips.

I sneaked into the tiny stage-side dressing room where a sweaty cocktail of adrenaline laced with a splash of elation oozed from the young rookies' pores, stimulated further by my brief resumé of the departed talent-spotter's favourable comments.

Taking time out, I excused myself as the acrid whiff of stale urine led the way to the gentlemen's toilet. Followed in by beefcake drummer Tom, I continued to rain down the morale-boosting compliments, distracting from the nose-pinching odour. 'You guys really pulled it off out there tonight – those scouts were well impressed,' I lauded.

Taking care not to splash on my shoes, I inadvertently glanced along the row of glossy white urinals as blokes do and caught sight of the musician's humongous truncheon wielded towards the comfort station in the dwarfed palm of his hand.

'Bloody hell – you're well blessed!' I exclaimed, clearing my throat, stricken by an overwhelming feeling of inadequacy.

'So everyone tells me; it's something I have to live with… To make matters worse my doctor warned me to not to lift anything heavy!' he immodestly joked, studying my reaction and emitting the filthiest of laughs.

I rejoined the freak of nature's bandmates in a mild state of shock and bade my goodbyes with a spate of hugs and handshakes. Giving the guys some space to wind down and gloat over a few beers, I swore to be in touch the minute a whisper leaked out of the big city.

Monday found me immersed in a pile of paperwork while the phones remained worryingly quiet, made up for the very next morning when a breathless, pleading voice urged into the blower: 'Dave, I urgently need photos, info and most importantly a demo of "Hair of the Dog"; my gaffer's well interested and I'm anxious to keep him on the boil!'

Acting with immediate effect, a pressing call followed to band vocalist and taskmaster Daryl, insisting the boys drop everything in preparation for a two-day studio session which I'd move mountains to organise, hopefully for the very next day.

'I don't believe this; we can't do it – Tom's gone off to see his girlfriend in Amsterdam and he's not due back until Friday!'

'Lucky girl… But seriously, we'll have to bring in a session drummer. I know a great player who, oddly enough, owes me a favour – I'll give him a shout. It's imperative I get that demo to Daniel by the weekend!' I stressed.

'Ooh, Tom won't be too happy about that: his ego's almost as big as his you-know-what,' gasped the guitarist, inhaling deeply.

'In which case you'll have to track him down and tell him to get his arse on the next flight back. I'll pick up the tab!' I resolved, bent on leaving nothing to chance.

Out of pocket to the tune of seven hundred quid and utterly zonked from a forty-eight-hour back-to-back session, clutching a sparkling portrayal of my protégés' modern classic on top of a wad of promo material I made it through the doors of the label's London headquarters just prior to the close of Friday's business. In moments flat the radio-friendly gem was booming joyously from the speakers of Daniel's ground-floor office.

'That's absolutely brilliant; I'll drop it over at my boss Ron's place first thing tomorrow morning – I just know it'll be right up his street!' the rep vowed, offering his mitt for a high five before rewinding the cassette and clunking play again.

I spent the entire weekend unable to get the tune out of my mind, aware a deal may be within touching distance. Monday morning inauspiciously arrived along with the winter's first snowfall as, rendered housebound and on tenterhooks, I impetuously put in a call to Daniel anxious to gauge the big chief's reaction.

'I'm still waiting for him to give it the green light; he loved the track but kept banging on about the guy with the frizzy hair, saying something about him being the spitting image of Todd Hardman,' the scout disclosed.

'Are you referring to the drummer...? Anyway, who the hell's Todd Hardman when he's at home?' I agonised, completely flummoxed.

'I thought you might ask that; I haven't got a clue either, but Ron said to hold fire before rushing into a decision. It appears your young protégé may have already made something of a name for himself!' the go-between unveiled, keeping his cards close to his chest.

After a bracing two-mile walk to clear away the cobwebs, imagination running wild, I returned to find an intermittent orange light flashing on the answerphone. A crackling message from a morose-sounding Daniel dealt my Svengali ambitions a crushing blow.

'I'm really sorry, Dave, but we've had a change of heart and decided against signing Boom-Boom; they're a talented little band but don't quite tick all the boxes. I've sent you some stuff in a sealed envelope, first class, that should hopefully explain everything!'

'What the f...? This is crazy!' I wailed, replaying the message and staring in disbelief at the machine. Barely able to take it all in, I angrily slammed the office door, crestfallen and hell bent on drowning my sorrows.

****

Forty-eight hours and a nagging hangover later, a card-backed envelope stuck out from amongst a jumble of post littered on the mat. I cast it aside along with a stack of junk mail to an empty space on my cluttered desktop, figuring the picky record company had at least bothered to return the bundle of unneeded paraphernalia.

Later, in an idle moment, I peeled back the package's sticky tab. Right before my eyes lay the centre spread of an explicit Dutch porn magazine, revealing a whole lot more than just the curly-topped locks of the well-endowed young percussionist I'd taken under my wing.

Knelt gleefully feasting on Tom's elephantine phallus, two black-rooted blondes glared lasciviously towards the camera, beneath which the caption read: '*Young stud Todd Hardman gives Heidi and Kirsten a "BIG" surprise!*'

Carving out an international career as an XXX-rated movie star and doubtless reaping in piles of cash as whopping as the tool of his trade, the prodigious talent looked to be in seventh heaven, partaking in a thrill-seeking escapade on foreign soil as opposed to a weekly stint in a run-down dive before a couple of dozen unappreciative deadbeats.

As I re-examined the images in all their carnal detail, flabbergasted at the leading man's libido, the penny finally dropped that, given similar circumstances, a majority of broad-minded, virile young guys scratching around on the breadline may easily have followed the same path as Tom. I couldn't help chuckling to myself at a gag the boy wonder had cracked just days before: 'I wish I had a ten-inch penis... I'm sick of lugging this bloody great thing around!' Boom-Boom!

Causes célèbres

Danny Grewcock – World Cup-winning rugby union player
Clive Owen – actor
Hazel O'Connor – singer/songwriter
Nigel Hawthorne – actor
Ian Bell – England cricketer
Richard Keys – TV presenter
Brian Matthew – ancient *Thank Your Lucky Stars* TV host
Laura Davies – golfer
Lee Child – author

Essential travelling band info

Favourite live music venue: Warwick Arts Centre, University of Warwick
Favourite curry house: Indian Empress, Binley Road – 62%
Favourite pub: Gatehouse Tavern, Hill Street – 54%
Don't miss: Coventry Cathedral – 60%
Sense of humour/friendly welcome: 42%

Chapter 19
Derby

'HI THERE, IT'S BBC RADIO Derby here; is that Dave?' the exaggerated baritone voice at the end of the line pronounced.

'Er, yes, it is,' I replied, in something of a stew.

'Our colleagues in Leicester kindly passed on your number; I'm calling on the off chance we could have an impromptu five-minute chat on air about your forthcoming show at the Derby Assembly Rooms?' the presenter fawned.

'I'm sorry mate, but I'm tied up right now; could you call back in ten minutes?' I implored into my newfangled cordless telephone.

'Don't worry, we won't keep you long… We're going live straight after the news,' the jock blabbed, ignoring my plea and annoyingly putting me on hold.

In a fourteen-year career teeming with TV appearances, radio promos and press interviews, being coerced into turning on the charm directly to an unsuspecting listening public while squatting firmly on the throne within an echoing bathroom represented a first.

Mind-numbing as it may be, technology waits for no one, with the bowel-loosening mid-eighties broadcast perhaps setting a precedent for future media interviews and business dealings conducted from some unimaginable locations; so much so that hereafter follows a chronicle of the top five most outlandish:

Wondrous place

As I stood breathing wheezily at altitude, fresh from a challenging climb for a photo opportunity above the ancient Inca civilisation of Machu Picchu in Peru, an unforeseen call arrived courtesy of a freelance journalist requesting a short tribute to a passing seventies star I'd barely known. Gazing down at the spectacular wonder of the world, waxing lyrical came easy, though curiously the departed celebrity's identity remains a mystery.

Caught in the act

I was delighting in a blissful afternoon romp with my dear wife when the cell phone stashed in the pocket of my disrobed jeans suddenly chirruped into life, eliciting the plummy-tongued chairperson of a local parish committee asking if I'd be good enough to fire the starting pistol at an upcoming charity wheelbarrow race.

'I'm really sorry, but I'm just in the middle of something right now; is there any chance I can call you back later?' I responded, remembering to do so the same evening after a period of much-needed recuperation.

Free willy

Fearing frostbite on a bitterly cold winter's day and taking refuge in a Leicester museum, I was warming my icy hands on a scalding radiator and killing time ahead of a solicitor's appointment when the weather-induced urge to take a leak took hold, hastening a visit to the nearby public lavatory.

Stood bolt upright in the centre of a row of overcoated patrons, as fate would have it the rock-'n'-roll tune preset as my mobile ringtone sprang to life in my top pocket, causing consternation amongst the peeing sightseers.

Briefcase grasped in one hand and cellular phone in the other, I thrashed out the logistics for a run of overseas dates. Meanwhile my unassisted, chilled appendage dangled roughly toward the urinary trough inattentively creating a rivulet of steaming liquid, revoltingly winding its way along a crack in the floor and underneath the loo's entrance.

Three-point wrong turn

Pulled into the roadside by a brace of macho traffic cops allegedly for the misuse of a mobile phone, I was brusquely summoned into the rear seat of a deluxe Range Rover patrol car and read the riot act. 'Looks like this one fancies himself as a tough guy, Charlie,' the non-driving officer mocked, squinting toward the in-car computer system. 'Best be on our guard eh, huh-huh… it says here he was convicted of GBH in 1982,' providing evidence to suggest the UK police force's idiot-proof database may not entirely be up to scratch.

After receiving a three-point penalty together with a hundred-pound fine for my sins, I called in at a close-by law shop seeking to clear my name. The hairy-lipped female supervisor snapped: 'That'll require a thirty-five-pound administration fee, sir,' adding insult to injury though ultimately expunging the stain from the record.

Colonic invitation

Recumbent on my side with a plastic tube attached to my jacksie during a spot of inner cleansing, as fate would have it the dreaded cell phone trilled into action: 'Dave, it's Richard. I hope you're having a better week than I am; everything's turned to shit – I need to get out and let off some steam!' my pal bellyached.

'Funny you should say that – the same could be said for me as we speak!' I quipped, anxious not to go into too much detail.

'Listen, I've heard you're not out gigging on Saturday night; are you free to join us… Are you okay, what the hell's that gurgling sound?' he enquired.

'I'm fine, in fact I'm just in the process of sorting out a load of crap myself; anyway, what's been getting your goat this week?' I replied ambiguously.

'You wouldn't believe it; business is going right down the tube. We're close to rock bottom. I'm sick and tired of dealing with arseholes who seem incapable of coming up with the goods,' he beefed rather aptly.

'I know exactly where you're coming from. The truth is, I've come a little unstuck myself this morning, so much so I'd better go as someone's causing a right stink – see you Saturday, thanks!' I signed off.

****

The A6 trunk road running between the southern tip of the city of Derby and the Leicestershire university town of Loughborough (where I served my secondary education) earned a dubious and somewhat hazardous notoriety towards the end of the 1960s due to the bizarre exhibitionism of a mentally troubled septuagenarian, succinctly dubbed by people in the know as 'A6 Lil'.

Rumblings abounded in the neighbourhood of the grotesque bony apparition clothed in nothing but an oversized gabardine raincoat and flimsy footwear caught in the headlights of many a passing gadabout, often known to veer into the path of oncoming vehicles, and the scores of morbidly curious peeping toms patrolling the route to take a snoop for themselves.

One afternoon at school a group of us were discussing the aged siren as we changed into shorts and black plimsolls in readiness for a character-building bout of 'murder ball' in preparation for an inter-schools football fixture the following evening. 'Rumour has it she's always out on a Tuesday night between nine and eleven,' broadcast classmate Colin – whose family resided close to the infamous stretch of tarmac – ahead of a potential spot of rubbernecking mischief with his scooter-riding chums.

Our curiosity had been foiled at the first attempt some weeks previously, and the latest escapade seemed destined to run similarly aground as we careered aimlessly up and down the outspread highway, chromium sidebars glinting in the moonlight. Just as we were beginning to tire of the game, we passed a pitch-black lay-by at the rear of which, trapped in a roadside hedgerow, a living thing of whatever description appeared to be in some distress. The rustling and grunting emanating from the lower dyke was made even more evident as the bikes' engines died.

'Go and take a look, Dave; you're an animal lover – it might be in a spot of bother,' urged lily-livered Colin, riveted to the spot in trepidation.

'Why me? There've been reports on the news of a black panther on the loose – I could get ripped to pieces!' I argued.

Plucking up enough courage to at least take a peek, I was barely able to believe my eyes. Slumped by the wayside, tangled in a twisted sheath of rusting barbed-wire fencing, lay the pathetic, gut-wrenching sight of a mangled, enfeebled human wreckage, rivulets of blood bespattering her exposed white limbs, striving desperately to free herself from the painful snarled mess.

'Keep still, for God's sake, you're only making it worse – my friends and I will get you out,' I assured the fearful babbling creature, wincing down at the troublesome, unsightly baring of gouged naked flesh. Squeamishly averting my eyes from the cadaverous figure I barked like a bossy sergeant-major: 'Graham, hop back on your scooter and get someone from the pub down the road to call an ambulance as a matter of urgency.'

I slithered down the miry bank, snagging my jeans on the jutting wiry spikes, to where the woman lay. I cradled her head and supported her curving spine, as agonised tears flowed down the casualty's hollow cheeks revealing the true torturous nature of her ordeal.

Assisted by my two equally queasy pals we unflinchingly applied ourselves to drag the ailing bag of bones clear of the rubbish-strewn gulley, careful to preserve the sufferer's dignity with the removal of my mud-coated Parka. A continuous blaring siren in the distance signalled help would soon be at hand, and shortly the ambulance came skidding to a halt on the shale surface, illuminating the murky sky with its intermittently flashing blue beam.

As the diligent task-force cut through the coiled web with a hefty pair of bolt-croppers, a soft-spoken paramedic knelt before the confused wretch holding an unwavering finger into the patient's line of sight. Eager to shed a little light on the mysterious circumstances leading to her fall, he carefully posed a handful of pertinent questions.

'Where did the bruises around your eyes and lower jaw come from, sweetheart? Don't worry, I'm only here to help, but I do need to know!'

'Thug… a nasty ruffian…' she disclosed. 'Crew cut… the eyes of the devil… I never…' Lost for words, hysterically sobbing, she reached out to her saviour,

131

who heartbreakingly embraced the forlorn figure.

'Bastard,' declared the furious helper, watching the orderlies lift the stretchered woman into the back of the ambulance, clearly hot and bothered by the sad case's condition.

'What happened?' I pressed, baffled by the sudden outburst.

'It would appear that some cowardly lowlife took exception to the lady's kerbside exhibition and saw fit to pull over and give her a good hiding... Not only that, he then dumped a defenceless seventy-odd-year-old into the ditch like a dead animal,' the guy bitterly denounced. He went on to stress that the poor wretch may easily have perished from exposure were it not for our timely intervention and subsequent fortitude.

A6 Lil's showboating days had reached a loathsome, brutal end, verified as the emergency vehicle's double doors slammed shut. Behind them lay a frail, punch-drunk old soul attached to a plexus of tubes and respiratory apparatus, bound for a hospital bed in the nearest available intensive care unit.

Beginning as nothing more than teenage high jinks, the unimaginable horror of the ghostly elder's wounds inflicted by a malevolent hooligan left a scar of their own, remaining hidden in the back of my mind only to reappear like a bad smell should I occasionally pass close to the newly modified scene of the injustice.

****

Spring 2012

Continuing in a not dissimilar vein, it's fair to say that the aftermath of one's dotage often bears an uncanny resemblance to that of a toddler's formative years, resulting in a distinct lack of bodily and mental acuity impaired by spasms of gaga-speech, round-the-clock supervision and the occasional need to strap on nappy-like incontinence pads.

I should make clear that I am in no way pointing the finger at either my working colleagues or indeed myself, none of whom has yet succumbed to the stultifying effects of premature dementia, notwithstanding the evidence of this journal and in particular the deluge of escapades while under the influence of brain-damaging quantities of alcohol.

The case in point, recounted directly from the lips of my good-humoured mother-in-law, involves a senior citizens' outing to hold dear the undulating Derbyshire countryside. The forty-strong party boarded the coach in the Nottinghamshire minster town of Southwell to which, sated from a day's sightseeing and an organised three-course dinner at a popular pub-restaurant on Derby's outskirts, the passengers would be returned the same evening. The trip's highlights included a leisurely drive through the renowned dales, stopping off for sustenance and a stretch of the legs in the historic town of Bakewell (aptly home to the famous tarts and puddings), amidst a throng of local residents converging on the centre for the weekly Monday market.

Divided into small groups fresh from disembarking the bus and under strict orders to realight by five o'clock sharp, the excursionists tottered off to freely pass an eye over the wealth of stalls and notable landmarks, the majority soon opting for a light bite and cake at one of a smattering of quaint tea houses.

Acting out of the goodness of her heart as chaperone to ninety-three-year-old Eileen whilst eager to sniff out a freshly prepared Bakewell Pudding directly from the dessert's place of origin, happening upon a comfortable riverside bench and instructing her elderly companion to rest and admire the blossoming springtime scenery, Dorothy – a sprightly seventy-six – hotfooted toward the town's busy main thoroughfare, content all would be well in her brief absence.

Temporarily left to her own devices, Eileen relished a moment's serenity basking in the temperate sunshine away from the wagging tongues of her daytripping playmates. As she did so, an attractive hostelry situated at the water's edge caught the great-granny's eye, creating a rare rush of blood to the head at the same time as unearthing a long-lost desire to act on impulse.

Scurrying back from her raid on the town's bakeries a sense of panic took hold of the normally reliable Dorothy, mindful her senior charge had to all intents and purposed vanished into thin air. This was the cue for a mad dash back and forth to scan every street and hidden alley in the immediate vicinity, aware the take-off hour was creeping ever nearer.

All of a hundred yards away at the bottom of the hill, a handsome young waiter catered to the revitalised Eileen's every whim as she settled into a deep-cushioned armchair, indulging in an infrequent drop of the hard stuff for the first time in many moons. She failed to escape the attentions of a dapper, similarly refined gentleman craving a little female company; and an engaging stroll down memory lane ensued, stimulated by the warming effects of a refill or two of top-notch French cognac, befuddling the engrossed dotard's mind as the grandfather clock right by her chimed five.

Back at the bus the fretful blue-rinse brigade urged the aggravated driver to summon the local police, envisioning a variety of conspiracy theories ranging from abduction by an organised gang to an unexpected dip in the River Wye. They were reassured by a fresh-faced bobby arriving on the scene that any act of a sinister nature would instantly put the townsfolk on red alert, guaranteeing all exit routes would be closely monitored whilst every single nook and cranny would be scoured with a fine-tooth comb.

Lightheadedly emerging from the watering hole with a hiccough and a wicked smile, assuming Dorothy and the famished wayfarers may already be halfway to the final port of call to strap on the nosebag, the mischievous Eileen summoned a taxi from just over the road and enquired as to the fare for the thirty-mile journey.

'That'll set you back all of forty-five pounds, love,' the upbeat cabbie responded, anticipating a welcome bonus.

'Forty-five pounds! You've got a nerve, young man; my grandson flew all the way to Barcelona with Rhino Air for much less than that recently!' the aged fusspot bickered, spurred by a touch of bravado from the afternoon binge.

Picking up a sign marked *Station Road* she put her best stick forward, hatching a plan to board the next Derby-bound train and surprise her long-gone friends. Sidling into the old railway building, exhausted from her efforts, the old girl crashed into a decrepit seating area and rested her head against the nicotine-stained wall to sleep off the effects of the liquid lunch.

Chancing upon the unconscious senior citizen, a young constable in the course of his daily beat and apparently unaware of any search in progress gently prodded the whistling lady and queried the purpose of her visit to the crumbling platform.

'I'm waiting for the next train to Derby; I missed my bus and need to catch up with the rest of the party,' the old dame informed him.

At that moment a piercing, hissing update came blasting through his walkie-talkie, causing the bobby to cotton on he may just have earned a few brownie points for solving the ongoing case in the nick of time.

'Are you now, madam? I'm afraid to say you'll be in for rather a long wait. Perhaps you'd like me to help you back to the coach park? It seems your friends were keen not to depart without you,' the recruit helpfully suggested.

'Oh dear, that wasn't such a good idea was it, officer; what time did the last train leave?' Eileen enquired, struggling to her feet.

'Forty-four years ago in 1968 madam!' the policeman answered, chuckling behind his hand and radioing for assistance.

Causes célèbres

Alan Bates – actor
Sir Henry Royce – Rolls Royce co-founder
David Brailsford – Britain's Olympic cycling guru
Jack O'Connell – actor (*Skins* etc)
Ellen MacArthur – record-breaking sailor
Joe Davis – snooker legend

John Hurt – actor (born in Shirebrook)
Florence Nightingale – nursing pioneer (brought up in Derby)

Essential travelling band info

Favourite live music venue: Flower Pot, King Street
Favourite curry house: Viceroy Derby, Midland Road – 62%
Favourite pub: Babington Arms, Babington Lane – 71%
Don't miss: Donington Park, Castle Donington – 70%
Sense of humour/friendly welcome: 48%

Chapter 20
Douglas

'YOU'RE BLOODY LUCKY TO HAVE me ferrying you around today; this is me last day as a cabbie... well, at least for the time being,' the unmistakably Liverpudlian taxi-driver revealed, testing the car's rocking suspension on the winding country lanes between Ronaldsway Airport and the band's hotel in Douglas, the Isle of Man's capital.

'It's a pain in the arse driving with matchsticks in your eyes 'til all hours of the night, we know all about that,' I responded indifferently.

'Oh, it's not the late nights – in fact I enjoy the driving; it's just that I got meself into a little spot of bother a few weeks back,' he admitted cagily.

'I take it that means you'd had a little tipple and got pulled in by the filth!' Geoff chimed in, stifling a yawn.

'Not at all mate, a professional driver would never do that! I can tell you're itching to know so I may as well give it to you straight: I beat a young hoodlum to within an inch of his life when he refused to pay his fare and got had up for assault,' he confessed.

'Oops!' I reacted, shifting uncomfortably in my seat.

'I wouldn't put meself down as a violent man, but the devious bastard had it coming. He'd only just puked his guts up outside of the club where I picked him up so I was watching him in the mirror like a hawk; then as I pulled in to drop him off he did a bloody runner,' he rambled on, almost spitting blood.

'How the hell did you catch up with him?' Rod intervened.

'I drove the car up onto the pavement and cornered the little git. Then he tried climbing onto the bonnet to get away but I banged her into reverse and sent the twat flying. All I wanted was me fare, but he had the nerve to take a pop at me; that was when I lost the plot and knocked seven bells of shit out of him!' he excitedly droned on.

'So I take it from what you're saying we'd be daft to mess with you!' I countered.

'Haha, don't worry lads – your fare's already sorted. Mind you, there was blood splattered all over the promenade. I knew I was handy in me day but it never occurred to me the magic might still be there,' he boasted.

'I'd have thought scrapping was part of the school curriculum on Merseyside?' I jested, continuing to wind him up.

'You could say that, pal,' the Liverpudlian nodded, suddenly squealing on two wheels into the car park of the incongruously named Palace Hotel.

In reality, and due largely to its geographical position cut adrift in the Irish Sea, the self-governing crown dependency attracts an annual influx of unskilled migrants predominantly from England's north-west region, most of whom make the notoriously turbulent crossing from May onwards seeking short-term employment to coincide with the island's renowned TT Week (Tourist Trophy) extending through the busy summer holiday season.

With the island playing host to the celebrated two-wheel extravaganza for in excess of a hundred years whilst opening its arms to the elite of the biking world, frequent hops over to the Manx capital Douglas often found the troupe rubbing shoulders with revered title-holders such as Mike Hailwood, Joey Dunlop and latterly Steve Hislop, swapping tales and unwinding in the dungeon-like downstairs bar of reputedly the isle's premier hotel establishment.

Rising majestically from the rear of the hotel's sprawling car park prior to its demolition in 1994 stood the now legendary 'Palace Lido Ballroom'. Considered one of Europe's foremost live music venues throughout its sixties and seventies heyday, it accommodated close on six thousand well-oiled pleasuremongers who crammed into its gaping main hall to get a load of the big-name artists of the day jetted in from over on the mainland. The lofty mantelpiece of a stage was sandwiched between a towering multi-stacked sound system which delivered a cacophony of kilowatts to every corner of the vast auditorium, raising both the temperature and the hair on the back of each performer's neck, spurred on by an animated mass gathering of hankering carousers.

With the band beset by a flu epidemic sweeping the nation ahead of our first visit to the island in 1974, the propeller-powered plane lifting out of Liverpool airport bumped and juddered above the lashing whitecaps thousands of feet below accompanied by a fanfare of hacking coughs, splutters and snorting noses before touching down onto Manx soil. My worst fears were confirmed when, as I descended the clattering aluminium steps amid a swirling wind, a bout of jelly-legged feverishness swept through my whole body.

Figuring an afternoon siesta may provide the perfect antidote, I took to the comfortable hotel bed. Within minutes of my blacking out, the sharp ringtone of the bedside phone interrupted a profound, blissful slumber. The het-up receptionist's garbled message implied that a passenger on a later flight, purporting to be the band's manager, had been detained by airport security officers and carted off for questioning by police at the main Douglas headquarters.

'They were very insistent that a representative from your party should go along to help with their enquiries,' the girl went on, offering to call a taxi. Putting two and two together I deduced that the alleged felon could be none other than tour manager Tony arriving from Manchester.

Calling on Rod for a little moral support, I dressed quickly. The cab sped to an austere-looking building where, within moments, a welcoming committee escorted the ailing pair to the outside of a tiny holding cell. Inside, slumped disconsolately into a wooden chair, sat the hapless Tony coiled up like a spring.

'Can you identify this man as a key member of your touring party?' the chief officer prodded, belittlingly pointing through the door's small pane.

'A key member… hmm, that's interesting; but yes, he is with us. What on earth has he done wrong?' I inquired, utterly bemused.

'The gentleman has attempted to import a holdall laden with substances which contravene the Isle of Man's medications and drugs act,' the official reported.

'Really? Is it okay to go in and have a word? He's usually as straight as a dye and despises that kind of thing!' I implored. Briefed as to the routine security measures, I entered the room with a case of the jitters.

'I don't bloody believe this!' Tony sighed, puffing out his cheeks.

'You're being accused of importing drugs – have you lost your mind? What the hell were you carrying?' pumped Rod.

'I had a call this morning telling me two or three of you were laid low with the flu, so I thought I'd stock up with Benylin to be on the safe side,' he grieved.

'What – and they've pulled you in for possession of a bloody cough mixture?' I gasped, hardly able to believe my ears.

'Twenty bottles to be exact; there's enough there to concoct a very potent and lethal cocktail, sir!' the policeman cut in sternly.

Receiving a light rap on the knuckles and released without too much further ado, the flustered Man Friday hunched into the return cab launching into a bitter diatribe against the Manx authorities, insisting the constabulary should concentrate on catching real criminals, and relieved of seventeen bottles of confiscated expectorant.

Backstage in the oppressive, grubby changing room I put on a brave face, dosed up to the eyeballs with a cache of magic potions and tablets legally purchased from a nearby pharmacy. The pounding rhythms emanating from the upstairs hall visibly shook the huge structure's foundations precipitating a hot flush washing over my brow, foisted by a rush of the shivers ahead of tearing out before the hyperactive multitude.

Roughly four songs into the set I strapped on a black Fender Telecaster and strutted forward to the mike, a melee of outstretched hands grabbing ferociously at my pink-socked ankles, hankering for the briefest whiff of acknowledgement during the opening lines of the next tune. As I hollered like a man possessed, egged on by the boisterous crowd, a delayed sneeze fomented in my congested sinuses, ultimately exploding like a light bulb and coating my upper lip and cheek with a revolting pea-green layer of mucus. This effectively poured cold water on the prospect of any further hero worship from the more fickle onlookers, who viewed each swivel of the hips with suspicion for the remainder of the evening's performance.

Dead on my feet, I turned in ahead of the gang. A sound night's sleep worked wonders, and I rejoined my fractious, bleary-eyed pals in the lobby rejuvenated and chirpy as the cock crowed for the red-eye flight home.

'Ah, you've come down at last; you're the only one I haven't got – would you mind signing these?' a zit-faced devotee muscled in, sloping upwards out of a tucked away sofa from where he'd seemingly spent the night and shoving a felt-tip pen in my face.

'Not at all,' I responded. Flipping through a wad of glossy Polaroid snaps taken the evening before, I was aghast to come across a shot of my slime-spattered face. 'Do you mind if I hang onto this one as a souvenir? It's our first visit to the island,' I asked, resolutely clutching the offensive image.

'Which one is it?' the weirdo queried. Peeping over my shoulder he exclaimed: 'Oh no, I want to keep that one – it's my favourite!'

'What the hell is there to like about that shot?' I pleaded, desperate not to let such a damning manifestation slip from my grasp.

'It shows that you're human!' he astoundingly replied.

Reminiscing with a grimace, I count my blessings that the intrusive era of social networking had yet to be thrust upon an addictive global audience. Had the incriminating evidence been provided in the modern age, I shudder at the stark image of a degrading snotty-nosed snapshot circulating through cyberspace for all and sundry to deride.

****

To the majority of more mature Manx residents the name of the Summerlands Leisure Centre evokes painful memories of a horrific fire which tragically claimed the lives of fifty-one people during the peak holiday season of 1973. The original site provided the setting for the band's penultimate trip to the island in the late nineties, once again as part of TT Week.

An early afternoon arrival at the reconstructed venue to acquaint the band with the hired-in rig preceded a relaxing stroll to the chock-full hotel, admiring on the way a battalion of ostentatious superbikes stretching for miles along the promenade, most of which still gleamed in the fading light of day on the return leg.

Raring to go and designated two makeshift partitioned booths for changing in the dusty backstage area, we engaged in an acoustic mini-rehearsal for a short recap of a new song in the set. Our efforts were drowned out by the voice of Sinatra crooning 'New York, New York' blaring from the powerful PA system, cueing a wander back out into the passage to locate the tea-making facilities set aside in a tiny box-room.

'Come and take a look at this, lads,' exulted tubby crew-member Penny (a.k.a. Keith), clearly distracted from his stage rigging duties and dashing back to the wings ahead of the flock of sheep following in his wake.

'Very nice – mine's the blonde,' vied Trevor, as we feasted our eyes on a quartet of scantily clad strippers seen strutting their stuff to the visible delight of a multitude of hairy, red-blooded bikers foaming at the mouth at the stage's brow.

'Shit! Is that a fucking python?' gasped Romeo, spotting one of the girls moving in circles half-throttled by an enormous slithery beast.

'I hate the bastards,' blurted Geoff, whose fear of the reptiles was well known amongst his fellow musicians.

'What, strippers or snakes?' I quipped.

'Very funny. Look at its bloody tongue! I hope she doesn't bring it back here or you won't see me for dust,' the ashen-faced ophidiophobe warned.

'Never mind the bloody doped-up python; what about the totty?' drooled Penny, eyeballs popping out of their sockets.

Backstage post-performance any fears or hidden phobias vanished in a puff of smoke as the four hour-glass-figured females adorned in nothing but their high-heeled shoes unblushingly introduced themselves to their open-mouthed co-performers. The social pleasantries were nipped in the bud by a prudish gopher with steamed-up glasses who ushered the foursome to the confines of their cabin in a bid to preserve the girls' modesty.

Stereotyped as showing a preference towards a hard-edged metallic din, the leather-clad fraternity inexplicably warmed to the band's energetic driving rhythms, culminating in a rewarding night's work, upheld by the pleased-as-Punch promoter who responded in kind by laying on a shedload of booze in the cramped changing area.

As we perched on a line of makeshift benches like a post-match football team, a minor eruption of exploding ring-pulls and popping corks filled the room. I wet my own whistle with a half-decent Chilean Merlot sluiced into my glass by an over-eager Romeo. Abetted by our lager-swigging buddies, we gloated over the unexpected reaction well into the night.

'Correct me if I'm wrong, or maybe it's just a trick of the light, but I swear I just saw your suit-bag move,' perceived Romeo, pointing to a heap of luggage stashed beneath the pew upon which Geoff was slouched.

'How many glasses of that red piss have you had?' the bassist replied.

'Ro's right – there's definitely something moving in that pile of crap behind your legs!' I interrupted, ducking down to take a closer look.

'If this is a wind-up you're both making a crap job of it,' snapped Geoff, fidgeting uncomfortably in his seat.

'No seriously, it's not a piss-take – check under your bag,' suggested Romeo.

Jerking the holdall to one side, Geoff gave vent to a bloodcurdling scream before disappearing in a flash. Curled up beneath the bench, a heavy-bodied boa constrictor reared its ugly striped head, cold-bloodedly peering into the room curious as to what all the fuss was about, rendering the remaining observers still as stone.

'Keep quiet, don't antagonise it – everyone knows reptiles can be unpredictable,' advised the scaredy-cat promoter, backing tentatively out of the doorway.

'Norman, Norman, come out wherever you are,' a female voice squeaked from the corridor, pursuing a male friend of some description, oblivious to the fossilized bill-toppers sat just a few feet away.

Summoning up the courage to sneak into the narrow corridor and judging the expression of the concerned exotic dancer, in hushed tones I articulated: 'Norman wouldn't happen to be your pet python, would he?'

'Why are you whispering? He's as deaf as a post – all snakes are. I take it he's crawled into your dressing room?' she surmised, peeping through the gap in the door.

'Yes – he's curled up underneath a pile of bags,' I mumbled.

'He's always creeping off looking for somewhere to take a nap,' she sighed, alerting her fearsome friend which slithered towards its keeper.

'Good boy! See, he's just a pussycat really,' she smilingly heeded, crouching low to gather the beast up and planting a kiss on its head.

'If he's "Mutton Jeff" how come he heard you calling him?' I asked, frozen to the spot as Norman's wriggling tail slid dauntingly over my toes.

'It wasn't until he picked up my scent that he realised I was searching for him. I'm really sorry if anyone was alarmed,' the girl relayed sweetly, bidding the gang a fond farewell to a gust of relieved sighs and concealing the provocateur in a soft-leather case before heading off with her curvaceous colleagues.

We returned to the hotel lounge for a late nightcap. Propping up the bar perched upon a stool, a wary-looking Geoff greeted our arrival with some suspicion, having shown a clean pair of heels roughly two hours earlier in some distress.

'You've not brought those bloody strippers back here, have you? If that fucking snake's anywhere near this hotel I won't sleep a wink tonight!' he bellyached.

'No, you daft sod, they went off on their own. Anyway, the dancer that owns him said he's just a pussycat and wouldn't hurt anyone. Apparently they only react to smell,' I pointed out, quoting the words of the serpent's attractive owner.

'Did I just hear you right, Mr B – snakes only react to the smell of pussy?' remarked upbeat chauvinist pig Penny upon entering the bar.

'In a nutshell, yes; much like yourself Penny, much like yourself!' I reminded him, making my excuses and turning in.

****

A hard December frost clung tenaciously to the rooftops and bare deciduous trees lining the streets of Leicester city centre where, entering into the spirit of Christmas and warming my hands on an idle workman's brazier, a hummed rendition of 'Jingle Bells' quivered on my lips prior to a spot of Yuletide shopping.

'Dave, fancy seeing you – I was only talking about the band to my flatmate this morning,' chirped a disgraced ex-crew worker, pausing for a moment to exchange pleasantries.

'Dipstick, how are you? I bet you were giving us a right slagging,' I reacted, anxious to curtail the conversation as quickly as possible.

'Have you had a Christmas card from Penny yet… you lucky bunch of bastards?' the one-time lackey expressed, eyes lighting up.

'No, I haven't. I'm not quite with you,' I responded.

Reaching inside his duffle coat he retrieved a card-backed envelope and carefully removed a glossy photo pasted onto a plain white greetings card. The blissful features of the heavyset stagehand canoodling before the camera with four nude burlesque artists on a balmy summer's evening in Douglas filled the threatening sky with a warm glow.

'Nice! And we were paying him too. If you hadn't been such a naughty boy all those years ago it might just have been you; merry Christmas Dipstick!' I bade him in a cloud of steamy breath, jogging over to the shops.

Causes célèbres

Mark Cavendish – champion sprint cyclist
The Bee Gees – tragedy-tinged tunesmiths
Norman Wisdom – lived on the island for many years until his death in 2010

Essential travelling band info

Favourite live music venue: Gaiety Theatre, Harris Promenade
Favourite curry house: Taj Mahal, Esplanade Lane – 43%
Favourite pub: Rover's Return, Church Street – 53%
Don't miss: Trike Tour – 82%
Sense of humour/friendly welcome: 38%

Chapter 21
Dundee

RESPONDING TO A THUNDEROUS KNOCK, I sheepishly peered through a narrow gap before leaping back in alarm as the hotel-room door almost swung from its hinges heralding the arrival of a high-handed policeman whose bright red complexion and alarmingly protruding veins suggested all may not be well.

Storming inside uninvited, the bad-tempered chief barked dictatorially: 'Should either of you clowns go anywhere near that window again I'm arresting the pair of you, and you can spend the night banged up in rather less comfortable surroundings!'

'We're only acknowledging our fans,' I pleaded a trifle timorously, again incurring the officer's wrath:

'I don't give a monkey's what you say you're doing – all I know is you're inciting a riot, so less of your lip, laddie!'

The agitator's second-in-command strode across to the window and aggressively drew the curtains (meeting with an audible chorus of boos and groans sent forth from around four hundred highly excited kids gathered on the street below) before nodding to his senior who strongly advised: 'I'd also urge you to stay put in the hotel and have a few drinks or whatever it is you people do, as opposed to stirring things up outside where you're likely to get ripped to bits. Now, just bloody well behave!' he ordered, making a dramatic exit and slamming the door.

The day had begun on a high, with spirits soaring after the schedule's opening date in Carlisle where the ear-splitting crowd noise and rousing reception heralded the dawning of exciting times ahead for the band as a genuine headlining act; but we were soon brought crashing down to earth by engine trouble and lashing rain on the tedious morning trek north.

Pulling off the main drag into a public car park at the rear of the landmark and cavernous Caird Hall, we instantly recognised an arm-flapping crew member afforded the task of looking out for his employers. The scruffy labourer efficiently let on: 'The soundcheck's cancelled; we were late getting in, and besides there's a posse of thirty or forty screaming kids blocking the route to the stage door. The day manager said you should go to the hotel until somebody calls and they'll provide transport to get you back here later!'

Picking us up in a rattletrap of a minibus the maniac of a driver hightailed through the busy city streets, tyres squealing, and turned on a sixpence onto a paved area to the front of the arena. The vehicle hurtled noisily up a metallic ramp before mercifully drawing to a halt at a concealed side-entrance where help was at hand following an urgent radio message.

Getting wind of the unjust diversionary tactics and darting towards a well-known short cut the huge gathering of wily followers made for the alternative access point, foiled in the nick of time by our equally cunning chaperon whose presence of mind, not to mention athleticism, ensured safe passage into the huge building.

From the raucous opening: 'Good Evening Dundee', scores of crazed young females attempted to scale the high-rise stage, thwarted by a formation of strapping security men who ungraciously despatched the offenders' skinny frames back into the stalls. I lapped up the adulation and laid it on thick, every swivel of the hips or sudden jerk giving rise to a shrill, frenzied outcry camouflaging any efforts to attune to the thrashing guitars pumping out of the onstage amps, but in truth proving of little consequence.

Plucking a handkerchief from one of a flood of outstretched hands, I audaciously tucked it into the waistband of my drainpipe trousers and tantalisingly tugged the offering little by little through my unzipped fly. As I did so a deafening, penetrating salvo of girlish screams reverberated about the packed hall, increasing the excitement level – etched deliriously on the expanse of impassioned adolescent faces – to fever pitch.

As we fled into the waiting minibus in a trance-like stupor, the sense of awe quickly turned to elation, paraphrased from the lips of Romeo: 'What an amazing gig! I hope there's plenty more where that came from,' corroborated by the self-satisfied, flushed faces of the guys contemplating a post-gig wingding, perhaps in the company of a bevy of local beauties. That was until PC Plod and his clan arrived on the scene!

****

December 1977

'I'll be perfectly honest, if it was left to me you wouldn't be staying here; we've had nothing but trouble from pop groups in the past. I sincerely hope my suspicions are ill-founded and you'll all be on your best behaviour,' disparaged the narrow-minded reception manager of the town's supposedly most prestigious hotel, unnecessarily reading the riot act prior to handing out the keys to our rooms with an air of reluctance.

'As long as there's a late bar you won't hear a peep out of us,' advocated guitarist Russ, gathering up his belongings and making every effort to placate the pompous Scot, before turning tail and hastily summoning the lift.

'We put up a scruffy, long-haired heavy-rock group a few months ago; I think they were called "Leonard Skinhead" or something similar. I personally had never seen anything like it. An almighty fracas broke out between their drunken personnel and a group of gentleman residents; there was furniture flying all over the place!' the man bickered, snatching back the registration form bearing my details.

'I take it you're referring to the American band Lynyrd Skynyrd…? Well, I wouldn't go losing too much sleep over them showing up here again – three of their members were killed in an ill-fated plane crash only a few weeks ago!' I corrected him.

'Oh my good God, I didn't know that; well, let's just hope it's not a bad omen,' the upstart needlessly remarked, skulking into the adjoining office.

Over vegetable broth and a pot of stewed tea in the deserted coffee shop, Geoff's mumbled rendition of the tragic Floridian band's signature tune 'Sweet Home Alabama' raised the subject of the tumultuous rockers, frequently vilified as hard-drinking brawlers with a penchant for trouble, and their notorious on-the-road antics.

'Did you hear about the time they tried to gatecrash a private function at the Holiday Inn in Birmingham?' Geoff asked.

'No, but it sounds like you're about to tell us anyway,' said Romeo cynically.

'Word has it the hotel bar was empty when they arrived back from a gig up the road, but right next door in the conference hall a helluva knees-up was taking place, so they decided to try their luck at gatecrashing the party. Apparently a scuffle broke out when the doormen knocked them back, with the band having the upper hand at first – that was until a section of the guests got wind and came to the rescue,' the bass player related, taking a slurp of tea.

'Is that it?' I countered, making a wry face.

'Guess whose annual bash was going on inside… it was the official awards ceremony of the Amateur Boxing Association! Need I say more? All I know is they got their arses well and truly kicked,' he chuckled.

'It sounds as if those guys were jinxed from the word go,' observed a pensive Romeo, interrupted by our snooty friend the reception manager who was back on our case.

146

'Gentlemen, though you may be blissfully unaware, the coffee lounge closed fully thirty minutes ago; the cleaners are waiting to get on with their job, so I must request that you vacate the area immediately. Unlike you some people have to work for a living and don't have time to sit around all day making the place look untidy!' the idiot derided.

'That jumped-up prick is getting on my tits!' Geoff snarled, offering a two-fingered salute as the flunky spun around and minced out of earshot.

'With a bit of luck he'll have finished his shift by the time we get back from the gig,' I responded hopefully.

'I must stress that the bar will remain open until 1.30am and not a moment longer; also that any such service will be strictly for residents only!' our new adversary snapped, traipsing down the staircase from his lair at the first-floor reception desk and carrying on where he'd pigheadedly left off to a disgruntled chorus of contemptuous groans.

'Oh, that's so kind of you, how thoughtful; I'm sure we're in for a right barrel of laughs if you're still on duty when we arrive back,' I cussed sarcastically, meeting the man's eyes with a chilling glare of disapproval.

****

'What say we indulge in a bit of monkey-business when we get back to the hotel?' Geoff suggested artfully, emptying an excess of ketchup onto a plateful of chips wheeled backstage by two friendly Scots lassies along with an assortment of fast food.

'What, with that over-officious twat on the prowl? What exactly do you have in mind?' I asked with a hint of foreboding.

'Anything to bring that arrogant prick down a peg or two,' he growled, setting my mind racing in an effort to dream up a prankish master-plan.

Buoyed by a typically moonstruck Dundee concert, we nonetheless managed to keep our post-gig destination well under wraps. Just a handful of guileful aficionados lay in wait in the first-floor lounge bar, complemented by a brace of journalists granted permission to tag along, all asked to leave within thirty minutes by the uncompromising tub-thumper.

After socialising briefly with a group of guests and knocking back a swift heart-starter while the guys made their way down in dribs and drabs, Geoff's stealthy wink from the doorway signalled the coast was clear and hinted the time for some fun and games had arrived. Undetected by the happy gathering we surreptitiously sloped off together and tiptoed downstairs.

Yelling at the top of my voice to ensure maximum effect for the audience on the upper level, I abrasively ranted: 'You bastard!' followed by a stream of angry expletives, before Geoff retaliated with a few choice profanities of his own. All this was accompanied by a tumult of bangs, crashes and violent slaps designed to simulate a full-on bout of fisticuffs.

As the feigned altercation shifted into the opening lift the audible assault intensified, fists pounding like a jackhammer against the metallic bulkhead to create a disturbance of almost seismic proportions. Retrieving from his jacket pocket the bottle of ketchup pilfered earlier, Geoff smothered his face with the sticky goo causing his features to take on the look of an unfortunate car-crash victim. Meanwhile the lift jerked hesitantly to the first floor where a small crowd had assembled on the landing to watch the doors part.

Geoff flung his body dramatically forwards onto the tartan carpet to gasps of horror from the onlookers concerned at the scrapper's blood-spattered features, while I resumed the pretence by way of a carefully restrained boot aimed at my collaborator's derriere. Playing to the gallery I raised my fists, hovering intimidatingly above my playmate and theatrically snarling: 'I can't believe you did that, you scumbag; just make sure it never happens again!'

'No more, no more, please – I'm sorry,' my pal wheezed like an Oscar nominee.

The performance was observed with shock-horror by the panic-stricken manager. Cowering away from the battle zone, he whined: 'This is a disgrace! I'm calling the police – you'll all have to leave!'

'This is for your benefit, you conceited arsehole; it's a complete hoax cooked up to teach you a lesson in manners,' I fiercely berated, watching Geoff crawl to his knees licking his lips before collapsing again in a heap of unrestrained laughter.

Creating havoc on top of the desired impression, unable to contain themselves the enthralled mix of spectators broke into a spontaneous ripple of applause, howling uproariously and delighting in the hilarious charade. The chaotic scene was pricelessly abetted by a watery-eyed lady who, in handing a clump of tissues to the besmirched bass player, tripped and joined him on the floor.

'This is outrageous! I'm going to have to ask you all to return to your rooms. The bar is now closed; and as for you lot, consider yourselves fortunate you're not out on the street,' carped the less than genial host.

'The lads are right – you are a pompous ass; lighten up, man!' chided a sharp-suited executive busy entertaining a party of associates. 'Haven't you got a sense of humour? My company books rooms in this hotel all year round; and, if that bar doesn't stay open until my friends and I are ready to turn in, we'll be taking our business elsewhere in future.'

'I'm terribly sorry sir, but I fail to see how you can side with this bunch of reprobates; surely you can see their behaviour is beyond contempt!' the prig bickered.

'They happen to be a rock-'n'-roll band and a bloody good one at that. What's more, you should be privileged to have them staying here. It's high time this place was livened up; it's like a bloody morgue every time we come here!' the bigwig flatteringly reprimanded.

'You and your colleagues are most welcome to remain in the bar sir; however, I refuse to serve this rabble,' the stick-in-the-mud maintained defiantly.

'Just shut the fuck up and get the lads a round of drinks on my bill,' glowered the hospitable tycoon, finally getting through to the killjoy who, disappearing with his tail between his legs, left his more than capable deputy to do the honours through to 4am.

Causes célèbres

Brian Cox – actor
George Galloway – politician
The View – rock band
Robbie McIntosh – Average White Band drummer

Essential travelling band info

Favourite live music venue: Caird Hall, Crichton Street
Favourite curry house: Malabar, Perth Road – 36%
Favourite pub: Bank Bar, Union Street – 60%
Don't miss: Battlefield Live, Kingsway East Leisure Park– 72%
Sense of humour/friendly welcome: 66%

Chapter 22
Durham

'I'VE HAD ALL MY STUFF nicked,' shouted Rod, zipping up his chinos and feeling inside the pockets, prompting Romeo to anxiously reach for his jeans before hollering: 'The thieving bastards – some fucker's been rifling through our gear while we've been on stage!'

'You should have been more sensible and kept your cash with you at all times like I did,' perked up penny-pinching lead guitarist Russ in a holier-than-thou tone, meeting with a stony silence from his colleagues frantically rummaging through their stuff.

After drying off the beads of post-gig perspiration I checked my own trouser pockets. Predictably the wad of notes I'd stashed inside had also disappeared, along with the keys to the Ford Granada in which I and three co-musicians had journeyed north, presumably pilfered by a light-fingered student who had deliberately fought shy of attending the gig with the ulterior motive of accessing the dormitory earmarked for changing. Potentially stranded, we had little choice but to inform the organisers and instigate a thorough search of the campus buildings while, adding salt to the wound, the four unaffected band members gathered up their stuff ready to make themselves scarce. They would be sticking to the original plan of heading back to base, thus cutting the travelling time in half by avoiding the morning traffic on the busy A1 trunk road. The rest of us were left in the lurch looking daggers.

Without any introduction a striped-jacketed, self-important scholar all of twenty years of age sprang through the ajar door, launching into an uppity tongue-lashing in an overcooked la-di-da accent: 'I'm afraid any complaints will fall on deaf ears; all personal effects left in this building were done so at your own risk, and furthermore no culpability whatsoever lies with the SU organisers!'

'Well how in fuck's name are we supposed to get home, you toffee-nosed git? The thieving bastards have even stolen the ignition keys to our car!' Trevor uncharacteristically swiped, balling up his fists and thumping the wall in frustration.

'And what in God's name do you expect me to do about that?' the high and mighty mouthpiece harangued looking down his nose, incurring the wrath of Romeo who from the look of pure loathing in his eyes had other things on his mind.

'Listen up for a moment, sunshine,' I intervened, fearing for the upstart's well-being. 'I think perhaps you need to check the wording of the band's rider that was signed either by yourself or one of your SU chums. One of the clauses clearly states that the employer shall provide two "LOCKABLE" dressing rooms that are to be made secure at all times!'

'I don't have a copy to hand, I'm afraid,' the spokesperson timorously admitted, caught off guard and doing an about-face, moving his sorry backside out of the door presumably to summon assistance and get onto the case.

Outside, a procession of heavy boxes were being heaved back on board the waiting truck. Getting wind of a suspicious-looking character lurking around the loading bay and detecting the individual prodding a set of jangling keys into the lock of one of the band's cars, lighting engineer Steve reacted quickest of all, sounding the alarm to a posse of burly, grim-faced stagehands who within seconds had the plunderer surrounded. As he vainly attempted to make a bolt for it, amidst a stream of profanities a one-sided scuffle ensued. It culminated in Steve landing a ripping right uppercut squarely onto the delinquent's jaw, all before the eyes of the passing union rep.

'God forbid! All hell is breaking loose out there, but I'm relieved to say the main culprit seems to have been apprehended!' crowed the melodramatic buffoon, bursting breathlessly into our quarters to underhandedly seize the chance of covering himself in glory.

The bloody-nosed punk hit the deck with a loud crack as he was slung head first through the changing-room door. Dangling the car keys before our noses and cuffing the hoodlum to the side of the head, the lighting man gruffly elicited: 'Now, perhaps you'd like to explain your actions to these pissed-off gentlemen here!'

'I'm sorry,' whimpered the guilty party.

'Is that the best you can come up with, you piece of shit? How about handing back the rest of the stuff you nicked?' snarled Steve, shoving the scumbag with his right boot.

'Argh… I said I'm sorry. I haven't eaten properly in three days and spent it on some food,' the flinching rogue lied.

'Bullshit, there's nothing around here for miles. Come on, you snivelling little bastard, where's the cash?' urged the incensed Romeo.

'I'm skint and haven't got a pot to piss in; there's a burger van round the back of the main hall,' the low-life fabricated, cowering in fear.

'I reckon he's hidden it up his arse,' implied Steve, aggressively twisting the youth's arm halfway up his back.

'There's an old broom-handle in the kitchenette – perhaps we could try shoving that up to see if we can extract anything,' I piped up intimidatingly.

'Come on, let's get his trousers off and teach him a lesson,' encouraged Steve with a treacherous glint in his eye, clearly relishing every minute as he jostled his prey and tugged at the waistband with a little help from assistant Martin.

'No, no, get off please! I've got most of it but I spent a tenner on fags and booze,' the rat panicked, reaching down into a woolly sock to magically retrieve his rich pickings. The contents were quickly snatched from his hand and distributed amongst the injured parties.

'Thanks to your employees and my own efforts it would seem this unsavoury matter has been resolved with a minimum of fuss!' the aloof SU rep interjected, wearing a smug, self-satisfied smile, meeting with an incredulous response from the stupefied gathering who, in a booming, unified chorus, asserted:

'FUCK OFF!'

****

Escaping Durham town's effervescent streets in pursuit of the magnificent cathedral on a later visit to the region, I squatted down in a verdant corner known as Palace Green as a blast of sun pleasingly emerged from behind the clouds, creating a golden hue over the towering landmark whilst lightly caressing my anaemic skin.

As I munched on an M&S sandwich and eavesdropped on an indecipherable altercation between two Japanese tourists, just a few yards away resting his head against an old hessian sack lay a rustic-looking man of around sixty twitching uneasily in his slumber. Coming to with a splutter and a shake of the head, he struggled groggily to his feet and, as he did so, I noticed a faded white logo ingrained on the sack and honed in to take a closer look.

Telepathically twisting on a dime the old codger bade: 'What's up lad?'

'I'm sorry, I didn't mean to be nosy; I was trying to make out what it says on the sack – I'm just curious that's all,' I reciprocated.

'Ah, no problem boy, feel free to have a gander; it reads "The Pied Piper", and that's the telephone number underneath.'

'You're not a flautist by any chance, are you?' I pried.

'Pardon me, a bloody what?' he fired back in a state of confusion.

'Do you play the flute – it says "The Pied Piper" on your sack?' I reasoned, warming to the man.

'Oh, I get you! No lad, the only thing I'm any good at playing is the fool. You can come and see what's hidden inside if you like,' he offered half in jest.

Collecting up my things, I crept over with no inkling as to what lay in store. Untying the string securing the bag the man boasted: 'Just take a look at them beauties, lad!'

Poking in my nose and balking at the deathly odour before reeling backwards in horror I screeched: 'What the bloody... hell?'

Huddled together resembling a litter of decaying stillborn puppies, a quick headcount revealed a dozen or more revolting, furry, long-tailed creatures nevermore destined to follow in the wake of this or any other self-proclaimed Pied Piper.

'What on earth are you doing carting those bloody horrible things around?' I queried, feeling my stomach turn at the vile sight.

'I'm a rat-catcher lad, that's what I do for a living!' he explained.

'What, and you're expecting me to believe that putrid plague is this morning's catch?' I asked almost retching.

'Ah now, that might be pushing it a bit far; you see, they're not exactly today's,' he unveiled with a hint of cunning.

'I'm really not with you – why would anyone of sound mind be carrying around a sack of dead rats?' I dubiously probed.

'Let's just say that's my little secret – though I might be willing to let you in on it if you promise me faithfully you won't say a word to Mrs Maitland!' he sniggered, mischievously tapping the side of his nose.

'Who the f... I mean hell's Mrs Maitland? I don't know anyone of that name,' I replied, tickled by the odd request.

'That's strange, I thought everyone in these parts knew the old goat!' he exclaimed, stroking the whiskers on his chin.

Wallowing in the devilry, sniffing a twist in the tail and mocking the knave's north-eastern twang I mimicked: 'Why-aye man, that's just it, I'm nay from round 'ere!'

'You're not Welsh are you? I don't trust those bloody weirdoes,' he chortled in a xenophobic tone, before proceeding to let the cat (or even rat) out of the bag. Paying heed to the captivating yarn unravelling in my ears, I tried hard not to laugh as the scallywag brought to light the most enterprising of schemes. It seemed the rodents were hunted down courtesy of a wicked scam conducted in a disused grain barn close to his modest country retreat literally crawling with the much-maligned creatures.

'First I lure 'em out by spreading a few peanut butter sandwiches around the place; then as they're tucking in I smack 'em on the head with a stick, bag 'em up and dump the little buggers in the back of my van. When a customer such as

Mrs Maitland calls, I nip along to put some pellets down and go back a couple of days later!' he recounted.

'Hang on a sec; so you get paid according to the number of rats you catch, but how do you get the dead ones inside without being sussed?' I queried, bedazzled.

'You see that wax jacket over there? It has what we call "poacher's pockets" where I can hide a dozen or more rats. Basically I just walk onto the premises carrying the empty sack and transfer the vermin into it out of harm's way, then I present the satisfied customer with the evidence. They're usually happy to settle up on the spot… In ten years of doing it I can count the actual rats I caught on one hand!' he fiendishly cackled.

'You crafty old git,' I chuckled disbelievingly, shaking the trickster's filthy mitt whilst offering my gratitude for the entertainment in total awe.

I watched him lurch off, sack on his back, towards a disfigured old rattletrap parked close by. Roughly halfway he startled me by spinning on his heels to combatively lay down the law: 'Now don't you be going telling that old bat Mrs Maitland, do you hear me?' waving an admonishing finger before disappearing behind a row of trees.

Causes célèbres

Rowan Atkinson – *Mr Bean, Blackadder* et al
Tony Blair – George Bush's old pal and partner in crime
Pat Barker – author
Paul Collingwood – England cricketer
Trevor Horn – successful '80s/'90s record producer
Sir Bobby Robson – legendary England football manager
Wendy Craig – TV actress

Essential travelling band info

Favourite live music venue: Gala Theatre, Millennium Place
Favourite curry house: Alishaan, North Road – 61%
Favourite pub: Olde Elm Tree, Crossgate – 77%
Don't miss: the cathedral – 90%
Sense of humour/friendly welcome: 79%

Chapter 23
Edinburgh

SCOTLAND'S MUCH-ADMIRED CAPITAL CITY APTLY plays host to a variety of top-notch theatres, none more so than Usher Hall situated on Lothian Road. Its grandeur is underlined by a well-impressed Romeo's reaction upon idling slowly by the landmark's stately frontage for the very first time: 'Now that's what you call a proper gig!'

The venue indeed exudes all the pomp and splendour associated with a bastion of cultural excellence, and is capable of housing close to three thousand baying Scots. As the band struck up for a pre-gig run-through, the drummer's sentiments resounded through the vast auditorium like an orchestra playing, spelling out that the evening ahead promised to be something out of the ordinary.

Dominating the elevated skyline atop a gargantuan mound casting a dark clinging shadow over the encompassing gardens and old town, the imposing castle fortress glares toward the hive of activity known the world over as Princes Street, which serves as a foothold for scores of smitten sightseers eager to capture the renowned setting on film.

Poles apart from Europe's chicer capitals such as Paris, London or Berlin, the Caledonian mini-metropolis harbours a measured kindliness whereby, in the thick of the constant daily hullabaloo, the huddled masses take time out to linger and chat, affably acknowledging their friends and colleagues amidst a backdrop fused with disparate cultures.

****

At a time when fierce swarms of impassioned teenage females north of the border looked to add locks of hair or perhaps even body parts to their souvenir collections, the attendees cooped up in the Usher Hall appeared to be similarly outgoing; so much so that, following an electrifying grand finale, any ideas of a hasty retreat to our tarrying transport became pie in the sky with every escape route from the building's rear blockaded by a wall-to-wall shoal of juveniles.

'We'll have to create a diversion,' panicked a member of staff. Dishing out strict orders to an underling, he beckoned for the ensnared party to follow in his footsteps through a maze of narrow tunnels back towards the now deserted auditorium, where we hurriedly shimmied through the stalls out into the expansive arched foyer. 'Wait here gents, and don't move a muscle or we can't be responsible for your safety; I'll be back in a jiffy,' warned the uneasy employee.

Steeped in perspiration, the shivering bill-toppers waited restlessly, drainpipe trousers clinging like a second skin. A few moments later the flushed errand boy dashed back from his heroic assignment. 'There's a minibus on the street at the bottom of the steps – I suggest you get your arses inside it,' he urged. Sensing our discomfort, he added: '… and get out of those wet things at the earliest opportunity.'

'What happened to the lynch mob? There were hundreds of them!' Romeo flapped, peering through an ornate lead-light window onto the forecourt.

'Don't worry, they're taken care of. Half a dozen of the crew boys sprinted out of the stage door into two waiting cars smothered in blankets covering their heads; the fans were going crazy. C'mon, there's no time to lose, 'cause in my experience they're not stupid and have probably already sussed out what's going on,' our saviour pressed.

Meeting up with the boys in the open-plan bar of the Royal Scot Hotel on the edge of town, libation in hand to settle the nerves having weathered the earlier storm, I overheard a masquerading crew-hand holding court before a clique of mildly interested patrons, boastfully detailing his five minutes of adulation: 'All this young totty was going apeshit, pulling at our clothes and grabbing at our hair and nuts; it was fantastic!'

'You must have about as much meat in your pants as a veggie's fridge,' I interrupted, entering the confab. 'Nobody in their right mind would want their gonads groped by a cranky female, and believe me I know!'

'Ah, come on – I bet you can't get enough of it,' crowed the hireling.

'That's precisely where you're wrong. I've never forgotten being dragged out of a car by my hair in Leeds a couple of years ago. There were hands all over my body taking lumps out of me. When I got back to the hotel my balls were black and blue – I had to sit in a cold bath to ease the swelling,' I painfully recalled, reinforcing the argument.

In truth most 'fan-handling' incidents proved not only hair-raising but downright scary, spawned by irrational groups of overexcited kids carried on a wave of hysteria and displaying an alarming propensity towards exacting actual bodily harm. Straying too close to a stage's brow to engage in a fierce tug-o'-war with an extended sea of hands was fraught with danger, inflamed by manic females seeking to extract blood samples, slashing sharp fingernails into the tiniest strip of exposed flesh or perilously lassoing items of loose clothing around a get-at-able ankle.

'I can assure you there's nothing sexually arousing about being torn to shreds by what amounts to a pack of wild animals,' I quibbled, 'and besides, they're nothing more than kids, so there's absolutely no likelihood of any late-night shenanigans!'

'Well, it's a darn sight more exciting than lugging bloody great boxes around and getting covered in dust and shit in the process,' the unconvinced roadie beefed.

Cutting him short, a sharp-dressed, distinguished-looking man interjected: 'Excuse me, lads, I'm sorry to bother you but I'm up here with a group of delegates and we've just been to your show, which by the way was brilliant. If it's not too much to ask, there are a couple of young lady associates who'd love to meet you; I know it's cheeky but could I bring them over?'

'Perhaps we could come and join you,' I suggested, catching sight of two radiant, head-turning blondes attracting the entire bar's attention.

'Hey, I was enjoying our chat – can I come too?' the dumbfounded crew-man begged, eyes straining in their sockets.

'I wasn't, so I think perhaps it's best if you stay put,' I reciprocated, turning to acknowledge the co-guests and beckoning to Rod.

'This is Lena and Annika,' mine host acquainted. 'They're over from Stockholm in Sweden for the Volvo conference.'

'Can't life be a bitch sometimes?' I mocked, wearing a self-satisfied smirk and catching the ear of the envious stagehand. Muttering an incomprehensible diatribe of expletives he supped up the dregs of his pint and made straight for the exit.

****

Satisfying an abiding wanderlust, recent years have seen me celebrating the dawning of a new year in a sprinkling of exotic worldly destinations. A number of highlights immediately spring to mind, ranging from the civilised composure of Auckland, New Zealand to the foolhardy pyromania of Peru's capital Lima (where, said to bring good fortune, everyone including my wife and me sported yellow underwear), whilst not forgetting the spectacular annual firework display detonating o'er the rooftops and harbour of Madeira's capital city Funchal at the stroke of midnight.

One that has so far fallen between the cracks, due for the most part to festive work commitments over three and a half decades, is the celebration acclaimed as 'the world's greatest street party'. More specifically known as Hogmanay, it remains firmly on the radar as an experience to savour on at least one future occasion, having regrettably declined an invitation just prior to the turn of the century from an old friend. The omission was atoned for by an impromptu spring visit, only to find myself on the receiving end of an iniquitous prank.

After taking the bumpy one-hour hop north out of Stansted airport, I hailed an overpriced cab for the additional jaunt to the sprawling capital's suburbs. A speedy check-in to a modest B&B establishment paved the way for an early visit to the bar run by old pal Bobby Smith.*

'Hey big man, it's great to see you,' my pint-sized friend effervesced, greeting me with a hug and wasting no time in offering a wee dram of typical Scottish hospitality.

'I'll think I'll leave that 'til later; I've a gut feeling we could be in for a heavy night. A cuppa will do just fine for now,' I balked, mindful of the man's reputation.

'You're looking good, big Davy, though the barnet's beginning to go a wee bit thin at the back,' he cheekily teased.

'Typical of you to notice that; it's nothing more than an excess of testosterone. Besides, we're in the middle of a recession,' I jested, enviously eyeing up the brown curly locks very much in evidence on the top of my buddy's think-tank.

'You've still got more than enough to do a rescue job. What you need is a dose of Auntie Val's magic potion. A regular customer of ours called Hughie gave it a try and all his hair grew back. I tell you, it's amazing stuff!' he enthused a trifle too convincingly.

'Pull the other one, mate, it's got bells on,' I scoffed, slurping avidly at the hot tea, oddly perceiving on my taste buds a fiery additive of some description.

'It'll be your loss Davy, especially being in the game you're in. The locals have been using it up here for nigh on five hundred years,' he persisted. I responded with a sceptical shrug of the shoulders as I sensed the time may be ripe to return to my lodgings, conscious a degree of staying power may be requisite for the evening ahead.

I returned refreshed from a shave, shower and change of shirt, and a compendium of nostalgic yarns ensued, focusing on Bob's time south of the border getting on for twenty years before. With the drink flowing freely the storytelling began ratcheting up a few notches, further enhanced by a sprinkling of local scallywags weighing in with a tale or two of their own.

I was engaged in a smidgen of people-watching during an idle moment

---

* Ex-Leicester City footballer and friend Bobby Smith died of cancer at the age of 56 in 2010. Such was the magnetism of the impish Scot's personality, the funeral service was beamed to an overflow in excess of a hundred attendees obliged to pay their respects outside of the church.

when a mystical auburn-haired woman bedecked from head to toe in black robes swaggered into the bar. From an old leather bag she proceeded to unearth an archaic Bunsen burner, accompanied by a Tupperware sandwich box containing a hideous-looking gooey grey mixture.

Having a quiet word in the wee man's ear, I whispered: 'What the fuck's going on? This has all the makings of a bout of witchcraft!'

'That there is Auntie Val, big man; she's a real one-off!' he replied, full of the devil all those around him had come to know and admire.

'Let me just get this straight,' I inquired, cottoning on I may be the butt of a wind-up. 'That wouldn't happen to be her magic potion… would it?'

'Now, which one of you lot is big Davy?' the woman asked gruffly.

Looking daggers at Bobby I growled: 'You scheming little runt – you never were one to be trusted! Perhaps you'd like to let me in on exactly what's going on?'

'There's no way I could allow you to come all this way without offering a proper Edinburgh-style welcome; after all, we're known for our hospitality up here,' he babbled, fighting back the laughter and introducing me to the resident sorceress.

'Sit yourself down, sonny boy – in no time at all you'll experience just how efficacious this remedy is!' she proffered in a persuasive Scots tongue, scraping the concoction onto a ceramic plate and placing it on a mini-tripod above the burner.

Deciding to play along with what could only be a practical joke, I grudgingly parked my backside. The obvious question beckoned: 'Would you mind telling me what's actually in the elixir? I don't want the rest of my hair to fall out!'

'Stop bickering, laddie!' the wild-haired sibyl gestured, firmly putting me in my place. 'Don't be ridiculous; it's nothing more than a few natural ingredients hand-picked from my garden!' Drawing out a small paintbrush from a hidden pocket in her robes, much to the delight of the sniggering onlookers the wicked witch warned: 'Now, don't move a muscle; and consider yourself privileged – this restorative would cost you an arm and a leg elsewhere!'

'That's what I'm afraid of! The stench is absolutely disgusting. I just hope I'll get out of here in one piece,' I complained, freezing in the chair.

'Just sit still and stop whining, laddie, you'll be thanking me in a few months' time!' she scolded, removing the frothing pot from the flame.

'I'm not sure I can go through with this; that fucking stuff smells like rotting cow-dung,' I grumbled. While Bob was with some difficulty restraining a high-pitched girlish titter, my remark triggered off an uproarious chorus of unrestrained laughter amongst his partners in crime, including Harry Potter's grandmother.

'You bunch of haggis-bashing bastards – it *is* shit isn't it?' I bawled, springing like a cat out of the seat. Feeling the heated compound trickle onto my pate, I shrank away from the enchantress and stood my ground.

'That it may well be, but this isn't just any kind of shit,' she chided. 'It has magical healing powers. I collected it fresh from my dovecote this very evening!'

'Magical powers my arse – that stuff is nothing more than stinking birdshit and you wanted to daub it onto my bloody head. What kind of a welcome do you call this!' I bellyached. I intimated towards the polished cranium of another watery-eyed customer beaming beneath the lights, trying desperately to contain himself. 'Why don't you try it out on him and, if it works, next time I'm up in this neck of the woods I'll gladly give it a go!' I vowed.

'We already have, big man; that's Hughie who I was telling you about earlier,' Bob snickered, unable to keep the lid on another fit of laughter.

'What, he's the one whose hair you said grew back?' I concluded, seeing the funny side and joining in with the mirthful outpouring.

'That's him, Davy, the very man,' the wicked host affirmed, doubling up. 'Let's just say I was being a tad economical with the truth!'

The practical joke at my expense proved the ideal icebreaker, and a predictably boozy night ensued. At one point I was cornered by hairless Hughie who spelled out the whys and wherefores of an ancient tradition said to date back to the sixteenth century, which had supposedly worked wonders for a diversity of thinning Celtic scalps.

'Without wishing to be rude, it didn't exactly work for you; it's just a load of bullshit!' I contended, not mincing my words.

'Dove shit, to be precise. I was the exception, big fella; this stuff's been solving follicle disorders for nearly five hundred years!' insisted the slapheaded Scot, stoutly defending the potion's mythical powers and falling from his stool.

Causes célèbres

Sean Connery – the original and most celebrated James Bond
Alexander Graham Bell – 'Hey baby I'm your telephone man!'
Robert Louis Stevenson – author of *Kidnapped* and many other classics
Sir Walter Scott – poet/novelist
Sir Arthur Conan Doyle – Sherlock Holmes creator
Bay City Rollers – '70s heart-throbs
Ronnie Corbett – the sole remaining Ronnie
Alastair Sim – character actor
Ken Stott – actor

Iain Banks – author
Ludovic Kennedy – broadcaster
Alexander McCall Smith – novelist (*The No. 1 Ladies Detective Agency*)
J.K. Rowling – Harry Potter creator
Irvine Welsh – novelist
David Wilkie – Olympic gold medallist swimmer

Essential travelling band info

Favourite live music venue: Usher Hall, Lothian Road
Favourite curry house: Gurkha Café and Restaurant, Cockburn Street – 85%
Favourite pub: Café Royal, West Register Street – 80%
Don't miss: Arthur's Seat, Holyrood Park – 82% (spectacular views)
Sense of humour/friendly welcome: 76%

Chapter 24
Ely

Spring 1984

'THIS IS MANFRED; HE'S a Baader-Meinhof terrorist and is staying with us for a while to visit Anna,' my one-time neighbour 'Wobbly Bob' jokingly revealed over a pint in the village pub. He was introducing me to a mild-mannered, frizzy-haired young German his beloved daughter had taken a shine to at a university ball only months previously.

'Good to meet you, or should I say *willkommen* or even "Prada Meinhof",' I responded, grasping his hand and doing my level best to make him feel at home.

'They're not giving much away, but I can smell romance in the air!' Bob hinted, raising a glass to the young couple and patting the Deutschlander heartily on the back to confirm his approval of Anna's taste in young men. As he waxed lyrical as to how two pairs of wandering eyes had met across a room on a balmy summer's night, the conversation turned to the outlander's future prospects. To my surprise I learned that Manfred not only ticked all the boxes as a perfect suitor but also excelled as an accomplished organist, studying music at London's prestigious Royal Academy of Music.

In stark contrast to the George Orwell novel *1984* the year would mark one of the happiest and most significant occasions of my own thirty-two years of existence to date, in that on Sunday August 25th I would at last take the wedding vows together with my beautiful bride-to-be, Cathy. After a low-key service conducted in the village church by the eccentric local preacher, we would move on to an upmarket reception to be held in a lavish marquee set in the lush gardens of a renowned, historic Cambridgeshire hotel.

Proving to be a thorn in the side during the painstaking organisational build-up to the big day, the limited ability of the well-meaning but bumbling parish church organist was creating nightmares of a different kind, in which I imagined J.S. Bach's glorious 'Jesu, Joy of Man's Desiring' and the John Stanley classic 'Trumpet Voluntary' put to the sword at the ceremony's inception by the misguided fingers of a ham-fisted soloist.

'When are you likely to return to Germany?' I asked Manfred, visualising an opening staring me in the face whilst also sensing the perfect excuse to dig me out of a hole.

'I have no plans to go back until Christmas,' the student replied. 'First I have to sit my exams, and zen I must spend some time with Anna… and her family.'

'Would you do me the service of playing the organ at my forthcoming wedding?' I eagerly posed, jumping straight in at the deep end.

'Zis vud be a great honour for me,' he responded, answering my every prayer. 'To play at such an important occasion, especially for a fellow musician, vill be – how do you say – zee icing on zee cake; sank you so much for asking me!'

'That's absolutely fantastic, or as your fellow countrymen say "*wunderbar*"; but you must allow me to pay for your services,' I added.

'Not at all, zis vill not be necessary; I don't need payment. Perhaps though zere is one favour you could do for me,' he hinted.

'Anything, you only have to ask – I'm over the moon you've agreed!'

'Do you know of a place called Ely? I vould love to go and visit zee cathedral; zee organ zere is said to be werry special!' he explained.

'Done; it's only around sixty miles from here. What about one day next week? We can even pack a picnic and make a day of it!' I enthused, striking up a gentlemen's agreement before stumbling home to awaken the future Mrs Bartram with the wonderful news.

****

The sparsely populated, yet oddly attractive Cambridgeshire fens exude a discomfiting aura of bad chemistry, even toward interlopers from the neighbouring county, or so I was rudely reminded halfway through a charity bike ride some two years previously. Essentially to pick up some water and rehydrate, I called into a remote village one-stop shop where the reception afforded bore all the hallmarks of hostile hillbilly country much as depicted in an overkill of weird American road-movies.

'Bloody cyclists, we don't like 'em round 'ere; they're nothing but a bloody nuisance and prevent the bloody farmers from gettin' on with their bloody work!' a cherry-faced customer garbed in a boiler suit cursed provocatively as I ambled to the counter.

'And a very good afternoon to you too; lovely day isn't it?' I sarcastically replied.

Knocked off his stride, the dishevelled rustic ignored me completely as he shuffled towards the exit muttering to the lady assistant: 'I can't stand bloody cocky Londoners; any road Madge, I'll see you tomorrow morning mate!'

'He's a barrel-load of laughs; did he just call you mate?' I puzzled, placing the items onto the cluttered counter.

'He's my brother,' the unfriendly woman grunted. 'Is that all?' She snatched away my money with a look of pure evil, kicking my imagination into overdrive.

'Perhaps I should've guessed,' I retorted, eyeing a kaleidoscopic poster advertising 'THE ELY FOLK FESTIVAL', envisioning scandalous tidings of incest and other bizarre goings-on emerging out of such an unsettled backwater.

The city itself sweeps upward from the middle of hectare upon hectare of marshy fenland. Its name reputedly derived from the proliferation of eels found nesting in the surrounding shallow waters in years gone by when, going under the name 'The Isle of Ely', the region bore the distinction of being a county in its own right, prior to joining forces with Cambridgeshire in 1974. Ascending into prominence out of the flat horizon the pre-eminent 'Ship of the Fens', as the cathedral is known, looms large to the naked eye from as far as twenty miles away, visible from any of the narrow, winding approach roads as it gazes commandingly across a massive expanse of horizontal nothingness.

'There it is – it's huge!' cried Cathy, pointing to the edifice growing ever larger on the skyline, creating a false impression of being closer than it actually was. This was attested to around an hour later when, after being stuck behind a snail-like combine harvester even a nuisance cyclist could have overtaken, an extended terrace of higgledy-piggledy, multi-coloured two-up, two-down cottages revealed themselves on the township's main street, signalling the tedious journey had reached its end.

I was determined that Anna and in particular Manfred would wallow in their all too brief visit, and followed directions to the Vice Dean's office within the cathedral grounds. An affable, dignified-looking clerk exhibiting a neatly trimmed grey beard extended the warmest of welcomes, going out of his way to be helpful before transmuting into a mild state of shock at the merest mention of the young German experimenting on the prodigious organ. He proceeded to blind me with science, banging on about an extensive programme of restoration work completed just eight or nine years earlier. 'And then there's the revamped console and action lovingly repaired by...' the man babbled in full flow.

'This guy is not just any old Tom, Dick or for that matter Harry; he's a serious musician studying at London's Royal Academy,' I pleaded. 'Not only that, he's come all the way over here from Germany and it would mean the world to him!'

'I'm not promising anything, but if you can come back in around an hour I'll have a little chat with our Director of Music; he's an extremely understanding man, so fingers crossed!' the notary pledged optimistically.

Re-energised by an impromptu snack spread out on a nearby strip of newly mown grass, roughly ninety minutes later we found ourselves back in the cathedral where, within earshot of a spellbound small gathering, the vast sets of pipes pumped and resonated majestically throughout the holy place's interior expanse, magnified tenfold by the inspired Manfred's admirable handiwork. Blissfully throwing his hands at the tiered banks of ivory keys he belted out the most joyous cacophony as Cathy, Anna and I listened in the knowledge our mission had been perfectly accomplished.

****

Beneath a cloudless, azure August sky our wedding day passed in a dreamlike trance, free of any dramas or hitches whatever. Amidst a great deal of pomp and circumstance a thirty-strong local choral society mellifluously filtered through the resounding aisles, jubilantly drowning out the discordant vicar, whilst Manfred at the peak of his powers literally pulled out all the stops, doing myself and my new bride proud.

Causes célèbres

Oliver Cromwell – Lord Protector after overthrowing Charles 1st
Sir Clive Woodward – England Rugby Union World Cup-winning coach
Guy Pearce – Australian émigré actor (*LA Confidential*, *Memento*)

Essential travelling band info

Favourite live music venue: The Royal Standard, Fore Hill
Favourite curry house: Le Spice, Fore Hill – 41%
Favourite pub: Prince Albert, Silver Street – 70%
Don't miss: Oliver Cromwell's house – 66%
Sense of humour/friendly welcome: 55% (in the neighbouring villages 20%)

Chapter 25
Exeter

AUGUST FORTNIGHT! THE HIGHLIGHT OF ANY calendar year for most diligent, working-class people and their families, especially prior to the overseas, sunshine-filled package holiday boom of the seventies. The fourteen days when most high-powered corporations and manufacturers temporarily shut up shop signified not only a welcome change of air, but a mass exodus to the coastal resorts of Devon and Cornwall by way of a lengthy annual pilgrimage that clogged up every route south-west.

Many of the hordes of liberated holidaymakers indulged themselves by adding a short stopover en route, anxious to break up the gruelling nine-hour journey and allow their tuckered-out, overheating engines a well-earned breather whilst also seeking to push the boat out. Often centring on the city of Exeter and its close proximity to their final destination, these brief stays proved equally popular with a number of savvy guest-house owners and hoteliers who, rubbing their hands together, cashed in by hoicking up the room rates in a bid to make a quick killing.

Partially sated by an unappetising cooked breakfast complete with thinly buttered bread curling at the edges from being left out all night, the come-rain-come-shine house rules dictated that all guests would be required to vacate the premises for anything up to seven hours, ostensibly for cleaning purposes, though effectively to afford the overwrought owners a little precious downtime. Arriving back en masse at five o'clock on the dot battered and windswept by the unpredictable English summer elements, visitors took shelter in the flea-bitten TV lounge where fully ninety minutes of incessant whingeing ensued, mostly from the tongues of grizzly, snivelling children complaining of hunger pangs, until the sonorous clang of the six-thirty dinner gong triggered a stampede for the designated tables and two courses of unpalatable slop served up to fulfil the proprietor's obligations.

The completion of the M5 motorway in 1977, coupled with two major road construction projects to upgrade the existing A30 and A38 trunk roads into high-capacity dual carriageways, spelled the end of the gravy train. Most of the town's profiteers found themselves bypassed in droves by the ever-loyal bucket-and-spade brigade, in tandem with a glut of surfer dudes and adventuring city slickers moving full steam ahead in the direction of the Cornish Riviera.

****

Serving as a blessing in disguise after what seemed an eternity of diversions and contraflows, the modernised highways virtually halved the travelling time to seasonal theatre dates in tourist traps such as Barnstaple, Paignton and St Austell, putting an end to unbearably wearisome jaunts south-west soured by petty squabbling and short-temperedness amongst griping band-members fidgeting like bored brats constantly at each other's throats.

Showaddywaddy were tagged the 'darlings' of the college circuit by student-union bookers for much of the 1980s when, harking back to their misspent early teens, the in-house brainboxes revealed their true musical colours (along with a delightful excess of female flesh whilst scaling the stage). A sea change in musical fads put paid to Freshers' Balls and the like until inexplicably, in 2003 following a fourteen-year hiatus, we found ourselves booked to play a prestigious New Year's Ball on campus at the University of Exeter.

'It's bloody light years since we did a college gig; I'd have thought the more recent intakes would've been into all that plink-plonk electronic shit!' asserted Geoff, settling into his seat ready for the final instalment of an uneventful twelve-month period.

'Things move a little more slowly down in that part of the world, Geoffrey. Some of the locals still point up to the sky if a plane flies overhead!' Romeo piped up, making reference to his frequent trips to visit family based in Cornwall.

'I tell you what, I'm glad we're not flying – the weather's really cutting up rough,' I apprised with a degree of caution as I hit the accelerator, all set to raise Cain and ring in the New Year taking Devon's undergraduates by storm.

We reached the M5 motorway in good time and well on schedule for an 11pm performance; but the wintry elements took a turn for the worse, as gale-force winds rocked the people-carrier from side to side in cahoots with an incessant barrage of rain hardening into sleet and lashing down onto the windscreen, making visibility nigh on impossible.

'I forgot to mention, we've been asked to perform "Auld Lang Syne" on the stroke of midnight,' I recollected as the vehicle was reduced to a crawl in a quagmire of slush. 'Does anybody know the chords?'

This spurred guitarist Danny into a spontaneous detailed rendition:

'Should C acquaintance be G7?

167

And C brought to F,
Should C, A minor be G7?
And F lang C... it's a piece of piss!' he claimed.

Although our arrival was cut a little too close for comfort, the treacherous conditions outside were soon forgotten three hours later when, aided by a miked-up radio, the resonant chimes of Big Ben clanged through the mighty loudspeakers, heralding the dawning of a new epoch, followed hot on the heels by an undisciplined interpretation of the ancient Scots anthem.

Linking arms in a confusion of circles below, an intelligentsia of professors and lecturers garbed up to the nines in penguin suits and evening dresses (in complete contrast to the boisterous merrymakers envisaged) exercised their vocal talents. As the song reached its climax they broke away from their chains to plant kisses on their bosom buddies' cheeks, before rolling back the years with some nifty footwork whilst harbouring fond memories of their own unfettered university days.

The gig marked the band's thirty-first year in existence on a sustained high note. Little did anyone know the return passage would be just as unforgettable, for all the wrong reasons!

****

Departing into a glistening, less intense icy drizzle via the uni's main gates, we anticipated a trouble-free journey on notoriously the year's quietest night on the roads. Scarcely a mile from the M5 junction, however, a scene of utter turmoil emerged in the headlights, underlined by twenty or thirty animated bodies in all their finery zigzagging any which way out of a snarl-up of discarded vehicles strewn at all angles in our path.

Pounding like rolling thunder above the idling engine noise, in the blink of an eye an uncontrollable herd of stampeding horses careered wildly from a concealed side lane, cutting loose down the main street like a destruction of fleeing wildebeest on the African plains, whilst frightening the life out of all and sundry.

We observed the un-mounted chaos for all of thirty minutes, as a disarray of flashing blue lights lit up the sky intermingled with the unoccupied jeeps and Chelsea tractors congesting the main thoroughfare and grass verges. The gridlock was aggravated further by groups of headless chickens vainly attempting to shepherd the beasts into a roadside paddock.

'Fucking horses, they should be kept in stables together with their stuck-up owners, not running amok on the roads spreading shit everywhere,' beefed city boy Danny. He was jolted back in his seat as driver Rod cleverly seized upon an opportunity to tail a departing ambulance, weaving through the narrowest of gaps accompanied by the sarcastic cry of 'Happy New Year!' bellowed hoarsely from out of an open window.

'Not even wild horses could stop us getting home tonight!' I japed just south of Bristol.

I had perhaps spoken a little too soon as, checking the rear-view mirror, Rod picked up on another blue light flickering way in the distance. He eased off the throttle to allow the speeding patrol vehicle to pass unimpeded; but unbelievably we found ourselves under surveillance and subsequently flagged down onto the hard shoulder.

Leaping like stuntmen from a souped-up station wagon, four tooled-up, heavily padded officers resembling a US SWAT team dramatically encircled the vehicle, bossed by a macho leading man squawking sibilantly into a loudhailer: 'Okay, step out of the vehicle one at a time and spread your hands against the side windows… slowly!'

'What's with all this gung-ho bollocks – is this some kind of wind-up?' I argued, wrestling free of the open door and shrieking above the howling wind.

'Keep your mouth shut until you're spoken to, and refrain from using any further bad language or I'll book you here and now,' the brawny cop sniped.

Unnecessarily using brute force by kicking apart our legs, the three remaining officers conducted a vigorous body-search on each individual, before the patrolman in charge of the trio demanded: 'Now, remove each item of baggage from the tailgate – slowly!'

'Take it easy, buddy – we're just a bunch of humble musicians on the way back from a New Year's gig in Exeter; why all the fuss?' Romeo pleaded.

'All you need to know is that we received a tip-off around an hour ago. Now, if you'd kindly oblige by opening up your things,' the top dog insisted, rummaging inside a suit bag prior to feasting his eyes on a scarlet stage outfit. 'What's this, have you just come from a fancy dress party?' the screw queried curiously, looking askance at rhythm guitarist Trevor.

'No – it's a Showaddywaddy suit!' the performer stressed.

'I haven't heard of them in years; did you bid for it at a vintage clothes auction?' the senior bobby drolly enquired, taking the heat out of the situation whilst pointing Rod in the direction of the patrol car to undergo a breath test.

'Okay fellers, you're free to go… you don't look much like a gang of organised jewellery thieves to me!' barked the head honcho, giving Rod the all-clear and racing through the deteriorating blizzard to reunite with his chums huddled in the four-by-four.

****

'What the fuck!' yelped Rod only minutes later as, fresh from a brief pit-stop, he swerved to avoid a urinating carouser halfway along the slip road. 'What a prick – I could easily have hit him.' Pulling sharply over to the side he implored: 'Do you mind taking over? I'm knackered and the snow's playing tricks with my eyes!'

Approaching the M42 junction with the never-ending schlep's end finally in sight, I squinted through a torrent of mesmerising hailstones as a seemingly impenetrable barrier of white appeared like an illusion, blocking off the entire highway. Drawing nearer I could make out the shape of a gigantic articulated truck sprawled in an elongated L-shape across all three carriageways, doubtless having jackknifed on the treacherous road surface.

Glissading to a halt, I leaped incautiously from the driver's door. Flickering dimly within the lorry's cab, barely visible in the midst of the unmerciful salvo, a shadowy, sporadic light reminiscent of an age-old Toc H lamp outlined an upraised arm, presumably putting out an SOS and in desperate need of a helping hand.

Battling manfully through the gale-force wind I saw that a further obstacle presented itself in the shape of a heavy folding step tucked beneath the driver's side door. Released by means of a sturdy safety-catch, with a thudding jolt it slammed down, narrowly missing the transporter's fender. Thrusting my feet onto the knurled rundles, I pulled forcefully at the cab's door-handle. Caught in a savage gust, the bulky metal frame thrashed wide open, almost taking off my head, revealing a shaven-headed man collapsed over the huge steering wheel.

'*Pomoch-me...* I no Engleski...' the foreigner stammered in a husky Eastern European tongue, gazing helplessly through a glassy-eyed oblivion.

'What's that, buddy? Are you in a spot of bother? Methinks you need a doctor,' I urged, making out the poor guy's deathly-white features and punching 999 into my cell phone to summon the emergency services.

Squeezing into the passenger seat alongside the bloodless carcass, I took the strain as his body slumped to one side. The sound of irregular breathing quivering into my chest set my own pulse racing, genuinely fearing for the ailing stranger's wellness. Patting a comforting hand between his broad shoulder blades I whispered: 'Hang on in there, buddy!'

Without delay, as if by a miracle a squealing ambulance sloshed hurriedly onto the scene, its agile paramedics springing from the rear doors and scaling the steps with a true sense of urgency. Affixing an oxygen mask to the patient's mouth and placing an arm over his chest, they efficiently went about their business with cool-handed aplomb.

'The left side of his face has dropped; he's suffered a stroke, that's for sure!' diagnosed the older medic.

His view was backed up by his boyish assistant, intimating: 'Someone up above was looking over him tonight. It's a good job we were only up the road in Bromsgrove when the call came in, and that you were on hand to calm him down!'

Back inside the people-carrier five unconscious shivering wrecks obliviously blew snooze bubbles into the air. They were awakened by the screeching sound of a giant tow-truck winching the humungous beast of burden sideways towards the hard shoulder, creating a gap for the marathon expedition to continue, accompanied by just three other waiting vehicles along with the tetchy whinges and moans of the revived passengers.

'All we need now is for a horde of wailing red Indians to swoop out of the night and take us all hostage before setting fire to the wagon!' Romeo elaborated.

'What, then tie us up, whip off our scalps and roger the lot of us?' chipped in Geoff, imagination working overtime.

'There won't be many screaming Indians out in Leicester tonight, especially in this weather. Anyway their big celebration is Diwali, and that was back in November,' a half-asleep Danny concluded, misinterpreting the sordid banter.

Damned by the devil's own luck, as if things could get any worse, incredibly just five miles from going our separate ways a violent juddering sound warned of yet another setback, wreaked by a puncture to the front passenger-side tyre. It was fixed with surprising alacrity by grease-monkey Danny, surrounded by a handful of sodden, disconsolate figures.

As the dawn began to break, we ultimately disembarked at the hotel rendezvous point where a scattering of half-buried cars sat forlornly on the pearly-white driveway. One final, superhuman effort was required to bring an end to the year's inauspicious start.

'By the way, I forgot to wish you all a Happy New Year,' I bade satirically through the open window as I slid away over the frosted surface, tuning into an ungracious reply fluttering on the chilling breeze:

'Yeah, and fuck you too!'

****

Harking back to my younger years, few comedians ever split my sides in quite the same way as the blundering and achingly funny Tommy Cooper. Although born in Caerphilly, Wales, he spent the best part of his upbringing in the small town of Crediton some eight miles from Exeter, having relocated to Devon with his English mother and Welsh father at the age of three.

Renowned throughout Christendom for his wacky antics on the small screen, the flat-footed and ungainly character's unique brand of humour took the lucrative seventies and eighties club circuit by storm. He possessed an uncanny gift to render an audience hysterical without so much as moving a muscle or uttering a single word, and as a result played to packed houses seven nights a week, often for months on end.

I was once privileged to meet the one-off icon backstage during a stint in my home town of Leicester. Sipping at a tumbler of Scotch the amiable big fella impassively complimented: 'What was that number one song you had? I really liked that…'

'You must mean "Under the Moon of Love",' I responded, half expecting a sting in the tail which, silencing the room, duly arrived bang on cue.

'No, not that rubbish… wasn't it called "Bohemian Parody" or something like that?' he teased, convincing the sceptical onlookers I'd been mistaken for Freddie Mercury from Queen.

'Just ignore him, he's pulling your leg and knows exactly who you are,' admonished PA Mary, tearing a strip off the funny man, whose huge raised palms and 'what, me?' expression reduced the small captive audience to watery-eyed wrecks.

The mirthful encounter was one I will cherish forever, particularly in the light of Tommy's extraordinary death seven years later; and the man's legend lives on through countless TV reruns and conflicting accounts of his private life. His inborn inability to take life at all seriously was substantiated to me at first hand by a Bournemouth hotelier from whom the jester rented a room for the duration of a sell-out three-month summer season whilst at the peak of his popularity.

Wiping away the fatty excess from a freshly cooked breakfast each morning with a starched white serviette, the big man requested two boiled eggs to take up to his quarters. The order was fulfilled with a smile on a daily basis by the obliging kitchen staff, presuming he needed something to keep the hunger pangs at bay as the hours wore on.

'Tommy's agent stipulated he'd like a lockable wardrobe when the booking was made, which naturally we were more than happy to provide,' the manager recollected, grinning from ear to ear prior to unleashing a gut-busting guffaw.

'Go on,' I urged, captivated.

'The morning he checked out he went out of his way to personally thank every member of staff, handing out a signed photo and shaking each one by the hand. That's the kind of guy he was!' the proprietor lauded, taking a sip from a cup of tea.

'Surely that's not it!' I quizzed impatiently.

'No, no, it's not. Guess what happened when Beryl the housekeeper unlocked the wardrobe door?' the guy chuckled, removing his steamed-up glasses.

'C'mon, don't leave me in suspense,' I pressed.

'A mountain of hard-boiled eggs tumbled like golf balls over her feet and legs, scattering all across the room! The stench took days to get rid of. The poor woman was in such a flap,' the manager proclaimed, beside himself with laughter.

'Did she see the funny side?' I asked, close to wetting myself picturing the comic's deadpan, self-satisfied features all the way home.

'Oh yes, she was fine about it; we were all in stitches for weeks. They sure don't make 'em like that any more!' the man concluded.

The bungling 1.93-metre comedy genius collapsed in a heap live on stage at London's Her Majesty's Theatre on April 15th 1984, at the age of sixty-three. He had suffered a fatal heart attack before a multi-million TV audience, the majority of whom were creasing up in the privacy of their living rooms, blissfully unaware their comedy idol had sadly made his final bow.

Causes célèbres

Henry Chadwick – father of baseball
Tommy Cooper – comedian (raised in the city from the age of three)
Chris Martin – Coldplay frontman
Beth Gibbons – Portishead vocalist
Tony Burrows – renowned '60s session singer, whose voice was featured on
    many hit records

Essential travelling band info

Favourite live music venue: Phoenix Theatre, Gandy Street
Favourite curry house: Pukka Indian, South Street – 58%
Favourite pub: Mill on the Exe, St David's – 74%
Don't miss: Haldon Belvedere (or Lawrence Castle) – 77%
Sense of humour/friendly welcome: 48%

Chapter 26
Glasgow

A DEPRESSING PHALANX OF BEDRAGGLED, malnourished deadbeats stretched for fully thirty metres along the crumbling pavement outside of an open hatch to a primeval soup kitchen. Pulling into the adjacent loading bay of the famous old Apollo Theatre, the boys and I gasped at such a forlorn and disturbing reality.

Recent years have seen Glasgow rescued by a large-scale, freethinking programme of regeneration outlined to address the city's ailing decline whilst turning round its economic fortunes. In the early seventies, however, the city painted a wholly different picture, soured by high unemployment and street violence amidst a grim backdrop of run-down tenement blocks and council flats, a far cry from the leading-edge, thriving metropolis of the twenty-first century.

'Now that's what you call being down on your uppers,' I commented, having assumed the days of the poorhouse belonged to a bygone era.

'I didn't realise soup kitchens still existed in Britain… if I hadn't seen it with my own eyes I'd never have believed it,' choked an equally astounded Rod.

Downtrodden but unbroken a dishevelled, bearded man gruffly hollered from the queue: 'Aye ye got a couple o' bob for a cup o' tea?'

Heeding his request, I reached into my pocket and handed over a five-pound note. Within a split second a dozen or more lingering itinerants lunged towards the beneficiary seeking a share of the spoils, knocking the man to the ground in a desperate scramble to lay their hands on the booty.

They were quickly thwarted by the intervention of an authoritative overseer who, weighing up the situation, angrily snapped: 'What in creation is going on here? Get back in line now or you'll all go hungry!' Sniffing a rat and giving the sheepish recipient the evil eye, he bellowed: 'What's that in your hand…? Come on, I wasn't born yesterday; it's money isn't it? Where in God's name did you steal it from, you filthy scum?' Grabbing the culprit's arm, the supervisor forcibly prised open his clenched fist to extract the screwed-up fiver.

'It's okay… I realise I probably shouldn't have… but I gave it to him!' I admitted, immediately raising the boss-man's hackles.

'Five fucking pounds? Are you trying to incite a riot, son?' the man ranted, witnessing a clean pair of heels disappearing up a metal ramp and through the theatre's rear fire-doors into the less hostile confines of the backstage area.

In the sphere of concert halls the Apollo stood head and shoulders above the rest. A magical energy pervaded beneath the splintering multi-tiered rafters, guaranteed to serve up an exhilarating cocktail of adrenaline fused with tingling goosebumps unrivalled in any other theatre on the planet.

Out on stage the duration of the show passed in a kind of blur, galvanised by three and a half thousand vociferous Glaswegians passionately belting out the lyrics to the band's entire repertoire, whilst casting one's eyes upwards to the gods the gravity-defying balcony rocked capriciously on its support columns.

Physically unable to scale the five-metre-high stage in the thick of the evening performance, early influxes of tenacious young females bent on getting to grips with their heroes used every trick in the book to outsmart the system. Incredibly, some had infiltrated the camp during the lunchtime load-in to lurk away for hours inside a range of empty equipment flight-cases strewn in the wings, dementedly unearthing themselves mid-show to rocket out onstage and accost their mystified idols in a state of wonderstruck delirium.

The legendary venue poignantly closed for business on June 16th 1985, subsequently going under the wrecking ball in 1987 after being deemed by the local authorities as structurally unsafe. The modern-day site now houses a multiscreen cinema complex.

****

The band's first brief foray north of the border dropped anchor in the town of Rutherglen close to the Glasgow boundary, where on a chilly spring evening back in 1974 a greyhound-racing track known as Shawfield Stadium (also the home of Clyde FC) provided the setting for a markedly bittersweet curtain-raiser.

We had been booked to play warm-up to egotistical pretty-boy actor David Cassidy as part of a much-publicised three-night whistle-stop tour, and were champing at the bit to give a good account of ourselves in front of an estimated collective audience of ninety thousand teenagers. An early arrival soon hit the skids, however, evoked by the condescending tone of a high-handed organiser insisting no dressing-room facilities had been set aside for any support artists, and further inflamed by a bright idea to partition off a small section of the terracing as an emergency measure.

'What happens if we need to take a crap?' posed regular-as-clockwork guitarist Trevor, meeting with a disinterested 'as if I really give a shit' shoulder shrug from the jumped-up gofer amid a stream of discontented mutterings.

Debuting at the giddy heights of number forty-four on the latest chart with our first single 'Hey Rock and Roll', and further boosted by predictions suggesting a coveted top thirty entry may be on the cards the following Tuesday morning, our firm resolve to impress the arriving crush far outweighed any thoughts of redress, and we slipped gingerly into our glittering stage-suits left out in the cold on a tiered concrete plateau with nothing more than a jug of water and a pineapple-shaped bucket of unthawing ice for refreshment.

Maltreated but in no way downhearted, we received an ovation from the pubescent hordes that more than atoned for the earlier humiliation. It was one that would live long in the memory, together with a smidgen of devilish retribution unleashed upon our disobliging hosts when, chilled to the bone, the group of bag-carrying nonentities broke camp.

Exiting via a shabbily erected lean-to assigned as a catering area for the production staff and crew and bedecked with a mouth-watering selection of goodies, grovelling to a backroom boy equipped with an *Access All Areas* laminate I enquired: 'Any chance of nabbing a can of Coke mate?'

'I suppose so,' replied the youth indifferently.

Grabbing an infamous red can from the table and glancing shiftily to either side, I surreptitiously removed the ice-bucket from a concealed carrier-bag. In a split second the plastic item of fruit took pride of place planted in the middle of the spread, unnoticed by the officious staff preparing for the headliner's performance. The hushed yet speedy farewell which followed unsurprisingly fell on deaf ears.

'What are you sniggering at?' inquired Rod, curious as to a spontaneous snorting sound which emanated from my nostrils before shifting mid-course into a girlish titter.

'I'm just amused by a little stink I caused back there… it's nothing really,' I ambiguously fabricated.

I felt Trevor's hand tugging lightly at my upper arm. 'Guess what I did in the ice-bucket when I got taken short…? One of those snotty-nosed gits has got to clear up the mess!' the rogue uttered with a defiant grin.

'I know exactly what you did, you dirty bastard, and you should be ashamed of yourself!' I chided, struggling to contain myself.

Wincing, a disgusted Rod reacted: 'Oh, that's gross! What the hell did you do with it?'

'I just replaced the lid and left it on the terrace steps behind the partition. Anyway,' Trevor bellyached, 'it serves the arrogant twats right!'

'Well, actually no, you didn't; in fact, as we speak it should be sat right in the middle of the promoter's scrumptious little banquet!' I confessed to an outpouring of horrified gasps, followed by sporadic fits of raucous laughter all the way home.

****

Preparing to take root in Scotland's largest, metamorphosing city for a seven-night stretch at the capacious King's Theatre in the late nineties, I checked into a moderately stylish hotel a stone's throw from the central labyrinth of streets encompassing the fashionable West End. Much to my chagrin, whilst lingering at the main desk I found myself confronted by an aggressive, stubbly ruffian whose faded Metallica T-shirt and oil-stained jeans sorely conflicted with the day's overcast, bone-chilling elements.

'I recognise you. You're that fuckin' nancy boy from the Showaddywaddy band, aren't you?' he intimidatingly grunted.

'How graphically put… I'm not sure I quite fit that description, but yes, I am. Was there something you wanted?' I skittishly responded.

'Don't fuck with me, son, I'm originally from the Gorbals; just gimme your autograph for the wife!' he coarsely demanded.

'Well they obviously didn't teach you any manners in the Gorbals – a please wouldn't go amiss!' I rapped, finding his attitude worrisome.

'Och, never mind that bollocks sonny, just gimme a signed photee for the dragon. She says you have a sexy voice, but I told her that's 'cause you sing like a c***… How's that for a crackin' put-down?' the roughneck vilified, taking the cheapest of shots.

Sizing up a character bearing all the hallmarks of a human time-bomb and anxious not to rock the boat, I reached inside my bag to retrieve a picture-postcard handout. 'Okay, Rambo,' I begged, 'what's your good lady's Christian name?'

'What the fuck's that gottee dae wi' you?' he snarled viciously.

'I was going to dedicate the card to her! Do you want this autograph or not?' I rallied, sticking my neck out.

'Aye, make it out to Barbara, then I'll be on a promise; personally I don't know what the fuck she sees in you!' the ignoramus growled.

'You know, I was just thinking exactly the same thing!' I retaliated, scrawling an untidy moniker across the photo.

I was caught off balance as, snatching up the souvenir, my new acquaintance tore up the adjacent staircase like Usain Bolt. His hasty retreat was clearly prompted by the arrival of a helmeted task force of armed policemen, who animatedly crashed into the open-plan lobby to reconnoitre the immediate area, evidently in hot pursuit of a desperado on the loose.

'What happened to that man you were just conversing with?' a barrel-chested officer bellowed in a frighteningly abrupt tone.

'Ugh… he legged it up the stairs the very second you guys showed up…' I faltered.

Ascending the steps three at a time, the officer barked down authoritatively to an underling: 'Take that man aside for questioning!'

I was detained in a box room to the side of the reception area and instructed to park my backside. A brace of menacing boys in blue launched into a good-cop-bad-cop routine in not-so-glorious stereo either side of my battered ears, but cottoned on lickety-split that the suspected accomplice was nothing more than an innocent bystander simply picking up a keycard.

'Reinforcements to level six immediately,' a distorted voice blurted out through their crackling radio sets, putting the kibosh on the grilling. As the head man marshalled his troops from the upper level, my interrogators intimated I was free to go.

As I fled towards the lift hoping to distance myself from the ensuing chaos, the commotion stemming from the descending elevator resembled World War Three. The shuddering doors parted revealing a pitched battle within as five bloodied officers went for broke, grappling desperately to suppress the uncontrollable madman who in a flash gave them the slip, bounding towards the main doors. He was thwarted ultimately by a scrum of macho back-up troops, relishing the challenge to brutally wrestle their prey to the ground and clapping a pair of handcuffs onto his wrists.

'Get that fucking animal in a cage where he belongs!' demanded the senior bluecoat, giddily clutching at the handrail for support and exhaling deeply as he dejectedly looked on at his comrades manhandling the psycho from the building.

'Bloody hell, that was like Armageddon! I was only signing an autograph for him a few minutes ago. What the hell did he do?' I asked the recuperating bobby.

'I'm sorry to say he not only robbed a nearby convenience store, but smashed the Asian owner's head to a pulp with a hammer,' he shockingly conveyed. 'I gather the poor victim's already on a life support system in the Royal Infirmary. I only hope he pulls through!' Shoulders hunched, he slouched away in despair.

****

'Excuse me sir, but there's an Inspector Patterson on the line for you,' the hotel receptionist bade, kindly interrupting an irritating Saturday-morning cookery programme ahead of the week's sell-out grand finale.

'Okay, put him on… Hello!' I answered sleepily.

'I thought you may be interested to know the shopkeeper's come through his ordeal… but I'm still bloody livid,' the officer complained.

'Why? Aren't you pleased?' I asked.

'Of course I am. It's just that the perpetrator should be up for attempted murder, but now it seems more likely he'll get off with armed robbery… I tell you, the law in this country's a bloody joke!' he bickered, snapping at the hand that feeds.

'I can understand your frustration; anyway, thanks for letting me know,' I concurred, putting down the receiver, prone not to disagree.

Causes célèbres

James McAvoy – actor
Robert Carlyle – actor
Billy Connolly – comedian
David McCallum – actor
Gordon Ramsay – foul-mouthed TV chef
Gordon Jackson – actor
Stanley Baxter – comedy legend
Lulu – singer
Angus Young – AC/DC guitarist
Andrew Marr – broadcaster
Frankie Boyle – comedian
Mark Knopfler – Dire Straits guitarist
Lorraine Kelly – TV presenter
Ken Bruce – radio presenter
Biffy Clyro – alt-rock band
Alex Harvey – 'The Sensational Alex Harvey Band'
Paulo Nutini – singer
The Blue Nile – sophisticated rock band

Essential travelling band info

Favourite live music venue: Royal Concert Hall, Sauchiehall Street
Favourite curry house: Mother India, Argyle Street – 90%
Favourite pub: Pot Still, Hope Street – 77%
Don't miss: Kelvingrove Art Gallery and Museum, Argyle Street – 72%
Sense of humour/friendly welcome: 79%

Chapter 27
Gloucester

LAUNCHED IN LATE 2012, OPERATION YEWTREE is the ongoing police investigation into a string of allegations against an ever-increasing list of high-profile celebrities, including amongst others Rolf Harris, Freddie Starr, PR guru Max Clifford, former Radio One DJ Dave Lee Travis and the late, disgraced predatory paedophile Jimmy Savile.

****

Midway through 2013, an extraordinary email popped up on my office computer screen. It urged a company representative to contact one of a team of investigating officers with regard to an incident alleged to have taken place at a venue at which the band had performed some thirty-five years previously, stressing that no current or former members were in any way implicated.

Deeply curious as what possible role either I or my colleagues may have to play in such a newsworthy inquiry, I put in a call to the number at the foot of the page. The dense fog of mind-numbing doubt that descended into my mind was thankfully pacified by the understanding inspector's robust opening gambit: 'Just to put your mind at rest, no individuals are in any way pointing the finger at you or your co-performers and, what's more, we are extremely grateful for your cooperation.'

I was asked to cast my mind back some three and a half decades to a one-off concert staged in a disused aircraft-hangar close to the town of Stroud in Gloucestershire. Incredibly the date – June 17th 1978 – rang a bell, as cradling the receiver between my chin and shoulder I typed the digits into a web page I regularly used for a spot of research.

'That's amazing, I knew there was something – it was the day I visited Lords Cricket ground for the very first time to see a test match!' I enthused, chuffed to bits with my own piece of detective work whilst picturing England heroes Bob Willis and Ian Botham ripping through a strong Pakistani batting line-up for a paltry 105 runs prior to my frantic dash along the M4 motorway to the old airfield located a dozen miles to the south of Gloucester.

Billed as 'A Midsummer Night's Rock & Roll Dream', the evening's entertainment was hosted by renowned *Top of the Pops* presenter and radio DJ Dave Lee Travis who, clearly not content to play second fiddle, saw fit to encroach on our own headlining performance, taking to the stage as an uninvited guest and setting about make a thorough nuisance of himself.

Climbing up onto one of two drum kits used as part of the live spectacle and grabbing a pair of sticks, the 'hairy monster' laid into the skins, banging loudly out of sync for all he was worth, backed up by eighteen-plus stones of muscle and blubber.

The obvious displeasure of a cranked-up crowd clearly indicated that he had outstayed his welcome so, seeking to nip the intrusion in the bud, I politely conveyed into the mike: 'Okay everybody, let's hear it for the one and only DLT!'

Taking a bow to a clamour of ironic cheers and jeers, the thick-skinned DJ withdrew, only to leap back onto the spare kit as the pounding percussive intro to the next song shifted the air like a hurricane. He proceeded to add a few unrhythmical patterns of his own more akin to the building of a shed than anything likely to lend weight to the proceedings.

'Whoa, whoa, easy tiger,' I yelled into the mike, watching the cringing Romeo draw to a temporary halt whilst the self-absorbed 'hairy cornflake' continued unabated.

'Dave… Dave, either play in time or fuck off,' I berated. After staring me down with malicious narrowing eyes, the offended hulk banished his lumbering frame from the stage, trading a few profanities of his own.

Charged on fourteen counts of sexual assault and one of indecent groping under Operation Yewtree, David Patrick Griffin a.k.a. Dave Lee Travis stood trial at Southwark Crown Court on Tuesday January 14th 2014. I was personally summoned as a witness for the prosecution, essentially to confirm the accused's presence at the said airfield in June 1978. Sworn in and apprehensively taking to the stand under the watchful eyes of a hushed, packed courtroom, I gave my full name as requested before a genial lady prosecutor took up the reins, entering into a detailed, flattering resumé of the band's life history inclusive of my own role together with the true purpose of my subpoena.

Staring straight ahead, a dozen stoical jurors impartially pored over the oddly random deposition in total contrast to the vortex of journalistic vultures seated to my right hastily scribbling down notes whilst hanging on every word, primed to pounce upon the merest crumbs of sensationalism set to make a splash in the tabloid headlines.

Perceived as devil-may-care, or as one national newspaper reported 'a surreal intervention', the fifteen-minute testimony more resembled a light-hearted scene from a TV sitcom, highlighted during the line of questioning put forward by the defence counsel:

'Mr Bartram, how can you be one hundred per cent certain the defendant performed alongside your group all those years ago?'

'Once the police contacted me, I tapped into an internet search engine I use for research, then checked the date on my band's website. I remember the show vividly, especially when DLT ventured onstage and proceeded to make a nuisance of himself!'

'I see; in what way did my client, as you put it, make a nuisance of himself?'

'By climbing up onto the second drum kit and making an awful racket!' (Rumbles of laughter in the courtroom)

'I take it his drumming wasn't much to your liking!'

'Indeed it wasn't; he didn't have a clue and was asked in no uncertain terms to leave the stage!' (The DJ bursts into laughter from his position behind a glass partition)

'Well, we're not here today to discuss Mr Travis's ability as a drummer!'

'We should be – it was criminal!' I shot back to a kerfuffle of mirthful laughter, nipped in the bud with a swift rebuke from the distinguished red-robed judge.

Cutting a forlorn figure on the steps of Southwark Crown Court before a gaggle of reporters and photographers some twenty-eight days later, the browbeaten sixty-eight-year-old DJ delivered a dour speech vilifying the injudicious press at the announcement of his acquittal on twelve of fourteen charges and describing his ordeal, etched on his ageing, withdrawn features, as 'eighteen months of hell'. He was later to receive a three-month suspended sentence following a guilty verdict on one count of indecent assault at a retrial held in September 2014.

Such is the weight of public opinion that the ongoing fascination with celebrity misdeeds and unhealthy lust for revenge have in recent times provoked a series of awkward questions from acquaintances and friends along the lines of: 'You must have got to know Savile, you worked with him enough times!' or: 'Those bloody *Top of the Pops* presenters weren't content with money and fame; they thought everything in a skirt worshipped the ground they walked on!' – implying that, in addition to the two cited parties, almost every radio or TV host known to grace the seventies airwaves must at some point in their careers have been similarly culpable.

So to set the record straight and dispel any urban myths, for what it may be worth I hereby offer a personal appraisal of the best-known proponents of a much maligned species:

Simon Bates

Nasally voiced, gossipy narrator with a face for radio if ever there was one! Renowned for reducing innumerable housewives and sentimentalists to tears on a daily basis, with his ever-poignant 'Our Tune' feature. Clean as a whistle.

Tony Blackburn

Self-absorbed old-fashioned disc jockey, whose personal life was never brought into question, as opposed to his genuine love of music!

Paul Burnett

Likeable, chirpy northerner whom the band only worked with on a couple of occasions.

Noel Edmonds

The canny, ever-approachable Noel's record speaks volumes for itself. Ambitious, supremely professional and a gentleman.

'Diddy' David Hamilton

Silky-smooth diminutive presenter with a big personality and a cheeky but never seedy sense of humour.

David 'Kid' Jensen

Diffident and knowledgeable, Kid's distinctive Canadian tones set him apart from the crowd. A thoroughly decent guy.

Andy Peebles

A sociable, down-to-earth broadcaster known for occasional sojourns into the field of cricket commentary. Sound as a pound.

Peter Powell

'Nice guy' Peter heaped regular praise on the band, often lauding our best efforts as his 'Record of the Week' as well as attending a number of our London shows. Friendly, enthusiastic and never up himself.

Mike Read

Friend and Cliff Richard lookalike, Mike's ultra-polished, educated style endeared him to countless listeners, with a constant demand for his services to the present day. A good egg and a family man.

Emperor Rosko

A personal favourite, always full of surprises but not outside the field of music! Modelled what was thought to be a unique style on the legendary American DJ 'Wolfman Jack'.

Ed 'Stewpot' Stewart

Articulate and straitlaced, Ed's uncontentious, robust delivery was ideally suited to either TV or radio. Married for more than thirty years before divorcing in 2006. Known to spend much of his time on the golf course.

Tommy Vance

The late, great Tommy's first love was rock music, though – blessed with an appreciation of most genres – his constructive, music-minded approach earned the respect of the listening public and his peers alike. A master craftsman, Tommy's irreplaceably resonant tones graced the airwaves for the final time in 2005 when a huge stroke sadly took his life.

Johnnie Walker

Probably my least favourite of all the seventies DJs, Walker's uncalled-for spiky comments and total disregard for the successful 'pop' artists of the day drew harsh criticism from many quarters, though on a personal level his cringingly sycophantic recent interviews with a host of big names may have been likened to a bout of Japanese water torture.

Jimmy Savile

Conclusive evidence points to this opportunistic, vile, slippery character severely abusing his position as the most high-profile DJ of a generation, heinously stripping his young and naïve victims of their innocence over a period of more than fifty years.

I worked with the blond-locked rat on more occasions than I'd care to mention, and found his associates' tongues were constantly set wagging by the man's tasteless flamboyance and air of untouchability. Exhibiting a total lack of sociability away from the studio floor, he stooped to unimaginable depths in a depraved and unrelenting assault on human dignity.

****

I guess you could say I led a charmed life when it came to dealing with the trifling few hecklers the boys and I were ever exposed to, shielded by a barrage of sound bringing up the rear to drown out the majority of loose-lipped clever dicks, unlike many blighted stand-up performers forced into toughing it out face to face with their adversaries. There remains, however, one particular gig that will probably forever stick in my craw, the show in question which at best could be summarised as acutely embarrassing having taken place during an early-eighties tour at the cavernous, clattering Gloucester Leisure Centre.

On the infrequent occasions when a loud-mouthed prankster cried out something derogatory in the course of the band's set, I'd generally shrug my shoulders and smile, often taking a pop back with a curt put-down such as: 'Let's swap places, you come up here and sing and I'll play the arsehole!' or simply: 'I'd love to help you out… exactly the same way that you came in!'; but in truth there were odd instances when my feathers became a little more ruffled, where seething inside I opted to go for the jugular, reacting with something caustic, perhaps along the lines of: 'You give a whole new meaning to the word *TWAT*!'

On the singular night in the West Country city things were somewhat different when, during each of my links between songs, a loud, undisguised expletive echoed from the rear stalls close to the back of the hall.

'If you're not enjoying the show, just bugger off!' I retaliated. Bafflingly, the audience remained strangely subdued.

'Wankers! Arseholes!' the punk continued to holler, putting me distinctly on edge, wishing the stage would open up and swallow me whole and dreading each song's finale. 'Twat!' he bellowed, somehow stifled in the process.

'No, my friend, you're the irritating twat round here,' I responded cuttingly, 'and what's more, your moronic remarks are upsetting the other people who are trying to enjoy the show; now for Christ's sake put a sock in it!' Again, I sensed the crowd fidgeting uneasily in their seats.

Unknowingly, I had encountered the debilitating effects of Tourette's syndrome for the first time ever, well ahead of any national media coverage. The weight of guilt like a threatening raincloud lingered darkly overhead for days, tempered only by a heartfelt wave of compassion for the afflicted fall guy's loved ones.

Movingly, a month or so after the event a handwritten letter dropped through the post, forwarded on via the concert's promoter, scrawled by the pen of the unfortunate sufferer's mother. I anticipated a tongue-lashing for my abrupt response but the content was astonishingly apologetic, oddly praising me for my understanding and explaining that the frequent outbursts were simply born of sheer excitement, adding that her stricken son in truth had loved every minute of his favourite band's performance.

****

Viewed as an occupational hazard amongst most seasoned pros, a sprinkling of other transgressors muscled in on the occasional performance, more often than not blabbermouths under the influence of alcohol seeing fit to audibly express themselves. This frequently led to the extreme displeasure of other show-goers, resulting in heated verbal exchanges, or (less often) the odd bout of fisticuffs, as a rule quelled by brawny security guards accompanied by an arsenal of disparaging put-downs from the stage.

Midway through a nineties visit to the United Arab Emirates and following an excruciatingly bumpy coach ride to a dust-ridden oil-camp social club somewhere in the middle of the desert, the disembarking touring company pitched camp in a quadrangle of basic, converted outbuildings. Later, we happened upon a male-dominated pack of wolves embarking on an all-out mission to drink one another under the table.

Chirpy comedian Jeff Stevenson endured a nightmare in his thirty-minute supporting routine, coming close to throwing in the towel as he was continually heckled by the apathetic majority's foul-mouthed taunts. His efforts largely falling on deaf ears, the tenacious cockney nonetheless toughed it out before scurrying back behind the scenes brandishing a few choice words of his own.

As the band struck up uneasily, the jaunty up-tempo rhythms sparked a remarkable change of body language amongst the rowdy mob spreading to all four corners of the glorified canteen. A half dozen physically capable souls were even inspired to leap to their feet, working up a sweat bopping in the aisles between the Formica-topped tables.

Engaging in a touch of light-hearted banter with a table of ex-pats midway into the performance, I briefly alighted from the stage. Grabbing at my arm, an attention-seeking poseur garbed in a pair of oversized shades complemented by a dandruff-flecked duck's arse rudely interrupted: 'Why don't you play some proper rock 'n' roll? Let's have some Elvis!'

'Have no fear, we'll be paying a tribute to the great man a little later on,' I affirmed, making every effort to appease the diehard.

'You're not listening; play an Elvis tune now – I've heard enough of this shit!' he persisted, forgetting his manners.

'What the f...? Just be patient and put a sock in it,' I responded, getting hot under the collar to his obvious dissatisfaction.

'Huh, I could show you a fucking thing or two when it comes to singing some real rock 'n' roll,' he boasted, brassily slicking back his hair with a comb.

Deliberately cold-shouldering the intruder, eager not to be drawn, the boys thrust into another upbeat hit tune, overpowering the uncalled-for torrent of abuse whilst riling the far-gone narcissist now positioned intimidatingly in my eyeline scowling and going through his own repertoire of obscene hand gestures.

'Hey asshole, what's the big deal? Let me do an Elvis song... or are you worried about being upstaged?' the meddler challenged at the song's conclusion, sticking in my craw like a bitter pill and necessitating a little payback at his expense.

'So, let me get this straight: you'd like to perform an Elvis Presley song, right? Any particular choice you have in mind?' I inquired, edging towards bass player Rod to discreetly unveil a plan hatched on the spur of the moment.

' "Heartbreak Hotel",' the numpty grunted, mistiming his uninvited ascent onstage and teetering clumsily towards the drum kit.

'What's your name, pal?' I asked, offering a steadying hand.

'Ricky; everybody knows me around here – I'm the local karaoke legend,' he slurred, attempting to wrestle the mike from my hand.

'No, no, I don't want your dog breath contaminating this one – try using the spare mike over there,' I advised, keeping a firm grip on the tool of my trade. 'Ladies and gentlemen,' I announced, 'here's the moment you've all been waiting for: the one and only Ricky is about to perform his own dynamic version of the Elvis classic "Heartbreak Hotel"!' Placing the mike into the stand, I nodded back to the boys to follow suit by exiting the stage into the box room situated to the side.

Unhappy at the disruption and smelling blood, the spectators issued a rising storm of booing and hissing which degenerated into bitter verbal abuse, nipped in the bud by two beefy policemen in khaki uniforms acting on impulse to remove the incensed sucker out of harm's way.

'Is there anyone else that fancies their chances at giving us all a song…?' I teased, re-emerging from the wings to a hubbub of relieved cheers, spared any further interruptions from the strangely revitalised onlookers. 'No? Well in that case, next up is a genuine classic from the undisputed King of Rock and Roll… no, I don't mean Ricky! It's Elvis's "Jailhouse Rock"!'

Causes célèbres

Henry Cecil Booth – inventor of the vacuum cleaner
Simon Pegg – actor
Alastair Cook – England cricketer
Nathan Sykes – member of 'The Wanted'
Dick Whittington – legendary Lord Mayor of London and pantomime hero
    (who actually did exist)

Essential travelling band info

Best live music venue: Guildhall, Eastgate Street
Favourite curry house: Polash Indian Restaurant, Mead Road – 71%
Favourite pub: Pelican Inn, St Mary's Street – 86%
Don't miss: Prinknash Bird and Deer Park – 56%
Sense of humour/friendly welcome: 42%

Chapter 28
Hereford

'I ONCE SIGNED THE OFFICIAL SECRETS Act… I was only sixteen,' I unfolded to a yawning studio engineer guzzling noisily at a moonlit caffeine boost prior to downing tools following a marathon albeit productive eighteen-hour session.

'Blimey, were you working in an undercover government department or something? Whatever job it was, it sounds more exciting than slogging your guts out at every hour God sends for bloody peanuts,' he sleepily retorted.

'Fat chance; I was a trainee technician for Post Office Telephones, which you'd know better these days as British Telecom,' I countered, quietly confident the formal process of keeping mum had by now elapsed.

So, without fear of retribution, the information about to be disclosed should strictly speaking remain confidential. It was recounted directly from the lips of an ex-SAS soldier – also named Dave – previously stationed in the city of Hereford, and focuses on a tragic yet uplifting story inexcusably soured by the bitter aftertaste of a military career forcibly cut short.

****

Posted on a covert tour of duty to Iraq in the thick of the hostilities in 2003 and stationed close to Basra in the southern territory's governorate, within days of Dave's arrival misfortune struck, casting a dark cloud over the remote patrol base when news leaked out of the tragic deaths of two soldiers from the same unit. Both men met their fate in the act of fleeing from mass gunfire, caught unawares while recceing an enemy outpost.

Holed up in the outlying, oil-rich province for getting on six months and spending much of his time patrolling the area for mine activity, the stocky military man's main duties focused on acting as an armed guard to various dignitaries passing through the province, ensuring each VIP's safe passage through the unforgiving, dangerous terrain.

Assigned to a clandestine mission principally to usher a team of high-level American diplomats on a fact-finding mission to locate weapons of mass destruction manufactured in the region – notably found to be non-existent – the six-vehicle cavalcade met with an unexpected hindrance in the shape of a beaten-up red van conspicuously blocking the single-track carriageway midway between Basra and Baghdad. Slowing to a crawl, they observed a roadside fracas involving a gang of local policemen and the agitated obstruction's owner. The leading pair of armoured cars (the second driven by Dave) radioed back to the motorcade following behind before cautiously deviating from the bituminous surface, bumping onto the dune-ridged verge to steer well clear of the abandoned vehicle.

'The only thing I remember is a bloody enormous blast which was the last thing I'd hear for going on two years!' Dave opened up. Stirred by emotion, mind wandering, he strived to refocus and continue filling in the blanks.

Coming into contact with an IED of cataclysmic power, the armoured car to the front of the convoy whipped wildly into the air as if caught up in a swirling twister, descending directly onto the top of Dave's ill-fated Snatch Land Rover.

'My gaffer told me when I came round they were certain I was a goner, until a German medic detected a shred of a pulse… after which I was airlifted to the closest medical facility and kept under twenty-four-hour surveillance,' the warhorse recalled, crediting divine intervention for limiting the fatalities to just the driver and helmsman in the front vehicle. 'God was looking out for me that day!' he reflected with a rueful smile, sighing and drifting off into a daydream.

Cut adrift in a coma for the best part of three months, the battle-scarred soldier had no memory of the journey back onto British soil, only of regaining consciousness in a hospital bed surrounded by a huddle of familiar faces, trapped inside a ghostly closet of silence.

'It was otherworldly; for a moment I thought I'd been transported to hell. I know I can be a bugger sometimes but I never thought I'd committed enough wrong deeds to be sent packing down there!' he remarked whimsically.

He was discharged from hospital stricken with mild traumatic brain injury, mollified only by the unrelenting support of a closeknit family. Eager to escape the patronising distractions of their West Country neighbours Dave and his Leicestershire-born wife uprooted to the East Midlands county, taking up residence close to my own home, where perhaps unsurprisingly we first rubbed shoulders over a flagon of ale in a local pub.

Mercilessly put out to grass he harboured no discernible trace of animosity, but a simmering wave of hostility far removed from the events in Iraq lurked disturbingly beneath the surface, provoked by the pitiable disservice afforded injured soldiers by the Ministry of Defence. It amounted to nothing less than negligence, pooh-poohing those who so proudly served their country.

'I knew when I got on the plane there was every chance I'd get blown to smithereens but you accept that as part of the job; besides, I didn't come home in a body bag did I…? What hurts most of all is I've been ignored and forgotten, as have my family. I get a measly pension which is nowhere near enough to live on, so my better half has to work so we can make ends meet. I've put in all sorts of claims for compensation, but so far I've never received a bloody penny!' he grieved, supping cheerlessly from his pint pot.

'So you're telling me they just looked the other way?' I probed incredulously.

'That just about sums it up. They're well aware I suffered brain damage and probably think I'm bonkers,' he speculated, sighing heavily.

'Where do you go from here?' I asked.

'I've got lawyers on it as we speak, but I've already been refused legal aid; it's just not fair! I've got my loved ones to consider and I like to think a few more years ahead of me. It's just typical of this sodding country – they hand out money to every Tom, Dick and Harry coming over here yet choose to ignore anyone home-grown!'

Our paths crossed at regular intervals over the ensuing months as, bogged down in red tape and bureaucracy, the case dragged on at a snail's pace. Dave's painful history of rejected compensation claims served against the authorities raised serious questions as to his chances of success in the impending action.

'I like to think I've presented the bastards with a far and away sterner proposition,' the pit bull terrier of a man belligerently scowled, convincing those in his company that, despite the odds stacked against him, sheer tenacity would surely win through in the end.

Heeding a request from the organisers of a local committee to fire the starting pistol for a charity wheelbarrow race, I again clapped eyes on the not-so-old soldier togged up in a Fred Flintstone costume, wife Wilma perched in the bucket, preparing to run through hoops of fire to support the underprivileged. Heavily sponsored and raising a huge amount, Dave modestly reflected: 'I don't know for the life of me why everybody keeps saying I deserve a pat on the back; just look at those lads who had their limbs blown off in combat strapping on their blades to compete in marathons and the like – they're the real heroes! All I got was a bump on the head!'

****

I have always been unimpressed, by and large, by wacky individuals juggling chainsaws on a unicycle or going to other extremes to produce the heaviest pumpkin on the planet purely in order to grace the pages of the *Guinness Book of Records*, nor for that matter did I especially harbour any ambitions to do so. So when the band were requested to attend a fundraising event at Hereford's Courtyard Leisure Centre on a March afternoon in 1989, little could I have imagined that we were to partake in an attempt to specifically do just that! It was to prove one of the most extraordinary performances of our entire careers.

'On top of making a bundle of cash for a roster of worthy causes, there is a method behind the madness,' expressed the presumptuous voice at the end of the line, making the initial somewhat bizarre request.

'So where do we fit in?' I replied, oddly intrigued.

'We'd like you guys to front the whole thing. It'll help us with TV and press coverage. The plan is to assemble a record number of guitarists and create the longest ever rendition of a rock-'n'-roll classic,' the caller elaborated.

'What's the choice of song and how long will we have to play for?' I delved.

'We're unanimous it should be Bill Haley's fifties hit "Shake Rattle and Roll". You'll need to play for sixty-five minutes without a single pause!' he stated, signing off.

We arrived in Hereford ahead of schedule to see a lengthy queue stretched around the leisure centre's perimeter consisting of local musicians from all walks of life, clinging onto combos and instruments of all shape and sizes.

'Look at the guy on the bike,' squealed Rod, gleefully pointing out a flush-faced kid ferrying a vintage VOX AC30 amp on the handlebars of his rusting bicycle and providing a sentimental throwback to the years in which our careers had been shaped.

Inside the main hall a cacophony of sound hurtled from wall to wall, ricocheting like blasts of gunfire in a western movie, as a multiplicity of 'axe-men' diligently tuned up their guitars, hoicking up the volume knobs to number eleven.

'What a fucking racket! Have we really got to put up with that for more than an hour?' bickered Geoff inarticulately, shielding his ears.

'Afraid so,' I responded, under no illusions whatever the rumpus would further deteriorate as the record-breaking attempt got under way.

'Okay everybody, pipe down please; I need to brief you all as to the rules and regulations…' screeched the official adjudicator, taking centre stage and digging in his heels before rambling on: 'We kindly suggest that every participant restricts their volume to an acceptable level in keeping with the recommended guidelines…'

'How about sticking in a five-minute drum solo to relieve the monotony?' I put to Romeo in the wings, receiving a two-fingered salute for my trouble.

'Furthermore, I need to make you aware of the safety procedures plastered on the rear of every fire exit…' the arbiter jabbered *ad infinitum*.

'I think he's going for a double whammy and wants the record for the longest speech too!' seethed a fidgety Rod, becoming bored of the never-ending address which by now had moved on to a long list of eminent sponsors.

'Okay, that's about it; good luck everybody. Now, without further ado, please welcome on stage our most charitable special guests – *Showaddywaddy!*' the creep revealed to a placated round of warm applause. Jigging up onto the portable platform, the front-liners were greeted by a unique sight to behold as five hundred or more hairy denim-clad wannabes awaited the green light to offer up a diverse range of musical styles and proficiency. Still not done, the overactive emcee returned in a rush, once again grabbing at the microphone and squawking: 'Okay all you record breakers, this is it: 10… 9… 8… 7… 6…'

He was drowned out by Romeo who hollered, '1, 2, a 1-2-3-4,' to set the clock ticking.

Tantamount to a seismic eruption the thunderous commotion hit the roof, shaking the whole complex on its foundations in addition to parting the hair of each half-deafened partaker pounding dissonantly in all directions.

'*Get out of that kitchen and rattle those pots and pans,*' I belted out, setting in motion a seemingly endless assault on the anthem, strangely dragged beyond my comfort zone with zero likelihood of turning back.

20 minutes: As I craned my neck to check out the elevated stop-clock the discordant, hair-parting racket bore the hallmarks of a clamorous factory-floor shift, pounding at the temples like a battering ram; but what the heck, this was a charity event and, regardless of any musical misgivings, could scarcely go down as a black mark on the band's CV.

45 minutes: Strutting from the stage to relieve the tedium, I hoarsely mouthed the verses for the umpteenth time. A mix of spotty-faced punks and greying old rockers hid behind their contrasting locks, motoring along like a runaway train blissfully unaffected by the selfsameness yet inspiring a blob of mischief soon to take the form of a few alternative lyrics.

55 minutes: I vaulted back up on stage predisposed to breathe new life into the enduring rendition. By virtue of a couple of improvised verses, the bastardised golden oldie explored a new tone, coming out something like:

'Get outta that toilet and wash your piss-stained hands,
Get outta that toilet and wash those piss-stained hands,
Well you never do nothin' but stroke your swollen gland.
Wearin' those dresses with your hair done up so right,
Wearin' those dresses with your hair done up so right,
I can tell by the stubble that you're a transvestite.'

It temporarily relieved the monotony and my flagging companions on stage reacted with a lukewarm smile. A moment later an announcement blared from the in-house PA: 'One hour completed; come on guys, we're almost part of Hereford folklore!' Thanks to the presence of a sprinkling of vain local councillors seizing upon a photo opportunity to enhance their charitable reputations in the local rags, thirty or more animated hangers-on spilt out onto the stage from the wings ready to witness history in the making and bask in the limelight of the defining moment.

As we headed towards the big countdown, every eye in the building suddenly diverted to a cloud of black smoke ascending towards the ceiling, kindled by the comical sight of an overburdened amplifier engulfed in flames amidst the hodgepodge of gizmos resounding in the auditorium. Miraculously it failed to trigger the fire alarms, but proved too much to take for the undisciplined band who coughed and spluttered our way through the song's final bars, entering the prestigious Guinness book busting a gut.

The record was predictably short-lived, owing to the staggering number of eccentrics vying for recognition in the celebrated who's who. All of twelve months later the achievement slipped quietly into oblivion, eclipsed presumably by a half-deafened throng amassed in some distant amphitheatre, fulfilling their ambitions well out of earshot from the previous year's special guests.

Causes célèbres

Nell Gwynn – actress and mistress of Charles II
The Pretenders – melodic rock band (with the exception of vocalist Chrissie
    Hynde, who is from Ohio)
Mott the Hoople – '70s rock band
Ellie Goulding – singer
Gilbert Harding – broadcaster
Beryl Reid – legendary comedy actress
Horatio Nelson – the famous sailor became a freeman of the city

Essential travelling band info

Favourite live music venue: The Courtyard, Edgar Street
Favourite curry house: Razbari Restaurant, Eign Street – 70%
Favourite pub: Barrels, St Owen Street – 82%
Don't miss: Hereford Cider Museum, Rylands Street – 64%
Sense of humour/friendly welcome: 70%

Chapter 29
Inverness

THE TRIALS AND TRIBULATIONS OF a professional singer bear many similarities to pretty nearly any line of work, steeped in exhilarating highs whilst at times blemished by humbling lows. The latter can as often as not be attributed to a complex, temperamental vocal mechanism, noted for playing dirty tricks on even the most consummate of powerhouses.

Flexing my muscles along with my bandmates in a bellyful of music halls sullied by a thick fog of smoke reminiscent of 1940s London, I managed to lead a charmed life for the best part of thirty years. Though periodically hindered by the odd sore throat, influenza and fatigue, lady luck forgivingly warded off any malignant demons lurking unseen. However, an aggressive style combined with inhuman yawping between songs meant that perhaps inevitably something had to give, ultimately leading to my own fair share of complications.

In the midst of a week-long tour of the Scottish highlands in 1985 which fascinatingly included a one-night stand off the beaten track in the Shetland Islands, I found myself afflicted with an acute bout of laryngitis. A short hop from the main island's southern airstrip into Inverness the next morning foreran a mad dash to a doctor's surgery for a pre-booked consultation with a senior practitioner. I arrived thirty minutes late at the modern, albeit snug, health centre and was ushered hastily into a spartan office where a bespectacled, professorial-looking elderly sawbones endowed with an impeccable English accent greeted me with a firm handshake, enquiring: 'Now, what seems to be the problem young man?'

'I suppose you could call it an occupational hazard,' I croaked.

'Oh, I'm awfully sorry, perhaps I should draw the blind – the sun can be a damn nuisance at times. So, what is it that's bothering you?' he asked mind-bogglingly.

'Forgive me, but I'm not quite with you?' I wheezed.

'You implied you were dazzled by the sunlight leaking in through the window,' he maintained, removing his glasses and scratching his brow.

'Did I? Well, not to worry... Anyway, I seem to be laid low with a nasty attack of laryngitis!' I huskily replied, sidestepping the comment.

'Oh, goodness me; perhaps you'd care to slip off your jeans and underpants and pop onto the couch in the corner – I'll be back in a few moments,' he answered ever more confusingly whilst rising from his seat.

'Excuse me, but contrary to what some people may think I don't normally sing out of my arse, so why do I need to remove my underwear?' I pleaded, begging the obvious question.

'Because I need to take a peep at that dangerous weapon you're concealing down there,' he brashly responded.

Summoning a deep breath, with all the strength I could muster I rasped: 'What, for laryngitis? Surely you want to take a look at my throat!'

'Goodness gracious... I say, that's rather amusing, young man; I could have sworn I heard you say *balanitis*!'

'What in heaven's name is balanitis?' I roared, finally catching on that the old brainbox may be a trifle hard of hearing.

'Oh, it's inflammation of the corona of the penis – a most unpleasant infection. I'm told it can cause extreme discomfort!'

'In a way I wish it was that – at least I'd be able to sing tonight!' I reflected, returning to the hotel laden with a bag full of medicinal goodies, along with strict instructions to rest up and remain silent until the performance time.

****

As I joined the party at the preset breakfast table the morning after, an uncomfortable silence fell over the room, serving as a harsh reminder of a performance maddeningly curtailed just hours before due solely to my ailing, over-exerted larynx, rescued only by a sympathetic audience content to settle for a costly rescheduled show at a later date.

'How's the Hobson's,* Dave? I had to take my hat off to you for getting as far into the show as you did,' praised roadie Gargoyle (real name Martin), at least showing a hint of concern for my well-being.

'Even worse I'm afraid; I'll need to follow the doctor's orders and keep my big gob shut for a few days,' I jested in the hoarsest of tones.

'Shame we won't be on the road – that would've made for a pleasant change,' carped Trevor, stifling an extended yawn.

'You won't believe what happened to me when I was tucked up last night,' Martin cut in, gaining the ear of the chomping pack.

'Michael Barrymore entered the room and gave you the best blow job you've

---

* Rhyming slang, as in Hobson's choice

ever had,' Geoff offered in jest.

'Ha bloody ha. You know that long-black-haired guy that never says a word who's been working on the crew all week? Well, I drew the short straw and got to share a room with him. He's a bloody animal!' he explained.

'Is that it?' was the best I could muster.

'No… There I was dead to the world when he barged in and switched on the light… Anyway, he dumped his kit bag onto the mattress and rooted around in it 'til he came out with a bloody hammer!' he expanded, shovelling half a fried egg onto his upturned fork.

'Go on,' Geoff urged.

'I was shitting myself – there were all kinds of things going through my head,' he continued, becoming animated. 'Then he stripped down to his vest and underpants and clicked off the main light before switching on the bedside lamp and climbing into bed.'

'What the fuck did he do with the hammer?' asked Rod on tenterhooks, eyeing Gargoyle lapping up the attention.

'He looked across at me with madness in his eyes, still clutching the bloody thing, and just said "Goodnight"; guess what he did then?'

'What?' the expectant chorus rang out.

'He smashed the sodding light bulb to smithereens and was snoring his head off within a couple of minutes! There's absolutely no way I'll be bunking up with him again!' he closed, rising from the table and bidding his gobsmacked audience farewell.

'Did you hear about Gargoyle's room-mate and the episode with the bedside lamp? I hope we don't receive a bill for the damage!' I later croaked to crew boss Ian, busy settling his hotel extras ahead of setting off for the long trek south.

'You must mean Grunt – he's a mental case,' he disparaged. 'That's nothing compared to what he did a few nights ago after the gig in Newcastle; he just hates hotels!'

Still subdued on the back of a difficult weekend, I didn't dare ask!

****

I had been cudgelling my brain to come up with something unforgettable to mark my darling wife's landmark fortieth birthday. An out-of-the-ordinary 'foodie' experience figured high on the list, preferably endowed with a Michelin star or two and huddled away off the beaten track in an unashamedly romantic setting.

Trawling through a number of websites and food guides galore prior to drawing up a shortlist fit for purpose, a much lauded gourmet's paradise caught my eye, standing head and shoulders above the rest by virtue of its idyllic location on the bonnie banks of a little-known Scottish loch, accessed exclusively by a private boat.

Having boxed clever to keep the adventure under wraps for months on end, bright and early on a parky March morning all roads led to Luton airport, destination unknown. Parking up the car, we joined the crowds assembled in the departures area.

Studying a pair of juxtaposed orange display boards mounted directly above the check-in desks, the excited birthday girl tagged onto the end of the Nice-bound queue shuffling gently forwards to the left before being urged by an admonishing gesture from me to veer off to the shorter queue over to the right.

'Inverness? What on earth's there other than the Loch Ness monster?' she bickered, frowning up at the board, showing signs of disappointment along with a clear preference towards a trip to the French Riviera.

'You'll just have to wait and see!' I forewarned, intent on giving nothing away.

Next morning, after pottering around in the UK's northernmost city savouring a complaisant aperitif of Highland hospitality prior to an early night, the moment arrived to finally reveal the true significance of such a long journey north. I unveiled a swanky brochure received by post months in advance, and eyeballed my enraptured wife as she drooled over the mouthwatering contents between tucking into a hearty Caledonian breakfast.

We continued northwards, unweariedly soaking up the striking, rugged wilderness where sheep outnumbered humans by a hundred to one. The sleepy coastal town of Ullapool drew ever closer, gilded by curious rock formations and snow-capped mountain peaks captured beneath an endless, glorious azure sky and providing the perfect *hors d'oeuvre* for what lay ahead.

'There's even a private boat laid on which ferries the guests across the loch right to the hotel's doorstep!' I enthused.

'Wow, you shouldn't have! How much is this all costing?' she pried.

'Never you mind; it's not every day you get to celebrate the beginnings of a mid-life crisis,' I joked, receiving a light jab to my left bicep.

****

The Altnaharrie Inn nestled tantalisingly in the midst of a scenic landscape of rolling green hills, sheltered away behind a thicket of trees on the south side of Loch Broom whilst protected from the inclement winter elements by the warm Gulf Stream currents. It looked every inch the ideal retreat for an evening of overindulgence.

Although tempted into making an early crossing, we opted instead to dilly-dally around the smattering of pubs and pricey gift-shops making up the tiny town of Ullapool. An overabundance of tartan kilts and scarves scattered amongst a range of touristy preserves proved of little interest, impelling a bracing stroll along the waterfront. Gazing out over the loch's blue waters, I sighted a light vessel bearing the hotel's name puttering slowly into the wee harbour.

'Come on, let's get a move on – the ferry's about to dock!' I urged.

'I'm sure it'll wait awhile before it sets sail again; besides, I want to pick up a little something for Holly' (our young daughter), Cathy stalled.

'Best make it quick, or they'll leave without us!' I fussed.

As I glared through squinted eyes along the promenade, the small packet-boat precariously wobbled to a halt, collecting up a group of hyperactive gourmands eager to set sail for 'Scotland's best-kept secret' before promptly lilting round and rocking unevenly over the choppy waters bound for the banks of our anticipated slice of heaven.

'Shit, I don't believe it!' I scoffed, striding over to a nearby kiosk to enquire as to when the next crossing might be.

'Nay for a good two hours, laddie; but there's a bumpy back road that winds all the way round there if you fancy taking a drive,' he helpfully let on, sketching out the directions on the back of a glossy pamphlet.

The jewel of a residence smacked of an idealistic hideaway. A dozen guests occupied the main building with the remainder, including the birthday girl and yours truly, accommodated in a handful of delightful individual cottages set within the grounds and bedecked in the highest quality fabrics and furnishings.

Pricking my ears in the doorway whilst taking a breather, the surreal calm and serenity seemed strangely at odds with the overriding lap of luxury, stirring my senses beneath a yellowing crescent moon, nullified only by a grumbling stomach beckoning me to lurch back inside and don my best bib and tucker.

Bewitched by a milieu exuding elegance and tranquillity the exquisite four-course dinner exceeded every expectation. It was presented impeccably free from unnecessary formalities, tainted only by the perturbing sight of a heavy snowfall embellishing the loch's banks with a coating of virginal white through the tableside window.

'I wouldn't worry too much: we haven't had more than a dusting up here in over twenty years,' the proprietor reassuringly verified. Heeding his advice we focused our attentions solely on the banquet so awe-inspiringly laid before us. Meanwhile, persisting in earnest, a torrent of flakes the size of saucers tumbled from the sky, forming a giant sheet draped over the water's surface, cutting adrift the isolated headland in a luminescent sea of whiteness amplified by the in-house generator fast approaching overload.

Intoxicated by the evening's perfection and latching onto a clique of similarly ecstatic tipsy inmates we relaxed in a charming cubbyhole, chatting over a fine cognac and imagining ourselves stranded in a foodies' paradise until, mindful of the intensifying avalanche and anticipating a morning delay, we donned a pair of wellington boots apiece to briefly brave the elements and trudge the few yards back to our lavish hideout.

I parted the curtains at first light to a blinding surge of brightness. The branches buckled on the trees, drooping beneath the weight of a pristine snowfall, and transforming the bucolic landscape of the day before into a winter wonderland.

'Doesn't it look beautiful?' extolled Cathy, carefully lining up her camera to capture a memento of the striking picture-postcard backdrop.

'Normally I'd agree, but I can't for the life of me see how we're going to get out of here and make the flight back,' I surmised in a flap.

The unperturbed steady ticking of the antique grandfather clock in the hallway was obscured by a loud revving tractor churning its way down the slippery slope, signalling the one-man cavalry's arrival to save the day. He attached a sturdy chain to the tow ring of the rented Ford and climbed back into his cab. Skidding and skewing up the treacherous incline, the thick-treaded agricultural tyres dug in deep, finally making light work of hauling the swaying Mondeo's chassis to the summit. With a valedictory wave as the wheels set in motion, the friendly rustic shouted: 'You'll be okay from here – safe journey!'

Half a mile ahead a breathtaking Utopian dreamland opened up, stretching for miles like a never-ending ocean of virginal alabaster visually enhanced for an arctic adventure movie, rendering its wide-mouthed visitors speechless. A heavenly glade of maturing Scots pine and Douglas fir saplings trembled transfixed in the frozen silence broken only by the humming vehicle gliding haphazardly through a hallucinatory fantasy world, beautified further by a proud horned stag prancing between the wildwood like an enchanted, fictional unicorn.

'The best things in life are free,' roared John Lennon on the Beatle's defining cover of the sixties Tamla hit 'Money (That's What I Want)', words which now came springing to mind as we marvelled at this serendipitous brush with Arcadia in marked contrast to the preceding hours of unadulterated luxury. Perhaps it was never our destiny to cross the loch and the hand of fate intervened, setting aside a surreal diversion to round off an extraordinary twenty-four hours, forever etched in the memories of two grateful, satiated recipients.

Causes célèbres

Charles Kennedy – ex Lib-Dem leader
Yvette Cooper – politician (Mrs Balls)
Ian Mackintosh – writer
Nessie – the Loch Ness monster

Essential travelling band info

Favourite live music venue: Eden Court Theatre, Bishop's Road
Favourite curry house: Gathering Place, Academy Street – 44%
Favourite pub: Castle Tavern, View Place – 68%
Don't miss: Loch and River Ness – 77%
Sense of humour/friendly welcome: 75%

Chapter 30
Kingston upon Hull

TREADING THE BOARDS CONTINUOUSLY FOR the best part of half a century, plying his vocation in theatre productions, summer seasons, pantomimes and a wide range of club venues, suave sixties crooner Craig knew virtually every trick in the book, and proved the canniest of characters when it came to getting by on a tight budget. Shrewdly maintaining a silky-smooth, breezy air of finesse more often associated with the privileged classes, the streetwise Londoner manoeuvred this way and that pulling all kinds of strokes to cut down on unnecessary overheads, relying heavily on a tattered, yellowing little black book of lady friends spreading to every distant corner of the UK.

Featuring alongside the band as part of a nostalgic package thrown together shortly after the turn of the century, the guileful sweet-talker took pains to plan each charted course, frequently delving into an index of old flames and acquaintances perhaps willing to put him up for the night, saving a small fortune on accommodation costs in the process.

Taking in the tour's northerly stint midway through the schedule, Craig's success rate at cutting back on board and lodgings amazingly extended through Aberdeen, Dundee and Sunderland, though as we chatted backstage at the latter's soundcheck I gathered the charmer faced something of a dilemma ahead of his arrival in the city of Hull the following day.

'I've got to be honest, I'm chancing my arm a bit with this one. I haven't even spoken to the lady in thirty-seven years aside from not having the faintest clue what she looks like; what do you reckon?' he posed in a quandary.

'It doesn't matter what I think, but one thing's for certain – you've got the gift of the gab; plus it'll save you around fifty quid, so why not give it a shot? It's not as if you *have* to sleep with her!' I advocated, glad not to be in his shoes.

The day following the Hull gig, after trooping south for a Midlands show, an unusually dishevelled-looking Craig surfaced from his dressing room, dusting himself down fresh from a catnap, not at all resembling the debonair old pro we'd come to admire.

'You look absolutely knackered; am I right in assuming everything didn't go according to plan last night?' I queried, greeting him with a handshake.

'Don't ask; what a fucking nightmare!' he rued, mumbling beneath his breath, for once looking like a man in his early seventies.

'Aren't you going to fill me in with the gory details?' I asked, intrigued.

'It's not funny. I dossed down in her fucking garage on a pile of sacks and now every muscle in my body's aching!' he complained.

'So I take it she didn't like the look of you after thirty-odd years?' I ribbed.

'No, it wasn't that at all. I arrived fearing the worst, but couldn't help noticing how tidy she looked when she answered the door, especially for a woman in her mid sixties. I nipped back to the car to get a bottle from my stash and one thing led to another!' he enlarged, stalling to take a slurp from his mug of tea.

'Keep going – it was just starting to get interesting,' I pressed.

'Oh, very little happened. Just as we were becoming reacquainted, a bloody car pulled onto the drive – her old man had returned home unexpectedly. In seconds flat I was back downstairs being shoved through a side door into the garage, which as you may have guessed is where I spent the night until he pissed off again at five o'clock this morning!' he admitted.

'Didn't she tell you she was married?' I probed.

'Not until he showed up completely out of the blue. Apparently he was due out on a trawler which was delayed 'cause of bad weather, so he decided to come back to the house to get his head down for a couple of hours!' Craig unfolded.

'Bloody Nora, that's what you'd call a close shave!' I gulped.

'You're not kidding. I saw him through the upstairs window – he was a bloody brute of a man; and I haven't mentioned the dog yet!' he revealed, getting a little hot under the collar.

'What dog?' I asked, gawping like a fish.

'A fucking great Alsatian whose slobbery, stinking breath kept me awake half the night. Look at the evidence – there's hairs all over my jacket!' he ranted, brushing away a few remaining whiskers with the back of his hand.

'You should consider yourself lucky; that's nowhere near as bad as one of our lads a few years ago. He went back to a bird's flat and while he was busy on the job her dog started licking his balls!' I chuckled, recounting a gory, well-worn tale.

'Sounds like a double act I once saw in Thailand!' the crooner quipped, quickening my departure to the catering area for a spot of refreshment.

****

'According to a recently held nationwide poll the city of Hull has been declared the worst town in Britain,' claimed a 2003 BBC news report, supported by vox-pops from a random selection of seething local residents. These included a prim and proper female dweller who was quoted as saying: 'The place is a sad story of unemployment, teenage pregnancy, heroin addiction, crime, violence and rampant self-neglect!'

Few would argue the UK's busiest seaport manifests an appealing façade. Long portraying a rough-hewn, gritty image frequently associated with harbour towns, in recent times (and regardless of the damning poll) it has benefited from an ambitious programme of redevelopment, turning the coastal city's tarnished aspect on its head. A modernised waterfront awash with jazzy bars and restaurants now lines up alongside an epidemic of individual, arty shops refreshingly at odds with the humdrum multiples to be found further afield.

Away from the remodelled focal point, the huge derricks and decrepit rusting vessels which dominated the skyline on the band's early visits (not to mention the lingering whiff of fish) remain, relocated in part to the north bank of the Humber Estuary in an ambitious two-hundred-million-pound project which hopefully marks the beginnings of a prosperous future for the city.

At our debut theatre date in the town's attractive City Hall building back in 1976, a largely working-class crowd bordered on running riot. The tumultuous reception left a lump the size of a golf ball in the throats of each band member, and spread to the city streets where the hotel's frontage resembled a mini-mass in the Vatican's St Peter's Square prior to the papal Sunday-morning blessing. The heaving throng was dispersed in part by a body of indignant policemen, who nonetheless managed to overlook a nest of snakelike stragglers who slipped unnoticed through the net.

We had gathered in the mezzanine bar for the matter-of-course post gig get-together, happy to sign album sleeves and merchandise belonging to the chosen few. Ordering an early nightcap to take to his room, guitarist Russ mooched on the spot bearing a look of concern.

'Anybody know where Bill is? He was going to lend me the book he just finished!' the tall guy asked, referring to the conspicuously absent bass vocalist.

'I spotted him sneaking into the lift with a leather-jacketed young lady only moments ago,' interjected Geoff, signifying his tubby bandmate may be requiring a little privacy in his sixth-floor bedchamber.

'Who are your mates?' I put to crew boss Ian, relating to a pair of shaven-headed, sinister-looking characters lurking with intent amongst the posse of familiar faces.

'I don't know them from Adam; I assumed they'd been invited back by you lot. Perhaps I'd better have a quiet word in someone's ear!' he offered cagily, making off to attract the attention of the duty manager.

'Does anyone have any idea who that pair of thugs are? It seems as if they blagged their way in for whatever reason,' I forewarned the boys. Mindful of the undesirables busy turning the screws on a bewildered Geoff all of a few yards away, I reacted quickly and shoved through the human traffic backed up by Rod and Romeo.

'These… gentlemen are looking for Bill; he's in 612, isn't he?' the bass player let slip.

'612!' the taller hoodlum repeated aggressively, excitedly making his way towards the lifts.

His way was barred briefly by a green-jacketed member of staff. 'Can I help you gentlemen – are you residents?' the man asked timidly.

'Yes, we're in room 612,' the lout snapped.

'You lying sod – I only just told you that's the room number of one of the band members!' Geoff retaliated, wary of his blunder.

'There's some fucking arsehole in this band named Buddy who came back here with my missus, and if I lay my hands on him he'll rue the day he fucked with me!' the same guy snarled, baring his teeth like a rabid dog.

'Somebody needs to call Bill's room urgently to warn him that the shit's about to hit the fan!' I whispered to Rod, cautiously stepping to one side as I sensed something may be about to erupt.

'Leave it with me,' he mumbled, slinking off unseen.

Leaving a bloodied undermanager reeling on his knees with a handkerchief over his nose, the vicious scumbags strode towards the lift. Ascending to the sixth floor, they proceeded to create panic amongst the stunned guests and night staff, one of whom gathered himself sufficiently to scamper to reception and summon yet again the overworked boys in blue.

Fast losing the plot, the angry bruisers hammered violently at the door of 612, where inside the fully clothed scarlet woman had been pouring her heart out to a snuggled-down Bill. She fell silent as the bowing woodwork shook on its hinges.

'Shit, that'll be him,' shrieked the girl, urging the performer to either make himself scarce or face up to the consequences.

'It's not as if there was anything was going on,' Bill revealed shortly after the dust had settled. 'She was just a fan who said she needed someone to talk to. She'd been considering dumping him for ages 'cause of the violent outbursts. I was shitting myself!'

Situated to the forefront of the room's sliding windows and running the length of the building's perimeter lay a narrow tiled ledge barely capable of withstanding a child's weight let alone that of a stocky, traumatised adult.

Clambering out onto the precarious rim in near-zero temperatures clad in just an XL pair of white undergarments and suffering the dizzying effects of vertigo, Bill shuffled gingerly towards the adjoining room and tapped at the window, disorienting guitarist Russ who, forced into looking twice, lay down his paperback to come speedily to the rescue.

Back in the downstairs bar area a trio of macho police officers stormed dramatically onto the scene insisting the absent hotel manager be called. Fresh from his bed and put out of his stride, he arrived in minutes flat.

'We have a rather delicate situation on our hands; I'm not sure you're aware, but there's a man balanced on the top floor of this building dressed only in a pair of Y-fronts – we have reason to believe it may be a suicide attempt!' the director of operations stated, playing not only to the staff but the dumbfounded gallery.

'I did my best to stop them Mark, but two skinheaded hooligans in white T-shirts forced their way into the elevator and went up to the sixth floor. This is what I got for my trouble!' the blood-spattered deputy intervened, uncovering his damaged conk.

'What on earth is going on?' exclaimed the hotelier. 'First we have a nutter trying to top himself, and now there's couple of psychos on the loose!'

A group of curious observers (band members included) who had been earwigging the conversation dashed onto the street, where they joined a small crowd of alarmed onlookers craning their necks to see Bill edging nervously along the ledge before oddly disappearing from view.

Meanwhile, the police had muscled in on the heated exchange unsettling all and sundry on the top floor and intervened to keep the peace. Briefly escaping the clutches of the officer restraining him the incensed cuckold threw a vicious uppercut, missing the guilt-free woman's chin by a hair's breadth, and receiving a size nine boot to the midriff as he stumbled to the floor.

'That's your problem – you think everything can be sorted out with your fists! Can't you see I'm still fully dressed? I was just glad to get away from you!' the girl bleated, calmly closing the door to 612 and pressing the lift button.

'You fucking bitch, I'm having you when I get home!' the thug threatened, this time foaming at the mouth.

'Promises, promises… I didn't tell you I've had the locks changed, so don't bother coming home – you're history!' the woman bowed out, before descending to the lobby.

****

Following a lengthy illness Bill 'Buddy' Gask passed peacefully away in 2011 at the age of sixty-five, bequeathing amongst other things the enduring memory of a farcical brush with danger, teetering on the brink of a multi-storey hotel's sixth-floor ledge, goose-pimpled and terror-stricken, clad only in a pair of unflattering Y-fronts, surviving the ordeal with a short, sharp slap on the wrists from a team of tickled-pink boys in blue.

Causes célèbres

The Housemartins – '80s hitmakers (of which Fatboy Slim was a member)
Maureen Lipman – actress
John Alderton – actor
Amy Johnson – aviator
Mick Ronson – David Bowie's 'Ziggy Stardust' sidekick
Tom Courtenay – actor

Essential travelling band info

Favourite live music venue: New Theatre, Kingston Square
Favourite curry house: Ray's Place, Princes Avenue – 53%
Favourite pub: Olde White Harte, Silver Street – 74%
Don't miss: Hull Maritime Museum, Queen Victoria Square – 74%
Sense of humour/friendly welcome: 63%

Chapter 31
Lancaster

THE PHONE ALARM UNFORGIVINGLY CHIRPED at the unearthly hour of 7.30am. Recognising in a bleary-eyed stupor I'd clean forgot to reset the beeping contraption, I testily punched in *STOP* and turned over to grab at least another hour prior to scurrying downstairs for the last available breakfast just ahead of the 9.30am deadline.

After fidgeting restlessly beneath the sheets for all of ten minutes I chucked in the towel and, using the pillows from the unused bed to prop up my back, I zapped on the TV remote. Flicking through a cornucopia of satellite channels, for some inexplicable reason I stopped at a cookery programme featuring celebrity chef Rick Stein. As I slothfully observed the balding gastronome eulogising over a container brimming with potted shrimps, lauding the delicacies as 'the finest to be found on British shores', my own taste buds were set a-tingling by a fleeting reference to the seaside town of Morecambe, the self-same locale as the day's scheduled port of call. There and then I determined to put the presenter's recommendation to the test in the wake of the two-hour trek south from Glasgow.

****

Acknowledged as part of the city of Lancaster, Morecambe epitomises an honest-to-goodness bucket-and-spade resort, displaying little in the way of airs and graces. Its 'what you see is what you get' aura is further boosted by an especially welcoming local community notable for exhibiting an exemplary tolerance towards the annual influx of visitors, directly opposed to the bulk of the UK's dispassionate, money-grabbing tourist traps.

Under the directions of sax player Dave's Android cell phone we headed off the beaten path through a matrix of side roads. Setting a brisk pace, the posse of ravenous day trippers tore through a mini-cyclone, observing the inhabitants' burgundy complexions undoubtedly ingrained as a result of the exposed coastline's blustery climate.

'It blows a lot up here,' understated the jovial, florid-faced fishmonger as he diligently spooned the curly crustaceans into half a dozen disposable cartons. Strongly advising the delicacy should be sampled warm, he popped the contents into a microwave oven to the accompaniment of my chirruping mobile phone.

'The gear's all set; the staff over here mucked in, so you can soundcheck earlier than usual if you like,' gushed front-of-house engineer Ollie. He was speaking from one of the nation's more unique venues: 'The Platform', which as the name implies served as the town's railway station between 1907 and 1994. Moulded just three years after its closure into a quirky entertainment complex, it is characterised by the intact, original exterior.

Wolfing down the lip-smacking fare whilst mulling over the ailing fortunes of the town's football league club – aptly nicknamed 'The Shrimpers'- a darkening sky foreshadowed a trot back towards the promenade. An even tougher battle against the gusty elements was thankfully aborted by a blast of sunshine over the mudflats of Morecambe Bay, rekindling memories of the tragic events of 2004 where, trapped by a killer tide, twenty-three exploited Chinese cockle-pickers perished in a stretch of dangerous sand fished by locals for generations.

We moved on, and the mood quickly lightened as we posed for an impromptu snapshot kneeling by the statue of legendary comedian Eric Morecambe (who took his name from the town),unveiled by the Queen in 1999 and situated on the sea front.

'Our old mate Trevor modelled himself on Eric, you know!' I remarked, making reference to the band's recently retired ex-rhythm guitarist.

'How the hell do you work that one out? There was nothing remotely amusing about his playing!' queried Rod, pulling a long face.

'He played all the right notes but not necessarily in the right order!' I chuckled wickedly, borrowing one of the comic genius's famous quotes.

'You evil bugger; mind you, you're not wrong!' Rod snickered, reminded of his former colleague's uniquely undisciplined style and U-turning back towards the venue.

****

A once thriving and prosperous northern town, Lancaster presents something of an enigma. Brimming with impressive though sorely neglected Georgian stone architecture which doubtless lent an air of sophistication to the picturesque undulating streets in erstwhile times, in the modern era it is scandalously repressed by a lack of investment and foresight attributed largely to a city council culpable of resting on its laurels.

As I came to a halt in busy traffic on the Penny Street Bridge ahead of parking up to the rear of the commanding town hall, small pellets of hail patted against the car roof. These were brushed off by the hardy, undeterred locals going about their daily business, who conceivably knew better as the threatening sky abated in no time at all to put on a happier face.

A man garbed in football shorts and a pair of flip-flops, seemingly unaffected by the bitter outside temperatures, lay prostrate on the surround of a monument dedicated to Queen Victoria. He stirred briefly as a trio of pebble-throwing street urchins used his recumbent figure for target practice, scattering like beetles exposed beneath an upturned rock at the encroaching sound of the out-of-towner's purposeful footsteps.

I forged ahead towards the central hub, where what may once have been individual butcher's, baker's, or perhaps candlestick-maker's stores gave way to a phalanx of seedy takeaway joints, pound shops and reeking amusement halls interspersed with dismal boarded-up outlets, deserted like rats from a sinking ship by their struggling previous owners.

The atmospheric bustle of Market Street provided a welcome relief, smattered with robust outdoor traders vending cheeses, bread, vegetables and other staples, though the blackened façade of the city's museum would hardly have tempted anyone through its doors. I gave it a wide berth as, with an audible sigh, I strode hurriedly by.

As I walked on muttering cantankerously, a bewitching old pub came into view. Bearing the name 'Merchants 1688', it was furbished with a roaring log fire spreading its warmth through the flagstoned, low-ceilinged bar, and provided an ideal stop-off for a swift caffeine boost.

'I'll have a cappuccino, please,' I politely requested, settling into my seat, a trifle miffed by an icy draught leaking in through an ill-fitting window.

'Is that it – a coffee?' the waiter curtly replied, getting up my nose in a flash.

'I tell you what mate, if it's too much hassle I won't bother!' I disdainfully snorted, rising from my seat and skulking back out onto the street, furious at shooting myself in the foot and missing out on a warm by the fire.

I curved right into a steep lane where a huge, sinister-looking stronghold stood rooted to the spot. This proved to be the city's castle, though – astutely acting in recent times as the city's prison – it arguably served as one of Her Majesty's most sought-after institutions, by reason of a large proportion of the facility's cells enjoying an advantageous 'room with a view', commandingly gazing out over the surrounding panorama.

Somewhere in the distance, an authoritative male voice could be heard echoing: 'Garden…! Garden…!' I presumed this to be discharged by a trader vending horticultural produce or a selection of exotic plants until, to my extreme amusement, upon turning a corner the cry was revealed to belong to one of a dying breed of newspaper salesmen, hollering forcefully from a wooden booth on which a sign boldly advertised '*Lancaster Guardian*'!

Per head of population Lancashire's county town surely tops the UK's list for its profusion of fast-food outlets. Every access route into town is bestrewn by a succession of kebab houses, Southern fried chicken, tandoori, Chinese and countless pizza takeaways, implying the lion's share of the city's inhabitants survive on unhealthy fare, whilst accounting for an excess of disposable boxes and cartons overflowing into the gutters of virtually every street.

Taking a peek through the door of the decaying cathedral, I decided against entering, just as a flurry of raindrops cascaded from a foreboding sky. Abetted by a sudden crash of thunderclaps making the earth shudder, it was the cue for a final mad dash to the shelter of the car.

Causes célèbres

Joe Abercrombie – author
Jim Bowen – comedian and former host of TV's *Bullseye*
Steve Kemp – drummer with Hard-Fi
John Waite – '80s singer ('Missin' You')

Essential travelling band info

Best live music venue: Dukes Playhouse, Moor Lane
Favourite curry house: Sultan of Lancaster, Brock Street (a unique converted old chapel) – 66%
Favourite pub: The Borough, Dalton Square – 57%
Don't miss: Statesman Rail Scenic Railroad from Settle to Carlisle – 80%
Sense of humour/friendly welcome: 56%

Chapter 32
Leeds

AFTER PULLING THROUGH THE MANNED gates of the imposing Yorkshire Television building, bass player Rod and I were waiting to be called for a live TV interview on the early-evening magazine programme *Calendar*, hosted by *Countdown* presenter Richard Whitely. Left to our own devices, we whiled away the minutes plied with tea and coffee in an open-plan waiting area, eavesdropping in on a belligerent, nitpicking voice emerging from the adjoining corridor.

'I'm not accustomed to this kind of treatment; I'm already late for meetings and was due on air fifteen minutes ago,' remonstrated a disruptive loudmouth enveloped by a small body of heavies, laying into a timid, dainty go-between armed with an earpiece and clipboard who was plainly coming off second best. 'Somebody's head will roll for this!' claimed the objectionable character. Unwilling to listen to any excuses from the flustered aide, he ranted on without a single breath, turning the air blue before strutting to a private room close to where we were seated.

'Well, we are honoured – look who it is!' I voiced cynically, getting a brief glimpse of the pedantic firebrand's scouring-pad-style comb-over.

'Sorry, I got distracted; who was it?' Rod responded.

'It's that gabby miners' leader, Arthur Scargill; talk about full of himself! That girl would've been quite within her rights to have whacked him round the head with her clipboard!' I intimated, half wishing she'd done exactly that.

'You couldn't swing a bloody cat in there!' the union man resumed, stepping back into the corridor and overdramatically throwing his hands into the air before being led by his long-suffering minders to at long last complete his piece to camera.

I watched on an elevated monitor as the hard-done-by Arthur ripped into a fierce tirade of well-rehearsed rhetoric unlikely to evoke the sympathy of any sceptical viewers. It brought his true autocratic colours to the fore, whilst earning the despot few friends away from the NUM's downtrodden membership.

'No wonder he needs protection; that guy sure knows how to rub people up the wrong way!' the exhausted coordinator conceded, patently relieved to see the back of the headline-grabbing rabble-rouser as he was ushered at a rate of knots from the building by his army of bodyguards, leaving Rod and his disgruntled frontman to take up the mantle.

'So what brings you both up to our neck of the woods?' Richard Whitely posed in his diffident, matter-of-fact manner.

'As opposed to the motormouth just seen gracing our screens, who refers to a march through the streets with his sheep as "a day of action", there will be a genuine night of action not far away in Batley tonight!' I carped, still miffed at the unionist's lack of decorum and catching the ashen anchorman way off guard.

'What Dave means to say is, we're playing at the old Batley Variety Club, now known as The Frontier. It's always been one of our favourite gigs!' Rod intervened, anxious to take the heat out of the situation.

'Well, thank you for coming in, guys… Break a leg and all that,' the host mumbled incoherently, abruptly cutting the piece short and urged frantically by the rattled floor-manager to improvise ahead of the next item.

As we gathered our stuff from the rest area the programme's director dashed from his post. Wagging a reproachful finger in my face, he delivered a stinging rebuke: 'That was bang out of order; you completely threw Richard. You're bloody well here to publicise your tour dates, not make uncalled-for political statements!'

'I'm as entitled to an opinion as anybody; you didn't see the way he talked down to your assistant – he made her life hell,' I offered in defence.

'That's beside the point. I can't say I'm a great admirer of the guy myself, but to unnerve Richard like that is just not on!' he concluded, hotfooting it back into the control room without a hint of a farewell gesture.

On our way back out to the car park, we handed back our temporary passes to a giant of a security man. 'Would you mind autographing this?' the guard asked, presenting a crumpled album sleeve brought in especially to coincide with our visit.

'Not at all,' I replied, scribbling an illegible signature across my body and handing the collector's item to Rod.

'So you're not entirely in agreement with Mr Scargill's motives then?' the man bade, impassively referring to the curtailed interview.

'Oh, I just got a bit hot under the collar, that's all. Don't get me wrong, I sympathise with the workers' suffering families; but that oaf's prolonging their agony – plus it's about time he learnt some manners!' I tactfully responded.

212

'Oh, he's a stroppy so-and-so, that's for sure. What's more, he couldn't lick Joe Gormley's˙ boots. You'd have enjoyed what happened out there around fifteen minutes ago,' he teased, beckoning towards the exit.

'Go on,' I prompted, lending an ear.

'There's a massive dumper truck that comes on site every week, but it was a different driver today who scraped along the side of a lady's car parked next to the barrier; the way out was blocked for ages. Your new mate was going apeshit, pacing up and down effing and blinding like there was no tomorrow. I couldn't help laughing my socks off!' he chuckled.

'Serves him bloody well right. Would his language have been offensive to miners?' I retorted, playing the smart-aleck and waiting for the penny to drop.

'Haha, you're a bloody wag – you should be on the stage. Go on, sod off!' the hulk chortled, clicking open the automatic lock.

****

During a two-night temporary residence in the Roundhay district of the city as part of a run of late-eighties dates, guitarist Ray ('86-'95) lumbered into the hotel's breakfast room one morning looking irritable and oddly out of sorts.

'What's up – did the bedbugs bite?' I inquired, feeling the bench seat quake at the added weight of his lethargic frame.

'The inconsiderate bastard in the adjoining room was up at five-thirty this morning with his telly blaring out at full volume. I just hope he's not booked in tonight or there'll be a whole heap of trouble!' he complained bitterly.

As we sauntered back to our ground-floor quarters grimacing at the effects of the baked beans, a pair of sprightly chambermaids flitted from one room to the next carrying pillowcases, detergent and replacement toiletries, neglecting to gather up a lone vacuum-cleaner cast aside in the middle of the corridor.

'That should do the trick,' the sleepless guitar-man remarked. After checking the coast was clear, he requisitioned the appliance, puzzlingly making off into his spotless bedchamber and bolting the inner latch.

'Excuse me, sir, but you don't happen to have seen a stray Hoover on the loose do you? I could've sworn I left it here in the hallway,' a baffled housemaid pondered, forcing open the door to an adjacent room.

'I… don't think so!' I fibbed, dodging the issue, completely in the dark as to the cunning musician's intentions.

'Ah, not to worry, one of my colleagues must have taken it,' she intimated, before being summoned by the canny Ray whose balding pate popped out into the corridor.

˙ Scargill's predecessor as President of the National Union of Mineworkers

'Pardon me, love, but have you got a pass key to the adjoining door? My friend in there borrowed my shaver a little earlier on and forgot to give it back,' he fabricated, giving a thumbs-up from the doorframe as the girl released the catch.

'What are you up to, you crafty bugger?' I whispered, shuffling barefoot across the hall carpet, deeply curious as the plot thickened.

'It's nothing really – I'll tell you later,' the smart cookie insisted.

We partook in a lively post-gig soirée on the back of a satisfactory albeit overly formal corporate bash, and an extended session looked to be developing courtesy of a tireless night-man content to keep the bar open 'til all hours.

'Oh well, it's time for some shut-eye and a bit of payback; I'll see you in the morning!' uttered Ray, checking his watch and ascending from his seat with a sly grin as 2am approached. Half ignoring the veiled threat, I reciprocated in kind through blurry eyes before stumbling over to a bar stool to join the other inebriates.

I was mopping up the juices from yet another greasy fry-up with a stale piece of wholemeal bread when an unconventionally chipper Ray breezed into the dining room well aware he may be late. The kitchen staff confirmed that the chef had just knocked off.

'No worries, Big Ears;* I'll make do with some cereal and toast!' he blithely reacted without a trace of irritation.

'You're in a better mood this morning; did you win the lottery?' I remarked.

'No such luck, but I had a much better night's sleep… with a bit of fun thrown in before lights out,' he uncovered, grinning from ear to ear.

'What, was Miss World waiting upstairs for you?' I quipped.

'Funny you should mention that… but if it's any consolation, I was rolling around on the bed… in stitches!' he crowed.

'Perhaps you'd care to enlighten me,' I prompted.

'You remember me telling you yesterday about the guy in the adjoining room who kept me awake half the night?' he harked back, becoming animated.

'Yeah, the bloke whose telly was on full blast at five o'clock in the morning,' I recalled.

'Well, I got him back good and proper; so much so I'd have loved to have been a fly on the wall!' he cackled with an evil look of condemnation.

'Pray continue – you have my undivided attention,' I urged, well and truly hooked.

Using a nail file to remove the three-pin plug attached to the end of the Hoover's cable, the plucky guitar-man stashed the contraption behind his

---

* A regular term of endearment

neighbour's clothes dangling on hangers inside the wardrobe, feeding the line from the machine's pulley into a gap at the rear of the cabinet and beneath the interconnecting door, meticulously tucking the plastic sheath under the carpet's edge to carefully conceal the appliance's trail.

Replacing the plug and forcing the pins into his bedside wall socket, the devious old rocker switched on the device for a trial run before, sensing the sweet smell of retribution, he locked the adjoining door from the inside, content to await the nightfall.

Creeping back to his room, buoyed by the alcohol, he listened at the abutting door. A light sonorous snore whinnied from the adversary's quarters, suggesting the guest may be sound asleep, goading Ray to reach for the switch.

'You should've heard it – what a bloody racket! It sounded like a bloody pneumatic drill,' he wickedly guffawed, splashing tea onto his lap.

'You evil sod,' I remarked, completely enthralled.

'Every time I figured he'd dropped off again I fired it back up, five times in total, until I heard him on the phone swearing at the night porter, banging on about workmen on the night shift at 3am. He was bloody livid!' he surmised, lapping it up.

Later that day, when we were some fifty miles north of Leeds, Ray asked: 'Any chance I can borrow your mobile phone for a sec Dave? I need to call the hotel.'

'Yeah, no problem at all.' I passed over the handset, assuming he'd left something behind, perhaps in the form of an unpaid bar-bill.

'Oh yes, I was with the party that left not long ago. Just in case you've lost one, I thought I should mention there was a stray vacuum-cleaner hidden away in my wardrobe; the room was 314!' the rogue pointed out, before passing back the receiver with a contented chuckle.

****

As the first decade of the twenty-first century petered to a close, the end of an era beckoned. After battling constantly with my demons for going on eighteen months, I opened up to my long-standing bandmates and close friends Rod and Romeo, stressing the time was nigh to hang up my rock-and-roll shoes and consider quitting the band after a professional career spanning thirty-seven eventful years.

Breathing difficulties wrongly diagnosed as asthma-related had long played havoc with my singing ability, leading to bouts of depression and occasional nightmares made maddeningly worse by the uncertainty of the attacks, not knowing how or when any upcoming performance may be affected if indeed at all.

A succession of specialists fell well short in unearthing the root of the problem. Poring over MRI scans, X-rays and endoscopies, they each concluded that, other than the odd spot of wear and tear, my vocal chords remained very much intact, confusingly giving the green light to a further, sustained period plying my beloved trade.

Although rallied by rapturous receptions at the bulk of the band's performances, the crushing reality of an altered existence far removed from what I'd known and loved for so long reached into the pit of my stomach, curdling beneath the surface in a lather of mixed emotions. Ruminating long and hard, I concluded that a further twelve months may at worst allow a period of transition, after which my colourful costumes and scuffed brothel-creepers would be forever consigned to the roof space of my house, attracting nothing more than dust.

Bringing to fruition a rock-'n'-roll journey comprising four thousand live gigs (an educated guess), just a singular two-hour performance remained. It took place on December 3rd 2011 in the charming Yorkshire spa town of Ilkley close to Leeds where, running out on stage to an unprecedented standing ovation, I finally reached the end of the road.

Backstage, flower arrangements, chocolates and oversized greetings cards cluttered the spacious changing rooms, augmented by a startling array of farewell trinkets and keepsakes, sending out a poignant reminder of a calling that had struck a chord with a multiplicity of devotees stretching all the way back to their schooldays.

Holding it together with cool aplomb, I breezed through the set like a finely tuned old piano as a sea of glassy-eyed faces peered upwards to the centre mike analysing every wavering expression for a flicker of emotion whilst awaiting the merest hint of acknowledgement, gratified with a knowing, impassive smile.

Returning to the stage for a valedictory encore and plucking finger-style at the strings of my guitar to complete silence, I proceeded to reel off a couple of lines of my favourite self-penned song, an album track aptly entitled 'Swansong': '*Tonight's the night I'll get stage fright for the last time/I pray it will be a night of nights.*'

It was sufficient, and after pausing for a moment I succinctly ad-libbed: 'It truly has been a night of nights. Thank you all for the last thirty-eight years – it's been an absolute blast!'

Ripping into the last hurrah – an impassioned rendition of Bob Seger's 'Old Time Rock and Roll' – the adrenaline gushed through my system like a waterfall, almost tearing out my lungs. As my heart pounded like a sledgehammer, all at once my emotions succumbed, adding a tremulous quiver to the razor blades already savaging my throat.

I reached the song's final bars pogoing up and down like a spaced-out teenager; and a realisation hit home that the party was over, closed out by a prolonged, room-filling crescendo bouncing from the rafters in a fist-pumping climax. A near lifetime of rock and roll had indeed been a blast, of seismic proportions!

Causes célèbres

John Simm – actor (*Life on Mars*)
Mel B – Spice Girl
Vic Reeves – of Reeves and Mortimer
Gabby Logan – TV presenter
Alan Bennett – dramatist and writer
Ernie Wise – straight man of Morecambe and Wise
Corinne Bailey Rae – singer
Marco Pierre White – celebrity chef
Chris Moyles – ex-DJ
Jeremy Paxman – argumentative TV presenter
Peter O'Toole – veteran actor
Malcolm McDowell – actor

Essential travelling band info

Favourite live music venue: Grand Theatre and Opera House, New Briggate
Favourite curry house: The Corner Café, Burley Road – 66%
Favourite pub: The Hop, Granary Wharf – 69%
Don't miss: City Varieties Music Hall (home of TV's *The Good Old Days*) – 85%
Sense of humour/friendly welcome: 64%

Chapter 33
Lichfield

THERE'S AN AGE-OLD MUSIC GAG that goes like this:

Q) What's the difference between a jazz musician and a rock-and-roll star?

A) A jazz musician plays thousands of chords to three people but a rock-and-roll star plays three chords to thousands of people!

Lending credence to the joke's sentiment, jazz fans in general make up the most esoteric and snobbish of all musical aficionados, theorising affectedly over dynamic contrasts, experimental phrasing and complex rhythmical patterns, hypocritically turned on its head by a dearth of purported fans who rarely venture out in force to support the cluster of struggling die-hard exponents practising the genre.

The term 'jazz' encompasses a diverse range of styles, varying between acid jazz, fusion, avant-garde, traditional, Latin, smooth… the list goes on and on – as indeed do many of the windbag devotees, precious few of whom possess even a basic knowledge of the rudiments affecting the majority of the forms.

A case in point befell a drummer pal of mine named Rob, an experienced old pro in every respect, kept busy with studio sessions and working alongside a whole host of esteemed musicians for many years, well in advance of the formation of our own band. Booked to team up with a quartet of seasoned stalwarts reforming to play the long-standing Lichfield Real Ale, Jazz and Blues Festival but delayed by heavy traffic on the dreaded M6 motorway, he showed up too late for even the briefest of run-throughs. However, spotting a short hiatus between bands, the ultra-professional Rob rushed to the supplied kit and, closing his ears to an eccentric glittery-shirted pairing apparently conducting an extraordinary soundcheck, puffing at a saxophone and tinkering on a keyboard making all manner of discordant squeaks and unpleasant clangs, he positioned the tom-toms and adjusted the snare to his satisfaction whilst tap-tapping at the drumheads, throwing in a few busy rolls and thumping at the bass drum with his heavy right boot.

An anxious looking stage-manager appeared behind the percussionist and placed a gentle hand on his shoulder. 'I'm sorry, I realise you've not had much time to prepare, but would you mind waiting until they've finished their set?' the official admonished.

'Are you serious? I thought they were just fucking about!' Rob replied, clearly nonplussed and not budging an inch.

'I'm afraid it's no joke; they are actually a well-respected jazz duo from France, and will only be doing thirty minutes, so if you wouldn't mind keeping the noise down, there's a good feller,' the gofer patronised.

'You could've knocked me over with a feather,' Rob later told me. 'I honestly thought it was a piss-take!' Feeling obligated at the time to tune in to the duo's offbeat repertoire, he learnt little in the process. 'What a load of pretentious bollocks – it was just a mishmash of blue notes and improvised chords!' With that, the drummer convulsed into a contagious fit of the giggles, his analysis also proving too much for his enraptured listener.

****

Having put down roots in a leafy Leicestershire village at the age of twenty-three thanks to three big-selling singles and a prestigious top ten debut album, even from beneath my permanently attached shades the future looked brighter than sunshine. I settled in as the proud owner of a mind-blowing detached bachelor pad, wedged in between a backbreaking schedule of tour dates, TV appearances and round-the-clock studio sessions. The resulting lead single from the band's forthcoming second album, a cover of Eddie Cochran's 'Three Steps to Heaven', changed everything.

Casting an eye over the property's roadside frontage, little could I have known that the bus stop situated adjacent to the entrance gate doubled as a secondary-school pick-up and drop-off point, from where a dozen or more uniformed kids made their way on a daily basis to and from a noteworthy faculty based in the soon-to-be university town of Loughborough.

As I arrived back at the house on a weekday afternoon fresh from a recent *Top of the Pops* performance and with the band riding high in the charts, a gaggle of pimply teenagers alighted from a red bus briefly blocking the driveway.

'It's him... it's him!' yelled a pigtailed damsel in distress, looking through my car window. This created mayhem amongst the other kids lining the pavement, who animatedly poured into the front garden chanting the lyrics to the band's current chart success.

'If I give you all a signed photo, will you promise to let me have some privacy? I've been touring for weeks and I'm really knackered,' I pleaded, rushing indoors to grab a wad of pictures and sending the gleeful gathering packing.

With the months progressing and the list of achievements reaching a new high, a morning chorus of greatest hits overpowered the birdsong, waking me each day from a brief period of slumber induced by a hectic wee-small-hours lifestyle. More often than not I would leave the building to avoid a repeat performance come 4.15 in the afternoon.

In all fairness, other than the occasional minor breach of the peace, the well-meaning kids created little in the way of real headaches, sporadically turning up unannounced proudly clutching the band's latest seven-inch single for signing. Often they would be escorted by salivating mid-thirties mums, some of whose out-of-earshot compliments left little to the imagination.

One morning in December '76 as we topped the charts with the million-selling 'Under the Moon of Love', a joyous sound emerging from the entryway below rang in my ears, interrupting a sound sleep. Naked as a jaybird, I grabbed a towel and rushed to the window to gaze down on thirty or forty beaming kids gathered en masse like carol singers on the drive to mark the final day of school's autumn term.

'*We wish you a merry Christmas, we wish you a merry Christmas, we wish you a merry Christmas and a happy new year,*' the teenagers hollered. I waved sleepily whilst carefully concealing a flicker of emotion forming in the corners of both eyes.

'Merry Christmas to you all too; I'll no doubt be seeing you next term,' I yelled through the skylight, perhaps a trifle disingenuously, knowing full well an intensive programme of house-hunting had been set in motion for early in the new year.

****

Transporting hero worship into a parallel universe, pasty-faced Paula from Lichfield opened a vastly different can of worms. Turning a series of intrusions into a family outing, she would habitually roll up alongside a neck-braced father and shrimp of a mother, dragging two ill-at-ease younger boys plausibly aware of the error of their senior's ways.

'Good morning Dave, it's Jim your friendly neighbourhood policeman here; can you please explain why there's a tent pitched directly across the road from your house on another resident's back lawn? The infringing parties claim to have your permission!' the local bobby probed.

'With all due respect, Jim, why the hell would I give some weirdoes the green light to park their arses on a strip of land I don't own?' I reacted.

'I did wonder that, but I have to pose the question. Would you like me to get them to move on?' the amiable bluebottle suggested.

'If you would, please, Jim… and thanks,' I signed off. Reaching for a set of binoculars to spy on the trespassers from an upstairs window and seeing Staffordshire's answer to the Addams Family camped out just yards away from my doormat, I kept a low profile behind closed curtains for the remainder of the afternoon.

A string of other disturbing incidents followed, ignored at my peril and coming back to bite me on the bum in the form of a mountain of hate mail personally delivered to the property alleging all manner of things. Freakily, they included an outrageous claim professing I may be in some way related to the unsavoury tribe, attributed to a long-lost ancestor somewhere in the lineage tenuously connected to a dear late aunt.

'Dave, we have a telegram that's just arrived at the office which I think you need to take very seriously,' announced co-manager Les some months later, finally bringing the matter to a head. 'It's from a lady called Paula; would you like me to read it out in its entirety?' he asked.

*'DEAR DAVE – (STOP) – I CANNOT BELIEVE YOU CONTINUE
TO AVOID ME AT ALL COSTS – (STOP) – I MUST SEE YOU AS
A MATTER OF URGENCY – (STOP) – SHOULD YOU NOT AGREE
TO THIS BY 6PM WEDNESDAY – (STOP) – I WILL BE FORCED
TO CONTEMPLATE SUICIDE BY SLASHING MY THROAT
PAULA'*

'This is getting out of hand, Les,' I grieved, becoming deeply concerned. 'I think it's high time I consulted a lawyer. We can't go on like this – it's bloody harassment; and even worse the whole bloody thing's turning my world upside down!'

Some weeks later I was copied in on a legal document warning of impending action should the flagrant invasion of privacy continue. A welcome period of calm ensued, brought to a close by a letter of apology winging its way into my mailbox via the band's office and evidently written with the aid of rose-coloured spectacles:

'Dear Dave, whilst we regret any offence caused we are extremely sorry your father feels this way and has seen fit to involve solicitors. We are after all not only fans but also have family ties. We realise this is none of your doing but due to the nature of the complaint will not be bothering you again in the future.'

'Cruel as it may sound, my personal view is they're all stark raving bonkers. I doubt you'll either see or hear of them again!' remarked friend and legal eagle James. He was proven wrong on both counts in just a matter of weeks when, portraying the true fickleness of infatuation, the anaemic-looking Paula showed up at a Birmingham concert pledging her undying affections towards the unsuspecting Trevor… later changing course to Geoff… and then on to Rod.

Causes célèbres

Samuel Johnson – originator of the English Dictionary
Gary Mason – superbike champion
David Garrick – actor

Essential travelling band info

Favourite live music venue: Garrick Theatre, Castle Dyke
Favourite curry house: Le Jardin Punjabi, Bird Street – 72%
Favourite pub: Bowling Green, Friary – 67%
Don't miss: National Memorial Arboretum, Alrewas – 80%
Sense of humour/friendly welcome: 48%

Chapter 34
Lincoln

NEVER COULD IT BE SAID I came from a musical family, though my mum occasionally enjoyed carving out a tune on the family's antique 'nicely out of tune' upright piano in a carefree style only a past generation could master. Perched bolt upright on the wooden stool, she would throw her more dextrous right hand at the upper keys whilst randomly plonking at the bass clef notes with the thumb and pinkie of her spanned left hand.

Banished to the dustbin of nostalgia, the pre-TV days of family gatherings clustered around the ivories primed for a shambolic sing-song happily made way to the swinging sixties, opening the floodgates to a brave new world of rock-'n'-roll and electric guitars leaping out from the overtaxed speakers of a multi-coloured range of Dansette record players.

Caring little for passing trends whilst taking note of her younger son's budding aptitude for tinkling the 'black and whites', come the tender age of eight and despite a number of protests my beloved mother packed me off for a spun-out series of piano lessons supervised by a 'teacher' whose credentials in truth barely outshone her own, unaware that the budding maestro tied in the weekly ordeal with a visit on the way home to an older friend's house to gleefully strum on his battered acoustic guitar. I was banging out tunes from both instruments in no time at all; but the piano tutor's limited dexterity coupled with an obsession with theory spelt the end for the old joanna, as I opted alternatively to save a few shillings and quit the multi-keyed instrument to concentrate solely on the magical in-vogue six-stringer.

Friday nights huddled together in front of a fourteen-inch black-and-white screen brought another unwelcome distraction, with the family members encouraged to sit through what I now believe to be my late mum's favourite ever TV programme: a show entitled *My Music* hosted by the dashing, ultra-smooth Steve Race. 'That man knows how to play the piano,' she'd eulogise, prior to the outrageous downgrading of the show to a radio-only slot years later when the penny finally dropped the old girl nurtured a secret crush on the receding ivory-keyed wizard.

Born in Lincoln in 1921, Steve Race earned the distinction of being one of just a handful of TV stars ever to provide my dear mother with a diversion from hours of seemingly endless housework, thus creating a nostalgic lump in my throat upon the announcement of his passing in the obituary section of a Nottinghamshire news journal in 2009.

****

As the ageing process takes hold and a catalogue of childhood memories diminishes into a mere jotting-pad of trivial flashbacks, almost bizarrely the bulk of abiding thoughts seem to centre on the more distasteful episodes of one's adolescence, visualising every scrape and minor setback befalling pretty much every schoolkid, goody-goodies included. The first punch-up, the first kiss on the lips from a girl reeking of halitosis, the introductory knee-trembler, bumps on the head, six of the best... all overshadowed by the humiliation of being dumped by a girlfriend for the first time. None of these, however, remain as firmly implanted in my mind as a humbling loss of face suffered on a cultural outing to the city of Lincoln.

Afforded the luxury of an entire day freed from the shackles of a stuffy classroom, the school's history department went to great lengths to organise a meaningful excursion. They plumped for a day trip to set eyes on the revolutionary Magna Carta in the city's Castle buildings, side by side with a leisurely stroll around the magnificent Gothic cathedral. Also provided for a small stipend were close on forty packed lunches squeezed into Tupperware containers along with a crateful of third-pint milk bottles to wet each pupil's whistle.

We scampered aboard the coach like a herd of elephants and made for the prized back-row seats, more preoccupied with mischief-making as opposed to actually learning something. Within moments of lift-off the rustling sound of greaseproof paper let slip that obligatory 'big-boned' fat kid Christopher could stall no longer, chomping greedily into his inadequate lunch pack and polishing off the lot in five minutes flat.

'What's wrong with the apple, fatso?' commented one of the boys, alluding to the sole remaining healthy option languishing on the container's lid.

'Oh, I'm allergic to fruit,' the glutton falsified, sparking a mini-stampede to claim the ripe green Granny Smith going spare. Unsurprisingly it was nabbed by school bully Harvey and stashed into the net pocket in front of him.

Detecting the first rumblings of irritation within barely thirty minutes and grabbing the intercom system's mike situated to the driver's left, history teacher Mr Williams patronisingly announced: 'Boys and girls, we will soon be pulling over for a short five-minute break to allow those of you wishing to use the toilet to relieve yourselves in the roadside facilities… After all, we don't want any little accidents, now do we?'

A million miles from the twenty-first century's state-of-the-art service stations decked out with hamburger joints, newsagents and M&S 'Simply Food' outlets, the truckers' refuge boasted little in the way of amenities other than a basic café offering chipped mugs of builder's tea to accompany bacon or fried-egg sandwiches, all ignored by the desperate youngsters snaking through the tables to the reeking loos.

'Time's up, children; let's have everybody back on the bus as quickly as possible, please… Bartram, where the hell do you think you're going? You'll be on detention if you continue to disobey my orders,' barked the dictatorial Mr Williams.

'The queue for the bog… sorry, toilets was ridiculous, sir. Is it okay if I water the hedge over there? I promise I'll be quick!' I fawned, receiving the teacher's approval and scurrying out of sight tailed by a half-dozen equally stricken delinquents.

Reinvigorated by the pit-stop (or rather piss-stop) we reboarded the coach in haste. The insatiable Christopher tucked into a mysteriously purchased Mars Bar, munching away to the envy of the self-disciplined majority, most of whose families refused to lavish their hard-earned pay on such non-essential luxuries. Safe in our seats, we busily emptied the contents of our lunch-boxes as, taking up the mike again, the petulant lecturer-cum-tour-guide pointed out a number of not-to-be-missed sights and ancient relics waiting only miles away at our final destination.

He broke off his tedious address in order to scold a pair of bashful girls who were dissolving into a fit of the giggles, muffled by the tissues pressed hard to their noses. 'Okay everyone, I want the name or names of those responsible for letting off a stink bomb,' the authoritarian bleated, referring to the farmyard smell thickening the air and threatening a hundred lines for every last pupil should the culprit fail to come forward.

'It's not a prank sir, it's Tubby Hayes over there – I think he needs his nappy changing!' revealed teacher's pet Colin, spilling the beans on the watery-eyed human dustbin clutching his stomach in the seat opposite.

'What he means to say is he's crapped his pants, sir,' interrupted another smart aleck, pinching his nostrils in disgust to cries of 'Pooh!' and 'Oh my god!' with the odd anonymous expletive chucked in for good measure.

'I know exactly what he means, lad; now pipe down, the lot of you,' the master ordered. Distracted by the awe-inspiring cathedral looming large on the right-hand side and shirking his duties as the party's guardian, he tripped self-importantly from the bus.

****

Scribbling down notes in preparation for a mandatory homework essay expected in during the following morning's history lesson, the day took a fascinating turn for the better as we trailed in the footsteps of a humorous, well-versed guide. Scouring the grounds animatedly for any relevant scraps of information, we marvelled at the sheer enormity of the towering Gothic masterpiece while, perhaps more importantly, maintaining a healthy distance from the discredited Christopher, cast out like a leper at the back of the group.

'How much longer? I've had enough and I want to go home!' the porker lamented, trudging dejectedly towards the edifice hounded by a bombardment of vicious catcalls. Paradoxically, however, he was later destined to have the last laugh.

Prodded by an impatient coach-driver whose clocking-off time appeared to be fast approaching, we got cracking on the inbound journey. Rapidly hitting the outskirts of town, a jangle of sighs and moans permeated the foul-smelling charabanc as a band of restless classmates complained bitterly of stomach cramps, sorely in need of a breath of fresh air along with a top-priority toilet visit.

'I don't get paid to make unscheduled stops. I'm due back at the depot at 6pm sharp,' the jobsworth bickered, bloody-mindedly keeping his toe to the floor and patently getting the simmering Mr Williams's goat. Meanwhile, I gently rubbed at my own distended paunch, all the signs pointing towards a similarly embarrassing problem.

Lounging back in his seat seemingly unaffected by the root of his earlier misfortune, a surprisingly upbeat Christopher gnawed into yet another Mars Bar retrieved from his hidden cache. Devouring the treat in an instant, he closed his eyes contentedly, evidently oblivious to the pained snivelling coming forth from the dirty dozen in dire straits.

'Can you boys please put a sock in it? The driver has refused flatly to make another stop and is apparently perfectly happy for his bus to smell like a pigsty, so grin and bear it for crying out loud!' the seething Welshman lashed out.

'It's just that Perkins has soiled himself, sir!' squealed shit-stirring pipsqueak Robert, attracting the irked teacher's attention.

'So have I, sir!' close friend Nick conceded, coolly raising his hand.

For once forgetting the microphone and standing tall in the aisle the teacher challenged: 'How many of you have poorly tummies?'

Ten hands, including my own, rocketed into the air amongst a hail of whines and moans.

'Lord, give me strength; this is unbelievable! Some of the food in the lunch-packs must have been well past its prime!' the tutor inferred, before attempting to reason with the road-runner once more to make an emergency stop and allow his wards a moment of respite.

'Hang on a minute, Einstein, if you can't keep a bunch of kids under control it's hardly my fault,' the driver griped, gasping for air through the open window whilst continuing resolute in his quest to churn up the miles.

Back at school, waddling from the coach like a team of pregnant ducks, we were whisked off to the changing rooms to shower and clean up. As we quickly stripped off, a dung heap of discarded jockey briefs accumulated on the tiled floor. Slipping bareback into our unsullied outer garments feeling human again, we trooped out into the evening for a pre-organised ride home.

'Hello son; blimey, you look as white as a sheet... Did you have an interesting day?' my father asked, clunking the car into gear and pulling slowly away.

'Oh, it was certainly that, Dad. Some of it was great and some of it... well... crap, if I'm honest!' I reflected, shifting uneasily in the passenger seat.

****

'On behalf of the governors and trustees I would like to offer a sincere apology to all the pupils experiencing difficulties during the recent Lincoln Cathedral excursion,' announced a remorseful headmaster two days later, coerced into eating humble pie before a stunned, chock-full school assembly. 'It appears that, due to an oversight, the pre-packed lunchboxes were foolishly left exposed to the sun by the kitchen staff prior to being distributed amongst the passengers, unhappily becoming contaminated as a result and causing a sudden outbreak of diarrhoea in the camp. Rest assured we will be writing to your parents with a full explanation along with an official apology,' the principal pledged to rumblings of derisive laughter from the floor. 'Silence! Salmonella is no laughing matter!' he bawled as he deserted his post, happy to see the back of the insubordinate throng overflowing into the foyer, the large majority of whose mirthful expressions suggested otherwise.

'Sam who?' posed Nick on the way to the day's opening maths lesson, still a little queasy and failing to see the funny side.

'I'm pretty sure he meant food poisoning,' I responded, carefully reining in a bellyful of trapped wind... just in case!

Causes célèbres

Lord Alfred Tennyson – poet
Hereward the Wake
Sybil Thorndike – actress
Patricia Hodge – actress
Steve Race – '60s TV and radio DJ
Jennifer Saunders – comedienne and actress
Jim Broadbent – actor
Margaret Thatcher – former PM was born in the county

Essential travelling band info

Best live music venue: Terry O'Toole Theatre, North Hykeham (six miles away)
Best and worst curry house: The Bombay, The Strait (I was informed it was the best) – 22%
Favourite pub: Wig and Mitre, Steep Hill – 77%
Don't miss: Lincoln Castle (including a copy of the Magna Carta), Castle Hill – 66%
Sense of humour/friendly welcome: 51%

Chapter 35
Lisburn

I JUST KNEW IT WAS going to be one of those days. From drawing back the curtains to near darkness cast by a giant black rock barely a metre from the windowpane to pogoing around the bedroom on one leg struggling into my skintight Levis and painfully stubbing my toe against the TV stand, all the signs pointed toward a daily grind of nightmarish proportions.

Upon reflection the penny should have dropped much sooner, when I checked into my room to find a black-and-white cat lying sound asleep on the bed, apparently unperturbed by the all too familiar sound of guests interrupting its peace.

Juddering down just one floor in the ill-maintained lift to search out a non-existent breakfast nook, I ambled to the unmanned reception desk where a dearth of human activity forged an image of the Marie Celeste in my mind's eye. There did not appear even to be a kitchenette where at least I could make use of the tea-making facilities. With neither hide nor hair of a single soul, and figuring the boys would still be counting sheep after the mandatory post gig binge, I threw in the towel and, scaling the stairs to pick up my coat, plumped to take Shanks's pony into town, fantasising over a bacon sarnie and refreshing cuppa lying in wait just yards away at a welcoming roadside hostelry.

As I walked, I relived the previous night's free-for-all in a ramshackle ballroom-cum-pub gig not far from the city, at which we encountered a hostile group of Sinn Fein 'delegates' busy winding down from an all-day conference in the selfsame venue. At a post-performance heart-to-heart, the dance hall's manager diplomatically complimented the band on its professionalism whilst expressing his genuine satisfaction at a larger than usual turnout.

'I thought you guys did really well out there tonight. That bunch of wankers seemed hell-bent on giving you a hard time, but you even won them over in the end, and believe me that takes some doing,' the Ulsterman eulogised backstage.

'We've had better nights, but thanks anyway. Incidentally, have you seen Seamus the promoter?' I asked quizzically. 'I was meant to meet him here.'

'He was here earlier on to collect your fee but disappeared about an hour ago,' the owner retorted, setting the alarm bells ringing.

'He didn't happen to say where he was going… did he?' I begged, freezing on the spot with all kinds of thoughts entering my head.

'He mentioned something about calling in to see the band Bagatelle in Armagh, and also that he'd be making his way over to Cavan for a meeting with the Brady brothers in the morning on his way back to Cork,' the man snitched.

'*Cavan?* The lying bastard! He was supposed to settle up for the final three shows tonight because he couldn't make it along to the last gig tomorrow, which as you may have guessed is in the very same town…!' I agonised, lost for words.

'Cavan… The man's a fucking scoundrel – he'd sell his own mother down the river if he thought it'd save his skin. I think I'd best buy you all a jar!' he altruistically offered, taken full advantage of by the thirsty, aggrieved gang.

Recalling the conversation now as I wandered in search of breakfast, a sudden thought struck me. 'The Brady brothers… an important meeting… Mary mother of God – this may just be a lifeline,' I blasphemed, before doubling back along the leafy Lisburn back road towards the glorified guest house at full throttle, driven by a savage lust for revenge and fixed upon wreaking havoc upon the unscrupulous Seamus Collins.

****

'How the hell can Directory Enquiries be engaged?' I cussed, slamming down the phone and hunting high and low in vain for a set of Yellow Pages. Foiled in my efforts to glean the Cavan venue's number, I wandered downstairs to the miraculously tended reception desk, making a bad job of hiding my amazement at finding a girl busily scribbling into a page-a-day diary.

'I'm sorry to disturb you, but is there any chance you could help me find the telephone number for a hotel in Cavan? My party are due to check in there later and I urgently need to speak to someone before we set off,' I pleaded, perhaps a tad overeagerly.

'I'm awfully sorry, I'm just helping out this morning – Mrs Flaherty's been taken ill and won't be in for the rest of the day!' the ginger-headed temp explained.

'I'm sorry to hear that; perhaps you've got a phone book back there I could borrow? It'll only be for a few seconds!' I begged.

She reached to the bottom of a heavy pile, surprisingly appearing to come up trumps.

'Oh no, this one is only for the Province. I could call my sister who lives in Monaghan, not far from Cavan? It's been ages since I phoned her so she'll be pleased as punch to hear from me; then I can kill two birds with one stone and get her to find the number… if you'll allow around fifteen minutes for a quick catch-up!' the girl helpfully vowed.

I scribbled down the details for her and sloped off outside to wait. The sound of two siblings prattling incessantly leaked through the open skylight, continuing unabated for fully twenty minutes until, becoming restless, I stepped back inside and the relief receptionist slid over a smudged 'with compliments' slip bearing the required number.

I vaulted up the stairs three steps at a time and frantically unlocked the room door. Within seconds of my picking up the phone the lilting mannerly tones of a competent desk clerk announced the hotel's name, adding: 'Now, how may I help you sir?'

'Could I speak to Mr Brady please? I'm calling on behalf of the band Showaddywaddy and need to get hold of him desperately,' I affirmed, recalling how I'd hit it off with the canny proprietor some two years earlier and figuring myself well enough acquainted to prewarn him of the devious promoter's intended chicanery.

'I'm afraid Mr Brady's not due in for a while yet – he had rather a late night last night. Would you like me to pass on a message?' the girl offered.

'I really need to speak to Thomas personally. It's a matter of urgency,' I stressed.

'If it's regarding tonight's show I'm afraid we're all sold out, there's not a single ticket left,' the girl emphasised semi-apologetically.

'No, no, I don't need tickets, I just need Thomas – I'm one of the band!' I repeated.

'There's only one band on tonight and they just showed up with all their equipment; would you like to speak to one of them?' she suggested, referring to the recently arrived crew and totally getting the wrong end of the stick.

'There might not be a show this evening if I don't get to talk to Mr Brady!' I exclaimed, becoming a tad hysterical.

'You wouldn't…! The show's a complete sell-out! Look, he's due in for a meeting at twelve o'clock but I'll do my best to get a message to him beforehand,' the girl steadfastly promised, making a note of the Lisburn number.

Zapping on the minuscule TV, I tuned into a preview of a Gaelic football fixture set to take place the same afternoon. The harsh trill of the bedside phone signified a swift response from the day's destination, and I snatched up the phone in an instant.

'There's a Mr Brady on the line – would you like me to put him through?' the sisterly temp beckoned, indicating the caller sounded none too happy.

'Hello, is that Thomas? Thanks for getting…' I answered, excitedly holding the phone to my ear only to be abruptly shot down in flames.

'Mr Brady to you son; what in God's name is this about you cancelling tonight's show? We've sold every last ticket!' the boss-man angrily confirmed, proceeding to read the riot act.

'Whoa, hold on a sec, I never threatened any such thing! Your receptionist got it all wrong. I wouldn't pull out at this late stage!' I assured him. Detailing the issues raised with the shyster promoter and begging the man not to part with any funds at the midday meeting, I promised to rally the troops and leave at the earliest opportunity.

'You have my word, son. I like to think of myself as an honourable man; besides, I can't stand that fucking crook. Get over here as soon as you can and take the matter up with him yourself. It's about time he had his comeuppance!' he advocated, signing off.

We navigated the invisible borderline from north to south in good time but, with a notable deterioration in the road surfaces, the journey's final thirty miles dragged tediously by, crawling at a snail's pace behind a scourge of hayricks and jalopies. We eventually passed a sign indicating *Cavan 3 Kilometres* just the wrong side of midday.

'We'll catch the bastard with his pants down,' I growled, sniffing blood and clenching my fist, intent on outfoxing the con artist. Soon manoeuvring onto the hotel's drive, I sprinted hell-for-leather through the swing doors into the crowded reception area.

'I need to see Mr Brady – he's expecting me!' I implored, discourteously ignoring a sizeable party busy filling in a wad of registration forms.

'Mr Brady is tied up in a meeting, sir; perhaps you'd be kind enough to wait in line until I've attended to these customers!' she answered curtly, turning back to her work.

Forced into toeing the line and blowing hard, I honed in on an altercation spilling over from a nearby office. The familiar southern twang of the villainous Mr Collins instantly set my skin crawling; and, slipping stealthily out of eyeshot, I sneaked along the carpeted hallway.

'Come on in, David!' proclaimed a rasping Irish voice as its owner heard a light rap at the oak-panelled door. This signalled the sudden exit of the chiselling charlatan who, grabbing at his briefcase, galloped like a thoroughbred up the corridor and out of harm's way.

'Did you just see Collins rushing out of here?' I shouted over to the boys assembled by the entrance, meeting with glum-faced expressions all round.

'Don't tell me he's done a runner… please!' Rod exclaimed.

'He was out of that office like a rat up a drainpipe,' I owned up.

A manhunt reminiscent of a Keystone Cops movie ensued, with the band splintering into pairs and coiling every which way. The chase quickly gathered momentum with the ranks swelled by a body of nimble staff-members flying up staircases with the agility of an SAS crack unit.

'No sign of the bloody rogue anywhere! He's a slippery customer that one,' adjudged Thomas, calling off the search roughly thirty minutes later and offering the dejected lynch mob a drop of the hard stuff to atone for the setback. We assumed the swindler had shown the posse a clean pair of heels and inconceivably gone to ground.

'Don't fret, David – I have your fee for tonight safely under lock and key, so all's not lost!' the chieftain boomed, attempting to make light of the situation.

His attention was caught by an apologetic member of staff decked out in black-and-white checked pants. 'Excuse me, Mr Brady, I'm sorry to interrupt but there's a man lying unconscious in the kitchens,' the stubbly guy disclosed.

'You don't think… ?' I stammered.

'I think we'd better go and take a look!' urged the resolute boss, leading the way through a network of grimy tunnels.

'He slipped on the greasy surface and went crashing head first into the sinks. He was out for the count when I found him!' revealed a makeshift nurse in the process of reviving the fugitive, who was slumped semi-conscious against a giant metallic oven.

'So he's not dead then; what a pity,' barked Thomas cynically, spotting fear in the eyes of the dazed fraudster who, shifting uncomfortably, made the feeblest of attempts to lift up his carcass and make another bolt for it.

'Save your breath, Seamus – you're well and truly fucked this time… or perhaps you'd prefer it if I leave you to the mercy of these gentlemen!' the hotel owner advised, glowering down at the pathetic, whimpering wreck.

'If it's sympathy you're looking for, forget it, you snivelling piece of shit,' I spat viciously. 'Perhaps you'd like to explain where the six grand is that you owe me!'

'There's some in Mr Brady's safe; other than that I'm on me uppers – I haven't got another fuckin' penny,' he insinuated, lying through his teeth.

'So where's the money you collected on our behalf last night, before you slunk off without as much as a word?' I chided, balling my fist.

'Every last penny went to Bagatelle! The shows haven't been going at all well and I haven't got a pot to piss in,' he fabricated.

'You lying piece of scum – we've played to full houses every night bar one,' I argued, lining up my right boot.

'Just take it easy… business is way down on last year and it's a case of robbing Peter to pay Paul,' the rascal lamented, persisting with a catalogue of stock excuses.

'Never mind Peter, Paul or fucking Mary, empty your pockets you bloody weasel!' I demanded, spitting blood.

At this point Thomas intervened. 'I have two more bands booked through your sleazy set-up Seamus, and for obvious reasons they will be the last. I'm going to deduct what David's owed from their fees and I'll hold onto the rest to err on the side of caution. While we're on the subject, God forbid neither band shows up or I'll break your fucking legs!'

Close to tears, Collins bleated, 'I'm ruined,' scratching around on his knees for the remnants from his pockets and collapsing back into a heap on the floor, to the utter disgust of the retreating Thomas Brady whose swift toe-poke into the ribs spelt the end of the proceedings, sealed with the parting shot:

'Just be thankful you're still alive; now get up and fuck off, Seamus, and crawl back into the hole you came out of!'

Causes célèbres

John McMichael – former leader of the Ulster Defence Association
John Hallam – actor (*Robin Hood: Prince of Thieves* and many more)
Ray Stevenson – actor

Essential travelling band info

Live music venue: Island Arts Centre, Civic Centre, The Island
Favourite curry house: Spice, Bridgewater House, Bridge Street – 25%
Favourite pub: Tap Room, Hilden Brewery – 61%
Don't miss: Lisburn Leisure Park – 41%
Sense of humour/friendly welcome: 11%

Chapter 36
Liverpool

PULLING UP OUTSIDE OF LIVERPOOL'S oddly shaped 'Wookey Hollow Club' back in 1973, the band were heartened by the previous seven nights roughing it in the Lancashire town of Oldham. The ecstatic introduction to the band's professional career came tumbling down to earth as our eyes fell on a giant advertising hoarding, displaying in brightly coloured lettering:

TONIGHT TIL SATURDAY
SENSATIONAL NEW COMEDY SHOWGROUP
SHOW-WADDY-WADDY

'Fucking comedy show-group? They haven't even spelt the name right!' beefed Trevor, climbing out of the vehicle to take a leak on the forecourt, followed by the remaining disgruntled passengers sidestepping the shameful urinary trail.

'We're looking forward to a right good knees-up tonight lads, and we've near enough a full house all week!' commented the garrulous club manager, cracking a series of indecipherable gags whilst conducting a brief guided tour of the venue.

'The board outside is wrong,' I bade, sticking in my oar. 'I don't know who gave you the information, but we shouldn't be billed as a comedy show-group.'

'I spoke to your agents and they seemed okay with the idea, plus I saw you on *New Faces* a few months back and thought you were hilarious!' the wag verified.

'That's crazy – we're just a rock-and-roll band,' insisted an incredulous Romeo. 'There's nothing remotely funny about what we do!'

'That's a matter of opinion, mate; all I know is our customers love a good laugh and you'll have them rolling in the aisles before the night's out,' the character retorted, flitting away to continue about his daily routine.

With the city touted in many quarters as the 'home of comedy' (and thievery), the band's introduction onto a Liverpool stage fully lived up to expectations, trumpeted by the farcical sight of a colourful eight-strong outfit trooping like Muppets across an ill-conceived wooden humpback bridge beneath which lay an equally absurd fibreglass water feature, finally reaching the main platform to be welcomed by a finger-pointing assortment of grinning night owls.

As we pummelled through an uptempo repertoire of fifties and sixties covers gussied up with a series of recently rehearsed, energy-sapping dance routines, bounding across the boards in a sideways formation, the booker's flippant words began to ring true in our ears. A curiously jollified reaction seemed to be lighting up the room, with large sections of the audience bordering on wetting themselves, crippled by the antics of the flummoxed bill-toppers, at the same time putting paid to any big ideas of being taken seriously.

Tempering the mood in an impassioned (albeit hammed-up) tribute to the much lauded Buddy Holly, I stepped forward to the microphone amidst a pitter-patter guitar pattern echoing like raindrops in the background and sombrely recited:

'On February the third 1959 in Fargo, North Dakota, three rock-and-roll stars were tragically killed in a plane crash: J.P. Richardson, known as the Big Bopper; seventeen-year-old Ritchie Valens; and the one, the only, *Buddy Holly.*'

I paused briefly at the mike, silhouetted in near darkness, allowing ample time for the eulogy to strike the desired chord. A confused silence was broken by an astonishingly penetrating smoker's cackle resounding upwards to the overhead rafters, erupting into an uncontrollable hiccoughing fit gripping the stage-side tableful of abettors.

Notwithstanding the misleading billing, I assumed the outburst to be drink-related. Unsettled and biting my lip as I shook myself down, I exclaimed: 'Excuse me for asking, but what's so funny?'

'Ah-ha-ha-ha-hah!' the rabid hyena howled, triggering off a similarly mirthful response from one end of the floor to the other.

'Just look at his face!' another female yelled, zeroing in on the stage and splitting her sides, craving the support of her equally paralysed other half.

I never quite got my head around what sparked such an uproarious reception, but the idiom 'throw enough shit at the wall and some of it will stick' brought into question the exterior billboard's misbegotten hard-sell. As if by magic, following repeated requests the sign was transfigured from 'comedy' to 'rock-and-roll' show-group, shifting at once any preconceived notions of slapstick towards a fast-moving nostalgia-tinged musical spectacle.

****

Rummaging through a hoard of weighty boxes hoisted down from my loft in preparation for a major downsizing operation in 2013, my attention was caught by a clutch of A4 diaries dating back to the early seventies. Hesitating briefly, I brushed the dust from the shiny hardback covers whilst considering dumping the entire collection.

As I browsed through the yellowing pages, a boundless number of references to the city of Liverpool made for not only interesting but amusing reading, detailing the band's ups and downs in the shrine of British pop culture. A few of these anecdotes follow in their original form, updated with a brief resumé of my recollections of each event:

1973

Played at the birthplace of the Beatles i.e. The Cavern, what a night, the adrenaline was pumping like crazy. Risked life and limb mentioning Liverpool FC, the place was crawling with Everton fans!

Unforgettable, despite the stiflingly clammy atmosphere, but oh how I wish I'd asked someone, anyone to capture a moment in time on camera for posterity!

1974

I finally went the whole hog and had my long locks shorn off, falling victim to an effeminate hair-stylist working in a trendy salon situated on the ground floor of the shopping mall close to Bailey's nightclub where we were playing for six nights.

Following a few nudges from the boys I plucked up the courage to uncover my youthful features, hidden for eons behind a chestnut-brown mane reaching right down to the small of my back, prior to the release of the band's debut single in April. As the pile of shiny tresses accumulated strand by strand on the floor of a swank city-centre hair and beauty parlour, a would-be rock anachronism was transformed into a budding overnight sensation in an overdue nod to the future.

1976

LIVERPOOL 5, LEICESTER CITY 1, Frank 'Elvis' Worthington opened the scoring, but then the home side shifted up a gear and started playing. The highlight of the night was meeting Liverpool manager Bill Shankly, whose witty comments, particularly at the expense of my pal Jeff, left a lasting impression.

'Some people believe football is a matter of life and death. Let me assure you it's much more important than that!' coined (allegedly) the much revered 'Reds' manager known affectionately as 'Shanks', summing up in but a few words the strength of feeling for the beautiful game up on Merseyside where the sport is deified as something of a religion.

Having trekked northwards along with sidelined Leicester City skipper and friend Jeff Blockley (unable to play in the game due to a fractured jaw sustained the previous week), we made our way through a spine-tingling maze of corridors lurking beneath the bleachers of the compelling Anfield stadium which opened up to a roomy hospitality area filled with a who's who of familiar faces, many of whom had at one time graced the hallowed turf with their silky skills.

Eavesdropping in on a nearby conversation, I heard a droll, raspy voice dryly jabber: 'Gardening, what a waste of any man's time that is; just concrete it over and paint it green and it'll never grow... or give you backache!' I looked on agog as, splitting from the pack, the spiky-haired folk hero laid eyes on the unsuspecting Jeff. 'Why aren't you playing, son?' the gritty Scot posed to the injured player following an unexpectedly cordial introduction.

'I broke my jaw in a game last week and it's wired up, Bill!' Jeff acknowledged, stifling a pained smile and stroking the whiskers obscuring his battle scars.

'Yes son, but why aren't you playing?' The lightning response, lapped up in a chorus of howls by all and sundry within earshot, displayed a sharpness of wit rarely associated with the modern game's humourless hierarchy, perhaps also explaining the extraordinary strength of character attributed to his all-conquering seventies heroes on the field of play.

1977

Rolling up mid-afternoon for a one-off gig at the city's Empire Theatre where two guitars had been snatched from the back of the truck during the load-in. 3 band members including myself were whisked off to the main Police depot to make a statement, giving the details of the stolen items to two mischievous local bobbies in the hope of submitting an insurance claim to atone for our losses, not exactly setting the finest of examples themselves in putting together the necessary documentation.

Throughout much of the band's existence I led a relatively charmed life in terms of pilfered items of equipment, but the notoriously light-fingered environs of Liverpool struck a nonetheless calculable blow evident from a gaggle of animated crew-members and staff gathered in the loading bay of the prominent Empire Theatre.

'They've nicked the spare Strat and Trevor's black Les Paul. The pigs want you down at the station to make an official report, like now!' crew boss Ian urged, prompting a swift U-turn towards the police headquarters located just a stone's throw away. I was greeted by a chirpy double act of lanky, insouciant constables and escorted to a stark albeit private backroom. Shuffling through a wad of forms the attention turned to the band's recent on-the-road conquests as opposed to the boring formalities of paperwork.

'So roughly how many young ladies would you guys get to have your wicked way with in a calendar year…?' the younger man snooped.

'Rough ones? Oh, hundreds… but don't believe everything you read!' I censured, hinting towards sarcasm.

'Everybody from afar thinks all the women round here are the spitting image of the "Liver Birds", but some of them are really tasty… and right goers!' the senior plod chipped in.

'I'm sure we could chat about the subject for hours, but unfortunately we've got a gig to do just up the road,' I just happened to mention.

'Oh yeah, well anyway what do you reckon the replacement value of these stolen instruments would be… purely for insurance purposes that is?' voiced the younger bobby, finally getting down to brass tacks.

'Well, the Gibson's easily worth a couple of grand,' Russ estimated, taking a stab in the dark, 'and as for the Stratocaster, at least fifteen hundred quid.'

'And didn't you lose a valuable acoustic guitar; plus you guys use a saxophone, don't you?' hinted the senior accomplice.

'Then there's the amplifiers to make the instruments work… surely a couple of those must've gone missing!' his playmate insinuated, punching the digits into a desk calculator and jotting down the total on a pad. 'That takes it well past five grand and I don't doubt them robbing bastards have got some kind of excess on the policy, so realistically speaking I'd say that just about covers it – what do you reckon?' the wide-boy intimated.

'But that's fraud… isn't it?' I implied.

'Bloody fraud – have you seen the size of their headquarters in London? I'm sure the pittance you're about to claim won't make a ha'porth of difference to their deep pockets, and besides they're all bleeding crooks!' he bit back with a knowing wink.

Subsequent visits to Merseyside unearthed a treasure trove of similarly outlandish encounters, including an offbeat TV makeover featured on the *This Morning* magazine programme (cruelly tagged the Pinch and Judy show by the taxi driver). It was designed to transform an outmoded bunch of seventies teddy-boys into a chic, twenty-first-century coterie of revamped catwalk kings, but in the process we fell foul of frumpy co-presenter Judy Finnegan, whose caustic, indiscreet 'And who might these old fossils be?' received a justifiably spiky 'pot calling the kettle black' response, creating a mini-ruction amongst the bawdy camera crew.

****

And last but not least my sincere thanks go out to 'Liverpool Lou', whoever she

– or perhaps he – may be (a prostitute according to a cynical musician friend from the region), for saving the day at a packed Dublin concert disrupted by an untimely blackout.

As I grabbed an acoustic guitar and shuffled to the brow of the stage, an Irish folk song I'd learnt as a boy scout spontaneously fell from my lips:

'*Oh Liverpool Lou lovely Liverpool Lou*
Why don't you behave just like other girls do?
Why must my poor heart keep following you?
Oh stay home and love me my Liverpool Lou.'

Generating their own unique brand of electricity, the effervescent crowd took up the mantle, stretching into a half-dozen extra verses and choruses, linked arms swaying to and fro silhouetted in the hall's flickering twilight. The moment ended on a scintillating high note as the telescopic lighting-towers blazed blindingly into action.

'And there you have it. Many hands do indeed make light work!' I quipped to a humungous cheer, soon drowned out by the meaty intro to the next song up.

Causes célèbres

John Lennon, Paul McCartney, George Harrison and Ringo Starr
Billy J. Kramer and the Dakotas – '60s outfit
Gerry and the Pacemakers – '60s outfit
Kim Cattrall – *Sex and the City* actress
Paul McGann – actor
Alison Steadman – actress and 'Loose Woman'
John Bishop – comedian
Ken Dodd – comedian
Jimmy Tarbuck – comedian
Rita Tushingham – actress
Jimmy McGovern – writer
Cilla Black – '60s singer/TV personality
Steven Gerrard – former England Captain
Brian Epstein – late Beatles manager
Kenny Everett – zany DJ and comedian
Patricia Routledge – 'Mrs Bucket' in TV's *Keeping Up Appearances*
Frankie Vaughan – '50s/'60s crooner

And many more…

Essential travelling band info

Best live music venue: Philharmonic Hall, Hope Street
Favourite curry house: Spiceways, Childwall Road – 67%
Favourite pub: Dispensary, Renshaw Street – 82%
Don't miss: 'Mendips', John Lennon's childhood home, Menlove Avenue – 77%
Sense of humour/friendly welcome: 90%

Chapter 37
London (The City of)

WHILE IN NO WAY PROFESSING to be an expert in all things relating to the annals of rock-and-roll history, I would guess that perhaps the singularly most bizarre piece of billing on record hit the stage of Kilburn's now defunct National Ballroom on September 7th 1987. It was cooked up by a scatterbrained impresario of dubious origin who, in pairing German Goth-rockers 'Einstürzende Neubauten' with retro chart-toppers Showaddywaddy, effectively threw the British contenders to the lions while smugly sitting back on his senatorial perch to observe the modern equivalent of a bloodbath. The evening's entertainment went on to scale the giddy heights of number fifty-six in *Time Out* magazine's Top 100 London gigs of all time.*

Egged on by a body of upbeat aficionados (strangely intermingled with a variety of heavily pierced, ashen-faced freaks) we took up the gauntlet with rebellious aplomb, galvanising not only the partying mainstreamers but the ocean of onlookers garbed from head to toe in black. '*ENGLAND 4 GERMANY 2*' proclaimed *Melody Maker* one week later, panning the industrial Germans for failing miserably to come to terms with following a band who had simply upped the ante out of sheer bloody-mindedness.

Using jackhammers, building implements and scrap metal (including a supermarket trolley pilfered from the local Sainsbury's), the Teutonic hubbub left large sections of the twelve-hundred-strong crowd unimpressed as they turned their backs and headed in their droves for the bars, eyeballed from the wings by the disbelieving albeit self-satisfied first band up.

'We pulled into the loading bay in a truck when we arrived, but then the Krauts arrived with a fucking skip!' mocked lighting technician Steve in a backhanded slight at the humiliated Berliners, stealing the plaudits for the evening's best comment.

Serving later as an evangelical church, the National Ballroom closed its

---

* Live Aid reached number fifty

doors as an entertainment venue in 1999, following – perhaps unsurprisingly – a long legal battle over noise levels.

****

Partaking in a musicians' mini-pool tournament in the recreational area of Wembley's Music Centre studio complex and smarting from a sound thrashing at the hands of hirsute session guitarist Big Jim Sullivan, I sauntered disconsolately to the bar to lick my wounds and ordered up a fizzy drink, taking the load off to await the next frame.

'Your turn up, Dave – there's no stopping Jim today,' Geoff summoned, laying down his cue in disgust and resetting the balls.

'Hey, kid… can I have a quiet word?' a strange voice beckoned, spelt out by a stubby hand clawing at my right arm.

'Sure, what was it you wanted?' I asked, weighing up a broad-shouldered guy squeezed into a tight-fitting shiny suit.

'Miss Massey was wondering if you might like to join her for a drink and a chat?' the burly minder grunted from the roof of his mouth. His eyes shifted towards a headscarfed, dusky-faced middle-aged woman, seductively drawing an extended gold cigarette holder to her pursed lips, poised and confident in every aloof movement.

'I don't think so, buddy; I'm in the middle of a pool game with the lads and there's a few quid hinging on the next frame, but please give her my thanks for the offer,' I responded.

I felt his grip become noticeably firmer. 'I don't think you heard me correctly, son. No one in their right mind refuses an offer from Miss Massey, or they have me to answer to!' he inarticulately threatened.

'Please take your hand off of my arm or this cue may accidentally get wrapped around your head. I told you politely – I'm otherwise engaged,' I retaliated, wriggling from his grasp and raising the pool-stick aggressively.

'Easy, kid… Have you any idea who that lady is?' he faltered, revealing the full extent of a wretched speech disorder.

'The Queen of fucking Sheba, I'd imagine. To be honest I don't give a monkey's!' I exclaimed, turning tail as, veins standing out on her neck, the temptress stormed from the bar, followed by her shamed bodyguard, tail between his legs.

'What the bloody hell was that all about?' asked Jim, pumping out his chest buoyed by yet another triumph.

'Did you see the old diva sat in the corner on the bar stool? Well, her babysitter threw a right strop when I refused to join her for a drink,' I confessed.

243

'Who – Ron? Shirley's man? Jim gasped, whispering the star's true identity in my ear.

'You're kidding…! But I thought…' I sputtered, referring to a spate of recent rumours coming out of the gutter press.

'And so did I… Anyway, are you ready for another thrashing?' the guitarist challenged, eager to change the subject.

****

I feel impelled at this point to name-drop a couple of international heavyweights, as the self-same Music Centre again burnished its reputation as a hallowed stamping ground all of a few months later. I was nibbling at a plate of Marmite on toast during an idle moment when the voice of complex owner Louis beckoned me over to the bar's seating area to meet two equally sophisticated greying men whose faces seemed vaguely familiar.

'Young Dave, let me introduce you to a couple of friends of mine… This is Fred… and this is Bing – they're over from across the pond for a few days to do some recording with a big band in studio one,' Louis drooled.

I was greeted warmly by the celebrated old hands and we engaged in a chummy confab; but not until I was taking lunch with my parents the following Sunday did the penny drop how privileged I'd been to share a few moments in such exalted company, as I launched what proved to be a bombshell into my normally bulletproof father's ears.

'You're a fan of the old-timer Bing Crosby, aren't you Dad?'

'Indeed I am. That's what you call a proper singing voice; he never felt the need to yawp in his entire career!' he blustered in a pernickety tone.

'I had a cup of tea with him and his mate Fred at the studio last Friday,' I boasted, watching his jaw drop almost to the floor.

'You don't mean Fred… A… Astaire and Bing Crosby… you've got to be pulling my leg son… surely!' he remarked, utterly gobsmacked.

'The very same; what's more, they'd both seen us on last week's *Top of the Pops*!' I added, laying it on even thicker.

'Well, I just hope some of Fred's magic has rubbed off on you… Talk about having two left feet!' the old boy disparaged, rising from the table rubbing at his back and collapsing into an armchair for a post-prandial snooze.

****

I admit to being something of a royalist at heart, so far be it from me to be in any way critical of the world's most famous family; but, running the risk of sticking my head on the chopping block, it must be said HRH Prince Edward is a bloody awful dancer.

The band were booked to perform at a ritzy charity bash held in the capacious ballroom of the swank Dorchester Hotel on Park Lane, at which London's *crème de la crème* turned out in force to lavish a king's ransom on a noble cause. Swigging extortionately priced Krug champers and flaunting stupidly expensive creations by Vivienne Westwood, Lagerfeld and Valentino et al, they were all incredibly eclipsed by the straight-laced royal's awkward lack of rhythm.

Within moments of our running out on stage to an unexpectedly ebullient reception from the moneyed crowd, the animated gathering overflowed onto the dance floor, delighting to the driving rhythms of a string of hits taking most of them back to their schooldays, punching the air and ready to party all night long.

'Look who's down there!' Rod yelled into my ear above the pandemonium, nodding towards a scrum of gyrating bodies amongst whom the balding Prince and his animated wife Sophie frolicked beneath the psychedelic lighting.

Taking on the role of an embarrassing uncle at a family wedding, the sprightly royal (flanked by fellow noble the Right Honourable Charles Spencer) threw caution to the wind, cavorting uncoordinatedly as if dancing on hot coals, much to the disapproval of a sprinkling of jostled revellers despairingly attempting to give the foursome a wide berth.

'Tonight brings a whole new meaning to the phrase a right royal knees-up!' I cornily cracked, opting not to dwell on the subject and launching into the next song, giving the nod for the turbo-charged Duke to fling his bumbling arms every which way whilst jogging on the spot in some kind of military drill gone awfully wrong.

'At least he seemed to be enjoying the band,' I offered in the extrovert Prince's defence, towelling off backstage.

'That's as may be, but can you imagine the choice comments his old man would've come out with if he'd laid eyes on him?' hinted Romeo, alluding to the caustic tongue belonging to Her Majesty the Queen's gaffe-ridden husband Philip.

****

The bulk of the band's early sojourns into the capital zeroed in on a string of nightclub/fun-pubs owned by a conglomeration known as Wheatley Taverns. Astutely spreading their wings to attract the plethora of artists storming the burgeoning cabaret-club circuit north of Watford, they anticipated a similar explosion in the south of England and beyond.

With the band at that time operating on a shoestring budget, an inexpensive albeit dingy east London hotel simply named The Hartley came to the rescue, offering an affordable deal for bed and lodgings stretching over a concerted nine-week period and owned by stern-faced taskmistress Dorothy, running a tight ship with no time for shirkers.

We soon found ourselves on first-name terms with the sedulous staff, made up of a young-middle-aged in-house couple and a trio of part-time domestics. A shortage of front-door keys meant that late-night access was restricted to the roadside lounge window, under strict instructions from the proprietor to slide the bolt firmly into place once the final guest was safely inside.

In permanent residence and always on the go, attractive receptionist-cum-housemaid-cum-waitress Cherie kept a dutiful eye on everything hotel-related. She was ably assisted by husband Doug in the role of general dogsbody, attending to maintenance issues and the like, amiably coming and going at all hours decked out like an out-of-work PT instructor.

Revelling in the spotlight, buxom Cherie's flirty, outgoing nature stirred the loins of each red-blooded occupant, but she chose to focus her attentions solely on swarthy young back-line roadie Rob, who – at nineteen years of age and with no regular girlfriend – seemed ripe for plucking. He could scarcely believe his luck.

'She's not bad for an old 'un, but I can hardly try anything on while he's around,' the lad commented, aroused from a quick fondle whilst taking afternoon tea in the lounge, though admirably opting to do the decent thing.

Fresh from a late-night gig in the Seven Kings area and designated the task of wrenching open the cumbersome sash window, I squeezed through the narrow gap before fumbling through the dimly lit lounge. The curvy contours of a stock-still Cherie stood tantalisingly in my path, finger to her lips whilst motioning toward other half Doug flat out on the sofa.

'Shush, he's just finished a twelve-hour shift – let him sleep… Is Robert outside with the others?' the enchantress whispered hopefully, cautiously sneaking into the hallway out of earshot and anxiously awaiting my reply.

'No, he won't be back for another half-hour or so; the crew were still packing the gear away when we scarpered,' I informed her before unlatching the front door, signalling a stampede in the direction of the boys' sleeping quarters.

Digging into my bag for a six-pack of insipid lager plundered from the dressing room, I sloped off to Rod's slightly larger cubbyhole to wind down from another energetic night's work. The rumble of the outside traffic shook the wafer-thin partitions, intensified an hour or more into the conversation by a rhythmical metallic creaking sound reminiscent of an overplayed park see-saw dating back to our misspent childhoods.

Spotting Geoff in the corridor draining the last remnants of his own precious tinny, I called out, 'Who's in the room two doors down from here?'

'That'll be one of the crew; why, what's up?' the bass player replied, letting rip with a resounding belch.

'Come and get a load of this – there's some randy twosome going at it like rabbits,' I urged, gesturing with my hand.

'I heard that myself a few minutes ago,' a refreshed, snowed-under Doug remarked from nearby. 'It would seem one of your lads got lucky tonight!' With that, he leaned into a store cupboard to retrieve a bag of tools and vanished again in a cloud of dust.

'I'm assuming it was you keeping everyone awake half the night, you dirty little git!' I put to the haggard-looking Rob, observing his bloodhound eyes and pulling up a chair to join the gang for breakfast just a handful of hours later.

'Morning lads!' said an equally burned-out Doug, entering the room with the morning papers. 'I'm not sure which one of you it was, but I have to take my hat off to you; I was up half the night fixing a plumbing problem and some lucky young couple were banging away for hours. I only wish I had half your energy!' he complimented before continuing on about his chores.

'What the f...? I assumed he was tucked up and out for the count...!' spluttered Rob, almost choking on his cornflakes, eyes bulging from their sockets.

'Okay, out with it – who was the lucky lady?' I pried, holding everyone's interest.

'Promise me none of you will say a word or I'll be in deep shit. It was his missus – she can't get enough!' he owned up, insisting that, in refusing to take no for an answer, the insatiable Cherie had in fact seduced the lad.

'You lucky bastard, I wouldn't have minded a pop at that myself,' Rod piped up enviously. With nods of admiration at the young stud's redoubtable libido, our lips remained sealed for the final two weeks in residence.

****

'Just like me you've been around a while, Dave; tell me, what in your experience is the most poscd question put to you in your long career?' probed veteran DJ Mike Read during a fairly recent in-depth interview for his Radio Berkshire show.

'Hmm, that's a very uncommon question in itself Mike. I've been asked numerous times where the band's name originated from; but giving it some thought it has to be: "What was it like appearing on *Top of the Pops*?" '

So perhaps the time is apt to set the record straight in portraying a chronological, warts-and-all case history of a day spent leading up to and recording a slot for the most celebrated of music shows, beginning in the words of the renowned voiceover:

'Yes, it's number one, it's… Top of the Pops!'

7.30am: Assemble at rendezvous point and scramble into two band-owned vehicles, taking the southbound carriageway of the M1 motorway in convoy.

10am: Arrive at main gates to the BBC Television Centre, Shepherds Bush. Twiddle thumbs whilst an over-officious uniformed guard radios ahead to confirm the authenticity of our claim to be part of the show, barking orders to an underling to direct the car to an out-of-the-way overflow facility. From there, laden with items of bulky luggage, the boys and myself undertake a strenuous half-mile hike to the main entrance.

10.15am: Enter reception and pick up laminated passes issued to each visitor. Follow youthful member of production staff through a labyrinth of corridors to a hallway of frugal dressing rooms, one of which will act as the party's base for the remainder of the day.

10.30am: Report on set. Meet up with the show's director and producer to discuss requirements in terms of live mikes, foldback and props. Rehearse positions in civvies, check pre-recorded backing track to confirm sound quality.

11am: Coffee break – down tools en masse for union-stipulated twenty-minute interval, taking refreshment in one of various locations scattered throughout the multi-storey structure of studios and offices.

Midday: Report back to studio for initial performance run-through, lining up camera angles and detailing stage routine in synch with backing track, inspiring director into becoming creative and providing input.

12.45pm: Return to dressing room instructed to be back on set in full regalia at 4.30pm sharp for final dress run.

1pm: Lunchtime. The entire workforce knocks off for a one-hour break, rushing to the huge, clattering main canteen to strap on the nose-bag.

1.30pm: Twiddle thumbs, scan through the newly published *Melody Maker*, strum acoustic guitar, attempt newspaper crossword and take a welcome nap.

2.30pm: Stroll into Shepherds Bush to pick up dry cleaning dropped off earlier by record company gofer; fall into line behind members of the Bay City Rollers and DJ Ed Stewart.

3pm: Return to TV Centre. Change into stage costumes for photo session for use in conjunction with chart rundown and BBC promotional publications.

4pm: Tea break (everything yet again grinds to a standstill).

4.30pm: Full dress run. Socialise off set with co-performers for longer than expected, killing time while bitchy choreographer tears lumps off of Legs & Co, attempting for the umpteenth time to perfect a recorded insert for the show.

6pm: Ushered to top-floor BBC bar, issued with temporary passes; swap stories and socialise over a beer with a veritable who's who of TV personalities from Patrick Moore to Noel Edmonds, Ronnie Corbett to Sting and any other straggling personalities – the indisputable highlight of a long-drawn-out day.

6.45pm: Make-up call – receive a going-over from one of a line of skilled cosmetologists waiting to slap on foundation, eyeliner and mascara, completing the task by meticulously coiffuring a healthy head of plentiful locks.

7.15pm: Pace up and down corridor outside dressing room, nervously awaiting floor manager's call to assemble outside studio.

7.30pm: 'Live' recording commences, red studio light ablaze.

7.45pm: Tiptoe behind drape curtains, clocking heavily made-up David Bowie waiting in the wings cool as a cucumber.

7.50pm: Perform latest chart single before an invited studio gathering of approximately fifty guests, strutting our stuff before an astonishing estimated TV viewing audience purported to be in excess of sixteen million people.

9.15pm: Change, scrub off make-up and head back to base, arriving in the East Midlands just shy of midnight.

And there you have it: no glitzy after-show parties, no delirious hordes of fans waiting to rip their heroes to bits, no fraternising with Pan's People or Legs & Co, simply a hard day's graft prolonged by a helluva lot of hanging around, culminating in an end result nothing short of astonishing as record sales rocketed in some cases to a staggering 100,000 copies per day, making (or in some cases breaking) an artist literally overnight.

Top of the Pops was and remains the most influential music show of all time, sadly gracing the nation's TV screens for the final time on July 30th 2006, destined never to return.

(N.B. Showaddywaddy's debut appearance on *Top of the Pops* in March 1974 was performed on a Morecambe and Wise set without any musical instruments whatever, due to industrial action enforced by the scene shifters' union.)

Causes célèbres

Actors: Tom Hardy, Daniel Day-Lewis, Benedict Cumberbatch, Damian Lewis, Robert Pattinson, Naomie Harris, Helena Bonham Carter, Jude Law, Sacha Baron Cohen, Gary Oldman, Daniel Radcliffe, Alan Rickman, Emma Thompson, Helen Mirren, Hugh Grant, Paul Bettany, Michael Caine, Christopher Lee, Stephen Fry, Emily Watson, Ray Winstone, Dev Patel, Vanessa Redgrave, Terence Stamp, Roger Moore – to name but a few!
Musicians: David Bowie, Adele, Amy Winehouse, Fleetwood Mac, Dizzee

Rascal, Ed Sheeran, The Kinks, Mumford & Sons, Dusty Springfield, Rod Stewart, Sex Pistols, Status Quo, Queen, Peter Gabriel, The Who – and many more, with apologies to the wealth of remarkable artists excluded.

Others: Barry Norman, David Beckham, Ben Elton, Bruce Forsyth, Charlie Chaplin, Dame Vera Lynn, David Attenborough, David Jason, Jimmy Carr, Claudia Winkleman, Sebastian Coe, Queen Elizabeth II, Henry VIII – et al.

Special mention: Fanny Cradock – the first lady of food (whose husband Johnnie coined the immortal phrase: 'I hope your doughnuts end up looking like Fanny's')

Essential travelling band info

Best live music venues: The Royal Albert Hall; Wembley Arena; Union Chapel, Compton Avenue N1; Barbican, Silk Street EC2

Favourite curry house: Ma Goa, Putney – 82% (one of numerous excellent restaurants)

Favourite pub: Dispensary, Leman Street E1 – 80%

Don't miss: The Royal Opera House, Covent Garden – 90%

Sense of humour/friendly welcome: 41%

Chapter 38
Londonderry (Derry)

'WE'VE HAD A REQUEST FROM an Irish newspaper for the band to meet up and have a photograph taken with the Reverend Ian Paisley… what shall I tell them?' the office PA relayed through the crackling earpiece of my cell phone, briefly delaying preparations to head west out of Belfast during a late-nineties whistle-stop visit to the province.

'Why the hell would he want to meet up with us?' I replied, contemplating rubbing shoulders with the vociferous Democratic Unionist and already having my doubts.

'They seem to think it's a great idea, plus they're willing to do a short interview to give the tour dates a plug!' she mentioned, implying a little extra publicity may help put a few additional bums on any unsold seats.

'Leave it with me for an hour or two; I'll need to okay it with the promoter first. I'll call you back when we get to the hotel,' I signed off, intrigued at the thought of such an odd encounter and scrolling through my cell phone's list of contacts.

'Steer well clear of that gobshite,' tour promoter Michael warned, viciously turning on the dog-collared politician in an abusive tirade and stressing in no uncertain terms that any contact should be avoided at all costs. 'He'll be up to no good, I tell you. The man's a fraud and not even an officially ordained priest; you don't stand to gain anything out of such a scheme!' he blasphemed, ranting into the mouthpiece like a man possessed.

'Mickey… for God's sake, don't blow a fuse; I'll say we're not available and that should put an end to it!' I proposed, eager to nip the conversation in the bud.

'It's a fucking hare-brained idea,' he started up again. 'I'd like to know who came up with it in the first place. That loudmouth's a disgrace to the cloth!'

'*Michael*…! Shut the fuck up; it's not going to happen. Consider the matter dead and buried – forget I ever even mentioned it,' I bawled, reaching boiling point.

'Well, I'm glad that's sorted then. I'll buy you all a pint when I get to the hotel,' he atoned in a sudden change of tack.

****

Dwelling for a while longer on the subject of Ireland's priesthood, again bringing into question the integrity of a small minority of less scrupulous clerics, a particular encounter at the mercy of a corrupt man of the cloth springs immediately to mind. It occurred in the rough and ready town of Strabane, all of fifteen miles south of Londonderry, midway through a mid-eighties tour taking in both sides of the border.

Billed as a fundraising event for an unspecified church-related charity, a bumper evening appeared to be in prospect as, swinging round towards the rear of the building, I caught sight of a 'HOUSE FULL' notice clearly visible by the entrance doors to the ballroom. With the deal based on a high percentage of the door take against a guaranteed fixed sum to cover running costs, as I peeped through the curtains to conduct a rough head-count a satisfactory evening seemed assured.

Refreshed from a post-gig sluice amid a flare-up of popping ring pulls, I sloped off ahead of schedule to the kitchen area for a pre-arranged soirée with the fat friar. Caught flat-footed with a group of henchmen counting out a stack of crumpled banknotes, the shrinking priest's body language spoke volumes.

'Ah yes, I wasn't too sure how long you'd be, young man. I hope you noticed we left some cans of lager in your dressing room,' the padre fudged in an abrasive Ulster tone, handing over a rather lighter brown envelope than I'd imagined, which after a quick skim through I twigged to be no more than the guarantee alone.

'I take it you haven't calculated the percentage figure yet; when were you planning to give me the rest?' I queried, instantly suspicious.

'That's all there is, son – we only just managed to cover the set fee!' he fabricated, shrugging his shoulders and holding his palms face up.

'Obviously maths isn't your strongest subject; the place was heaving out there. What's the point in trying to pull a fast one?' I reasoned, aware I was being taken for a mug and staring him right in the eye.

'Don't try to be clever, son. Perhaps I should remind you our little deal allowed for guests of the sister hotel to enter for free, which made a large dent in the gate receipts,' he fired back, unmoved and lying through his teeth.

'So that would account for around half a dozen,' I argued.

'Two hundred to be exact!' he barefacedly plucked out of thin air, displaying a brazen effrontery belying the cloth.

'*Two fucking hundred…?*' I aggressively responded. 'Do I look like I was born yesterday? The hotel only holds fifty people – you're talking absolute bollocks!'

'Just take it easy, you piece of scum; how dare you question the Father's integrity?' a pudgy lackey burst in, menacingly baring his teeth.

'Keep your nose out of it, Tubs; my agreement was with Rasputin over there, not you!' I snarled, aware I could be treading on dangerous ground, a suspicion which was upheld as the brawny bootlicker made towards me, fists balled up.

'Show some fucking respect,' the man bellowed, 'or I'll…' He was cut off in his prime by a turning Formica-topped table luckily striking him squarely on the knee and sending the bully toppling to the floor clutching at his injured leg.

'That animal should be kept on a lead,' I remonstrated with the preacher, just as the door flew open to reveal a detachment of crew and band members obviously getting wind something may be about to kick off.

'Now, now, boys, there's no need for any trouble; we had precious little time to count the takings – perhaps there could have been a slight miscalculation,' the perjuring priest feigned, grudgingly handing over a second envelope and disappearing in a jiffy, stalked by a scowling, hobbling lapdog bringing up the rear.

****

Last in line at reception, I dilly-dallied briefly to admire the autumnal scenery to the rear of a picturesque riverside hotel situated on the edge of town. A disorganised rabble of green-suited females made hard work of checking in the eight-strong party, dealing confusedly with one customer at a time and degenerating into something of a tangle. As I mulled over the resulting chaos, enjoying a minute's peace, the grind of heavy luggage dragging across the floor killed the moment and I ambled up to the desk. I was grabbing a pen to fill in my details when Rod, fresh from inspecting his room, reappeared at my side.

'Excuse me, I just checked into my room and there's a bit of a problem; do you think you could get someone to take a look at my telly?' the bass man griped, oblivious to the fact his close companion was next up.

'What was that sir? I'm not quite with you. You're supposed to be looking at it *yerself!*' the girl astonishingly replied in a lilting southern tone.

As Rod and I acknowledged one another in total wonderment, I made an effort to speak, but the words wouldn't come, underlined by his inarticulate reaction: 'Did you…? I can't be… that was just… oh, I bloody give up!'

'Talk about ask a stupid question… Now, sir, were you looking to check in – what was the name?' the girl queried, seemingly unruffled.

'B… Bar…' I spluttered, equally dumbfounded, tears welling in my eyes.

Plagued throughout the performance with technical problems due largely to an inadequate sound system, a disappointing evening's work influenced a restless, alcohol-induced night's sleep, rudely interrupted at the unearthly hour of six-thirty by a juddering pneumatic drill, presumably attempting to come through the wall. Squinting at my watch in shock-horror, I hopped out of bed to root through my bag. Retrieving a pair of army issue earplugs kept for such emergencies, I shoved the foam accessories into my lugholes and a further period of fitful shut-eye eventually befell.

Stirring heavy-headedly not long after nine o'clock and slipping quickly into my clothes I made a dash for the last breakfast. Upon reaching the open-plan snack-bar the heavenly whiff of sizzling bacon teased my nostrils, and I prepared to sit at the nearest empty table.

'I'm not sure what it is that you want, but breakfast finished at nine-fifteen,' a gaunt, acne-faced waitress said gormlessly.

'Oh, did it really? Well, we'll see about that,' I bleated crabbily, turning and striding in the direction of the reception desk.

'Sorry to bother you; I don't wish to sound unreasonable but I was awoken by a helluva racket made by a gang of workmen at six-thirty this morning, yet after oversleeping by just eight minutes I've been told that I'm too late for breakfast!' I complained, adding hopefully: 'All I'm asking for is a pot of tea and some toast!'

'Ah well, if you were awake at six-thirty and had taken your breakfast at that time, you could easily have gone back for some more sleep afterwards!' the greying, middle-aged assistant astoundingly replied, knocking me for six.

'Are you for real – did you hear the bloody racket? Is it honestly too much to ask for a pot of tea… please?' I begged.

'Let me remind you, sir, this is a three-star establishment and not a five-star. The cafeteria opens promptly at 11am if you'd care to wait, though should you be desperate there are tea-making facilities in your room,' she quibbled, fobbing me off to attend to a matter far more pressing than a fractious, dissatisfied resident.

Causes célèbres

Amanda Burton – actress (*Silent Witness* et al)
Nadine Coyle – former 'Girls Aloud' performer
Feargal Sharkey – Undertones singer ('A Good Heart' solo No. 1)
Josef Locke – '40s and '50s singing star
Neil Hannon – Divine Comedy vocalist/songwriter
Martin O'Neill – ex Leicester City, Aston Villa and Sunderland manager

Essential travelling band info

Best live music venue: Millennium Forum, Newmarket Street
Favourite curry house: Chilli's, Strand Road – 66%
Favourite pub: Ice Wharf, Strand Road – 43%
Don't miss: The city walls – 72%
Sense of humour: 50%
Friendly welcome: 14%

Chapter 39
Manchester

OUTRAGEOUSLY DUMPED OUT ON THE STREET by virtue of a bigoted B&B landlady taking a dislike to Romeo's skin colour, a post-Christmas visit to Greater Manchester's northern environs began on the sourest of notes. The band and crew were coerced into scampering from pillar to post attempting to find affordable lodgings for an eleven-man party ahead of a five-night stint, effectively to bid farewell to a an arduous albeit trailblazing 1973.

Wowing sell-out, revved-up crowds frolicking beneath the galleried roof of an extravagantly renovated church for much of the week, we were all geared up for an electrifying New Year's Eve finale. Having heeded a request to lead the customary rendition of 'Auld Lang Syne', ably assisted by a traditional Scottish piper scheduled to appear from the wings on the stroke of midnight, the stage seemed set for a glittering crescendo.

Accessed precariously by a narrow winding staircase wholly unsuitable for the band's standard issue 'brothel creepers', the converted bell-tower assigned as the main dressing room posed problems of a different kind. Hemmed in by a corkscrew of coarse exposed-brick walls, there was precious little space to manoeuvre to and from the wings, where yet another hazard awaited in the shape of a nine-inch-wide chasm, requiring a sharp-witted and sure-footed approach to finally make it onto the jutting stage platform.

Roughly forty-five minutes shy of the bewitching hour, we cut loose with a back-to-back blitz of rocked-up fifties covers and a colony of penguin-suited worshippers swept out onto the dance floor, throwing caution to the wind in a blaze of unbridled exuberance led by a glinting array of easy-on-the-eye bling-bling soulmates. Spotting an Afro-permed man gesturing from the stage's brow and acknowledging with a thumbs-up, I stretched out the song in progress with a spot of ad-libbing and one eye on the clock as the big countdown drew ever closer.

'In just sixty seconds' time, it's out with the old and in with the new; is everybody ready?' I yelled to a resounding cheer, before making way amidst a surge in excitement to a radio broadcast 'live' from Big Ben pumped relentlessly through the overworked PA system.

'Ten... nine... eight... seven...' the crowd roared, overwhelmed by the clanging chimes tolling from the nation's capital, permeating the joyful room.

'*Happy New Year, Manchester!*' I hollered, cueing the arrival of an immaculately clad kilted piper bellowing out the annual send-off's opening bars highlighted by a blinding Super Trouper picking him out to stage right. The soloist had taken just two paces forward when, evidently unsighted by the inflated windbag attached to his chest, his spindly legs calamitously plummeted into the crevice, ripping his uncovered knees to shreds amid a gore of torn skin and blood, serenaded by a disharmonious skirl simulating a clutter of stray cats at nightfall.

As he slumped on the edge of the stage receiving emergency treatment from a female member of staff, family jewels exposed to the arm-linked throng of onlookers intent on fulfilling the annual ritual, the pitiful sight of the bruised and bloodied Scot rendered the band helpless. The anthem's dwindling refrain cruelly descended into farce, bidding farewell to an extraordinary year with a deafening honk and painful clatter.

****

In defiance of a volley of social network notices posted during 2007's nostalgic 'Once in a Lifetime' arena tour, mostly suggesting the opposite, I feel I should at last set the record straight in stating unreservedly that I never at any time bore any resentment whatsoever towards American entertainers 'The Osmonds'.

'How in tarnation did you manage to rub those guys up the wrong way? They wouldn't normally say boo to a goose... well, not to your face, anyway,' howled an agent pal upon getting wind of an altercation that had kicked off midway into the ten-day run.

'You may well ask, but in truth the whole episode's been blown out of all proportion; in fact, it was more akin to a lovers' tiff!' I clarified.

Putting aside the fixated smiles and squeaky-clean image (not to mention the irritating seventies smash hit 'Long Haired Lover from Liverpool' by *enfant terrible* Little Jimmy Osmond), the Mormon boys' finely honed, albeit cheesy, vaudevillian flair resonated with a global audience through a handful of massive-selling singles between 1972 and 1975, and saw them content to unashamedly trade on past glories some three decades later.

Coming off the back of surviving on measly rations in the Australian outback as a participant in the prime-time TV reality show *I'm A Celebrity Get Me Out of Here*, the not-so-'Little' Jimmy was basking in a rekindled flicker of the limelight; and he and his band of portly siblings (at one time a seven-piece but stripped back to a trio) breezed in on a new high, jetting in from across the pond pumped up and ready to roll back the years.

Fresh from a zappy, crowd-pleasing opening set of our own, I was downing a well-earned bevvy in the multipurpose catering area when the unmistakeably pulsating rhythms to 'Crazy Horses' echoed out into the arena. Keen to check out the Utah boys 'live', I sprinted to the wings to catch sight of the beaming trio indulging in a neatly choreographed step-over routine, discouragingly mouthing the tune's lyrics badly out of synch with a full-playback rehash of the original recording. Even more mystifyingly, they were 'accompanied' by a band of glum-faced dummies doing little more than going through the motions.

Wholly unimpressed by the lifeless mock-up, and reinforced by a justifiably subdued audience reaction, I reported back to SWW's website guru, Paul. The result was that a less than gratifying account of the spurious charade found its way into cyberspace, essentially to allow fans an exclusive insight into the day-to-day rigours of life on the road, but provoking an unseen spate of Chinese whispers as to rumblings of disharmony within the touring company.

'The stage is all yours if you want an early run-through,' briefed sound man Chris upon the band's arrival at Manchester's MEN Arena (currently known as the Phones 4U Arena) the following day. Intimating the Americans' allotted slot remained unfulfilled, verified by an unsurprising dearth of grinning Cheshire cats anywhere near the building, he added, 'That's by far the easiest soundcheck I've ever been party to – it was just a matter of making sure everything was cool with the minidisc player!'

The engineer's light-hearted dig was cut short by my cell phone's warbling signature tune. 'Dave, I'm bloody furious. I've been negotiating for months to bring Jimmy and the guys over from the States, and what happens? You go spouting your mouth off unfairly criticising them on your band's website for every Tom, Dick and Harry to see!' griped the tour's promoter, getting rather hot under the collar.

'It wasn't unfair criticism; I saw the sham of a spectacle with my own eyes from the wings. Besides, any comments I made were posted for our own fans to read. Who the hell's been telling tales out of school anyway?' I asked in a huff.

'Jimmy, that's who – he spends all his time on the tour bus surfing the web and took a look at your site; he's not best pleased I can tell you. I want you to clear the air and apologise to him before tonight's gig,' the taskmaster insisted.

'Why should I? It's none of his business what I wrote,' I grouched defiantly. 'I meant every word; I hate seeing artists who don't give a shit about their audiences!'

'Look, you know how sensitive some performers can be, especially the Yanks. Get it sorted or we could have a problem,' he ordered bossily, cutting me straight off.

Locating the surviving siblings' dressing room through a winding labyrinth of backstage corridors, I tapped apprehensively at the door. A strained atmosphere pervaded the room, deepened by spokesman Jimmy's refusal to acknowledge an offered mitt.

'Isn't this all a bit over-the-top? I'm just an old rocker who's never used playback – I hate it; plus, I thought you guys could do it live, so what's the point? "Crazy Horses" alone would be a hundred times more exciting played live!' I bandied, cutting to the chase.

'Surely you can see we're missing some key members? The band's been plagued with bad luck and illness recently but the last thing we wanted to do was let the fans down. You guys know how it works, so why would you want to go saying nasty things about us?' Jimmy reasoned a trifle oversensitively.

'What's with the "nastiness"? All I said was you weren't playing live; I was as disappointed as some of the fans. I was just being honest!' I countered.

'Well, there's no way we'd say any hateful things about your band on our site!' he maintained with a hint of backhandedness.

'What more can I say? It certainly wasn't my intention to upset anyone; if I've caused any offence I'm truly sorry,' I upheld. 'What say we just drop the matter and move on – after all, there's another week's touring to complete!'

With that, I found myself smothered in a lovey-dovey three-way man-hug, out of which I came unscathed and strode back purposefully through the echoing passageway, yearning to be a fly on the wall.

****

Conceitedly referred to as the 'Second City' or 'Capital of the North' by native upstarts, twenty-first-century Manchester paints a vastly different picture to its unstable 1970s equivalent, embodied in a purlieu of modernistic glitzy architecture and new-fangled trappings becoming of a go-ahead, thriving economic centre.

Amid a fall into decline attributed primarily to the ailing textile and cotton industries and subsequent closure of the forsaken dockyards, the blunted city's long-standing reputation for nightlife prospered regardless. The kudos of the most fashionable 'discotheque' of the day belonged to the nightclub 'Millionaires', renowned for playing host to the area's elite who were regularly seen rubbing shoulders with a sprinkling of northern celebrities.

In the city for a sell-out performance at the Apollo Theatre during the build-up to 1978's silly season and on cloud nine following an ego-massaging reception, we were afforded a VIP invitation to unwind at the notorious club. Jumping full of beans into two cabs, a small contingent of band members headed out for a night on the town.

We were received by the venue's condescending manager and escorted to a roped-off area. Rudely snapping his fingers, the overseer beckoned a pair of gum-chewing waitresses, allotted the task of catering to our every whim.

'You see where the queue of young ladies is on the far side of the room? That's Rod Stewart and his entourage; he's also been performing in town!' the weasel boasted.

'Perhaps we should go over and say hello – I met his mate Ronnie from the Faces not long ago and he was a smashing bloke,' I propositioned.

'That makes perfect sense; give me a minute and I'll pop across and make sure it's okay,' he replied. The official minced across the tartan-patterned carpet before returning to sheepishly report, 'I'm afraid Mr Stewart is busy,' implying the crooner may be otherwise engaged.

'You mean to say he's cold-shouldering us, is that it?' I sussed, relaying the message to the boys above the incessant din.

'He doesn't look very busy to me; he's just sat there on his fat arse trying to play it cool,' Geoff vilified, invoking a salvo of stinging comments from the remainder of the gang as we slunk back to our own secluded hideaway.

Suddenly, thanks to a subtle hint dropped in passing by the wheedling toady, we began attracting oodles of attention from the opposite end of the room. Unsettled by a total lack of TLC from the hoarse whisperer and deciding to cramp his style in an unforeseen moment of reprisal, a bevy of mini-skirted beauties flocked to the more cordial confines of the 'Wads' zone, shunning the standoffish pantomime in favour of a more festive approach across the way.

'He only likes blonde bimbos anyway!' commented a stunning brunette in a thick Lancashire accent, delighted to be granted entry.

'Maybe we caught him on a bad night,' I rationalised as, flanked by a small body of henchmen, the wizened rocker flounced across the club's upper tier, not about to be upstaged and heading largely unnoticed to the exit.

'Well, I don't think he's fucking sexy!' Geoff rapped, taking a dig at the hit-maker's recent chart-topper, dismissively slugging back a drop of the hard stuff and jigging from side to side – coincidentally to the rhythms of the hit tune 'Hey Fatty Bum-Bum'.

Causes célèbres (abridged)

Albert Finney – actor
Oasis – rock band
Danny Boyle – film and Olympic opening ceremony director
Steve Coogan – actor

Mike Leigh – film director
John Thaw – late great actor
Karl Pilkington – *An Idiot Abroad*
Sarah Harding – 'Girls Aloud'
Bill Tarmey – *Coronation Street* legend
Victoria Wood – comedienne
The Smiths – influential rock band
Caroline Aherne – Mrs Merton/Royle Family actress
Happy Mondays – '80s band
Les Dawson – legendary comedian
Russell Watson – singer
10CC – '70s band
Martin Lewis – TV news presenter
Baron Norman Foster – Britain's most celebrated architect
The Hollies – '60s hit-makers

Essential travelling band info

Favourite live music venue: MENA, Victoria Station
Favourite curry house: Coriander, Chorlton-cum-Hardy – 79%
Favourite pub: Marble Arch, Rochdale Road – 83%
Don't miss: National Football Museum, Cathedral Gardens – 77%
Sense of humour/friendly welcome: 42%

Chapter 40
Newcastle upon Tyne

'*YOUR SONS AND YOUR DAUGHTERS are beyond your command,*' forewarned Bob Dylan in the prophetic sixties folk song 'The Times They Are a-Changin'', doubtless inspired by an escalation in permissive attitudes that flew in the face of authoritarian parents trapped in a time loop born of outmoded formalities and military service.

Turning a deaf ear to the sentiments of the visionary tunesmith, even a decade later the granite-hard traditions of Britain's northern counties remained as staunch as ever. Born out of a generation of maturing 'war babies' built of the same pious stiff-upper-lipped stuff, they remained impervious to ephemeral hare-brained ideas and irreverent behaviour, whilst often finding themselves offhandedly dismissed as sadly out of touch by a burgeoning so-called tolerant society.

Pigeonholed unjustly under 'fast and loose', the band often bore the brunt of the narrow-minded prejudice prevalent amongst a breed of spiteful private hoteliers hell-bent on doing away with 'bimbos' invitated for a late-night soirée, stymieing in the process the fringe benefits associated with a rock-'n'-roll lifestyle. Not to be outdone, a sense of cunning infused the ranks, paving the way to a mixed bag of Machiavellian ruses and ploys designed to outsmart the killjoys, and smuggle members of the opposite sex onto the premises.

****

Revelling in the plaudits earned from a rewarding headlining debut at the Newcastle City Hall on a bitter night in '75 and stalked all the way back to a modest hostelry off the beaten track by a carload of teenage girls, a formidable adversary lay in wait taking the form of a finicky twenty-stone-plus Asian hotelier.

'Will you gentlemen be requiring a late bar service when you arrive back from your evening's work?' the scheming titan had fawned earlier, playing up to the sizeable gathering preparing to depart and intent on making a quick killing upon our return.

'I think we'd better give that a miss, mate – we can't afford rip-off hotel prices,' Geoff swiped, declining the offer on the band's behalf. The refusal immediately aroused the suspicions of the testy owner totting up the cost of an unexpected rebuff, yet patently aware of a lurking ulterior motive.

Specifying a list of beverages tantamount to a brewery inventory (in addition to a half-dozen pages of technical jargon), an addendum tagged the contract rider provided ample means for a post-gig piss-up, shipped back surreptitiously in the boot of tour manager Tony's car to a designated hotel room. There, out of range of the prying eyes of any on-duty party-poopers, the recuperative effects of a wee dram could be savoured in private. Such ruses were known on the odd occasion to unfold into an insidious battle of wits; but the oppressive 'Genghis Khan personified' presented a tougher than usual proposition, equipped as he was with X-ray vision supported by an uncanny sixth sense. A deviously thought-out plan would be necessary even to contemplate outfoxing such an obsessive control freak.

Boxing clever, we dropped Trevor and Rod a short distance from the hotel's entrance, their assignment being to sidetrack the big chief before sneaking off to unlatch the rear fire-doors which backed onto a makeshift car-park. Meanwhile, the four remaining band members – hotly pursued by the rotting totty-mobile – bumped warily onto the muddy wasteland, taking pains not to arouse suspicion by keeping the clatter to a minimum.

As we meandered across the mini-wilderness, careful to sidestep a formation of puddles and ever anxious the decoys would cut us some slack and throw the man-mountain off the scent, I squinted to survey the building's rear walls. In the splash of light reflected from the massed banks of symmetrical windows, not one but two alternative entry points looked to be in use, situated to either end of a potholed loading bay. One was perched atop a sturdy wrought iron staircase, while the other was reached by a rusty, precarious-looking spiralling framework.

'It doesn't look as if that rickety thing at the far end's been used in years. Surely this one here's the main emergency route?' I figured out.

'I don't think they've had a chance to open it yet,' Geoff sighed.

'I reckon both entrances are still bolted,' Romeo observed.

'That sadistic bastard must've caught them in the act,' Geoff speculated, needlessly shushing the girls as Tony's whining Datsun screeched onto the rutted earth like a thing possessed, threatening to blow everyone's cover and sliding to a halt in a hail of grime and sludge, much to the consternation of the cringing onlookers.

As we tiptoed up the tinny staircase like a mischief of mice, a minute shaft of light leaking out onto the top landing intimated that, as planned, the exit door had indeed been left slightly ajar, giving just cause for optimism.

I briefly observed a breathless Tony blundering up the steps laden with two chock-full brown paper bags of booze retrieved from his illicit stash, before coming a cropper halfway up the metallic flight, on account of the bottom dropping out of one of the Man Friday's carriers. The calamitous clatter of breaking glass echoed into the distance like an audacious smash and grab, rendering the started interlopers motionless.

'Hush a little while longer… It seems as if we may have got away with it; maybe the big boss-man's unconscious in his snore-bag!' I pondered after an eternity, breaking the deafening silence.

Ignoring me at his peril, the overeager Geoff impetuously shoved and kicked at the wood planted firmly in the hole. 'It won't budge a bloody inch! There's a smell of brick dust; I reckon there may be some cement bags or a pile of builder's shit blocking the way,' the bassist surmised, failing hopelessly to dislodge the unyielding portal.

'Here, let me give it a go,' I bade, playing the human battering-ram and charging shoulder-first at the entrance. As I did so, the door suddenly flew open and I catapulted head over heels, coming to rest at the feet of the humongous proprietor.

'What in the name of Allah is going on here?' the big unfriendly giant boomed. Receiving nothing in the way of a credible response he continued: 'It would appear, gentlemen, you are attempting to smuggle alcohol onto my premises. Of course it goes without saying I will have to charge you corkage. Then there's the little matter of your lady friends who to my knowledge haven't yet registered as guests!' the ogre implied, wearing a smug, gloating leer.

'We're nay checking in, man; we've just come along to get our souvenirs signed!' a cute Geordie voice perked up.

'I'm afraid all non-residents are barred from entering the premises after licensing hours, so should you set foot inside I will be left no choice but to apply the double-room rate!' the avaricious hulk shot back.

'Ah well, I suppose we should be making tracks, 'cause two of us have school in the morning,' the leader of the pack unveiled.

'School…? B-b-but you said you were nineteen!' exclaimed Geoff in horror.

'Perhaps I was exaggerating a little, but we will be in three years,' the brunette giggled, finally knuckling under.

'Oh well, it looks as if that's that,' I denounced, ready to give up the ghost, attempting to squeeze past the fat controller's portly stomach.

'Jailbait – let's just sign their posters and let them be on their way; they're not even old enough to drive!' pronounced Romeo, eyeing up the unroadworthy rattletrap littering up the unimpressive surrounds.

'I'll have you know I'm just turned seventeen. My dad bought me that little runabout over there for me birthday; I'm driving it legally on a provisional driving licence!' the matriarch of the tribe boldly pointed out.

'But you're not supposed to drive without… oh, never mind,' I harped on.

Out of nowhere, Rod's tiny head popped to one side of the host's midriff, comically eclipsed in the doorway by the man's mountainous frame. 'I've been hanging around for bloody ages at the other door; mind you it looks as if the plan's gone tits up anyway!' the freckly member lamented.

'What the hell happened to that fucking selfish accomplice of yours?' I threw in nastily, alluding to the missing Trevor.

'Him? You don't want to know; maybe I'll tell you later!' Rod fumed.

We stood watching as the female foursome clanked down the staircase and scrambled into the jalopy, blowing a flurry of kisses through the wound-down windows whilst the car skidded haphazardly over the uneven surface and disappeared in a billow of mud and gravel.

'Now then, gentlemen, if you'd care to follow me to the reception desk there is the small matter of the corkage to be settled!' proclaimed the hotelier, studying the boys' crestfallen body language and rubbing salt into the wounds.

'What? You're taking the piss!' Romeo griped despairingly.

'Fuck him, he's dreaming; if we get a move on we can get a late one at that shithole just up the road,' Geoff rapped, paying little heed to the tightwad's request and stomping towards the sliding doors in haste.

'I tell you what, you money-grabbing git, you can keep the lot for your trouble… Oh and, by the way, don't forget to clean up the broken glass on the fire escape – we wouldn't want any health and safety officers prowling around in the morning… now would we?' I sardonically hinted, eyeing the priggish owner clutching remorsefully onto the remaining carrier bag, before scurrying out of the lobby in pursuit of the gang.

'Well, that ingenious plot literally backfired,' commented Geoff, reflecting upon the evening's events in the seedy joint while clearing away a handful of used glasses to make space for a tray of lagers provided courtesy of an overgenerous Rod.

'This'll piss you all off big time: not long after you dropped us off, an old Vauxhall drew up and pulled right outside of the hotel reception… Guess who waltzed straight inside and up to his room with the ugly bird driving it?' Rod snitched.

'*Trevor!*' denounced a pack of howling wolves in unison, lent support by a line of shaking heads choreographed in utter disbelief.

****

Based within spitting distance of the Geordie metropolis of Newcastle and initially saddled with the absurd handle of *SAS Artistes* (a far cry from the crack unit cited in the Hereford chapter), a team of beyond-their-depths agents assumed control of the band's affairs from 1973 onwards. Alarmingly, they were found wanting in most matters relating to actually managing a bunch of musicians whose ambitions lay way beyond the northern club circuit, a situation which culminated in the appointment of a likeable straight-talking Ulsterman known as Les McSheffery.

Au fait with the basic mechanics of the music industry and sharing a vision extending way beyond a full calendar of UK performances, the gritty Irishman fought his protégés' corner against a domineering organisation, steadfastly maintaining that a policy of endless touring, albeit profitable, would only result in one thing: burnout. He insisted that the band were far too readily available, and advised his hard-to-please employers to think again.

'I told them to take a listen to some of the material from the forthcoming album;* how many artists are blessed with an awesome live show on top of a songwriting ability to rival anyone around at the moment? There's a ready-made worldwide audience out there waiting to hear this stuff!' the Svengali complimented, touching upon a work in progress that veered away from a winning formula of reworking versions of Eddie Cochran's 'Three Steps To Heaven' and Buddy Holly's 'Heartbeat' which, despite shifting shedloads of copies, had failed to stir the affections of music journalists or the media alike.

Upping the ante with the release of an appetizer from the soon-to-follow *pièce de résistance*, in the form of an infectious self-penned effort entitled 'Heavenly', a rising tide of optimism spread throughout the camp, lent support by a selection of high-profile DJs enthusing over the radio-friendly single's hypnotic rhythm and strident acoustic guitars, endorsed as: '*Back to their exuberant best!*' by a well-known weekly rock and pop journal.

It raised our spirits tremendously, with bandied predictions pointing toward an ego-boosting chart-topper whilst also spelling out good things for the eclectic mix of tunes comprising the newly completed masterwork. Hopes ran at an all-time high, sustained by an exciting albeit hectic schedule on the horizon ahead of a cooling-off period to top up our tans and get the creative juices flowing. Little could we have predicted, however, that an enormous gaffe by the overweening Les was set to cost both the man himself and the band he represented dearly.

---

* *Trocadero*, released in 1976

****

With the single making a surprising showing in the chart's nether regions purely on the strength of just two days' sales and with optimism justifiably running high, the promotional wheels of a major label ground into motion. No stone was left unturned in ensuring the record's success, backed up by regular airplay on the nation's most listened-to radio stations.

'We've got *TOTP* – the record's a cert to go top ten next week!' whooped the jubilant company rep, virtually guaranteeing a sure-fire smash should the band impress on the BBC's influential Thursday countdown broadcast to millions of music fans.

'I'm afraid the boys aren't available; they're due to fly out to Brussels to take part in the country's National Lottery TV show. There's always next week!' Les replied complacently, spurning the gilt-edged invitation in an astonishing move. It was one that would come back to bite the whole shebang on the bum as the single disastrously plummeted two places on the following week's chart, subsequently killing off all hopes of a prestigious slot on the prime-time show and putting paid to a potentially huge-selling top ten record.

Having scrutinised Les's every move for some time and seizing upon the fatal error of judgement to remove the uncompromising, bungling Svengali from his tenure in one fell swoop, an *ad hoc* meeting of the powers that be saw the Ulsterman relieved of his duties with immediate effect, rashly neglecting to consult a single band-member prior to wielding the axe.

'What kind of idiot wants to work for a fucking organisation called *Spot a Star* anyway?' barked a truculent Les as he relayed the disquieting news, as ever seeing the funny side in what was sadly to be our final conversation prior to the Irishman's untimely death as a result of a tragic boating accident out at sea off the Spanish coast.

'You're taking the piss! SAS stands for spot a bloody star?' I responded, catching flies. 'No wonder they wanted to keep that one under wraps!' Thanking the man for his sterling efforts on the band's behalf, I pledged an unfulfilled promise to keep in touch.

Locked into a watertight agreement until 1983, the hard-earned lessons of a ten-year pact led to a speedy parting of the ways once our obligations to the agency were fulfilled. Overwhelmingly the band members decided it was in our own best interests to ditch the renamed SAS and go it alone, culminating in the formation of a thriving, hands-on enterprise still up and running to this day.

Causes célèbres

Lindisfarne – Geordie band ('Fog on the Tyne'etc.)
Cheryl Cole – *X Factor* judge et al
Jack Douglas – comedy actor
Ant and Dec – TV presenters
The Animals – legendary '60s band
Sting – Police frontman and solo star
Hank Marvin – Shadows guitar legend
Alan Shearer – ex England football star/TV pundit
Miriam Stoppard – agony aunt/TV doctor

Essential travelling band info

Favourite live music venue: Newcastle City Hall, Northumberland Road
Favourite curry house: Solomons, Denton Road – 79%
Favourite pub: Pleased to Meet You, High Bridge – 82%
Don't miss: The Quayside, the place to be by night – 70%
Sense of humour/friendly welcome – 80%

Chapter 41
Newport

BASKING IN THE SOLITUDE OF an anomalous nature reserve known as the Wetlands on the edge of the reviled Welsh town of Newport and fascinatedly poring over an ambit of unfettered winged creatures, the region's reputation for disused mines and unsightly slagheaps seemed all of a million miles away, replaced by a panoramic expanse of green-belt land gently rolling towards the nearby Vale of Usk.

Awarded city status as recently as 2002, the town's unremarkable central streets appeared deserted as I pulled up outside the dingy railway station. I was there to pick up a session pianist who, having missed his connection from London and subsequently been delayed three hours, bundled grumpily into the car for the twenty-five-mile trek to Monnow Valley studios in deepest darkest Monmouthshire for an intensive period of recording.

Home to a striking number of musicians per head of population attributed to an uninterrupted sweep of undulating hills and hollows, the Gwent countryside consequently plays host to a pick-'n'-mix of high-tech studio facilities. Transformed at no little expense from a wide-ranging rubble of neglected farm buildings, they attract scores of esteemed artists seeking inspiration from the unique isolation, many holing up for months on end in the thick of a malodorous essence of arable crops and livestock manure.

Such establishments are also, of course, a dwelling place for the endangered lesser-spotted audio engineer, renowned for indulging in long-drawn-out periods of sleepless activity and easily distinguishable by a cadaverous physique and hollow-eyed ghostlike pigmentation commonly referred to as a studio tan. Most of the band's creative assignments from 1977 onwards evolved in the company of one such specimen, namely close friend John Acock, whose tireless efforts through ninety percent of SWW's sessions for close on a decade came blessed with an uncanny, ultra-placid temperament as he laboured diligently way beyond the call of duty, imperturbably continuing about his business seemingly immune to all manner of outrageous distractions.

Unsettling alcohol-induced brawls straying rather too close to the sound-desk, young fillies in a state of undress unashamedly displaying their assets for every-man-jack to see, aromatic feasts shipped in from the local curry house soon magnified by malodorous after-effects, sex toys placed on the mixing console, bunfights involving items of fruit (and, in one instance, a session-halting fresh farm egg) and a host of other childish pranks are all dismissed with an impassive shrug of the shoulders by a uniquely unflappable model professional.

'It was all water off a duck's back to me... Mind you, I wasn't too pleased when I laid my hand on a certain someone's pecker placed over the talkback button a few years ago,' the iceman reflected during a late-night conversation, referring to a distasteful piece of tomfoolery, before frowning deeply and proceeding to unveil the details of a nightmare experience at the hands of the Bee Gees' frontman Barry Gibb.

'He was really difficult to work with – he'd spit his dummy out at the drop of a hat!' a strangely out-of-character John diplomatically disclosed, pressed into unravelling the full unabridged account of the moment his staunch resolve finally cracked. 'I hated every minute of that session; he was such a know-it-all, I was permanently on edge!' the hapless engineer explained, criticising the hirsute Gibb brother's unbuttoned, macho dress-sense along with an egocentric lack of tolerance. 'He was trying to lay down a vocal track and was in the foulest of moods. A line in the song included the word "hypnotise", which came out sounding like "*hyp-m-otise*", so I thought I'd better subtly give it a mention,' John recalled.

'What, and he didn't like you pulling him up?' I pried.

'You can say that again; he flew right off the handle, screaming and shouting like a spoilt brat, telling me I should keep my effing nose out!' he enlightened.

'Did he do a retake?' I probed.

'No, he sacked me there and then on the spot. The thing is, I made a point of listening to the track's final mix a few months later and the bearded wanker was still singing *hypmotised*!' the usually mild-mannered engineer badmouthed.

Commissioned to record a moderately successful Christmas single written exclusively for the GAS (Germany, Austria & Switzerland) territories in 1998, the band jetted over for a three-day session to the Swiss city of Lucerne. Rolling back the years in a gladsome reunion, the ever-meticulous John once again proved his worth, sprinkling his unique brand of fairy dust onto a run-of-the-mill yuletide ditty, sadly working with the band for the final time.

****

Booked for a run of four consecutive early-nineties dates at a remote bread-

and-butter cabaret club situated ten miles to the north east of Newport, a master plan to return to base following each performance quickly hit the skids, scuppered by an unexpected onslaught of heavy snow creating treacherous nationwide road conditions. The Friday-night show had to be abandoned entirely, much to the disappointment of a flood of coach parties unable to make the trip from a breadth of upcountry locations.

Left little option other than to bed down in a terrace of grubby chalets lying adjacent to the ice-bound car park as news leaked out of the gig's cancellation, the seedy unheated confines bore more resemblance to a primitive cellblock than a motel, equipped with two exposed single mattresses, a grimy washbasin and an ill-fitting wardrobe, but worst of all devoid of any form of central heating to stifle the perishing outside temperatures.

Catching the club's caretaker in the act of locking up the premises, I blagged an electric fire from a lone store-cupboard. As I switched on the appliance, a mini-explosion plunged the entire wing into darkness, affirmed by a storm of abusive catcalls penetrating the paper-thin walls from the shivering, wrathful bedfellows overloading the grid with their own devices.

'It's fucking freezing in my room; how's about finding a pub in town with a roaring log fire?' a voice echoed in the doorway, as a heavily wrapped-up Geoff extended an invitation way too good to pass up.

Trudging the three quarters of a mile to the charming little town, an air of congeniality filled the mesh of streets and alleyways as locals in a similar boat traipsed to and from a multifarious overabundance of drinking establishments in need of a reinvigorating flagon of winter warmer and a friendly confab.

Chancing our arm by descending upon a side-street pub hopeful of a nightcap as the nearby church clock chimed eleven, an unexpectedly hearty welcome awaited, afforded by a mid-thirties muscular landlord abetted by a rogue's gallery of musicians and personnel primarily in employment at the club, making the most of a serendipitous weekend get-together far removed from the humdrum nightly grind.

'Hey, it's the top-of-the-bill boys! Why don't you pull up a chair and join us, lads?' beckoned plummy emcee Roddy, rearranging the furniture along with his pals to accommodate the illustrious duck-out-of-water gatecrashers.

'We'd love to, but have you seen the time? It's already past closing!' I stated a trifle naively, setting in motion a jangle of rapturous laughter.

'We never call time in this place boyo… it's far too dangerous,' the barman interjected, smiling broadly from ear to ear.

'Really, why's that?' I posed, a little intrigued.

'I used to be the Welsh middleweight ABA boxing champion and every time I hear a bell I kick off – there's no stopping me boyo!' the bruiser joked, raising up his fists and dancing on the spot to the delight of the captive audience, sparking a rambunctious session stretching well into the night packed with a compendium of ribald tales.

'Have you ever worked with Greg Lake? I used to be friends with his ex-roadie, Ralph,' the in-house band's pianist gushed. Winding back the clock to the halcyon days of a topsy-turvy career, he claimed to have rubbed shoulders with the ELP vocalist and bass player extraordinaire prior to his sidekick's unanticipated dismissal.

'Not really our field, though I used to be a big fan in my youth; Keith Emerson was an incredible performer,' I eulogised, lending an ear along with the gang as the chaperone's extraordinary story began to take shape.

Dubbed the original 'supergroup' and regarded by many music fans as the architects of progressive rock, Emerson, Lake and Palmer's trademark classical-influenced style resonated with a global audience amounting to mega-millions, taking the band to a spectrum of far-flung destinations. They were buttressed by an entourage rivalling that of a military machine, rumoured to include a priest, caterers, translators, medics, masseurs et al, in addition to a multitudinous sound and lighting crew, and incorporating an elite minority of manservants designated the task of catering to the headlining threesome's every whim.

Earning the respect of a number of musicians throughout a decade or more of extensive touring, likeable rogue Ralph knew the ropes well. Working with an impressive roster of big names and landing a plum job with one of the world's most prominent bands, he figured that, with his foot in the door, the good times had finally arrived.

During a gruelling schedule of worldwide dates, handed a considerable monthly budget to purchase multiple packs of assorted bass and acoustic guitar strings likely to amount to thousands of pounds, Ralph devised a sneaky get-rich-quick scheme guaranteed to deceive even his taskmasters' finely tuned ears, utilising a primitive method of recycling cooked up by hard-up musicians aplenty to save precious pennies. Brushing aside the bosses' orders to replenish each instrument with a glinting new set of strings prior to every performance, the conniving Ralph opted to steam-clean every last batch, figuring changing the little beauties at alternate gigs would go unnoticed, thus allowing him to pocket the difference.

Acquiring a porter's trolley the morning after the curtain-raiser and stashing Greg's prized collection of guitars safely in the confines of the hotel room, Ralph set out his stall by double-locking the door and pouring boiling water from an electric kettle into the bathroom sink before removing the used strings from the previous night's gig with the utmost care and carefully poaching the nickel-wound steel. Upon close inspection the age-old trick appeared to have worked wonders, and thumping the air the smug dogsbody meticulously restrung each instrument with a good-as-new set, adding the finishing touch by polishing the fret-board with a well-known product to give the strings an ultra-clean, smooth-as-silk feel.

Cheered by the potentially astute piece of profiteering, he fraternised briefly with a group of riggers in the vast echoing auditorium and gave directions to a brace of lackeys wheeling in the flight-cased instruments before swaggering behind to the double doors marked 'MR LAKE', where the self-satisfied Ralph settled methodically into the process of suspending each buffed-up guitar onto its own individual stand. Stepping back, he admired his slick handiwork confident everything was in order and headed straight to the catering wing to feed his face.

Chauffeured in by limousine all geared up for a rigorous pre-gig workout, the headlining band were ushered by a body of security staff to the privacy of their personalised dressing rooms. After running up and down a series of vocal arpeggios in quick succession, eager to flex his fingers the contented Greg drew up a chair and reached for his favourite bass.

On tenterhooks in the adjoining room with the door ajar, Ralph waited anxiously for the virtuoso to begin his warm-up routine. As he picked up the first instrument and thumbed a solitary bottom E note, a deafening silence ensued.

'*R-a-a-a-alph!* These fucking strings haven't been changed!' the ex-King Crimson man thundered, shaking the walls in summoning the lily-livered scammer who, fearing the worst, knew the game may be well and truly up.

'B… b… but I did it an hour ago!' the jabbering lackey faltered.

'Never mind the bullshit; get them done in double quick time – and when you've finished, book a flight back to London!' the sharp-eared musician asserted, shattering the trickster's illusions of a healthy windfall in a single resonant thrum, whilst also putting paid to a vocation most technicians could only dream about.

****

Slipping and sliding through the glacial conditions on our way back from the pub like misdirected Eskimos teetering between igloos, we eventually espied the row of weatherbeaten shacks standing forlorn in the distance. Reaching them at the second attempt by hurdling over the roadside fence, cushioned by the anaesthetising effects of the alcohol, we bade one another goodnight.

As I unlocked the chalet door in a fuddled haze, the fetid stench of unwashed socks and fouled linen permeated my icy nostrils. I put it down to the room's recent lack of use and thought little of it before collapsing onto the bed.

Some thirty minutes later I awoke, shaking like a leaf, and climbed beneath the sullied sheets still fully clothed. Upon closing my eyes I sensed a presence in the room, as a confusing sow-like snuffle fluttered within earshot. Figuring it to be one of the guys out cold in an adjoining hovel, the sound served as little more than a temporary distraction prior to my passing out again.

I came to with a pounding headache intensified by a sudden burst of sunlight streaming through the unlined curtains. Unnerved by a foul smell wafting from beneath the mattress I leapt out of bed to investigate, lifting up the valance in trepidation. A badly scuffed pair of leather boots stuck out from under the bed, attached to the body of an unhealthy-sounding intruder bedevilled by a vicious chesty cough.

'Who's there? Is this a wind-up?' I gasped, reaching for my coat and backing up against the door, looking on aghast as a flea-bitten individual shuffled from his refuge.

'Surely you wouldn't expect me to sleep outside in this bloody awful weather? Give me the price of a cup of tea and maybe something to eat and I'll be on my way without another word!' the stinking vagabond spluttered, staggering to his feet and releasing yet another guttural, retching bark from the back of his throat.

'How the hell did you get in?' I asked, completely baffled. 'I checked all the windows and locked the door securely before I went out!'

'Never you mind, laddie; but don't worry, I won't be bothering you again,' the crafty hobo pledged, snatching the fiver retrieved from my jeans pocket out of my hand and lumbering unsteadily into the snowbound yard.

'Who was that you were talking to…? Do you fancy a walk into town?' asked Rod, appearing in the doorframe, nose twitching.

'Oh, just some old-age traveller. I take it you're hungry; shall we head for the café on the main street – I could murder a bacon sandwich!' I suggested.

'Good idea… Mind you, I think we desperately need to find a chemist before we do anything else!' the bass player retorted.

'Why's that – have you picked up a dose of scabies from last night's bedding?' I jested, scratching at my neck in sympathy.

'No… we urgently need to buy you some bloody deodorant!' my pal fired back, screwing up his nose in utter disgust.

Causes célèbres

Johnny Morris – legendary *Animal Magic* TV presenter
Leslie Thomas – author
Michael Sheen – actor
Joe Strummer – The Clash frontman
Grant Nicholas – Feeder frontman
Nicky Wire – Manic Street Preachers bass player
David Davies – Tory MP
Tony Pulis – current manager Crystal Palace FC
Darren Campbell – athlete

Essential travelling band info

Best live music venue: The Riverfront, Kingsway
Favourite curry house: Delhi, Caerleon Road – 55%
Favourite pub: Lamb, Bridge Street – 71%
Don't miss: National Roman Legion Museum, High Street, Caerleon – 71%
Sense of humour/friendly welcome: 47%

Chapter 42
Newry

GAZING OUT ONTO THE MEAN streets of the valley township of Newry from the sixth-floor window of the plush centrally situated Canal Court Hotel, the hideous Saturday night/Sunday morning backdrop resembled a battleground, underlined by two shaven-headed bullies kicking mercilessly at the unprotected skull of a defenceless youth. Fearfully, he curled up into a ball to preserve his bloodied cranium from the assault, before athletically springing to his feet to show his assailants a clean pair of heels.

Run ragged from a laborious two-hour set before an apathetic six-hundred-strong audience, I had looked in briefly on the crowded ground-floor bar, but in no mood to suffer fools gladly I had opted for the solitude of a comfortable hotel room. A wave of optimism, born of giant strides made towards a peace agreement, was said to be sweeping the province; but right now it looked to be pie in the sky, compromised as ever by an unruly minority.

Floundering on the far pavement, two scrawny females displaying way too much flesh yanked at each other's hair and clothes like savages, much to the sordid delight of yet another group of drunks getting in on the act by pitching into the mix a merry clink of empty beer bottles, which smashed close to the combatants in a flurry of jagged shards.

Clinging to the bars of the hotel's front gate, a wavering young inebriate paused briefly to unleash a vile torrent of his night's excesses, which decorated the metal rungs and forecourt. He was egged on by a pot-valiant accomplice yelling an incomprehensible tirade of abuse for the benefit of the dormant guests on the upper floors, blending in perfectly with the shameful spectacle representative of a fun-filled Saturday night out in Ulster.

Stepping away from the vantage point and stretching out on top of the pillow-stacked bed, I reached for the paperback thriller lying on the night table and scanned through the next chapter. All hell had broken loose in a remote corner of Estonia where, fighting for his life in a nail-biting climax, the indestructible hero of the piece appeared to have finally met his match. The stark parallels to the blood and guts spilt only metres away proved too much to stomach, and I replaced the bookmark and switched out the light.

****

Giving Newry the slip, we headed due south towards the northern shoreline of Carlingford Lough for a one-off spring date in the quaint settlement of Warrenpoint, County Down. A sorrowful, tight-knit community was bracing itself for a day of mourning brought about by events just days before, when on April 12th 1989 an indiscriminate IRA bomb attack carried out at the headquarters of the Royal Ulster Constabulary tragically and prematurely claimed the life of a twenty-year-old shop assistant named Joanne Reilly.

In an unprecedented outpouring of grief roused by a shattering sense of loss and injustice, the town's honest-to-goodness traders temporarily shut up shop, putting a lucrative Saturday's business on hold to take to the streets in a sombre-faced funeral procession befitting a head of state. It was witnessed from the kerbside by a trio of band members, like-manneredly paying our respects whilst acknowledging local resident and tour promoter Michael treading a similarly desolate path with his wife and teenage children.

'Those murdering bastards proclaim to defend every Catholic in the province, when in reality they've butchered far more people of their own faith than the sum total of the armed forces and loyalists put together,' a passionate Michael denounced, dabbing at a faint trickle of emotion with a white handkerchief backstage at the evening's gig, fully demonstrating the depth of feeling directed at a cowardly and evil minority.

****

Afflicted by a dose of the munchies upon returning to base, and unlikely to find repose in the hotel bar where a shooting match of boisterous aficionados gawped at a giant TV screen airing a remorseless hurling fixture, Geoff and I headed back onto the street, escaping the rowdy confines to wander aimlessly in the crisp midday sun as the town's resolute traders and residents began to pick up the pieces, ruefully going about their daily business.

We stumbled across a shabby side-street emporium doubling as a clothes boutique and souvenir store. Itching to take a shufti inside, compulsive spender Geoff ducked through the door, promising to be no more than a jiffy but followed nonetheless by my good self, biding a little time prior to a welcome lunchtime snack.

Selecting an embroidered two-tone blue retro bowling shirt from a rail of fusty-smelling second-hand garments and slipping the silky fabric over his plain T-shirt, Geoff paraded before the full-length mirror before giving a self-satisfied nod and making towards the counter.

'Is this a genuine vintage Da Vinci mate?' my pal tentatively asked, replacing the item back on its hanger.

'That it is; it came all the way on a boat from the USA,' the dusky-faced salesman endearingly replied in a lilting half-Indian, half-Irish accent.

'How much is it?' Geoff enquired.

'Now, that particular one would be ten pounds,' the settler verified.

'I'll give you eight for it!' Geoff bid.

'Twelve!' the shopkeeper smartly retorted.

'Ten!' Geoff shot back, caught unawares.

'Done! Let me put it in a bag for you,' the shifty character chirped, rising up from his seat and ringing the purchase into the till.

Scarcely able to believe my ears, hand to mouth concealing a wide grin, I spoke up. 'Hold on a sec – he's having you over!'

'How do you work that one out?' the bass player puzzled, failing to cotton on.

'He originally quoted you a tenner, and that's exactly what you're about to pay!' I spelt out, chuckling contentedly.

'Bloody hell, you're right; the crafty old so-and-so,' Geoff suddenly grasped, seeking to take issue with the streetsmart character.

'That'll be ten pounds precisely; or perhaps you'd like to try on a matching pair of slacks?' the scamp nervily proposed.

'I don't think so; I can see you're a very shrewd businessman – you got me there hook, line and sinker,' Geoff owned up, admitting defeat.

'Well, I like to think so; my partner taught me almost everything I know,' he revealed, shoving the cash drawer to.

'So I take it this co-conspirator friend of yours is every bit as savvy as you are!' I chimed in with a knowing wink.

'He is that… the only problem being he didn't teach me everything *he* bloody well knows, or muggins here wouldn't be the only one working on a sunny Saturday afternoon!' the rogue concluded, bidding us both a fond farewell as the doorbell ting-tinged on our way out onto the street.

****

The honour of city status was bestowed upon Newry as part of the Queen's Golden Jubilee celebrations in 2002; and a whistle-stop visit a half-dozen years later, essentially to partake in a finger-numbing festive frolic marking the big switch-on of the Christmas lights, unmasked a resuscitated locality exhibiting a new-found confidence, poles apart from the demoralising turn of events witnessed from a bird's-eye view during the previous stopover.

'From bomb to boom,' reported a BBC news feature, praising a post-ceasefire change in attitudes that was transforming a town once surrounded by military watchtowers and barbed wire into a vibrant, thriving economic centre, reverberating to all parts of a peaceable province for which the core of its long-suffering patriots deserve enormous credit.

Causes célèbres

Pat Jennings – ex Northern Ireland goalkeeper (119 caps)
Christine Bleakley – TV presenter (*The One Show*) and potential footballer's wife
Michael Legge – actor (*Shameless* and *Angela's Ashes*)
Ronan Rafferty – professional golfer

Essential travelling band info

Best live music venue: Bellini's, Merchants Quay
Curry house: Tinley Tandoori, Monaghan Street (not for the faint hearted) – 19%
Favourite pub: The Harbour Inn, Harbour Drive – 31%
Sense of humour/friendly welcome: 40%

Chapter 43
Norwich

'SO NOW YOU'VE HAD AN hour to mull things over, do you think going out on a pub crawl in a strange city is a good idea?' the senior policeman pressed at around 4am, perched on the end of a tiny bed in a holding cell in the basement of the Norfolk Constabulary.

'All I can say is it seemed like a good enough plan when we started out,' I babbled, coming to after falling into a coma on the rock-hard mattress.

'Do you think it was a good idea to urinate onto an old lady's flower beds in full view of the passing public at two in the morning?' the bobby continued.

'Perhaps not… I can only apologise,' I crawled, 'but I was pissed out of my head and didn't have a clue what I was doing.'

'I should also inform you that you could well be had up on a murder charge!' the grim-faced officer startlingly revealed.

'M… murder! What are you saying?' I hesitated, scared witless.

'You were stood in the middle of a major road crucifying Frank Sinatra's "My Way" – or perhaps it may have slipped your mind!' the chief derided.

'I couldn't find the guest house I'm supposed to be staying in. I'd had about six pints of that jungle juice called Old Growler!' I rued.

'That just about sums up what I was saying. Now, I suggest you bugger off and find your B&B, unless you'd prefer to continue gracing us with your presence that is,' the bluecoat sniggered, unbolting the cell door and escorting me to the exit.

****

Pleased as punch to be reuniting with a pair of old pals who had relocated their business to the city just a couple of years previously, I had headed east having prearranged to check out an indie band who were on my managerial radar before catching up in the quieter surrounds of a favoured alehouse. Meeting up with the quartet of young hopefuls for a scheduled late-afternoon soundcheck, an unexpected glitch cast doubts over the evening's performance.

'The cellar underneath the stage was flooded out last night and that's where the bleeding electrics are located. We're doing our best to get it sorted, so what say you come back in an hour?' the venue manager recommended, clutching onto a mop and bucket and pointing in the direction of a string of fast-food joints and pubs in close proximity.

'This'll do!' hinted one of the boys, forging ahead of the pack and spotting an old Victorian watering hole at the top of the street, identified by a weather-beaten sign shifting precariously in the strong breeze above the crumbling building's façade.

Conjuring up images of a Wild West saloon whilst also reminiscent of the spine-chilling seventies horror movie *The Hills Have Eyes*, a cannibalistic-looking posse of locals fixed their penetrating, crazed peepers on the quintet of unwelcome strangers in a chilling display of hostility, epitomised by a pair of burly, intimidating roughnecks blocking the exit route to discourage the gatecrashers from attempting a U-turn.

'Bad manners to come into a place without buying a drink!' the vested landlord growled, sticking out his whiskery chin and flexing his chunky biceps, goaded by a pack of equally hirsute, slobbering nodding dogs.

Glancing furtively to either side, we edged up to the bar as if over hot coals. A rush of watery suds sloshed into a handful of sullied half-pint glasses; and, twitching nervously, we relocated to a vacant table to guardedly plan the next move. As we consumed the flavourless slop amid a restless feeling of unease, a toothless hag of a woman burst in from an adjoining snug and entered into a furious slanging match with a badly bruised individual perched at the bar, adding a black eye to his collection with a thumping right hook and sending the deadbeat crashing to the terracotta-tiled floor.

'Get the fuck out of my life, you bloodsucking witch,' the man responded in kind, thinking better than to pursue the matter any further and attempting to struggle to his feet, assisted by a painfully thin shell-suited youth.

On the far side of the barroom a guy in a frayed black T-shirt indiscriminately flung an arm across a bench-top table, clearing the decks and smashing an accumulation of used pint pots to the floor before launching into a tirade of abuse directed at the incensed gruesome twosome keeping a watchful eye on the incomings and outgoings. As they impulsively weighed in, deserting their post in the process, a sorely craved chance opening presented itself on a plate and we fled for our lives from the snake pit to the relative safety of the street, thankful for a slice of good fortune.

****

'Let's have a good blowout and do the Triangle followed by a Ruby Murray!'

bade old mucker John, receiving the green light from business partner Bill. His suggestion was an alternative to the washed-out showcase which had bitten the dust on the grounds of 'safety issues', with the promise of a rebooking once the problems had been addressed.

'Shame about the boys' gig; I just hope that old banger of a van gets them back in one piece... Now, what's this Triangle place you were banging on about?' I put to my pals as we pulled into the tiny car park of a smart-looking centrally located guest house in spitting distance of the city's main hub of trendy bars and restaurants.

'Haha, it's not a nightclub or anything like that; the Triangle's a well-known pub crawl – not to be taken lightly, Davy boy!' Bill unravelled, implying the evening may be more than I'd bargained for with a thick head at the end of it.

'I hope and pray the pubs are a darned sight friendlier than the one we called into earlier; what a den of iniquity that was!' I conveyed.

'I wouldn't recommend any of the hellholes on that side of town to my worst enemy. Anyway, it's time we got started,' urged John, putting his best foot forward.

'I like Norwich – it's got an uncluttered feel; it surely must be a decent place to live,' I lauded over a sparkling jar of real ale. This clearly struck a nerve as John and partner in crime Bill proceeded to rip the place to shreds.

'Small-town mentality, that's what it is. Most out-of-towners see it as a desirable neighbourhood, but I can assure you it's not the town it used to be; plus it's full of druggies these days,' said John, becoming hot and bothered.

'And what about the chavs who terrorise the shopping malls?' Bill added.

'There's loads of inbreeding here, too; the place is crawling with weirdoes. And then there's the bloody road system – it's crazy! There's one-way streets that take you all round the houses – even the locals get lost!'

'And we've no motorways or dual carriageways, apart from the horrendous ring road; plus it's a nightmare trying to park on weekdays!'

'I hate the ridiculous accent; outsiders are always taking the piss. I tell you, that stupid bloody Singing Postman's got a lot to answer for!' John created, pausing for breath to take a sup from his pint before reigniting the fuse. 'You don't know the half, Davy. You mentioned that rough pub you happened upon? Well, some of the estates are exactly like that. You wouldn't find me hanging around Anglia Square at any time of night – I'd be scared shitless!' the curmudgeon jabbered on.

'Then there's the green-welly brigade all garbed up in their wax jackets and jodhpurs, ferrying their snotty-nosed kids to school in their brand new Range Rovers; half of them wouldn't know one end of a horse from the other!' Bill grieved.

'Enough, enough! There's plenty of run-down cities in this country but I wouldn't have put Norwich amongst them; it doesn't look much like a shithole to me,' I contested. 'Surely there has to be a good side – or is this it?'

'You got it in one, Davy. Other than some ancient architecture there's an abundance of bloody good pubs; and, that said, it's time we were moving on to the next. You'll like this one: it's called the Mad Moose Arms after the landlady!' John exhorted.

The rest, as they say, is history, and the wee small hours found me wandering the streets in a state of disrepair, aggravated by a disgusting late-night Indian curry curdling amongst the flagons of hops and barley poured down my neck during the preceding hours. Incapable of locating my board and lodgings and pulled up by the boys in blue for wantonly watering a sleepless pensioner's garden, I received the part-sobering dressing down recounted at the head of this chapter. What happened to my pals remains a mystery to this day.

****

On any given weekend afternoon between mid-August and May, Norwich City's Carrow Road stadium offers the setting for eleven canary-clad footballers to engage in a battle royal with a similar number of opponents, swinging a boot in anger at a leather windbag on a lush green surface resembling a giant billiard table.

Breaking with tradition on a baking hot mid-nineties summer's day, the hallowed turf set the scene for a nostalgic retro music festival, purporting to feature a host of big names synonymous with the 1970s who would grace the historic city's theatre of dreams with a diverse range of sounds from the charts of yesteryear.

The event was scheduled for a lunchtime kick-off, and to start the ball rolling an overkill of counterfeit bands did their own takes on Abba, Queen and Earth, Wind and Fire. Meanwhile, arriving in dribs and drabs throughout the afternoon, a variety of familiar, forgotten faces trod the concourse linking the behind-the-scenes area, greeting their old contemporaries like long-lost friends, cranked up for a sizzling evening's work under a reddening sky.

At a loose end, I passed the time observing the Bay City Rollers belting out 'Shang-A-Lang' and 'Bye-Bye Baby' to a receptive crowd, many of whom were obliviously exposing their lily-white ribcages to the sun's penetrating rays while mouthing the cheesy lyrics. Suitably satisfied with the band's seven o'clock slot, I deviated to the backstage toilets to find a quiet cubicle and indulge in a habitual warm-up routine.

I put a stop to a tuneful arpeggio as the echoing sound of footsteps suggested I was not alone. 'Dave, are you in here? It's Geoff; the promoter's been looking everywhere for you – they're asking if we can go on stage an hour earlier,' my bandmate revealed, precipitating a mad gallop to the production office close to the band's dressing room.

'What's happened, Jason; has somebody failed to turn up?' I asked, catching sight of the flustered organiser pacing through the corridor past the loos.

'Oh, it's that sodding Beatles bootleg outfit – they think everyone's coming to see them and want to go on later; their leader's kicking up a right stink!' he explained.

'They should have considered that well in advance of the day! Besides, what's it got to do with us?' I reasoned.

'You wouldn't help me out by doing the six o'clock slot would you... please? the flustered top dog pleaded.

'Much as I'd like to do you a favour, the guys are still tuning up, let alone changed and ready; we can't just drop everything!' I quibbled.

'I understand perfectly, it's already been a long day; don't worry, I'll go and get it sorted,' he sighed, puffing out his cheeks and making for the fab four's dressing room.

'We've decided in our wisdom to stick to the original running order, so assuming you're all present and correct can you be ready by six?' the promoter conveyed diplomatically, overheard by yours truly eavesdropping in the corridor.

'Everybody's here man, but by rights we should be headlining this event; look at all the hits in our set list compared to their measly half-dozen! Surely it's a no-brainer we should be on after them?' the faceless, mop-haired copyist astoundingly asserted.

Unable to keep it in, I strode into the room and viciously sounded off. '*What!* If I hadn't heard that with my own ears I'd never have believed it. You're living in a fantasy world buddy...! Do the later slot if you must... and incidentally, we've had twenty-three chart hits all of our very own, you jumped-up twats!' With that I left, slamming the door on the way out.

'Um... Dave... I take it from what you just said – and by the way I agreed with every word – that you've decided to run with the six o'clock slot?' the hesitant promoter cross-examined, poking his head through the doorframe, startled to find the band adorned in a rainbow of vivid pastel shades, along with a vengeful sense of purpose.

'Let's just say that's the general idea; nobody in this room can believe what that fucking upstart said. What a bunch of prima donnas!' I belligerently snarled.

'Me neither! Well, in that case, if you'd like to follow me, let's... as they say... get this show on the road,' the official brownnosed.

'Come on you lot, let's stick it to the fuckers and see if they're capable of following a real band!' Romeo vilified, promptly stepping up to the plate to pound out a pulsating rhythm to set the tone for what lay ahead.

'Follow that!' challenged a pumped-up Trevor, throwing down a gauntlet to the mop-topped foursome idling in the wings as we came off stage fresh from wowing an enraptured audience with an adrenaline-fuelled forty-five-minute set, pausing briefly to acknowledge a sprinkling of co-performers offering a pat on the back for a job well done.

Changed and ready for the off, I lingered at the stage side to bid a few goodbyes. As I peered out towards the grandstand, lending a critical ear to a lacklustre portrayal of 'Strawberry Fields Forever', I experienced the sweet scent of retribution permeating the air, yet strangely also a twinge of sympathy for the largely ignored pseudo John, Paul, George and Ringo, providing little more than background music for the less-than-impressed throng seeking shelter from the rays and dispersing to the bar areas in their droves to rehydrate.

Causes célèbres

Admiral Horatio Nelson
Elizabeth Fry – social reformer
Edith Cavell – legendary nurse
Cathy Dennis – singer/songwriter
Beth Orton – Mercury Prize winner
Ruth Madoc – *Hi-de-Hi!* actress
The Singing Postman – 'Hev You Gotta Loight Boy' (brought up in
    Sheringham)
Delia Smith – celebrity cook and chairperson of Norwich City FC, who
    although born in Surrey is regarded as the city's favourite adopted daughter

Essential travelling band info

Best live music venue: Waterfront, King Street
Favourite curry house: Spice of India, Holt Road, Horsford – 81%
Favourite pub: Fat Cat, West End Street – 79%
Don't miss: Norwich Castle, Castle Meadow – 66%
Sense of humour/friendly welcome: 64%

Chapter 44
Nottingham

HAILING FROM THE BEESTON DISTRICT of Nottingham (notorious as the home to the estate of pharmacy giants Boots the Chemists) and fresh from completing a successful college education in electrical engineering, bespectacled beanpole Bob Rankin felt the need to spread his wings and distance himself from the clutches of a bullying stepfather. He wound up renting a dilapidated basement bedsit close to the city's bustling centre.

Instantly endearing himself to scores of musicians holed up in crannies the length and breadth of the East Midlands, Bob's wizardry in the field of electronics kept him busy 'til all hours. He displayed an uncanny ability to pinpoint the root cause of a problematical amplifier, fuzz box or guitar pick-up at the drop of a hat, straining his ears for a brief second and removing the offending device's rear cover to diagnose the problem with a contented chuckle, before waving his index finger and using his stock quote: 'Eureka!'

As a struggling guitarist in the late sixties, I dropped by at Bob's run-down living quarters on more than one occasion, reclining in a daze on the moth-eaten sofa entranced by epic tracks from 'Love' or 'Moby Grape' whilst the budding Einstein busied himself beneath a dim lamp in the corner of the flat, hovering above his workbench repairing the troublesome gizmo encircled by a pungent fog of tobacco smoke.

'Pardon me for saying this, Bob, but there's a horrible rancid smell of piss coming from the window over here,' I pointed out on an emergency visit, pinching my nose and indicating a rivulet of mildew running alongside the bare skirting board.

'All under control, David; I've been working on something recently that I'm sure will unravel that particular can of worms,' he replied, resting a glowing soldering-iron on its metallic stand before going into detail in a shocking admission: 'I'm not sure if you know, but many of the inebriated clubgoers piling out of the joint on the top road use the lane as a short cut to the nearby taxi rank. The problem is that when they find themselves caught short they tend to take a leak into the metallic grille situated above the skylight, which then oozes its way into the apartment,' the boffin explained.

The plan, masterfully hatched, involved tacking a concealed length of cable running vertically upwards to the ground floor and affixing the exposed wires to the railing's framework, then meticulously attaching the opposite ends to a fully charged twelve-volt car battery. At around 2am, prepared for the usual stream of drunken louts passing through the alley, the scheming 'Mad Professor' intended to put his feet up on the window sill and lie in wait for the first transgressor, anxious to nip the problem in the bud with an electrifying form of punishment.

'I'll be celebrating going "live" this coming Friday night with a bottle of Bull's Blood if you're in the vicinity and fancy a good laugh!' the brainbox offered, rubbing his hands together, clearly relishing the moment of truth.

'I've actually got a gig, Bob, but I'll be back over any time soon to pick up my spare amp… that is, if you can fix it!' I responded with a seed of doubt.

A few weeks later, bound for a Miner's Welfare gig close to the town of Mansfield, I paid Bob a flying visit. 'I'm afraid your amplifier has seen better days, David; the truth is it's ready for the knacker's yard!' the whizz-kid determined, before changing the subject with a wide grin at the merest mention of the pissing passers-by.

'David, you should have been here; I haven't laughed so much in years – I almost wet my pants!' he drooled, taking a seat to further elaborate. 'There I was, curled up in a ball in my pyjamas near enough at kicking-out time with a little bit of Lebanese on the go, both crocodile clips in place on the battery terminals; and hey presto – in moments I'd hit the jackpot. The bloodcurdling yell from the first wretch was like something from a horror movie; but the bonehead carried on regardless, screaming the place down before running off down the alley. I counted eleven in total including two women, who were that wasted they just fell on top of one another. Perhaps it was a little bit mean to let them suffer, and looking back I should probably have disconnected it before I did,' he said humanely.

'Have the golden showers stopped?' I queried.

'Oh yeah, everything's drying out nicely. Two weeks later there was a knock at the door which turned out to be a sparky from the council sniffing around with a meter, but he wasn't in any way suspicious, even though the battery was on charge in the kitchenette. A couple of days after that the landlord showed up with a builder who patched up the wall with cement inside and out, and Bob's your uncle – there's no more damp seeping in at all,' he croaked, lighting yet another cigarette.

'I take it there must've been a string of complaints for him to act so swiftly,' I analysed, wafting away the smoke.

'Indeed there was; the people upstairs were banging on about "dodgy" wiring and saying the place was an accident waiting to happen, threatening to call the environmental health people, so in a way it's done everyone a favour,' he hacked.

'You're a genius, Bob! Now, about my flagging amp: what exactly is wrong with it?' I inquired, getting ready to leave.

'There's an old technical term that explains fully why that box of tricks is on the blink,' he replied with a smirk.

'Go on then, blind me with science,' I urged.

'In my expert opinion, the fucking fucker's fucked,' he concluded, disregarding his usual eloquence and cackling into a smoker's cough.

Embarking on my worldly travels with SWW roughly a year later, I lost touch with the genial wizard; but a heart-warming tale reached me via a musician friend hinting the ace had amazingly found love, relocating from the city to a northern town to assume a full-time post working alongside a crack team of researchers in a university laboratory. This was followed only months later with the melancholy tidings that the heavy-smoking human dynamo had fallen victim to the deadliest killer of them all, lung cancer, which tragically claimed my old pal's life only weeks later when he passed away in the arms of his inconsolable sweetheart at the age of forty-two.

Lamenting the Mad Professor's sad demise and raising a glass to his all-too-brief existence, a rueful smile crossed my lips as I envisaged the dastardly hotshot dreaming up one final devilish ploy, perhaps taking the form of a hair-raising electrical storm designed to scare the gathered mourners out of their wits as they ducked for cover beneath the pews, observed from the heavens above by the much-loved mischief-maker hacking his last laugh.

****

Residing no more than a forty-five-minute drive from the lively haunts of the 'Lace City' for the best part of the seventies and early eighties, the lure of the East Midland town's atmospheric hub often proved irresistible. This was not in any way restricted to my own circle of friends: scores of red-blooded males were magnetised by a statistic claiming the neighbourhood's fair sex outnumbered their male counterparts by an astonishing four to one.

A number of acquaintances made hay in the city's flourishing nightclub scene, and I witnessed first-hand the lavish 'work hard, play hard' lifestyle associated with reaping in wads of cash. Sibling business-partners Gordon and John displayed a more grounded approach, transforming an old cinema complex into an all-purpose entertainment venue and extending regular invitations to a variety of sponsored sporting events, which I grasped with both hands in the knowledge an evening of top-notch entertainment lay in store.

'I'll have to take you up for a spin in my private plane; maybe we could do lunch in Paris!' lovable rogue and elder brother John proudly offered, having obtained a coveted pilot's licence and champing at the bit to indulge in a spot of channel-hopping fresh from forking out a small fortune on a swanky Piper Comanche.

Inexplicably invited along as one of two 'guests of honour' to a charity boxing event held at the club on a foggy autumn night, I took my place at a ringside table, easily distinguishable in a snazzy white tuxedo. I was introduced to a group of cliquey sponsors, but both the brothers grim seemed oddly conspicuous by their absence.

'I suppose John's off somewhere gallivanting in his private plane,' I put to right-hand man Alan, curious as to the co-owner's whereabouts.

'I'd best keep my lip buttoned on that one, Dave; the magnificent man and his flying machine have been experiencing a spot of turbulence of late, which to put it lightly is something of a sore point,' he answered with raised eyebrows.

'Don't tell me he's been blowing a load of dosh on that Beaujolais Nouveau piss the Frogs have the nerve to call wine? This year's crop is worse than ever,' I insinuated, making reference to the most fatuous exercise of one-upmanship ever known to mankind, ripening into an annual November cross-channel charade amongst the idle rich.

'No, he's a little more savvy than that; let's just say it's a rather more delicate situation,' Alan responded knowingly, tapping the side of his nose.

I was announced in my celebrity capacity to a farrago of polite applause and mocking wolf-whistles from the well-oiled all-male audience, acknowledged in kind with a belligerent smile and a middle finger. Once these pleasantries had been completed, the evening's first combatants climbed into the ring, flexing their muscles and dancing on tiptoes, and set about staging the mismatch of the century.

Seconds into the fight the substantially beefier West Indian pugilist thrust a wicked right uppercut to his punier Caucasian opponent's jaw, followed at lightning speed by a crushing left hook catching the underdog squarely on the nose. As if in slow motion, a zigzagging torrent of bright red blood soared airborne towards my pristine tux, bespattering the garment's rear in spite of my last-ditch efforts to take evasive action.

'Gentlemen, it seems our esteemed guest of honour may have been expecting an evening of karate, as – for those of you who can or can't see – he is now proudly draped in a Japanese flag!' emcee Ronnie (previously known to me) caustically cracked, raising the victor's hand aloft to an eruption of cutting laughter. This triggered off a spate of further cheap shots between contests, which I took on the chin like a champ (or perhaps chump) until the final bell tolled to signal the end of the evening's entertainment and I was spared any further punishment.

Tail between legs, I was ushered into the relative calm of the VIP bar, where the semi-drunken chit-chat turned to the indiscretions of the absent top gun John (referred to in jest as the flying Notts-man), yielding a no-holds-barred account of a recent business trip gone awry, ostensibly to an unattractively grim location in the north of England. Dropped off at the airport by his devoted long-standing better half, John said farewell to his good lady with a loving smack on the lips.

'You surely haven't forgotten it's our wedding anniversary on Friday; you will be back, won't you?' she pined.

'I wouldn't miss it for the world, darling,' the entrepreneur replied, despite the red-letter day having somehow slipped his mind.

Once airborne, the plane's course was altered to Nice in the south of France, while a well-turned-out lady passenger also seen boarding the aircraft busied herself cancelling all John's scheduled meetings for the next forty-eight hours, claiming her burnt-out boss urgently needed some time to recharge the batteries, whilst insidiously preparing the potentially stony home ground by means of a forest of flowers bedecked in a glorious display throughout the husband and wife's home, thus narrowing the risk of an unwanted rift upon the moonlighting couple's return.

Touching down a little late at East Midlands Airport south of Derby, refreshed but pale as a ghost from deliberately avoiding the Mediterranean rays, the adulterous twosome marched arm-in-arm into the arrivals hall and indulged in a passionate embrace, planting a farewell kiss and contriving to go their own separate ways.

Champagne on ice, perched seductively on a bar stool armed with a bevy of surprise goodies to make special her husband's homecoming, who should happen to witness the heart-rending send-off but the wronged woman herself. Simmering with hatred, screaming blue murder and flipping into an uncontrollable fit of rage, she littered the busy forecourt with a shower of airborne gifts, much to the astonishment of the influx of arriving passengers and their welcoming parties.

'She was mad as hell; I'm told it took three members of the airport security staff to restrain her. In all honesty it could only end in tears, with most of them shed by John when the settlement was announced,' a pie-eyed confederate surmised, suggesting the romantic interlude may have proved costly in more ways than one.

Causes célèbres

John Bird – comedy actor
Jake Bugg – singer/guitarist
Su Pollard – *Hi-de-Hi!* comedy actress
Jesse Boot – Boots the Chemist creator
Paul Smith – fashion designer
Alvin Lee – legendary Ten Years After guitar man
Ian Paice – Deep Purple drummer
Bruce Dickinson – Iron Maiden frontman
D.H. Lawrence – novelist and poet
Robert Harris – author
Carl Froch – boxer
Stuart Broad – England cricketer
Torvill and Dean – gold-medal-winning ice skaters

Essential travelling band info

Best live music venue: Royal Concert Hall, Theatre Square
Favourite curry house: 4550 Miles from Delhi, Maid Marian Way – 77%
Favourite pub: Olde Trip To Jerusalem, Brewhouse Yard – 90%
Don't miss: Goose Fair, held annually in early October and possibly the best fair in the UK – 90%
Sense of humour/friendly welcome: 71%

Chapter 45
Oxford

December 1976

THE WARBLING OF THE BEDSIDE TELEPHONE washed over me like cold water, waking me from a deep slumber at the stroke of 9am. Bare shoulders chilled to the bone in the heatless room and still feeling the effects of the previous night's show, I fumbled for the handset. The puzzling sound of silence failed to grab my attention.

'What?' I answered abruptly, temporarily forgetting my manners.

'Dave, it's Bill. It sounds as if you're still in bed; are you able to talk?' the familiar voice articulated, failing to take effect.

'Let me call you back in an hour, Bill,' I grunted antisocially. 'I'm still half asleep. It may have slipped your mind, but we were gigging last night!'

'Don't hang up – I've a feeling you might want to hear this,' the lilting Geordie voice enthused, not at all registering.

'Go on then, but make it quick!' I urged, still keen to get a little more shut-eye.

'I've got some good news and some bad news; which would you like first?' the annoyingly wheeler-dealer added, continuing the wind-up.

'For God's sake stop pissing about Bill, just give it to me loud and clear; the good news first, please!' I agitatedly responded.

' "Under the Moon of Love" is number one in the charts,' he gleefully enlightened, at last bringing me to my senses.

'Bloody hell, that's incredible,' I gasped, punching the air and bracing myself for a spur-of-the-moment dash along the M40 to acknowledge the achievement at the London studios of a TV news channel. 'But what the hell can the bad news be?'

'Ah, every silver lining has a cloud and all that; you've been banned from every Trust House Forte hotel in the country,' he advised, pouring scorn onto the glad tidings. It appeared Sir Charles Forte's ever-expanding empire of upmarket establishments was definitely crossed off the Christmas card list, thus creating a dilemma in booking our future accommodation needs.

'What's the big deal, Bill? Charlie may not be one of our biggest fans, but it's months since we stayed in one of their hotels!' I remonstrated, determined to savour the moment and fobbing off the potential inconvenience.

'How about last night in Oxford?' Bill challenged. 'I had the manager on the phone at 8.30 this morning giving me a right ear-bashing.'

'But we only used two rooms for changing and left straight after the gig; some of the staff even asked for autographs!' I upheld.

'Ah, there's the rub. Nobody's pointing the finger at the band members, but you were registered as a block booking… which included the crew!' he ratted.

'You're kidding! What the hell could they have done to get a whole party of regular customers banned?' I despaired.

'Apparently the one named Ernie triggered the hotel's fire alarm system at four in the morning, after a blazing row with his wife had already woken a number of the guests. Every single resident had to be ushered out onto the street, with the majority of them stood freezing their nuts off in nightgowns and pyjamas,' Bill decried.

'Did you explain it was the crew responsible, and that it had nothing whatsoever to do with the band?' I contended.

'I tried, but they weren't listening. I'm afraid that's the price of being number one in the charts – you're all tarred with the same brush. What's done is done, and it would seem there's not a lot we can do!' he intimated, leaving me resigned to our fate.

'Well, it doesn't take the shine off being top of the charts: it's wonderful news. In future we'll just have to bed down in Holiday Inns, which I prefer anyway!' I signed off, rolling over for another hour's blissful kip.

****

The second oldest[*] though arguably most revered university city of them all, Oxford's compact mediaeval heart exudes a carefree, captivating air. Happy-snapping sightseers descend in their multitudes on the county town for twelve months of the year, enraptured by the jaunty, ethnically diverse hustle and bustle and the stunning backdrop of college buildings harmoniously scattered in all their architectural glory in the thick of the attractive streets and alleyways.

Bestrewing the elevated banks of the River Thames and within shouting distance of the vibrant maze of shops and major attractions, a succession of picturesque gastropubs, upmarket apartments and idyllic residences complete

[*] Bologna tops the list

with private moorings spiral downstream into unspoilt countryside, marking the route for London commuters and townies wishing to walk their dogs or stroll hand in hand to the accompaniment of a variety of chuntering outboard motors propelling a flotilla of wide-ranging river-craft.

Taking advantage of a discounted pamper weekend and bedding down in the lap of luxury on the city's outskirts, I peered from the hotel room window across open fields and slipped into a pair of chequered shorts more conducive to the soaring Indian summer temperatures. Content to leave my wife and daughter lavished with a facial mudpack apiece resembling an isolated Amazonian tribe and letting myself out through a nearby fire-door, I set about an afternoon of sun-kissed therapy of my own making.

I picked up a trampled-down footpath, presumably put to use by a bunch of similarly cooped-up guests, cussing at a profusion of brambly offshoots obstructing the route. The famous river rippled in the distance, soon drowned out by a piercing loudhailer indicative of a regatta or some other aquatic event in progress.

To the bottom of a short bridle road a robust red-brick hostelry loomed large at the water's edge, overflowing with families and smiling couples perched upon wooden picnic benches tucking into a Sunday roast accompanied by all the trimmings. On a heaven-sent early September's afternoon it proved too tempting to resist, and I zigzagged between a throng of merrymaking patrons to a pleasant seating area next to a wooden boathouse which straddled an old substructure jutting out into the shallow water. A tubby man revealing a builder's cleavage at the hem of his red football shorts wrestled comically with a striped deck chair, encumbered by a pint clutched in his left mitt, before angrily giving up the ghost and kicking out at the cumbersome recliner to which I quickly staked my claim.

I ordered up a 'Bluebeard's Special' club sandwich, washed down with a pint of strong local ale. By-and-by the soporific effects of the alcohol kicked in and, resting my head, I floated into a beatific slumber to the see-sawing rhythms of an assortment of vessels puttering gently over the golden-brown water's rippling surface.

My reverie was broken by a man of between seventy and eighty tapping me lightly on the shoulder. 'Excuse me w... waking you,' he said apologetically, 'b... b... but I couldn't help noticing that your face is a little flushed and it's not Red N... Nose Day until November!'

'I'm sorry, I was completely gone there; what was it you wanted?' I asked, a trifle startled.

'I think you may be b... b... burning in the sunshine; your c... conk appears to be t... turning a bright pink colour,' he observed.

'Oh – thanks for telling me!' I replied. 'It sure is a scorcher today; the temperature must be well up in the eighties. Ah well, I suppose I should be making tracks.'

'There's n... n... no rush; why don't you c... c... come and k... keep an old fart company in the shade for a while? C... can I get you a drink?' he offered hesitantly.

'That's very kind of you; okay, if you insist I'll have a pint of the Old Speckled Codger – in a jug if you don't mind,' I agreed.

'Huh – it sounds as if they b... brewed that concoction with me in mind! B... but I'd b... best stick with the G and T's,' he jested, struggling to cope with an excess of b's. Leaning back in his seat to summon a waiter, he almost toppled over.

Moving into the shadow of the boat shack and plonking his paunchy frame down next to my good self, the old boy set about detailing an abbreviated personal history. It continued in earnest for all of five minutes during which he failed to pause for a single breath.

'That's m... my problem, I talk too b... bloody much,' he admitted, sussing my attention wandering toward a gaggle of underdressed young fillies.

'Really? I hadn't noticed. By the way, the name's Dave,' I quipped, gathering myself and offering a hand.

'P... p... pleased to meet you; I'm C... C... C... Chris,' he reciprocated.

'Do you mind if I call you Christopher for short?' I joked.

'Haha! A man with a sense of humour – I like that. Your legs and arms are extremely tanned; have you b... been away recently?' he pried, beginning to relax.

'I have a place over in Portugal,' I crowed. 'I've been spending a lot of time over there this summer; I got back a couple of weeks ago.'

'I'm not long back from holiday myself, though the weather was b... bloody awful – it r... rained every day b... but one!' he bemoaned.

'Ah, that's bad luck; where did you go?' I delved.

'B... B... Belfast,' he surprisingly proclaimed.

'Do you have relations over there?' I asked, slightly baffled.

'N... no, I j... just fancied a change and it was somewhere I'd n... never b... been; and b... believe it or not it was quite interesting!' he verified.

'I've been on several occasions; there's a fantastic pub in the city centre, but in truth it's not exactly a magnet for tourists!' I commented.

'I take your point, b... but the escorted "Troubles Tour" they took us on was absolutely fascinating!' he continued rambling.

'Bloody hell, you know how to enjoy yourself!' I cracked.

'Goodness me – you don't get many of those to the pound; she's hardly g...

got a stitch on!' my new acquaintance gasped, eyes averting along with those of every other stallion to a luxury yacht cutting gently through the water's surface, adorned by a busty blonde in the skimpiest of bikinis. Clinging to a polished walnut mast she revelled in the attention, flaunting her sizeable assets to an indebted, salivating audience.

'Calm down, you'll give yourself a coronary! She's lapping it up – just look at her; plus, the yacht's not too shabby either,' I observed.

'Don't worry, it'd take a lot more than a pair of p… pumped-up tits to get me excited. I'm afraid I'm a little past it in that department; I suffered a b… bout of prostate cancer only last year and since then I haven't really felt a stirring in my loins,' he admitted.

'Sorry to hear that. You can get tablets to make it stand to attention – surely you must know that?' I preached.

'Oh, I'm *au fait* with all that; I went to my lady doctor and she recommended a course of tablets, which she said I'd have to take for the rest of my life!' he uttered impassively.

'Well, what's the problem then?' I snooped.

'She only gave me four!' he hilariously countered.

'You old bugger! Let me get you another G and T?' I suggested, knees cracking like a Geiger counter as I rose from the low-backed chair.

'That would be marvellous; you're both a gentleman and a scholar, and there aren't many of us left!' the oldster flatteringly retorted.

I made my way inside to order and settle the bill. A huddle of bulked-up beefcakes presumably belonging to a rugby team littered the bar, getting in the first of what would doubtless be many rounds in a feat of endurance destined to reach its conclusion when each recipient's hollow legs buckled under.

As I punched the four-digit PIN code of my credit card into a whining gizmo, a shrill, spine-chilling scream resonated from the outdoor decking area, climaxed by a young pigtailed waitress scampering up to the hatch panting like an asthmatic dog.

'Mr Norton, one of the customers out in the garden has collapsed into a heap; I hate to say it but I think he may be… Heaven help me, I don't know what to do!' the clearly shaken girl heaved breathlessly.

'Go to the staff room, get a glass of water and take a break Mandy – I'll take care of it,' the manager urged. 'I'm sure it can't be as serious as you're making out.' Putting on a brave face, he dashed outside in something of a dither to join a small crowd of panic-stricken underlings gathered around the prostrate carcass.

I stood motionless in the doorway, drinks in hand, peering above a caboodle of anguished onlookers as a half-dressed bystander leaped from a table close by and pumped vigorously at the inanimate figure's ribcage. Catching sight of the casualty's liver-spotted features, the realisation hit me that this was the man I'd laughed along with just moments ago. I was overcome by an odd sense of responsibility, coupled with a quivering bottom lip.

'Poor bugger – I think that huge pair of knockers was too much for him,' prated a sunburnt shirtless guy, outwardly wallowing in the excitement and wildly gesticulating to his friends as a summoned ambulance screamed into the adjacent car park.

Replaying the afternoon's events in the grey mist of my subconscious, the old-timer's light-hearted banter augmented by an engaging deadpan expression echoed repeatedly in my brain. I traipsed around the hotel gardens in something of a trance, silently rooting for a team of heroic medics to weave a little magic and inspire a happy ending.

****

In 1985 on a memorably stifling hot July day, ex-Genesis drummer turned solo artist Phil Collins earned the distinction of becoming the first rock musician to perform live on two continents in the same twenty-four-hour period, crossing the pond by means of a transatlantic flight in between running out before appreciative audiences in London and Philadelphia for the benefit of the mega-profile Live Aid charity appeal. The balding Londoner's unprecedented feat of endurance received favourable press along with tributes flowing in from far and wide; but the achievement, albeit impressive in many ways, paled into insignificance when compared with my own band's similarly superhuman efforts all but two years previously during the midsummer of 1983.

Renowned for pushing the boat out in profligate style in orchestrating the daddy of the summer balls, the deep-pocketed Oxford University colleges saw fit to lavish hugely extravagant budgets on luxury marquees, fine champagne, gourmet cuisine, fairground attractions etc. Complementing all this was a glittering diversity of top-notch live entertainment, ranging from the odd thirty-piece orchestra heard bashing out lush arrangements of modern rock classics to the pop heroes of the students' early teens. This latter category gratifyingly extended to the so-called 'darlings of the university circuit' back in '83: none other than Showaddywaddy.

We were approached late on in the previous semester with an enquiry as to the band's availability for not one but two individual proms by an adept agent friend who had been set the task of providing a mouth-watering bill for umpteen such occasions. Excited at the prospect of a profitable night's work, a further chat ensued as to the logistics of the double whammy.

'If we keep the nine o'clock set at Wadham down to an hour, there'll be ample time to shift your backline gear* across town for the 4am dawn chorus over at Magdalen,† with the added incentive of being a few grand to the good and all tucked up in your snore-bags by 7am!' the man gabbled, making the initial request just prior to the Christmas break.

'The road crew are a little apprehensive, but I'll bung them all a few quid which should more than compensate for the extra workload,' I pledged, ready to dot the i's and cross the t's upon reaching agreement. He clinched the deal with an undertaking to provide a contingent of clued-in assistants to ease the burden placed on our own technical team.

'Good morning and a happy new year,' an unfamiliar voice proclaimed on a miserable January day. 'I'm contacting you on behalf of the organising committee for Trinity College in Oxford. I have a proposal to put to you!'

'If this has anything to do with the college's summer ball, I hate to disappoint you but the band are already contracted for two gigs on the very same night!' I spelt out.

'Ah yes, so I understand; in fact that's the reason for my call. I was rather hoping you may be able to squeeze a third performance in during the interim period? We'd make it well worth your while!' the man said persuasively.

'I'm afraid that would be both physically and logistically impossible!' I explained, pouring cold water on the idea.

'What are your scheduled onstage times at the other colleges?' the coordinator inquired.

'Nine o'clock at Wadham and four in the morning at Magdalen,' I clarified.

'Hmm, that's interesting; so it's not beyond the realms of possibility to squeeze the band into the 11.30pm slot,' he optimistically implied.

'Whoa, hold your horses a sec – three gigs in the same night is a helluva tough ask. Apart from bringing the band to its knees, it would be inconceivable for the road crew to get everything set up in time!' I contended.

'Why not bring in an alternative crew? We'd be more than happy to pick up the costs to make it happen,' he enticingly put forward.

I needed to make a couple of calls but promised faithfully to confirm either way before close of business. The crew manager's blunt reaction reinforced my suspicions, submitting that not only was the idea hare-brained but in reality unworkable, leaving far too much to chance with every likelihood of the wheels coming off.

'I just thought we could all grit our teeth and make a few extra quid in the process. Not to worry, I'll go back and tell the guy it's a no-goer!' I ceded.

---

* Onstage amps etc.
† Curiously pronounced 'maudlin'

'Hold on, let's not be too hasty,' he stalled, suddenly reconsidering his options at the mention of a bumper pay day. 'If the gigs are not far from one another, with a few extra bodies on board we may just be able to pull it off.' Deeming the strategic nightmare as far from out of the question, he dismissed the physical hardship as 'water off a duck's back'.

Clean forgetting the small matter of a fourth performance within the space of twenty-four hours due to take place the next evening in the Northamptonshire backwoods, the triathlon was given a green light. I trod carefully whilst relaying the true size of the task ahead and any rumblings of discontent subsided in a flash.

Chaotic as they come, the Wadham College gig in part provided an insight as to the true nature of the challenge we had taken on. The makeshift interlocking stage was crammed full with a mountain of amplification, instruments and props belonging to a half-dozen disparate bands, providing precious little elbow room for a fast-paced animated spectacle. Happily, nevertheless, it panned out into a rip-roaring hour-long frolic, abetted by the ebullient acclamation of well in excess of a thousand impeccably decked out soon-to-be graduates.

Darting across town for the night's second instalment over at Trinity, we hooked up with the hired-in crew to find a sense of panic filling the roped-off backstage area. The programme was running well behind schedule; and, to make matters worse, there were grave concerns as to the stability of the ply-board platform contorting beneath the excessive poundage of a thirty-strong gospel choir.

Swaying joyfully from side to side as they belted out glittering white-teethed renditions of the Bee Gees' 'How Deep is Your Love' and the popular hymn 'Amazing Grace', the harmonious happy-clappers drummed up a mesmerising outcry, percussively stomping the soles of their shoes in sync with the hypnotic rhythms, until – like an earth-shattering thunderclap – the impoverished timber succumbed under the excessive strain. The singing was transposed forthwith into an agonised ruckus of wails and groans emanating from a mountainous confusion of torsos, limbs and splintering debris.

A flock of uniformed St John Ambulance staff climbed amongst the rubble, fearing the worst whilst anxious to assess the choristers' injuries. As they tended to a hodgepodge of bumps and bruises on the spot, the army of bodies sluggishly dispersed, miraculously reporting no serious casualties.

As I looked on in trepidation, seemingly from out of nowhere a hard-hatted assemblage of carpenters armed with wooden boards, giant spirit levels, saws, hammers and nails honed in on the wreckage and diligently set about reconstructing the ruptured bandstand while crew personnel repositioned the lopsided PA equipment hovering perilously above the stunned, half-cut revellers wedged together close to the area of destruction.

Fully seventy-five minutes behind schedule and with no hope whatever of checking out the provided gear, compelled into biting the bullet and going for broke, the band pounded into a salvo of upbeat rock and roll, taking the animated and hugely relieved students by storm. The hitch-free performance owed a debt of gratitude to the surrogate technical bods who, like clockwork, proved more than equal to the task.

A brief period of respite to freshen up and change clothes was followed by yet another mercy dash back in the direction of the city centre, experiencing pangs of *déjà vu* and swallowing razor blades as the most uplifting of grand finales awaited.

We cruised through the gates of Magdalen and were ushered into our allocated parking spaces by a dapper, white-gloved attendant. The architectural gems and stunning landscaped gardens of the college glowed beneath the first signs of daybreak, embellished by the yellow halo of the sun peeping its head above a sparse patchwork of whitening clouds. Shuffling heavy-legged into a cordoned-off passageway lying to the rear of a jumbo marquee, we were led to a spacious holding area set aside for changing. Plonking down a tray of scrambled eggs and smoked salmon topped off with a magnum of pricey bubbly and oodles of orange juice, a small, half-cut welcoming committee provided ample succour for the band's endmost assault on the elite gathering of wasted collegians. The goodies were devoured with aplomb and added a much needed sparkle to the jaded, bone-weary company.

I took a snoop outside. The setting resembled a raunchy adaptation of an *Inspector Morse* episode, accentuated by a scattering of amorous young couples unashamedly copulating in the shadows of a colonnade of sandstone archways. Close by, a less fussy pairing camouflaged behind a collection of shrubs and flower beds begrimed their designer ballgown and tuxedo with mud and grass stains, impervious to any peeping passers-by. Overlooked by the ancient glaring majesty of the houses of learning, a trio of teetering good-for-nothings squawking plummy obscenities devised their own version of a game of pitch and toss, recklessly aiming a stream of piss toward a row of empty Bollinger bottles before falling to the ground heehawing like a drove of seaside donkeys.

Ready and waiting backstage enlivened by the hospitable reception, the scintillating hue of a lazy sunrise oozed through the ill-fitting shelter's seams etching a fiery glow of rekindled brio onto the boys' faces. It boded well for a journey into unfamiliar terrain as the introductory fanfare blasted through the elevated banks of speakers.

Disoriented by a surreal, light-headed sensation, we took up the reins once more. The hour-long set veered between the real and the imaginary, stirred by a delirious crowd resolved to bow out on a high, energised by a dawn chorus of throbbing pop anthems. After extracting every last joule of energy from the frazzled carcasses of everyone present, we left the stage physically and emotionally drained from an unforgettable last hurrah.

'Three gigs in one night… that takes some bloody doing… Unbelievable!' I babbled to myself, journeying back to base gripped in the jaws of fatigue, serenaded by a chorus of whistles and porcine breathing patterns sent forth from my mummified bandmates out cold in the rear and passenger seats. Slapping at my cheeks to remain alert, I enviously hit the gas, finally making it back to the comfort of my own bed.

'I've done brunch to keep you going for the rest of the day… Only one more to go!' my wife sweetly conveyed just before midday, gently tapping my shoulder and placing a welcome cup of tea on the bedside table.

'Did you just say one more…?' I faltered, rubbing the sleep from my eyes. 'Oh lord, you're right… and here was me thinking it was Sunday…' In only a matter of hours, my spent bag of bones and overstretched larynx would yet again be subjected to the sternest of tests, entertaining a barn full of cherry-complexioned Northamptonshire Young Farmers expecting great things of their Midlands neighbours at an annual charity hoedown.

A far cry from the dewy fragrance of first light, a balmy rustic evening unearthed the pungent stench of rural ordure permeating every whiff of air. The effect was partially nullified by the hoppy aroma of gallon upon gallon of potent ale, vended to a swarm of wholehearted country cousins from a stainless-steel army of beer barrels lining the outbuilding's rear wall.

Mindfully sidestepping a thousand and one empty pint pots carelessly dumped on the brim of a pair of abutting trailers doubling as a stage, adrenaline tingling in the thick of a magnanimous buzz of animated bodies merrily careening back and forth, I looked up to the heavens and, running on empty, summoned up the last reserves of energy to see the task through.

'Phew, that's it!' I exclaimed, hobbling back toward the converted stable block set aside as a dressing area, heart pumping nineteen to the dozen amid a wave of euphoria, determined never to repeat such a crazy feat of human endurance.

Causes célèbres

Radiohead – 'The Bends' and 'OK Computer' geniuses
Lord Baden Powell – founder of the Boy Scouts
Hugh Laurie – actor

Lewis Carroll – author of *Alice in Wonderland* and other classic fantasies
Sir Winston Churchill – the fearless leader
Martin Amis – author
T.E. Lawrence – Lawrence of Arabia

Essential travelling band info

Best live music venue: The Junction, Park End Street
Favourite curry house: Spice Lounge, Banbury Road – 76%
Favourite pub: Far From the Madding Crowd, Friars Entry – 76%
Don't miss: University of Oxford – 83%
Sense of humour/friendly welcome: 46%

Chapter 46
Perth

IDLING IMPATIENTLY IN A CAVALCADE of thrumming motor vehicles past the crumbling landmark Lovat Hotel, I observed palpable signs of a recent (or perhaps imminent) celebration lining the roadside, taking the form of a trail of multi-coloured bunting flapping aloft the gusty March breeze and piloting the way into the centre of town.

Playing hide and seek as it flickered behind a scattering of wispy clouds, the sun's intermittent rays made scant impression on the blocks of sturdy, blackening buildings, jauntily dodging up and down a gridiron of symmetrical streets in creating a checkerboard effect complete with moving pieces dotting hither and thither going about their daily chores.

Accidentally – and outrageously – stripped of its long-standing city status by an inadvertent clerical foul-up uncovered in the late nineties, the 'town' chose to ride roughshod over the culpable 'powers-that-be', its stalwart residents remaining unmoved. Their steadfast resolve to cold-shoulder any such transition and simply leave things be was evident from the profusion of mounted road-signs pointing towards the 'City Centre'.

Following an irksome roadwork-plagued two-hour journey from Glasgow, I was keen to keep the hunger pangs at bay, and after pumping a pocketful of loose change into a parking meter abreast of the main shopping zone I happened instantly upon a chintzy café where I ordered up a stodgy snack together with a milky coffee. In double-quick time the fare arrived, dished up by a fulsome, attentive serving wench perhaps in her early forties.

'Is something exciting about to take place in Perth over the next few days?' I enquired.

'Indeed it is; we've been reinstated as a city in recognition of Her Majesty the Queen's Diamond Jubilee celebrations... and not before time,' she staunchly replied.

'That's excellent – though, if my eyes didn't deceive me, most of the directions seem to suggest it already *is* a city; but whatever, it would be rude not to offer my congratulations,' I extolled, eager to get into the spirit of things.

'That's very kind of you. If you're stopping over there'll be a few bottles of bubbly popping down at "That Bar" tonight; maybe you'd like to accompany me?' she offered, leaning forward provocatively to tempt my eyes in the direction of her ample cleavage.

'Ah, you wouldn't want one of the auld enemy swinging on your arm...! Besides, I'm not staying the night, as I'm on my way up to Elgin,' I balked, declining the invitation, well aware that given half a chance such a strapping lass would eat me alive.

'Elgin! What a godforsaken place that is if ever there was one. Why don't you delay your trip until tomorrow and indulge yourself in some proper Scottish hospitality... I could even put you up for the night,' she proposed, audaciously plonking her robust posterior on my knee and gently caressing the back of my head.

'I have some important business to attend to up that way first thing in the morning... plus I'm a happily married man,' I revealed to no avail as, rising to show the sole remaining customer to the door, the undaunted scarlet woman snapped on the latch.

'We officially close at two-thirty and it's almost that now; I thought perhaps you might like some afters... on the house, of course!' she insinuated, removing her pinafore and lustfully pouting her glossed lips.

What are you, Bartram, man or mouse? I mused, staring the wanton hussy down with a look of pure loathing, shaping to wrongfoot her and make a bolt for the door.

'I could cry rape, you know!' she exasperatingly warned. This proved the final straw as, grabbing at a handily placed giant peppermill, I stood my ground.

'Get out of my way, you ugly fat cow, or it'll be me that calls the police,' I retaliated, breathing fire. I brushed belligerently past her, making light contact, and yanked at the Yale catch to make good my getaway.

'Are you alright buddy? You look like you just saw a ghost,' a strutting, slicked-back-haired John Travolta lookalike analysed, observing my overtaxed lungs wreaking havoc as, using the car for support, I inhaled some life-saving fresh air.

'Help! Stop that English pig – he just tried to molest me!' the vamp startlingly interrupted, screaming herself hoarse from the café doorway, turning my legs to jelly amid a malicious and unfounded verbal assault.

'Huh, I'd say that's an extreme case of wishful thinking on your part, you old hag,' the young rocker retorted to my momentous relief. 'The goings-on in your café are common knowledge around here – you should be closed down. Now leave the poor guy alone!' Having delivered this riposte, he studied my expression, enquiring again as to my well-being.

Accelerating out onto the main carriageway, tyres squealing, shaking in my shoes at the potential ramifications of such a brush with misfortune, I doubled back towards town intent on stretching my legs ahead of the journey's final leg. Squeezing the car into a vacant space and still smarting from the ordeal, I strode manfully across the street to an old stone bridge where I gazed down upon a cluster of fly-fisherman trying their luck at tickling a trout or two. My mood quickly lightened as I acknowledged a small gang of young jacketless Scots braving the cutting temperatures clad only in skimpy T-shirts and jeans, their milky-white, unhealthy features evoking images of a band of forgotten prisoners banged up in a Soviet gulag.

Having fallen short in polishing off the flavourless pickings back at the licentious pit stop, I abandoned the Tay River to duck inside a side-street convenience store. Opting to nibble on a Mars Bar, I found myself confronted by a blotchy-faced checkout girl exhibiting an array of piercings including a weighty-looking metal ball in the middle of her tongue, who saw fit to lecture me as to the lack of nutritional value and exact number of calories contained in the treat.

'I'm just one of many lacking a bit of willpower when the munchies kick in. Besides, while we're on the subject, doesn't that piece of shrapnel on your tongue get in the way when you chew your food?' I posed out of genuine interest.

'Not really – I'm a vegetarian; on the rare occasions any meat passes through these lips the guys lap it up, if you catch my drift!' she brazenly hinted.

'I haven't a clue what you're talking about,' I bluffed. 'I'd best just settle up for my chocolate fix; how much do I owe you?'

'There's a lot you can do with a Mars Bar,' she lewdly implied, fluttering her eyelashes. 'You surely know the story about Mick Jagger?'

'Is there some kind of aphrodisiac in the water up here, or is it just that there's bugger all else goes on?' I retorted, giving her the exact change and tugging at the heavily sprung door, anxious to avoid any further innuendos.

Impressed by the new-found nattiness of the central hub, which had plainly undergone a concerted clean-up campaign since my previous visit aeons ago, I wandered aimlessly by an array of restored apartments and offices en route to the paved High Street. An angry voice from four storeys up hurled a diatribe of abuse across the square, inflamed as a downpour of polluted water gushed from a bucket onto the flagstones below, scattering the horrified passers-by taking evasive action to avoid the sluice of cascading filth.

Reacting in a dither, jeans and feet soaked to the skin, I peered skywards and launched a bitter tirade up towards the perpetrator. The apartment window slammed shut, rendering me high but by no means dry and with no alternative but to slosh over to a vacant bench to remove my sodden footwear, grumpily discarding the hose into a handy rubbish-bin.

I ventured into M&S anticipating picking up a crisp new replacement pair. Rushing to my aid, overcome by a hot flush, the awe-stricken assistant led her unexpected guest across to a network of neatly laid out racks displaying a wide range of products, where she stood aside, hands on hips, taking stock of my every move.

'I just suffered the misfortune of getting wet through and had to dump the pair I was wearing into a rubbish bin; is there somewhere I can pop these on right away?' I asked.

'The fitting rooms on this floor are currently out of service, but you can use the staffroom,' said my helpmate, leading me to a cubbyhole tucked away in the corner of the store and pointing to a padded footstool covered in the discarded packaging from a recently tried-on garment. 'I used to be a massive fan you know!' she let on.

'That's fantastic; I remember the wild audiences over at the old City Hall. They were great days!' I reminisced with fondness.

'If you need to slip off your trousers, don't worry about me – I'm very broad-minded!' she rather forwardly suggested.

'So it would seem are all the females in Perth, but I honestly don't think that's necessary to put on a pair of socks,' I responded with a knowing wink.

'Maybe you're right; not to worry. You'll find me over at the till when you're done,' she sighed, a wee bit disappointed.

'Are there any famous people you know of that come from Perth?' I asked, waylaying her in the hope of extracting some information to assist in my research.

'Hmm, I'll need to think on that one; I'll see who I can come up with while you're trying on the socks,' she pledged, at a loss.

A few minutes later, while ringing in the cash, she proffered: 'The famous actor Heath Ledger from the film *Brokeback Mountain* was born in Perth. What a hunk; it's such a shame he was gay!' I thanked her, jotting down the ex-cowboy's identity on my notepad.

Making my way back to the car shaking my head, I stopped briefly on the pavement to tap into Google on my cell phone, swayed by a wave of uncertainty stemming from the cheeky Scots lassie's pearl of wisdom. I smiled broadly at the screen as the facts stared me in the face, verifying the recently departed Hollywood star was indeed from Perth – in Australia!

Causes célèbres

Ewan McGregor – actor
Stuart Cosgrove – broadcaster
John Buchan – author (*The 39 Steps*)
Colin McCredie – actor

Essential travelling band info

Live music venue: Perth Concert Hall, Mill Street
Favourite curry house: Tabla, South Street – 74%
Favourite pub: Capital Asset, Tay Street – 61%
Don't miss: The Museum of the Black Watch, Balhousie Castle – 69%
Sense of humour/friendly welcome: 77%

Chapter 47
Peterborough

MUCH MALIGNED BY A LARGE majority of 'serious' bandsmen and virtuosos, the broad diversity of tribute bands found muscling in on the 'live' music bandwagon in recent years more often than not bear little comparison to the genuine article. Frequently pitched together in a mad rush by semi-professionals giving up on a sniff of the big time, they opt for an easier and more profitable means of survival by paying homage to a variety of superstars hardly likely to experience one sleepless night as a result of their existence.

Fair to say the genre boasts a smattering of adroit exponents, with a couple of exceptions to the rule being 'The Australian Pink Floyd' and the Abba alternative 'Bjorn Again', both setting the bar higher in terms of attention to detail whilst earning the plaudits of the original artists and performing sell-out concerts in their own right.

Even, perhaps flatteringly, extending to a pastiche of Showaddywaddy rip-offs (including the likes of 'Showmaddymaddy' and 'The Heartbeats', both of whom by all accounts feign an acceptable imitation), the list of tongue-in-cheek plagiarists goes on and on, perchance stretching into the thousands. Most manage to thrive in a world of counterfeit or copied goods, becoming part and parcel of the modern-day entertainment industry.

Approached for management by a seventies tribute band going under the half-baked name of 'Not Chocolate', I showed up at a reeking town-centre sports bar to judge for myself. An hour of lacklustre cover versions provided little more than background music for a huddle of around forty punters far more interested in a non-league football fixture gracing a bank of TV screens, paying no heed to the lifeless spectacle up on stage.

'If you don't mind me saying, wouldn't you be better off with a shaven-headed black guy on lead vocals as opposed to a Johnny Rotten lookalike?' I put to bandleader Lee at the bar, at worst offering a few words of advice.

'What, and get rid of Phil? He's a better singer than Errol Brown ever was… and besides, he owns the van!' the guitarist argued, hardly making a case for his buddy.

'So why do you need management if you've got it all figured out?' I pooh-poohed, convinced the band were not for me.

'Because we thought you'd be able to fill up the diary on the strength of the name!' he blurted out, clearly away with the fairies.

'*The name* – are you kidding? It's bloody awful!' I bleated incredulously, skedaddling out of the venue as fast as my legs would carry me.

Which, purely for fun, leads me on to a variety of similarly absurd pseudonyms in existence at the time of writing:

'50 Pence' (50 Cent)
'Fake Bush' (Kate Bush)
'You Too' (U2)
'Motorheadache' (Motorhead)
'Pink Fraud' (Pink Floyd)
'Deaf Shepherd' (Def Leppard)
'Fred Zeppelin' (Led Zeppelin)
'By Jovi' (Bon Jovi)
'No Way Sis'/'Oasisn't' (Oasis)
'Phoney M' (Boney M)
'Pete Loaf' (Meat Loaf)
'Red Hot Chilli Pipers' (Red Hot Chili Peppers with bagpipes)
'Aerochix' (Aerosmith all-girl tribute)
'Slack Babbath' (Black Sabbath)
'Nearvana' (Nirvana)

I accepted a kind invitation to a notable car dealer's midsummer barbecue bash held in the lush gardens of his country estate on the outskirts of Peterborough where I touched base with a few mutual friends, hindered by a mouthy DJ generating an over-the-top hullabaloo. A brief pause in the proceedings brought a welcome period of calm, regrettably soon to be broken by a further barrage of exaggerated blather.

'Guys and gals, not forgetting the offspring of course, it's cabaret time,' (interspersed by a deafening fanfare). 'I've worked with this guy on a number of occasions and you'd hardly know him from the real thing. Please welcome: *Blobby Williams!*'

Bounding onto the paved area set aside for the spectacle flaunting a blubbery waistline bedecked by a miscellany of grotesque tattoos, the larger-than-life character pirouetted on the spot like a circus elephant, soon sweating like a pregnant nun as he launched into a rib-tickling adaptation of the kosher Robbie's hit 'Let *Meat* Entertain You', working his pudgy guts out to win over the dumbfounded gathering.

He continued for thirty minutes on a similar theme, rehashing his idol's original titles into foodie alternatives such as 'Let *Grub* [Love] Be Your Energy', 'Veal' (Feel), and a rousing take on 'Angels' (cornily incorporating the word 'Delight'). Taking his bow to a flutter of polite applause, the imitator sped to the safety of the swimming-pool changing room.

'More... more!' bellowed the DJ, goading the captive audience into baying for an unwarranted encore. The strains of another Williams song 'Radio' blared out of the overtaxed PA to hail the wacko's big party piece as he stumbled back to the performance area garbed in a blow-up Mr Blobby outfit.

'Who does he think he's kidding? That fat twat doesn't need any extra padding!' the cynic beside me indelicately chided.

The mimic made a beeline for a gaggle of unwitting female guests who staunchly resisted the screwball's advances. Undeterred, he gave chase, hunting down the terror-stricken young mums fleeing into the adjoining rose garden before thinking twice and doubling back towards the walled pool area to the main body of mostly displeased spectators shielding their pommeled ears to muffle the cacophonous din.

By now the entertainer was being hotly pursued by an unruly lynch mob of gleeful youngsters who tagged along armed with a potpourri of ammunition swiped from the salad bar and sweet table. The mischief makers set about shellacking him from head to toe, which the soft touch accepted in good part as he precariously encircled the pool's perimeter.

As the chase reached fever pitch it was bound to end in tears. Overcome with excitement at catching up with his prey, a similarly chubby boy pitched the buffoon headlong into the chlorinated blue water, soaking any bystanders through to the skin.

'Help! A-a-ah...! I can't swim... Somebody... please... help me... I'm going to drown,' the bobbing impersonator overreacted, wildly flapping his arms, unaware the buoyant inflatable about his person would keep him afloat all day long.

Dashing to the poolside with a half-dozen grown-ups in tow, a bunch of hyperactive water babies made merry concocting a wicked game of push and pull, roughly shoving the floating plaything to and fro to further incense the hapless chump.

'Are you okay?' a male guest hollered.

'No, I'm bloody well not, I'm shitting myself,' the lame duck yelled in desperation. 'Somebody get me out of here, for pity's sake!'

Stripping down to our boxer shorts amidst a clutter of kids scattering like flies at the unbidden show of adult flesh, a group of us dived into the deep end to assist the basket case. The chore of hoisting the buoyant garb upright proved a step too far, however, leaving little other option than to release the outfit's stop valve in order to complete the rescue.

'How do you deflate it? Where's the air hole?' I gasped, grabbing at the costume's derrière jouncing below the eddying water.

'Tug at the pink Velcro flap at the arse end – there should be a rubber plug hidden underneath it; quick, hurry!' he panicked, whimpering like a baby.

'Stop being such a bloody scaredy-cat, and for God's sake keep still or we'll never get you out of here,' another of the emergency lifeguards said firmly, finally putting a stop to the chicken-hearted drama queen's constant clucking.

The heroics were left to a 'Man from Atlantis' lookalike who vanished athletically beneath the water with barely a ripple. Displaying a Herculean lung capacity, the superman worked at freeing the troublesome rubber bung before dramatically resurfacing gasping for breath.

'It's no good,' he exclaimed, coughing up water, 'I'm going to need a pair of pliers or something similar to get the damn thing to budge.'

'Here, see if this'll do the trick,' offered a slovenly out-of-towner, observing the pink and yellow lifebuoy drifting towards the pool surround and stubbing out a thick cigar butt on the costume's shoulder.

'A-a-a-argh! What the hell have you done…? Help!' the clown snivelled, capsizing into three pairs of waiting arms amidst a mighty gush of deflating air which hilariously blasted skywards like a giant farting raspberry. As he sloshed awkwardly up the pool steps the tub of lard bickered, 'Oh, that's fucking great! Two hundred quid down the drain just like that!'

'That's the price of fame, my friend; besides, Mr Blobby is a little bit old hat these days, don't you think? Judging by that performance in the pool you'd be better suited as a female impersonator,' I cuttingly remarked, returning briskly to the party horrified at the caked mess glazed over the once pristine gardens.

****

Later, with the kids safely flaked out in a makeshift crèche, the adults chilled out on the veranda, soothed by the balmy temperatures and mystical twilight. Unexpectedly, the benevolent man of the house appeared on the terrace oddly attired in a white towelling bathrobe.

'Are you going in for a moonlight dip, Mike?' an inquisitive guest probed, puzzled as to his buddy's baffling state of undress.

'Afraid not, Paul; I hate to say it, but the show's over and I'm about ready to turn in,' the sour-faced lord of the manor declared.

'What a shame; it's been such a great day. Mind you, I don't envy you one bit – there's one helluva lot of shit to clean up. Perhaps we should all muck in!'

the man pitched, placing a comforting hand on his pal's shoulder.

'No, no, that won't be necessary – we've got a professional company coming in first thing to straighten the place up; it's just that something else has really pissed me off, which I'd rather not discuss,' the party pooper expressed. Lowering his voice to a murmur, he took me to one side as the unsettled circle of friends began to disperse. 'Dave, you live just up the road from Stewart who left an hour or so ago – do you happen to have a number for him logged in your mobile?'

'Yeah, I'm pretty sure I have – shall I Bluetooth it over to you? Is there a problem?' I pried, scrolling through my list of contacts.

'Best not to go into detail right now, but that'd be great. Now, perhaps you and Cathy would care for a little nightcap before you tootle off?' he kindly offered.

'It's such a lovely night it'd be rude not to, Mike,' I said gratefully, catching my good lady's attention to indicate that she should delay picking up our zonked-out daughter.

The peaceful moonlight tipple was interrupted by the genial host rising up from his wooden rocker. 'Why the hell should I keep it to myself any longer?' he trumpeted.

'Go on, spit it out mate,' close friend Martin urged.

'What say we teach that snivelling little bastard a lesson?' Mike confusingly advocated. Punching a series of digits into a landline extension, he switched it through to the speakerphone to the astonishment of the listening stragglers.

'Is that Stewart?'

'*Yes, it is…*'

'So this is Stewart the freeloading, pilfering wanker?'

'*I beg your pardon! Who's that?*'

'You know full well who it is, so before you make any excuses, get your car loaded up with the stuff you nicked and make sure it's back here within the hour!'

'*But I've had too much to drink…*'

'I don't care if you've had your eyes gouged out or even if you're shagging Miss World as we speak, get my bloody liquor back here pronto – that is, if you don't want to spend the night in a hospital bed.'

'*B-b-b-but…!*' the thief babbled.

'Put it back exactly where you found it and make sure your sorry arse never comes anywhere near this place again… and think yourself lucky you've escaped a bloody good hiding!' Mike harangued, slamming down the phone.

It transpired that a co-guest's eagle-eyed teenage son had earlier caught sight of the deceitful scoundrel seriously abusing the host's hospitality by loading his car boot full of a selection of booze earmarked for the partygoers before skulking quietly off the drive. Meanwhile, the hidden youngster studied his every move, returning to his father's side to squeal like a pig.

As the small hours approached, a pack of voyeurs lying low in a darkened office huddled around an in-house closed-circuit TV screen watching as a pair of headlights shone into the lens. Little suspecting he was being closely observed, a hooded figure unloaded crate after crate of alcoholic goodies.

'Come on, lads, let's have some fun; we wouldn't want him to mistake my kindness for weakness, would we now?' the owner playfully chuckled, quoting the notorious Al Capone and beckoning to the gang to follow the leader.

'Surely you're not planning on giving the lad a good pasting… are you Mike?' I muttered, fearing for the poacher's well-being.

'Not likely; I like to think of myself as a generous man, Dave. I just figured he might like to round the weekend off with a midnight dip!' the wheeler-dealer implied.

****

Never the most alluring of places, yet just a forty-five-minute train ride from London's Kings Cross station, Peterborough has fast become a sought-after location for an abundance of upwardly mobile commuters. Simultaneously it has bucked the trend of post-millennium economic uncertainty in attracting a succession of major businesses to the area, from online giants Amazon to a host of big-name financial institutions, thus bringing a renewed sense of prosperity to a region lambasted as dull and unexciting by local killjoys.

Residing all of eighteen miles from the city for nigh on twenty-one years, I have a whole portfolio of happy memories of the place, from the wintry radiance of our rosy-cheeked young daughter captivated by the dazzling magic of the Christmas lights lavished upon the commodious Queensgate shopping centre, to the summer afternoon food fights aboard the Nene Valley steam train, where an overexcited caboodle of kids waged war on one another before being slapped firmly on the wrists by their flustered mothers, all the while ignored by the muster of dads turning a deaf ear, hankering to be in the nearest taproom.

Under wraps amidst a leafy, wooded terrain of undulating countryside, many surrounding villages bear an uncanny resemblance to the much lauded Cotswolds district, complete with chocolate-box sandstone cottages and ancient remnants steeped in olde-worlde rustic charm, though remarkably without the endless streams of traffic and coachloads seen frequenting the commercially viable West Country equivalent.

I was meeting friends in one of many excellent pub-diners close to the city for a bite of lunch when, in the midst of catching up, the topic of conversation fascinatingly took a different twist as the bizarre subject of the neighbourhood's WCs reared its tasteless head.

'I don't suppose you heard on the grapevine, but Peterborough has just won the prestigious "Loo of the Year Award" for 2011 from more than thirteen hundred entrants,' my pal quoted.

'No shit…? Surely you're talking out of your arse!' I wisecracked. Though acutely unaware any such accolade existed, I at least showed some interest as to which esteemed dumping ground had walked off with the dubious distinction.

'The Car Haven Welcome Centre!' he gloatingly announced.

'Perhaps next time we paint the town we can do a curry first, then go and put it to the test,' I suggested with a hint of sarcasm.

'You can't bloody well take anything seriously… By the way, did you see the documentary on Prince William the other night?' my buddy queried, keen to change the subject.

'Yeah, he comes across as a grounded kind of guy. Do you think he'll ever take his rightful place on the throne?' I posed, breaking into a snigger.

'I think Charles will probably… Oh for God's sake, don't you ever put a sock in it?' he huffed despairingly, summoning a waiter.

Causes célèbres

Aston Merrygold – singer with boy band JLS
Luke Pasqualino – actor (*Skins* etc.)
Paul Nicholas – actor/singer
Jake Humphrey – sports presenter
Andy Bell – Erasure vocalist
John Clare – poet
Adrian Lyne – film director
Catherine of Aragon – first wife of Henry VIII was buried in the cathedral

Essential travelling band info

Best live music venue: The Cresset Centre, Bretton Centre
Favourite curry house: The Banyan Tree, Westgate – 71%
Favourite pub: Charters, Town Bridge – 58%
Don't miss: the cathedral buildings – 77%
Sense of humour/friendly welcome: 62%

Chapter 48
Plymouth

Munching on a pre-packed lunch during an excursion to a Leicester museum at the tender age of thirteen, I eavesdropped in on a conversation between two sex-starved naval recruits referring to a field of activity known as a 'red light district'. I was at once distracted from catching up on a backlog of homework, as fleeting references to illustrious ports of call such as Amsterdam, Ostend and Hamburg evoked wondrous visions of a glittering world far removed from a dull, depressing hellhole brimming with decaying artefacts.

Feasibly more intriguing, particularly for a gullible prepubescent schoolkid, allusions to 'big ripe melons', 'nipples like raspberries' and 'shaved fish' to name but a few embedded themselves unwaveringly in my memory banks, as I pretty soon cottoned on that the juicy banter in fact pertained to female body parts, doubtless uncovered by a wide variety of 'ladies of the night'.

A few years later, at the still impressionable age of seventeen, I fronted a short-lived outfit blighted by the ornithological tag of 'Ptarmigan'. Offered a prestigious one-off gig at a Royal Navy airbase close to the town of Yeovil, with two additional pub dates tagged on essentially to cover costs, the long trek south-west led us to Plymouth's infamous Union Street.

We checked into a downmarket B&B handily placed for the first pub venue, albeit in an area of town renowned for petty theft. The unkempt, string-vested landlord reluctantly unlatched a back entrance accessed via a narrow wooden-fenced alley, activating a strenuous route march lugging a stack of equipment up three flights of stairs to an insanely cramped three-bedded fleapit.

Wearied and in need of sustenance following an hour's kip, the meagre kitty stretched to a greaseproof bag of soggy, curry-covered chips apiece in advance of yet more fun and games carting the kit in the opposite direction for the short hop to the venue.

Rough beyond measure with a clientele to match, the run-down pub's equally bedraggled manager clattered open the bar's rear fire-doors, unexpectedly mucking in to ensure a speedy load-in ahead of offering a welcome cuppa hidden away in a smoke-filled backroom.

'You'd be wise not to play any of your own stuff and stick to something they know,' the guvnor advised. 'They can be a funny lot here, so be warned.' Cranking up the volume, we toed the line with two sets of crowd-pleasing rock classics, even earning faint ripples of applause from sections of the well-oiled, glassy-eyed mob.

'I'm going to leg it to the digs – it's only at the bottom of the road!' I called out as we heaved the final piece of gadgetry into the asphyxiating, untaxed old Bedford van chucking out an unhealthy excess of reeking emissions.

'Well, don't forget we've got to cart the stuff up to the room when we get back, you skiving git,' the bass player yelled.

'I'll be there before you know it!' I countered, putting my best foot forward.

A discomfiting feeling of unpredictability hung heavy in the air, emphasised by a sprinkling of roughnecks openly urinating in full view of a group of passing females who crossed to the opposite pavement. All in all I inferred that Union Street may not be the most salubrious part of town in which to hang out, especially the wrong side of midnight.

'What are you looking at, you dirty bitch?' a pissing thug bellowed, grinning and thinking himself smart by confronting the disinterested honey.

'I thought it was a cock, only it's way too small!' the girl retorted, wiping the smile from the stunned hooligan's face before scurrying away with her tittering friends.

Minding my own business, I reached a less busy part of the lengthy street where a youngish, oriental-featured female of around twenty-five stepped from a shop doorway, taking me by surprise whilst giving me the once-over.

'Hello Cherry, you looking for good time?' she asked in broken English.

'Why, is something about to happen?' I naively replied.

'I give you good time; you very cute Cherry boy, I like you – maybe I offer you special half price!' she said smilingly, inching a little closer.

'Half price! I take it you're selling something,' I foolishly responded.

'I do anything you like; you come with me to my apartment!' the dusky damsel persevered, curiously looking the picture of innocence.

'Ah, I get it… N-no thanks,' I nervously stammered, at long last cottoning on. 'In all honesty I'm a little bit similar to those guys up the road and haven't got a pot to piss in; maybe I'll come back when I'm famous!'

'Ah, that's a shame, you are so cute; I here tomorrow if you change your mind, and I make cheap deal for you,' she persisted, winking at me.

'So this is what a red light district looks like!' I reasoned, curiously harking back to the rookie sailors' enlightening confab in those callow schooldays, chuckling beneath my breath and moving on with a spring in my step.

As I approached the side street where the bedbugs, let alone the B&B, lay in wait, an old-timer midway through his nightly stroll paused for a breather. Sizing up the young stranger treading a similar path, he drew a handkerchief from his pocket.

'Good evening; nothing like a breath of fresh air, is there?' I bade agreeably.

'Good evening? What's so bloody good about it? Let me tell you, young man, this part of town used to be *the* place to live in Plymouth. It wasn't so long ago the shops were thriving and the pubs were bursting at the seams, but look at it now – full of tarts, transvestites and yobs. The gutters are awash with spew and there's litter lying everywhere. I blame it all on the bloody Navy!' the man bitterly griped, waving an admonishing finger under my nose. Muttering discontentedly to himself, he crossed the road.

'Sorry I spoke, mate… Goodnight!' I puzzled, submitting to a mild twinge of sympathy, which faded fast at the prospect of a backbreaking last act.

****

Revisiting the maritime city and curiously enough Union Street around a dozen years later, little on the surface seemed to have changed (other than my own musical fortunes, that is), a fact underlined during an impromptu rehearsal at the once prominent Palace Theatre, latterly transformed into a rollicking purpose-built rock venue known as The Academy.

After running through a couple of new tunes, which sounded well up to scratch in the rambling acoustically sound old hall, the band were set to kick our heels for the remainder of the day, and the delights of the Devonian town's insalubrious eateries awaited our presence.

We were immediately waylaid by a shady-looking dude slinking out of a concealed back alley in a second-hand cloud of smoke. Taking a crafty peek into the dark depths of the town's underworld from whence he came, the boys and I shaped to move on.

'Hey gents, how about checking out a blue movie show? These are the real McCoy from Sweden, plus it'll only set you back a fiver apiece!' the barefaced peddler wheezed, nervously fidgeting on the spot and cagily taking a look around.

'We've got bugger all else to do; how about fifteen quid for the four of us?' Geoff quibbled, ever the barterer.

'Go on then; you drive a hard bargain son,' the dodgy geezer acceded. 'But you'll have to hold fire for a couple of minutes 'cause there's a show on as we speak.'

We pursued the sweet-talker back along the passageway to a weather-ravaged double door which sprung on its hinges, clattering against the brick wall, to reveal two sheepish customers presumably keen to make a low-profile exit.

'Just a few seconds more, boys, while Auntie Val tidies up,' the man balked to gasps of disbelief as a plump middle-aged woman carting a mop and bucket brushed past the party, tootling contentedly into the darkened room.

'For crying out loud, I'm not fucking going in there; you don't know what germs you might pick up!' protested a surprisingly repulsed Rod, sticking two fingers toward his throat and screwing up his face in utter disgust.

'Rod's right; besides, we shouldn't be seen dead in a dump like that!' I empathised, ignoring the hustler's pleas and beating a hasty retreat.

'Hold up lads, what the fuck's going on? Where's my twenty quid?' the seedy character bleated, giving chase.

'Down the drain along with the dregs in the bottom of Auntie Val's bucket,' I answered back, quickly disappearing from view.

****

With all due respect to the residents of Plymouth, the notorious Union Street forms an insignificant part of what in truth is an attractive and blossoming city, highlighted by the spacious Hoe area frequented by visitors and natives alike taking a leisurely stroll with the kids on a pleasant summer's evening, evoking visions of the heroic Sir Francis Drake biding his time playing bowls as the Spanish Armada drew ever nearer.

Frequented by myriad tourists and scores of local motorists seeking a diversion from the airless city, a number of winsome small towns such as Totnes, Salcombe and the lower-key Kingsbridge pepper a region rightfully designated as an area of outstanding beauty, best visited out of the peak season when the herding frogs go to ground.

All of a few miles to the west lies a tiny dot in the ocean known as Burgh Island where literally time and tide stand still. Doggedly shunning the trappings of the modern world and thus beckoning scores of sightseers on foot by means of a large stretch of sand accessed from the village of Bigbury-on-Sea, it was sampled unexpectedly by my other half and me during a weekend escape to Devon in the recent past.

Steeped in character, the local pub 'The Pilchard Inn' immediately aroused my imagination, stirring images of days of old when Blackbeard and his rascally pirates plausibly dropped anchor, consuming ewers of paint-stripping rum and pitchers of mead accompanied by the pipe and drum ahead of planning the next dastardly move.

In keeping with the buccaneering tradition, a covey of hirsute local yokels (no doubt boasting a history of the high seas) loitered at the public bar decked out in a range of chunky home-knitted pullovers designed to cover their portly bellies.

'If I were you I'd plump for the crab sandwiches, they're handsome,' a wizened man recommended with a roguish wink and a smile, prompting the pair of us to heed his advice whilst resting awhile in the uniquely welcoming setting.

'Where do I know your face from? You're not from round these parts, are you?' the bulbous-beaked landlord inquired, placing the scrumptious fare on the table.

'No, we're from the wilds of Northamptonshire, but that said I wouldn't mind investing in a place down this way; it's beautiful around here!' I complimented.

'House prices in Devon have gone through the roof of late. It'll set you back an arm and a leg to buy something in this locality, plus a lot of the older properties that outsiders seem to go for are haunted,' a wily old fox eerily warned, stimulating a small arsenal of well-spun tales of woe cooked up to scare the living daylights out the pub's rapt visitors.

Entering into the spirit of things by consuming an efficacious tankard or two of the local hops and barley, we whiled away an hour or more until, after struggling from our seats to return the empty glasses and plates to the bar, my good lady and I made for the exit, bidding the pack of friendly scallywags a fond farewell.

'I don't think you'll be heading off anywhere for a while yet, young feller – the afternoon tide's well in by now and the last tractor left more than fifteen minutes ago!' the innkeeper snickered, removing a breadcrumb from his upper lip.

I peered through the stone mullion window frame. Sure enough, there in the distance, a heavily laden agricultural vehicle tugging a trailer load of windswept passengers bobbed up and down in perfect rhythm with the turbulent ocean's ebb and flow, seemingly fighting a losing battle against the inexorable force of the incoming current.

'Those tractors are on stilts, matey; you won't find anything like that up in your posh neck of the woods!' a buck-toothed old rascal broadcast.

'What's more, that laggard won't be back for a dog's age; I'd order up another pint if I were you, son,' his cackling partner in crime advised.

'That's very kind of you to offer!' I joked, instantly wiping the smile from the old boy's face to the unbridled amusement of his pals.

'The last time he bought anybody a drink Cornwall was still a bloody kingdom in its own right!' the jovial landlord jibed in the endearing local tongue.

'It's a little bit potent, that stuff; perhaps I should give it a miss while my legs are still functioning. I think we'll go and take a leisurely stroll around your little piece of paradise until the ferryman arrives back,' I deferred.

I was halfway out of the door when, amidst a sudden rumble of thunder, the heavens opened.

'Second thoughts,' I chortled, scurrying back inside and ordering up another pint pot of loopy juice, along with a fizzy water for my unimpressed female co-pilot.

Causes célèbres

Sir Francis Drake – who was actually from Tavistock, close by
Beryl Cook – one of my favourite all-time artists, died in 2008
Michael Foot – unkempt former leader of the Labour party
David Owen – floating politician
Tom Daley – Olympic pin-up diver
Wayne Sleep – dancer
Richard Greene – TV's original Robin Hood
John Inverdale – media journalist/presenter
Captain William Bligh – the 'Mutiny on the Bounty' legend

Essential travelling band info

Best live music venues: Plymouth Pavilions, Millbay Road
Favourite curry house: Jaipur Palace, Vauxhall Street – 54%
Favourite pub: Dolphin Hotel (Beryl Cook's former local), The Barbican – 75%
Don't miss: Plymouth Hoe – 77%
Sense of humour/friendly welcome: 70%

Chapter 49
Portsmouth

'HOW THE BLOODY HELL ARE we supposed to sell gigs out when there's not a sodding poster anywhere in sight?' complained one of the boys, picking up on a dearth of local advertising as we crawled nose to bumper along the winding coastal road to the south of Portsmouth's city centre.

'That's a very valid point,' I acknowledged, muting the daytime radio host babbling the news headlines for the umpteenth time, spotting the parochial theatre to the left and hanging the people-carrier into a concealed car park.

We were afforded a fawning welcome by a corpulent young chap decked out in a tight-fitting golf sweater in the middle of June. Clanging open the rear fire exit, he guided the tuckered-out party down into the catacombs doubling as our dressing area where, huffing and puffing like an asthmatic donkey, the ailing lard-bucket paused for breath.

'If you fancy a cuppa, there are tea-making facilities in the green room over to stage left; I'll make sure your sandwiches are delivered down here by 6pm,' he efficiently briefed before shimmying out of sight leaving the heavily sprung door to slam noisily on its hinges. Behind it, a bright red laminated sign attracted my attention:

IN THE EVENT OF FIRE
Important notice to all staff and visiting companies
KEEP CLEAR EXIT FROM EMERGENCY ESCAPE ROUTE
STAIRCASE MUST BE KEPT CLEAR AT ALL TIMES
During performance times the emergency alert code for staff, artists and crew is:
'MR SWIFT IS IN THE BUILDING'

'Have you seen this? I wonder what would happen if Mr and Mrs Swift attended tonight's gig and there was an urgent message for them!' I deviously intimated, alerting the band and crew as to the warning's crucial content.

'Don't even think about it!' barked Rod, reading me like a book and sensing a piece of tomfoolery may just be on the cards.

'Come on, what do you take me for – I'd never fuck a gig up intentionally!' I assured the gang, hands held high in mocked surprise.

I was lethargically stretched out on the dressing-room sofa hindered by the remaining half-dozen clues of the *Telegraph* crossword when the out-of-place wall-clock chimed four, signalling teatime. As I stirred from the couch, my mobile chirruped into life displaying Geoff's moniker on the screen, presumably from somewhere close by.

'What's up?' I yapped into the mouthpiece.

'Can you come and let Trevor and myself in? The fucking jobsworth on the door doesn't believe we're members of the band!' he carped back, throwing a cantankerous wobbly, instantly cutting me off dead in his frustration.

A gangly man in a shabby black suit sized up the stranger shooting to the top of the staircase. 'And who might you be?' he discourteously inquired.

'I'm the band leader, pal, and I understand you've refused entry to a couple of my colleagues,' I responded in kind, much to his chagrin.

'What, surely not those two old stagers out there on the street; aren't they a little long in the tooth to be gallivanting around in a pop group?' he harshly chided, clearly amused by his own brand of caustic wit.

'Where's your bosom buddy gone, who was here earlier? At least he was efficient *and* helpful!' I taunted, eager not to take the bait.

'Oh, you mean Graham, my tubby subordinate; he's gone home to Mummy for his tea. Anyway, I'm in charge around here and everything has to come through me!' he self-importantly sneered, nose stuck in the air.

'Well, in that case, perhaps you could start by letting my fellow performers in, or there's a strong possibility we may not have a show tonight!' I threatened.

'We've only sold two hundred and forty-three tickets when everyone was told to expect a full house; maybe your group are not as popular as you were years ago!' he argued defiantly, incapable of looking me in the eye.

'If you don't open that bloody door soon there'll be almost two hundred and fifty disgruntled people requesting a refund; and while we're on the subject, whatever happened to any advertising? There wasn't a poster to be seen on the way into town; perhaps you should take that up with your marketing underlings,' I fiercely retorted.

Agitated at my response and continuing to give me the brush-off the bigot finally shoved the release bar, revealing the band's grumpy old men looking daggers. Tramping forlornly into the building, they paid no heed to the contrary numpty.

Back down in the dungeon, a hot-under-the-collar Geoff was still furious at the man's unnecessary stance. 'That lanky piece of shit was being awkward out of spite; he'd be out on his ear if I ran this gaff. Just look at the place – it's a shithole!' he bickered.

'The theatre director's name is Alan and he came across as a thoroughly decent guy. He said he'd be in at five; I could always have a quiet word?' I hinted.

'Why not? That arsehole needs bringing down a peg or two!' Geoff affirmed.

As we continued tearing lumps out of the day manager, a huge clatter echoed on the stairs winding down to the black hole. Tugging open the cumbersome door revealed an empty metal platter gleaming on the flagstone floor outside, trailed by several rounds of buttered bread and a selection of sandwich fillings strewn from top to bottom of the granite staircase.

'I'm not paid to do this, you know, and don't think I'm making any more!' bawled a blue-rinsed biddy from the stairwell, implying the mishap was no fault of her own with a dismissive gesture before turning tail and sloping off.

Tiptoeing gingerly up the flight of steps, warily avoiding a hash of foodstuffs still scattered in my path some twenty minutes later, I located an unmarked side-door, perhaps leading to Alan the director's office. As I tugged at the handle I received yet another tongue-lashing.

'What the hell is it now? You lot have worked my wife up into a frenzy!' the man (whom we had christened 'Lurch' after the Addams Family character) bellyached, stepping out from the shadows like the walking dead, silhouetted in near darkness at the stage side.

'Where's your boss, Alan?' I asked firmly, looking the prophet of doom directly in the eye. 'I want to see him!'

'Oh, how remiss of me; he called asking me to pass on his apologies – he's been out all day attending to some rather more important business and won't be in tonight. It goes without saying I'm the man in charge as of now, so any concerns should be addressed to me!' the unctuous idiot crowed.

'How good of you to let me know! Well, you could start by organising for a plate of sandwiches to be delivered to our dressing room as per the band's contractual rider, perhaps without decorating the staircase this time!' I pressed.

'Huh, you've got another think coming, sonny. My wife Janet went to a heap of trouble to make the last lot for you; we've completely fulfilled our obligations and with no thanks from you or your jumped-up companions,' he jibed.

'Unless I'm seriously mistaken, the clumsy battleaxe didn't even make it halfway down the steps, so get your bloody facts right!' I growled, finally flipping my lid.

'I'm not used to being spoken to…!' he faltered, scrutinising my every move whilst quaking in his shoes as I edged towards him.

'I haven't even started, pal; now get me a loaf of bread and some cheese and we'll make our own fucking sandwiches!' I truculently demanded, storming onto the stage to compose myself and taking it out on one of the acoustic guitars.

****

The band settled pleasingly into the evening's show, bolstered by a healthy walk-up of bored holidaymakers seeking shelter from the persistent afternoon drizzle. True to form, midway through an incessant burst of rowdier tunes the beanpole of an acting manager rushed theatrically up in front of the stage flaunting his spindly arms in full view of the crowd and harping on about the decibel levels soaring beyond the pale.

'Is everybody enjoying the show?' I called out, fighting the urge to plant my right brothel-creeper beneath his jaw as the song in progress drew to a close.

'Yeah…!' yelled the crowd spontaneously.

'Well, I'm afraid "creeping paralysis" down there doesn't seem to agree and is insisting we turn the volume down as it's playing merry hell with his hearing aid!' I responded in jest, bowled over by a section of heated onlookers venting their fury at the sourpuss with a volley of boos, catcalls and clenched fists. 'It would appear you're outvoted, buddy; now do us all a favour and piss off back into the hole you crawled out of!' I scowled, belligerently thrashing into the next song mindful I may well have stirred up a hornet's nest.

I was indulging in a spot of horseplay with a flamboyantly attired hen party just minutes later when there, bang on cue vying for my attention, the irksome Lurch appeared at the brow of the stage, clutching onto a handheld radio set armed and ready to spoil the party.

'Hang on a moment, everybody, we appear to have a rather bothersome king bee in our midst, and we wouldn't want a nasty prick to go spoiling things… now would we?' I scoffed, kneeling forward to lend an ear.

'If you don't turn it down right now I'm going to pull the plug,' he overzealously barked, echoing through the microphone to further incense the crowd. Fearing for his own safety, the pantomime villain fled via a side door.

'Perhaps I should save you the trouble, you interfering knobhead!' I whispered under my breath, blood boiling at the provocative threat and coiled up like a spring determined to extract an overdue pound of flesh. 'For those of you that enjoy a spot of literature, we're honoured have a celebrated author with us in tonight's audience; I recently read an excellent novel written by him called *Last Orders*,' I fabricated, fully prepared to wreak a little havoc. 'Please show your appreciation for… Graham Swift!' Into the stunned silence that followed, I bawled at the top of my voice: 'Yes folks, *MR SWIFT IS IN THE BUILDING!*'

I figured the warning would more than likely pass unnoticed, only to be

324

seriously mistaken as within an instant all hell broke loose. Flapping like dragonflies, a posse of panic-stricken staff dashed hither and thither amid a state of chaos, herding up four hundred confused souls and ushering each attendee toward a variety of escape routes. Deafened by the shrill whirr of the hall's fire alarm, Lurch's impromptu fag break was cut short and the band were left with little choice but to clear the stage.

'What the fuck did you do that for?' cried Romeo as we clambered through the fire doors and huddled together in the rear of one of the trucks.

'That bastard insisted he was going to pull the plug if the volume wasn't turned down, so I thought I'd call his bluff!' I explained, endeavouring to justify my actions.

'Boys… We just got the all-clear – everyone's making their way back inside as we speak; can you be ready to roll in five minutes?' a torch-bearing assistant politely enquired.

'That's fine – let's go for it!' I confirmed.

'What a stroke of bad luck; fancy there being someone in the audience with the name of Mr Swift – that's our emergency code, you know!' she rued.

'Goodness, is it really? What a coincidence!' I unconvincingly gasped, mouth dropping to the floor in mock disbelief.

'In all honesty, the duty manager wouldn't really have hit the power switch; he's full of bluster that one, and, as for his dragon of a wife, what can I say other than the pair of them think they own the place. Our boss Alan would've had his guts for garters if we'd had to offer refunds; he'll be on the carpet first thing tomorrow, that's for sure,' the street-smart madam implied. 'Anyway, ten minutes lads – break a leg!' With a knowing nod, she rushed off to go about her duties.

'Where's that twat, Lurch? It's about time he had a piece of my mind,' Geoff scolded, slinging a deaf 'un due to a bout of selective hearing.

'Ah yes, the one and only Lurch. I have a gut feeling we won't be seeing hide nor hair of that jumped-up pain in the arse, at least for the rest of this gig,' I replied, watching the curtain rise and readying myself for action.

Causes célèbres

Charles Dickens – surely Britain's greatest ever author
Roland Orzabal – Tears for Fears musician
Amanda Lamb – TV personality
Gerald Flood – actor
Mike Rutherford – Genesis/ Mike and the Mechanics
Roger Black – former athlete

Mark Austin – news presenter
Sir Arthur Conan Doyle – Sherlock Holmes novelist
Rudyard Kipling – *Jungle Book* author
Peter Sellers – comedy genius (born in Southsea)
James Callaghan – former Prime Minister
Isambard Kingdom Brunel – engineer extraordinaire
Nevil Shute – novelist

Essential travelling band info

Best live music venue: New Theatre Royal, Guildhall Walk
Favourite curry house: Blue Cobra, London Road, Northend – 81%
Favourite pub: Hole in the Wall, Great Southsea Road – 71%
Don't miss: Portsmouth Historic Dockyard, Victory Gate – 68%
Sense of humour/friendly welcome: 44%

Chapter 50
Preston

Moving mountains to promote my one and only solo single 'Black Ice' in the thick of a savage early-eighties winter, I made my way out of Preston's 'Red Rose Radio' station (currently known as Magic 999), and stopped briefly to stock up on a few goodies for the lengthy trek home. As I entered the bum-tapping supermarket, an unfortunate encounter with a distraught female turned my whole world upside down.

'I only left her for five minutes! I knew this would happen; some bastard must've been following me!' the bundle of nerves babbled in an uncultured northern dialect, referring, I presumed, to an unaccounted-for child.

'Is there anything I can do to help?' I offered, hurrying to the young mother's side to play the white knight whilst failing fully to grasp the gravity of the situation. 'There's a payphone over there – have you called the police?'

'Where in fuck's name are you from? What a weird accent!' she ungratefully snapped.

Two bulky staff members clad in yellow jerkins sprinted red-faced to her side and stood surveying the scene, hands on hips. 'Are you alright, love?' the beefier helpmate panted. 'We just received word there's been an incident – something to do with a missing child!'

'It's me daughter Becky, she's only five,' she spluttered, fighting back what appeared to be crocodile tears. 'I told her to wait 'ere while I had a quick whizz round – I get me shopping done in half the time if I'm on me own. Somebody must've run off with her!'

'And you sir, who might you be?' the acne-spattered second guard pumped, intimidatingly tapping at the truncheon attached to his waistband.

'He's not from round 'ere, that's for sure; he was hanging around over there in the car park looking suspicious!' the woman shockingly claimed. This provoked an over-the-top reaction from both security men, one seizing my arms in a painful hammerlock while his scowling co-conspirator proceeded to read the riot act.

'This is madness – I was only trying to help!' I ranted. My protestations of innocence were silenced by an unwelcome knee thrust into my lower back.

'Huh, we'll see what Mr Plod has to say about that… Now move, you scumbag!' the bulkier guard ordered, forcing my body through the automatic doors and into the store to the consternation of a small gathering of interested spectators.

I remained under lock and key in a stuffy closet full of brooms, buckets, mops and feather dusters for fully two hours before at long last the boys in blue made a dramatic entry, heavy-handedly crashing into the storeroom like bulls at a gate.

'I think you've got some serious explaining to do, sonny; now be a good boy and tell us where your accomplice has taken the girl?' the armed officer barked sadistically.

'This is bang out of order; I'd only stopped off to pick up some things for the trip home and thought I'd do my good deed for the day only to find myself wrongly accused and imprisoned in a claustrophobic rabbit-hutch!' I grieved in pure frustration.

'Where on earth are you from?' the frowning bobby pressed, perceiving I may have dropped in from another planet.

'I'm from Leicestershire, which judging by your reaction is somewhere close to Mars!' I carped in utter frustration.

'Don't get fucking cocky; you're in deep shit, son,' snarled cop one, evidently pitching for the starring role in a Lancastrian adaptation of *Miami Vice*.

'I was of the understanding that on these shores you are innocent until proven guilty,' I retaliated, before suddenly smarting from a short sharp slap to the back of my head. 'What the f…?' I screeched. 'That's way out of line… Whatever happened to good old-fashioned British jus…' I was cut off by an elbow to the small of my back, causing me to leap from the chair screaming out in shock horror.

'Cuff him!' directed the senior man. 'He fancies himself as some kind of smart-arse; let's get him down to the station.'

All at once he bowed his head in deference at the arrival of a plain-clothes detective who squeezed his slender frame into the cramped cell.

'Well fuck my old boots, look who we've got here – it's that bloke from Mud, Les what's-'is-name! This'll make the front pages tomorrow, boys!' the top dog announced, studying my features with a contemptuous huff.

'My name's not Les and nobody appears to be taking me at all seriously; do you honestly think I'd fuck up a glittering career by allowing myself to be involved in a bloody abduction?' I groaned in desperation, receiving little sympathy from the po-faced trio.

'That's right, that's right, that's right, that's right, I really love your tiger feet,' the brain-dead junior officer inanely hummed, meeting with the disapproving eyes of his boss gazing right through him and bringing the lunacy to an abrupt halt.

'I regret to say the young lady in question is adamant you were acting in a suspicious manner, and if her daughter isn't found soon I'm afraid this could spell big trouble for you, no matter who you are!' the deadpan chief maintained.

'What in God's name is suspicious about parking my car and walking into a supermarket?' I roared back, at my wit's end. 'Normal law-abiding citizens do it every day of the week! The only difference, or so it would seem, is that I'm from another fucking solar system!'

'He really does have a weird lingo, don't you think, sir?' interrupted cop two, bowing and scraping to the superior officer.

'So that makes me guilty of being party to a kidnapping does it, you bloody idiot? Don't you ever get out of Preston? Besides, I love kids!' I avowed in a softer tone.

'There you go sir, he's as good as admitted it – he says he loves kids!' remarked the boneheaded cop, thinking himself clever.

'Do you have to wear a dunce's cap when they fit you for a helmet?' I mocked, dreading a slap albeit highly unlikely in the presence of the DI.

'Parker, Jennings, why don't you both piss off home – I'm sure I can handle Elvis here without your invaluable assistance,' the head honcho barked sarcastically. Taking the hint, Batman and Robin thankfully did a runner.

'I have to admit, that double act are not the sharpest knives in the drawer. Now, let's try and make some sense of all this,' the DI mooted in a far more agreeable tone, taking the heat out of the situation in a flash.

An hour or so later, the wiry duty sergeant poked his head into the interview room, cradling his right hand into an imaginary handset. 'Sorry to disturb you, guv, but there's an important call for you,' he relayed, giving rise to a further period of inactivity shuffling uneasily in my seat whilst the interrogator left the room for what seemed an age.

'Okay son, you're free to go. Thanks for your cooperation!' an elderly policeman clad in a navy pullover announced out of the blue, sneaking in through the door to mumble the words I'd figured would be music to my ears.

'What, you mean that's it – no explanation or apology, just sod all?' I beefed, gobsmacked and understandably still a little on edge.

'Yep, that's all son; I'll organise for one of my colleagues to give you a lift back to your car… Off you go, now, you're making the place look untidy!' the old-timer bade.

Outside in the corridor, oblivious to my presence, the plain-clothes inspector chatted amiably with a blue-shirted constable, content to bury his head in the sand as I passed by unacknowledged. Mystified at being blanked, I doubled back.

'Don't I at least get an explanation as to why I was wrongfully arrested, never mind clipped round the ear?' I interrupted, at last grabbing his attention.

'Just a sec, Tom… Can't you just be happy you're off the hook? Everything's been sorted; these things happen from time to time,' he loftily pointed out, clearly nonplussed at my own lack of propriety and taking up where he left off with his lackey.

'Happy? I've just been detained for over three hours and you expect me to be… happy!' I carped, busting a gut. 'I'm sure you can see I'm dancing on air! I'd simply like to know why I was arrested, not to mention the sudden change of heart!'

'You take care of this Tom, I'm way too busy to deal with this crap,' the self-important big shot sighed, strutting away like a peacock, clearly believing such a trivial matter to be well beneath a man of his undoubted standing.

The missing child, it transpired, had been snatched in the blink of an eye by the tot's estranged father, who had been carefully monitoring his ex-partner's movements for some weeks. Following a stressful hour or two with his hyperactive daughter, the wayward dad sought refuge at the grieving mother's council flat where he received a sound thrashing at the hands of the woman's new live-in boyfriend, retaliating in kind by pressing charges against the bully for aggravated assault.

'They're on their way over here in a squad car as we speak… It's all getting rather messy; that's why the guv was a little snappy!' the constable chattered, making his excuses and escorting me into the station's lobby and offering an apologetic hand.

'Excuse me, but are you Dave?' a strapping WPC called over from behind the main desk. 'There's a gentleman on the phone from Red Rose Radio who'd like a quick word.'

'Really…? What the f… hell does he want?' I retorted, careful to readjust my Ps and Qs.

'Hello again, Dave; a little birdie has told us you've been in a scrape with the local authorities since you left us earlier on! Is there any chance you could pop back in? We'd love to chat about it live on air,' the nasally familiar voice enthused, clearly thrilled at the prospect of a hot-off-the-presses exclusive with a fugitive celebrity.

'Me…? Oh, Chinese whispers and all that; I think it's a case of mistaken identity as I'm led to believe it was Les from Mud who they actually arrested.

Try contacting the officer in charge of the investigation – he'd be delighted to talk to you. Take care – see you soon!' I signed off, getting the hell outta Dodge.

Causes célèbres

Roy Barraclough – actor (*Coronation Street/Les Dawson Show*)
Eddie Calvert – 'the man with the golden trumpet'
Andrew 'Freddie' Flintoff – England cricketing legend
John Inman – camp actor (*Are You Being Served*)
Nick Park – *Wallace and Gromit* creator
Tom Finney – '50s and '60s football legend
John Thomson – actor (*The Fast Show* and more)

Essential travelling band info

Best live music venue: The Guildhall, Lancaster Road
Favourite curry house: Sylhet Bangla, Liverpool Road – 58%
Favourite pub: Market Tavern, Market Street – 70%
Don't miss: Bowland Wild Boar Park – 76%
Sense of humour: 62%
Friendly welcome: 31% (largely due to a young mother and two thick policemen)

Chapter 51
Ripon

BORED WITH THE QUARTERLY TREK north to the offices of the band's accountants (inconveniently based in the old Lancashire mill town of Burnley), I had mapped out an infinitely more attractive route via the panoramic Yorkshire Dales. I was hankering for an invigorating rush of untainted air, and the rolling hills of the English uplands awaited.

Dumping the car on a patch of scrubland next to a designated National Trust trail abutting the quaint village-cum-town of Grassington and double-lacing my scuffed walking boots which had been slung onto the back seat amongst a hodgepodge of ledgers and invoices, in good spirits and ready to ramble I put my best foot forward.

A giant yellow sun peeked above the horizon, casting laser-like beams of flickering light over a sparse grove of copper beech, ash and silver birch trees, creating an autumnal picture book of pastel shades festooning the moist, glistening foliage swaying softly to and fro in the energising breeze. Shackles removed and savouring every minute, I negotiated stiles and fences with youthful aplomb, spurred on by the far-reaching landscape's beautiful nothingness. The lightly blushing skyline uncovered the first signs of a beckoning dusk descending over a criss-cross of silver stone dwellings nestled in the near distance.

As I scrambled over a nettle-bound dyke leading back towards the village, on the path ahead a mature lady garbed in an olive-green wax jacket lay slumped on the ground clutching at her shoeless right foot amongst a scattering of lingering dust and debris, showing clear signs of discomfort, body rocking from side to side. Picking up the pace and careening through the remnants of a collapsed garden wall which had buckled beneath the unhappy wanderer's efforts to surmount the obstacle, I stooped to offer a few crumbs of comfort.

'Are you okay? Have you sprained your ankle?' I asked as our eyes met, clocking the tell-tale signs of agonising pain etched in the old girl's withered features.

'I think my ankle may be broken – it's throbbing like hell; but no matter, it's my own stupid fault,' she humbly confessed.

'If it's broken, you'll need an ambulance. What say we get it checked over by a local doctor first; do you know if there's a surgery in the town?' I pondered, uncertain as to whether the casualty should be moved at all.

'No need to fuss; if I could just rest up for a second then perhaps you could help me hobble back to the village and we can ask in the Post Office,' she surmised.

'Whenever you're ready. I take it you were trying to climb over the wall; is there a shortcut that way?' I queried.

'No… I was just being nosey, that's all. Like I said, it's all of my own doing!' she avowed, overtly anxious to change the subject.

Detecting a clattering piece of horticultural machinery which I took to be a cultivator churning up the earth on the far side of the disintegrating wall, I sprang up onto the adjacent embankment to take a peep. Startled by a gunshot-like blast backfiring through the contraption's exhaust, I lurched in reverse onto the heath, dying with laughter.

Clinging to a whopping petrol-driven lawnmower, a pipe-smoking silver-haired man of advanced years dawdled in the machine's wake naked as the day he was born, adorned only by a pair apiece of white trainers and army surplus ear-defenders and afflicted by an outbreak of goosebumps the size of marbles.

I dusted myself down and trotted back to the walking wounded. As I approached, the biddy coyly turned the other cheek, a wry glint in her eye.

'Who's a naughty girl, then?' I admonished.

'I am, aren't I? He must be a nudist or an exhibitionist, don't you think? I could see his bare chest from the top of the steep mound over there,' she admitted, pointing to an intrepid trekker stood atop the same rock formation.

'Ah well, it doesn't hurt to look I suppose – seeing is believing… Fancy cutting the grass in your birthday suit… in early November… He must be freezing his nuts off!' I inferred, laughing along with my playful new lady friend.

I placed a steadying arm around the red-faced granny's waist, and together we limped step by step back to the little town's well-stocked Post Office. It was about to shut up shop, but the helpful assistant directed us to a charming nearby inn and promised faithfully to summon the district nurse, vowing help would be at hand in just a matter of minutes.

True to the official's word, in no time a smiling uniformed auxiliary darted through the entrance and crouched to remove a pair of bike clips before immediately setting to work. Diagnosing a sprained ankle or at worst a hairline fracture, she insisted the patient get plenty of rest and go along to the minor injuries unit at Ripon hospital first thing. While she strapped a tight-fitting bandage onto the sufferer's foot with the utmost care, a friendly chat as to the accident's cause took an unruly turn for the worse as the conversation's tone began veering toward ribaldry.

'That's the weediest hand tool I've ever seen... or maybe it was his garden hose!' the debilitated minx jested.

'It seems as if it wasn't... *hard* to spot and hadn't been used in a while!' the care provider cornily retorted, guffawing like a hyena.

'From what I saw it was just some limp dick arsing about with a lawnmower,' I intervened. Receiving a glower of disapproval from both ladies, I instantly seized upon the opportunity to cut and run, wishing my fleeting acquaintance a speedy recovery and legging it back to the car for the final leg of my journey to the cathedral city of Ripon.

****

Coming courtesy of a wide variety of wandering minstrels, whose dietary requirements rely heavily on a superabundance of Asian cuisine generally consumed at all hours of the day or night, perhaps I should stress I cannot in any way be held accountable for roughly fifty per cent of the recommendations contained in this journal.

The curry has been long regarded as the preferred fodder of countless itinerant musicians known to keep the hunger pangs at bay in a diverse range of outlets, but the unwelcoming tandoori restaurant close to Ripon's centre most certainly seemed to have slipped through the net.

Skulking through a pair of saloon swing-doors and relieving himself of a burdensome pile of tablecloths on the counter top, a gaunt, strangely out-of-place white waiter stopped dead in his tracks, evidently stunned by the arrival of the evening's first potential customer.

'Can I help you?' he edgily inquired, sizing me up in the manner of an undertaker.

'Maybe; I was thinking about chancing my arm and eating here tonight?' I hinted, slipping off my weatherproof and draping it around the first available chair.

'Really? What, now?' he asked, mouth open wide.

'Well, now would be preferable, or perhaps I could take a look at the Christmas menu and come back in a few weeks' time!' I derided.

'It's just that we don't normally get any customers in before clearing out time at the local pubs, so you caught me unawares!' he whined.

As I watched him slouch apathetically back to the ornate mahogany bar, crumpled suit hanging on his gangly frame like a half-empty sack, trouser turn-ups gathering dirt on the smeared floor, a gut feeling suggested the individual may not be entirely happy with his lot.

'So what's it to be then?' the misery guts enquired, gripping a ballpoint pen in his nicotine-stained fingers, poised to jot down my order.

'I think I'll go for the tandoori mixed grill with boiled rice and some spicy Bombay potatoes,' I replied, feeling my stomach rumble.

'And…?' he pressed.

'Sorry… did I forget my manners?' I bade repentantly.

'No, no… What would you like to drink?' he sighed, getting a tad uppity.

'That's very kind of you; I'd like a pomegranate and kiwi fruit margarita with a dash of African lime if it's not too much trouble!' I jibed, attempting to lighten the mood.

'You what…?' he yawped in surprise.

'Just a pint of Cobra if you don't mind… and thank you,' I patronised, eyeing the grumpy ragamuffin ambling into the kitchen.

'You don't very often find an Englishman working in an Indian restaurant!' I remarked upon his return, grimacing at the sight of the bowlful of chewed-up nibbles plonked down on the table alongside a flat pint of amber swill.

'That's as may be, but let me assure you it won't be for much longer!' he grumbled, making no bones about his dissatisfaction in the position.

'So is this just a temporary thing?' I blabbed on.

'No, I've been offered a job at the new Tesco store and start in two weeks. It'll be heaven to be out of this smelly dump!' he bleated maliciously.

'Surely it can't be that bad; most of the Indian guys I know have a wacky sense of humour – you must have a few laughs along the way!' I added tactfully.

'You wouldn't be laughing if you saw the state of the kitchen – they should be reported to those environmental people!' he rapped, muscles tensing.

'You might have told me that before I bloody well ordered,' I quibbled, almost choking on the insipid beer.

'I wouldn't worry; disgusting as it is we haven't had any fatalities…' he hesitated, '… yet!' With that, he traipsed back toward the creaking swing-doors.

Placing a fiver on the table to cover any costs, I made a bolt for the exit. A trio of startled Asian faces peered from the kitchen doorway watching my every move, shoved aside by the astounded soon-to-be ex-employee.

'Good luck at Tesco… oh, and thanks for warning me in the nick of time!' I bade, bounding through the door, instantly lured by the heavenly aroma of fresh fish and chips wafting through the air from a nearby fat-fryer.

****

As I walked off the stodgy fare navigating my way through a patchwork of cottage-lined streets, strains of raucous laughter leaking from the open skylights of a nearby watering-hole prompted a swift about-turn. Following my nose towards the jovial commotion, I ascended a small flight of stone steps into the packed public bar.

Inside, I was confronted with a wall-to-wall delusion of octogenarian fully paid-up members to heaven's waiting room, squeezed together like sardines in a can. The inn's kindly, affable hubbub persuaded me into staying put, and I fought my way to the bar through an aluminium confusion of walking frames amidst a thick cloud of swirling smoke.

Above an almighty racket of cackling old maids bawling over one another, I ordered up a pint of the frothy local bitter and, feeling very much the spring chicken, found some elbow room by an upright serving hatch where a bout of people-watching ensued. I found myself revelling in a good old-fashioned Yorkshire night out, taking my hat off to the roomful of shiny-skulled, blue-rinsed citizens enjoying nothing more than a customary get-together.

Pulling up a stool to a yellow-keyed, battered old piano stuck in the corner, a cigarette-smoking old-timer plonked rigidly at a succession of nicely out-of-tune melodies, cueing a rambunctious spur-of-the-moment sing-song. As the merry patrons swayed erratically from side to side, their movement stirred the tarnished, antique chandelier fluctuating perilously above a coconut shy of beaming, nodding heads.

Spreading contagiously to every corner of the bar the dissonant, tumultuous racket continued unremittingly, dominated by a brood of tuneless would-be sopranos tremulously whining: '*You made me love you, I didn't wanna do it, I didn't wanna do it…*' Jolted by a neighbourly elbow in the ribs from a toothless old rascal, an overwhelming urge to pitch in took hold; and I stretched my own trusty vocal chords through a repertoire of nostalgic gems my parents used to belt out, gathered around the piano in my childhood days.

Saved by a clanging bell, accompanied by a hoarse cry of 'time, gentlemen please', the ensemble promptly hushed and, in orderly fashion, the happy watch of nightingales headed straight for the door, clearing the lounge in seconds flat. Downing the remnants of my pint and helping a giddy old boy up from his seat, I followed suit.

Pulling at the brightly polished door handle, I stalled while a crush of tipsy proletarians exited the smoke room on the opposite side. A familiar voice sounded to the rear of the pack, belonging to a lame 'golden ager' gabbling to a bunch of companions.

'Not a stitch on, I tell you,' she rambled on, 'other than a pair of tatty old running shoes; he could've got frostbite on his wink…' Suddenly she froze on the spot. 'It's him – this is the chap I was telling you about! Would you believe it?' the old she-devil unleashed, shrieking with unbridled joy.

'What, he was the one mowing his lawn in the altogether?' gasped one of her playmates, hand over mouth to restrain a fit of the giggles.

'Don't be silly, Mavis, not him! I might have seen something worth a broken ankle if it had been. He's the one who rushed to my rescue and most likely saved me from catching hypothermia! This is my knight in shining armour!' she exaggerated.

'Don't be silly! I couldn't have just left you lying there to rot; anyone would've acted the way I did!' I reasoned, flattered by the praise.

'Maybe so, but you're special,' she fawned, losing her stick and planting a sloppy kiss on my unguarded lips, wantonly attempting to ram her tongue down my throat.

'Take it easy or you'll do yourself another mischief,' I howled, staunchly resisting her advances yet coerced into clinging on to break her fall.

'Spoilsport – I was rather hoping you might offer to come and mow my lawn tomorrow as I'll be laid up for a few days!' she intimated, eyes twinkling.

'You saucy so-and-so; I know exactly where you're coming from. You're old enough to be my mum!' I chided. Having bid the tipsy threesome a warm farewell, I looked back to chuckle, observing their unsteady gait arm in arm along the street.

'It's number thirty-one if you change your mind!' I made out, carrying on the breeze, as I strained every nerve to scurry back to the safety of the hotel.

Causes célèbres

Lewis Carroll – author of *Alice in Wonderland* etc.
Richard Hammond – *Top Gear* TV presenter
Bruce Oldfield – fashion designer
Simon Grayson – football club manager

Essential travelling band info

Best live music venue: The Royal Hall in neighbouring Harrogate
Favourite curry house: Balti House Bangladeshi, Kirkgate – 33%
Favourite pub: One-Eyed Rat, Allhallowgate – 68%
Don't miss: Fountains Abbey, near Aldfield (approx 3 miles away) – 81%
Sense of humour/friendly welcome: 66%

Chapter 52
Salford

HAILING FROM THE RENOWNED NEMESIS of many a visiting Rugby Union side, for an uninitiated Leicester lad like yours truly the macho sport of Rugby League held little interest, and I was never quite able to get my head around the abundance of overly complicated rules bearing more resemblance to American Football than to the traditional and, to my mind, superior alternative.

Historically the League game has been regarded as a northerly spectacle, predominantly for the entertainment of a dogged minority of flat-capped traditionalists seeking a welcome diversion from an afternoon at the allotment. An unexpected invitation to witness first hand a blood-and-thunder encounter at Salford's historic stadium The Willows arrived via a friend of a friend during the inaugural Super League season of 1996, fitting in with a performance in my own professional capacity due to take place in the stadium's spruce entertainment complex the very same night.

Taking to the field for a clash billed as a cliffhanger between the Salford Reds (now known as the Salford Red Devils) and the sport's elite club St Helens (The Saints), the eighty-minute contest put to rest a number of previous theories thanks to the slick organisation and exceptional fitness of both sides, rallied by an ardent air of optimism sweeping through the old ground's populous tiers of wooden bleachers.

'These lads are athletes, not bloody lard-arses like those beer-bellied Union thugs,' opined partisan Reds devotee Archie from the seat adjacent, voicing his true feelings as to the rival code as the twenty-six wedge-shaped participants glided silkily across the scarring turf, making a beeline for the opposition's try-line by instalments.

'Union's changing, Archie,' I contended. 'There's a real buzz at every Tigers* game I go to; plus the new crop of players are as fit as fiddles.' Giving me the brush-off, my biased host proceeded to leap to his feet at regular intervals to

---

* Leicester Tigers

contest every debatable decision, sending himself hoarse to little avail as the masterful, table-topping Saints ran out victors by the convincing margin of thirty points to twelve.

****

Housed beneath the stadium's main stand and capable of seating six hundred and forty ebullient night owls, The Willows Variety Centre played host to a miscellany of prominent artists for nigh on half a century, earning a reputation as one of the top bread-and-butter gigs on the circuit. It was blighted by a distinct lack of ventilation when full to bursting, rendering it particularly oppressive during the humid summer months.

While preparing for a weekend stint at the club in the course of a September heatwave, at the crew's request I had packed a set of bathroom scales to check the weight of a few essential items of equipment ahead of a forthcoming overseas excursion. As I removed the device from my on-the-road suit bag, a row of perplexed faces awaited my next move.

'What the fuck have you brought those along for – are you on a diet or something?' barked Romeo, more than a little intrigued.

Renowned for enjoying a good wind-up, I invited each contender to take turns hopping onto the scales clad only in their undergarments. 'It's high time we established exactly who puts the most graft in on stage!' I taunted, suggesting that we compare each band member's measured weight before and after the gig.

'What a load of bullshit,' claimed senior member Trevor. 'You might sweat like Gary Glitter's newsboy but that doesn't mean you do work the hardest; it's all about being fit!' Sniffing humiliation, he sloped off out of harm's way to survey the evening's talent.

Amazingly, figuring the experiment to be basically just another wacky stunt to pass the time prior to the acid test onstage in the stifling show hall, and obviously curious as to the amount of bodily fluid shed during an hour plus of drudgery, the rest of the band played ball by stripping down to their smalls before each willing guinea pig stepped up to the plate in turn.

Reduced to a pulp from seventy-five minutes of menial labour, I teetered step by step down into the catacombs, unbuttoning my drenched black shirt and wringing out the excess toil into a nearby sink. The usual post-gig analysis made way for a sustained period of much-needed rehydration in addition to a well-earned breather.

'Okay, let's see how much weight everybody's offloaded,' urged a surprisingly sprightly Romeo, bounding into the room dressed only in his underclothes, keen to unveil the results of the pre-gig case study.

'Bloody hell, I'm so knackered I'd forgotten all about that,' I gabbled, dragging the scales from beneath my pile of belongings.

Shedding a staggering eight pounds apiece the energetic drummer and his weary frontman stepped aside, gloating from our joint efforts, to pore over the remaining pairing of Rod and Danny picking up the gauntlet and losing three and four pounds respectively.

'What a bunch of vain nancy-boys you lot are! Mincing about like a bunch of tarts weighing your bloody selves in the dressing room... Now I've seen it all!' seventeen-stone backline roadie 'Big Steve' bickered, lumbering through the door loaded down with a pile of old album sleeves and CDs passed backstage for signing.

'That's bloody rich coming from you! When was the last time your fat arse went anywhere near a set of scales?' Rod fired back insultingly.

'Do you honestly think I give a shit about my weight? I'm just big-boned, that's all,' the big feller insinuated. 'It's everyone else who seems to be more bothered!'

'What you mean to say is, you haven't got the will power to go on a diet; plus, you're too fucking lazy anyway! Go on, hop on the scales and give us all a good laugh!' Geoff challenged, joining in the fun in his own inimitable fashion.

'What the fuck for? What are you trying to prove?' Steve rallied with a hint of malice in his native Wearside tongue.

'That we're obviously paying you too much – you weren't half that bloody size when you started working for the band, and besides the set of scales are here to weigh the gear for the Polish trip next month,' I made plain.

'What happened to the guy who was supposed to deliver the drinks?' Rod enquired, veering off the subject. 'I'm dehydrated and all the water's gone!'

'Steve's probably eaten him,' joked Geoff to the roadie's obvious displeasure, staring down the barrel of an explosive temper and taking a pace backwards.

'Okay, you bunch of piss-takers, I'll get on the fucking scales and if I'm more than seventeen stone two pounds I'll go on a bloody diet!' the BFG announced. Stunning all and sundry, he proceeded to peel off his own sweat-soaked quadruple XL T-shirt followed by his chunky boots and ankle socks to reveal a gargantuan sun-starved blubbery chassis.

'Put your clothes back on Steve, we were only winding you up!' I reasoned. The crew hand turned a deaf ear, however; and I stood dumbfounded and transfixed as he pulled off his tracksuit bottoms, tramping onto the burdened weighing device naked as the day he was born whilst at the same time recording the exact figure he'd predicted.

'Gentlemen, your meet-and-greet have arrived... What the bloody hell...? please hang on a sec, ladies!' squawked assistant manager Ronnie, barging into the dressing room accompanied by three horrified female guests at the precise moment Big Steve stepped from the bowing scales encircled by his mickey-taking workmates.

'Oh lord, I think we've come at a bad time!' attested one of the ladies, putting a hand to her mouth in genuine astonishment.

'That's disgusting!' yelped her outraged sidekick. 'What the dickens is going on? I think we'd better leave!'

She backpedalled into the hallway in shock, leaving the loose-tongued Ronnie rendered for once speechless as, plonking down the drinks, he slid down the wall panting hysterically with tears streaming down his face.

'What's the matter? Have you never seen a naked man before?' Steve protested, clearly put out by the intrusion and reaching for his tracksuit bottoms.

'Not that fucking size I haven't! What a horrible sight – I'll be having nightmares for weeks!' Ronnie reacted, removing his glasses to wipe away the excess moisture in his eyes and leaving the room in a state of helplessness.

'I suppose I should make the effort to lose a bit of weight. The problem is I'm just a lazy fat bastard; Geoff was right!' the roly-poly man coyly conceded, bending forward to relace his boots with a great degree of difficulty.

'What you need to do is get yourself into a rock-and-roll band and jump around like a complete ass for seventy minutes in that bloody sauna out there!' I conceived, placing an empathetic hand on his shoulder in a sudden shift of tone.

As I drove homewards beneath a clear night sky, the uplifting signs of a new dawn loomed over the bleary horizon with all but one of the clammy-skinned troupe either sawing wood or grunting in their seats like old sows.

'I think we're in for a lovely sunrise!' I put to guitarist Danny.

'You might be right… What do you reckon that trio of meet-and-greeters had to say after they left the dressing room earlier on?' the musician speculated, changing course, still a little on tenterhooks from the ill-timed intrusion.

'Oh to be a fly on the wall sometimes! We blotted our copybook with that little contingent, that's for sure; there'll probably be rumours circulating around the Salford area for weeks, or who knows how long!' I conceded.

'Oh well, it's one for your book when you finally get round to it!' he chuckled, eyes closing and dead to the world in no time at all.

****

Falling victim to the biting recession towards the end of the new century's first decade and left little choice but to enter into liquidation, the ailing nightspot opened its doors to a diminished band of dignitaries and loyal customers for the final time ever on Saturday January 28th 2012, expedited some months before by the controversial departure of Archie's beloved Salford City Reds to a new purpose-built stadium located in Barton, Eccles.

Bringing down the curtain on forty-six years of rollicking non-stop entertainment, yet another long-standing, much-loved venue bit the dust, consigned to the annals of history by a smug developer's merciless wrecking ball.

Causes célèbres

Sir Ben Kingsley – Oscar-winning actor
Christopher Eccleston – actor
Al Read – TV/radio comedian ('50s and '60s)
Emmeline Pankhurst – notorious suffragette
Elkie Brooks – singer
Albert Finney – actor
Graham Nash – Crosby, Stills, Nash and Young musician
L.S. Lowry – famous 'matchstick men' artist
Mike Leigh – wonderful film director/writer
Peter Hook – Joy Division/New Order bassist
Robert Powell – actor
Russell Watson – tenor
Tony Warren – *Coronation Street* creator
Ryan Giggs – Manchester United footballer

Essential travelling band info

Best live music venue: The Lowry Centre, Salford Quays
Curry house: Bilash Balti House, Swinton – 31%
Favourite pub: Salford Arms, Chapel Street – 48%
Don't miss: Ordsall Hall, Ordsall Lane – 45%
Sense of humour/friendly welcome: 74%

Chapter 53
Salisbury

PORTRAYED AS 'THE CITY IN the countryside', Wiltshire's ambrosial county town possesses much to admire. It affords scores of visitors found wandering its charming lanes a warm welcome, offering up a potpourri of individual outlets vending anything from cakes to trinkets, mostly housed in quaint half-timbered buildings. It all makes for an undemanding shopping experience, rarely associated with bigger, bustling hubs where nondescript, lifeless malls full of multiple chains engulf a festering eyesore of one-time architectural gems.

A far cry from the gentle see-saw of the town's heartbeat, the aforementioned* annual summer exodus south-west towards the popular seaside resorts of Devon and Cornwall gives rise to an unenviable can of worms, taking the form of an endless stream of mobile holidaymakers bringing every surrounding highway to a complete standstill, easily rivalling that of a densely populated major metropolis.

A simple solution to the nightmare exists, but it is routinely ignored by intransigent local planners closeted dispassionately in their ivory towers. Content to overlook Salisbury's unique standing as a city with no bypasses, they push aside various proposals whilst carloads of indignant tourists converge on the pastoral municipality in their droves.

'It's a huge problem, but the people here don't like change... of any kind!' the stage manager of the acoustically challenging City Hall condemned, before recommending a peaceful riverside walk far removed from the gridlock where Rod, Danny and I could while away a couple of hours midway through another arduous nationwide tour.

Paving the way wrestling with a windswept tourist map gleaned from a display unit in the gig's foyer, keen gadabout Danny stepped on the gas and soon gained on a rubicund gathering of silver-mopped ramblers stood admiring a flapping creature of considerable size which was trampling

---

* See Chapter 25 – Exeter

uncertainly over the furrowed watery flats.

'Get a move on, boys – it looks as if the wan… I mean walkers have sighted a blooming pelican!' the guitarist bellowed, gesticulating with an arm.

'A penguin… no way,' I cried out, experiencing a bout of selective hearing thanks to thirty-odd years of rock 'n' roll.

'Not a sodding penguin – a *pelican*, you dummy. But I suspect he may also have it wrong; they're coastal birds, aren't they?' surmised ornithological expert Rod.

'Now you're asking, but I don't recall seeing one outside of a zoo in this country,' I contemplated, assuming my pal to be spot on with his analysis.

'Hurry up, lads, he's a beauty,' shouted Danny, closing in on the billed critter, goading the pair of us to up the pace until – doing a bird impression of its own – Rod's mobile sprang into life, compelling the bass player to temporarily hang back.

Purposefully bearing down on the animated pack up ahead, revitalised by a waft of humid air gently caressing my dehydrated skin, I reached the hoary gaggle as a bald, bushy-moustached man preached to a captive band of old-timers, making several references to the half-dozen or more species of pelicans in a long-drawn-out address. He was still ranting to himself as the main group thankfully made tracks.

'Ah, are you sorry to see them go, buddy? I can see a huge lump in your throat!' mocked Danny, moving perilously close to the feathered friend, glad of the chance to marvel at the living thing unhampered by the guild of jabbering retirees.

'Do you think he's escaped from a nearby bird sanctuary?' I inferred.

'Who knows? The old boy with the handlebars thinks he's strayed well off his patch, but said there weren't enough fish in these waters to interest him for long… What a bloody know-it-all; he was beginning to get on my tits!' bitched the guitar player.

'Dan, Dave – is he still there?' echoed Rod's voice on the wind, somehow unsettling the muddled vertebrate which responded in aggressive fashion by flapping his wings violently and leaping into the centre of the footpath.

'Whoa, easy now boy,' an apprehensive Dan said guardedly, shrinking away from the waterbird an inch at a time.

'Something seems to have upset him; perhaps he can't stand grey-haired people,' I kidded, referring to the walking group in close proximity as opposed to my frosty-topped bandmate waddling along the footpath.

Amidst a sudden flutter of feathers and a piercing squawk the short-fused pelican launched into a vicious attack, pecking at Rod's face and arms in a wild frenzy and sending the alarmed bassist crashing to the ground curled up into a protective ball, bleeding profusely from a deep cut to his own sizeable beak.

'Shit, he really took a dislike to you! I felt so bloody helpless. Perhaps we should get you to a doctor,' I panicked, rushing to the sitting duck's side while dependable Dan shooed the assailing critter out of mischief's way with a dead branch.

'There's no need; I'll be okay, I'm just startled that's all. What the hell did I do to upset him?' he reflected, visibly shaken from the ordeal.

'I reckon he'd had enough of those babbling old farts and got pissed off when he saw another one coming!' commented Dan, attempting to cushion the blow.

'Perhaps he spotted the size of your bugle as you were meandering up the track and saw you as some kind of threat!' I ribbed.

'Something freaked him out, that's for sure. Maybe he thought you were a bald eagle!' Dan jibed, making reference to Rod's aquiline profile.

'Maybe it's the mating season and he took a fancy to you?' I jested, before at last cottoning on that Rod wasn't exactly seeing the funny side.

'Did he have a pop at you?' queried the hairy-lipped smart-arse, arriving back on the scene. 'They can be very temperamental you know…' he droned. 'In fact, in the breeding line…'

'Just slow down a minute, Mr Attenborough; it's no good you telling us that after the event,' snapped Dan, cutting him off dead. Taking the hint, the gasbag shuffled off along the trail without so much as another word.

Back at the theatre, with a large pink plaster applied to the gash, victim Rod received little if any sympathy from the touring company gathered for pre-show refreshments, finding himself the butt of a batch of cruel jokes. The worst came from tour manager Claude who, whilst dressing the wound, remarked: 'They're both intelligent and fussy, these pelicans, you know; they only go for the "top of the bill" – *touché*!'

****

Where possibly in this green and pleasant land could one find a more mind-blowing backdrop for an ambitious young band's trailblazing photo shoot than the otherworldly primeval site of Stonehenge?

Loaded up to the gunnels with a wide assortment of tents, sleeping bags and camping accessories – not forgetting a 'borrowed' parent's camera – a quartet of sixteen-year-old wannabes together with an acne-ridden would-be paparazzo rendezvoused in a pub car park. As they sat champing at the bit astride a cluster of Lambretta and Vespa deathtraps, ahead of them lay a three-hundred-mile round trip to the magical and mysterious Salisbury Plain. Freed from the shackles of parenthood on a shoestring budget scrimped and scraped from a range of part-time jobs, they got under way, oblivious to contingency plans or potential dangers.

Before long, like a mirage in the murky distance, the arcane rock formation rose out of the ground in all its mystery, bringing the bikes to an unscheduled halt, the riders unsettled by a ghostly, howling wind sweeping ruthlessly across the plain's open expanse.

'Let's get off the main drag at the next side road,' shouted self-appointed leader Lee above the squall. 'There should be loads of campers in the fields nearby!'

Getting on for an hour later he was eating his words as the search for the faintest sign of life continued in vain; and, out of desperation, the troupe opted for a muddy track leading through an open gate into a rocky, undulating meadow bespattered with sheep and rabbit droppings.

'This'll have to do,' bawled Lee, cutting the first turf and shimmying through a trail of rutted, muddy tyre-tracks, oblivious to the calamity unfolding behind him as my own scooter's front wheel smashed into a protruding rock, flipping the mechanism onto its side while my lean frame spiralled head over heels into a patch of nettles. After briefly squealing like a castrated pig the ailing engine rumbled to a halt, unnoticed by my bandmates juddering across the uneven surface without a care in the world, assuming my stroke of misfortune to be nothing more a blip on the radar.

I hoisted my pride and joy up onto its stand to survey the wreckage. To my dismay, a problem with the steering column stared me in the face: it had shifted badly out of kilter, most likely rendering the vehicle unroadworthy. To make matters worse, the chromium luggage rack carting the sleeping arrangements had sheared its bolts and separated from the bike's rear end, dragging the rucksack across the sludgy surface and through a train of yellowy cowpats.

'Hey you lot – I've got a major problem over here and need some assistance!' I yelped, hoping against hope at least one of my buddies would rush to help me out. Yet again I received short shrift from the feckless, gabbling bunch and was left with little choice but to plough on freewheeling to the chosen place of rest.

'What kept you…? Oh no, for fuck's sake, look at the tent – it's covered in shit!' brattish vocalist Chris remonstrated to a chorus of furious groans.

'Never mind the pissing tent; my scooter's knackered and, barring a bloody miracle, I won't be astride the sodding thing going home!' I retorted, flying into a fit of rage and slinging the bundles of camping equipment onto the boggy earth.

In a nutshell the groundbreaking photo shoot failed to pan out, attributed chiefly to a mini-whirlwind of hailstones and youthful petulance as the equally unmanageable tent flapped from east to west, ripping at the seams and proving impossible to erect, fraying tempers to boiling point with the young guns disbanding on the spot.

'You selfish bunch of bastards – not one of you gives a shit how I'll make it back. I hope it chucks it down all the way home!' I hollered, left high and not so dry in the middle of a Wiltshire field without a pot to piss in or a roof over my head, nursing a busted-up scooter, a bruised toe and a veil of shattered dreams.

As I slumped disconsolately against a wooden stile with the twisted crate propped up to the side, the coarse yap of a barking dog briefly lifted the sombreness. The animal came into view tracked by an ageing rustic seemingly trapped in a parallel universe.

'Are you okay, son? You seem a little down on your luck,' the avuncular countryman posed, a tad put out of his stride.

'I'm afraid I'm just having one of those days. I skidded into a boulder and came off my scooter as I turned into the field. I think the steering may be shot!' I let on, spilling the beans as to how my self-styled friends had upped and abandoned their smitten colleague.

'I've had my fill of days like that recently. If you can push it about a half-mile to my yard, I have a workshop over there in a converted stable where I'd be more than happy to give it the once-over,' he kindly offered.

'Do you know if there's a barn close by where I could doss down until the morning?' I pleaded, dragging the cumbersome machine along the craggy track. 'Oh, and I could do with knowing where the nearest phone box is as I'll need to call my parents at some point – that's when the shit will well and truly hit the fan!'

'I've got a spare room I can put you up in; you can call your folks from there. Don't worry, you'll be safe with me, and to be honest I'd be glad of the company… I lost my wife recently – she died of cancer a month ago to the day…' he confessed.

The rookie widower worked diligently into the night wielding screwdrivers, spanners, pliers and belatedly a rusting claw hammer, all beneath a low-wattage naked bulb suspended from the joist of an adjoining outbuilding, leaving no stone unturned as he bobbed and weaved obsessed with identifying the root cause of the problem.

'There's a small round casting in the centre of the column that appears to have been knocked out of shape and needs re-welding. I can try putting a blowtorch on it first thing if you like, but I wouldn't go getting your hopes up as I doubt you'll be able to ride her tomorrow. What say we go inside and have a nightcap?' he urged. 'My eyes are on the blink!'

'I bet you never had a drop of this stuff before, but I have a feeling you may like it!' my cordial host announced, placing two ballooned cut-crystal glasses side by side, soon awash with a honey-coloured liquid poured from a black bottle bearing the label 'Remy Martin'.

I coughed and spluttered at the first gulp, sending the hospitable old soul into a mirthful fit. As he replenished my glass I received orders to sip the dark nectar; and, in doing so, I felt a velvety sensation caress my palate, reaching warmly into the pit of my stomach. After three further generous refills I passed out on the sofa.

As the daybreak blinked through a crack in the curtains trammelled by a not-so-magic sleep fairy, all at once my senses were stirred by a joyless, fluctuating whimper seeping in from the adjoining room. Tiptoeing over the creaking floorboards and stealthily twisting the doorknob, I found my grieving host knelt at the bedside, weeping uncontrollably as he cradled a framed photograph of his recently departed loved one.

Touched by the Good Samaritan's kindness and wishful of reciprocating in the smallest way possible, I gripped a clump of tissues from a cardboard box on the night table and slunk into the master bedroom. The poignant, pitiful sight made my heart melt, and I crouched down beside him on a tattered rug, gently patting the small of his back.

'I figured these might come in handy,' I softly motioned.

'Thank you, that is so kind; sometimes I just feel the need to let it all out... I take it I've kept you awake – I really can't apologise enough,' he croaked unnecessarily. Leafing open a discoloured family album, he poured out his heart.

After grabbing another couple of hours' kip I was welcomed downstairs to a hearty plateful of baked beans on toast. Kick-starting the scooter and taking a spin around the yard, reality struck as I discovered the handlebars were pointing off-centre, well out of alignment. I realised the journey home may at best be torturous, but I was dead set against abandoning the bike.

'I think you straightened it out sufficiently to make it fit to ride; if I take it easy I should be home by teatime,' I lied, preparing to tough it out and flee the Wiltshire plains, as I grasped the man's hand and climbed astride the potential deathtrap.

'You will be very careful now, won't you?' he fussed, waving a cautionary finger in the manner of a concerned grandparent.

'I'll just take it one step at a time – there's no rush. I don't know how to thank you for helping me out and putting me up for the night,' I acknowledged, afflicted by a tinge of sadness at leaving him alone to wallow in his grief.

'There is one thing you could do before you go,' he implied.

'Just say it, anything,' I pleaded.

'If it's not too much to ask, will you promise me that, if you're ever down this way again, you'll come and look me up?' he craved, suddenly ill at ease.

'You have my word!' I replied, intent on keeping it.

****

Six years later on an overcast spring afternoon, I crunched the gear lever of my MGB-GT into first. The car had been purchased thanks to a busy year on the club circuit; and now, as a maze of Wiltshire country lanes close to a tourist-plagued Stonehenge opened up before me, my surroundings fortuitously took on a familiar look and I plumped for a concealed turning. At the bottom of an overgrown driveway, the boarded-up farmhouse stood desolate and forlorn, confusingly distinguished by a multi-coloured 'FOR SALE BY AUCTION' sign staked into the grass frontage.

Recalling a picturesque village post office I'd wobbled by on the torturous trek home way back in 1968, I pulled onto the kerb and leaped up the steps. A jovial postmaster attended to a local yokel taking eons to decide upon his choice of ice-cream, before opting instead for a giant bar of Cadbury's milk chocolate and digging in his pocket for a variety of coins.

'Sorry to rush you,' I implored, butting in, 'but I'm trying to find old John – I think his name is Crook – who used to live at the derelict farm building up the road. I noticed the place was on the market and wondered if you might know where he's moved to?'

'Well, I never – you're the lad that was on the goggle-box recently. John said you'd be coming over to see him; but I'm sorry to say you've missed the old fellow!' the bespectacled official disclosed, removing his glasses and rubbing at his eyes.

'What a shame, I've been intending paying him a visit for ages now; surely he can't have moved away from the area?' I insinuated.

'I'm awfully sorry to say, young man, that John passed away just over a month ago. You couldn't get near the church on the day of his funeral!' he lamented, offering a hand of sympathy which I accepted with a heavy heart.

Setting forth from the village and passing a tiny moss-covered church, I parked close to the gate and clunked open the weighty door. Inside, I whispered a short prayer devoted to a man I'd barely known, but whose humanity had touched both my heart and my liver, almost tasting the complex oaky delights of the fine cognac sampled in his genial company. I bade a final farewell to an altruistic old acquaintance and journeyed back to base in solemn silence.

Causes célèbres

Joseph Fiennes – actor
Michael Crawford – *Some Mothers Do 'Ave 'Em* legend
David Mitchell – comedian
Dave Dee – late friend and frontman of Dave Dee, Dozy, Beaky, Mick and Tich

Essential travelling band info

Best live music venue: City Hall, Malthouse Lane
Favourite curry house: Anokaa, Fisherton Street – 79%
Favourite pub: Wyndham Arms – 69%
Don't miss: The Close, West Walk Street – 77%
Sense of humour/friendly welcome: 60%

Chapter 54
Sheffield

BEARING LEFT FROM THE FIRST main exit route for Sheffield city centre whilst heading north on the M1 motorway just prior to rush hour and bumping along a notorious stretch of unobstructed dual carriageway known simply as 'The Parkway', I felt the urge to hit the throttle of the deluxe Ford Granada and enjoyed a brief surge of power from the thirsty three-litre engine. It didn't last long. Eyeing the driver's mirror, I detected a flashing blue light gaining on us at great speed, and duly eased on the loud pedal in advance of being shepherded onto the hard shoulder.

'I just clocked you at seventy-two miles per hour when the statutory limit is fifty,' barked the authoritative traffic cop, notepad at the ready and all set to unleash a stern ticking-off as I staggered from the vehicle.

'Don't you think that's a little over the top for a main drag like this? The road's every bit as good as the motorway, and besides there's precious little traffic around so it couldn't be said I was doing any harm,' I offered in my own defence.

'The limits are put in place for a reason; there could've been a group of kids playing innocently at the roadside. What's more, you don't have to scrape up the mess!' he overdramatized, jotting down the registration.

'You've got to be having a laugh; just take a look around you – the entire road is fenced off. If there were any children out here they'd be committing suicide!' I snapped back.

'That's as may be, but the law is the law; now, what is the purpose of your visit to the city, sir? the officer brusquely enquired.

'We're a rock-and-roll band and will be performing in concert at the City Hall tonight; in fact, we're running a little late, which perhaps explains why I was in something of a hurry,' I reasoned a touch remorsefully.

'You wouldn't happen to be Showaddywaddy, would you? My fifteen-year-old daughter's going along to see you – she's been full of it for days,' he said, lightening up.

'Perhaps I could give her a namecheck on stage to atone for being a little bit heavy-footed on the accelerator?' I grovelled.

'That would be fantastic! Her name's Kim. She'll know it's my doing; I can't wait to see her face when she gets home,' the cop hee-hawed, changing his tune entirely, albeit a tad too smugly for my liking.

'Okay, well that's that sorted then; anyway, we must be getting a move on,' I smiled, jangling the keys in my hand.

'Hey, not so hasty – is there any chance I could have a signed photo of you and the lads?' he queried, beginning to push his luck.

'Let me see… Have we got any promo pictures on board?' I shouted into the car window. 'If so, can you scribble your monikers on one for the officer?'

'Just a sec – I've got a wad in my jacket pocket,' Trevor yelled from the back seat, pretty soon coming up trumps.

'There you go, mate; I hope it makes her night,' I purred, slowly scrawling the name Kim on the card and giving a thumbs-up to the boys to suggest all was well.

'That'll be brilliant – I'll be the toast of the household later on. Anyway, I suppose I'd better ask you for your driving documents,' he requested, shifting back to a stern tone.

'I always keep them safely under lock and key at home. Do you need me to produce them at my local law-shop?' I queried.

'Yes, you'll have to do that, but I need to take down a few particulars for the summons; you mentioned you were in a rush, so best we get started!' he cajoled.

'What – you're still booking me?' I yelped incredulously.

'Of course I am,' he stated authoritatively. 'That's what I'm paid to do!'

Receiving a pink sheet ripped from a perforated pad all of five minutes later containing every last detail, anticipating yet another blemish on my licence I moodily turned to walk, shoulders slouched, back to the car.

'Whoa, hang on… That's the unpleasant stuff out of the way, now have you got that signed photo?' the cop boldly fished.

'Excuse me, but are you for real?' I sniffed, struggling to get my head around such an audacious request.

'What are you getting at?' he flouted.

'Do you honestly think I'm going to give you the time of day after you just booked me? I tell you one thing, you'll be the toast of your wife and kids alright after I've namechecked your daughter at tonight's gig!' I snapped, climbing back into the car in a fury.

Oh to have been a fly on the wall in the PC's humble abode when his stroppy teenage daughter arrived home fresh from witnessing her pin-ups live in concert, during which – before two and a half thousand fans hanging on every word – hell bent on keeping my promise I sauntered to the mike to exact a little revenge.

'I'd like to dedicate the next song to a young lady going by the name of Kim, whose daddy just so happens to be the policeman that nicked me for speeding on the way into the city,' I announced, getting it off my chest. 'Sadly, his actions cost you a signed photo… Do me a favour when you get home, Kim, and make his life hell!'

****

In the steel city again for a stint at the fabulously plush Fiesta Club some two years down the road, the band took residence at a rather grand city-centre hotel bearing the upmarket name of the Grosvenor. The high and mighty manager took time out to lay down the law for the benefit of the nightbirds assembled in the crowded lounge bar, warning that all non-residents were to vacate the premises by 11.30pm and that, should they fail to do so, the going room rate would be applied to the bills of the guests responsible.

We paid precious little heed to the headmasterly lecture, but sure enough at the stipulated time the shifty-eyed barman locked the shutters into place, stranding around thirty invitees and hangers-on forced out onto the street, acutely aware the boys and I had little or no intention of footing the bill for their presence.

'We may as well get hammered; there's sod all else to do!' carped Geoff, craning his neck to eyeball Trevor surreptitiously smuggling a young lady into a nearby lift, somehow managing to give the head of staff the slip.

'My shout – let's get the night porter over,' I announced to a racket of ironic cheers.

'He'd just disappeared into his hole at the side of the reception desk the last time I spotted him,' Rod chipped in.

'I thought this was a bloody five-star hotel; what the bloody hell's going on?' I said, becoming a little agitated. 'I'd better go and find the lazy git.'

In my efforts to fast-track into the foyer I almost collided with the manager. 'Would you please thank your party on my behalf for their understanding? I'm about to go off duty now, so if there's anything you need just ring the bell and Derek will see to it. Anyway, I'll bid you all goodnight,' he fawned, eager to make a bolt for it, patently aware his draconian actions had proven somewhat unpopular.

'Thankfully Adolph has buggered off for the night,' I explained, rejoining the parched mob. 'Grandpa was taking a nap cooped up in his hutch – he says he'll be over shortly.'

Meanwhile in the back of my mind I was dreaming up a childish prank, hatched whilst I had been killing time pacing to and fro at the night-man's desk, studying a perforated felt letter-board perched on top of a tall easel on which the interchangeable characters read:

FOR LATE NIGHT CHECK IN AND OTHER ENQUIRIES PLEASE ASK AT THE PORTERS DESK
WITH COMPLIMENTS THE MANAGER

Long possessing a fascination with words and anagrams, whilst at the same time peeved at the top dog effectively putting paid to any libidinous shenanigans, I weighed up the phrases on the display panel, puzzling over a few alternatives. Sporting a mischievous smirk I returned to my seat, thinking better than to rock the boat.

Ultimately served by the arthritic Derek, who quickly made himself scarce and crawled back into his cubbyhole, at a loose end I jotted down a concise selection of words on a handy hotel comp slip, focusing my attention on 'CHECK IN', 'DESK', 'ENQUIRIES' and 'COMPLIMENTS', soon coming up with a range of options including 'SUCK' and 'COCK' and smiling to myself at the thought of poking a little fun at the unfortunate concierge.

'What are you up to, Bartram?' asked Geoff, peeping over my shoulder.

'Oh, I got bored and came up with this hare-brained idea, but I think perhaps it's best to give it a miss,' I responded, losing my bottle.

'Why have you written down "suck" and "cock" on that scrap of paper?' he persisted.

'I was just pissing around mentally rearranging some of the letters on the noticeboard by the night porter's cubbyhole,' I came clean.

'Really... Do you fancy a refill?' he replied, failing to disguise a devilish glint in his eye and flitting back into the reception area.

'These have been signed for by your colleague with the green eye,' the janitor advised minutes later, blundering into the lounge shoving a metal trolley loaded up with a fresh round of drinks before skedaddling back to his post, passing a self-satisfied Geoff on the way.

'Cheers!' the bass man proposed, raising his glass. Leaning down, he whispered in my ear: 'Don't say another word, just go and take a shufti at that display board – you'll piss yourself laughing when you see it!'

Emerging from my seat feigning a trip to the loo, I crept furtively into the lobby where, fighting the urge to dissolve into hysterics, I clamped both hands to my mouth. There, leaping out from the board, were the words:

LATE AT NIGHT PLEASE SUCK THE PORTERS COCK
PETER FORESKIN THE SHIT MANAGER

In stitches at the wordsmith's slick improvisation, I teetered backwards into the doorway unable to keep a straight face, summoning the guys into the lobby to get a piece of the action just as a distinguished, well-to-do-looking couple clattered through the revolving doors hampered by a suitcase apiece and stalling at the reception desk.

'Bloody hell, this could be interesting,' observed a sheepish Geoff.

'Norman, there doesn't seem to be a soul around; how on earth are we supposed to register and get the key to our suite?' the refined lady quibbled, clearly feeling the ill effects of a lengthy journey into the night.

'Don't worry, I'll ring the bell darling, although it appears there's some information regarding late-night check-in on the board over there,' he implied, blissfully unaware his good lady may be in for the shock of her life.

Shuffling towards the noticeboard, the queen bee stopped dead in her tracks. 'Goodness me, Norman – what kind of a hotel is this? Come and take a look at what's posted on this stand; it's absolutely frightful!' she chastised.

'What's on earth's wrong, darling…?' the good husband inquired, turning on a sixpence only to find himself confronted by the fawning night porter.

'You must be Lord and Lady Kettleborough; I'm so sorry to have kept you,' Derek pandered. 'We've been expecting you – your room is all prepared!'

'Really Norman, I think we should be staying elsewhere; my eyes are far from deceiving me and I can honestly say I've never witnessed anything quite as obscene!' the lady bickered, taking a seat to recuperate.

'Darling, it's much too late to go gallivanting around the city looking for another hotel. Besides, I've stayed here before and it's perfectly acceptable,' the immaculately spoken peer maintained. 'What on earth is bothering you?' He turned to the bulletin board and perused its contents. 'Hahahahahaha, that's the funniest thing I've seen in years,' the toff rat-a-tat-tatted like a human machine gun, reaching for the seat beside his wife to catch his breath.

'Norman…! Really, you can be so coarse sometimes; you're not in the company of your military friends now!' the woman bleated.

'Don't be such a stick-in-the-mud, darling, let me have my fun… Have you had any takers yet?' his Lordship cackled in the direction of the oblivious, flummoxed concierge, wiping away the tears of joy welling in his eyes.

'I'm not at all with you sir, though I'm pleased to see that everything's to your liking and that something seems to have amused you!' the night-man obsequiously responded, watched with interest by the dillydallying bystanders.

'From the looks of it you've had a few rather creative guests in here this evening, who it would appear have been erring on the side of playful,' the nobleman wryly chuckled. 'Don't you just love a rascally sense of humour? I know I do!' Collecting his key, he wandered to the lift with her ladyship in tow.

'I think perhaps your next job should be to amend the wording,' a fellow resident remarked, skipping up the stairs bidding everyone goodnight, heralding a mass exodus into the bar where before long the session moved into overdrive.

'I thought his old dear was going to kick off big time – her face was as white as snow,' inferred Rod as we chewed over the aristocrat's broadminded wit which had earned the admiration of a bunch of rather less sophisticated drifters.

'He seemed like a worldly-wise guy to me; I'd lay money he used to be a brigadier or some high-ranking military man!' I observed.

'It's called breeding,' Geoff elaborated, releasing a contemptuous sigh and raising his eyes to the ceiling as Trevor waltzed into the bar resembling a hobo, clad in a moth-eaten yellow running vest and frayed tracksuit bottoms, bitterly complaining that room service had failed to heed his call.

Causes célèbres

Joe Cocker – gravelly voiced singing legend
Jarvis Cocker – ex Pulp frontman
Michael Palin – globetrotting Python funny man
Brian Glover – actor
Alex Turner – Arctic Monkeys gobby frontman
A.S. Byatt – author
Joanne Harris – author
Richard Hawley – the Sheffield Sinatra
Paul Carrack – classy singer
Alastair Burnet – newscaster
Bruce Oldfield – fashion designer
Leslie Ash – comedy actress
Eddie Izzard – comedian
Patrick McGoohan – *The Prisoner* legend
Sebastian Coe – Olympic hero in more ways than one

Essential travelling band info

Best live music venue: Motorpoint Arena, Broughton Lane
Favourite curry house: Viraaj, Chesterfield Road – 68%
Favourite pub: Henry's Café Bar, Cambridge Street – 73%
Don't miss: Botanical Gardens, Clarkehouse Road – 49%
Sense of humour/friendly welcome: 67%

Chapter 55
Southampton

BY THE MIDDLE OF THE 1990s the pursuit of cruise holiday-making hitherto associated with a well-heeled breed of passenger took a tilt toward a more mainstream clientele, becoming affordable to industrious career-minded adventurers and energetic working couples seeking alternatives to a banal 'all-inclusive' recess languishing in a purpose-built Mediterranean or similarly predictable beach resort. In consequence, as setting sail caught on as the in-vogue thing to do, many leading shipping lines received a deluge of booking requests and enquiries, thus creating a major upsurge in business and all-out war as rival companies dreamed up new ideas and offered large discounts in a bid to blow the competition out of the water.

As the staid and stuffy clients of yesteryear made way for hordes of ocean-going, new-money party animals in search of a hedonistic experience living it large on the high seas, the cabin doors were opened to a who's who of celebrity chefs, renowned gardeners, daytime TV hosts and retired sportsmen fronting a variety of themed cruises, all tempted on board by unthrifty fees and luxury suites.

Next in line a host of internationally renowned musicians and artistes ascended the gangplank, roped into headlining 'Fifties', 'Sixties' and 'Seventies' packages. This culminated in an approach to the band to perform four shows over just two nights as part of a fourteen-day junket aboard P&O's *Oriana*. It proved far too tantalising a prospect to resist, and we grabbed it with both hands, setting the stage for an undemanding career first.

As the ship put out to sea from the port of Southampton a booming baritone horn resonated, buoying a scattering of wayside onlookers into waving and gesticulating to the happy seafarers, bidding *bon voyage* to the vessel gliding gracefully from its berth into open water.

Disappointingly, the performances were reined in by decibel restrictions, essentially to avoid giving offence to a small number of nitpicking elderly passengers; but, oddly in keeping with the nautical drift, the watered-down shows fell short of dampening either audience's or band's spirits, and provided us with the perfect fillip far away from the rough and tumble of the road as we donned our formal dinner suits and enjoyed a revival of the camaraderie that had been somewhat cast adrift in recent times.

We found ourselves mingling in with a bunch of entertainers and crew well acquainted with the ins and outs of life on board, and pretty soon invitations flew back and forth requesting my own and the boys' presence below sea level in the staff's private facilities, shut off from the social graces of the upper decks and happily where a round of drinks came in at a third of the price of the public areas.

Escorted on one such excursion by a smart young officer attired in navy whites and cap, I spotted an out-of-place red sign pointing off toward the port side indicating '*Mortuary*', which more than aroused a morbid curiosity.

'I suppose you could call that vault the dead centre of the ship. Do you ever find a use for it?' I pressed, afflicted by an outbreak of the jitters.

'You'd be surprised at how many passengers we do lose, especially on the three-month-long world cruises where more often than not some old stager pops their clogs,' he responded, passing it off with an insouciant air of inevitability.

'Doesn't it feel a bit spooky, carrying dead bodies on board for weeks on end?' I enquired, suffering a minor outbreak of goose pimples.

'To be honest, you don't really think about it; though there was one episode that touched the hearts of the whole crew,' he relayed with a hint of sadness. Over a beer he opened up and recounted a heart-wrenching, achingly poignant tale.

****

Hailing from the Lancashire town of Ashton-under-Lyne, Jack and Margaret Hargreaves came from an era where a couple's marriage vows remained etched in stone, and they shared a life of wedded bliss like two peas in a pod for in excess of forty-nine years.

Jack had served as a rookie naval officer towards the end of the Second World War, and cherished a long-term ambition to return to the briny with his childhood sweetheart in the duo's autumn years. Envisaging the trip of a lifetime and following his heart, at the age of seventy-six the intrepid Jack took the plunge, seizing the opportunity to lavish a large chunk of the couple's life savings on the abiding dream of a world cruise, timed to coincide with the couple's golden wedding anniversary looming on the horizon. The proposed itinerary of faraway destinations encompassed the likes of Australia and New Zealand whilst also realising Margaret's enduring ambition to visit the

Polynesian paradise of Tahiti.

'You get to know most of the passengers pretty well on a ninety-nine day trip, plus Jack was renowned as a generous tipper which made him very popular with the staff; but even so we all held a soft spot for the pair of them, though it was clear from the outset that Mrs Hargreaves wasn't in the best of health,' the seaman enlightened.

After celebrating the big fiftieth with a spectacular day's sightseeing on the island of Bali, the golden couple returned to the ship for a low-key romantic dinner. An evening of unashamed indulgence awaited them, inspired by scores of homespun greetings along with cards and trinkets from the well-wishing crew and fellow voyagers alike, crowned by a sumptuous feast at the captain's table. An enormous handcrafted cake was unveiled, and the never-to-be-forgotten occasion was brought to a close with a commemorative toast led by the ship's top dog.

'The pair of them stayed holed up in their cabin for days after the big blowout, which most of us figured was likely due to exhaustion,' the salty dog continued. 'Then a member of the admin team got wind of an alteration to their booking, confirming that the couple would now be disembarking in Kuala Lumpur in Malaysia in just a few days' time, which albeit a little out of the ordinary failed to trigger off any alarm bells.'

Having disregarded the 'do not disturb' sign and entered the cabin by way of a pass key to provide fresh towels and bed linen, a young Asian steward alerted his seniors stressing that the inhabitants had tidied up after themselves and vacated their suite. They had left behind a range of fully packed suitcases and three sealed envelopes, marked for the attention of the captain and crew, the housekeeper and Douglas Hargreaves, Jack's brother and sole living relative.

'A whole crowd of us gathered in here till all hours that night, mostly in floods of tears, doing our best to come to terms with what had happened,' the guy confided, his voice cracking with emotion as the outcome unfolded.

Three months prior to setting sail and fulfilling their dream, following months of tests a team of specialists had tragically diagnosed Margaret Hargreaves as riddled with cervical cancer, the silent killer being too far gone for any form of treatment to prove effective and resigning the lady to a maximum of six months to live.

'The letter broke everyone's hearts. I can remember one line vividly which really brought home Jack's total devastation, saying: *I cannot and will not go on living without my lifeblood and one true love. To attempt to do so would be meaningless, painful and utterly futile!*' the young mariner recited from memory to a chorus of snivels and frogs in throat.

According to eyewitnesses, having attended the luxurious midnight buffet dressed in their most elegant finery, Jack and Margaret Hargreaves were last seen at around 2am embracing beneath a starlit sky with the wind in their hair, casting a lovers' shadow silhouetting across the foaming wake aback of the ship's stern.

Hand in hand, reminiscent of a Shakespearian tragedy, the devoted couple doggedly scaled the high-reaching safety rail before taking flight together like angels into the boundless Neptunian abyss, their souls bonded, unendingly inseparable.

****

Despite a checklist of professional misgivings, the maiden voyage more than lived up to the cruise line's expectations as, in flattering tones, impressed by our performances, the P&O representatives came knocking again just eighteen months later. They agreed to ship on board a few additional items of equipment to up the ante and give the shows a more familiar feel.

Once again we put to sea out of Southampton. The labyrinthine docks teemed with haulage vehicles unloading freight trailers onto cargo vessels, overlooked by a formation of high-rise derricks and inactive hoists which towered above the melee of roof-racked cars weaving through the mass of activity towards the big ship.

'The Jewels of the Atlantic', as the cruise had exotically been dubbed, focused its attentions on the year-round sunshine of the Canary Islands, taking in popular ports of call such as Tenerife, Lanzarote and the lesser known enclave of La Palma ahead of docking in Portugal's capital Lisbon and the Galician city of Vigo on the return passage.

We were hopping into one of a line of taxis idling at the ship in the port of La Palma when the unmistakeably bronzed – though in recent times worryingly antisocial – figure of Trevor sauntered past his fellow explorers.

'Do you want to tag along with us?' offered Danny.

'No... I'd rather walk,' the football-shorted sun-worshipper laconically snapped, refusing the offer with a resounding thumbs-down.

'It very long way, mister – maybe five kilometres!' the cabbie called out to him in pidgin English. Finding himself completely ignored, he accelerated toward the unkempt little town. It turned out to be not improved in any way by a rabble of tourist-unfriendly locals and street vendors, and we soon hurried back to the port for an afternoon dip in the quietude of the uninhabited ship.

'Where the fuck's Trevor? We're supposed to set sail at six and it's twenty to now!' crabbed Geoff nervously. As the clock tumbled towards the hour our reclusive bandmate was still missing, leaving us little choice but to contact the cruise director.

'I'm afraid the port authority allows us very little leeway and we'd probably only be able to delay by a maximum of fifteen minutes. That said, it's impossible to get lost on La Palma – it's just a dot in the ocean!' the helmsman chided.

I was pacing anxiously back and forth on the top deck and peering over the polished handrail when, at ten minutes past the hour, a yellow cab screeching into the harbour at long last announced Trevor's late arrival, welcomed with a sigh of relief. Springing from the passenger seat the guitarist hot-footed it up the sole remaining gangplank.

'You cut that a bit fine; where the fuck have you been?' Geoff admonished, stepping out into the hallway in the midst of a row of heads protruding from their own quarters. Ignoring him, the guitarist let himself into his berth in a tense silence.

'Trevor, let me in – we need to talk,' I pleaded, tapping lightly on his cabin door, anxious to get to the bottom of his air of despondency along with a few facts as to the mysterious island escapade that had so nearly cost us dear.

'Look, I just got lost, that's all. I don't know what all the fuss is about – I made it back in time, didn't I?' he belligerently upheld.

'That's not good enough,' I persisted. 'You almost literally missed the boat; why the hell were you so late? It seems like you don't give a shit.'

'You wouldn't believe me if I told you, so what's the point?' he groaned.

'Try me!' I urged…

As Trevor strutted purposefully in the direction of the small capital of Santa Cruz de la Palma, a swarthy Spaniard pulling out of the port in a dusty Volkswagen had struck a deal with the ageing rocker, offering him a lift to any part of the island in return for his assistance in lugging a bootload of supplies to a colleague's nearby property.

'The sacks weighed a bloody ton; but he was keen to keep his part of the bargain, so I asked him to drop me off at the nearest beach and we wound up at this amazing hacienda-style gaff with steps leading down to a private beach,' Trevor gushed.

'And?' I pressed.

'He kept banging on about his friend being a famous singer in Ireland, saying that he was on his way over tomorrow on his yacht. Anyway, that's basically it; I couldn't get a taxi back and got lost!' he claimed, suddenly curtailing the conversation.

'Hang on – why didn't he give you a lift the same way you came? This tale just doesn't ring true; come on, out with it!' I urged, unwilling to be fobbed off.

'Look, he plied me with a load of booze and I fell asleep; when I came round he was gone – that's it,' he admitted in a strop. 'Now for fuck's sake leave me alone!' Clearly ruffled, he leaned back onto the pillow, hands behind his head.

'It still doesn't add up; why would he leave you at his house and just piss off into thin air?' I probed, refusing to let him off the hook.

'Because it wasn't his place at all! The bastard had nicked my watch and all my money,' he finally owned up. 'When I woke up there were two blokes stood on the terrace asking what the fuck I was doing there, one who only spoke Spanish and the other with an Irish accent, both pointing to a dead body bobbing up and down in the sea!'

'A dead body... and they thought you had something to do with it?' I gasped.

'Precisely... but the Paddy seemed more concerned as to what I was doing at his friend's house. I knew I recognised him from somewhere, and then clicked that he was the Irish singer the thieving dago had mentioned,' he continued.

'You don't think the dead body was him, do you?' I contrived.

'I didn't wait to find out. The real owner thought he may have been the gardener delivering some topsoil. Whoever he was, I could've murdered him with my own bare hands, the light-fingered twat!' Trevor complained.

'So you couldn't afford a taxi back to the ship?' I surmised.

'You're quick on the uptake. Before I knew it, the pair of them had stripped off and were jumping around in the pool stark bollock naked; they even asked me to join them, but I was out of there like a shot. The area was crawling with coppers so I just kept on walking until I found a screwed-up ten-euro note in the swimming pouch of my shorts, otherwise there's no way I'd ever have made it back in time,' he vented, fishing for a pat on the back.

'Actually, you do look kind of gay in those tight shorts! So is there a warrant out for your arrest in La Palma?' I jested.

'Let's just say I won't be going back there in a hurry!' he closed, leaping up and mincing out of the cabin in the direction of the cafeteria.

Causes célèbres

Benny Hill – legendary TV comedian
Ken Russell – film director
Craig David – singer
Howard Jones – electronic '80s hitmaker
Mike Batt – Wombles mastermind
Will Champion – Coldplay drummer

Essential travelling band info

Live music venue: Mayflower Theatre, Commercial Road
Favourite curry house: Royal Bengal, Coronation Parade, Hamble – 70%
Favourite pub: Guide Dog, Earl's Road – 81%
Don't miss: The Old Cemetery, Cemetery Lane (especially for *Titanic* enthusiasts) – 74%
Sense of humour/friendly welcome: 54%

Chapter 56
St Albans

LYING JUST TO THE NORTH of the M25 motorway, the sprawling overspill of England's capital enshrouds a conglomeration of prosaic quasi-satellite new towns, all bearing a striking resemblance to one another in both the concrete-dominated architecture and humdrum high streets. Regardless of serving a purpose, they hold little sway for any visiting out-of-towners, often found taking a wrong turn only to feel the effects of *déjà vu*.

In stark contrast to the likes of Hemel Hempstead, Hatfield, Stevenage, Welwyn Garden City, Braintree, Harlow and the labyrinthine confusion of Milton Keynes just to the north, the delightful upmarket settlement of St Albans instantly breaks the mould, offering a pleasant diversion whilst constituting the county town of Hertfordshire.

Lauded for its location and amenities (including the deceptively named 850-capacity Alban Arena where the band performed on a number of occasions) in addition to lying well within London's renowned stockbroker belt, the agreeable small city acts as a magnet for scores of high-earning city slickers, a fact duly reflected in the affordability of the domain's ever-rising property prices, peaking at amongst the highest in the UK.

****

During a late-eighties run of Middle Eastern dates, the band were preparing to live it large in an opulent five-star Abu Dhabi hotel when a rough-diamond Englishman going under the name of Ken Harris instantaneously latched onto the party. Supposedly eager for a bit of craic with a bunch of fellow nationals, he was clearly at loggerheads with the powers that be who quizzically scrutinised his every move, suggesting the man had few admirers in these parts.

Hailing from St Albans and undoubtedly pigeonholed into the dubious category of a 'likeable rogue', the oil-rigger bubbled over with enthusiasm as the troupe checked in at the ornate reception desk, briefly stepping aside to allow a scruffy, obsequious local man to greet the gang with a welcoming gift of a small hamper. It was quickly found to contain two bottles of white spirit together with a wide variety of Arabian nuts.

'It is customary in my country to greet foreign visitors with an offering of nuts and vodka,' the buck-toothed Muslim generously announced, hastening to add: 'But on this occasion you can keep the nuts and I'll have the vodka!' Grabbing the bottles, he beat a hasty retreat from the premises in a disorientating fast-forward blur, fortunate not to receive the waiting boot of a burly security guard lurking close by.

'Where's your mate gone with the vodka?' Geoff put to our new pal.

'What, Ali Baba? He's no friend of mine; he just seized on the opportunity of a buckshee tipple. That freeloading git's always hanging around in here!' the ink-gunned compatriot explained, much to his countrymen's disappointment. 'I've been looking forward to you lads arriving; I love a bit of rock and roll, and this place desperately needs livening up… I'll get a few bevvies lined up in the bar later after the show's over, 'cause I bet you'll be gagging for a few beers by then,' he spouted like a long-lost buddy. He appeared harmless enough, and our heads nodded in the affirmative, believing the invitation may at least provide a modicum of mirth.

Surpassing everyone's expectations, the lavish outdoor extravaganza worked the partygoers up into a frenzy. A circle of dish-dash-clad natives were mind-bogglingly enticed up onto the dance floor gagging to shake a leg with a bevy of French air hostesses staying the night in the hotel, doubtless in the hope of getting lucky as the night progressed. Meanwhile, vying for our attention, a gang of demonstrative ex-pats situated to the rear of the Arabian ocean of white whooped and hollered, climbing onto their seats and raising a red-lettered makeshift banner bearing the greeting:

'*SHAWADIWADI WELCOME TO ABU DERBY*'

Sticking out a mile with its flagrant misspellings, it warranted a mirthful response from the boys and punters alike and was signalled out for special attention. The energetic clique lapped it up, snaking between the tables with reckless abandon, all adding up to a night to remember cavorting beneath a coruscating star-studded sky.

As we entered the palatial cocktail lounge to a ripple of applause post-performance, a cross-section of exuberant ex-pat guys stood propping up the bar, perspiring heavily in their light-coloured linen suits. Meanwhile their evenly tanned spouses flaunted themselves within spitting distance, gaily adorned in a kaleidoscopic array of strappy summer dresses.

'Have you seen those "Frog" air stewardesses? I've got my eye on one of those little beauties!' the irrepressible Ken fantasised as he welcomed us over to the bar. He had clearly missed out big time on impressing in the fashion stakes, being outrageously bedecked in a pair of loud, pocketed combat trousers together with a black 'AC-DC' T-shirt.

'You're bloody dreaming! What would they want with a tattooed English drunk?' Geoff lashed out, a trifle over-familiarly.

'You cheeky sod! The night is still young; a few G&Ts and they won't be able to keep their hands off me. Anyway, it's your shout – get the bloody drinks in, you tight git!' the rascal coerced, jabbing his new drinking partner in the ribs.

As midnight approached, the gathering whittled down dramatically to a sprinkling of addled laggards. Stripping to the waist and flexing his biceps in a vainglorious effort to impress a lingering pair of Air France trolley dollies, the incorrigible Ken cockily reeled off a stockpile of tall stories as to the reasons behind his badges of courage.

'I'm afraid I find them utterly repulsive; were you in the merchant navy or something?' an unsteady, refined ex-pat lady slurred.

'What, me, a bum-bandit sailor? Not likely! But I am a well-travelled man, mainly through working on the oil rigs,' Ken expounded.

'I've got a tattoo on my old boy that says "MARY"!' I tipsily contributed.

'Really, have you?' the inquisitive gentlewoman asked, turning in my direction with raised eyebrows and a wry smile.

'Yes, and when I get aroused it says "Merry Christmas Everybody", hahaha!' I inanely jibed, wishing I'd kept my big mouth shut.

'I like that, but I can go one better; I've got two W's on the cheeks of my arse... for real!' the topless rabble-rouser boasted.

'Do the letters stand for William Wordsworth, or perhaps William Wallace?' enquired the lady, adding a cultural tone to the conversation.

'William who...? I'll show you if you like!' offered Ken. Needing little encouragement he jumped onto a glass coffee table before dropping his Swiss Army slacks in true exhibitionist style, revealing a blue inked letter 'W' emblazoned on each of his pallid buttocks. 'Do you get the picture, or do I need to spell it out?' he challenged, pulling his cheeks apart and roaring 'WOW!'

This prompted a distinguished-looking suited man to rush onto the scene frantically gesticulating with his arms.

'This kind of behaviour is unacceptable in our country; I will be forced to call the police if you don't put your clothes back on immediately, sir. Please do try and show just a shred of respect to the other guests!' the official insisted, ordering two burly members of staff to escort the flaunter to a nearby lavatory to make himself decent.

'I'm terribly sorry, ladies and gentlemen, but I'm going to have to ask you all to vacate the bar area with immediate effect. If the local police got wind of tonight's events we would almost certainly be closed down,' the manager claimed, shepherding the unimpressed band of residents towards the open-plan reception area.

'That's the only wow factor that odious man will ever possess!' the piqued lady signed off, making for the lift and bidding everyone goodnight.

****

Seven days later we arrived by light aircraft into an oil camp close to the Yemeni border in the Sultanate of Oman. Picking up his bag from the back of a pick-up truck and strolling towards our chalets, an artful-looking Geoff caught my attention.

'Our old mate Ken from Abu Dhabi was transferred over here the day we left, so no doubt we'll be in for some fun and games later on!' he chuckled to a muted reaction. Dropping down his belongings, he wandered off to seek out the head case.

'Did you find him?' I put to Geoff as we met up in the canteen for supper, ignoring the leering glances from a bunch of strangely effeminate riggers.

'I didn't actually find him, but he's really gone and done it this time. He had to make a speedy exit before the rag-heads came and lynched him. They put him on the first plane out of here yesterday… he's been deported!' the bassist croaked, hacking a smoker's cough ahead of filling in the blanks.

Picking up from where he'd left off in the UAE, the hell-raiser had partaken in a vodka-fuelled session at the members' clubhouse until 3am. Stumbling back to his quarters, he had seen fit to ascend the gallery of a nearby minaret (used five times daily for the sacred Islamic call to prayer), blasphemously bellowing out his own take on Jennifer Rush's 'The Power Of Love' through the mounted loudspeaker in a shrill, raucous tone, soon finding himself manhandled from his position by a group of oil company employees fearing for his safety.

A full-scale enquiry was set in motion, conducted by the Omani authorities who showed up at the camp the very next morning in the form of a team of grim-faced armed officers. Upon learning of the perpetrator's defection only minutes prior to their arrival they came down hard on all and sundry, desperately looking for a scapegoat; but their efforts to prevent the individual from fleeing the Sultanate unscathed were thwarted once again.

Rumours swirled concerning a London-bound flight out of Oman's Muscat airport taking to the skies above the heads of an incensed battalion of security forces dashing onto the tarmac resolved to apprehend the malefactor. By the skin of his teeth he had avoided trial, along with a guilty verdict punishable by the most draconian penalty of all… death by beheading!

Causes célèbres

Francis Bacon – philosopher
Rod Argent – The Zombies and Argent musician
Steve Collins – ex-boxer
Nicholas Breakspear – the one and only English pope (1154AD)

Essential travelling band info

Live music venue: Alban Arena, Civic Centre
Favourite curry house: Abbey Spice, Stanhope Road – 62%
Favourite pub: Mermaid, Hatfield Road – 68%
Don't miss: Organ Theatre and Museum, Camp Road – 77%
Sense of humour/friendly welcome: 64%

Chapter 57
St Asaph

'THERE WAS SOMETHING ON THE news earlier this morning about three towns being awarded city status to mark the Queen's Jubilee year in 2012,' my wife Cathy revealed over breakfast, provoking a mad dash to the computer. Anxious to glean a little more information, I clicked on the Google icon, leading me to a Reuters piece which reported:

'The British towns of Chelmsford, Perth and St Asaph are poised to gain city status to mark the Queen's Diamond Jubilee, beating off competition from twenty-two others to win the "civic honours" accolade under the royal prerogative, following advice from Deputy Prime Minister Nick Clegg.'

'How do you fancy a day trip to St Asaph in North Wales?' I suggested, fresh from poring over an AA atlas lying about close to my desk and grabbing a tea towel to assist a rubber-gloved Cathy slaving over the kitchen sink washing the dishes.

'What's there?' she asked with a puzzled look.

'I'm not at all sure; all I know is it's the only UK city I've never been to, so if my book is intended as a comprehensive guide I really need to go!' I vowed.

****

Passing a black-and-white sign specifying *'St Asaph, 4 Miles'* around two weeks later, a sense of familiarity suggested the expedition into Denbighshire may not after all be my first trek into the vicinity, having made regular trips to the nearby bucket-and-spade resort of Rhyl and once stopping off in neighbouring Rhuddlan more than thirty years previously during an ill-fated jaunt* to Holyhead in Anglesey.

Hanging the car left from the A55 dual carriageway and drifting past a ramshackle store vending a range of specialist fishing tackle, the penny dropped I'd actually trodden these streets only a handful of years earlier, accompanying

---

* See Chapter 4 – Bangor

guitarist Danny in his quest to acquire a colourful assortment of floats and spinners for use in pursuing his favourite pastime whiling away the hours on the Leicestershire river banks.

As the road trundled over a delightful old humpback bridge traversing the river Elwy and slanted down towards an outwardly non-existent city centre, overhead a conspicuous display of coloured banners and bunting rippled in the gentle breeze suspended above a variety of pubs and shops, presumably to celebrate the Deputy Prime Minister's recommendation, though somewhat confusingly also hailing the locality as the '*City of Music*'!

Glued to the wheel, I wracked my brain as to the vagaries of the town's prestigious new status; and later perusing my notes a thought occurred that I'd visited any number of villages vastly more populated than the three-and-a-half-thousand-strong Welsh community. The journey thus seemed to be something of a wild goose chase, though having travelled so far I wasn't about to cut and run without at least giving the place a chance.

One is hardly likely to miss the ancient cathedral languishing at the top end of town and I navigated a narrow pathway meandering through the neatly mown frontage, passing beneath an ornate arched entrance into the oddly inconspicuous structure. As if sensing my bewilderment upon encountering several rows of IKEA-style upright chairs more akin to a provincial church hall, a delightful silver-topped lady asked politely if I required any information.

'Ah yes, if you don't mind; what happened to the original pews?' I probed, noticing an absence of fixing holes on the flagstoned floor.

'There were none; the area you're referring to was actually where the hordes of paupers stood for hours on end, well out of smelling distance from the citizens of more noble origin, most of whom would have been comfortably seated at the top end of the nave, close to the chancel,' she informatively explained.

'So I take it similarly poorer families don't attend the services any more?' I delved, veering towards a potentially touchy subject.

'That's actually a very good question; these days it's a constant struggle to attract people from any walk of life to the services... but then again that didn't prevent us from getting city status ahead of that dreadful place twenty-five miles up the road, did it now?' she answered defiantly, proudly perking up mid-sentence.

'I'm sorry, which town is that?' I asked.

'Wrexham, of course; just saying the blessed name makes me go cold!' she huffed, crossing herself at the mild indiscretion.

'Don't you like people from Wrexham? My brother-in-law lives there!' I teased.

'I'm sure he's a perfectly good human being, though it's fair to say there's always been a healthy rivalry between the two towns… In any case they didn't deserve the accolade; they've only got a rubbishy parish church, which compared to this divine building I'm sure swung the balance… Let's be honest, it was really no contest!' she boasted, excusing herself to attend to a batch of new visitors, who judging by their piercing full-mouthed comments reverberating to all four corners of the holy place hailed from across the pond.

****

Stop-starting in a never-ending stream of traffic descending into gridlock on the town's narrow main street, I located a vacant parking berth close to the Translator's Monument (commemorating the adaption of the Bible into Welsh) and reversed into the space. As I alighted from the car, an oddball character clutching onto a young girl's hand appeared to take issue, blocking my path and looking fixedly into my eyes.

'What the bloody hell are you doing here?' the man boldly pried.

'Excuse me, but do I know you?' I inquired, slightly taken aback.

'No, but I bloody well know who you are; I've got every one of your records going all the way back to 1974 on vinyl and CD!' the fanatic replied.

'Wow, some of them must have gathered a little dust by now!' I commented, offering my hand in gratitude and winking at the youngster.

'This man here used to be more famous than Wetshite you know!' he derided, rattling the obviously long-suffering girl's cage.

'You know they're called Westlife, and that's a stupid joke!' she retaliated, wheeling away in her embarrassment.

A trifle belittled by the odd comparison to the Irish boys who'd once blanked the band on the set of a German TV show, I slipped away to leave father and irate daughter to battle it out on the pavement. As I hurried back to the car to get the hell outta Dodge a small roadside patisserie directly opposite caused my stomach to rumble, and I weaved through the line of cars to grab some sustenance ahead of the journey's second leg to Manchester.

'Tuna and sweetcorn please, on brown bread if you don't mind,' I requested. Leaving the plastic-gloved assistant to slice into the chunky loaf, I whiled away the time scanning a flyer-littered noticeboard advertising the town's forthcoming events.

'That'll be two pounds and thirty pee including the Lucozade,' the serving wench confirmed. The door's sharp ping heralded the arrival of another hungry patron, almost inevitably turning out to be my new best friend.

'I knew I'd find you in 'ere, 'cause it's by far the best sandwich bar in town!' he tattled, grovelling like a lapdog.

'Isn't this the only sandwich bar in town?' I flippantly countered.

'Haha, I'd have to get up early to catch you out… Yes, I think you're right!' he squirmed, grabbing a thick wad of paper napkins from the glass worktop to plainly alienate the jumbled hash of gawping customers waiting in line. 'Can you put your moniker on these eighteen times? One for David, that's me… one for Caron, that's my daughter here… one for Bethany, another one for Ewan… oh and I mustn't forget…' he slobbered outside of the shop, counting his every living relative on his fingers though balking at my raised right hand.

'Listen mate, I appreciate you being a fan and all that, but I really haven't got all day. I'll do two, one for you and one for your daughter – though in all honesty I'm not sure she's that fussed – but that's it!' I scolded, drawing the line.

'On no, that's a bloody shame, it's not every day you meet a leg-end in St Asaph; do you get it – leg… end?' he nauseatingly spelt out.

'And it's not every day I meet a knob-end in St Asaph, so we're all square,' I disparagingly shot back, tugging at the car door. I slid down into the seat, pulled on a pair of shades and made every effort possible to distance myself from the pain in the neck, before eventually sinking my teeth into the crusty bread.

Hopelessly trapped behind a six-wheeler bus attempting to manoeuvre around an inconsiderately parked Chelsea tractor, I clicked on the radio to catch up on the Saturday football scores. Unbelievably, a bothersome tap-tap-tapping akin to the sound of a woodpecker jabbed at the passenger side window; and to my left I clocked the out-to-lunch douchebag fussily brandishing the wad of serviettes.

'Come on boyo, just a couple more!' he badgered.

'*I'M A CELEBRITY GET ME OUTTA HERE!*' I screamed. As I raised a despairing hand to my brow, mercifully I observed the coach edging around the shiny black Range Rover. It was tailed by my own BMW, practically attached to the driver's bumper.

Causes célèbres

Ian Rush – ex-Liverpool and Welsh International footballer
Henry Morton Stanley – explorer who coined the phrase 'Doctor Livingstone, I presume?'
Felicia Hemans – poet ('The boy stood on the burning deck')

Essential travelling band info

Live music venue: Pavilion, East Parade, Rhyl
Favourite curry house: Chilli Pink, Queen Street, Rhyl (there isn't one in
    St Asaph) – 43%
Favourite pub: The Plough, The Roe – 36%
Don't miss: the smallest cathedral in Britain – 51%
Sense of humour/friendly welcome: 58%

Chapter 58
St Davids

YET AGAIN CASTING AN EYE back to my younger years, earning a weekly stipend courtesy of a 'proper job', in hindsight I probably owe an enormous, yet ironic debt of gratitude to a beanpole of a Welsh whinger proud of his deep-seated roots in the county of Pembrokeshire, close to the chocolate-box miniature city of St Davids.

While I learned the ropes as a telecommunications apprentice cooped up in a small telephone exchange on the outskirts of Leicester, each hard-earned tea break took on a similar tone to the previous one, detracted from by Taff's incessant grumbling. Whether the subject be politics, football or even sex (which he referred to as overrated), he persistently laid any constructive arguments to waste with a sure-fire diatribe of negative bunkum. Always sharp to form a biased opinion and give rise for further bellyaching, the contrary Taff rarely found a good word to say on any subject, berating this and finding fault with that in between reluctantly putting on the kettle (I don't believe I ever saw him do any other work) in the small works canteen, making endless references to the incomparable beauty of his native county and the genuine warmth of the people he so sorely missed, despite not having set foot in his homeland for over forty years.

'That rock-and-roll stuff is the music of the devil,' the wiry caretaker carped as if straight out of the pious American 'Bible Belt', where in all likelihood he may well have felt much more at home. 'I don't know how you can listen to it let alone play the bloody crap! Give me a proper singer like Harry Secombe any day!'

'You'll no doubt be pleased to know I've decided to quit the Post Office and follow my dream of becoming a professional singer-guitarist... I just can't bloody well listen to any more of your griping!' I announced out of the blue as I entered the mess room one morning, calculably earning a wrathful response from the irascible caretaker.

'You'll never make a proper living doing that; you're just a dreamer, boy, and a fucking idiot to boot!' the Welshman abusively ranted, giving me a piece of his mind.

'Look, it's something I really want to do, and if I don't give it a go while I'm young I may well live to regret it; you just don't get it, do you?' I argued.

'Fuck off, I understand perfectly well; you've got a good steady job here that you could be doing for the next forty-odd years!' he quarrelled, instantly nullifying any reservations entering my head in but a few ill-chosen words. The harrowing vision of a group of ageing curmudgeons gathered at the same table four decades down the line, putting the world to rights over a pot of stewed tea, was all it took to deem the decision a no-brainer.

****

Irrefutably one of a kind, Great Britain's own small slice of Lilliput in truth presents a geographical nightmare. Jutting out by itself at Wales's westernmost tip, it is easily bypassed by travellers cutting the corner in search of Fishguard Harbour, whilst also neglected by scores of holidaymakers heading eastwards during the summer months into Carmarthenshire and the 'sweet shire' of Cardigan to seek out the region's unspoilt beaches.

Slightly afield of the sand dunes and seashells, the charismatic picture-postcard one-horse town radiates a gentle timelessness all of its own, from the manneredly village-like main street to the historic twelfth-century cathedral buildings rising from the ashes of an ancient monastery founded by the city's eponymous patron saint in the sixth century.

I visited the pocket-sized metropolis once only, on August 26th 2005. Much to my good lady's chagrin, the celebrations for my twenty-first wedding anniversary had been put temporarily on hold, with the call of duty taking precedence in the shape of a nightmarish tour of thirty-three caravan parks the length and breadth of Great Britain, the events of which remain documented in my previous literary masterpiece *The Boys of Summer*. In need of a little solace from the perpetual chaos of one holiday camp to the next and keen to tick off yet another UK city in my little black book, I followed the forty-mile route away from the tourist honeypot of Tenby with the sole intention of restoring a modicum of sanity. What lay in store made the hop doubly worthwhile.

Emblazoned in bold lettering on a sizeable metallic plate the sign read: '*The City of St Davids*'. The suggestion of a conurbation of sturdy buildings, sprawling industrial estates and all the usual city trappings was contradicted in seconds flat as I idled along a civilised main street adorned with colourful hanging baskets, quaintness and charm.

As one might expect to find in the majority of towns on a Friday afternoon, a swarm of happy shoppers littered the streets occupying every designated parking space. I got lucky as an exhausted old couple laden with goods returned to their Ford Fiesta, though it took an age for them to load up their boot and reverse at a crawl into an ever-growing tailback of traffic.

By now I was in need of a restorative pick-me-up and, though clearly spoilt for choice, a charming little converted cottage took my fancy, tucked away behind a tasteful façade offering 'home-cooked staples' and fitting the bill perfectly. A mild-mannered elderly lady sheathed in an off-pink housecoat afforded the warmest of welcomes into the captivating tearoom-cum-gift-shop.

'Hello there, what can I tempt you with?' she coaxed with a softly spoken lilt.

'A cappuccino and a slice of carrot cake, please,' I replied, adjusting the cushion on the chair and shuffling closer to the table.

'I'd highly recommend the Welsh cakes, they're just fresh out of the oven and we think they're the best in Wales here in St David's; besides, the carrot cake has been on the go for a few days and is probably past its prime!' she admitted.

'I only ever tried a Welsh cake once and it was as heavy as a brick!' I let on, evoking a reaction filled with shock horror.

'Ooh, I don't know where you 'ad that, it's unforgivable!' she tut-tutted. 'Ours here are wonderful; it's our own secret recipe, see!'

'Well, if they're that good, it would be rude not to wash one down with my cappuccino,' I acquiesced, licking my lips.

Smiling pleasantly, she sauntered back to the tiny kitchen humming to herself. I felt very much at home, and entered into a discussion with a rather partisan Welshman as to the current state of affairs in an 'Ashes' test match then in progress. Before I knew it she was back, competing with a tray laden with three currant cakes, together with a bone china tea service complete with pot, cup, saucer and sugar bowl.

'I'm really sorry about this – there seems to be some kind of mistake; I actually ordered a coffee with the cakes,' I murmured contritely.

'No you didn't, you naughty boy, I distinctly 'eard you with my own ears. You said, "I'll 'ave a cuppa tea now and a slice of carrot cake," ' she reproached, giving me a light slap on the wrists and standing her ground.

'That's brilliant…!' I cracked up, restraining a loud guffaw. 'Though I think we have a slight breakdown in communication here – I asked for an Italian coffee, a capp-ooh-chino, not a cup-of-tea-now; but don't worry, it'll do just fine.'

'Oh dearie me, I'm ever so sorry, I am. I must be gettin' 'ard of 'earin' in my old age. Do you want me to change it for a milky coffee?' she backtracked.

'Honestly, that won't be necessary; I almost ordered a pot of tea anyway, and I like to think the bone china brings the flavour out more,' I mediated.

'Oh my goodness… Had you said you wanted a proper frothy coffee in a proper coffee cup I may well have got it right, but that funny name you said completely threw me,' she tongue-twistingly bade. 'How did you pronounce it again?'

'C-A-P-P-U-C-C-I-N-O, as in cappuccino,' I clarified, chuckling lightly under my breath. 'Have you never been to Italy?'

'I went to an island called Corfu once; I think that was near to Italy!' she charmingly responded, all at sixes and sevens and pausing to fan herself with a tea towel. Whilst almost choking on the Welsh cake, I nudged myself to restore a little decorum as the little lady asked my opinion of the freshly baked house speciality.

'Absolutely delicious – I can't believe the difference between these and the previous ones I sampled years ago,' I complimented. I placed a five-pound note underneath the handwritten bill and followed her wiggling backside towards the tiny kitchenette.

'As a small token of our gratitude for being so understanding, here's a teeny-weeny reminder of your visit to our little city,' the delightful woman expressed, returning with my change and carefully placing a small vellum envelope to one side.

Tucked neatly inside, a folded sheet of letterheaded paper containing the secret recipe of the house read as follows:

Mrs Morgan's Picau Ar Y Maen (1 Dozen)

Ingredients
200 grams plain flour
50 grams diced butter
40 grams diced lard
1 teaspoon baking powder
70 grams sugar
1 quarter pint of milk
50 grams currants
1 well beaten egg
1 tablespoon cooking sherry
2 teaspoons honey

Dice the butter and lard into small pieces and add to sifted flour and baking powder, then rub with fingers to fine consistency.

Mix in the currants, sugar, honey and sherry and add the beaten egg with milk to make the dough good and solid.

Roll out the dough, flour your hands and knead the dough in your hands until the mixture is smooth as silk.

On a bed of flour roll out the dough to a quarter of an inch thickness and use a fluted pastry cutter to cut the dough into 3-inch rounded shapes and put in the oven to bake straight away.

Bake until golden brown on a greased baking tray for 4 minutes either side.

Sprinkle over sugar and cinnamon.

Enjoy the cakes warm.

I recently rediscovered the envelope used as a bookmark in an unfinished novel. Never professing to be especially dextrous around the kitchen (other than the odd bout of washing-up), the delights of Mrs Morgan's mini-feast have still to be sampled, though should the delicacy come anywhere close to the real McCoy savoured in St David's, they'll be well worth the wait!

Causes célèbres

As far as I am aware, other than the eponymous patron saint, the only notable person to hail from St David's is the author Richard Llewellyn; although, perhaps somewhat dubiously, Hillary Clinton's claims to a Welsh ancestry also refer to this small corner of the UK.

Essential travelling band info

Live music venue: The only place you'd be likely to hear live music of any kind would be the choral variety at the yearly St David's Cathedral Festival, although it is said to be expanding the programme of events in the near future which will include more diverse musical performances.

Favourite curry house: Saffron, Nunn Street (the only one) – 49%

Favourite pub: The Farmers Arms, Goat Street – 61%

Don't miss: Venture Jet – an exhilarating jet boat adventure – 80%

Sense of humour/friendly welcome: 84%

Chapter 59
Stirling

I ONCE SIGHTED ONE ON the Sydney Harbour Bridge clad in all his patchwork glory struggling to protect his modesty from a near gale force wind. There were two perched behind me on an open-top tourist bus in Washington DC, and yet another of the species juggling cocktails behind the bar of an Irish pub in the Peruvian city of Cusco.

Begging forgiveness for the over-the-top outburst of place-dropping, the curious fact remains that wherever one cares to tread on this golden planet the likelihood of a chance encounter with a tartan-clad, milky-fleshed 'sweaty sock' appears almost inevitable, regardless of a population only slightly in excess of five million. Glitzy corporate functions, private wingdings or pretty much any excuse for an organised piss-up could never be complete without a drunken Scotsman clambering onto the stage to inextricably reveal his hindquarters from beneath a patriotic 'Jock frock', often giving horrified onlookers a little more than they bargained for.

Which leads me on to a Stirling resident (known rather aptly as Big Jim) who, during the course of a high-society bash held at Perthshire's celebrated Gleneagles Hotel in the late eighties, unashamedly felt the urge to uncover his prodigious manhood, frightening the life out of a goggle-eyed audience part way through SWW's performance.

The gig had started decorously enough and, with the loudness moderated to a level more attuned to the tinkling piano music accompanying the culinary feast, a sprinkling of immaculately attired party animals soon took to the floor. As we cranked things up a gear, they went through a repertoire of nifty moves in tandem with their partners directly in the band's line of sight to the forefront of the stage, and we encouraged a handful of them to join us atop the buckling platform to exhibit their jiving skills amid the spectrum of multi-coloured bandsmen.

Suddenly, from out of the shadows, a hirsute, lumbering kilted man barged aggressively through the revellers, hogging the spotlight and yelling a chest-thumping, animalistic cry in advance of lifting up the tartan sarong to reveal the pendulous reproductive organs drooping beneath.

'Fucking hell,' shouted a disbelieving Trevor, blocking my view with his body, whilst at the brow of the stage a group of shocked beholders gazed up at the brute of a man's nether regions with similarly wide-eyed expressions.

'What's going on – did I miss something?' I yelled within range of the microphone, at something of a loss as to what was taking place, before spinning round towards the drum kit to catch Romeo's eyeballs also straining in their sockets.

Giving the onstage revellers a wide berth, I regained my place to the platform's fore. There taking centre stage stood the mighty Jim, kilt aloft exhibiting an unimaginably elephantine man-pole, outrageously wielding the monstrosity for all to see.

Having failed to impress a section of indifferent bystanders including a trio of envious male escorts gesticulating angrily at the titan to cover up, the belligerent freak simply turned the other cheek, wiggling his pallid buttocks in the mud-slinger's faces and revealing a drooping set of dangly bits, showing a total disregard for propriety whilst raising the temperature of a small circle of flushed females leaving their seats to take a closer look.

'Now ye know why they call me Big Jim, lads,' the flashing Scotsman boasted as he savoured his five minutes of fame back in the dressing room. Referring to his foot-long weaponry as 'Jimmy's Joystick' and pig-headedly shooting off his mouth as to his innumerable conquests, he was gratifyingly quelled by a sharp rap at the door.

'Sorry to bother you… Ah, that's who we've been searching for!' one of two well-groomed middle-aged ladies gasped as the pair sidled foxily into the underground hideout, focusing their attentions solely on the shaggy highlander. 'We were wondering if you might like to join us for a wee drop of the hard stuff… We just need to settle a little argument,' the spokesperson intimated, leering back at her excited playmate who was foaming at the mouth.

'There's a room next door that's not in use if you'd prefer a little privacy,' the mischievous Geoff helpfully offered.

'Perfect… By the way, you boys were very good out there, although without wishing to be rude there's little doubt as to who stole tonight's show… if you know what I mean!' the devilish cougar hinted with a licentious sparkle in her eye. Taking the big guy by the hand, she led him in the direction of the nearby den of iniquity.

'Well, that's a first – fancy playing second fiddle to a gigantic prick!' I remarked, turning towards my grinning colleagues.

'What about the tour we did with David Cassidy…?' Geoff sharply retorted, as ever on hand with a caustic, albeit merited, riposte.

⋈⋈⋈

In the thick of a hectic four-day schedule, I was running on empty. It had commenced with a two-hour flight out to Denmark for a one-off outdoor festival, returning starved of shuteye into Manchester the next morning at the crack of dawn. A 230-mile trek north to the recently sanctioned city of Stirling awaited, together with the band's first ever concert in the one-time Scots capital, some thirty-seven years in the making.

Badly in need of forty winks, I relocated to a small side-room backstage where I removed the shoes from my malodorous feet and stretched out across a rock-hard old Chesterfield sofa. My eyes closed, and a split second later everything turned to black.

'DB… where the hell are you?' a gruff, familiar voice called out, stirring me from the sound nap. The trim-bearded noodle of Scottish-born sax player Davy G peeped around the door to disturb the peace. 'I've been bloody well looking for you everywhere; you said you wanted to do a spot of sightseeing!' the musician contended.

'Phew, I was well gone there,' I harped, coming to in a trancelike stupor. 'Is it time for the soundcheck?'

'No, not yet; the crew guys said they won't be ready until five – we've got a good hour. Come on, off your arse, let's get some fresh air!' he harangued. Glancing at my watch, I kicked up a stink at being awakened after just five minutes.

An avenue of stalwart stone buildings safeguarded our passage into town as a trail of conspicuous brown signs earmarking the route upwards to the notorious castle added impetus to the sortie. Hanging left, we ascended a picturesque part-cobbled lane flanked by a row of small terraced houses interspersed with gift shops and tea rooms. It led us toward the impressive statue of Robert the Bruce, mounted close to the fortification which legendary Scot besieged to foil the auld enemy in the twelfth century.

'DB, I hate to say it but there's somebody following us; he's been tailing us ever since we left the gig!' Dave mumbled halfway up the steep ascent. Diverting my eyes to the left I spotted a tall, lank-haired man sporting several days of stubble growth, carrying a larger than average violin case and lingering suspiciously behind.

'Bloody hell, he looks well dodgy – a bit of a weirdo I'd say; plus you can almost smell him from here,' I commented, whiffing the air.

'Perhaps if we upped the ante a bit we might be able to lose him,' suggested Dave, stepping on the gas into a light jog. To our joint surprise the pursuer

381

quickened his own pace to remain within spitting distance.

'I'd love to know what's in the case,' I pondered a little edgily. 'I'm convinced it's not a bloody musical instrument.'

'Do you think he might be packed? You know, a complete nutter who watches too much TV?' Dave speculated, narrowing his eyes.

'What, a pistol? Surely not; he's probably just trying to get rid of some illicit gear or even a batch of porn DVDs,' I panted, hazarding a wild guess.

'Well, whatever he's up to, it doesn't feel right to me. Worst of all, everybody else seems to have done a vanishing act,' my buddy worryingly observed.

'Let's make a bolt for it – we can lose him at the castle and he doesn't look that fit to me,' I bade optimistically. Like a fleeing antelope I galloped up the incline, hot on the heels of the pacier, more youthful saxophonist.

'C'mon DB, we're losing him,' Dave excitedly goaded, noticing the pursuer lagging behind and again upping the tempo.

'*Stop – stop now!*' the stalker's loud cry echoed as he dropped onto one knee honking like a goose, seemingly in the midst of a mild seizure.

'Fuck him, Dave… Keep going, we're nearly at the top,' I urged, keeping my pal on the radar and pumping even harder.

'*Stop*… please stop – I mean you no harm!' the man heaved hysterically, clearly coming to the end of his tether.

'What the fuck does he want?' Dave brooded as he reached the castle entrance, crouching forward hands on thighs and blowing hard.

'I honestly wish I knew, but he looks out on his feet to me; plus there are two of us – surely he won't try anything stupid!' I boldly surmised.

Feeling we had little choice but to confront the grubby individual, we crept tentatively back down the slope. Slumped to his knees, the man breathed a huge, exhausted sigh as he stared upwards through hollow eyes.

'I've waited thirty years for this moment, Dave; I'm one of your biggest fans… It's been my life's ambition to meet you!' the stranger wheezed, struggling to regain his composure and seemingly on the verge of keeling over.

'What…? Then why did you act so sheepishly… and what's with the viola case?' I pressed, thrown off guard. Still unconvinced as to the true motives behind his dogged pursuit, I was intent on giving the oddball the third degree.

'I spotted you both coming out of the stage door at the hall so I tried to tag along, but you were walking so quickly I could barely keep up. All I wanted was to get my stuff signed,' he admitted, unlatching the case to reveal a pile of vinyl singles, CDs, tour programmes, posters, a mug and other stuff I'd long forgotten ever existed.

'And we thought you might be a hitman,' I disclosed half in jest roughly thirty minutes later as I knelt on the cobblestones outside of the castle gates, adding the crowning signatures to the devotee's extensive collection of outdated keepsakes.

'Shit, we're late for the soundcheck – it's almost half five!' a spooked Davy G shrieked, checking his watch and scrambling to his feet.

'See you mate, sorry for the misunderstanding. I take it you'll be at tonight's gig?' I bade him, making my way down the craggy slope.

'I will that, I'll be sat right on the front row. You'd better be good… or else!' the admirer spoofed, taking aim with an imaginary six-shooter.

Causes célèbres

Kirsty Young – TV presenter
Willie Carson – ex-champion jockey/TV personality
Billy Bremner – former Scotland football captain
Mary Queen of Scots – beheaded ex-resident

Essential travelling band info

Live music venue: Albert Halls, Dumbarton Road
Favourite curry house: Green Gate Indian Restaurant, Queen Street – 80%
Favourite pub: Portcullis, Castle Wyne – 64%
Don't miss: National Wallace Monument – 72%
Sense of humour/friendly welcome: 73%

Chapter 60
Stoke-on-Trent

'How can you describe Stoke-on-Trent? Well, if the world needed an enema, Stoke would be where they'd shove the pipe!' – a quote from an ex-resident of the city.

****

RENOWNED AS AN ERA OF harsh change in conjunction with economic upheaval, few survivors of the troubled decade comprising the 1970s would ever look back with fondness to a dark age tainted by innumerable national strikes, financial hardship and pre-organised riots virtually bringing the United Kingdom to its knees.

Sparked off by a faction of militant ITV technicians shunning working with new-fangled colour television equipment during early negotiations for a pay increase, an ensuing sense of foreboding proved the catalyst for a major disruption to the service, resulting in a unanimous call for strike action by union representatives.

The rest as they say is history, with the much publicised and unsettlingly violent miners' strikes of '72 and '74 foregoing '78 and '79's 'winter of discontent' consisting of a three-day working week purportedly to conserve energy, an ineffectual postal service, rubbish piled high on every street as a result of dustmen coming out in sympathy, and worst of all the maddeningly frequent electricity blackouts timed to coincide with the country's hard-done-by workers tucking into their evening meals side by side with their families.

Inevitably and eventually something had to give – though not before arguably the most extraordinary walk-out of them all, by virtue of a mini-revolt which perhaps just as well received no media coverage whatsoever.

****

Unique in its constitution, the spreadeagled West Midlands city of Stoke-on-Trent is made up of the six towns of Hanley, Burslem, Fenton, Longton,

Tunstall and not forgetting Stoke itself, together commonly referred to as the Staffordshire Potteries. It was in Hanley that, in the mid seventies, a large, all-singing all-dancing venue going by the name of 'Baileys' first opened its doors to cash in on the thriving club scene sweeping the nation; and, with the band sitting pretty in the top ten with our sixth hit single, we were booked to play yet another Monday-to-Friday stint at the new nightspot.

The thought of flogging our guts out in but one more sweatshop owned by the directors of our management company gave rise to simmering tensions which threatened to boil over from behind closed doors. We were bitterly critical of a take-home pay that in no way reflected the band's ongoing success and current high profile, but any attempts to express our concerns fell very much on deaf ears.

We opted wisely to cut back on running costs (and hangovers) by commuting the fifty or so miles to Hanley on a nightly basis. Assembled and ready at the rural rendezvous point ahead of the Friday-evening jaunt, a quick headcount revealed that the usually punctual Trevor was conspicuous by his absence.

'Where the fucking hell is he?' bickered Geoff. Just then, a high-pitched squealing sound could be heard in the distance; and pretty soon the late arrival's ancient vehicle came whining its way along the uneven mud-track, enshrouded in a cloud of carbon monoxide fumes pumping from the farting, grumbling exhaust.

'It's time you got rid of that old rot-box,' advised Romeo, offering a few words of wisdom as his ruffled, tracksuited bandmate clambered out of the car.

'The sodding fan belt snapped just as I was leaving,' Trevor complained. 'I had to borrow one from a neighbour up the street and it's slipping like crazy.'

'Let me get this right… you borrowed a fan belt…? So do you intend returning it to its rightful owner when you get back home?' I asked incredulously.

'Don't be daft… I didn't have time to get a new one; and anyway I'm skint 'til the wages go in,' the whiner agonised, picking up his stuff.

'Tell me about it,' rued Geoff. 'It's fucking embarrassing – everyone else thinks we're loaded after being on *Top of the Pops* every other week!' His heartfelt gripe set the tone for the journey ahead; and the mood continued on into the gig's dressing room.

'What's wrong with you lot? They're hanging off the rafters out there – you're in for a wild night!' sound engineer Ian drooled as he bounded into the room full of beans, shaken out of his stride at the rumblings of discontent.

'How many people do you reckon they've crammed into this place?' I queried. 'Well over the fire limit, I'm sure.'

'Ooh, I'd say there's getting on two thousand,' Ian estimated. 'It's absolutely rammed; and, like you said, God forbid the authorities get wind of it!'

'Those bastards have got a licence to print money; the only problem is, we aren't seeing a bloody cent of it,' Rod carped, up in arms.

'How many more hits do we need under our belts before we make any dosh? I'm on my bloody uppers and could have missed the gig because of a dodgy fan belt!' Trevor bellyached, still rattled by his mechanical problems.

'All I know is, those tight-fisted gits up in Newcastle are fobbing us off and nothing's likely to change until we make a stand,' I beefed, unknowingly igniting the fuse.

'Are you suggesting we go on strike? Surely that's a little extreme?' guitarist Russ chipped in, sporting a look of concern.

'It's their funeral – they must know we're not happy, and it would serve them bloody well right; I'm all for it,' Romeo boldly hinted.

'That wasn't quite what I had in mind, although there's little doubt it would hit them right where it hurts – especially with a full house out there in one of their own bloody clubs!' I speculated, warming to the idea.

'Yeah, let's get out of here,' no-nonsense bass vocalist Bill pitched in, already busily repacking his stage suit and brothel-creepers.

'But what about the punters? You can't just piss off and leave a couple of thousand paying customers in the lurch!' Ian contended.

'Who can't? They'll just go potty at the venue and ask for their money back,' Geoff countered, lighting a cigarette to calm his nerves. 'Like Dave says, there's no better time than right now if we really want to ruffle their feathers.'

'If we're deadly serious about doing this there are bound to be repercussions, so just for once we have to be united; how about a show of hands?' I proposed, taking a leaf out of a troubleshooting firebrand's book.

Following a display of unified solidarity akin to a hard-nosed, one-out-all-out strike ballot, we gathered up our belongings and, marching in single file from the building to the startled looks of the backstage staff, the embittered boycotters hit the bricks, laying the groundwork for an irate crowd to hit the roof… big time!

The phone rang just after 9am. 'Mr Smith will be arriving at the Holiday Inn Hotel in Leicester at twelve o'clock sharp for an urgent meeting; please make sure you are there… on the dot!' a female voice barked authoritatively down the line, indicating the incensed MD may already have hit the trail, heading due south from Newcastle all guns blazing.

'Oh yes, you're booked into the conference suite on the first floor; you can rant and rave as much as you like up there!' the receptionist affirmed as she greeted my comrades and I to the plush hotel, pointing to the lifts situated on the foyer's far side and seemingly anticipating a few fireworks ahead of the midday showdown.

Peering unnoticed from an upstairs window, I observed the chauffeur-driven Rolls Royce cruising inaudibly onto the hotel forecourt. 'He's here – his driver just dropped him right by the entrance,' I relayed back to the meeting room.

'There seem to be some nice cars parked outside!' the small-framed executive snapped, striding into the conference suite with a face like thunder and slamming his briefcase down onto the table without a single word of acknowledgement.

'Well one of them doesn't bloody well belong to me – I had to borrow a sodding fan b…' stuttered Trevor, only to be rudely interrupted.

'You're fucking yourselves up!' the usually mild-mannered big cheese bellowed, causing everyone to sit bolt upright.

'Whoa, we're not here for a full-scale war! You swan into town in your bloody Roller, yet the monthly pittance you're paying us is a joke… Let's get real,' I argued with the boys' full backing, not content to concede the upper ground.

'And I had to work my balls off for many years to achieve that! Perhaps that's a lesson you should all learn… and quickly,' the boss-man preached.

'That's bang out of order,' I indignantly struck back. 'We're out working your venues every night of the week while you're turning punters away, yet we still haven't got a pot to piss in; how do you explain that one away?'

'And we're onto our sixth hit single with two big-selling albums… It just doesn't add up!' Rod squabbled, lending weight to the conversation.

'How dare you let all those people down?' he ranted dictatorially, unwilling to hear our own side of the story. 'The reputation of my clubs is at stake. Any thoughts you had of a pay rise went out the window last night!'

'Okay, if that's the case then maybe we should cancel tonight's gig too!' stated Romeo to a stunned silence, at last grabbing the exec's attention.

Over the next hour or more we unlocked horns, with the powwow taking on a vastly more constructive tone. All talk of impending action soon petered out into oblivion, and agreement was reached on a revised pay structure to be put into immediate effect and handled by a firm of independent accountants answerable exclusively to the band members, thus transforming a cluster of wildcats into a purring pride of animated young lions.

Bearing many similarities to a newsworthy industrial dispute, magnified by the aggrieved employees forcing the hand of the intransigent hierarchy, the siege of Stoke at worst proved the true value of togetherness – never the band's strongest suit – and not only boosted the members' personal coffers but added a touch of self-esteem for the rocky road ahead.

****

My first musical memory goes all the way back to the black-and-white days of 1956, when as a four-year-old kid I laid eyes on the goofy, toothsome entertainer Tommy Steele singing his anglicised rendition of the Guy Mitchell ditty 'Singing the Blues' on a 14-inch GEC television screen in a darkened living room. Although I took note of the chirpy cockney swivelling his hips to his one and only chart-topper, the accolade of my first ever boyhood hero oddly went instead to a magnificent western lowland primate inhabiting London's Regent's Park zoo and going under the name of Guy the Gorilla. I was instantly captivated by the powerful silverback eyeballing me with a curious, strained excitement through the toughened glass window of his living quarters; and the experience left me with a lifelong inherent fascination with apes and monkeys.

A rare opportunity to satisfy my interest presented itself while preparing for a summer festival on the outskirts of Stoke-on-Trent, when I picked up on signs to the adjacent Monkey Forest all of a half-mile stroll away and took a couple of hours out to investigate.

'How many different species of apes are there in the park?' I queried, disturbing the gateman in the midst of a debate on his portable radio.

'None... they're monkeys, not apes; and it's a forest, not a park!' the man brusquely retorted, almost biting off my head.

'So there aren't any gorillas?' I persisted.

'Hardly likely, though a couple of the staff might fall into that category,' he sardonically huffed, mildly convulsing at his own line of wit.

'What kind of... *monkeys* might I see swinging from tree to tree in the *forest*?' I testily over-emphasised, getting the man's back up further.

'If you'd care to cough up the sum of seven pounds fifty, the day staff will be more than happy to answer your questions,' the paymaster abruptly wrangled, giving me change from a tenner and turning back to the broadcast.

Caught in the act of raking up a scattering of doings from the pebble pathway, an amiable, khaki-shorted girl brushed away the flyaway hair from her glowing features. 'All of the monkeys here are Barbary macaques,' she explained, urging me to hurry on ahead and tag along with a guided tour which had departed all of five minutes before.

I caught up with the party in a small clearing where a group of chattering humanoids looked on spellbound at a quartet of playful primates and fired a barrage of inane questions at the female escort. These mostly related to the protruding pink penis of one of the inmates, which the show-off was contentedly caressing in full view of the fascinated spectators.

'Look at him – 'e doesn't give a monkey's what anyone finks,' cracked the senior man of the clique, guffawing gruffly along with his partner-in-crime.

'Ah, he's just fiddling around with his nuts!' his henchman reacted, creasing up at his own attempt at humour. Despite the muted reaction, this sparked off an onslaught of childish puns and cringeworthy *double entendres* to the annoyance of the rest of the group.

'Look girls, there's a baby one… he's a chimp off the old block if ever I saw one,' jested the first guy, unrestrainedly creasing in two.

'Oh, don't go upsetting the little 'un or his parents might go apeshit,' his stooge giggled, beside himself with mirth.

'Put a sock in it, you daft 'apeth… that's enough monkeying around for one afternoon,' the folly went on.

As I bent to my knees to study the exhibitionist macaque, the creature suddenly bounded forwards, confronting me with bared teeth in a fierce display of unfettered aggression. Taking evasive action I rolled into a jumble of legs, almost trampled upon by the scaredy-cat caboodle understandably shrinking away. The perturbed critter meanwhile continued its blood-curdling screech, livid I'd strayed too close to his territory.

'Blimey, that little feller just went bananas,' the humourist stupidly yawped. He was shoved aside by the rattled guide who rushed to the fore, urging the party to take a step backwards whilst she shooed the primates into the nearby shrubs.

'What the hell did I do to upset him?' I queried, taken aback.

'Don't worry, you didn't do anything wrong,' she said reassuringly, keeping one eye on my simian foe nervously scampering up a tall cedar tree. 'You may have reminded him of someone who was unkind to him in the past, or perhaps he thought it was you cracking those awful jokes; they are very sensitive creatures.'

'If you hadn't been here, darling, he may well have had a monkey on his back,' the life and soul of the party snorted, refusing to let up and plainly getting the goat of the mild-mannered assistant, who it seemed had bottled things up long enough.

'Very witty, sir; do you know which animal is the macaque's worst enemy?' the girl quizzed, staring her prey down.

'I wouldn't have a clue, darling,' the man dumbly responded.

'There are actually two answers, the first being a puma; however, they also have a distinct dislike for jackasses, so be careful to watch your back when you're walking under the trees,' she unleashed with both barrels, moving on ahead.

'That's the first genuinely witty comment I've heard all day… but then again you are from a town nicknamed Joke-on-Trent,' I commented as she passed.

'Me… from this dump…? Now you *are* joking!' she derided.

Causes célèbres

Captain E.J. Smith – captain of the *Titanic*
Stanley Matthews – legendary footballer
Robbie Williams – singer
Arnold Bennett – novelist
Lemmy – from Motorhead
Phil Taylor – darts world champion
Neil Morrissey – actor

Essential travelling band info

Favourite live music venue: Victoria Hall, Bagnall Street
Favourite curry house: Planet Bollywood, Glebe Street – 62%
Favourite pub: Coachmaker's Arms, Lichfield Street – 49%
Don't miss: Trentham Monkey Forest, Stone Road – 66%
Sense of humour/friendly welcome: 58%

Chapter 61
Swansea

'NOT THE MOST ATTRACTIVE OF skylines, is it?' observed Rod from the passenger seat. An unwholesome yellowish hue dominated the Port Talbot horizon, etched by a forest of blast furnaces and smoking towers pumping out gases into the atmosphere, broken up by a herd of dinosaur-like mammoth cranes. The spectacle afforded a grim welcome to the line of cars hanging left towards Wales' second city from the westbound M4 motorway.

Disregarding the region's unwanted distinction as the most polluted in Britain, Swansea is very much a city of contrasts. Away from the noxious picture painted by the neighbouring steelworks and smelting urns, in no time at all the air of gloom is replaced by the spectacular landscape of an expanse designated as an 'Area of Outstanding Natural Beauty', namely the Gower Peninsula which lies in all its glory on the city's fringes.

'According to a national survey I read recently, this place is one of the hardest towns in the entire UK to find work,' I pointed out as we cruised through the humdrum centre blighted by a glut of boarded-up shop frontages. My words fell on deaf ears as I took a right towards the classic old Victorian Grand Theatre, anticipating a wild night ahead before a crowd of vociferous Welsh dragons.

✳✳✳✳

Few if any journeying musicians will ever have escaped what is known in the trade as 'a nightmare gig'. The Swansea Grand was the setting for co-performer Alvin Stardust* to spit out his dummy midway through the soundcheck of a nineties package tour, moping in his dressing room and refusing flatly to cooperate or even talk to any of the on-site crew as the headliners arrived at the theatre to a strained atmosphere.

---

* Alvin Stardust (a.k.a. Bernard Jewry) died after a short illness at the age of 72 just prior to the completion of this journal. Purely by coincidence, his funeral service took place in the city of Swansea.

'Go and have a word, will you Davy? At least he'll give you the time of day,' pleaded tour director Bob, still smarting from a severe tongue-lashing from the evidently perturbed artist. Referring to Alvin's manager he added: 'Shirley won't be arriving 'til later.'

'What's up, matey?' I murmured, knocking tentatively at the crooner's door and entering uninvited. I found him sulking over a steaming mug of boiling water clutched tightly between his whitening knuckles.

'I'll tell you what's up – there's no fucking mirrorball!' he wrathfully exploded, slamming down the mug and thumping a balled fist on the table.

'Whoa, whoa, take it easy... I'm on your side; is this what all the fuss is about – a bloody mirrorball?' I replied, finding the outburst most out of character.

'Listen... it's an important part of my show and there's no way I'm going on if they don't provide one,' he threatened petulantly.

'What the fuck's gotten into you today? There has to be another theatre in town that'll have one hidden away – though how you expect to get it sorted out by blanking everybody is beyond me?' I semi-tactfully reasoned.

'I'm not talking to that lot out there; they're a bunch of bloody idiots and I've said my piece. What's more, if they don't come up with something soon you won't be seeing my arse for dust!' he warned, fast losing the plot.

'Never mind the crew, what about the punters that have paid good money to see you?' I reflected, treating the singer with kid gloves, though somewhat disconcerted to see my normally approachable buddy's nose put out of joint.

'I overheard one of those bastards say I've got an inflated ego and should show them more respect... I'm not putting up with that; they're here to do a job, not criticise the artists paying their wages,' he persisted.

'Ah, come on Alvin... you've been around long enough to know what crew workers are like – sometimes they're a law unto themselves; but in all fairness they do have to put up with a lot of shit. I'm more than happy to have a word on your behalf if you think it might help,' I offered, playing the role of the diplomat.

'You know, in the old days just after "Jealous Mind" had gone to number one, I was staying in a top hotel in Birmingham and insisted they change the carpet in the lift 'cause I hated the colours; now *that's* when I had an ego!' he recalled.

'Haha, that's what's called being slightly up oneself... Did the staff agree to have a new one fitted?' I posed, genuinely interested.

'Of course they didn't, but you know where I'm coming from – I'm sure you've been in similar situations. Look, all I'm asking for is a bloody mirrorball; surely they can find one... somewhere,' he maintained, coming down from his high horse.

'I heard a tale recently from a PR guy who worked on the last Mariah Carey tour; now there's an ego to be reckoned with from the sound of it,' I recapped, relieved to be indulging in a spot of light tittle-tattle. 'Rumour has it she'd taken up the entire top floor of one of the swanky London hotels and insisted her suite be decked out with two hundred little fluffy white bunny-rabbits there to greet her when she arrived. Put in a nutshell, when she entered the room she found her luggage covered in rabbit shit and threw a right wobbler. The stink was so bad she refused flatly to stay there!' I gossiped, laying it on thick.

'That's absolutely brilliant… and you're right, that is probably taking the ego thing to new extremes!' he chortled, lightening up sufficiently to stick on the kettle and talk things over to at least make an effort to resolve the situation.

As I peeked from the wings in full regalia ahead of the upcoming hour's spectacle, an array of glittering shapes encircled the full house's greying pates, used to good effect in the pitch-black auditorium and gussying up Alvin's retch-inducing rendition of his song 'I Feel Like Buddy Holly' complete with the reflective prop stipulated in the performer's contract, which had been uncovered in a dusty basement by a flea-bitten member of the theatre staff.

'Thanks for your help in sorting the little spot of bother earlier on, Dave… oh shit!' yammered the melodramatic Shirley (a nickname bestowed in the tour's opening week). Watching Alvin's already fraught day go from bad to worse, he dashed into the auditorium to attend to yet another minor catastrophe taking place.

'Fucking hell, that was hilarious… Is he having a bad day or what?' chuckled Geoff, walking back to the dressing room in stitches.

'I couldn't see… What happened?' I probed.

'He was about to do that corny stunt with the shaken-up champagne bottle and the cork popped sooner than expected; some dapper guy on the front row got absolutely saturated and was going potty at Alvin,' the bassist spluttered.

'*Second half beginners, this is your one-minute call,*' the announcement blared through the backstage intercom. The colourful sextet filed out to the stage side, coming across the bubbly-spattered whipping boy remonstrating in the corridor with the hapless Alvin and his preening manager.

'Don't even think about fobbing me off with a bottle of champagne – I think I've had more than enough for one night! I want a new suit to the tune of a hundred and fifty quid,' the man squabbled. Spotting us in his peripheral vision, the complainant theatrically bitched: 'And you'd better make it quick, 'cause I only came to see these guys, not some burned-out old fossil; if I miss a second of their show I'll sue your bollocks off!'

Upon leaving the stage I spotting the busy tour director scuttling along the hallway to his hideout. 'Bob… did Alvin manage to sort something out as regards the guy's spattered suit?' I beckoned, breathing heavily.

'I believe so, Davy… Far be it from me to go spreading any scurrilous rumours but the gentleman in question seemed well satisfied with the outcome… By the way, you boys were on top form tonight!' he answered diplomatically.

'Would you care to expand?' I pressed.

'Let me put it this way… The injured party seemed to be, should I say, "a little limp-wristed"… but after fifteen minutes in the dressing room with Shirley he reappeared with a cheque for a hundred quid and a broad smile on his face… See you tomorrow matey!' the beaming Bob acknowledged, raising his bushy eyebrows and scarpering.

****

Hero worship… a weird yet often wonderful phenomenon, coming in many different guises from – in my own experience – valuable items of jewellery, stars suspended in the heavens bearing my own monogram and fine vintage wines to piles of fan mail containing soiled panties (the feminine variety), cuddly toys and innumerable bags of jelly babies, along with stamped addressed Jiffy bags requesting such oddities as toenail clippings, old (unwashed) socks or other garments which may at some time have been about my person.

The aforementioned items apart, without a doubt the most laudatory and extraordinary act of adulation came courtesy of a likeable regular visitor to the band's gigs named Stefan Morgan from Pontypridd in the Welsh valleys, with whom I often engaged in brief but interesting chats at the stage door upon making an exit at the show's end.

'I thought you might like to know I expanded my business recently, but more importantly the new company's named after you,' the Welshman proudly announced by the stage door of Swansea's most renowned theatre.

'Really, what have you called it?' I asked inquisitively.

'None other than "Bartram Design"; it's got a nice ring to it, and I think it'll be good for business,' he replied contentedly.

'But what was wrong with your own name?' I posed quizzically.

'Ah, there are far too many bloody Morgans in this area; I wanted something a little bit different, so I thought it'd be great to name it after my idol… You don't mind, do you?' he pondered in an endearing tone right out of the valleys.

'I don't mind at all, in fact I'm very flattered,' I replied, ambling to the bus bowled over by the extraordinary piece of adulation.

'How uncanny is that?' I remarked to Rod, positioning my rear end into the passenger seat still a tad dumbfounded.

'I could see you were deep in conversation; what was it he was saying?' Rod nosed, turning the key in the ignition.

'He's only gone and named his bedroom design business after me!' I gasped.

'What the bloody hell's he done that for? It'll go tits up in no time!' squawked a disdainful Trevor from the rear seat, popping a pull-ring from a can and covering himself in Coke much to everyone's amusement.

'For fuck's sake, Trevor… Hmm, bedroom design, so I assume that makes you a sleeping partner?' Romeo offered in jest.

'That bird Lyndsey up in Manchester's into a bit of bedroom design – you should've seen her place; there were whips, masks and all kinds of kinky clobber hanging on the walls!' Geoff pitched in, to uproarious laughter.

'Alright, alright, I just thought it was something out of the ordinary. I only hope his company goes from strength to strength,' I countered.

'In his dreams,' quipped Romeo a trifle too disparagingly.

'Just like any business it'll be no bed of roses, that's for sure!' Danny chipped in as the comments rained down hard and fast.

'Oh, for God's sake… Well, let's just say I won't be having any sleepless nights, nor will there be any tears shed on my pillow should it turn into a nightmare,' I retaliated, finally putting an end to the childishness.

In true keeping with most bedtime stories the tale pleasingly has a happy ending, bolstered by several updates from the man himself who reliably informs me the business continues to prosper. I did put my oar in to suggest the alternative name of 'Bedshaped' on the back of the more modern Keane song, only to receive a flea in my ear from the implacable Welshman, who dismissed the idea out of hand with a scornful wave of his index finger.

Causes célèbres

The Storys – underrated vocal harmony band
Harry Secombe – The Goons legend and tenor
Catherine Zeta-Jones – actress (Mrs Douglas)
Rob Brydon – comedy actor /TV host
Ian Hislop – *Private Eye* editor and TV panellist
Martyn Lewis – news broadcaster
Spencer Davis – from the eponymous '60s band
Badfinger – tragic '60s band
Dylan Thomas – legendary playwright
Martin Amis – novelist

Essential travelling band info

Live music venue: Grand Theatre, Singleton Street
Favourite curry house: Rose Indienne, St Helens Road – 48%
Favourite pub: No Sign Bar, Wind Street – 62%
Don't miss: Rhossili Bay (especially the sunset) – 85%
Sense of humour/friendly welcome: 72%

Chapter 62
Truro

THE SUMMER OF 2006 USHERED great excitement into the camp with the anticipated release of the band's first new studio album in fifteen years, excitingly ramped up by a national TV advertising campaign to virtually guarantee a top-thirty chart entry, all rounded off with a reworking of the band's debut hit 'Hey Rock and Roll' into an uplifting football anthem ahead of the World Cup in Germany entitled 'Hey England'.

Having spent the harsh winter months cooped up in a Welsh backcountry studio for as much as eighteen hours a day, interspersed with the odd weekend gig to keep the bank balance ticking over, I was suffering the effects of sleep starvation; but, with the project almost complete, an invitation to appear on Jonathan Ross's popular Saturday-morning radio show started the nerve ends tingling. We performed a 'live' acoustic version of our 1975 hit 'Three Steps To Heaven', crowned with an exclusive preview of the forthcoming 'footie' single.

We had envisaged a slating from the cynical press for blatantly cashing in on the *pièce de résistance*, offering nothing more imaginative than a trite rehash; but a surprisingly favourable reaction from media and public alike rendered confidence high, heralding the prospect of our first hit single in more than twenty years and hastening preparations for a concerted push, set to include the recording of a promotional video.

'This is a football tournament, so let's not try to be too clever,' the director advised. 'What I suggest we do is shoot the band performing "as live" in your jazzy stage suits, and then do a retake with each of you togged up in an England strip!' Looking through the band's tour dates he surprisingly plumped for Truro's 'Hall For Cornwall', roughly a fortnight in advance of the big kick-off, as the preferred venue; and we agreed to an afternoon of filming set to roll into action during an extended pre-organised soundcheck.

****

'You should've reminded me – we're already down at the gig,' beefed crew boss

Steve. He was speaking on his mobile from the diminutive city, shirking responsibility for failing to load the trunk of props and England strips – key to the video's plot – which had been left languishing behind some two hundred and fifty miles away in a Leicestershire warehouse.

'There's only one thing for it… we'll have to go shopping!' I surmised. An impromptu spree followed our arrival in town, as we scrambled around a sprinkling of sportswear stores like a posse of compulsive spenders, returning to the venue weighed down with shirts, shorts and a stack of paraphernalia bearing the George cross.

'Hold on a minute… the badge on that polo shirt is the bloody stars and stripes, you dodo,' observed an astounded, bare-chested Rod staring over at the dishevelled-looking Trevor pulling on his togs in readiness for the shoot.

'It's the same colours and was less than half the price of the official ones, so I thought I'd save the band a few quid!' the guitar player reasoned, fresh from wandering off to acquire his own goods in a nearby department store.

'Have you got half a brain? That's a bloody USA shirt; I know they qualified for the tournament but that doesn't mean we'll be supporting them! The song's called "Hey England" not "Hey Yankee Doodle Fucking Dandy"!' I boomed across the room, expediting a helpful crew-hand into tearing across the street to pick up a suitable replacement.

We demonstrated a few inept ball skills on camera in an end product tailor-made for yobs of all ages and primed to hit the small screen alongside a quirky TV ad in just a matter of days. As we boarded a Berlin-bound plane the following weekend, the stage looked set for a comeback of Lazarus-style proportions, briefly put on hold by twenty thousand beer-swilling, sausage-munching Germans gathered in a huge Romanesque amphitheatre ready to make merry on a balmy late-spring evening in the capital of the Fatherland.

Opting for a breath of fresh air as against catching up on some shuteye, I was strolling alone along the capital's busy main street, the Kurfurstendamm, when a trembling sensation deep within my trouser pocket heralded a call from the UK.

'I realise you're out of the country, but are you able to talk?' posed a tremulous voice which I recognised as belonging to the record company's artist liaison manager.

'No problem at all, Michael… Is something wrong? You sound a little down on your luck,' I inferred, somewhat apprehensively.

'I think you need to sit down,' he said nervously. 'I just came out of an emergency production meeting, and it's not good news I'm afraid!'

'Go on, spit it out… there's little point in beating about the bush,' I pushed, preparing myself for the worst.

'The marketing team don't get the project; they see it as uncool,' he relayed. 'We've been arguing the toss for two hours, but without their backing the whole game plan's in tatters. Consequently the company has decided to pull the plug!'

I felt as though I'd been crushed by a sharp hammer blow ripping into the pit of my stomach. 'What the fuck do they know? I bet they haven't even listened to the album!' I belligerently snarled, visualising a bunch of coke-sniffing, high-rolling whippersnappers laying waste to months of toil and sleepless nights based on nothing more than a whim.

Just days later I returned home, tail between legs, to a busy schedule of fatuous promotional appearances still to be fulfilled. 'That football single could well be a big hit for you boys,' predicted *X Factor* judge Louis Walsh as we chatted in the green room of ITV's breakfast show *GMTV* on the eve of the tournament's opening game.

'I don't like to disagree with you, but that's about as likely as England winning the World Cup!' I mocked, eating sour grapes ahead of a campaign which also, despite huge expectations, died a not dissimilar death.

****

On any given Sunday between the years of '62 and '72 a large majority of music-minded teenagers switched on their transistor radios at the hour of 4pm, waiting with bated breath as iconic DJ Alan 'Fluff' Freeman introduced the exclusive countdown to the brand new chart on his cherished *Pick of the Pops* broadcast.

Fast-forward to a digital age of MP3s and ever-changing formats, where even diehards fostering a genuine passion for music succumb to the split-second option of online purchases, and the one-time obsession with facts, figures and authentic collectables pales into insignificance amid a confusion of ephemeral downloads and other high-tech distractions. The old-fashioned record shop, known to millions, is now rendered as something of a black rhino, whilst by the same token a similarly dying breed of eminent High Street emporiums once found in every major UK town and city is threatened perilously close to extinction.

Flying in the face of new-fangled fads, the Cornish town of Falmouth clings tenaciously onto the days of yore, harbouring a one-off trading post known as Jam Records which provides its customers with a throwback to a bygone era. On entering I was transported back to a misspent youth in which I passed hour upon hour skimming through shelves and racks of psychedelic gatefold-sleeved vinyl gems and donning a pair of headphones in a soundproof booth before blowing my hard-earned pay from a variety of part-time jobs on the latest sounds.

In a brief period of quiet reflection as I rested awhile on an old velour sofa studying the yellowing sleeve notes of an ancient imported treasure found hidden beneath a veneer of retro goodies, a collage of fond memories echoed in my head. They rekindled a frenetic heyday of youth putting every minute of every day to good use, scraping together just enough cash to stimulate a fantastical notion of a career in music.

A typical day in the life of a budding 14-year-old musician Anno Domini 1966

6.30am: A tap on the shoulder from Dad, whispering it's time to get up.

Wolf down a bowl of sugared Corn Flakes, before wrapping up warmly in a duffle coat or donkey jacket and scarf.

Walk a brisk quarter of a mile to the newsagent's shop.

Collect weighty newspaper sack and deliver morning papers (including on a Friday the men's magazine *Parade*, containing a bevy of topless ladies with retouched breasts, which I'd sneak off to ogle at, not realising until the age of fourteen and a half that the female species actually had nipples hidden beneath their bras.

Return home to change into school uniform; squeeze in 10 minutes of guitar practice.

Race to school bus meeting point for the thirty-minute journey to the school gates.

9am: The school day begins.

11am: Take a nap in the Biology lesson, hidden behind a partition handily in teacher Mr McClaren's blind spot.

12.30pm: Lunchtime; borrow friend Nick's guitar to learn a couple of new tunes in between munching at a pack of sandwiches.

3.50pm: Board bus for return trip home.

Back to newsagent's for the evening paper round.

Join family for seated evening meal.

Off to band rehearsal at friend's house (in a garden shed), returning home to rush through essential homework.

More guitar practice in bedroom whilst family tune into TV.

Retire to bed fingers and body frazzled.

The weekend picked up in similarly hectic style as I headed back to school heavy-legged from the news round for a crucial Saturday-morning football fixture, afterwards scampering home rosy-cheeked to make the fortnightly train ride into the big city, clad from head to toe in blue and white, to cheer on my beloved 'Filberts' ahead of another mad dash back to base to link up with my bandmates and set up the gear at a local village hop.

Snapping out of my reverie, sapped from turning back the clock and rising to rummage through a few more vinyl artefacts, I uttered a squeal of delight at laying my hands on a mint copy of Neil Young's masterpiece 'After the Gold Rush' (a record I'd originally purchased amid great hardship some four decades previously) and strode pleased as punch to the counter. Studying my features closely, the anaemic shop assistant rang the cash into the till.

'Do you buy old 78s?' I enquired. 'I've got a couple of dozen hidden in my attic, and I'll be down this way again later on in the summer.'

'If they're some of your band's old ones, I doubt they'll be worth a lot!' the cocky Jack the Lad unnecessarily joshed.

'Very funny, though they're actually from the forties and fifties, with quite a few them covered in scratch marks… no doubt like the bulk of your customers who take time out sitting on the flea-bitten settee over there!' I chatted back, rubbing at my exposed arms and making a quick exit into the healing sunshine's rays.

Causes célèbres

Roger Taylor – drummer with Queen
Robert Goddard – novelist
James Marsh – Academy award-winning film director (*Man On Wire*)
Barbara Joyce West – penultimate *Titanic* survivor

Essential travelling band info

Live music venue: Hall For Cornwall, Back Quay
Favourite curry house: Kathmandu Palace, Old Bridge Street – 80%
Favourite pub: Old Ale House, Quay Street – 67%
Don't miss: Healey's Cornish Cyder Farm, Penhallow – 74%
Sense of humour/friendly welcome: 45%

Chapter 63
Wakefield

AT THE EMERGENCE OF THE so-called 'Me Decade' marking the 1970s, the stereotyped woollen mills, cloth manufacturers and coal-mining industries of the West Yorkshire region made way for a totally different guise, harbouring the heartbeat of the prospering nightclub gravy train in the shape of two people-magnets just six miles apart. Both boasted ultramodern facilities; and both were set to remain at the forefront of the booming industry, casting their nets far and wide to attract a free-spending clientele shipped in by the coachload.

As I browsed through a glossy brochure in the reception area of the swish Wakefield Theatre Club (later to become the Pussycat Club) during a break from a deafening afternoon rehearsal midway into one of many weekly stints at the venue, an eyebrow-raising list of forthcoming attractions suggested the boys and I may indeed be in exalted company.

'Crikey, it must be costing a fortune to ship some of these artists over here,' I exclaimed, chatting to the lady at the bookings desk, scanning through an impressive line-up including Andy Williams, Tony Bennett and Stevie Wonder.

'Our policy is that anything Batley can do, we can do better,' she claimed, referring to the more conspicuous Batley Variety Club and the bitter rivalry between the two which involved fighting tooth and nail to upstage their near neighbours whatever the cost.

'I can only say I feel humbled to be treading the same boards as some of those guys... I bet you can't get a ticket for love nor money,' I implied.

'In all honesty, we make far more money out of home-grown artists like you lads than a lot of the international performers. It's just a game of dog-eat-dog really... but one we're determined to stay ahead of!' she confessed, boosting my ego tenfold as I swaggered back into the auditorium to exercise my vocal chords.

I was doing precisely that on a steamy autumn night back in '78, with the club packed to overflowing, when a small chorus line of mini-skirted females escaped the clutches of a tableful of virile young bucks and skipped a provocative light fandango to the fore of the stage, flaunting their skimpy undies to the delight of every red-blooded male in the room. This, of course, only rubbed further salt into the wounds of their foaming-at-the-mouth admirers.

'Why don't you girls come up and join us…? Maybe you can teach us all a few nifty new moves,' I encouraged, triggering off a minor stampede amongst the half-plastered audience who climbed over one another to gatecrash the invitation.

'That was brilliant when that group of young stunners ran across the stage and wrapped their legs around your waist,' commented Geoff back in the dressing room, eyes lighting up as he towelled himself down.

'Yeah, you could see all their drawers… We should keep it in the show,' added Trevor with a lustful pout, harbouring some form of ulterior motive.

And so began a nightly ritual of untamed females taking a leap of faith to envelope my fatigued midriff, flashing varying degrees of exotic underwear ranging from stockings and suspenders to nothing at all, in a passage of unbridled mayhem guaranteed to send countless audiences away to their homes armed with a tale or two to tell.

****

I know not what it was I swallowed, nor the true intentions of whoever was responsible, or for that matter who would stoop so low as to go along with such a dastardly trick. All I really do know is that I awoke some sixteen hours later in a strange bed, confused and nauseous, recalling an impromptu all-nighter at a wealthy businessman's flash abode.

I looked away from the ornate bedside clock. Judging from the imprint and mysterious auburn hairs on the abutting pillow's surface, I'd also had company; but who? After all, I'd arrived alone intending to show my face before moving on to an old mucker's place in nearby Leeds, where the plan had been to bed down for the night.

Wracking my brain, I recalled that the day had begun well with a richly deserved 2-1 home victory over promotion favourites Sunderland at a packed Leicester stadium. Following the final whistle, I'd dashed north for the final night of four at the Theatre Club in Wakefield, where the work in progress concluded on a high and rambunctious note.

I was preparing to hit the road and shedding my sweaty glad-rags in favour of something a little less gaudy when a tap on the shoulder revealed pally venue owner Steve, lightly rubbing his hands together and offering his congratulations for a superb night's work prior to dragging me to one side for a brief chit-chat.

'I don't wish to be a pain in the arse, Dave, but would you say hello to a regular customer? He spends a small fortune in the club, though he's one of those types who loves to name-drop and mingle with the rich and famous!'

'I don't mind at all, mate; besides, I owe you a favour,' I replied, harking back to the man's bountiful hospitality during a previous visit to his home. I tied up my shoelaces and followed the top dog to a tucked-away lounge.

'My bloody missus would love to get her hands on you! She'd be as moist as an otter's pocket if she were here!' the animated scrap-metal baron crudely lauded, greeting me like a long-lost friend and thrusting an arm around my shoulder.

'Perhaps as well she's not then – I wouldn't want to be the source of any embarrassment... Isn't she here tonight?' I tentatively countered.

'She's in Paris... Anyway, young man Steve tells me you're not a bad snooker player; what about a couple of frames at my place before you go dashing off into the moonlight?' he pitched persuasively. Clearly not about to take no for an answer, he led the way through the rear fire-doors to a gleaming highly priced set of wheels.

Trailing in the Bentley's wake, I pulled off the road through a tall set of metallic gates and followed a sweeping driveway round to a stately frontage. A small covey of other late-birds gathered on the steps leading up to the imposing building's entrance.

'C'mon guys, let's leave the girls to have a natter while we grab a cue apiece downstairs,' the self-made host vaunted, summoning a green-jacketed manservant named Gerald and sauntering off to the oak-panelled snooker room.

'You're in esteemed company, lads; look at some of the wizards that have graced this table,' the owner boasted, pointing to a half-dozen legends of the green baize lined up in a mini-gallery of ornately framed signed photos.

I was distracted by a vastly more interesting print taking pride of place on the adjoining wall, depicting a stunning blonde draped in a tastefully placed fox fur reclining on a *chaise longue* in all her glory. 'Never mind bloody Alex "Hurricane" Higgins... who the hell is the delectable creature in the black-and-white shot over there?' I pried, gulping for breath.

'Oh, that's the missus, lad; like I said, she's living it up in Paris with a load of weirdos doing all this *avant-garde* modelling lark... which I call porn!' he blabbed, eyes narrowing and slugging back a sizeable gin and tonic.

'All I can say is, you're a very lucky guy... Anyway, whose break is it?' I responded, anxious not to dwell on an obviously touchy subject and taking up the invitation by smacking the white cue ball into the pack of reds.

Back between the sheets, my memory playing tricks, a light tapping sound drummed at the bedroom door. An attractive brunette entered with a tray of tea and buttered toast, gently placing the goodies on the bedside table.

'It's six-fifteen in the evening – I thought I'd better wake you. You've been out cold for around twelve hours!' she revealed in a blinding flash.

'Where the hell am I? Did I receive a bump on the head or something? What in creation happened last night?' I pleaded.

'Can't you remember?' she gasped, holding a hand to her mouth. 'That's so funny; you seemed to be having such a great time!'

'This must all be a bad dream… I need to use the phone urgently if that's okay!' I urged. I dressed in a hurry and called club-owner Steve in the master bedroom under the watchful gaze of the lightly giggling lady of the house.

'Dave, are you okay? You were almost out of control last night before I left… What the hell had you been on?' he blurted in a panic.

'I wish I knew; all I remember is having a couple of glasses of plonk and one of those sickly green cocktails and trotting downstairs to play snooker… After that it was as if someone switched out the lights!' I came clean.

'So you're saying you don't remember sniffing coke from the kitchen island dressed in just your pink stage socks and underpants?' he exposed.

'But I don't do coke… Oh good God, my mind's a complete blur – what the hell else did I get up to?' I shrieked, hyperventilating like crazy.

'Oh shit… some maniac must've spiked one of your drinks… There've been similar tales coming out of that place for years. His wife has a reputation for being a man-eater and throwing off-the-cuff wild parties. The locals have nicknamed the building "The House with Red Doors"!' he let slip, apologising for the introduction.

'It's a little bit late for that, don't you think! Who's the refined woman I was just talking to? She seems pretty normal.'

'Was she dark-haired…? Oh, that'd be Muriel, she's Jimmy's live-in lover… No one understands how she puts up with it all!' Steve disclosed.

'B… but I thought… oh, never mind,' I babbled, shaking my head in pure astonishment and hanging up in a state of total confusion.

'Chris… I'm really sorry I didn't show, mate; you're not going to believe this!' I gulped, making my next call. After filling in my estranged buddy over in Leeds with the gory details of the previous twenty-four hours I set off back to the Midlands in something of a trance, pondering what I may have put my body through.

I turned on the radio and tuned into an MOR choir demolishing a pastiche of recent chart hits. With visions of John Lennon's infamous albeit lengthier 'lost weekend' springing to mind, I shoved a cassette into the car's stereo system and whacked up the volume, soon mouthing the lyrics to an Eric Carmen song the band were about to cover.

'Well I was sixteen and sick of school; I didn't know what I wanted to do,' I warbled, pausing a moment to reflect on the irony of the tune's sentiment which pretty much summed up my demeanour. The title said it all: *'That's Rock 'n' Roll!'*

****

Heading in a westerly direction out of Wakefield and crossing the M1 motorway, the heavily built-up A638 leads out of the unkempt settlement of Dewsbury into the old mill-town of Batley, passing the priceless wall-mounted sign known to raise a chuckle on every visit: 'ERIC F. BOX, FUNERAL DIRECTORS'. Pretty soon, the inharmonious glittering lights over to the right hand side delineate the preeminent Variety Club.

I was hanging backstage savouring the electric atmosphere ahead of the band's debut performance at the club in early '75 when a beaming set of pearly whites shone in my direction, belonging to an amiable black artist psyching himself up for the imminent announcement. I met the man's eyes and felt my legs turn to jelly.

A moment later my theories were confirmed. 'Ladies and gentlemen, please give a warm welcome to the one and only "Mr Excitement"… yes, it's the wonderful *JACKIE WILSON*,' the compere broadcast, as I kicked myself to find such a legend on the same bill in a supporting role.

I peeped through the towering velvet drapes, drooling at the consummate ease with which his gilt-edged tones glided upwards to infinity, as the master craftsman belted out a thirty-minute repertoire of soul classics including 'Higher and Higher' and 'I Get the Sweetest Feeling', encoring with the later-to-be-rereleased 'Reet Petite'.* It was a showcase for what could only be termed as a God-given talent.

'That was brilliant, Jackie… I just wish you could've done longer,' I lauded, greeting the perspiring virtuoso at the side of the stage amid generous applause. Chatting fervently, we hit it off like a house on fire.

'Well, a little birdie tells me you guys put on a stage show not to be missed, so I'll be checking y'all out later and hope y'aint gonna let me down!' he humbly drawled, gripping my hand tightly and making off to change.

'Excuse me lads, but the Yankee singer who went on before you would like a word with David,' a muscular member of staff announced in a broad Yorkshire accent, shoving his head through the dressing-room door post performance

---

* 'Reet Petite' was to become Jackie Wilson's only ever number one hit two years after his death in 1986 following a pioneering plasticine-man TV advertising campaign very much in the mould of the award winning *Wallace and Gromit*.

whilst eclipsing a much shorter black guy standing back in his shadow.

'Jackie, come on in… Guys, this is Jackie Wilson… How was the show?' I enthused, rushing over in a state of undress to afford the artist a warm welcome.

'I loved it… you guys gave it absolutely everything out there, and David you have a fine set of tonsils,' the great man complimented, rendering the whole gang speechless in a moment I would forever treasure.

The UK tour of 1975 was tragically to be Jackie Wilson's last. In September of the same year the dynamic singer-songwriter suffered a massive heart attack, collapsing on stage during a performance at the Latin Casino in New Jersey, said to be while delivering the line '*my heart is crying*' part way into the song 'Lonely Teardrops'.

Spending the next eight and a half years in a semi-coma, the two-time Grammy Hall of Fame legend died penniless at the age of forty-nine in January 1984, hailed as one of the most influential artists of his generation and beyond.

****

In an age where the boundless demands of political correctness time and again override the ever-dwindling art of common sense, the plain-spoken Yorkshire citizen's 'to call a spade a shovel' ideology would doubtless rattle the cages of the numerous oversensitive do-gooders known to air their grievances on impulse, feasibly unused to the lack of diplomacy and bluntness part and parcel of daily life in the region.

Applying the selfsame 'shoot straight from the hip' approach, the cold-hearted curators of the city's former mental institution may well in latter-day times have landed themselves in seriously hot water and created a national outcry should the sinister-looking red-brick building's original roadside sign have remained in place. Constructed in 1818 essentially to put a roof over the heads of the 'insane poor', the notorious dinosaur of a sanatorium bolted up its doors for the final time as recently as 1995 to make way for a residential housing development, until which time it exhibited a monstrous and insensitive wooden board outside the main gates visible beneath the hospital's coat of arms, inconceivably describing the institution as: '*The Stanley Royd Pauper Asylum for Lunatics and Idiots*'.

Casting serious doubts over the actual saneness of the bureaucrats responsible for such a pitiless eyesore, the mounted plaque in truth differed little from a less ill-boding nameplate visible beneath the gaudy logo of a Florida joke shop aptly dubbed 'The Asylum', flippantly proclaiming: '*We're all here because we're not all there!*' – a description perhaps more pertinent to the inmates of HM Prison Wakefield (eerily nicknamed Monster Mansion).

Serving as Western Europe's largest maximum security penitentiary and in keeping with its sobriquet, it either incarcerates or has at some time accommodated a roll call of modern history's most despicable criminals, which makes for chilling reading:

Harold 'Fred' Shipman ('Dr Death') – hanged himself in the prison in 2004
Roy Whiting – depraved child-killer
Charles Bronson – 'the most violent prisoner in Great Britain'
Robert Black – evil serial child-killer
Mark Bridger – killer of five-year-old April Jones in Powys, Wales in 2012
Radislav Krstic – responsible for the genocide of eight thousand Bosnian
    civilians during the Srebrenica massacre of 1995
Ian Huntley – the vile Soham child-killer (later relocated to HM Prison
    Frankland in County Durham)
Michael 'Mick' Philpott – loudmouth slaughterer of his own six children in a
    pre-planned Derby house fire

Causes célèbres

Dame Barbara Hepworth – renowned sculptor
Jane McDonald – cruise-ship singer turned 'Loose Woman'
Andrew Burt – actor (*The Bill*)
Claire Cooper – *Hollyoaks* actress

Essential travelling band info

Best live music venue: Theatre Royal, Drury Lane
Favourite curry house: Kashmiri Aroma, Paragon Business Village, Herriot Way
    – 76%
Favourite pub: Fernandes Brewery Tap, Avison Yard, Kirkgate – 80%
Don't miss: The Hepworth Wakefield, Gallery Walk – 82%
Sense of humour/friendly welcome: 70%

Chapter 64
Wells

RENOWNED FOR ATTRACTING MORE THAN its fair share of unscrupulous rogues for over half a century, the 'get rich quick' perception of the music industry means that it continues to unearth a regular skulk of shady characters all looking to make a fast buck, usually at the expense of naïve, honest-to-goodness performers quite simply there for the taking.

I've managed to lead a charmed life for close on forty years, helped by an intuitive knack for sniffing out the odd fly-by-night; but perhaps I caught the law of averages on a bad day when, dropping my guard during a trumped-up phone conversation with a supposed organisational wizard, I gave the green light for the band to top the bill at a 'Party on the Pitch' event to be held at the local football ground of the tiny city of Wells in Somerset. Thus it was that a bacon-faced pair of have-a-go-merchants somehow managed to slip under the radar.

'We know all about putting on outdoor events down here, so you won't have any worries on that score,' the redneck purported. As he outlined the proposed details of the midsummer spectacular he made reference to plausibly the most high-profile festival on the rock music calendar – Glastonbury, barely six miles away – and purported to be a pillar of society by putting something back into the community.

Put bluntly, the West Country bumpkin 'promoters', hereinafter referred to as 'Mr Laurel' and 'Mr Hardy', amounted to nothing more than a ragtag-and-bobtail cowboy organisation, possessing little or no inkling as to the mechanics of staging a tea dance, let alone a moonlit extravaganza bandied to attract a crowd of between three and four thousand music fans. It was fated, perhaps inevitably, to result in one outcome – catastrophe!

****

'I've just spoken to the PA company providing the rig and apparently they've worked with the band before, so they know exactly what's required,' sound engineer Ollie briefed as the eleventh hour approached. He emphasised that, with a full programme of supporting artists scheduled to be cluttering up the stage from 5pm onwards, a physical run-through to check over the gear would be out of the question.

For the bulk of the journey south-west the traffic was nose to tail, while the few auspicious patches of blue sky were progressively concealed by a slowly shifting bank of darkening clouds overhead. Upon pulling in to refuel and climbing out of the people carrier, I felt a noticeable pre-autumnal dip in the temperature.

'I thought you were getting down here at three o'clock,' uttered Mr Laurel in his broad Somerset drawl through my mobile handset, enquiring as to the top of the bill's late arrival. Immediately, this set the alarms bells ringing.

'I think there's been a breakdown in communication somewhere; the crew you've hired in informed our guy a line check will suffice, saying they worked with the band a couple of years ago and are pretty much *au fait* with what's required,' I reassured him.

'That's as may be, but I've decided against sticking you on last as things often get a little bit out of hand in this neck of the woods,' he confusingly replied.

'How do you mean, out of hand?' I puzzled.

'Oh, it's just that the punters down here like a good tipple and these occasions often end up as an almighty free-for-all; so all told I'd rather get you on before anything untoward kicks off, then at least there can be no comebacks!' he babbled, pulling the originally designated slot forward to the twilit hour of 9pm.

Pulling off road through the gates of a sports-arena-cum-recreation-ground, we alighted from the bus to an over-the-top backslapping reception from a hulking, blood-pressure-flushed welcoming committee. The sycophantic Mr Hardy led the way to a communal dressing area crawling with youthful, black-clad musicians waging war against each other as they tuned up a range of instruments, creating a furore barely conducive to a few moments' recuperation following the wearisome afternoon hike.

'I can guess what you're thinking... but don't go chucking your toys out of the pram – we'll find you a room of your own when some of the workers on site have finished showering,' the gofer pledged, leaving us to it for the time being.

I ambled across to fraternise with the usually chirpy crew boys, only to find a rather subdued welcome awaiting. The guys seemed strangely out of sorts, nervously moving on the spot and avoiding all eye contact.

'What's up? Spit it out!' I urged Ollie, sniffing a rat.

'Where do I start? I don't want to upset the apple cart, but the PA is a pile of crap and then there's the sodding stage which has been slung together,' he cussed, clearly unhappy. 'I really don't like the feel of this one, Dave.'

'You're bloody joking… they swore blind they'd worked with us before! Is there anything you can do?' I asked hopefully.

'It'll be an uphill battle, that's for sure. I've got a few bits and pieces on the van, but it'll take ages to get everything up and running,' he whined dejectedly. 'Plus the riggers have been on the "afternoon delight" and are all half stoned!'

'Well, we've come all this way, so give it your best shot, buddy. Besides, I've a feeling the punters might go apeshit if we rain off this late in the day!' I reasoned.

'What a nightmare! I'll obviously do all I can, but it won't be a quick fix,' he grimly forewarned. 'Go and take a look at the trailers they've shoved together as an excuse for a stage; it's an accident waiting to happen. The health and safety inspectors would have a field day – some poor bugger's going to come to grief.'

I strolled over to the clubhouse to hunt down chief organiser Mr Laurel, ready to voice my concerns as to the inadequacies of the sound system. Raucous laughter boomed through the open windows as the merry dabbler held court before a posse of half-cut observers, enjoying a joke at the expense of his ruddy-faced, beer-spattered partner Mr Hardy whose drenched, slobber-coated polo shirt spoke volumes.

'Sorry to interrupt, but do you think I could have a quick word?' I quietly asked, attempting to keep a low profile.

'What's up, me old beauty?' the cherry-faced Mr Laurel enquired. He briefly pricked up his ears at my complaints as to the unsuitability of the gear supplied. 'Well, it seems to be working alright so far,' he chortled, referring to the cacophonous din emanating from the first band up in the background.

'Just go out there and take a listen; those bloody speakers won't see the day out – it sounds awful,' I disagreed, getting on my high horse.

'Calm down… there's no need to get so steamed up – I'm sure you boys can cope with a few teething problems. Here, let me buy you a pint?' he barked presumptuously. Taken aback at my refusal, he turned back to his tottering pals.

'This gig has disaster written all over it,' I bickered to Romeo, who was busy demonstrating a few nifty paradiddles on a rubber practice-pad back in the dressing area. 'I might as well have talked to the wall in there. No one gives a flying fuck!'

'Not exactly Glastonbury, is it? We'll just have to grit our teeth and make the best of a bad job,' he responded dolefully. He was interrupted by a booming commotion of ear-splitting distortion and feedback greeting the second band up, followed by a mishmash of energetic three-chord indie rock, more akin to a demolition than a wall of sound.

'For fuck's sake, that crappy PA system's on its last legs,' asserted sax player Davy G. 'I need to get out of here; anybody fancy a jaunt into town for a bit of peace and quiet?' His suggestion expedited a change of scene as a six-strong posse seized upon the opportunity to break free from the emerging turmoil.

'Perhaps in hindsight we should have just buggered off...' I reflected, savouring the brief respite offered by the city-in-miniature's enchanting streets before being drowned out by the gargantuan cathedral's heavy bells clanging seven.

'Hang on, I've got a text!' joked Davy G, signifying both the end of the chimes and a sharp about-turn. Watching our footing we made our way along a traffic-free cobbled street, reputed to be the oldest in England and no doubt providing the setting for any number of TV period dramas, as we headed back in trepidation to the wrong side of the tracks.

An appalling Frank Sinatra tribute tunelessly crooned 'New York, New York' accompanied by a disquieting din of crackles, whistles and other intermittent interference blasting forth from the disorderly stacks of speakers positioned to either side of the stage, adding fuel to an already simmering fire.

'Listen to that bloody racket,' Davy fretted. 'The old saying "you can't polish a turd" comes to mind, DB. What a fucking shambles this whole set-up is!'

'I feel for Ollie; he'll need a sodding miracle to get that pile of junk sounding any good... Somebody's head should swing for this!' I insinuated.

I unlocked the door to a separate changing room requested as per contract, relishing the thought of a spot of relaxation away from the ensuing mayhem. A downpour of powerful water-jets chucking out a head of steam indicated we may not be alone. Taking a stealthy peek into the cubicle I witnessed a naked, hairy-backed monster masturbating furiously amid a shifting fog of heavy mist. I balked in disgust and leapt back a proverbial mile.

'Who the fuck are you... and what do you want?' the individual scathingly barked, skidding on the polished enamel surface as he spun on his heels in annoyance and narrowly avoiding a nasty fall by gripping onto a handrail.

'We're tonight's headlining act and have just been informed we can use this room exclusively for changing... which, if I'm not mistaken, means there shouldn't be any other wankers in here having one off the wrist!' I hit back sarcastically.

'What the f...? Who are you calling a wanker? I'm one of the fuckin' organisers!' he scowled, covering up his manhood with a towel and pumping out his chest, balking slightly at the sight of Romeo lurking in the background.

'Organisers... wankers... it all adds up to the same thing!' I retaliated, hacked off at the stranger's tone and perhaps lighting the blue touch paper.

'Fuck you… Who do you think you are? I'm not here to be insulted by some jumped-up loser!' the bolshie individual ranted. He hurriedly dressed and stormed off in a huff, leaving the door rocking on its rusting hinges.

Meanwhile, soundman Ollie was charging from pillar to post patching a hodgepodge of cables into various rack-mounted gizmos and virtually rewiring the entire system in a race against the clock, eyeballed by a motley crew of oblivious weedheads. Their numbers were swelled at the completion of the preceding band's set by Mr Laurel and co impatiently urging everyone involved to get a move on, concerned at the agitated manner of the quivering gathering on an unforeseeably parky night.

Back at the locker room the thunderous pounding of a heavy fist almost dislodged the bolted door which flew open, pinning Davy G to the wall, to announce the unwanted arrival of a roseate, drunken moron standing pat wearing a look of pure venom.

'Get your fuckin' arses up on that stage right now or there'll be big trouble!' the rustic squawked intimidatingly.

Incensed by this unacceptable outburst, I reached my wits' end. 'How dare you?' I snarled. 'If you and your rat-arsed cider-drinking buddies had gone to the trouble of providing some decent gear, we'd be up there right now. So just fuck off and have another drink… you'll be the first to know when we're ready!'

'*Why are we waiting, why are we waiting,*' the restive crowd chanted tunelessly, putting untold pressure on the luckless crew boys striving manfully to work a little magic and rescue an impossible situation. Impeding their efforts still more, an unruly outbreak of fisticuffs kicked off big time in the segregated backstage area, dismantling the cordon of well-oiled 'security staff' and spilling over into the squelchy wings.

Fearing incurring the further wrath of the already disgruntled throng more than an hour on from the scheduled performance time, the band relayed a message to Ollie urging the techie to abandon all hope of making good the rig and to let fly on a wing and a prayer, forgoing any misgivings to help quell the unfolding pandemonium.

A hullabaloo of cynical cheers greeted the introductory music rumbling distortedly from the underpowered system. We warily took to the stage amid a stream of libellous insults and abuse hurled from the ireful mob, treading ultra-carefully into a hornets' nest of loose planks, empty guitar-cases, stray pieces of gadgetry and a huge metallic toolbox, all cast aside amongst an obstacle course of botched-up debris.

Faced with the unenviable task of winning over the antagonistic rabble, the boys and I hit the ground running, ably assisted by sound engineer Ollie who stepped up to the plate performing wonders with the subnormal rig. It all served to arouse a sudden shift in the baying crowd's demeanour and made inroads into atoning for the infuriating late start.

To the left, thirty or so fiery inebriates continued their tirade, seemingly on a mission to vent their fury with good reason against the shambolic 'organisers'. Overpowering the reinforced line of defence, they laid into anyone blocking their path in an all-out pitched battle, patently getting the better of the overwhelmed fly-by-nights.

Around forty minutes into the set, a blood-speckled oaf lumbered onto the stage and grabbed at one of the live mikes. 'Ladies and gentlemen, due to circumstances beyond our control tonight's entertainment will have to be brought to a premature close as of now,' he yawped incoherently, 'so if you could kindly make your way to the exits please!'

'Ignore the drunken twat, or we'll never get out of here alive...' I screeched in a quandary. 'The punters are lapping it up!' Concerned the announcement may only inflame the riot, I urged Romeo to crack on into the next song.

'Just take those old records off the shelf,' I unflinchingly hollered out, ripping into Bob Seger's rousing 'Old Time Rock and Roll' with lustful aplomb. A spontaneous fit of pogoing erupted amongst the bulk of the crowd, aided and abetted by the remaining droves swaying to and fro punching their hands into the air. *'Gimme that old time rock...'* I screamed, abruptly cut short by a loud clunk signalling the plug had been pulled, silencing the amplification and snuffing out the lights.

I gazed out from the darkness to a war-torn terrain to the left awash with blood-spattered casualties nursing head wounds and battered limbs, worryingly tainted by the odd serious case being attended to by a small army of police and medics who had arrived at the scene.

'Let's rev up and piss off out of here,' I cried to the guys, preparing to take flight and gathering up my belongings. We fled the rat's nest at a rate of knots and hit the road in something of a daze, content to count our blessings at coming through such a traumatic experience at least physically unscathed.

****

Scrawling a barely legible signature on the postman's handheld contraption some weeks later, I ripped open the large padded envelope to find a bundle of documents containing a court summons formally citing my partners and me for breach of contract. Laying it on thick, a farcical laundry list of alleged misdeeds mostly relating to the band's late arrival and subsequent delayed performance was complemented by an audacious claim holding ourselves solely responsible for a catalogue of injuries on top of sparking a near riot.

'There are more holes in this testimony than a Swiss cheese, Dave; plus they've omitted to address any issues regarding the equipment provided, which it would appear was the sole cause of any disruption to the evening's schedule!' my lawyer maintained, putting together an equally damning, watertight counterclaim.

I was informed that the outcome would be decided by a closed hearing based upon the factual evidence submitted, with neither party subpoenaed to attend. An impartial ruling effectively kicking the plaintiffs' case out of court brought the matter to a satisfactory conclusion, with common sense thankfully prevailing and all costs awarded in full.

Causes célèbres

Mary Rand – 1964 Olympic gold medallist
Harry Patch – the very last World War One veteran, who lived to the grand old
    age of 111
Edgar Wright – film director (*Hot Fuzz*)

Essential travelling band info

Live music venue: Glastonbury Festival (six miles away)
Favourite curry house: Riverside, Glastonbury Road – 55%
Favourite pub: City Arms, High Street – 55%
Don't miss: Wells Cathedral (one of the UK's very best) – 77%
Sense of humour/friendly welcome: 40%

Chapter 65
Westminster

'England swings like a pendulum do
Bobbies on bicycles two by two
Westminster Abbey, the tower of Big Ben
The rosy red cheeks of the little children'
– Roger Miller, 1965

****

DURING 2012 ALONE THE HISTORIC landmarks and infamous streets of England's capital acted as host to a staggering 16.9 million foreign travellers, intermingling with an equally overwhelming surfeit of sightseeing Brits taking a little time out to discover statistically the most popular city destination on the planet.

Unknown to a high percentage of the myriad visitors, in point of fact few ever set foot into the bona fide City of London, since the large majority of premier attractions are actually located in the central City of Westminster, created in 1965 upon the establishment of Greater London. Hyde Park, the Royal Albert Hall, Kew Gardens, Ladbroke Grove, Wormwood Scrubs, Kensington High Street, Buckingham Palace, the Houses of Parliament, Downing Street, Oxford Street, Piccadilly Circus and naturally Westminster Abbey all fall within the boundaries of the metropolis's invisible nerve centre, where in effect the term West (as in West End) relates to an abbreviated form of the later sanctioned Westminster, stretching geographically from the Royal Borough of Kensington and Chelsea to the easterly ancient City of London and extending southwards to a natural boundary fashioned by the meandering River Thames.

****

Nestled amongst the upmarket mansions of St John's Wood close to Lord's Cricket Ground lies a tiny stretch of tarmac arguably forming the world's most famous zebra crossing. It was immortalised by four Liverpool-born musicians captured on camera in 1969 taking a ten-minute break from recording to strut across the would-be hallowed ground, resulting in the iconic sleeve design of the Beatles' all-time classic *Abbey Road* album.

I was afforded an invitation to the high-profile launch of a bulky reference book entitled *The Guinness Book of 500 Number One Hits*, which aptly took place at the revered studio just yards from the black-and-white landmark. On arrival I tagged onto a short queue in the buzzing reception area where the budding bestseller's co-authors personally greeted a diverse who's who of erstwhile chart-toppers, all of whom had proudly occupied the coveted pinnacle at some time in their chequered careers going as far back as 1954. I found myself manoeuvring through a shoulder-to-shoulder throng of familiar faces and battle-hardened survivors from across the decades and chewing the fat with the likes of Sting (whom I knew well at the time), an ever-youthful Cliff Richard, the multi-talented Steve Winwood and my now sadly departed pal Mike Smith (from the Dave Clark Five).

An overkill of laudatory speeches ensued from the lips of the Guinness bigwigs and the tome's compilers, proposing a toast to the publication's future success and provoking a slow retreat toward the exits. Squeezing through a scattering of stragglers littering up the lobby at the top of the staircase, mostly queuing for cars and taxis, I accidentally stumbled across Paul McCartney chatting merrily away to one side and grabbed the opportunity to top the night off with a prized moniker on my souvenir copy. As I shuffled betwixt a small clique of loose-lipped hangers-on, somewhat distracted the ex-Beatle's eyes met my own.

'I don't wish to be a pain, but would you mind signing my book?' I pandered, vigorously flicking to the half title page.

'It would be a pleasure, mate… Just give me a sec, I've just been nabbed by someone from the press!' he answered humbly, taking the anthology and pen and stepping aside to make room for a bunch of departing guests.

'I wouldn't normally ask – I bet he gets sick of it… You know, I've only ever asked for one other autograph in my whole career!' I babbled, engaging in a brief chat with a good-natured fair-haired lady standing close by.

'He doesn't mind at all,' smiled the mysterious blonde, whom I realised to be none other than the star's then wife Linda. 'Who was the other honoured celebrity?'

'It was… um… Jack Howarth from *Coronation Street*, the old guy who played Albert Thingamabob!' I revealed, a little at sixes and sevens.

'He'll find that funny when I tell him…' she chuckled, before changing the subject midstream: 'How's the band going?'

'Oh, everything's pretty good thanks; we're just about to go back on the road for a marathon sixty-date tour,' I replied, pursing my lips.

'I can't stand your band,' she exclaimed from out of nowhere, glancing sideways to conceal the trace of a smirk in the corner of her mouth.

'Really…? Ah well, you can't win them all… I don't quite know what to say!' I recoiled, understandably taken aback.

'Please don't get me wrong, I'm not being nasty; it's just that me and the old fella over there get woken up every day to the sound of your music blaring out of the kids' stereo!' she let slip, seeing my jaw drop a mile.

'What, does he… get the… hump?' I stammered, fast losing the power of speech and pointing my thumb towards Paul.

'You bet we do; we often hammer on the floor yelling at the girls to turn it down… Anyway, it's been lovely talking to you,' she avowed, cutting the conversation short and bidding a fond farewell before trailing in the wake of her famous hubby out into the car park.

'Haha, I can just see it now: "Turn that bloody racket down!" That's just brilliant!' I jabbered, caught in a world of imagination and chuckling incessantly to myself.

'Dave… Dave… are you alright? Are you ready to go… Is something wrong?' enquired my record producer friend Phil, observing I was miles away.

'No, nothing's wrong… nothing at all. It's just that… well, I'm not sure you'll believe me if I tell you!' I rambled on, strolling past the legendary pedestrian crossing.

****

The Alexandra Palace (nicknamed 'Ally Pally') provided the setting for perhaps the shortest of all the band's historical live gigs. It was in the heady days of early 1979, at the no-expense-spared post-Christmas annual get-together of the voguish and notoriously boisterous 'Club 18-30' holiday group.

Leading off at breakneck pace in front of a wasted four-thousand-strong sea of party animals, I bellowed out the opening lines to 'Pretty Little Angel Eyes'; but, scarcely four songs into the set, a loaded metallic missile launched from the grip of an unidentified moron struck its target just above my right eye. I dropped the mike to the floor, almost out on my feet and clutching at a ballooning bump with blood-spattered hands.

I staggered from the stage seeing double and made it to the bottom of the exit ramp where a clear-sighted St John Ambulance volunteer rushed to my aid, stemming the flow of claret dousing my face and vivid yellow outfit before ushering my bowed frame towards a side room and urging a lackey to put out an urgent call for a doctor.

'You'd better get back out there – the crowd are going apeshit and the organisers are threatening to sue,' an unknown representative squawked, bursting into the dressing room to find the medical man shining a light into my eyes.

'This man's in no fit state to perform… he's mildly concussed and hardly knows the time of day. I strongly suggest you inform those coordinating this event as such!' barked the practitioner, tearing a strip off the man and effectively putting paid to any misconceptions the show may soon be up and running again.

****

Along with co-defendants Russ and Rod I was called upon to attend a potentially costly hearing at London's infamous law courts on the Strand (again in the city of Westminster), mystified as to the holiday company's outlandish claim for damages on top of a full refund of the prepaid fee. As battle commenced the arguments came thick and fast, disturbingly monopolised by the fabricated depositions of a string of unreliable witnesses, twisting the facts to insist the blame lay squarely on the band's shoulders for inciting the disruption.

'I'm afraid the dispute appears to be slipping from our grasp; my learned friend seems to have turned the whole thing completely on its head,' our stern-faced barrister implied two days into the hearing. He painted a bleak picture as to the case's likely outcome, but promised to readdress matters with a change of tack the following day.

I entered the dock on day three sprucely decked out in jacket and tie and was sworn in by a plummy notary. An intense grilling from the prosecution's brief ensued, pursuing a line of questioning based heavily on a pack of lies. My defence remained unshakeable and managed at last to uncover a few cracks to tilt the balance back in our own favour, though failing in any way to rouse the presiding judge from an abiding two-and-a-half-day reverie.

'Well done, young sir; we'll have them floundering on the ropes by the end of the day… though please remember you are still under oath,' our legal eagle smugly upheld as we gathered in a huddle just ahead of a two-hour recess, buoyed by a shift in the right direction and fully prepared to up the ante during the post-lunch showdown.

Pugnaciously springing to his feet from behind a lavish oak-panelled desk at the beginning of the afternoon session, the revitalised counsel launched into a fierce condemnation of the 'outrageously reckless' act of hooliganism leading up to the show's premature curtailment. Contesting the reliability of the prosecution witnesses' conflicting evidence and sniffing victory, he called for the defence's first witness.

Glancing to my left in between confirming a few necessary details pertinent to the case, I tried hard not to smile as the wigged moderator's liquid lunch seemed to be having a soporific effect. Slouched back on his perch he displayed a slothful contempt for such inconsequentialities, softly whistling in his renewed dormancy.

'Do members of the public often bombard the stage with an assortment of items during your performances, Mr Bartram?' the brief queried.

'Indeed they do, more or less at every show… though the articles they throw are usually intended as a token of their affections,' I explained.

'Could you please be more specific as to the type of objects the said audience members open fire with, Mr Bartram?' the advocate elicited.

'Cuddly toys, sweets, especially Jelly Babies, and more often than not an interesting mixture of undergarments,' I expanded.

'Really…? What exactly do you mean by undergarments?' the barrister pressed, stimulating a clearing of the throat from the learned bigwig himself.

'Oh, skimpy pairs of panties, G-strings, suspender belts, even the odd brassiere!' I responded, playing to the amused gallery who were hushed immediately by the rapping gavel of the spluttering and now fully alert judge.

'Panties… brassieres…! Would this behaviour be regarded as normal at your concerts, young man?' the authority barked with renewed vigour.

'Very much so, my lord; a large proportion of the female fans work themselves up into such a frenzy they'll do pretty much anything to attract a little attention,' I embellished, meeting the enraptured old boy's eyes above his glasses.

'How bizarre… Would I be right in assuming that these passionate young devotees have removed the said items from their person prior to peppering the stage with them?' the arbiter pried, clearly enjoying the exchange.

'Without a shadow of a doubt, my lord; I suppose you could call it one of the perks of the job!' I cheekily attested.

'Quite, young man, quite!' the learned man earnestly responded, handing the reins back to the upstanding defence brief.

Witnessing a decisive shift to gain the upper ground, succoured by the unshakeable evidence of Russ and Rod, the stout-hearted defence counsel remained in the ascendancy throughout the proceedings, battering the prosecution's wafer-thin case into submission and fending off the final arguments to win the day, which was topped off with a sly, self-satisfied wink in my direction from the wily old beak upon the announcement of the final judgement.

Noble causes célèbres

The Abbey became the final resting place to a number of monarchs including:
Edward the Confessor – 1066
Edward the First – 1307
Henry the Fifth – 1483
Henry the Seventh – 1509
Mary the First – 1558
Elizabeth the First – 1603
Mary Queen of Scots – 1587
James the First – 1625
George the Second – 1760

Other notable people buried in the Abbey:
Thomas Hardy – novelist (whose heart is buried in Dorset)
Rudyard Kipling – Nobel Prize-winning writer and poet
Neville Chamberlain – former Prime Minister
Clement Attlee – former Prime Minister
Sir Laurence Olivier – revered actor (died 1989)

Essential visitor information

Live music venues: Theatre Royal, Drury Lane; Adelphi Theatre, The Strand; Fortune Theatre, Russell Street; Jermyn Street Theatre; Soho Theatre, Dean Street; London Palladium, Argyll Street (to name but a few)
Favourite curry house: Silk, Great Marlborough Street – 77% (expensive but unique)
Favourite pub: Buckingham Arms, Petty France – 80%
Don't miss: A good tourist guide
Sense of humour/friendly welcome: 35%

Chapter 66
Winchester

'I'D GIVE THE ITCHEN PURE Gold a go, it's a cracking pint!' recommended a university undergraduate, slightly the worse for wear, perched on a stool at the bar of a characterful city-centre pub displaying a wide range of real ales.

'Thanks for that, I was feeling spoilt for choice… You don't also happen to know of any half decent restaurants nearby, do you?' I enquired.

'Ah, you might have me on that score,' the pale-faced student sighed. 'Pubs I'm a bit of an authority on, but when it comes to grub I tend to survive on junk food. Only a few more months to go, then I'm out of here… I can't wait!'

'It seems a really pleasant neck of the woods at first glance,' I complimented. 'In fact we were considering staying an extra night.'

'Everyone passing through thinks the same, but take it from me Winchester's the most boring place to live in the entire country… Nothing ever happens here!' the scholar lamented, lambasting Hampshire's by no means unattractive county town.

'Ah, come on, it can't be that bad; we were just looking in the windows of a few estate agents and the property prices are sky-high around here!' I argued.

'That's as may be, but the toffee-nosed gits forking out a fortune for them just move in and bury their heads in the sand,' he griped on. 'There's a handful of good pubs and that's it; you have to get pissed every night to stay sane!'

'Oh well, we're off to Russia first thing tomorrow so "Moscow"!' I joked, downing the dregs of my pint and making a hasty exit.

****

An early-morning stroll with Cathy along the River Itchen took us past a terrace of rickety old cottages backing onto the water's edge. A row of tall weeping willows shimmered in the autumnal sunlight, casting a long jagged shadow over the pebbled footpath which led into a peaceful side street. Here a wall-mounted plaque signified the humble abode of romantic novelist Jane Austen, conjuring up images of prim and proper ringlet-haired maidens draped in virginal white lace outfits, gently twirling their parasols whilst taking tea by the croquet lawn of a sun-kissed country manor and unfailingly attracting the attentions of a select few eligible male heirs looking dashingly handsome in a range of fashionable Beau Brummell Regency apparel.

Deviating off course into a hidden-away area of greenery we happened upon an elderly, silk-robed oriental character, impressively balanced on one leg, meticulously carving his hands and arms into a mystical array of shapes and moves. Seemingly in a trance, he appeared oblivious to the gruff commands of a tattooed, shaven-headed man who was full-bloodedly thrusting an orange Frisbee skywards to the obvious delight of a sturdily built Dobermann pinscher. Freed from its lead, the animal bounded powerfully across the meadow in pursuit of the airborne toy.

'Fetch it, Syn… there's a good lad,' shouted the animal's keeper. He repeated the process, this time carelessly propelling the chewed-up plaything within a whisker of the unperturbed Chinaman's left ear and onto the path by my wife's feet. 'Freeze… don't move a muscle and he won't hurt you!' the oaf bellowed, eyeing the beast sprinting towards the walkway.

At once, the alert Chinese guy stood firmly on both feet, glancing back in his peripheral vision to the damsel in distress. 'S-s-s-s-s-s-s-s-s,' the foreigner chillingly hissed, eyeballing the slobbering creature. Skidding to a halt it recoiled, whimpering a teeth-chattering cry, and shrank away from the enigmatic stranger and into the clutches of his bewildered master.

'There, there, Syndrome, just ignore the nasty man… Hey, Confucius, how the fuck did you do that?' the roughneck coarsely hounded. Finding himself blanked by the old boy, he dragged the animal well away from the creepy eccentric.

'I suggest you get that bloody thing on a lead where it belongs; you've scared my wife out of her wits!' I protested, a little shaken myself.

'Ah, there's no need to get uppity – he didn't mean any harm, he's just a big softy really… I'm sorry if he frightened you, love,' he atoned a tad reluctantly.

'Forget it… By the way, did I just hear you right… he's called Syndrome?' I double-checked, posing the obvious question.

'That's right; I came up with it when I was hammered in the local pub one night. You should hear it when I tell him to get down… Hey look, Fu Manchu's come back to life!' he fool-headedly sniped, falling silent as the mystical outlander passed close by, pausing momentarily to give the bonehead a piece of his mind.

'A-a-a-a-h… Me Fu Manchu… so you be careful!' the stranger spookily wailed, spinning round on a sixpence and startling both man and beast, causing the dog to wrap its lead around the owner's legs and sending the oaf crashing to the ground. With that, the yellow peril slipped on a pair of sandals and disappeared from view.

'If I were you, I'd do as he says… and while you're at it I'd change the dog's name before you really piss someone off!' I strongly advised. I grabbed the good lady's hand and we moved on in search of coffee and a sense of normality.

****

Treading new ground in England's ancient capital at a high-budget pre-Christmas ball held in the mid 1970s within the grounds of Winchester's renowned university, I ambled backstage for a sneaky peek to find a full-scale relocation of the band's gear apparently in progress, lugged by a body of brawny crew hands into the adjoining, appreciably smaller marquee.

'What's going on, Ian?' I yawped over to the clearly ruffled sound engineer, assuming the guys must have encountered a last-minute hitch.

'Don't ask; that flat-capped northern twat who was due on at ten has insisted all our gear is shifted so everyone can get a look at his ugly mug!' Ian bickered, hauling a large cabinet to one side and onto a waiting trolley.

'But there's no way we'll get everything into the other tent… it's tiny!' I quibbled, stating the obvious and stepping aside to make room for an additional bunch of helpers belatedly arriving on the scene.

'Tell me about it! We'll be running well over an hour late… I'll do my best to keep you up to speed,' the techie griped.

Gracing the expectant mob with his presence around thirty minutes behind schedule, the capped crusader fell way short of grabbing the restless crowd's attention, plink-plonking through a repertoire of pedestrian tunes unsuited to such an occasion and prompting a mass exodus into the wigwam next door, where packed together like sweaty sardines in a can the flushing revellers keenly awaited a rock-and-roll fix.

The band ducked beneath a raised flap to access the marquee's side entrance, prompting a dense swarm of reddening scholars to jostle forcefully for position. They were bulldozed backwards by a gang of burly security staff doing their level best to create a narrow inlet for the instrumentalists to squeeze through onto the wooden platform, where they instantly thundered into a hypnotic, percussive interpretation of the sixties classic 'Wipe Out'.

As I prepared along with Bill and Geoff to follow in the boys' footsteps upon the tune's conclusion, a delectable young filly slipping through the net raised the temperature still more, scaling the stage and tantalisingly beginning to disrobe. She was spared goosebumps and lecherous catcalls by a brute of a bodyguard draping his outsized jacket around her curvaceous assets, much to the displeasure of the drooling male onlookers.

The instrumental rumbled towards a close amid a cacophonous ovation and the chock-full mass of hyperventilating bodies dangerously surged forward. The trio of vocalists making ready to leap up to the vacant mikes were left stranded at the rear of an impenetrable crush, forced into doubling back whence we came to seek out an alternative route. Drummer Romeo was meanwhile craning his head this way and that, mystified at finding neither hide nor hair of the wayward trio of band personnel. 'Shit…! What the f…? Oh sod it… one, two, a-one-two-three-four,' he yelled, displaying admirable speed of thought as he grasped the nettle and proceeded to leather seven bells out of the kit's tom-toms in a purposeful reprise of the pounding refrain.

Crawling on our muddied hands and knees through an enforced gap at the marquee's back end and somersaulting onto the ply-board fringe, we shimmied over to the mikes to finally pick up the slack. A sea of pained expressions gazed longingly upwards, crushed together in a cauldron of utter chaos, spurring a scattering of fragile females into taking refuge around their partners' shoulders whilst a handful of adventurous types chanced their arm at monkey-walking up the central supporting poles, anxious to be freed from a claustrophobic hell.

'*You keep a-knocking, but you can't come in!*' the lyric frantically blasted out, augmented by the disintegrating crackle of splitting timber intensifying above the clamour. Like a felled tree, an overwhelmed beam gave way, ripping straight through the tent's canvas and toppling toward the gasping horde. It was heroically upheld by a posse of beefy young bucks clinging on for dear life to help make good the crowd's safe adjournment into the larger marquee.

'Guys, we desperately need you to dig us out of an enormous hole,' a flapping SU rep beseeched. 'Is there any way you could just go for broke on the rig in the adjoining tent? Otherwise, the event will be a total disaster.' The proposition was given the go-ahead by the crew boys and band alike and we pulled a rabbit out of the hat, culminating in an unforgettably spontaneous night's work, aided and abetted by the indebted, hugely relieved gathering.

After the gig we revelled in a spot of hospitality, with a wondrous feast of culinary delights juiced up by a plentiful supply of vintage Bollinger. With the hour approaching 4am and fast losing the power of speech, hankering for a breath of fresh air and forgoing the offer of a taxi to the hotel, the surviving foursome opted for an impromptu stroll. As we twisted through a side alley and onto the outspread main thoroughfare, the magnificent bronze statue of Alfred the Great imperiously glared back from his lofty perch close to the city's mediaeval East Gate, emboldened by the reddish hue of the moon and attracting the attention of the band of nocturnal songsters.

'Let's go and take a shufti at that monument just up the road,' I inarticulately proposed, laying eyes on the impressive mounted icon and wandering haphazardly over a patch of cobblestones tailed by three flatulent amigos.

'Who's it supposed to be?' Geoff slurred, teetering up to the plinth.

'It's Ethelred, isn't it…? Whoever it was, if it's life-size he was a helluva big bastard,' I jested, shushing my S's inarticulately.

'It's Alfred* the Great; I remember seeing him when I was a kid,' reminisced Rod, stifling a belch. 'My family used to drag me here on shopping trips every week… I think!'

'That's got to be bullshit… it say here the old cake-burner was erected in 1901, by which time you must have been well into your teens!' I lampooned, making every effort to wind up my senior of just four years.

'Ha bloody ha. It's true – we lived not far from here during my childhood; it's all coming back to me now!' he continued undeterred.

'I presume it was still part of Wessex then!' I persisted.

'You see that bloody great sword he's holding…? I'll wrap it round your head if you don't button it!' he warned, pausing to put one foot in front of the other and finally lurching in the general direction of the night's lodgings.

Causes célèbres

Colin Firth – Oscar-winning actor
Lucy Pinder – glamour model
Frank Turner – singer/songwriter
Christopher Cazenove – film and TV actor
Jane Austen – died in the city in 1817

Essential travelling band info

Live music venue: Theatre Royal, Jewry Street
Favourite curry house: Rimjhim Indian, City Road – 81%
Favourite pub: Fulflood Arms, Cheriton Road – 70%
Don't miss: Winchester Cathedral – 69%
Sense of humour/friendly welcome: 66%

---

* Or 'AELFRED' as inscribed on the granite pedestal

Chapter 67
Wolverhampton

'I'M DOWN YOUR WAY AT the weekend to attend a musical I've got in at Wolverhampton's Grand Theatre. I can put your name on the door and maybe we can go for a curry afterwards; there's an idea I'd like to run by you!' promoter friend Derek conveyed, enthusing over a groundbreaking new concept set to net us both a tidy sum.

'Wolverhampton… it's bloody miles away! That's the problem with you city slickers – you assume everything north of Watford is like a big village,' I squabbled. 'It's a seventy-mile journey and the M6 is a nightmare on a Friday night. What a shame it's not tonight; I'm only up the road in Birmingham as we speak!'

'Ah, I get it… that's your way of saying you'd like me to pay, you tight git. Well, don't worry, it'll be on me. There's a fabulous Indian called "The Spice Avenue"; we went there last time I was in town – you'll love it to bits,' he salivated.

'Don't forget it's a weekend night and if it's as good as you say we'll need to book a table,' I pointed out, feeling my own taste buds tingle.

'Can I leave that with you? I'm on my hands-free in the car,' Derek hinted. 'Make it for three – I'll bring my co-director John along.'

'I'm over at Central TV at the minute, so I'll get it sorted during the lunch break… Shall we say 10.30pm?' I proposed, promising to give him a shout back when everything was confirmed.

Supping at a mug of tea, I scanned through a well-used copy of the Yellow Pages on the cluttered desktop and paused at the restaurant section. A full half-page of establishments beginning with S oddly drew a blank, leaving me scratching my head to figure out the next move.

'That copy's years old, Dave; if there's a number you need I've got an up-to-date one here you can borrow,' news researcher Pam offered.

'You don't happen to know of a curry house called The Spice Avenue between Birmingham and Wolverhampton, do you?' I enquired, picking her brains. 'I'm back in the vicinity on Friday and my mate's asked me to reserve a table.'

'It doesn't ring any bells, but then again I live on the other side of the city. Why don't you try dialling 192?' she calmly suggested. Gulping down the lukewarm brew, I lifted the receiver to punch in the digits.

'*Directory Enquiries... Can oi 'elp yow?*' the broadest Black Country accent imaginable purred in the most lilting of tones.

'I sincerely hope so... Can you give me the number for The Spice Avenue in Wolverhampton, please?' I politely posed.

Would that be spice as in outer spice?' she mind-bogglingly responded.

'I'm sorry, but I'm not sure I heard you correctly; could you repeat that?' I urged, scarcely able to believe my ears.

'*I asked if you meant spice as in outer spice; yer know, rockeets and all that astronomy stuff!*' she astoundingly rehashed.

'No love, that's not what I said at all; its S-P-I-C-E – the Spice Avenue Indian Restaurant,' I snickered, spelling it out for her.

'*Ooer, I made a roight pig's ear of that one,*' she admitted apologetically. ' *'Ave yer gorra pen, 'cause oi've gorret eer in front of may?*' After articulating the digits surprisingly clearly, she offered another number for free.

'Actually you may be able to help me there... Second thoughts, not to worry,' I stopped short, noticing the name of lyricist Tim Rice scrawled on my pad whom I'd been asked to contact regarding a charity cricket match.

'*Would that be rice as in egg and spoon rice?*' I envisaged, imagining her response, as I rang off and dialled the restaurant's number.

****

Paying a flying visit to Wolverhampton for the ensemble's first headlining date at the cavernous City Hall in the mid-seventies, I was stricken with a feeling of wooziness attributed to a disgusting 2am takeaway the previous night. An appreciative, rowdy full house helped lighten the load, noisily chanting the hook lines to the encore 'Hey Rock and Roll' through the open dressing room windows as they dispersed from the building.

'When you're changed and ready, lads, there's a load of distinguished guests and press people waiting to meet you in the hospitality area just along the corridor, so for heaven's sake don't shoot straight off!' tour manager Tony prompted.

'Oh shit... I'm going rapidly downhill, Tone,' I quibbled, rubbing my stomach. 'I could've done without that, I need an early night!'

'It'll only be for half an hour... A couple of large brandies should help – they'll soon boost your immune system,' the Man Friday persuasively advised, presently leading the way to a plush suite awash with smartly attired guests.

'How's your Montezuma's revenge?' asked Geoff, handing over another large brandy and clutching onto a similar measure for his own medicinal purposes in between posing for photographs with the complimentary raised-pinkie-finger brigade.

'Oh, it's not the runs I've got; in fact it's quite the reverse – my legs are like jelly… Mind you, that cognac doesn't seem to have done any harm,' I contended, anaesthetised by the effects of the mollifying liquor.

'Gentlemen, may I just say it's been a pleasure having you here; however, your taxis are waiting by the main entrance ready to whisk you back to your hotel, so perhaps you could begin making tracks,' the venue supervisor announced, fresh from brown-nosing with the departing dignitaries and initiating a slow shift towards the exit.

Temporarily waylaid by a pigtailed blonde desperate for a souvenir snap, I was lagging behind the pack and taking it one step at a time down the marble staircase like an immobilised wreck when a fierce bout of stomach cramps stabbed dagger-like into my nether regions, diverting my attention to a sign for the public toilets.

Squatting agonisingly in the cubicle head in hands, fluid welling in the corners of my eyes, totally drained and resting my throbbing skull back against my overcoat, I breathed a demoralised sigh and fell into a deep, exhausted slumber.

Subconsciously picking up on a distant jangle, presumably from a set of keys, I came to in a nauseous stupor and sprang to my feet, plunged into darkness. I pulled up my trousers and blindly slid back the latch. Guided by a row of porcelain sinks I made my way to the outer door where, disbelievingly, I found myself under lock and key.

'Help! Is anybody there?' I screeched from the echoing chamber of horrors, repeatedly snapping down the handle, all to no avail. Eventually I threw in the towel and, facing up to the reality of spending the night in a cold, stinking WC, I dossed down on the tiled floor, soon mercifully again losing consciousness.

'*Aaargh!* What in God's name…?' cried the bucket lady, dropping her mop and standing her ground like an NFL quarterback. 'How the hell did you get in there? I'll have to report this to the management; are you a tramp?'

'No, I'm not a bloody tramp!' I bickered, gathering up my stuff. 'I got taken short last night and was locked in here by the inconsiderate caretaker.' Making for the door, I found myself impeded by a giant sweeping-brush thrown into my path.

'Just hold your horses, you might have vandalised the toilet or nicked something… Stay there while I fetch the manager,' she overzealously cautioned, disturbingly attempting to shove her own set of keys into the lock.

'Get out of my way, you fat cow; what the hell could I have taken?' I roared. 'Besides, you've run out of fucking bog-rolls!' Bulldozing my way through the door I hurtled down the stairs and out into the open air where, thankfully, I managed to hail a cab with little trouble.

'What've you been up to for the last ten and a half hours?' groused tour manager Tony, calling to make sure I was in the land of the living at 11am. 'Breakfast finished ages ago. We're leaving for Preston at midday on the dot!'

'Let's just say I've hardly had a wink of sleep and was waylaid by a brute of a woman; every muscle in my body's aching!' I explained.

'Well, don't expect any sympathy from me... you dirty bastard!' he responded, getting the wrong end of the stick and slamming down the phone.

****

Never the most glamorous of destinations, yet realistically a million miles from the fourth world, the downtrodden town found itself justifiably up in arms when, in 2009, the *Daily Mail* published a damning list of the world's top ten worst cities, compiled by the travel guide *Lonely Planet*, which unjustly and offensively marked down the Black Country conurbation in fifth place.

Provoking outrage in the local media on top of hitting the national headlines, the ill-considered feature begged many questions as to how exactly an earthy old industrial town could possibly bear comparison with the likes of the crime-tormented US city Detroit (which topped the poll), or for that matter be grouped alongside such poverty-stricken slums as San Salvador in El Salvador, rat-infested Chennai in India and the sprawling, degrading squalor making up Ghana's blighted capital Accra?

Dismissing the editorial as twaddle and conducting an immediate enquiry, the city council issued a statement claiming that no representatives from the publication had even bothered to set foot in the locality it saw fit to condemn, failing to support the malicious content with as much as a detailed write-up. Interestingly, they uncovered an alleged conversation purported to have influenced the city's inclusion, said to have taken place at New York's scene of devastation the day following the tragic events of September 11th 2001 between gaffe-prone American President George Bush and a pragmatic yam-yam tourist.

'Where are you from?' the Commander-in-chief asked.

'Wolverhampton, sir!' the man tersely replied.

'That's not a place I know; what state is it in?' the uninformed Bush enquired.

'Pretty much the same state as this in all honesty,' the journeyman sighed, baffling the sombre Texan who promptly moved on.

I'm reliably informed by a music industry veteran hailing from nearby Walsall that the argument continues to rage, with no hint of an apology or revocation ever forthcoming from the guide's callous compilers. Inevitably, this has resulted in a dearth of *Lonely Planet* publications occupying the shelves of the town's bookshops, perhaps summed up in the words of the same individual: 'They're as common round 'ere as rocking-horse shit!'

Which on a differing, sentimental note leads me on to one of the dearest living souls it was ever my pleasure to swap stories with, the lady in question being 'Lil', the mother of my wife's most cherished friend Sandra, who resided close to neighbouring West Bromwich for most of her long and happy life.

Lil's 'open house' mode of thinking afforded an unparalleled warmth and hospitality to a constant flow of visitors, born out of a kindly, good-hearted affection not only extending to her own sizeable brood, but lavished as a rule upon every friendly face fortunate enough to enter her cosy, genial parlour.

I relished my once-in-a-blue-moon social calls to the lady's charming, homely abode, where a moreish blend of extra strong tea and homemade fruitcake rapidly blew away the cobwebs. I would rise with difficulty from a deep-cushioned armchair, and the return crawl along the infamously congested M6 motorway would curiously pass without a hint of an angry word as I held dear an afternoon of good-natured companionable chit-chat.

Meeting up with a smattering of family members shortly after the much missed fairy godmother's passing, images of a heated stove brimming with pots and pans swamping the air with a fusion of mouth-watering aromas brushed past my nostrils as I mulled over the merits of the busy bee's distinctly satisfying 'special brew'.

'Oh Dave, I can't believe you never knew; she looked upon you as a special guest…' a close relative giggled, pausing mid-sentence to arouse my suspicions further. 'She always got the best bone china out when you showed up!'

'I can tell you're keeping something from me,' I sifted out, cottoning on I may be the butt of a long-standing joke.

'She had a bottle of fifteen-year-old Scotch hidden in the cupboard… Every time you came over she put a couple of tablespoons in your cuppa – that's probably why you left the place feeling so chipper!' she came clean, laughing uncontrollably.

'B… but I don't d… drink whisky… What's more I haven't touched a drop in more than twenty-five years!' I stammered, hesitating momentarily to take a whiff of the contents clinging to the insides of my teacup.

Causes célèbres

Johnny Briggs – actor
The Wonder Stuff – rock band
Slade – chart-topping seventies band
Robert Plant – former Led Zeppelin lead vocalist and solo performer
Ashley Young – Manchester United and England footballer
Eric Idle – Monty Python legend; went to school in the town and is a renowned
    Wolves supporter

Essential travelling band info

Live music venue: The Wulfrun Hall
Favourite curry house: Penn Tandoori, Penn Road – 69% (The Spice Avenue
    I'm told is still in the town, though its glory days are long gone)
Favourite pub: Hog's Head, Stafford Street – 66%
Don't miss: Closer to the Edge (Aerial Ropes Adventure) – 72%; a great day out
    for energetic kids
Sense of humour/friendly welcome: 95% (especially for Lil)

Chapter 68
Worcester

'DEARLY BELOVED, WE ARE GATHERED here together in the sight of this company to witness the union of a congregation of Worcestershire reprobates and a rock-and-roll band which is commended to be honourable among all men!'

Churlish or not, the sermon marked one of the more off-the-wall and borderline blasphemous introductions of my career. It was wryly intended to kick off the proceedings with a touch of devilry and win over a predominantly middle-aged crowd assembled within the unique Huntingdon Hall located in Worcester's city centre.

Taking its name from Leicestershire-born religious leader Selina Hastings, otherwise known as the Countess of Huntingdon, the one-of-a-kind theatre radiates an uncommon ambience, not only in having served as a thriving Methodist chapel during the eighteenth century (the final service took place in 1976), but by virtue of the original pews which make up the lion's share of the seating arrangements, equipping the worshippers with a bird's-eye view of the sturdy timber stage fashioned around the raised ancient pulpit from where, before a sea of confused faces, I delivered the tongue-in-cheek eulogy.

Half expecting a sinister volley of thunderclaps and streaks of lightning to horn in and disrupt the irreverent sermon, I tripped down from the lectern to take centre stage. Mercifully, nothing appeared likely to bring down the house other than the pulsating quake of a drum intro booming from the stacks of side-mounted speakers, underpinned by pockets of the five-hundred-strong crowd rising to their feet to boogie in the aisles, surfing on a wave of nostalgia remarkably some thirty-seven years in the making.

****

Overlooked by business-minded concert promoters generally plumping for larger capacity venues in easy-to-reach Gloucester and Cheltenham, of all the UK's sizeable cities Worcester's handful of repertory-style theatres never once featured on the band's calendar, other that is than the odd jaunt to the undulating splendour of the neighbouring Malvern hills. One visit in particular springs to mind, lingering fresh in the memory banks.

For the best part of six decades, the world of popular music has annually contrived to thrust a cast of unknowns mingled in amongst an extinction of over-the-hill dinosaurs onto the goggle-boxes of middle-of-the-road music fans in a pitched battle of musical imperfection known as 'The Eurovision Song Contest'. It keeps millions of TV viewers glued to their screens, from the north Russian arctic isles to the southernmost Red Sea settlements belonging to the western Asian state of Israel.

Approached to try my hand as a solo performer in 1984, I was subsequently castigated by business colleagues for knocking back the one-off 'golden opportunity'. Some twenty-three years later, a manufactured boy-girl quartet going under the name of 'Scooch' were mystifyingly selected to represent the UK at the 2007 event staged in Helsinki, Finland, and perhaps destined to be added to a perennial list of underachievers.

Media cynics harbouring reservations as to the credibility of the concept based on the uninspiring failure of the submitted songs to come up to scratch yet again proved spot-on, with the fresh-faced entrants' dismal portrayal of an insipid ditty entitled 'Flying the Flag (For You)' receiving a pitiable total of nineteen points whilst ignominiously voted into twenty-third out of twenty-four competing nations by their fellow Europeans. Never in the competition's lengthy history had a British entry suffered such humiliation, attested to by the familiar phrase hitherto most associated with Norway, *'nul points'* (zero points), ringing out from the hypocritical representatives of twenty-one countries before a TV audience approaching a staggering half a billion people.

Hot on the heels of the inglorious debacle and with the red-faced contestants clinging on to a cherished position in the nether regions of the UK singles chart, the sprawling Three Counties Showground in Malvern opened its gates to an unlikely pairing of the squeaky-clean dance-pop troupe together with our very own curmudgeonly ensemble, braving the unseasonably bone-chilling elements on an English late summer's evening.

Originally existing chiefly for the purpose of representing artists in as true a light as possible 'live' on television, to the bulk of touring musicians the term 'playback' typifies an easy way out for a more mercenary breed of performer, guilefully bolstering their bank balances scouring the country's club venues employing pre-recorded backing tracks as opposed to the uneconomical option of an entourage of session players. By the turn of the century the onset of 'hiss free' digital recording alternatives flooding the market brought an end to the stigma, giving rise to a deluge of get-rich-quick artists broken via prime-time

TV shows barefacedly vocalising karaoke-style over the original masters, leaving scores of 'warts and all' touring bands out in the cold scratching around for places to ply their trade understandably peeved at the downturn in fortunes.

Appearing on paper to be something of a mismatch, the Malvern gig harboured method behind the madness, seeking simply to impress both parents and infants alike by kicking off with a sprightly aperitif from the shamefaced Euro-poppers in advance of a nostalgic seventy-five-minute performance by the old hands to round off the evening's entertainment.

'Have the other band soundchecked yet?' I asked sound-man Steve as I carted my luggage to the changing facilities, itching to run through a couple of new tunes in the set and make familiar with the hired-in equipment rig.

'Huh! If you mean does their playback system work the answer is yeah. The only "live" thing they'll be using is a mike to introduce the bloody songs... That's what I call taking the piss!' the old-school engineer caustically replied.

'So I assume that means you're ready for us?' I enthused. Alerting the guys, I scaled the ramp to the lofty wooden structure, already noticing a few punters arriving early on the scene to secure a prized vantage point.

Failing to show until shortly before their allotted slot in a low-profile mode of transport suggesting the Euro gravy train may be fast drying up, the gaily attired young wannabes took nervously to the stage amid a muddle of high-pitched squeals and cynical howls. Waving exaggeratedly to a scattering of tots perched on their parent's shoulders, they skipped gingerly across the boards and jigged their way through a short repertoire of slickly choreographed routines, lip-synching to a mishmash of disco-hit covers thumping from the hefty sub-woofers, observed by the narrowing eyes of the stupefied band members trying to make some sense of it all.

'We'd like to thank everyone for coming; this is our last song and it's the band's biggest hit to date... You all know it, so sing along – it's "Flying the Flag"!' a goody-goody female voice babbled only minutes into the foursome's workout, fighting against a squawking loop of feedback pretty much giving the game away.

'Their biggest hit? It's their only fucking hit!' scoffed Geoff, making way for the unshaven, hot and bothered director of operations energetically springing up the access steps to ensure his ears had not deceived him.

'Has anyone seen this circus act's tour manager?' the coordinator huffed, clearly getting hot under the collar.

'I just spotted him walking back over to that beaten-up old minibus they came in,' lead guitarist Danny bawled above the din.

'Shit, they're booked to do thirty minutes! I'll be inundated with pissed-off punters asking for their money back if this is their final number. Listen, if this goes tits-up would you guys help me out and do an extra fifteen minutes? Please!' he panicked.

'Of course, but that won't help console any kids going off on one,' I reasoned, aware of the playback track fizzling out into oblivion, drawing a strangely muted reaction from the windswept and largely unimpressed crowd.

'You were booked to play for half an hour and I clocked you at eleven minutes thirty seconds – you've hardly broken sweat!' the coordinator blasted, chastening the light-footed troupe as they flitted zestfully from the stage.

'We're not with you; what exactly are you implying?' a spiky blonde-haired spokesperson flapped, shaking in his pink dancing shoes.

'I'm saying you'll have to get back out there and do some more! Those kids' parents have paid good money… What a bloody rip-off – just over ten minutes of prancing around like fairies!' the organiser demanded, losing his cool.

'But there are only four songs on the disk,' the mouthpiece admitted in a tizzy. Overheard in the wings, this remark accelerated a mad dash back to our own designated shelter to prepare for an extended short-notice slot.

Trousers at half-mast in the tiny loo and tinkering with a revised set list, I was caught completely off guard when the bass-heavy rig reignited into action, pumping out a distinctly familiar robotic rhythm and causing a distinct sense of *déjà vu* to sweep over the camp. Tucking in my shirt, I darted over to the stage-side and watched in disbelief as the mortified young quartet bunny-hopped and frolicked before a bewildered public, acting out an identical twelve-minute sham.

I did feel a twinge of sympathy as the ruffled bit players took their final bow before fleeing tails between legs back to the safe confines of a waiting minibus, making good a speedy getaway and leaving the wise old owls to pick up the pieces.

Causes célèbres

Sir Edward Elgar – English composer
Fay Weldon – writer
Dave Mason – musician and songwriter (Traffic)
Sir Charles Hastings – founder of the British Medical Association
William Morris – Morris motor company founder

Essential travelling band info

Live music venue: Huntingdon Hall/Swan Theatre, Crowngate
Favourite curry house: Monsoon, Foregate Street – 50%
Favourite pub: Cardinal's Hat, Friar Street – 71%
Don't miss: Elgar Birthplace Museum, Crown East Lane, Lower Broadheath –
    80%
Sense of humour/friendly welcome: 54%

Chapter 69
York

Encompassing a magical hodgepodge of overhanging timber buildings clustered around a stunning Minster and arguably two of the finest museums in the land, in any given calendar year the mediaeval walled city of York coaxes an average of around seven million tourists onto its winding cobbled streets, bewitched by the ancient county town's fascinating historical sights and steadfast character.

Having called in on the one-time Viking hangout on a number of occasions in my professional capacity I had often toyed with the idea of dropping anchor for a more sustained period, and finally took off with my wife and small daughter for an impromptu slice of olde-worlde England. It all seemed a far cry from a hectic schedule of crowded airports and delayed flights as we bumped leisurely along the uneven byways and even scaled the city walls (no mean feat clinging onto a pushchair), marvelling at a panoply of gravity-defying architecture.

We whiled away the hours wandering down memory lane on the recreated bygone thoroughfares of the unique Castle Museum before sauntering peacefully around the magnificent Minster, topping off a full day's sightseeing with an anticlimactic ride through the malodorous Jorvik Viking Centre ('It smells of pooh!' cried our little girl). After pigging out on a stodgy evening pizza we took the load off at the boutique-style hotel where, within moments, with the little 'un tucked in tight, my flagging missus followed suit.

Sneaking from the room on tiptoe looking to sample a jar in one of the city's renowned taverns, I stumbled upon a side-street hostelry and hopped onto a vacant bar-stool. Sidling up on an adjacent high chair a long-winded, red-nosed tyke picked up on my accent and unthinkingly began jumping down my throat.

'I take it you've come up from London to see what a pint of real bitter tastes like, lad!' the rascal taunted, seeking moral support from a band of roguish accomplices clearly the worse for drink littering up the old-fashioned taproom.

'I'm not from London, I come from the Midlands; but I like to think I know a good pint when I taste one, which in all honesty can't be said of this stuff – it's as weak as gnat's piss!' I shot back out of earshot of the busy, muscular landlord.

'Ye what lad…? The bloody beer down south is like something out of a sewer; it doesn't even have a head on it!' the man squabbled, again looking for backup from the group of nodding parasites grunting their approval.

'But the head's only air bubbles, which means you get another mouthful in your glass where I come from,' I rankled, standing my ground.

'Codswallop,' exclaimed the ticked-off agitator, thumping a fist on the counter.

He was joined at his side by an odd customer in a loud checked suit. 'I'm sorry to barge in, but you wouldn't happen to be a well-known singer would you…? If so, could I borrow you for ten minutes to help us out in the function room upstairs… please?' the guy begged with an effeminate lisp.

'What would you like me to do?' I asked, all at sea.

'We're holding our annual "sexy Santa" contest, but we've been dropped in it by the Yorkshire TV weather girl – she was supposed to be judging but she hasn't shown up… Is there any chance you could do the honours and fill in for her?' he pleaded. 'We've got a photographer here from the press and all sorts!'

'I don't mind one bit mate… Do you need me right away?' I asked.

'Wonderful, what a star you are – you've saved our bacon! There are eight entrants; we just need you to pick a winner and pose for a couple of pics for the local rag… that's all,' he urged, provoking an outbreak of cackles from my new acquaintances.

I was led up a narrow staircase and entered what appeared to be a dining area, where a row of scantily clad males garbed in red hats, thongs, furry boots and tinsel-trimmed waistcoats proceeded to strut the length and breadth of the floor, camping up every movement with gleeful aplomb to the strains of Slade's 'Merry Christmas Everybody'.

'Pardon me for saying, but when you said sexy Santas I was expecting to see a bevy of local beauties,' I commented, put well out of my stride.

'Oops, silly me – I forgot to mention it's the annual "Gay Sexy Santa" event. They take it ever so seriously you know!' my host pointed out.

'Will you excuse me for a sec…? I need the loo,' I balked. Out on a limb, I disappeared downstairs and uncharitably made my way back to the hotel, feeling perhaps I'd had more than enough stick for one evening.

****

The previous summer I was persuaded by a bunch of playmates to participate in a mini cricket tour set to take place within spitting distance of the city over a long weekend. Fancying my chances of putting leather on willow I packed my whites and, clambering onto a sizeable minibus, the shambolic eleven-strong party headed northwards.

Serving for the majority of the guys as an excuse to rid themselves of the stranglehold exerted by their henpecking better halves, the conversation on the outbound journey mostly centred upon the escapades of previous outings, and so we pulled into the village of Elvington near York without a hint of a master plan for the triathlon ahead.

Containing few surprises, the opening evening fixture perhaps predictably resulted in a sound thrashing at the hands of our vastly superior hosts. Chalking up a miserly total on the scoreboard, we scarpered to the B&B-cum-watering hole for a long-drawn-out post-match inquest over a barrel-load of the local tipple.

'You idle git, Bill; that was an easy single and you just leaned on your bat!' I carped, reflecting on my earlier run-out and holding the heftiest member of the party responsible for standing his ground and failing to heed my call.

'Davy boy, you're taking this far too seriously; for God's sake lighten up. When I said we'd be getting hammered, I meant on and off the pitch, so let's all just get ratted and enjoy a weekend of debauchery!' the fat man reacted, summing up the all-embracing insouciance sweeping through the disorganised ranks.

I joined my bloodshot-eyed, listless colleagues gathered around the refectory-style dining table for a late-morning fry-up with a thumping hangover serving as a painful reminder of the previous evening's overindulgence, accompanied only by the metallic clinking of cutlery on bone china as words seemed hard to find.

'Where's Martin? He's usually up with the lark,' captain and organiser John inquired, breaking the silence in referring to the squad's main strike bowler.

'I knocked on his door before I came down but there was no reply; he must be having a good lie in 'cause he buggered off early last night without buying a round,' clarified the absentee's regular drinking buddy, Eric.

'Hark who's talking. You haven't put your hand in your pocket since we left home, you bloody skinflint!' Bill hit back.

'Piss off, you bloody lard-arse,' Eric responded. 'Maybe we should ask the landlady for a pass key in case you've eaten him!'

'Stop bloody bickering,' chastised the skipper. 'I'll ask the old dear to unlock his door when we've finished breakfast.'

We were all assembled and ready to head off to the settlement of Hemingbrough close to the town of Selby when a concerned-looking John tripped down the staircase, cantankerously muttering a few well-chosen expletives beneath his breath.

'What's up, skip – has he gone AWOL?' I probed.

'It's a mystery; his stuff's still in there but he bloody well isn't, and his bed hasn't been slept in!' the head honcho unveiled.

'Y-you d-don't think…!' stammered Guy, the second youngest of the group, gaping over at Bill with a vexed expression.

'What, with that battle-axe of a serving wench? Not likely – her arse was twice the size of mine,' the tubby character flouted.

'And her moustache was bushier than Tom's,' kidded John, gesturing towards the hirsute six-footer and only decent bat.

'The bloody landlord told me she's nicknamed the Elephant Woman around these parts!' the cheery beanpole divulged.

'I've seen some of the lads in the band with a lot worse!' I honed in, surrounded by a roomful of gawping reprobates.

****

Sprinting back to the pavilion amid thunderclaps and lightning strikes after just thirty minutes' play in the second fixture, the team encountered an unexpected guest in the shape of an irate middle-aged woman sat taking shelter in the changing area, studying each individual with hateful eyes and manifestly simmering with rage.

'Where's my bloody husband? I'll kill him when I get hold of him!' she scowled, blasting at the unnerved John with both barrels.

'Oh no, Linda – you obviously haven't heard; he was rushed off to the local hospital last night complaining of chest pains. He was as white as a sheet and had to sit down in the bar, so we sent for an ambulance and they kept him in for tests,' Bill interrupted, bailing out his skipper with a hastily concocted tale.

'What kind of cock and bull story is that? Other than being unable to talk he was fine at 3am this morning when he called from a payphone saying he was lost and urgently needed picking up,' the woman contradicted.

'Really? He must've discharged himself and just wandered off into the night!' Bill prevailed, lying through his teeth.

'You expect me to believe that load of hogwash? The only time he swears his undying love for me is when he's drunk as a lord or riddled with guilt,' she sounded off, unaware of a dishevelled-looking ruffian stood in the doorway to her rear.

'Put a bloody sock in it woman, I've been through hell and high water since I last laid eyes on you. I was only with the boys for about an hour last night. It may sound far-fetched, but would you believe I got kidnapped?' he astoundingly unravelled.

'*Kidnapped?*' the chorus resounded from the stunned gathering.

'And I was born yesterday! What you mean to say is you slept with another woman, you bastard…' she flipped, cut short by her enraged hubby.

'*Shut the fuck up and listen for a second…!* I was in bloody agony – my piles were playing up like crazy. The big fat barmaid offered to take me to an imaginary chemist on the outskirts of York to pick up some ointment… and the next thing I knew I was taken prisoner in the battle-axe's house,' Martin conceded to a wave of stifled laughter.

'I never heard such crap in my entire life… You could easily have got directions and asked Eddie to take you to the chemists,' she persisted, referring to the group's driver. 'A grown man abducted by an old slapper of a barmaid? It just doesn't add up!'

'Eddie wouldn't have had a clue where to go, and besides he was busy downing a few pints with the lads… I'm telling the truth, for crying out loud; if you'd let me get a word in I'll give you the whole story!' he reasoned, at last silencing the woman.

Resisting the biddy's bullish advances upon stopping off at her place and purporting to need the loo to make good an escape, the hapless husband had found himself shoved inside a windowless bunk room under lock and key. After resting awhile leaning up against the wall, overcome by pain he crashed out on the floor, too knackered even to contemplate his next move, and spent half the night curled up in a ball, knees tight to his shivering chest.

'So how the hell did you get away if you were bolted inside?' the wronged spouse asked in a more forgiving tone.

'When I came round I spotted a small skylight in the roof and managed to squeeze through it from off the top bunk before climbing down the drainpipe, but I had no idea where we were staying and just headed back the way we came. Then I found a phone box and called you, which didn't exactly help, and wound up dossing down in a Dutch barn. By the time I woke and cadged a lift to the B&B the guys had cleared off without me. There you have it!' he recounted to a ripple of mocking applause from his pals.

'Oh my poor darling,' the woman lamented, softening in a flash and rushing towards her man to hug him in a tight embrace, though pulling away at once and bleating: 'Phew… what the devil is that godawful smell?'

'I was just about to explain. I hitched a ride on a trailer carrying two bloody great Tamworth pigs but was so knackered I nodded off,' he owned up. 'When I woke up I was laying there in a pile of shit in the middle of a field about five miles from here, but there wasn't a soul around so I had no choice but to leg it the rest of the way!'

'Well, I suggest you get showered and out of those stinking clothes, then we can all clear off to the pub!' proposed John to a raucous seal of approval.

'Not likely! Don't you think he's been through enough?' the good lady insinuated. 'I'm taking him home with me right now.'

'I don't think so, sweetheart; I came on this trip to get rat-arsed with the boys and still have every intention of doing just that. I'll be back late tomorrow anyway,' Martin upheld. 'Don't worry, I'll be fine; the Plymouth Argylls have settled down now!' After being allowed a little space to kiss and make up, he leapt onto the bus like a man on a mission ahead of joining our parched hosts for an extended soirée at the nearby inn.

****

Early the following afternoon, the minibus chuntered through the gates into a pristine, picture-postcard setting somewhere in the Lincolnshire backwaters. Sadly, however, the depressing sight of a waterlogged pitch pretty much spoke for itself. With little prospect of any play we were requested by the opposing captain to join his band of men for a pre-organised lunch.

'Well, it looks as if that's that,' skipper John bemoaned, hearing the pitter-patter of more rain splashing lightly onto the pavilion windows. 'It's been a bit of a washout this year to say the least, lads; perhaps we should all just piss off home,' signalling the cue for a mass exodus from the dampening premises.

Disappointedly going our separate ways following a melancholy pit-stop halfway home, I sought refuge in the local pub. An overfamiliar slap on the back from another cricketing acquaintance, Rupert, insinuated a session may well be in progress. He introduced me to a burly, bearded man with the firmest of handshakes.

'Please meet a pal of mine – Dominic. He does quite a bit of TV stuff; perhaps you've even worked together in the past?' Rupert hinted.

'I'm not sure we have, though I do know your face from somewhere; are you a comedian?' I pried out of genuine interest.

'Haha, some people might think so. No, I used to be the world champion memory man; I get invited onto a variety of programmes remembering barcodes and historic dates and all that poppycock,' the big man modestly made known.

'Are you the guy who's banned from every casino in the universe?' I inquired, recalling a newspaper story I'd once read.

'The very one!' he confirmed.

'Ah… who won the FA cup in 1923?' I questioned, getting down to business and barely giving the man time to breathe.

'That's way too easy: Bolton Wanderers beat West Ham United 2-0 in the first ever Wembley final,' he shot back.

443

'Okay, when was the first ever television broadcast?' a chirpy local chimed in.

'1926 from one room to another by John Logie Baird; the first transatlantic broadcast was two years later in 1928,' Dominic rattled off like a true pro.

Content to be put to the test, the genial brainbox endeared himself to the attentive, captive audience, conjuring up cricketing statistics and obscure battle dates in between slurping at the odd flagon of ale, before moving on to his barcode party piece. Finally he turned to the subject of pop music, apparently immune to the effects of the alcohol and again astounding the small gathering with a comprehensive stockpile of facts and figures.

'Okay then, clever clogs,' I interjected, winking over to the barman, 'who sang the top ten hit "Tits and Fanny" and what album did it come from?'

'Are you kidding? I can't recall that title,' the flummoxed intellectual stalled, scratching his head and entering into deep thought.

'Do you give up? I admit it is a toughie!' I elaborated.

'Yes, I'm afraid you've stumped me on that one,' Dominic sighed, suspecting a sting in the tail but nonetheless throwing in the towel.

'It was none other than Cliff Richard… Don't you remember it? *"Tits and fanny how we don't talk any more"*; it was taken from the album *I'm Nearly Famous*,' I teased, bursting into an impromptu rendition accompanied by an outbreak of loud guffawing.

'You silly sod, I thought you were being serious… You got me hook, line and sinker. What are you drinking?' he asked, sighing ruefully.

We continued shooting the breeze until one in the morning when landlord John finally called time.

'It's been great meeting you, Dave… I'll make sure Rupert drags me along here again when I'm next up this way,' the mastermind hinted, gripping my hand.

'The pleasure's all mine; it's been a hoot!' I concurred, picking up my coat and making slowly towards the door.

'Where the fuck did I park the car…? Bloody memory man – I've got a feeling my days may be numbered!' he rued, looking along the empty street.

Causes célèbres

Kate Atkinson – author
John Barry – composer of the *James Bond* theme and many classic film scores
Guy Fawkes – 'Remember, remember the fifth of November!'
Mark Addy – actor (*The Full Monty*)
Frankie Howerd – legendary camp comedian

Vince Cable – Lib Dem politician
Dame Judi Dench – lauded British actress

Essential travelling band info

Live music venue: The York Barbican, Paragon Street
Favourite curry house: Mumbai Lounge, Fossgate – 77%
Favourite pub: Maltings, Tanners Moat – 72%
Don't miss: York Castle Museum, Eye of York – 89%
Sense of humour/friendly welcome: 55%

Chapter 70
Leicester

TWO SHINY-FACED LADIES WITH DOTTED foreheads clad in brightly coloured saris sit animatedly chatting on a strip of rat-infested waste ground strewn with empty bottles and a hodgepodge of household rubbish inconsiderately dumped at the roadside. Meanwhile, a wreck of a Hyundai Atos carrying eight uncomfortable, babbling Asian passengers swerves sharply to avoid a clutch of toing and froing mopeds, almost obliterating a gaily turbaned youth perilously dodging between the cacophonous, haphazard bedlam.

Set back from the road amidst the mounting traffic chaos the access route to an overloaded bazaar – vending a huge variety of goods ranging from ornate filigree jewellery and carved wooden statuettes to roll upon roll of gaudy sequined fabrics – lies blocked off by a large, prostrate, horned water buffalo, creating a long tailback of old jalopies augmented by the frustrated gadabouts venting their fury in a cats' chorus of blaring horns.

From a side street an escorted elephant, adorned in an elaborate headdress, blunders into view leading an extravagant parade of bare-chested acrobatic dancers followed by a bevy of veiled would-be princesses daintily sidestepping the hazardous electricity cables flapping precariously in the humid breeze, placing one rhinestone-patterned shoe ahead of the other in celebrating an event of note on the Hindu calendar.

Okay, so I lied about the water buffalo; but in truth the harum-scarum backdrop depicted in all its eastern splendour actually came to pass on a baking hot, festive summer's afternoon in Leicester's cosmopolitan Melton Road district.

Representing the first city outside of Asia in which an influx of colourful subcontinentals outnumbers the indigenous population, the modern multi-cultural East Midlands metropolis understandably permeates a breezy air of exoticism. It contrasts greatly with the workaday albeit thriving manufacturing centre of the 1960s, which has been latterly reshaped by an idiosyncratic breed of good-humoured, diligent settlers putting down roots and turning the area into an all-embracing, commercially diverse hive of activity.

On the other side of the coin, legitimate arguments rage over the continuing evaporation of the changeful melting pot's Englishness, blamed on the failure of successive governments to control mass immigration to the region. These rows are underlined by increasingly frequent gatherings in the city's central hub by racist organisations such as the English Defence League (EDL), and further provoked by the rhetoric of shady local politicians and expenses-fiddling councillors only serving to exacerbate any underlying restlessness.

But when all is said and done my old home town boasts a shambolic individuality and togetherness more akin to an oversized village than a major city. It has moved on from the obsolete glory days of a prospering footwear and hosiery industry to mould itself into a cautiously optimistic role model for similarly mixed communities.

****

Following a successful driving test astride a gleaming cherry-red Lambretta SX 150 at the age of sixteen and dispatching my uncool L-plates into the nearest bin, the novelty of burning up the highways and byways on two wheels garbed in a modish, khaki-green parka rapidly wore thin, reined in as I was by the wind-chill of winter's frozen claws chafing at my rosy-red features.

Inexplicably, my test pass qualified me to three-wheel in a triangle-shaped motor vehicle, despite having no previous experience of handling an automobile of any description; and consequently I scoured the local rag's 'cars for sale' section on a daily basis, thrilled at the prospect of upping my profile from behind the wheel of an eye-catching skirt-magnet.

There in black and white a small advertisement grabbed my attention:

'For Sale: Bond Minicar Mark D De Luxe, 45000 Miles, Good Condition, Only One Previous Owner – £50'

This was it – the moment I'd longed for: an opportunity to hit the open road unperturbed by the battering elements, spared the teeth-chattering vulnerability of straddling a two-wheeled deathtrap. Keeping the details very much to myself and boosted by ample funds in my post office account, I picked up the phone in haste.

Venturing out into the unknown on a brutal February evening hampered by a heavy, merciless sleet shower, I parked the scooter on the pavement and battled towards a shabby council house stood forlornly to the rear of an overgrown jungle. As I made to ring the bell a cadaverous, ageing man clad only in an off-white string vest, stained black trousers and a pair of carpet slippers suddenly appeared from a side entry, seemingly immune to the biting cold.

'Have you come about the car? She's still garaged up at the minute; I took the little beauty out for a spin only yesterday and the engine was purring away as sweet as a nut!' he claimed in a gruff unsalesmanlike tone before doubling back along the alley.

Whilst I dashed beneath the tiny porch to take shelter, a clangorous rasping sound spluttered into life from behind the uprising garage door, silhouetting the ringer for Doctor Who and his highly improbable passion-wagon in a cloud of toxic smoke.

'I'm sorry, but it's not quite what I had in mind,' I tactfully implied, inwardly dismayed at the thought of blowing my hard-earned savings on a yucky brown house-painted wreck floundering on the brink of the knacker's yard.

'Why don't you take her out for a little run – you might be pleasantly surprised?' the guy persuasively wheezed. 'She may not look up to much, but I can guarantee it'll be the best fifty quid you ever parted with!'

Burdened by a sense of obligation, I tugged at the plummeting driver's-side door, feeling the dead weight in my hand before hunkering down into the sole front seat hindered by the oversized steering wheel rubbing at my chest.

Jerking upwards as an exposed spring came into contact with my clenched buttocks, I reached for a cushion lying to one side and shoved the comforter beneath my rear end. I clunked the stiff lever into gear and cautiously released my left foot. The aged rattletrap lurched suddenly forwards, jolting to a halt as my right boot stamped on the brakes.

'Increase the revs and ease out the clutch very gently,' the skinny drowned rat advised, soaked to the skin from the relentless howling squall, 'but whatever you do don't stall her 'cause she can be a bugger to start.'

Rocking and rolling out of the gateway onto the greasy road, the ailing Bond teetered this way and that, inducing a kind of seasickness in the pit of my stomach. Undeterred I drove on and slowly became acquainted with the stubborn old mule, swerving recklessly onto the main A6 trunk road to incur the wrath of a phalanx of tooting commuters taking evasive action to steer clear of the blundering crate and safely make their way home.

After bobbing up and down like a milk float for fully ten minutes, shaken to the core by a combination of rock-hard suspension and humiliating backfiring, I came to the end of my tether and hung her left to complete the circuit. I found myself in an uneven slip road running adjacent to an elongated trench sealed off by a formation of red-and-white wooden barriers, guarded by a set of temporary traffic lights which predictably turned to red.

I again jumped onto the brakes a tad too aggressively, and naively failed to depress the clutch with my left boot. The ailing engine kangarooed forwards, dying an abrupt death; and I realised the full extent of my blunder as the tousled owner's words of warning came back to haunt me: '*Whatever you do, don't stall her!*'

Tilting back and forth like a rudderless boat on a rough sea illuminated by the red, amber and green of the flickering lights penetrating the unrelenting blizzard, I frantically turned the key in the ignition, flinching at the incessant sleet pounding against the windscreen; but not as much as a peep came out of the dead duck.

To the rear a queue of impatient motorists wound down their windows, bellowing obscenities and leaning on their horns. It all added to the mounting pandemonium and left me little choice but to scamper from the vehicle, manfully attempting to unblock the escape lane by heaving the obstruction ever closer to the abyss.

As I braced myself to dump the bucket of bolts at the roadside ahead of legging it back to the man's house in the hope of making a speedy getaway, a leather-clad man astride a macho Harley Davidson drew to a halt and waved me over.

'I used to own one of those bloody contraptions but soon went back to a bike… You haven't stalled it, have you?' the man yelped in trepidation.

'Afraid so; I'm just in the middle of taking it for a test drive, but I can't get the sodding heap of scrap to restart!' I grieved.

'Aha, that's a common fault; what you'll need to do is lift up the bonnet and climb inside,' the biker advised, pursing his lips.

'And do what?' I jabbered.

'You should find a pedal down by the crankshaft which you'll have to jump down on to kick-start it. Anyway, must go – the best of British luck!' he yawped, zipping away in a flurry of spray as the lights once again flashed to green.

Fumbling like a giddy geriatric beneath the steering column inside the car, I yanked too hard at a rusting metal lever which came away in my hand. The bonnet scarily flew undone, flapping like a giant metallic vulture in the near gale-force winds and ripping away from its hinges. It cleared a fleeing Morris Minor by a hair's breadth and came to rest like a carbon-steel tepee pitched in the centre of the solitary carriageway.

'What a bleeding idiot – you could've taken some poor bugger's head off!' complained an irate motorist, backed up by the unsympathetic rabble inching along behind him, venting their inaudible fury in similarly invective tones.

Somehow holding it together and ignoring the caustic jibes, I climbed inside the tinny framework and quickly located the protruding pedal. As I did so, yet another freak gust caught hold of the detached bonnet which took flight once more and whipped narrowly above my head before smashing violently into a nearby greenhouse only yards from the roadworks.

'That fucking banger's not roadworthy,' bayed a hostile motorist, baring his teeth. 'The only proper place for that heap is the scrapyard!'

'I couldn't agree more,' I retorted, energetically bouncing on the foot pedal.

Umpteen attempts to start the wreck later, I was fading fast and breathing heavily when, sparing my blushes, the old girl screeched into life. Fearful of another humiliating seizure, I dived acrobatically into the driver's seat.

'Come back here, you little bastard – where the bloody hell do you think you're going?' a belligerent voice screamed from the abutting allotment. I eyed an incensed guy giving chase onto the main drag before clumsily toppling into a puddle of mud.

'Whoops, you should be more careful…! Sod off and take it up with the owner,' I reacted. Toeing the accelerator and getting the hell outta Dodge, I tore through the rows of weather-beaten, characterless houses to locate my own saturated two-wheeler, muttering to myself: 'So this bloody shit-heap does go, after all!'

****

'Blimey, I've not seen you in ages; how the hell are you?' I asked, greeting regular wag Mark upon entering the local village pub and watching him neck the dregs of a pint prior to dashing off for an early Sunday lunch.

'Haven't you heard…? I've been laid up in hospital for a week with a suspected case of appendicitis. It turned out to be a nasty case of gastric flu. I was over the moon when they gave me the news!' he curiously replied.

'Appendicitis can be really nasty. I got lucky when mine burst in the ambulance on the way to hospital… I was only nineteen, so I suppose it must have come as a relief to be laid low with a bout of the shits!' I chuckled unsympathetically.

'No, I'm not talking about the bug; when I was bedridden I didn't have a drink for seven days… which means I'm not an alcoholic. Yippee! Anyway, sorry I can't stay longer, we've got friends over – see you soon!' he enthused, bungling out of the door.

Light-hearted banter dashed with a dose of sharp wit and repartee were very much part of the staple diet of my local pub's constitution. As I eavesdropped in on the usual suspects' topic of the day, however, I found the conversation very much reflected the wintry gloom outside, uncannily turning to reincarnation without a trace of black humour.

'Bob swears blind the psychic was for real; she described the casket, pall-bearers even the flower arrangements to a tee, which in effect means the old boy must've been present at his own funeral!' unfolded a strangely macabre James. I listened, contemplating throwing my hat in the ring while warming my backside against the open fire.

'Can you imagine being there at your own funeral…? That's made me go cold!' chipped in long-time regular Gerald.

'Isn't it all a load of mumbo jumbo?' added the immaculately clad Toby. 'So many of these clairvoyants are fake; what's your take on it, Dave?'

'Incredibly, an uncle of mine did that very thing!' I revealed, confronted by half a dozen sagging jaws to suggest I had the circle's undivided attention.

****

Growing accustomed to a gentler pace of life on the back of twelve years of retirement, where funeral attendances sadly outweighed an ever-dwindling number of family get-togethers and social occasions, Uncle Ted (a.k.a. Edward Heathcote) habitually fine-combed the deaths and obituaries section of the local rag, the *Leicester Mercury*, curiously working his way through the newly departed to figure out whether some old acquaintance or former workmate may have drawn their final breath in readiness for a wooden suit.

Tuning into the six o'clock news on a pitch-black winter's evening betwixt flipping through the tabloid's pages spread out on his lap, he paused as per usual at the list of obits. A boldly inked tribute caused him to sit bolt upright:

EDWARD HEATHCOTE: Beloved husband and father of two sons, passed peacefully away on the morning of January 22nd at the age of 77 – Funeral arrangements to be advised.

'Brenda, come and look at this; it's uncanny – there's a fella here that's snuffed it with exactly the same name as me… What's more, he has two sons and is even the same bloody age!' he gasped, checking the wording for a second time.

'Are you wearing your reading glasses, love?' my aunt countered. Putting the dinner on hold she bustled in from the kitchen, stooping down at her man's side to take a shufti at the spooky announcement.

'You can see I am… How can we find out where the funeral's taking place?' Ted asked, much to his good lady's consternation.

'Why…? Surely you're not thinking of going!' Brenda implored, raising a hand to her mouth, understandably aghast.

'Oh, come on, love – it's not every day you get an opportunity like this! There may even be some people I know in the congregation,' he joked, morbidly fascinated at the prospect of witnessing his namesake's final outing.

Plagued by second thoughts and doubting anyway the wisdom of his gut instinct, Ted heeded his good lady's misgivings and banished all notions of attending the deceased's send-off. Only days later, however, midway through his nightly survey, there paraphrased in highlighted lettering loomed the full details of the remembrance service. It was scheduled to take place all of a few miles from his home, coincidentally at a parish church Ted knew well.

'Brenda, I've changed my mind; I'm going. I feel some kind of allegiance to this guy, and who knows – we may even be distantly related!' he insisted, spurred by an inexplicable urge to pay his respects to the late counterpart.

Entering the bitterly cold house of God on a bleak February afternoon decked out in his cashmere overcoat, sports jacket and black tie, Ted took a rear pew well away from the mournful gathering of family members and close friends and awaited the commencement of the ritual with head bowed, anxious to keep as low a profile as possible.

Glancing briefly to one side midway into the opening hymn, he met the eyes of a familiar-looking, prim and proper lady. Gasping in horror, the old girl collapsed into the aisle, prompting a quick reaction from two able-bodied pallbearers who helped her to her feet.

Thinking little of it and taking a second peek to keep tabs, Ted instantly recognised the sufferer as Dorothy from the accounts department of his former employers from which he'd retired so many moons previously. While mulling over the ex-bookkeeper's attendance, he noticed at least half a dozen other known faces amongst the concerned huddle.

'Goodness me, what the hell are that lot doing here?' Ted gasped, slowly growing wise to the fact the group of ex-colleagues had mistakenly shown up to pay tribute to muggins himself and not the corpse lying horizontal in the casket. It now became evident that the unfortunate Dorothy's blackout had been solely due to the apparition witnessed from the adjacent pew.

Under no false illusions as to the error of his ways and appreciating his presence may indeed be unwelcome, Ted shuffled with head hung low towards the exit. Seated to one side sipping at a life-saving beaker of water, the hapless Dorothy looked upwards, again identifying the face of the man to whom she'd come to pay her last respects before unleashing a blood-curdling scream and conking out for a second time.

Putting a spurt on at a pace belying his seniority, Ted cursed under his breath for as much as contemplating such a foolish act, fleeing the hundred yards or more back to his parked car before hitting the throttle like a boy racer.

'Is that you love?' asked a chirpy voice from the kitchen upon hearing the front door latch click open. 'You weren't long at all… How did it go?'

'I think you'd better sit down, Brenda – you're not going to believe this!' Ted replied, sheepishly entering the room.

Picking my roguish uncle's brains some months after the botch-up I found it nigh on impossible to keep a straight face, poking fun at the bizarre tale amid intermittent bouts of laughter. Eventually the time arrived to slip on my coat.

'You know, Dave, I often feel the odd pang of guilt that I didn't take the time to track down some of those old colleagues and come clean... but what concerns me most is there'll probably be nobody present at the service to pay their respects when it really is my turn!' Ted morosely reflected, showing me to the door.

'Don't worry, Ted – I'll be there... Mind you, I'll double-check they got the right man before I set foot inside the church!' I pledged, smiling and bidding him goodbye.

****

On December 10th 1987 the Leicestershire town of Market Harborough found itself put firmly on the map, courtesy of news channels the world over reporting an audacious prison break. It involved a hijacked helicopter being used to airlift gangland boss John Kendall and convicted murderer Sydney Draper from the sizeable exercise yard of Her Majesty's Prison Gartree, at the time a fully blown Category A institution. The outrageous movie-style getaway remains the one and only successful attempt of its kind to take place at a UK slammer, rendering the daredevil escapees temporarily at large whilst initiating an unprecedented nationwide manhunt.

Once the runaways had been dropped off at a location on the edge of town, the shaken pilot (admirably holding it all together despite being on the wrong end of a gun) was ordered to lift off in double-quick time and to remain airborne until his passengers had sufficient time to go to ground. After hovering for approximately ten minutes above the sprawling industrial estate, he was able to pinpoint a safe place to touch down and at last raise the alarm. Landing askew upon the forecourt of a machinery manufacturing plant, the disoriented pilot raced from the fluttering whirlybird in a mad panic and ducked beneath an open roller shutter, wildly flapping his arms and urgently requesting the assistance of the first helping hand available.

Coming up to retirement, curmudgeonly old-school character Derek Wilson worked flexible hours partaking in his daily duties as a glorified caretaker at the aforementioned works unit, in turn subsidising his modest income ferrying band member Geoff Betts to and from a string of rendezvous points, often in the dead of night. Priding himself to the nth degree on the virtues of punctuality and efficiency, he would regularly and bombastically remind his co-workers as to his seniority and invaluable experience. Treading a fine line to bypass any unnecessary conflict, Derek's colleagues avoided the grumpy old windbag like the plague, going out of their way to stagger lunch and coffee-breaks to give the old busybody a wide berth and make for a quiet life.

He was ensconced in his small side-office on a brisk winter's afternoon taking a well-earned statutory tea interval when, unhinging the old plodder in the midst of his all-too-brief respite, a disturbing, out-of-the-ordinary whoop-whoop-whooshing sound emanated from the adjoining courtyard and a thick swirl of grit spattered up onto the window.

'Bloody hell, I can't even have five minutes' peace!' he chuntered. Twisting round in his seat, he was startled to see a terror-stricken uniformed man rushing through the doorway.

'It's imperative I use your telephone, now!' the trembling newcomer demanded.

Briefly ignoring the unwanted visitor, the lethargic supervisor stepped out into the yard to take note of the disturbance in his official capacity.

'What the fuck…? Just hold your horses a minute,' Derek disbelievingly uttered.

'I said *now* – can't you see this is an emergency?' the airman furiously exclaimed. 'There are two wanted men on the loose!'

'If you think you're leaving that bloody thing parked there, you've got another think coming!' griped the dogged overseer, intent on following the rule book.

'Will you please get it into your thick head that I urgently need to contact the police?' the captain hollered, reaching his wit's end.

'Pipe down, Snoopy, and don't go raising your voice at me; I've got trucks coming in and out of here at all hours of the day. You'll have to get that heap of junk shifted… and now!' the unyielding foreman persisted.

'Look, I realise you're only doing your job but there's been a jailbreak from the nearby prison little more than twenty minutes ago, and it was that very helicopter with me piloting it that sprung the escapees; I must use your phone as a matter of national concern!' the aviator pleaded, opting for a less forceful tack.

'Bullshit, there's precious little goes on around here without me knowing,' Derek exaggerated.

He was cut short by a boiler-suited employee gasping for breath following a frantic obstacle race across the factory floor. 'Is that the chopper that…? I just heard on the radio… It's unbelievable!' he blurted. 'Sorry, do you need to use the phone? Quick, this way…' With a welcome sense of urgency the man directed the stranger to the workshop extension.

Peering out from his enclosure, hands on hips, the nonplussed Derek was observing the flying machine's blades continuously rotating, spreading a cloud of dust across the deserted clearing, when from the rear of the building the pilot reappeared, leaping athletically into the cockpit to put a stop to the whirring fan.

'Hey you, what the bloody hell's going on now?' Derek bickered. 'I told you already I've got ten-wheeler tractor-trailers coming in and…'

In the midst of overstepping the mark once again, he was interrupted by the hacked-off high-flier who wearily asserted: 'Shut the fuck up… please!'

Seated at the breakfast table the very next morning slurping at a mug of sweet tea and puffing at a habitual gasper, the gobsmacked jobsworth found two black-and-white mugshots plastered on the *Daily Mirror*'s front page boring into his eyes, complemented by the full story of two daring fugitives who had flown the coop into the international headlines, astonishingly putting the rural town of Market Harborough firmly under the national spotlight.

Although arch-villain John Kendall was tracked down after just ten days as a result of confidential police intelligence, the evasive Sydney Draper remained at large for thirteen months. He was eventually recaptured by a group of armed officers, prior to apprehending escape mastermind Andy Russell, who subsequently received a ten-year sentence in 1989.

****

Early 1973 portended the announcement by a leading international tobacco company of a large-scale nationwide search to unveil Britain's 'next big thing', aptly dubbed 'The Top Town Talent Competition'. The aim, among other things, was to sniff out a mini galaxy of budding young stars embarking on the first rung of the ladder toward a career in the world of music.

Getting the show on the road, a series of weekly heats were staged in a cartel of prominent club venues located the length and breadth of the land, whittling the numbers down to just sixteen contestants. Regional quarter- and semi-finals sought to determine the cream of the crop, culminating in a momentous Grand Final which was opportunely scheduled to take place at the chain's flagship nightspot in the band's home town of Leicester.

Sugar-coated with the opportunity to work alongside a top producer, ostensibly to open the door to a major record contract, the spoils of victory brought along a healthy windfall stretching to the tune of one thousand pounds (roughly the equivalent of ten grand in modern currency), further enhanced by a wealth of media exposure, all topped off with a chock-full diary courtesy of a bill-topping six-night stint in each of the participating venues.

Picking up the gauntlet in what appeared on the surface to be a no-lose situation, buoyed by the news the majority of Midlands heats would take place but a stone's throw from our homes, the band entered a sustained period of intense rehearsal, taking the bull by the horns to piece together a breathless routine designed to wow both judges and audience alike.

We progressed into the showcase's latter stages largely untroubled, in part attributed to the underwhelming stagecraft of the bulk of the contestants; and the merry month of May saw the newfangled eight-piece safely through to the prestigious finale, generating a huge stir among a rapidly accumulating band of supporters in local circles. As we chalked off the days leading up to the big night in anticipation of a thrilling climax, all the smart money was on the home-grown rock-and-rollers to come out on top.

The band grasped the nettle with both hands, coming out all guns blazing into a highly charged atmosphere reminiscent of a world title fight, with a fiercely partisan crowd in excess of three thousand psyching us into an exuberant thirty-minute performance up there with the most memorable of our careers. Following a few tense moments while the judges deliberated, we were crowned victorious in an aura of unbridled euphoria, described in Freudian terms by an articulate spokesperson as 'a cauldron full of seething excitation'. The seeds were sown for a long and adventurous journey far exceeding anyone's wildest dreams.

To the steadfast people of Leicester: I salute you. After all, this is where the story began and, fittingly, pretty much where it ends.

Causes célèbres

Richard III – the last Plantagenet king (buried in the city for 500 years)
Joseph Merrick – 'The Elephant Man'
Gok Wan – TV celebrity designer
Sue Townsend – late, great author and creator of Adrian Mole
Kasabian – rock band
Rosemary Conley – 'Hip and Thigh Diet' creator
Englebert Humperdinck – orange-faced crooner
Joe Orton – playwright
Gary Lineker – *Match of the Day* presenter
Kate O'Mara – actress
John Deacon – bass player from Queen
Julie Etchingham – newsreader
Mark Selby – snooker world champion
Michael Kitchen – actor
Thomas Cook – travel agency pioneer

Essential travelling band info

Live music venues: O₂ Academy, University Road; De Montfort Hall,
    Granville Road
Favourite curry house: Shimla Pinks, London Road – 88%
Favourite pub: The Old Horse, London Road – 76%
Don't miss: Richard III Exhibition, The Guildhall, Guildhall Lane – 81%
Sense of humour/friendly welcome: 72%

Epilogue

SO HERE I AM, PERCHED on a rickety wooden stool that will soon be used for firewood, surrounded by cardboard boxes, packing cases and polythene-wrapped items of furniture, staring admiringly at the verdant Leicestershire pastures I've known all my life, pondering what lies ahead in my new chosen home far away from here.

The view today looks more beautiful than ever, enriched by the morning sun casting shadows across the abutting meadow, creating an array of glistening dewdrops gently trickling from the neighbouring gabled rooftops.

I wander outside, quickly latching onto a wily old villager slowly idling by, waving a clenched fist from his open car window punctuated by a disparaging remark or two before disappearing beneath an avenue of trees. For sure I'll miss the blossoming hedgerows and bucolic characters I've shared a good many beers with after hours in the local pub, recognising life is full of goodbyes yet knowing deep down the time is right to move on.

The removal van pulls sluggishly from off of the drive, transporting the last remnants of our personal possessions to a convenient storage facility until further notice. Trudging back inside I see my wife Cathy stood forlornly at the bottom of the staircase, tears welling in her eyes. We cuddle and comfort one other, battling hard to keep our emotions in check, sobbing gently, endeavouring to smile through the heartbreak.

Perhaps privileged to have visited every city in the United Kingdom, I will always be a Brit through and through, bearing a strong sense of kinship not only to my fellow countrymen, but to the quirky neighbours making up the Union. The snobby English; the canny, thankfully non-independent Scots; the uncompromising Welsh; not forgetting the combative Northern Irish... All will forever hold a place in my heart, and will doubtless continue to feature in the odd crotchety dust-up during the course of a never-ending lust for travel, hopefully stretching further afield in the coming years.

There'll be parties to attend, complete with an obligatory kilted Glaswegian hankering to bare his blanched buttocks; sporting events where I'll be backed into a corner by a cantankerous Taff providing too much attention to detail. I'll listen to whinging Poms in airport queues complaining about this, that and the other (yet content to leave it at just that), on top of bumping into Ulstermen propping up the bar in Irish Pubs the world over.

The inhabitants of the UK are predominantly made of stern stuff, characterised on the whole as an accepting, open-minded society, boasting an enviable, ever-increasing tolerance towards multiculturalism boding well for the future.

Natural long-sufferers, we whine and complain about political correctness, government policies, the weather, myopic referees and pretty much everything else not to our liking, though in a country where free speech presides we have every right to do so. The persistent grey clouds overhead, brattish overpaid Premier League footballers, greedy bankers and violent mindless morons will continue to fill the headlines; but those living in a fantasy world auspiciously remain in the minority, whilst in essence the lion's share of Britons passively go about their daily chores desirous of a better life through hard work, common-sense and fairness.

In 2013 alone the rich heritages of the British Isles attracted well over thirty million tourists to its shores, a fact overlooked by a growing number of unpatriotic killjoys claiming the country may be going to the dogs, yet whose rare sojourns outside of their front doors stretch no further than a tacky, purpose-built resort on the Costa Fortuna.

From the Giant's Causeway to the mountains of Snowdonia and Loch Ness to Stonehenge lies a kingdom bursting at the seams with diversity and creativity, further exemplified by a unique sense of humour admired the world over.

Embrace your homeland and, should the opportunity arise, put yourself out there. See it, hear it, taste it and realise just how lucky you are!

Cause célèbre

Saint Christopher

THE END

Acknowledgements

FORGOING THE CUSTOMARY PROCESS OF compiling a list of names probably reaching into the hundreds, I offer my heartfelt gratitude to all the friends, relatives and acquaintances playing some part in this extraordinary rollercoaster ride, reserving a special mention for my unbelievably tolerant wife Cathy and wonderful daughter Holly-Ann.